UNDERSTANDING THE MATH YOU TEACH

Content and Methods for Prekindergarten Through Grade Four

Anita C. Burris

Youngstown State University

PEARSON

Merrill
Prentice Hall

Upper Saddle River, New Jersey
Columbus, Ohio

Library of Congress Cataloging in Publication Data

Burris, Anita C.
   Understanding the math you teach : content and methods for prekindergarten through grade four / Anita C. Burris.
       p. cm.
   Includes bibliographical references and index.
   ISBN 0-13-110737-2
   1.   Mathematics—Study and teaching (Preschool) 2.   Mathematics—Study and teaching (Elementary) I. Title.

QA135.6.B77 2005
372.7—dc22   2004002786

Vice President and Executive Publisher: Jeffery W. Johnston
Editor: Linda Ashe Montgomery
Editorial Assistant: Laura Weaver
Development Editor: Hope Madden
Production Editor: Mary M. Irvin
Design Coordinator: Diane C. Lorenzo
Cover Designer: Bryan Huber
Cover images: Corbis
Production Manager: Pamela D. Bennett
Director of Marketing: Ann Castel Davis
Marketing Manager: Darcy Betts Prybella
Marketing Coordinator: Tyra Poole

Microsoft® Word and Excel are registered trademarks of Microsoft Corporation in the United States and/or other countries.

This book was set in Times Roman by Carlisle Communications, Ltd. It was printed and bound by Courier Kendallville, Inc.The cover was printed by Coral Graphic Services, Inc.

Photo Credits: Karen Mancinelli/Pearson Learning: 2, 240; Scott Cunningham/Merrill: 22; Barbara Schwartz/Merrill: 46, 156, 178, 280; Todd Yarrington/Merrill: 70; Carmine Galasso/PH College: 92; Silver Burdett Ginn Needham: 126; Silver Burdett Ginn: 214.

Pearson Education Ltd.
Pearson Education Singapore Pte. Ltd.
Pearson Education Canada, Ltd.
Pearson Education—Japan

Pearson Education Australia Pty. Limited
Pearson Education North Asia Ltd.
Pearson Educación de Mexico, S.A. de C.V.
Pearson Education Malaysia Pte. Ltd.

10 9 8 7 6 5 4 3 2
ISBN: 0-13-110737-2

Preface

TEACHERS WHO ARE COMFORTABLE WITH MATHEMATICS DEVELOP CONFIDENT LEARNERS.

Understanding the Math You Teach: Content and Methods for Prekindergarten through Grade Four is the only text to combine methods and activities appropriate for the primary grade classroom with a constructivist presentation of the mathematical content that will enable you to teach math concepts effectively at the early childhood level. To teach math confidently, you need to feel comfortable with your own understanding of the mathematical content. You need to be familiar with the most appropriate content and field-tested teaching methods and strategies to share with Pre-K to grade 4 students. By building your understanding in each of these areas, this text will make math make sense for you and help you do the same for your future students.

Content

Each chapter scaffolds instruction in mathematics content knowledge, grounding your understanding and empowering your teaching. You'll have every opportunity to ensure that you fully understand math concepts while you learn appropriate methods for sharing this content with early grade students.

NCTM Standards The National Council of Teachers of Mathematics (NCTM) have provided teachers across the country with a comprehensive framework of the developmentally appropriate content for students. Your individual state has also contributed teaching standards you will need to understand and address in your classroom. Throughout all chapters you'll find Standards boxes that will help you understand how to integrate Standards-based material in your classroom.

- On the text's Companion Website you'll find quick access to all major mathematics standards, from NCTM's to your own state's. Look for the standards button on the navigation bar at *www.prenhall. com/burris*.

Problem Sets These appear after every major chapter section serve a dual purpose.

- *For Your Understanding* problems allow you to check your own comprehension of the math.
- *Applications in the Classroom* problems provide ideas and guide readers to generate materials to execute in early elementary math classrooms.

Methods

Learning the math content suitable for early grade classrooms will help you confidently teach the concepts. Familiarizing yourself with developmentally appropriate teaching methods and seeing how they play out in the classroom will enhance your understanding and better prepare you to teach primary grade students.

Activities *Activities* throughout all chapters model the kind of classroom teaching that will engage early grade students in mathematics, giving you the chance to see how to sequence the development of math concepts in the classroom.

Standards

NCTM

Pre-K–2

In addition to work with whole numbers, young students should also have some experience with simple fractions through connections to everyday situations and meaningful problems, starting with the common fractions expressed in the language they bring to the classroom, such as "half." . . . Although fractions are not a topic for major emphasis for pre-K–2 students, informal experiences at this age will help develop a foundation for deeper learning in higher grades.

NCTM, 2000, pp. 82–83

Standards are listed with the permission of the National Council of Teachers of Mathematics (NCTM). NCTM does not endorse the content or validity of these alignments.

Activity 9-2 — Grades 1–2

Birthday Pictograph

Materials: Birthday graph outline; a birthday cake or candle-shaped sticky note for each student.

Teacher Statement: We have studied the names of the months and are going to make a graph showing the birthdays in our class. You each have a sticky note. Write your name on the sticky note. When I call your table, you will come forward and place your note in the row of your birthday month.

What month has the most birthdays? What month has the fewest birthdays? Are there two months with the same number of birthdays? Is there a month with no birthdays? How many more birthdays were there in January than there were in March? And so on.

Manipulatives and Technology Manipulatives and technology each play an important role in today's math classrooms, and primary grade teachers need to know why and how to use these concrete instructional tools effectively. Each chapter in this book covers manipulatives and technology as appropriate to that chapter's mathematical topic. You'll find practical teaching instructions for employing manipulative and technology activities in early childhood classrooms.

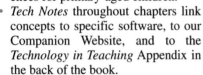

- *Math Manipulative* features help preservice teachers understand what manipulatives are and how to use them to provide concrete learning experiences for primary-aged children.
- *Tech Notes* throughout chapters link concepts to specific software, to our Companion Website, and to the *Technology in Teaching* Appendix in the back of the book.

Math Manipulative: Tangrams

The tangram set is an old Chinese puzzle. A set consists of two large triangles, one medium triangle, two small triangles, one square, and one parallelogram. The pieces fit together in a variety of ways. The set can be used to form one large square or several other interesting figures. See Blackline Master 2 in the Appendices for a pattern outline to create a homemade set. Sets may be purchased from teacher supply stores or catalogs and are available in a variety of materials. Overhead sets are also available.

Tangrams can be used for combining shapes to create other shapes and figures, completing fraction activities, reinforcing geometric terminology and ideas such as symmetry and congruence, and doing measurement activities.

Classroom Application

- *Using Literature in the Math Classroom* features suggest children's literature titles appropriate for chapter content and provide one or more specific strategies for using each title with young students. The reference section of each chapter provides an additional list of children's literature titles ideal for the content of the chapter.
- *Assessment* features model specific ways to assess student comprehension of mathematical concepts.
- *Lesson Plans* provide complete lessons on one mathematics topic appropriate for early grade classrooms.
- *Teaching Connections* sections in each chapter help you apply the math concepts being covered within the context of the early grade classroom.
- *Writing in Mathematics* sections in each chapter clearly illustrate the connection between math and writing.
- *Student artifacts* throughout chapters illustrate early grade students' work on topics specifically covered in this textbook.
- *Glimpse into the Classroom* features show real primary grade classrooms working successfully through a math concept.

Appendices

Burris's Preparation Materials for the PRAXIS I(R) Tests or Exams This appendix has been provided to help you prepare yourself for teacher credentialing. It contains concepts and content necessary for a full understanding of Pre-K to grade 4 material but is too advanced to be taught in Pre-K to grade 4 classrooms. You'll need to understand this math not only to deepen your understanding of the math you'll be teaching but also to be successful on your teacher credentialing exams.

Technology in Teaching This appendix contains a sampling of the most effective uses of technology in the primary grade classroom, including directions for teacher usage as well as specific examples and activities that may be used in the early childhood classroom.

Blackline Masters The final appendix includes many teacher resources appropriate for the classroom. These may be photocopied to create transparencies or to distribute to students in the classroom.

Supplements

Instructor's Manual This wealth of resources is free to adopters and includes chapter-by-chapter tools to simplify, broaden, and deepen the content being taught. You'll find teaching tips, including tips on teaching with technology and manipulatives, answers to even-numbered exercises from the text's Problem Sets, a complete test bank, and other chapter-specific comments.

Companion Website

A Companion Website has been created to build on and enhance what the textbook already offers. For this reason, the content for this website is organized by chapter and provides the professor and student with a variety of meaningful resources, including the following:

For the Student

- **Chapter Objectives**—outline key concepts from the text
- **Key terms and phrases**—focus study on the most important terms for each chapter
- **Interactive self-quizzes**—present hints and automatic grading that provide immediate feedback for students
- **Burris's Preparation for PRAXIS I(R) Tests or Exams**—presents a 40-question PPST—PRAXIS I(R) preparation quiz
- **Standards**—offers quick access to the NCTM Standards as well as each state's standards document
- **Web Destinations**—links to www sites that relate to chapter content
- **Message Board**—serves as a virtual bulletin board to post—or respond to—questions or comments to/from a national audience

For the Professor

Every Companion Website integrates **Syllabus Manager™**, an online syllabus creation and management utility.

- **Syllabus Manager™** provides you, the instructor, with an easy, step-by-step process to create and revise syllabi, with direct links into Companion Website and other online content without having to learn HTML.
- Students may log on to your syllabus during any study session. All they need to know is the web address for the Companion Website and the password you've assigned to your syllabus.
- After you have created a syllabus using **Syllabus Manager™**, students may enter the syllabus for their course section from any point in the Companion Website.
- Clicking on a date, the student is shown the list of activities for the assignment. The activities for each assignment are linked directly to actual content, saving time for students.
- Adding assignments consists of clicking on the desired due date, then filling in the details of the assignment—name of the assignment, instructions, and whether or not it is a one-time or repeating assignment.
- In addition, links to other activities can be created easily. If the activity is online, a URL can be entered in the space provided, and it will be linked automatically in the final syllabus.
- Your completed syllabus is hosted on our servers, allowing convenient updates from any computer on the Internet. Changes you make to your syllabus are immediately available to your students at their next log on.

Acknowledgments

I would like to thank the many people who made this project possible and who assisted in its preparation. I would especially like to acknowledge contributors Michelle Cicero and Cindy Morelli who both wrote wonderfully creative lessons, taught these lessons in their classrooms, and then wrote detailed lesson descriptions for inclusion in Chapters 3, 9, and 10.

I would also like to thank the administration, teaching faculty, staff, and students at West Point Elementary and Beaver Local Middle School for allowing me to observe and teach lessons and conduct numerous activities in grades 1 to 6 classrooms. This faculty-in-residence was made possible through the Tri-County Partnership for Excellence in Teacher Education Title II grant directed by Dr. Paul Gallagher.

A special thank you goes to the many students at Youngstown State University who provided valuable feedback and suggestions on a draft version of this textbook, and to the many family members, friends, and colleagues who provided invaluable support, ideas, and encouragement throughout the writing process.

Linda Montgomery (Editor C & I, Merrill Education/Prentice Hall), Hope Madden (Senior Development Editor, Merrill Education/Prentice Hall), and Emily Hatteberg (Production Editor, Carlisle Publishers Services) were all extremely helpful and patient, putting up with endless first-time author queries and concerns. They each had a large part in helping to shape this project.

I would also like to thank the following reviewers for their valuable comments and suggestions: Thomasenia Lott Adams, University of Florida; Linda Barron, Vanderbilt University; Patricia A. Brosnan, The Ohio State University; Mary Margaret Capraro, Texas A&M University; Yolanda De La Cruz, Arizona State University; William O. Lacefield, III, Mercer University; Chris Ohana, Western Washington University; Enrique Ortiz, University of Central Florida; Walter Ryan, Indiana University Southeast; Patrick Scott, New Mexico State University; Debra Shelt, Bowling Green State University; and Melvin Wilson, Virginia Tech.

Brief Contents

Contents

chapter 4

Understanding Place Value and Numeration Systems   70

chapter 5

Developing Concepts and Operations of Addition and Subtraction   92

chapter 6

Developing Concepts and Operations
of Multiplication and Division   126

chapter 7

Exploring Number Theory Concepts
and Operations   156

chapter 8

Developing Concepts and Operations
of Fractions and Decimals   178

chapter 9

Exploring Graphs, Data, Statistics, and Probability   214

chapter 10

Exploring Geometric Figures and Relationships   242

chapter 11

Developing Measurement Concepts and Operations 282

1

Teaching Early Childhood Mathematics: Influences and Methodology

Over the years, major changes have occurred in teaching methods in the field of elementary education, especially in the teaching of mathematics. National, state, and local standards have had a major impact on the curriculum. Today many mathematic concepts are introduced at an earlier age and in a different manner than when you were in elementary school. There may even be some topics covered in elementary school mathematics that you were never exposed to in your elementary school years.

You may need to teach differently from the way that you were taught. In today's classroom there is much less emphasis on drill and rote memorization and more emphasis on problem solving and conceptual understanding. Students are actively engaged in the learning process, and should be encouraged to estimate, to reason, and to explain their answers. Technology is an integral part of today's classroom. Most classrooms, even at the level of early childhood, come equipped with computers and are supplied with a variety of manipulatives.

This textbook provides the mathematical background that you will need to teach mathematics in an early childhood classroom. In some cases this will involve mathematics content beyond the material that you will be teaching. Content is presented conceptually, much in the same manner as it is presented in elementary classrooms, and is accompanied by classroom-tested activities and exercises. To refresh your own knowledge of the mathematics content, you should complete the exercises and work out examples as directed. If you suffer from "math anxiety," you will benefit from the conceptual approach used in this textbook; if you learn mathematics concepts with understanding, you will no longer need to fear them. Because a teacher must be comfortable and confident with content and familiar with instructional practices and techniques, this text will focus on both areas.

Objectives

After completing Chapter 1, you will be able to

- Discuss influences of the NCTM Principles and Standards on the practice of teaching mathematics in an early childhood classroom
- Describe the main principles of constructivism and conceptually based mathematics
- List and describe three levels of representation of knowledge
- List and describe three types of learning experiences
- Describe several considerations in planning or constructing an appropriate activity or learning experience
- Discuss considerations in the creation of an active classroom

1.1 A Brief History of Mathematics Education and the NCTM Standards

One of the defining events in the history of mathematics education was the launching of *Sputnik 1* by the Soviet Union in 1957. This marked the start of the space age and the space race between the United States and the Soviet Union. Concern that the United States was falling behind in the areas of math and science triggered major national reforms in these areas. These reforms brought about the "New Math" of the 1960s and 1970s. The emphasis of this New Math was on set language and properties, proof, and abstraction. However, the New Math curriculum failed to meet the challenge of increasing the nation's mathematical prowess as a whole. Some would even say that the New Math created more math confusion than it eliminated, which brought about the trend of Back to Basics in the late 1970s and early 1980s. Back to Basics emphasized arithmetic computation and rote memorization of algorithms and basic arithmetic facts.

Standards

NCTM

The K–4 curriculum should

- Be conceptually oriented
- Actively involve children in doing mathematics
- Emphasize the development of children's mathematical thinking and reasoning abilities
- Emphasize the application of mathematics
- Include a broad range of content
- Make appropriate and ongoing use of calculators and computers

NCTM, 1989, pp. 17–19

Standards are listed with the permission of the National Council of Teachers of Mathematics (NCTM). NCTM does not endorse the content or validity of these alignments.

Standards

NCTM

All students should

1. Learn to value mathematics
2. Become confident in the ability to do mathematics
3. Become mathematical problem solvers
4. Learn to communicate mathematically
5. Learn to reason mathematically

NCTM, 1989, p. 5

Standards are listed with the permission of the National Council of Teachers of Mathematics (NCTM). NCTM does not endorse the content or validity of these alignments.

The 1989 NCTM Standards

In the later 1980s the focus shifted to critical thinking. In 1989 the National Council of Teachers of Mathematics (NCTM) released a groundbreaking document, *Curriculum and Evaluation Standards for School Mathematics*. This publication, sometimes referred to as the "NCTM Standards," stresses problem solving, communication, connections, and reasoning. The key assumptions underlying the 1989 NCTM curriculum standards for Grades K–4, listed below, are addressed throughout this textbook.

A link to the 1989 standards and assumptions for Grades K–4 can be found at the textbook companion Web site.

The 1989 NCTM Standards include 13 curriculum standards addressing both content and emphasis. One theme common to the NCTM Standards and to the recent changes in mathematics education is that "the study of mathematics should emphasize reasoning so that students can believe that mathematics makes sense" (NCTM, 1989, p. 29). Although not discussed here, this document also includes similar sets of assumptions and standards for Grades 5 through 8 and for Grades 9 through 12.

The 1989 NCTM Standards list five goals for students. Although these are goals stated for elementary students, it is especially important that teachers of elementary students have attained them.

Professional and Assessment Standards for Teaching Mathematics

A second groundbreaking document released by the National Council of Teachers of Mathematics was *Professional Standards for Teaching Mathematics*. This set of standards "present[s] a vision of what teaching should entail to support the changes in curriculum set out in the Curriculum and Evaluation Standards. This document spells out what teachers need to know to teach toward new goals for mathematics education and how teaching should be evaluated for the purpose of improvement" (NCTM, 1991, p. vii). NCTM followed with the 1995 release of *Assessment Standards for Teaching Mathematics*. NCTM produced this important document because "new assessment strategies and practices need to be developed that will enable teachers and others to assess students' performance in a manner that reflects the NCTM's reform vision for school mathematics" (NCTM, 1995, p. 1). These assessment standards include criteria for judging the quality of mathematics assessment as listed in the box below.

In the 1990s the major focus of reform in mathematics education was directed toward teaching pedagogy. Numerous studies and articles promoted the use of manipulatives and technology in the classroom (Burns, 1996; Hatfield, 1994; National Association for the Education of Young Children [NAEYC], 1996; Roth, 1992). Key ideas of this era included the use of developmentally appropriate activities and the constructivist approach to teaching. The NCTM Standards continued to gain support and popularity among mathematics educators, and many states developed grade-level scope and sequences and competency-based model programs that reflected these standards. Proficiency testing became more widespread, with some states requiring a certain level of competency in subject areas such as mathematics for grade promotion.

Standards Update: The 2000 Principles and Standards for School Mathematics

In April 2000, the National Council of Teachers of Mathematics released its *Principles and Standards for School Mathematics.* This document updates the 1989 *Curriculum and Evaluation Standards* and includes some components of both *Professional Standards for Teaching Mathematics* and *Assessment Standards for Teaching Mathematics* as well.

With such far-reaching significant goals (see the standards box below), the 2000 *Principals and Standards* will certainly serve as a major influence in changes and trends in mathematics education and reform in the years to come. However, the focus of this document remains on curriculum, and so *Professional Standards for Teaching Mathematics* and *Assessment Standards for Teaching Mathematics* will both also continue to play major roles in math education and reform.

The 2000 *Principles and Standards* identifies six principles of high-quality mathematics education. (see the standards box on p. 6).

Content Standards
The 2000 *Principles and Standards* document describes in detail standards and expectations for grade levels Pre-K–2, 3–5, 6–8, and 9–12 for each of the five content strands:

- Number and Operations
- Algebra
- Geometry
- Measurement
- Data Analysis and Probability

Each of the content strands will be covered within the material of this textbook. Number and Operations is especially important in the early childhood curriculum, and will be covered mainly in Chapters 4–8. The Algebra strand includes patterns, relations, functions, and mathematical models. You may be surprised to see the various types of algebra that are included in today's early childhood curriculum. This strand will be covered in Chapters 2, 3, and 11. Geometry is covered in Chapter 10, Measurement in Chapter 11, and Data Analysis and Probability in Chapter 9.

Standards

NCTM

Assessment should:

1. Reflect the mathematics that all students need to know and be able to do
2. Enhance mathematics learning
3. Promote equity
4. Be an open process
5. Promote valid inferences about mathematics learning
6. Be a coherent process

NCTM, 1995, pp. 11–22

Standards are listed with the permission of the National Council of Teachers of Mathematics (NCTM). NCTM does not endorse the content or validity of these alignments.

Standards

NCTM

This document is intended to:

- Set forth a comprehensive and coherent set of goals for mathematics for all students from prekindergarten through Grade 12 that will orient curricular, teaching, and assessment efforts during the next decades
- Serve as a resource for teachers, education leaders, and policy makers to use in examining and improving the quality of mathematics instructional programs
- Guide the development of curriculum frameworks, assessments, and instructional materials
- Stimulate ideas and ongoing conversations at the national, provincial or state, and local levels about how best to help students gain a deep understanding of important mathematics

NCTM, 2000, p. 6

Standards are listed with the permission of the National Council of Teachers of Mathematics (NCTM). NCTM does not endorse the content or validity of these alignments.

Standards

NCTM

The six principles for school mathematics address overarching themes:

- *Equity.* Excellence in mathematics education requires equity—high expectations and strong support for all students.
- *Curriculum.* A curriculum is more than a collection of activities; it must be coherent, focused on important mathematics, and well articulated across the grades.
- *Teaching.* Effective mathematics teaching requires understanding what students know and need to learn and then challenging and supporting them to learn it well.
- *Learning.* Students must learn mathematics with understanding, actively building new knowledge from experience and prior knowledge.
- *Assessment.* Assessment should support the learning of important mathematics and furnish useful information to both teachers and students.
- *Technology.* Technology is essential in teaching and learning mathematics; it influences the mathematics that is taught and enhances students' learning.

NCTM, 2000, p. 11

Standards are listed with the permission of the National Council of Teachers of Mathematics (NCTM). NCTM does not endorse the content or validity of these alignments.

A link to the 2000 standards and expectations is provided at the companion Web site for this textbook.

Process Standards Process standards differ from content standards in that the process standards are not subject matter that can be learned but are the methods by which content knowledge can be acquired. The 2000 *Principles and Standards* document describes in detail the five process standards:

- Problem Solving
- Reasoning and Proof
- Communication
- Connections
- Representation

Although the title of Chapter 2 of this text contains the phrase "problem solving," problem solving is the heart of any solid mathematics curriculum and each chapter of this text will include some degree of problem solving. Reasoning is also stressed throughout this text. Students who are exposed to the logic behind mathematical procedures are more likely to be able to learn and correctly apply those procedures than students who attempt to apply rules without regard to their reasonableness (Carpenter, Franke, Jacobs, Fenemma, & Empson, 1998; Hiebert & Wearne, 1996; NCTM, 2003).

Communication is especially important for assessment. Students must learn to explain, write, draw, or otherwise show what they have learned. A variety of nonverbal forms of communication must be used in the early child-

hood classroom. Teachers must often devise alternate means of assessment and communication when dealing with students with disabilities or students who have limited-English abilities.

Connections refers to connections among mathematics topics as well as connections to other subject areas and to real-life situations. By stressing connections, one can show the relevance and importance of mathematics. Students must also be able to make connections among mathematical representations (Coxford, 1995).

There are often a variety of representations for a single mathematical concept. For example, to represent the amount twenty-five cents, one can use a word phrase such as "twenty-five cents" or "a quarter," use actual coins (or representations of coins) to show the amount in a variety of ways (one quarter, two dimes and a nickel, etc.), draw a pictorial representation, or use a symbolic expression such as 25¢ or $0.25. By learning several representations for a single concept, teachers can adapt their teaching methods to the needs and abilities of their students. Students should learn a variety of representations to best express and use their mathematical knowledge.

The Influence of Recent Legislation

The need for reform in mathematics education has not gone unnoticed by U.S. legislation. In 1994 Congress enacted into law the *Goals 2000 Educate America Act.* On January 8, 2002, President Bush signed into law the *No Child Left Behind Act* of 2001. These laws mandate that all states implement accountability systems and that teachers and schools are held accountable for the education of *all* students. The Goals 2000 Educate America Act includes the following terms and definitions:

(1) The terms "all students" and "all children" mean students or children from a broad range of backgrounds and circumstances, including disadvantaged students and children, students or children with diverse racial, ethnic, and cultural backgrounds, American Indians, Alaska Natives, Native Hawaiians, students or children with disabilities, students or children with limited-English proficiency, school-aged students or children who have dropped out of school, migratory students or children, and academically talented students and children;

(4) The term "content standards" means broad descriptions of the knowledge and skills students should acquire in a particular subject area;

Standards

NCTM

Number and Operations

Standard: Compute fluently and make reasonable estimates.

Expectation: In prekindergarten through grade 2 all students should use a variety of methods and tools to compute, including objects, mental computation, estimation, paper and pencil, and calculators.

NCTM, 2000, 78

Standards are listed with the permission of the National Council of Teachers of Mathematics (NCTM). NCTM does not endorse the content or validity of these alignments.

Standards

Scope and Sequence Document of West Point Elementary

Grade 2 First grading period:
V.15 Check problems by using a calculator.

Grade 2 Second grading period:
V.15 Symbolize a keying sequence on a calculator by adding 2 place numbers.

Grade 2 Fourth grading period:
V.15 Use a calculator to add and subtract 3 place numbers and predict the display.

Grade 3 Third grading period:
V.15 Symbolize a keying sequence on the calculator by adding, subtracting, multiplying, or dividing and predicting the display.

West Point Elementary Scope and Sequence, 2002

(9) The term "performance standards" means concrete examples and explicit definitions of what students have to know and be able to do to demonstrate that such students are proficient in the skills and knowledge framed by content standards;

(11) The term "State assessment" means measures of student performance which include at least one instrument of evaluation, and may include other measures of student performance, for a specific purpose and use which are intended to evaluate the progress of all students in the State toward learning the material in State content standards in one or more subject areas

Goals 2000 Educate America Act, 1994

In compliance with these laws, nearly every state in the United States has developed its own set of content standards, performance standards, and assessment measures. At the time of this printing, the Eisenhower National Clearinghouse Web site provides links to the state frameworks for mathematics and science education for 49 of the 50 states. Many of these frameworks include

A link to the Eisenhower National Clearinghouse Web site is provided at the companion Web site for this textbook.

content standards that reflect the NCTM goals and standards. Some representative examples of objectives from state models or frameworks are provided within this text. You may wish to download or purchase the appropriate document for your state.

State and Local Standards

Many school districts have developed their own sets of standards and assessment measures. Such documents are generally based on the appropriate state model or framework or on the national standards set by the NCTM. Local district standards may break one national or state objective into several smaller objectives or specific tasks and may specify which objectives or tasks are to be covered during each grading period of the school year. Compare the Number and Operations NCTM standard versus the standard developed by West Point Elementary.

The tasks described by the West Point Elementary Scope and Sequence Document address the national standard expectation components of mental computation, estimation, and calculators. Other components of this expectation are addressed within other objectives (not reprinted here) from the West Point Scope and Sequence Document. Notice the progression of the difficulty level of the tasks throughout one year and into the next. This is typical of the teaching methods of today. A topic is not introduced, taught once, and then forgotten until the following year. Important instructional objectives are revisited and reinforced throughout the school year as necessary. Research indicates that an incremental approach, where concepts and skills build on prior concepts, skills, and knowledge, is highly effective in student retention of material (Klingele & Reed, 1984). This idea will be revisited in later sections of this textbook.

Problem Set 1.1

1. Consider the five goals for students given by the 1989 Standards. For each goal, make a list of two or three things that you, the teacher, can do to ensure that your students attain that goal.

2. Choose one of the five content strands given by the 2000 Standards. Compare the standards and expectations given for that strand for the Pre-K–2

and 3–5 grade levels to the corresponding curriculum standards for the same content strand for the K–4 grade level given by the 1989 Standards. Write a paragraph comparing and contrasting the 1989 standards to the 2000 standards for the content strand that you have chosen.

3. Choose one of the process standards: Problem Solving, Reasoning and Proof, Communication, Connections, or Representation. Write a paragraph comparing and contrasting the 1989 standards to the 2000 standards for the process standard that you have chosen.

4. Choose one of the five content strands given by the 2000 Standards. Select either the grade levels Pre-K–2 or 3–5. Obtain either a state model or a district scope and sequence document that describes the curriculum taught in local schools in your area. Write a paragraph that compares and contrasts the standards and expectations for the selected grade levels given by the 2000 Standards to those used in your local school district.

5. Choose one of the six principles for school mathematics given by the 2000 Standards. Research that principle and write a paragraph that summarizes what you have learned about it.

1.2 How Children Learn Mathematics

Suppose you were told that you must learn the "fact" $\Omega^{TM}\partial\_\Delta$. How would you learn it? You would probably need to repeat the sequence to yourself several times before you would be able to reproduce it without looking at it. Are all of the symbols used familiar to you? If not, you might make connections between unfamiliar symbols and objects that are familiar to you, perhaps calling Ω "horseshoe" or calling ∂ "backward six." Without some logic or meaning to the sequence of symbols, it would be difficult to commit this sequence to memory for more than a short period.

Constructivism and Conceptually Based Mathematics

Constructivism is a view of learning influenced by the works of Brownell, Piaget, Vygotsky, Dienes, and Bruner that asserts that children build or construct their own knowledge by integrating new concepts and procedures into existing mental structures. Children must create or recreate mathematical relationships in their own minds. For example, before a child learns the value of various U.S. coins, the child may believe that a nickel is more valuable than a dime because of the relative sizes of the coins. Once the child has assimilated the idea of coin value and has learned that a nickel is worth five cents while a dime is worth ten cents, the child will agree that a dime has more value than a nickel.

To process information, one must interpret it in relation to what is already known or believed. Children should be active in the learning experience in order to fully internalize the experience. Teachers who use the constructivist method of teaching encourage discovery learning and active experimentation by their students. With constructivism the emphasis is not on teaching, but on learning. Even very young children are capable of constructing mathematics concepts and algorithms (Cobb, 1994; Kamii & Ewing, 1996).

Procedural Learning and Conceptual Learning Various mathematics educators have compared two types of learning: procedural learning and conceptual learning (Hiebert & Lindquist, 1990; Skemp, 1971). Procedural learning involves learning processes or algorithms by rote. You may have learned how to divide one fraction by another by learning a rule like, invert the divisor and multiply. Section 8.4 in Chapter 8 shows several common student errors involving fractions and decimals, including errors that occur due to the incorrect application of the rule given above. Conceptual learning involves understanding the concepts and meanings underlying the operations as opposed to merely applying rules. The main tenet of conceptually based mathematics is that when students understand the concepts and reasoning underlying a process, they are more likely to be able to correctly apply that process. They are also more likely to be able to apply that process in learning related new skills and procedures. Let's use the example $3 \times 5 = 15$ to illustrate these ideas.

Three Levels of Representation of Knowledge

You probably do not recall learning that three times five is fifteen. This is a fact that you learned at approximately the second- or third-grade level. Yet you are able to retain this fact in your memory. Why? For one thing, this fact has been used hundreds, maybe thousands of times in your everyday life. Also, the symbols used in the representation of this fact ($3 \times 5 = 15$) are familiar to you. Most important, the fact makes sense. If you were to combine 3 piles of 5 blocks each, you would have a pile of 15 blocks—which explicitly shows that three times five is fifteen.

In learning this particular fact, you probably did not begin with the symbolic representation $3 \times 5 = 15$. You may have begun with a concrete representation such as the 3 piles of 5 blocks. Many elementary textbooks introduce addition or multiplication facts pictorially. For this particular example an elementary textbook might show a picture of 3 rows with 5 blocks in each row, and ask "How many blocks in all?" Skip counting can be used to see that in the 3 sets of 5 blocks there are 5, 10, 15 blocks in all. The fact $3 \times 5 = 15$ makes sense. Research indicates that, as this example illustrates, human beings tend to represent knowledge in basically three ways (Bruner, 1964; Piaget, 1952).

1. *Concrete:* The key component of the concrete level of representation is the performance of an action on an object or objects. At the concrete level, students use hands-on manipulatives to physically arrive at the solution. Consider the following problem: "My three dogs each have five fleas. How many fleas do they have all together?" A student at the kindergarten or first-grade level might solve this problem by first setting out three paper plates or three pages of paper to represent three dogs. They could then distribute five counters or "fleas" to each "dog" to solve the problem.

The solution described above would be possible only in a classroom where hands-on experimentation was encouraged. The idea of using plates or papers to represent dogs and counters to represent fleas shows great imagination and creativity on the part of the student. In Section 1.4 we explore how to create an atmosphere of openness and experimentation where students are comfortable using ordinary objects found in the classroom and other manipulatives to represent objects not in the room. Throughout this textbook you will find that as a new concept is introduced, it is often introduced through concrete activities that will help the student develop meaning for the concept.

2. *Pictorial:* At the pictorial level of representation the child no longer needs to physically manipulate objects to solve problems such as the one given above. The student may solve such a problem by drawing a picture of three dogs and drawing five fleas on each dog. In some elementary textbooks, several pictures are already drawn and the student is asked to choose the picture that matches a given problem situation. Often in a disposable textbook, part of a picture is drawn and the student is instructed to complete the drawing and use it to solve the given problem. The student may also solve the problem mentally by visualizing three sets of five and counting.

3. *Symbolic:* At the symbolic level of representation the student has acquired enough experience with the given problem type to represent it symbolically without using concrete operations or pictures or images. For the dog and flea problem discussed above, the student would merely write or state that $3 \times 5 = 15$.

When encountering a new problem type, students will need experiences at the concrete and pictorial levels before they are introduced to the symbolic representation of the problem. The concrete and pictorial experiences let the student acquire meaning for the concepts and operations involved in the problem. Many activities use a combination of the three levels of representation described. Students often use pictures as concrete objects, combining the levels concrete and pictorial. The pictorial level is combined with the symbolic or abstract level when students use pictures to arrive at an answer and then write or state a corresponding equation. Other combinations are also possible and will be encountered within our discussions of activities throughout this text.

Three Types of Learning Experiences

The type of learning experience or activity that you choose to use will depend on the objective of the activity or experience. We will focus on three types of learning experiences.

1. *Developmental:* Developmental activities are used to develop new ideas and introduce new concepts. Developmental activities should be conceptually based; the students should be able to acquire meaning for the concepts and operations that they are learning. These activities should be designed and presented in a way that will make the math understandable to the students.

2. *Reinforcement:* These activities are used to reinforce previously introduced skills and concepts. You may use developmental activities or modified developmental activities as reinforcement activities. You may also find or develop new activities to use as reinforcement activities.

3. *Drill and practice:* Drill and practice activities are used to practice or memorize previously learned skills, procedures, and concepts. When many people hear the phrase "drill and practice," they immediately think "flash cards." Although you may use flash cards in drill and practice activities, these are not your only option. These activities should not be boring. Pick activities that will engage the students. You can use contests, challenges, games, problems where the solution provides the answer to a riddle, and many other fun activities.

The type of learning experience or activity that you choose to use at a

---

Standards

NCTM

Algebra: Pre-K–2

Standard: Represent and analyze mathematical situations and structures using algebraic symbols.
Expectation: In prekindergarten through Grade 2 all students should use concrete, pictorial, and verbal representations to develop an understanding of invented and conventional symbolic notations.

NCTM, 2000, p. 90

Standards are listed with the permission of the National Council of Teachers of Mathematics (NCTM). NCTM does not endorse the content or validity of these alignments.

particular time will depend on your objectives at that time. Some activities fit more than one category. To classify an activity, consider your main objective or intent. An activity that is intended to introduce concept A is a developmental activity even if it reinforces concept B and contains practice in skill C. For example, suppose you wish to introduce the idea of calculating the value of a pile of coins containing two different types of coins. This developmental activity reinforces the value of a single coin and contains practice in the skill of skip counting.

In many cases, you will find appropriate activities to accomplish your objectives within the teacher's manual of your textbook series, in activity manuals that you have available, or in an activity file that you have created. In some cases you will need to modify a given activity so that it better suits your purposes. You may even create activities or learning experiences of your own to serve a certain purpose.

Teaching Connections

Designing a Learning Experience There are several things that should be considered when selecting or designing an activity or learning experience. Successful teaching involves extensive planning. In Section 1.3 we take a closer look at creating activities that are developmentally appropriate and conceptually based. We close this section with a list of some general considerations in selecting and presenting an activity or learning experience.

1. ***Decide upon a topic and select appropriate objectives for the lesson.*** It is not enough to know what topic you are teaching; you must also select explicit objectives within that topic. For example, suppose you wish to teach about bar graphs. An activity designed to achieve the objective "The student will be able to read and interpret bar graphs" will differ from an activity designed to achieve the objective "The student will be able to create a bar graph."

In choosing objectives, you may use guidelines set by your state model, your school district, other teachers, your own experiences, national organizations like the NCTM, or many other sources. You may be able to address more than one objective within a single lesson or activity, but do not attempt too many things at once. Children need time to assimilate new ideas and understandings (for example, see Piaget, 1952; Stigler & Hiebert, 1997; Suydam & Higgins, 1977).

2. ***Consider your students.*** Make sure that your topic and objectives are grade-level appropriate and that your students have the required background knowledge and skills. Reflect on the social characteristics, social and economic background, and interests of your class so that you can present the material in a manner that will be meaningful and interesting. Try to predict what difficulties your students might have with the material, and consider how you will handle such difficulties.

3. ***Choose appropriate vocabulary.*** Define vocabulary terms in grade-appropriate language. Refer to your textbook series, your state model, other teachers of your grade level or building, and other suitable sources to determine which terms and notations you should use. You might be surprised to learn that precise, mathematical terms such as *sum* and *addend* appear in elementary textbooks as early as the first-grade level. Do not refer only to the textbook series that you use in your classroom to determine appropriate terminology. Some state proficiency exams for a given grade level of elementary school students may include terminology that is not found in many of the textbook series for that grade level.

4. ***Choose a fitting motivation.*** To facilitate the process of assimilation of new material, relate material to the lives of the students and to other material that they are learning or have learned. Many teaching programs stress the creation of thematic units that integrate the teaching of all subject areas into a single theme or topic. Choose interesting problem stories that students can relate to so that they can incorporate the new material and knowledge into their own frames of reference. Children's literature provides a rich source of appropriate motivational stories. Select conceptually based activities and problem stories for your lesson that will make sense to the students and that will help them to construct meaning for the new material.

5. ***Collect manipulatives and materials.*** Decide exactly what activities will occur, and how they will flow into the lesson. It may be helpful to make a written list of all of the items that you will need for a lesson. Place items in the classroom so that they are easily accessible but not distracting to the students.

6. ***Plan for assessment.*** Select key places in the lesson where you will be able to ask questions or otherwise assess whether the students are understanding and are reaching the objectives you wish them to reach. Make a written list of the questions or types of questions you will ask. If this information is written down, it is easy to make notes that will aid you in teaching the lesson in future classes. Make sure that you are asking questions beyond those that can be answered with a simple "Yes" or "No." Ask questions that have more than one correct answer and questions that will challenge the students to think about the material, make observations, and draw conclusions.

Be prepared to give the students ample wait time. If students do not respond to a question, rephrase if possible in simpler terms so that you are sure that the students understand what it is that you are asking. Do not answer your own questions! Students will usually not provide textbook-perfect answers and comments. Let students answer in their own terms. Ask them to clarify their thoughts if necessary or ask other students for additional input, but avoid repeating what is said by a student. If some students indicate that they did not hear a comment, ask the student who made the comment to repeat it. If a student remark is incomplete or in need of correction, enlist the aid of the class to complete or correct the remark. You will want your students to acquire the habit of listening carefully to one another and to not always wait for you the teacher to be the final word and authority.

As well as the ongoing assessment described above, you may also wish to plan for some type of summative evaluation. Although this may include written handouts, quizzes, or tests, there are many other forms of assessment that will be described in Chapter 2 and throughout this textbook. Assessment tools may need to be appropriately modified for students with special needs.

7. *Observe students during the lesson.* Diagnose student progress. Were the students able to achieve all of the objectives of the lesson? What difficulties, if any, did they have that you had not planned for? Note any changes that need to be made in the lesson, and whether you have included enough assessment and appropriate assessment techniques within the lesson. Begin to plan follow-up or reinforcement activities.

The Value of Conceptually Based Activities

In the next section we consider the construction of developmentally appropriate and conceptually based activities. To illustrate the value of activities that are conceptually based, consider the following experiment: Without referring back to it, try to write down the "fact" that was given at the beginning of this section. After you have written something down, check to see whether you remembered it correctly. When this fact is given to a class of college students at the beginning of a 50-minute lecture on "How children learn mathematics," only about 13% of the students recall the fact correctly at the end of the lecture. The reason that so few students are able to recall this fact is that no basis or meaning for the fact was presented.

When students attempt to memorize concepts or procedures without being presented any logical basis or meaning, they are apt to make mistakes. Many of the students who were successful in remembering this sequence indicate that they did so by assigning some sort of meaning to the symbols. Some students use a pneumonic or other memory device to relate the sequence to a familiar experience or frame of reference, to incorporate it into their existing mental schema. If your teaching approach is conceptually based, your students will acquire meaning for the concepts behind the procedures and skills that you are teaching. Math that "makes sense" is more likely to be remembered, or if necessary recreated, than a random sequence of symbols and steps.

Problem Set 1.2

1. Using a subtraction fact example, describe how the fact could be represented at each of the three levels of representation.

2. Find three different examples or activities, one for each level of representation of knowledge, in an elementary school textbook. Photocopy or copy by hand the three examples and for each indicate which level of representation of knowledge it uses. Indicate the grade level of the textbook that you are using.

3. Find three different activities, one for each level of representation of knowledge, in this textbook. For each activity that you list, indicate which level of representation of knowledge it uses.

4. Find and print three different activities, one for each level of representation of knowledge, from a Web site containing classroom activities. For each activity indicate which level of representation of knowledge it uses.

5. Find three different examples or activities, one for each type of learning experience, in an elementary school textbook. Photocopy or copy by hand the three examples, and indicate for each how it could be used as the type of learning experience you have listed. Indicate the grade level of the textbook that you are using.

6. Look through the activities presented in Chapters 2 through 11 of this textbook. Select three different activities, one for each type of learning experience. For each activity that you list, indicate how it could be used as the type of learning experience you have listed.

7. Look through the activities presented on any Web site containing classroom activities. Select and print three different activities, one for each type of learning experience. For each activity that you list, indicate how it could be used as the type of learning experience you have listed.

1.3 CONSTRUCTING APPROPRIATE ACTIVITIES

In this section, money is used as the primary example for considering the construction of student activities. As mentioned in the previous section, you will find many suitable activities within the teacher's manual of your textbook series or in activity manuals that you have available. In some cases you will need to modify a given activity so that it better suits your purposes. You may also wish to create a file of additional activities to supplement those found in the traditional sources.

Preparing to Teach a Lesson About Money

Suppose that you are teaching a first-grade class, and presenting a unit for which it is natural to include money activities.

After looking at your state model and your teacher's manual, you decide to address the objective: The student will be able to count piles of money involving two types of coins. Children will need many experiences counting piles of coins involving two types of coins before they are ready to count piles involving three types of coins. In most textbook series and state models and frameworks there is a natural progression in the difficulty level and types of problems introduced.

You now have decided on the topic and selected an objective. Next, consider your students. Do they have the required background knowledge and skills? Background knowledge would include recognition of the coins involved and their values. This is something that you may wish to review, even if you think your students already know it. One important background skill is skip counting. Skip counting occurs when students count by twos, fives, tens, or some other value. If your students are not proficient in skip counting, they are not ready to count change.

Assume that you recently completed teaching a unit that involved drills in skip counting, and you are confident that your students are proficient in this skill. One potential difficulty in counting change is that you must begin skip counting by one quantity and then count by another quantity. For example, to count a pile involving nickels and pennies, you first count by fives and then you count by ones. This transition can be very difficult for some children. If all of the previous skip counting practice exercises began the counting at zero, your students are not ready to count change.

Assume that your students are proficient at skip counting even when the count does not begin at zero. You are now ready to choose vocabulary and notations. Use your textbook series, your state or district curriculum model, or other sources to determine appropriate terms and notations. If this is your students' first experience in counting piles of change that include two different coins, you will want to make sure that all of the amounts are less than one dollar and that you use cent sym-

Many first-grade-level curriculums will include only money activities with amounts that are less than one dollar. Most first-grade-level textbooks introduce the cent symbol notation only and do not present dollar symbol notation.

bol notation. Be careful with your notation. The quantity twenty-five cents should be written as 25¢ and not as .25¢.

It is relatively easy to select a fitting motivation for a money activity. Money is a part of the everyday lives of each of your students. Elementary students are usually eager to learn about money as they can see how this knowledge will be important to them in their own lives. There are several good children's books that include money concepts. See the children's literature references at the end of this chapter for some examples.

It is now time to plan specific activities and teaching strategies for the lesson. When counting a pile of change that includes two different types of coins, it is usually easier to begin by counting the coins of larger value. Will you tell this to your students, or let them discover this fact on their own? You might imagine a teacher-directed scenario such as the following:

Example Activity: Counting Money

Materials: Overhead projector, overhead coins (dimes, nickels, pennies), hundreds chart.

Each student (or each group) will need about six each of dimes, nickels, and pennies.

Teacher-Directed Example 1: Place four dimes and six pennies on the overhead projector.

Review the coins and their values and the counting of these coins using just the pile of pennies and then just the pile of dimes.

"Now we'll count all of the money on the overhead together."

Push the pile of dimes and pennies together.

"First we'll start with the dimes. How much is a dime worth? Right, ten cents."

Let the students count with you 10, 20, 30, 40, and slowly slide each dime as it is counted to another pile.

"How much money have we already counted? Right, forty cents. How much money is in this pile if I slide one penny here (to the pile of dimes)? Good, forty-one cents."

Let the students count with you as you slide each penny 42, 43, 44, 45, 46.

"We have forty-six cents."

Write 46¢ on the overhead.

"Do you think we would have the same amount of money if we started by counting the pennies first? Why do you think so?" Accept several responses.

Push the money back up to the top.

Let the students count with you—pennies first, then dimes. You may need to use a hundreds chart to illustrate 6 plus 10 when you transition from counting pennies to counting dimes.

Standards

Nevada Mathematics Content Standard

Measurement

Kindergarten: 3.K.4 Identify and sort pennies, nickels, and dimes.
Grade 1: 3.1.4 Determine the value of any set of pennies, nickels, and dimes.
Grade 2: 3.2.4 Determine the value of any given set of coins and bills.

Nevada Mathematics Content Standards, 2001

Using Literature in the Mathematics Classroom

Benny's Pennies

By Pat Brisson
Bantam Doubleday Dell, 1993

In this story, Benny begins with five new pennies. His mother, brother, sister, dog, and cat all give him suggestions for the type of items he should buy with his pennies. Benny spends his pennies buying five items for one penny each from neighbors and friends. He ends up with items exactly described by the suggestions, and gives each item to the person or pet that made the suggestion.

Classroom Activities:

1. As each penny is spent, children should explain how many pennies Benny has left to spend.
2. The teacher could make up related story problems for the children to solve.
3. The children could make up related story problems for the class to solve.

When finished, let the students comment that the amount was the same. Ask students which they thought was easier to find the overall amount, counting pennies first or dimes. You may wish to do an example that counts pennies and dimes without counting all of one set before counting the other. Ask students to explain why you skip counted by tens when counting dimes and counted by ones when counting pennies.

Repeat the process using the following example.

Teacher-Directed Example 2: Use six dimes and three nickels. Ask students to explain the skip counting process involved. Why did you skip count by tens and then by fives when first counting dimes and then counting nickels? Discuss starting the counting with the coin of largest value.

Teacher-Directed Example 3: "Can we make a pile of coins that is worth thirty-four cents? What coins should we use? How many of each coin? Yes, three dimes and four pennies does make thirty-four cents. Does anybody have another way?" Accept several answers. Let the students explain why their answers are correct.

Let students try some examples on their own or in groups.

Student examples:

Example 1: Four dimes and four nickels. How much?

Example 2: Five nickels and two pennies. How much?

Example 3: Three dimes, four nickels, and two pennies. How much? (This is for students who are proficient at counting piles of change involving two types of coins.)

Example 4: Make a pile worth forty-six cents. (Use smaller amounts if necessary.)

Check student work. Have students discuss answers and which type of coin that they began counting with. Then let students present different answers for Student Example 4.

Teaching Connections

Include Details in Your Lesson Plans Several comments about the envisioned scenario are in order. The scenario described above contains much more detail than would ordinarily be found in a teacher's manual or activity guide. When you first begin planning activities and lessons, you may wish to include such details. If you are reading this textbook as part of a preservice teacher education course, your instructor may have a specific lesson plan format that he or she wishes you to follow as you prepare lessons. It would not be too difficult to create a formal lesson plan based on the activity above. A formal lesson plan format is included in the Appendices.

From the pace and details included in the example, you may assume that this is intended as a developmental activity. The same activity could be used as a reinforcement activity if the students had already been introduced to the concept of counting piles of coins involving more than one type of coin. Notice the pause in the first teacher-directed example between counting the dimes and the beginning of counting the pennies. This is so that students have time to become aware of and register the thought that they should now be counting by a different value. Note that the original answer of 46¢ is written on the overhead so that it can be compared to the answer obtained when pennies were counted first. This writing of the answer is important. Otherwise, students may forget the original answer by the time the other part of the example is completed.

Notice that the teacher accepts several responses for open-ended questions and lets students explain their answers. Remember that student explanations will not always be perfect. If a student responds to the question "Which coin did you begin counting with?" by saying "The bigger one," you must get that student or others to clarify that "the bigger one" is the coin with the larger value. Otherwise, students may think that "the bigger one" refers to the size of the coin. One difficulty that children often have when learning about money is that the sizes of the coins do not accurately reflect their values. A dime is worth two nickels, yet a dime is smaller than a nickel.

In the example activity above, specific quantities of materials and specific examples are given. Often these details are omitted in teacher's manuals and activity guides. When using activities from these sources, you must often make these decisions yourself. As noted in the previous section, this information should be written in your plans. This lets you review the information following the lesson to make modifications as necessary. It is especially important to consider assessment before you teach a lesson. How will you determine whether students have achieved the objective? What types of questions will you ask? How will you modify the activity or assessment for students with special needs? In the above activity, students are asked to create piles of money that have a certain value as well as to count the value of a given pile of money. This variety of tasks is common in today's early childhood textbooks and materials. Many of the subsequent chapters will stress the idea of "the inverse problem." In a more condensed format, this activity might appear as shown in Activity 1-1.

Classifying the Type of Learning Experience of a Given Activity

Activity 1-1 could be used either as a developmental activity or as a reinforcement activity depending on the time allotted, number of examples given, amount of details provided, and other such factors. In a drill and practice activity, there is less emphasis on the meaning behind the computations. Activities 1-2 and 1-3 are drill and practice activities that give students practice in counting money.

In Activity 1-2 students create piles of money to match a given amount, and in Activity 1-3 students count a pictured amount. If desired, you could modify these activities to practice other skills or achieve other objectives. You must ensure that each student has a sufficient amount of play money avail-

able for Activity 1-2. Activity 1-3 requires mental math and speed in computation. It is labeled here as appropriate for Grades 1 to 4. The difficulty level of the deck of cards for each grade level should reflect the curriculum taught at that level.

Developmental or reinforcement activities such as Activity 1-1 should be conceptually based—students should be able to understand the underlying concepts and understand why each step makes sense, rather than merely performing the procedure. To count a pile of change involving two types of coins, you must skip count by two different values: the values of the coins. Students need to understand this relationship if they are to be successful in counting change involving two types of coins.

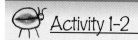

Activity 1-2   Grades 1–2

Money Bingo

Materials: Index cards with money amounts; Bingo cards with money amounts; play money for each student.

Example Bingo Card

23¢	31¢	17¢
30¢	12¢	9¢
25¢	13¢	28¢

Directions: The teacher draws a money amount card and writes the amount on the board or overhead. If this amount is on a student's Bingo card, he or she must cover that space with appropriate coins. A Bingo is three covered spaces in a row, vertically, horizontally, or diagonally. The student must have correctly covered the spaces with play money to win.

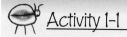

Activity 1-1   Grades K–1

Counting Change

Materials: Play money (six pennies, six nickels, and six dimes) for each student; overhead projector, money, and hundreds chart for teacher examples.

Directions:

a. Place four dimes and six pennies on the overhead projector. Review the coins, their values, and counting piles involving a single type of coin. Count the total—dimes first, then pennies. Count the total again—pennies first, then dimes.

b. Repeat the process using six dimes and three nickels.

c. Ask students to make a pile of coins worth thirty-four cents (accept various answers).

d. Discuss starting with the coin of the largest value.

Let students try examples on their own or in groups.

Activity 1-3   Grades 1–4

Five-Chair Money Counting

Materials: Index cards with money amounts pictured by a drawing of coins.

Setup: Line up five chairs. Five students sit in the chairs, five more students stand behind the chairs, and other students line up waiting to take their place behind a chair when one is available.

Directions: The teacher draws a money amount card and shows it to the student in a chair and the student behind that chair. The first of these two students to say the amount of money pictured sits in that chair, while the other student takes his or her place at the end of the line. Play continues down the row of chairs. Repeat for the entire stack of cards. The five students sitting in chairs at the end of play get a small reward.

Manipulatives often greatly increase students' understanding of math (Bruner, 1961; Dienes, 1960; Hiebert & Lindquest, 1990; Suydam & Higgins, 1977). Can you see how having money manipulatives on hand might facilitate students' learning of the process of counting change? We will further discuss the use of manipulatives in Section 1.4.

The NAEYC Definition of Developmentally Appropriate

All activities that you select or create for use in your classroom should be "developmentally appropriate" for your students. In a 1986 publication, the National Association for the Education of Young Children (NAEYC) described two dimensions of good practice: age appropriateness and individual appropriateness (1986, p. 2). Age appropriateness determines broad parameters based on the physical, emotional, and cognitive development of the age group involved. These parameters can help determine what is and is not appropriate for children of a certain age. For example, a three-year-old should not be expected to be able to count to 100. Individual appropriateness refers to the ability to connect the curriculum to the children's interests, background, and prior knowledge and experiences. This includes making sure that your students have acquired all the prerequisite skills and concepts before being introduced to a new skill or concept. It also includes making sure that the material is meaningful and significant to the students.

In the 1997 revised edition of this publication, the NAEYC expanded its description of developmentally appropriate practices (see the standards box on p. 16).

An increased awareness of social and cultural influences is also evident in many elementary textbook series and standardized test materials. Today these sources contain culturally diverse characters, examples, and problems not present in previous editions. Implicit in the vision presented in the Standards documents published by the National Council of Teachers of Mathematics is the premise that mathematics is for *all* students. Recent changes in textbook editions reflect progress toward achieving this vision.

Problem Set 1.3

1. Look up "money" in the index or table of contents of an elementary-level mathematics textbook. Photocopy or copy by hand an activity or problem involving money from within the textbook that you think is interesting or unusual and indicate why. Be sure to state the grade level of the textbook you are using. What objective from the NCTM model (or from your state or district model) does the activity or problem address?

2. Write a developmental activity that could be used to teach the value of a nickel and the value of a dime.

3. Write a detailed set of plans for a grocery store or shopping activity. Include a list of materials and appropriate vocabulary.

4. Write a grocery store or shopping activity using a condensed format such as Activities 1-1, 1-2, and 1-3.

5. Create a set of Bingo cards and teacher index cards that could be used with Activity 1-2.

6. Create a set of index cards that could be used with Activity 1-3.

7. Pick any math topic other than money and describe how to create a Bingo game to practice that topic. Show at least one example Bingo card and teacher index card. Indicate what objective from the NCTM model (or from your state or district model) the game addresses.

8. Pick any math topic other than money and describe how to create a five-chair game to practice that topic. Create a deck of cards for the game. Indicate what objective from the NCTM model (or from your state or district model) the game addresses.

9. Create a "Go Fish" game that practices a money concept. Indicate what objective from the NCTM model (or from your state or district model) the game addresses.

1.4 CREATING AN ACTIVE CLASSROOM

Today's classrooms may differ greatly from the elementary school classrooms that you remember. It is not unusual for a classroom to come equipped with computers and stocked with a variety of manipulatives. Research studies have shown that lessons using manipulatives are more likely to produce better mathematics achievement than lessons without manipulatives (Suydam & Higgins, 1977). Lessons with manipulatives can also increase student involvement and participation (Sowell, 1989). Some textbook series provide bags or buckets of student manipulatives so that *every* student has a set. Your school district will probably provide you with a budget so that you can order things you need that are not already provided. Many of the manipulatives and activity materials described in this textbook are easily made by hand. A good supply of manipulatives and classroom materials is essential to generate an active hands-on classroom atmosphere, but manipulatives alone do not teach mathematics.

Standards

NAEYC

Developmentally appropriate practices result from the process of professionals making decisions about the well-being and education of children based on at least three important kinds of information or knowledge:

1. *what is known about child development and learning*—knowledge of age-related human characteristics that permits general predictions within an age range about what activities, materials, interactions, or experiences will be safe, healthy, interesting, achievable, and also challenging to children;
2. *what is known about the strengths, interests, and needs of each individual child in the group*—to be able to adapt for and be responsive to inevitable individual variation; and
3. *knowledge of the social and cultural contexts in which children live*—to ensure that learning experiences are meaningful, relevant, and respectful for the participating children and their families.

NAEYC, 1997, p. 9

Using Manipulatives

There is a difference between using concrete materials to get an answer and using them to understand a process or problem. Children who use materials merely to get answers without reflecting on the process or meaning may become dependent on the manipulatives (Clements & McMillen, 1996; Thompson, 1994). The focus of the curriculum should be on understanding processes and answers and making math make sense, not on merely getting answers. Underlying concepts and processes must be fully understood before an attempt is made to transfer knowledge to a more symbolic form. Activities involving the pictorial level of representation can be helpful in this transition.

Students will need help in making the connections between manipulative activities and the mathematics they embody. Encouraging students to write about what they have done can help them formulate and formalize what they are learning (see Figure 1-1). Alexandra's work indicates that she understands that you may use the numerators to order fractions that have the same denominator. She correctly completes the challenge problem for which no fraction bars are available. This indicates that she understands the underlying concepts. A student's writings about a manipulative experience can also help you detect misunderstandings.

When introducing a manipulative for the first time it is a good idea to give students a few minutes to explore or play with the objects. A policy of "Don't touch them until I tell you exactly what to do" will stifle a child's natural curiosity about the manipulative. Such a "hands-off" policy discourages active student participation and experimentation. You will want students to learn to use the manipulative correctly, but they should also become comfortable enough with it that they will be able to use it with understanding and not just for imitating precisely the teacher's actions.

Suppose you are doing your first activity with base-ten blocks (described in Chapter 4). If no hands-off policy is declared, as the students receive their materials they will touch them, handle them, stack them, and so on. By the time the materials are distributed, and you have organized your own materials and notes for the activity, several of the students will have built elaborate towers with their materials. This should not be a problem. You want your students to become familiar with the objects. However, before you begin the lesson you may want to have the students knock over their towers. Otherwise, it is likely that one will fall as you are speaking. The traditional plastic or wooden sets of base ten blocks can be very noisy.

You may find several options when purchasing manipulatives. For example, base-ten blocks may be made of wood or plastic, or may be made of a foam material. Wooden or plastic sets are more durable than foam sets, whereas the foam sets are much quieter. Most manipulatives are available in overhead format. A teacher who wishes to use the overhead may wish to purchase manipulatives made specifically for the overhead. Overhead coins are particularly useful when the overhead is used in money lessons or activities. The face values of coins are not easily recognizable when actual coins are used on an overhead projector.

When certain amounts of a manipulative are necessary for each student, you may wish to prepackage the manipulatives for easier distribution. This will save time in the distribution and collection of materials. For example, in Activity 1-1 each student should have six pennies, six nickels, and six dimes. With student helpers passing out the materials, it would take a long time to count out these coins for each student in the class. Imagine how much faster it would be for the student helpers to pass out baggies that already contained six of each coin. Plastic zipper bags make an excellent container for individual student manipulatives. Prepackaging the materials also guarantees that you have enough manipulatives for each student. If you didn't prepackage, you might start distributing materials and then discover that you didn't have as many as you thought.

In using manipulatives, you the teacher need to be able to distinguish between what the children intend as their answer and extras that they may have lying on their desk. One solution is to give each child a paper plate to use as a manipulative mat (D. Pollack, personal communication, 1995). Students can be instructed to arrange the manipulatives that are part of their answer on the plate. Extra manipulatives should be left on the desk. A book or folder can be

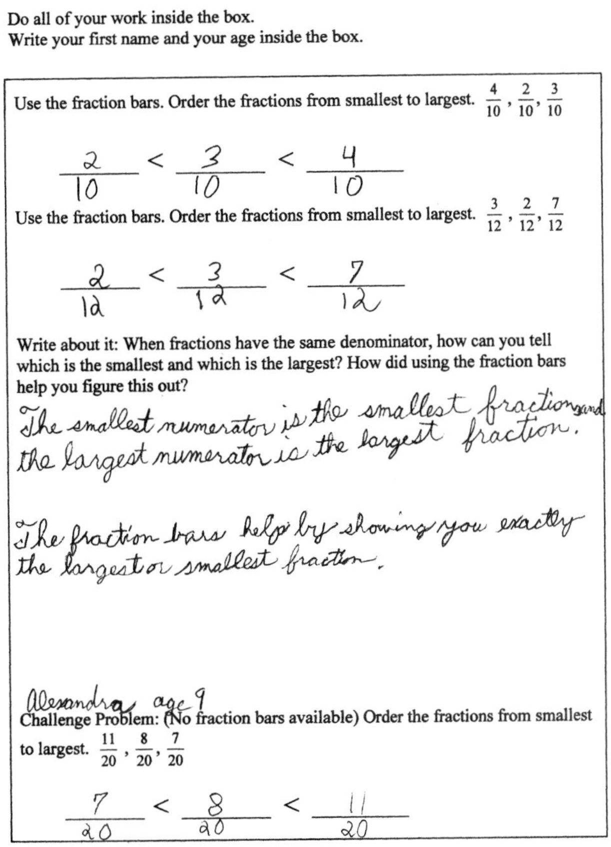

Do all of your work inside the box.
Write your first name and your age inside the box.

FIGURE 1-1 Writing about a manipulative experience.

Use the fraction bars. Order the fractions from smallest to largest. $\frac{4}{10}, \frac{2}{10}, \frac{3}{10}$

$$\frac{2}{10} < \frac{3}{10} < \frac{4}{10}$$

Use the fraction bars. Order the fractions from smallest to largest. $\frac{3}{12}, \frac{2}{12}, \frac{7}{12}$

$$\frac{2}{12} < \frac{3}{12} < \frac{7}{12}$$

Write about it: When fractions have the same denominator, how can you tell which is the smallest and which is the largest? How did using the fraction bars help you figure this out?

The smallest numerator is the smallest fraction and the largest numerator is the largest fraction.

The fraction bars help by showing you exactly the largest or smallest fraction.

Alexandra, age 9

Challenge Problem: (No fraction bars available) Order the fractions from smallest to largest. $\frac{11}{20}, \frac{8}{20}, \frac{7}{20}$

$$\frac{7}{20} < \frac{8}{20} < \frac{11}{20}$$

FIGURE 1-1 Writing about a manipulative experience.

---

used in place of a paper plate, but for ease of viewing it is best if the item used for the manipulative mat is a single color with no decorations. Paper plates are especially fitting for this purpose if the manipulative or the problem scenario involves food.

One final word of caution about using manipulatives: not all models will make sense to all children (Thompson, 1994). Remember that you as the teacher have already acquired the concept that you are teaching. If it is a concept that is new to your students, they may just see the manipulatives as the objects that they are, and not how they relate to the concept at hand. Communication is important. Have students explain what they are doing as they work with the manipulatives. Make sure that they understand the process and ideas and are not just repeating or imitating what you have done.

Write-On Boards

One idea that you may find useful in your classroom is for each student to have a small write-on wipe-off board or chalkboard. Students can hold up their boards with an answer to a problem. This allows you to easily check student work as well as to identify students who are having difficulty getting started on the problem. When write-on wipe-off boards are used, it is important that students al-

ways check that their marker is nonpermanent before beginning to write.

Writing in Mathematics

The idea of incorporating writing in mathematics simultaneously addresses both the Communication standard and the Connections standard set forth by the NCTM. Students may write to explain how they solved a problem, to explain why an answer makes sense, or to record the progress of an ongoing problem situation. Writing may be used to explain a solution or a concept, or may be reflective. Writing may be done in a journal or notebook or on loose paper. Many standardized exams and proficiency tests include problems for which a student must write to explain an answer or solution process.

You may wish to use writing prompts or stems to facilitate the writing process. Some examples of writing prompts include the following:

Reflective: What is your favorite number? Give reasons for your choice.
Explanatory: Explain your strategy in the Roll for $1.00 game.
Concept Assessment: What do you know about multiplication?

Some related writing stems are

My favorite number is ____. This is my favorite
    number because . . .
My strategy in the Race for $1.00 game was to . . .
Multiplication helps you solve the problem ____
    because . . .

Instruct students to write a word problem to fill in the blank.

Unless teachers at previous grade levels have encouraged writing in mathematics, your students may be unfamiliar with how to proceed and may need encouragement. Children at the prekindergarten to first-grade level can be encouraged to draw pictures to explain an answer or solution process. There are several excellent resources available that provide more details on incorporating writing into mathematics.

Children's Literature

Children's literature can be used to generate writing prompts and writing assignments. It is also a valuable resource for motivating or generating interest in a mathematical topic or lesson. Young children enjoy listening to stories. Many children's books explicitly contain math problems or questions. Other books may not explicitly contain mathematics problems, but may be easily incorporated into math lessons. Each chapter of this text will contain at least one literature connection activity and a brief list of some of the children's literature related to the topics of that chapter.

Collaborative Learning

Collaborative learning can be an effective tool in the process of shifting the focus from teacher as teller to students as active learners. Students will need practice and encouragement in the art of working together. Basic rules such as "A group may ask a question of the teacher only if all students in the group have the same question" and "Each member of the group must participate" must be established and enforced. One way to promote individual participation within a group is to let group members know that you may call on any one member of their group to explain the work of that group. If a group has a member that is quiet or not participating, other members of that group should ask that person to explain or rephrase what has thus far transpired within that group. All students should be held accountable for understanding what the group has accomplished.

Some teachers feel that it is best to group students by ability, whereas others prefer random group selections. You may want to vary groups for each activity, or you may wish to have the same groups working together for a period of time. Some activities work best with groups of three or four, whereas other activities are most successful when students are paired.

When using collaborative learning, it is a good idea to have an extension of the problem or task on hand for groups that finish early. There are several excellent teaching manuals and books listed in the references that can give you more direction in structuring and implementing collaborative learning activities.

 Teaching Connections

Generating an Active Hands-On, Minds-On Atmosphere
Each of the ideas and suggestions already discussed in this section can contribute toward generating an active hands-on, minds-on atmosphere in your classroom. You must create a safe environment where students are not afraid to ask questions and contribute to discussions. Let your students know that an incorrect answer is an opportunity for learning. When it is clear to the students that all ideas and thoughts related to a problem are valid contributions, they will be more willing to take the risk of being wrong. Students must realize that you do not expect every answer to be perfect.

For learning to take place, there must be an initial state of confusion. This confusion dissipates as children assimilate ideas and make sense of what they are studying. According to the constructivist view, this construction of knowledge is an integral part of the learning process. Students must be willing to think and to try new or untested ideas when presented with a new problem.

Attitudes and Values A teacher's attitudes and values can greatly affect students' attitudes and values. Again, here are the five goals for students as listed in the 1989 Standards (NCTM, 1989). All students should

1. Learn to value mathematics
2. Become confident in the ability to do mathematics
3. Become mathematical problem solvers
4. Learn to communicate mathematically
5. Learn to reason mathematically

For your students to attain these goals, it is imperative that you the teacher have attained these goals. The value of mathematics is apparent in its usefulness in everyday life and real-world applications. Look for these connections and help your students to recognize them. Success builds confidence. The purpose of a conceptually based, constructivist approach is to provide meaningful experiences relevant to the students involved. If mathematics is presented in a manner that makes sense to the students, they will be successful.

Math anxiety does exist, although it typically occurs with older children (Renga & Dalla, 1993). Primary students usually enjoy math and are eager to learn it. If you suffer from math anxiety you can benefit from the conceptually based, constructivist approach used in this textbook. If you learn mathematics concepts with understanding, you will no longer need to fear them. Caution parents about revealing negative attitudes toward mathematics. *Every* student can and should learn mathematics.

Learning to reason mathematically and learning to communicate mathematically are essential to becoming a mathematical problem solver. These three goals are a recurring theme throughout this textbook. To foster communicating mathematically, require students to explain their results either verbally or in written form. Do not ask for details or clarification only in the case of a wrong answer. Require students to verify or justify their own solutions. If students are to learn to use mathematics in the real world, they must not fall into the habit of depending on the teacher to verify results. It is well known that teacher expectations can influence student performance (Campbell & Langrall, 1993; Henningsen & Stein, 1997). Have high expectations both for your students and for yourself. Strive to make mathematics make sense for yourself as well as for your students.

Problem Set 1.4

1. Research the cost of play money. Visit teaching supply stores, local discount stores, or use mail-order catalogs or Internet resources. How much play money (list types and quantities) would you purchase for an average-size second- or third-grade classroom? What would your total cost be?

2. List possible advantages and disadvantages to using student write-on wipe-off boards versus using student chalkboards. Which of these would you prefer to use in your classroom? Explain your choice.

3. Read one of the articles listed as suggested reading at the end of this chapter. Write a paragraph that summarizes the main points of the article.

4. Choose one of the topics covered in this section. Do a search on the Internet using as keywords your chosen topic, "mathematics," and "early childhood." Write a paragraph that summarizes your findings.

References

Children's Literature References

Axelrod, Amy. (1997). *Pigs will be pigs.* New York: Simon & Schuster.

Brisson, Pat. (1993). *Benny's pennies.* New York: Bantam Doubleday Dell.

Hoban, Lillian. (1984). *Arthur's funny money* (I Can Read Book Series Level 2). New York: HarperCollins.

Hoban, Tana. (1995). *Twenty-six letters and ninety-nine cents.* New York: Econo-Clad Books.

Holtzman, Caren. (1995). *A quarter from the tooth fairy* (Hello Math Reader Level 3). New York: Scholastic Inc.

Merrill, Jean. (1972). *The toothpaste millionaire.* New York: Houghton Mifflin.

Murphy, Stuart. (1998). *The penny pot: Counting coins* (MathStart Level 3). New York: HarperCollins.

Schwartz, David. (1994). *If you made a million.* New York: William Morrow.

Silverstein, Shel. (1974). The googies are coming. *Where the sidewalk ends.* New York: HarperCollins.

Silverstein, Shel. (1974). Smart. *Where the sidewalk ends.* New York: HarperCollins.

Viorst, Judith. (1980). *Alexander, who used to be rich last Sunday.* New York: Simon & Schuster.

Wells, Rosemary. (2000). *Bunny money.* New York: Penguin Putnam Books for Young Readers.

Teacher Resources

Abrohms, A. (1992). *Literature-based math activities: An integrated approach.* New York: Scholastic Professional Books.

Artzt, A. F., & Newman, C. M. (1997). *How to use cooperative learning in the mathematics class* (2nd ed.). Reston, VA: National Council of Teachers of Mathematics.

Braddon, K. L., Hall, J. J., & Taylor, D. (1993). *Math through children's literature: Making the NCTM Standards come alive.* Englewood, CO: Teacher Ideas Press.

Brown, S. E. (1991). *Instant math for beginning skills and concepts: Hands-on manipulative activities.* Incentive.

Burns, M. (1992). *Math and literature (K–3)* (Book One) Sausalito, CA: Math Solutions.

Burns, M. (1995). Writing in the math class? Absolutely! *Instructor, 104*(7) 40–44, 47.

Burns, M. (1996). How to make the most of math manipulatives. *Instructor, 105*(7), 45–51.

Burns, M. (1999). *Writing in math class.* Sausalito, CA: Math Solutions.

Dacey, L. S., & Eston, R. (1999). *Growing mathematical ideas in kindergarten.* Sausalito, CA: Math Solutions.

Davidson, N. (Ed.). (1990). *Cooperative learning in mathematics: A handbook for teachers.* Menlo Park, CA: Addison-Wesley.

Goodnow, J., & Hoogeboom, S. (2000). *Doing basic math with manipulatives: Grades 1–3.* Grand Rapids, MI: Ideal School Supply.

Hechtman, J., Ellermeyer, D., & Grove S. F. (1998). *Teaching math with favorite picture books.* New York: Scholastic Professional Books.

Horne, S. (Ed.). (1997). *Mathtivities! Classroom activities for grades one through six.* Palo Alto, CA: Creative Publications.

Irvin, B. B. (1992). *K-3 overhead manipulatives in action.* Deerfield, SL: Learning Resources.

Jasmine, G., & Jasmine, J. (1995). *Primary cooperative learning activities for math.* Huntington Beach, CA: Teacher Created Materials.

Johnson, D. W., Johnson, R. T., & Holubec, E. J. (1993). *Circles of learning: Cooperation in the classroom* (4th ed.). Alexandria, VA: Association for Supervision and Curriculum Development.

Kagan, S. (1994). *Cooperative learning.* San Clemente, CA: Resources for Teachers.

National Association for the Education of Young Children. (1986, 1997). *Developmentally appropriate practice in early childhood programs serving children from birth through age 8.* Washington, DC: Author.

National Council of Teachers of Mathematics. (1989). *Curriculum and evaluation standards for school mathematics.* Reston, VA: Author.

National Council of Teachers of Mathematics. (1991). *Professional standards for teaching mathematics.* Reston, VA: Author.

National Council of Teachers of Mathematics. (1995). *Assessment standards for teaching mathematics.* Reston, VA: Author.

National Council of Teachers of Mathematics. (2000). *Principles and standards for school mathematics.* Reston, VA: Author.

National Council of Teachers of Mathematics. (2003). *A research companion to principles and standards for school mathematics.* Reston, VA: Author.

Nevada Mathematics Content Standards. (2001). Retrieved November 12, 2003 from http://www.leg.state.nv.us/interim/nonlegcom/academicstandards/Misc/Standards/Math.htm

Pattillo, J., & Vaughan, E. (1992). *Learning centers for child-centered classrooms* (NEA Early Childhood Education Series).

Peragine, D. B. (1991). *600 manipulatives and activities for early math.* New York: Scholastic Professional Books.

Reys, R. E., Bestgen, B., Coburn, T., Marcucci, R., Schoen, H., Shumway, R., et al. (1980). *Keystrokes: Calculator activities for young students.* Palo Alto, CA: Creative Publications.

Schielack, J. F., & Chancellor, D. (1995). *Uncovering mathematics with manipulatives and calculators: Level 1 (grades K–2).* Dallas: Texas Instruments.

Schielack, J. F., & Chancellor, D. (1995). *Uncovering mathematics with manipulatives and calculators: Levels 2–3 (grades 2–6).* Dallas: Texas Instruments.

Scope and Sequence Document (2002). Unpublished documents, Lisbon, OH: West Point Elementary School, Beaver Local School District.

Thiessen, D., Matthias, M., & Smith, J. (1998). *The wonderful world of mathematics: A critically annotated list of children's books in mathematics* (2nd ed.). Reston, VA: National Council of Teachers of Mathematics.

Whitin, D. J., & Wilde, S. (1992). *Read any good math lately? Children's books for mathematical learning, K-6.* Portsmouth, NH: Heinemann.

Whitin, D. J., & Wilde, S. (1995). *It's the story that counts: More children's books for mathematical learning, K-6.* Portsmouth, NH: Heinemann.

Selected Research Books and Articles

Bruner, J. (1961). *The process of education.* New York: Vintage Books.

Bruner, J. S. (1964). The course of cognitive growth. *American Psychologist, 19*(1), 1–15.

Campbell, P. F., & Langrall, C. (2002). Making equity a reality in classrooms. In D. L. Chambers (Ed.), *Putting research into practice in the elementary grades: Readings from NCTM journals* (pp. 294–298). Reston, VA: National Council of Teachers of Mathematics.

Carpenter, T. P., Franke, M. L., Jacobs, V. R., Fenemma, E., & Empson, S. B. (1998). A longitudinal study of inventions and understanding in children's multidigit addition and subtractions. *Journal for Research in Mathematics Education, 29,* 3–20.

Clements, D. H., & McMillen, S. (1996). Rethinking "concrete" manipulatives. *Teaching Children Mathematics, 2,* 270–279.

Cobb, P. (1994). Constructivism in mathematics and science education. *Educational Researcher, 23*(7), 4.

Coxford, A. F. (1995). The case for connections. In P. House (Ed.), *1995 yearbook: Connecting mathematics across the curriculum.* Reston, VA: National Council of Teachers of Mathematics.

Dienes, Z. (1960). *Building up mathematics.* London: Hutchinson Educational.

Hatfield, M. (1994). Use of manipulative devices: Elementary school cooperating teachers self-report. *School Science and Mathematics, 94*(6), 303–309.

Henningsen, M., & Stein, M. K. (1997). Mathematical tasks and student cognition: Classroom based factors that support and inhibit high-level mathematical thinking and reasoning. *Journal for Research in Mathematics Education, 28,* 534–549.

Hiebert, J., & Lindquist, M. M. (1990). Developing mathematical knowledge in the young child. In J. N. Payne (Ed.), *Mathematics for the young child* (pp. 17–36). Reston, VA: The National Council of Teachers of Mathematics.

Hiebert, J., & Wearne, D. (1996). Instruction, understanding and skill in multidigit addition and subtraction. *Cognition and Instruction, 14,* 251–283.

Kamii, C., & Ewing, J. K. (1996). Basing teaching on Piaget's constructivism. *Childhood Education, 72*(5), 260–64.

Klingele, W. E., & Reed, B. W. (1984, June). An examination of an incremental approach to mathematics. *Phi Delta Kappan,* 15–16.

Piaget, J. (1952). *The child's conception of number.* London: Routledge & Kegan Paul.

Renga, S., & Dalla, L. (1993). Affect: A critical component of mathematical learning in early childhood. In R. J. Jenson (Ed.), *Research ideas for the classroom: Early childhood mathematics* (pp. 22–39). Reston, VA.: NCTM, and New York: Macmillan.

Roth, W. M. (1992). Bridging the gap between school and real life: Toward an integration of science, mathematics, and technology in the context of authentic practice. *School Science and Mathematics, 92,* 307–317.

Skemp, R. S. (1971). *The psychology of learning mathematics.* Hammondsworth, England: Penguin Books.

Sowell, E. J. (1989). Effects of Manipulative Materials in Mathematics Instruction. *Journal for Research in Mathematics Education, 20,* 498–505.

Stigler, J. W., & Hiebert, J. C. (1997). Understanding and improving classroom mathematics instruction: An overview of the TIMSS video study. *Phi Delta Kappan, 79,* 14–21.

Suydam, M. N., & Higgins, J. L. (1977). *Activity-Based Learning in Elementary School Mathematics:*

Recommendations from Research. Columbus, OH: ERIC Clearinghouse for Science, Mathematics and Environmental Education.

Thompson, P. W. (1994). Concrete materials and teaching for mathematical understanding. *Arithmetic Teacher, 41,* 556–558.

U.S. Department of Education. (n.d.). *Definitions from Goals 2000 Educate America Act.* Retrieved November 12, 2003 from http://www.ed.gov/legislation/GOALS2000/TheAct/sec3.html

Further Reading

Battista, M. T. (1994). Calculators and computers: Tools for mathematical exploration and empowerment. *Arithmetic Teacher, 41,* 412–417.

Berk, L., & Winsler, A. (1995). *Scaffolding children's learning: Vygotsky and early childhood education.* Washington, DC: National Association for the Education of Young Children.

Burrill, G. (1998). Changes in your classroom: From the past to the present to the future. *Teaching Children Mathematics, 5,* 202–209.

Calvert, L. M. G. (1999). A dependence on technology and algorithms or a lack of number sense? *Teaching Children Mathematics, 6,* 6–7.

Campbell, P. F., & Stewart, E. L. (1993). Calculators and computers. In R. J. Jensen (Ed.), *Research ideas for the classroom: Early childhood mathematics* (pp. 251–268). New York: Macmillan.

Chambers, D. L. (Ed.). (2002). *Putting research into practice in the elementary grades: Readings from NCTM journals.* Reston, VA: National Council of Teachers of Mathematics.

Copley, J. V. (Ed.). (1999). *Mathematics in the early years.* Reston, VA: National Council of Teachers of Mathematics.

DeVries, R., & W. Kohlberg. (1990). *Constructivist early education: Overview and comparison with other programs.* Washington, DC: National Association for the Education of Young Children.

Drosdeck, C. C. (1995). Promoting calculator use in elementary classrooms. *Teaching Children Mathematics, 1,* 300–305.

Ginsburg, H. (Ed.). (1983). *The development of mathematical thinking.* New York: Academic Press.

Hiebert, J. (Ed.). (1986). *Conceptual and procedural knowledge: The case of mathematics.* Hillsdale, NJ: Erlbaum.

Hiebert, J., Carpenter, T. P., Fennema, E., Fuson, K. C., Wearne, D., Murray, H., et al. (1997). *Making sense: Teaching and learning mathematics with understanding.* Portsmouth, NH: Heinemann.

Kilman, M. (1993). Integrating mathematics and literature in the elementary classroom. *Arithmetic Teacher, 40*(6), 318–321.

Learning and teaching mathematics with technology [Focus issue]. (2002). *Teaching Children Mathematics 8*(6).

Mallory, B., & New, R. (1994). *Diversity and developmentally appropriate practices: Challenges for early childhood education.* New York: Teachers College Press.

Mathematical Sciences Education Board, National Research Council. 1989. *Everybody counts: A report to the nation on the future of mathematics education.* Washington, DC: National Academy Press.

McIntosh, M. (1997). 500+ writing formats. *Mathematics Teaching for the Middle School, 2*(5), 354–358.

NAEYC. (1996). NAEYC position statement: Technology and young children—Ages three through eight. *Young Children, 51*(6), 11–16.

Norwood, K. S., & Carter, G. (1994). Journal writing: An insight into students' understanding. *Teaching Children Mathematics, 1,* 146–148.

Ohanian, S. (1989). Readin', 'rithmetic—Using children's literature to teach math. *Learning, 18*(3), 32–35.

Payne, J. N. (Ed.). (1990). *Mathematics for the young child.* Reston, VA: National Council of Teachers of Mathematics.

Schifter, D. (Ed.). (1996). *What's happening in math class? Envisioning new practices through teacher narratives* (Series on School Reform, Vol. 1). New York: Teachers College Press.

Spann, M. B. (1992). Kindergarten clinic: Linking literature and math. *Instructor, 101*(8), 54.

Stiff, L. V. (Ed.). (1999). *Developing mathematical reasoning in grades K–12.* Reston, VA: National Council of Teachers of Mathematics.

Suydam, M. (1986). Research Report: Manipulative materials and achievement. *Arithmetic Teacher, 33*(6), 10, 32.

Vygotsky, L. (1978). *Mind in society: The development of higher psychological processes.* Cambridge, MA: Harvard University Press.

Wright, J., & Shade, D. (Eds.). (1994). *Young children: Active learners in a technological age.* Washington, DC: National Association for the Education of Young Children.

2

Problem Solving and Assessing Student Understanding

P roblem solving is the core of any good mathematics program and will be addressed throughout this text. In this chapter we begin with an introduction to Polya's four-step problem-solving process. We add one step to this process that is especially useful for current and prospective teachers and discuss several problem-solving strategies. A number of solved problems are included within this chapter to illustrate the problem-solving process and strategies. We also discuss the integration of problem solving into the early childhood curriculum.

A section on assessing student understanding is also included in this chapter. Chapter 1 briefly discussed assessment, but deferred a formal discussion of assessment until this chapter to focus on the assessment of problem solving in the classroom. Children frequently make errors in the mathematics classroom. To analyze and remediate these errors, the early childhood teacher must be able to detect the precise flaw within a faulty argument. The early childhood teacher must be proficient in providing counterexamples for false statements and justifications for true ones and must also assist children in developing these skills.

Building a solid foundation for logical reasoning and problem solving is especially important within the earliest grade levels. Problem solving is the cornerstone of the premise that mathematics makes sense. The National Council of Teachers of Mathematics placed great emphasis on problem solving in the 1989 Standards. This emphasis was continued and reinforced within the 2000 Standards.

Standards

NCTM

Mathematics as Problem Solving—Grades K–4

Problem solving should be the central focus of the mathematics curriculum. As such, it is a primary goal of all mathematics instruction and an integral part of all mathematical activity. Problem solving is not a distinct topic but a process that should permeate the entire program and provide the context in which concepts and skills can be learned.

NCTM, 1989, p. 23

Standards are listed with the permission of the National Council of Teachers of Mathematics (NCTM). NCTM does not endorse the content or validity of these alignments.

Standards

NCTM

Grades Pre-K–2

Problem solving is a hallmark of mathematical activity and a major means of developing mathematical knowledge. It is finding a way to reach a goal that is not immediately attainable. Problem solving is natural to young children because the world is new to them, and they exhibit curiosity, intelligence, and flexibility as they face new situations. The challenge at this level is to build on children's innate problem solving inclinations and to preserve and encourage a disposition that values problem solving.

NCTM, 2000 p. 116

Standards are listed with the permission of the National Council of Teachers of Mathematics (NCTM). NCTM does not endorse the content or validity of these alignments.

Objectives

After completing Chapter 2, you will be able to

- List and describe the five-step problem-solving process and several problem-solving strategies
- Solve problems using the five-step process
- Describe how to encourage problem solving in the early childhood classroom and how to create good problem-solving problems and activities
- Construct assessment tools to be used in the early childhood classroom

2.1 A Five-Step Problem-Solving Process

The Definition of a Problem

Before we discuss problem solving, we first probe into the definition of a *problem.* Is the following a problem? *Keefe has two cats and three dogs. How many pets does he have?* For many pre-school-aged children, this could be considered a problem. For the average second-grade student, this problem would be solved within a matter of seconds—no problem. To truly be considered a problem, a mathematical quest must contain some effort or thought on the part of the solver (Brownell, 1942; Polya, 1945). As a teacher you must remember that what is a problem for some students may be a mere exercise for others.

Problem solving involves a variety of skills.

> Problem-solving situations call upon children to retrieve previously learned information and apply it in *new* or *varying* situations. Knowing the basic arithmetic skills, knowing when to incorporate them into new contexts, and then being able to do so are three distinct skills. Having all three skills makes problem solving easier, but inability in one does not mean that a student does not understand a problem. It may mean that the student's learning style has not been addressed. Similarly, because students can carry out the operations in isolation does not mean they know when to apply them or how to interpret the numbers involved (Bley & Thornton, 2001, p. 37).

Good problems include modifications that may be made for students with varying skills, abilities, and learning styles. Multiple solutions and multiple methods of solution are encouraged in a classroom that fosters a problem-solving atmosphere. The challenges of creating good problems and maintaining a problem-solving atmosphere in the classroom will be addressed in the next section. In this section we focus on the process and strategies of problem solving.

Polya's Four-Step Process

Probably the most famous approach to problem solving is Polya's four-step process described below (Polya, 1945). Polya identifies the four principles as follows:

1. Understand the problem
2. Devise a plan
3. Carry out the plan
4. Look back

The problem-solving process is merely a general guide of how to proceed in solving problems. In many cases, steps of the process will overlap, thus it may not be possible to perform each step of the process in the order given above. These four principles appear in many elementary-level textbook series as early as the kindergarten grade level (see Figure 2-1).

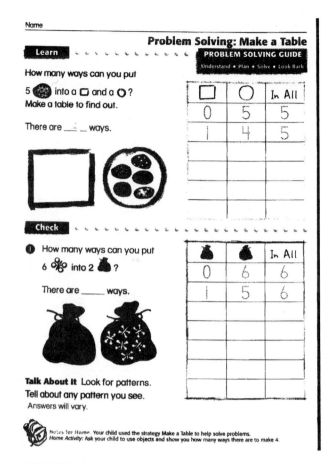

FIGURE 2-1 School book page.
Source: Page (61) from *Scott-Foresman—Addison Wesley Math Grade (1).* Copyright © 1999 by Addison Wesley Longman, Inc. Reprinted by permission of Pearson Education, Inc.

Use of the problem-solving process and specific strategies may be mentioned in a state or district model or framework.

After describing each of the four steps of Polya's problem-solving process in more detail below, we will discuss a fifth step. This is not suggesting that Polya's process is incomplete. In fact, the fifth step, *extend the problem,* is mentioned in Polya's manuscript as part of the fourth step— look back. These ideas are separated so that the process of extending the problem, especially relevant for teachers, does not become lost in the process of verifying the solution.

Step 1: Understand the problem. To correctly solve a problem, you must first *understand* the problem. Below are some questions that may help lead you (or a student) to an understanding of a given problem. Not every question will be appropriate for every problem.

What are you asked to find or show?

What type of answer do you expect?

What units will be used in the answer?

Can you give an estimate?

What information is given? Do you understand all the terms and conditions?

Are there any assumptions that need to be made or special conditions to be met?

Is there enough information given? If not, what information is needed?

Is there any extra information given? If so, what information is not needed?

Can you restate the problem in your own words?

Can you act out the problem?

Can you draw a picture, a diagram, or an illustration?

Can you calculate specific numerical instances that illustrate the problem?

Step 2: Devise a plan. Use **problem-solving strategies.** The "plan" used to solve a problem is often called a problem-solving *strategy.* For some problems, you may begin using one strategy and then realize that the strategy does not fit the given information or is not leading toward the desired solution; in this case, you must choose another strategy. In other cases you may need to use a combination of strategies. Several problem-solving strategies are described below (in no particular order). All of these strategies can be found in elementary-level mathematics textbooks at around the third- or fourth-grade level; many of these strategies are introduced as early as the prekindergarten level.

- **Use guess and check.** When a problem calls for a numerical answer, a student may make a random guess and then check the guess with the facts and information given within the problem. If the guess is incorrect, the student may make and check a new guess. Each subsequent guess should provide more insight into the problem and lead to a more appropriate guess. In some instances the guess and check strategy may also be used with problems for which the answer is non-numerical.

- **Draw a picture or a diagram/use a graph or number line.** A picture or graph may illustrate relationships between given facts and information that are not as easily seen in word or numerical form.

- **Use manipulatives or a model/act it out.** When a problem requires that elements be moved or rearranged, a physical model can be used to illustrate the solution.

- **Make a list or table.** A list or table may be helpful to organize the given information. It may be possible to make an orderly list or table of all possible solutions and then to choose the solution that best fits the given facts and information from this list. In some problems, the answer to the problem *is* a list or table of all possible solutions.

- **Eliminate possibilities.** When there is more than one possible solution to a problem, each possibility must be examined. Potential solutions that do not work are discarded from the list of possible solutions until an appropriate answer is determined.

- **Use cases.** It is possible to divide some problems into cases. Each case may be separately considered.

- **Solve an equivalent problem.** In some instances it is easier to solve a related or equivalent problem than it is to solve a given problem.

- **Solve a simpler problem.** It may be possible to formulate and solve a simpler problem than the given problem. The process used in the solution of the simpler problem can give insight into the more complex given problem.

Standards

Texas Essential Knowledge and Skills for Mathematics

Kindergarten (111.12)

(13) Underlying processes and mathematical tools. The student applies Kindergarten mathematics to solve problems connected to everyday experiences and activities in and outside of school. The student is expected to:

a. identify mathematics in everyday situations;

b. use a problem solving model, with guidance, that incorporates understanding the problem, making a plan, carrying out the plan, and evaluating the solution for reasonableness;

c. select or develop an appropriate problem solving strategy including drawing a picture, looking for a pattern, systematic guessing and checking, or acting it out in order to solve a problem; and

d. use tools such as real objects, manipulatives, and technology to solve problems.

Texas Education Agency, 1998

Standards

Mathematics Content Standards for California Public Schools

Mathematical Reasoning, Kindergarten

2.0 Students solve problems in reasonable ways and justify their reasoning:

2.1 Explain the reasoning used with concrete objects and/or pictorial representations.

2.2 Make precise calculations and check the validity of the results in the context of the problem.

California Department of Education, 2000

- **Look for a pattern.** Patterns are useful in many problem-solving situations. This strategy will be especially useful in solving many real-world problems. "Patterns are a way for young students to recognize order and to organize their world" (NCTM, 2000, p. 91).

- **Choose the operation/write a formula or number sentence.** Some problems are easily solved with the application of a known formula or number sentence. The difficulty often lies in choosing the appropriate formula or operation.

- **Make a prediction/use estimation.** One must closely consider all elements of a problem in order to make a prediction or use estimation. This careful consideration may provide useful insight into the problem solution.

- **Work the problem backward.** If the problem involves a sequence of steps that can be reversed, it may be useful to work the problem backward. Children at the early childhood level may already have some experience in working backward. In solving many mazes and puzzles, it is sometimes easier to begin at the end than to begin at the beginning.

- **Use logical reasoning.** One of the basic tenets of this textbook is that mathematics can and should make sense. Logical reasoning and careful consideration are sometimes all that is required to solve a mathematics problem.

Step 3: Carry out the plan. Once a problem has been carefully analyzed and a plan is devised, if the plan is a suitable one for the given problem, it is usually a relatively simple process to carry out the plan. However, in some cases the original plan does not succeed and another plan must be devised. The original strategy may need to be modified, or a new strategy may be selected. Students must realize that not every problem will be solved within the first attempt. A failed attempt can be viewed as a learning experience. Try to help students avoid getting frustrated or discouraged. Cooperative learning teams can be used to encourage and engage students. Computers, calculators, or other manipulatives may be useful tools when routine tasks are involved.

Step 4: Look back. Once an answer or solution is found, it is important to check that solution. Check all steps and calculations within the solution process. Below are some questions that you (or your students) may find useful in the looking back process.

Is the answer reasonable?

Is there another method of solution that will easily verify the answer?

Does the answer fit the problem data?

Does the answer fulfill all conditions or requirements of the problem?

Is there more than one answer?

Will the solution process used be valuable in solving similar or related problems?

Step 5: Extend the problem. For a classroom teacher, an important part of the problem-solving process should involve trying to create similar or related problems. A given problem may need to be simplified in order to be used at a specific classroom level or with students that have special needs. A teacher may wish to make a problem more complicated or to create similar related problems that are more difficult. Elementary school students often extend the problem as part of a journal writing exercise as they write their own story problems for a given situation.

It may be possible to generalize specific instances of a given problem. Teachers must be on the lookout for opportunities to have students generalize and make conjectures. Teachers should look for connections that can be made between given mathematics problems and solutions and real-life situations. Teachers should also look for connections between given mathematics problems and their solutions and other subject areas. There are many excellent articles that deal specifically with posing problems and extending textbook exercises. See, for example, the articles by Butts; Barnett, Sowder, and Vos; LeBlanc, Proudfit, and Putt; and Silver and Smith in the NCTM *1980 Yearbook: Problem Solving in School Mathematics.*

 Teaching Connections

Examples Using the Problem-Solving Process Several examples below illustrate the use of the problem-solving process and various problem-solving strategies. Read each example problem and attempt to solve it, making note of which problem-solving strategies you use. Then read the given solution.

Example 2-1: Find all three-digit numbers that meet these criteria: all digits are distinct, exactly one digit is odd, and the sum of the digits is seven.

Step 1: *Understand the problem.* First check to see that you understand what you are asked to find and whether any assumptions must be made. You are asked to find all three-digit numbers that satisfy the conditions above. The answer will be a set of whole numbers. The fact that you are looking for three-digit numbers indicates that the first digit is not zero.

Now analyze the given conditions. The condition that all digits must be distinct means that you are not allowed to repeat any digits within the number. For example, if you use 1 as the first digit, you are not allowed to use 1 as either the middle digit or the last digit. One of the digits must be odd; this condition could be confused with the condition that the number itself is odd. Be careful to use only one odd digit when constructing a number, although there is no restriction on where that odd digit can occur within the number. Recall that a *sum* is the answer to an addition problem. When you add the digits, the result must be seven.

Do you feel as though you understand the problem? Are all of the conditions clear? Do you know what type of answers to expect? If you have not already done so, see if you can find all of the three-digit numbers that satisfy the given conditions before reading further.

Step 2: *Devise a plan.* To devise a plan, start by looking over and considering the given list of strategies. You may use any one strategy or any combination of these strategies. You may even need to devise a plan or use a strategy not included in this list. The strategy of guess and check might be useful in creating or guessing appropriate three-digit numbers, but it would not ensure that you have found all such numbers. This does not appear to be a problem where a picture or manipulatives would be practical. It might be possible to make an organized, systematic list and to eliminate possibilities that do not fit the desired conditions. This may involve using cases to ensure that all valid numbers are discovered. There is no immediately apparent equivalent problem, but it might be possible to solve a simpler problem or to look for a pattern. The operation of addition will be necessary to check that that sum of the digits is seven. It is unclear at this time whether estimation or working backward will be necessary, but you may wish to use logical reasoning to ensure that you have discovered all possible answers.

A three-digit number can be written in three blanks (___ ___ ___) and numbers can be checked against the required conditions. You have already decided that the first digit is not zero. Now consider cases based on what number is chosen as the first digit. The conditions of the problem may be used to determine the possible remaining digits. The fact that the digits must be distinct and have a sum of seven implies that the largest first digit that must be considered is six. The attempt 7 ___ ___ could not be completed without incurring a sum larger than seven because two zero digits are not allowed.

Step 3: *Carry out the plan.* There will be six cases for first digits one through six.

- **Case 1: First digit equals one.** If the first digit is equal to one, the number will look like 1 ___ ___. The two unknown digits must have a sum of six. The possibilities are 0 and 6, 1 and 5, 2 and 4, or 3 and 3. Because you are not allowed to repeat any digits, you must eliminate the possibilities 1 and 5 and 3 and 3. This leads to four numbers: 106, 160, 124, and 142. Notice that each of these has exactly one odd digit as required.

- **Case 2: First digit equals two.** If the first digit is equal to two, the number will look like 2 ___ ___. The two unknown digits must have a sum of five. The possibilities are 0 and 5, 1 and 4, or 2 and 3. Because you are not allowed to repeat any digits, you must eliminate the possibility 2 and 3. This leads to four numbers: 205, 250, 214, and 241. Notice that each has exactly one odd digit as required.

- **Case 3: First digit equals three.** If the first digit is equal to three, the number will look like 3 ___ ___. The two unknown digits must have a sum of four. After eliminating answers that have duplicate digits, the only possibility is 0 and 4. This leads to two numbers: 304 and 340. Notice that both have exactly one odd digit as required.

- **Case 4: First digit equals four.** If the first digit is equal to four, the number will look like 4 ___ ___. The two unknown digits must have a sum of three. There are two possibilities: 0 and 3 and 1 and 2. This leads to four numbers: 403, 430, 412, and 421. Notice that each has exactly one odd digit as required.

- **Case 5: First digit equals five.** If the first digit is equal to five, the number will look like 5 ___ ___. The two unknown digits must have a sum of two. After eliminating 1 and 1 because of duplicate digits, the only possibility is 0 and 2. This leads to two numbers: 502 and 520. Notice that both have exactly one odd digit as required.

- **Case 6: First digit equals six.** If the first digit is equal to six, the number will look like 6 ___ ___. The two unknown digits must have a sum of one. The only possibility is 0 and 1. This leads to two numbers: 601 and 610. Notice that both have exactly one odd digit as required.

Step 4: *Look back.* You have found the following 18 solutions: {106, 160, 124, 142, 205, 250, 214, 241, 304, 340, 403, 430, 412, 421, 502, 520, 601, 610}. You can check that each of the 18 numbers listed in the set above does satisfy all of the conditions of the problem. The digit sum is seven, digits are distinct, and exactly one digit of each number is odd. By reviewing the process used, you are confident that all cases have been considered and all such numbers have been found.

You could verify this solution by solving in a different manner. You could consider sets of three distinct numbers that have a sum of seven. If you systematically list these sets by considering various combinations such as 0 and 1, 0 and 2, and so on, there are only four such sets: {0, 1, 6}, {0, 2, 5}, {0, 3, 4}, and {1, 2, 4}. Using a set that contains a zero, only four different three-digit numbers are possible. Using the set that does not contain a zero, there are six different three-digit numbers that can be formed. Because $3 \times 4 + 6 = 18$, this method yields 18 solutions. You can check that these are precisely the 18 solutions found above.

Step 5: *Extend the problem.* Due to the number of cases and conditions, the example given is approximately a fourth-grade-level problem. To modify the problem so that it could be used at an earlier level, you could change the sum of the digits requirement to five. This reduces the number of cases and solutions and results in a problem that could easily be used at the third-grade level. A similar problem involving only two digits could be written for use at the first- or second-grade level.

Example 2-2a: Sarah lives in an apartment building that has several floors. Sarah leaves her apartment and walks down two flights of stairs to visit a neighbor. She then walks up three flights of stairs to visit her grandmother. Sarah's grandmother lives on the fifth floor. What floor does Sarah live on? Solve this problem before reading the given solution.

Step 1: *Understand the problem.* You need to determine what floor Sarah's apartment is on from the clues given about the number of flights of stairs she walks. You must make the assumption that the third sentence implies that she walks up three flights of stairs *from her neighbor's apartment* to get to her grandmother's apartment without first returning to her own apartment.

Step 2: *Devise a plan.* For this problem, you could draw a picture or use manipulatives. You may also need the strategy of working backward because the clues end at Sarah's grandmother's apartment on the fifth floor, and you can retrace Sarah's steps.

Step 3: *Carry out the plan.* You draw a picture and record the fact that Sarah's grandmother lives on the fifth floor. Sarah had to walk up three flights from her neighbor's apartment to get to her grandmother's apart-

| 5 - gramma |
| 4 |
| 3 |
| 2 - neighbor |
| 1 |

ment. So the neighbor that Sarah was visiting lives on the second floor. You record that fact on the diagram. Sarah walked down two flights from her own apartment to get to her neighbor's apartment, so she must live two floors above her neighbor. You record this on the diagram. Sarah lives on the fourth floor.

Step 4: *Look back.* You can check the solution by following the clues. If Sarah begins on the fourth floor and walks down two flights of stairs, she will be able to visit a neighbor on the second floor. If she then walks up three flights of stairs, she will be on the fifth floor and can visit her grandmother. It appears correct that Sarah started on the fourth floor.

Step 5: *Extend the problem.* The problem as given is approximately a second-grade-level problem. It could be made easier if simpler clues or fewer clues were given. It could be made more difficult if more complicated clues or more clues were given. This would be a good type of problem to rewrite to include extraneous information. It could also be changed to a problem where not enough information is given. This problem contains a real-world situation, and many students will be able to relate to such

a problem. Another version of this type of problem (approximately third- or fourth-grade level) is shown below.

Example 2-2b: Kara is staying in a hotel. From her hotel room she walks down three fights of stairs to get to the ice machine. She buys a soda from the pop machine on the way back to her room. Later she takes the elevator to the 11th-floor restaurant. After eating dinner, she walks down four flights of stairs to return to her room. Which of the following can you answer?

a. On what floor is Kara's hotel room?
b. On what floor is the pop machine where Kara purchased her soda?
c. On what floor is the ice machine?

Example 2-3a: Faces 1 to 5 are shown. Extend the pattern by drawing and coloring four more faces. What would the 100th face in the pattern look like? Solve this problem before reading the given solution.

Step 1: *Understand the problem.* There are two patterns in the faces shown. The faces alternate between smiling and frowning and there is a repeating pattern of three colors—dark, striped, and light. You must draw four more faces, numbers 6 through 9. You must also determine whether face 100 would be smiling or frowning and what shade it would be.

Step 2: *Devise a plan.* This problem involves finding a pattern. It also involves prediction or estimation in finding the 100th face. A number sentence or logical reasoning may also be useful in determining the 100th face.

Step 3: *Carry out the plan.* The given faces alternate: smiling, frowning, smiling, frowning, and smiling. The next four faces should be frowning, smiling, frowning, and smiling, respectively. The given faces have a color pattern that repeats after every three faces: dark, striped, light, dark, striped. The next four faces should be light, dark, striped, and light, respectively. The row of the first nine faces is given below.

You can use the same type of logic to determine the 100th face. All of the odd-numbered faces are smiling and the even numbered faces are frowning. If the same pattern continues, the 100th face will be frowning. The color pattern repeats after every three faces. Because 99 is evenly divisible by 3, the 100th face will begin a new color pattern with a dark-colored face. Therefore, the 100th face should be dark and frowning. 😞

Step 4: *Look back.* Because the smiling–frowning pattern repeats after every two faces and the color pattern repeats after every three faces, it makes sense that the pattern involving both of these traits will repeat after every sixth face. Notice that faces 7 through 9 above are the same as faces 1 through 3. Faces 1 through 6 represent the six different possible faces that can be made by combining the two traits discussed. Now $100 \div 6 = 16$ with a remainder of 4, so within the first 100 faces, there are 16 full sets of the 6 different faces and a partial set of 4 faces. The 100th face is the fourth face of the set of 6 different faces. The numerical analysis confirms that the 100th face should be the dark, frowning face.

Step 5: *Extend the problem.* This problem could be altered by using a different number of colors or a different set of facial expressions. The problem could have been to determine a face other than the 100th face. A larger or smaller number could have been used. Similar problems could be devised using other objects such as pattern blocks or attribute blocks.

Example 2-3b: A line of attribute blocks is shown. Count the number of ways each block differs from the previous block in the sequence. Fill in the missing blocks. (Only the thin attribute blocks are used in this problem.)

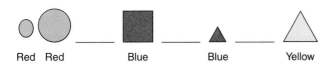

Red   Red   Blue   Blue   Yellow

Example 2-4: Use a set of tangram pieces to build the house that is shown.

Step 1: *Understand the problem.* You are to cover the outline of the house shown using all seven tangram pieces.

Step 2: *Devise a plan.* It may be possible to solve a simpler problem by covering part of the house using only some of the pieces and then covering the rest of the house using the remaining pieces.

Step 3: *Carry out the plan.* It is up to you to carry out the plan and cover the house with a set of tangram pieces. Trace and cut out the figure on the following page for a set of the appropriate size.

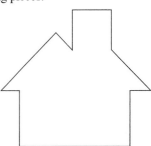

Step 4: *Look back.* Were you able to cover the house using all seven pieces? Which piece did you begin with? Many students will begin by using the square to build the chimney and a large triangle and the parallelogram to finish building the roof and top story of the house.

Step 5: *Extend the problem.* This problem could be made easier by providing an outline with some or all interior lines included. At the prekindergarten level, students should be provided with a pattern that includes all the necessary lines. Students can practice vocabulary terms while matching the tangram shapes to the outline. To make the problem more difficult, more complicated outlines could be provided. Similar problems could be devised using pattern blocks and pattern block outlines.

Example 2-5: The wall of the house shown in Example 2-4 is to be painted. The square chimney area requires 2 pints of paint. How much paint would be required to paint the entire wall shown?

Step 1: *Understand the problem.* You are to calculate how many pints of paint it would take to cover the entire wall shown. You are given that the square chimney requires 2 pints. You could first estimate the number of squares it would take to cover the area. One

Math Manipulative: Attribute Blocks

A standard set of attribute blocks contains 60 blocks with various combinations of the following attributes: color, shape, size, and thickness. There are three colors (red, blue, and yellow), five shapes (circle, square, triangle, hexagon, and rectangle), and two sizes (large and small). The blocks come in two thicknesses-thick and thin. Each block in a set is unique, but shares attributes

with other blocks in the set. In beginning activities, you may wish to use the smaller subsets of 30 thin blocks or 30 thick blocks.

Attribute blocks are useful for practice in the skill of distinguishing features. They may also be used in sorting, classifying, counting, and pattern activities. Logical reasoning must be used to determine attribute differences between blocks.

Math Manipulative: Tangrams

The tangram set is an old Chinese puzzle. A set consists of two large triangles, one medium triangle, two small triangles, one square, and one parallelogram. The pieces fit together in a variety of ways. The set can be used to form one large square or several other interesting figures. See Blackline Master 2 in the Appendices for a pattern outline to create a homemade set. Sets may be purchased from teacher supply stores or catalogs and are available in a variety of materials. Overhead sets are also available.

Tangrams can be used for combining shapes to create other shapes and figures, completing fraction activities, reinforcing geometric terminology and ideas such as symmetry and congruence, and doing measurement activities.

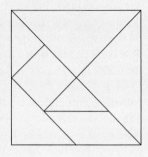

Math Manipulative: Pattern Blocks

A standard set of pattern blocks contains six different kinds of blocks: orange square, yellow hexagon, red trapezoid, tan rhombus, blue rhombus, and green triangle. A set contains several copies of each shape. Each side is 1 inch long, except for the long side of the trapezoid which is 2 inches long. This allows the blocks to fit together to create a multitude of patterns. Pattern blocks are available in wood and plastic, as well as in softer quieter materials. Overhead sets or sets that stick to a magnetic board are also available. See Blackline Master 4 in the Appendices for the pattern outline to create a homemade set, and Blackline Master 5 for a covering activity involving pattern blocks.

Pattern blocks may be used in sorting, counting, and shape recognition. They may also be used in extending and creating patterns, activities involving congruence, symmetry, and other topics of geometry, fraction activities, measurement activities, and activities involving algebra.

estimate is that it would take 7 or 8 squares to cover the wall. So you estimate that it will take 14 to 16 pints of paint to cover the wall.

Step 2: *Devise a plan.* An initial plan might be to use a set of square chimney-sized manipulatives and cover the house with these squares. You will quickly find that it is not possible to cover this shape using only squares of the given size. A revised plan might be to cover the square tangram piece using the two small triangular pieces. You know that each small triangular-sized area requires 1 pint of paint, thus it may be possible to solve the equivalent problem of covering the house with small triangular pieces. You could also solve the simpler problem of covering separately each of the tangram pieces using small triangles to determine the number of total small triangles that would be required to cover the entire house.

Step 3: *Carry out the plan.* It is easy to see that the medium-sized triangle is the same size as two small triangles. The large triangle is the size of two medium triangles, hence four small triangles. The parallelo-

gram can be covered with two small triangles. So the total number of small triangles in all of the tangram pieces is: 2 (small triangles) + 2 (square) + 2 (parallelogram) + 2 (medium triangle) + 8 (both large triangles) = 16. Each small triangle requires 1 pint of paint, so it will take 16 pints of paint to cover the wall.

Step 4: *Look back.* The answer is reasonable according to your estimate. It is also true that 16 pints is equivalent to 2 gallons, which seems to be a reasonable amount of paint for a large house wall.

Step 5: *Extend the problem.* The given problem deals with area. A similar perimeter problem could be devised. Students could also calculate the time it would take to paint the entire wall given the time required to paint one part or tangram-shaped area. This problem has a real-world connection that may be stressed.

Example 2-6: A child's rectangular wading pool is 3 feet wide and 5 feet long. It is filled with water 2 feet deep. A gallon of water is approximately 231 cubic inches. Determine how many gallons of water are in the pool.

Step 1: *Understand the problem.* You need to determine the amount of water in the pool. You can draw and label a picture: Pool dimensions are given in feet, but the amount of water in a gallon is given in terms of inches. You have to be careful with units.

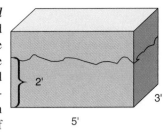

Step 2: *Devise a plan.* You can calculate the amount of water in feet, convert this number to inches, and divide by 231 to determine the number of gallons.

Step 3: *Carry out the plan.* The pool contains $3 \times 5 \times 2 = 30$ cubic feet of water. There are 12 inches in a foot, so there are $30 \times 12 = 360$ cubic inches of water in the pool. Because $360 \div 231 = 1.5584415$, there are about 1.6 gallons of water in the pool.

Step 4: *Look back.* What? Only 1.6 gallons of water? In a pool that is 3 by 5 feet that amount of water wouldn't even cover the bottom of the pool! The water is supposed to be 2 feet deep. You must have made a mistake.

You should have begun with an estimate. Visualize a 3 by 5-foot table top. How many gallon jugs do you think you could fit side by side on this table top? A rough estimate is that you could fit about 5 jugs in one direction and 8 in the other. You could fit about 40 gallon jugs into the bottom layer of the pool. If water were poured out of 40 gallon jugs, how deep do you think the water would be? The water will fill the entire space, so the height of the water is much less than the height of a gallon jug. A reasonable estimate is that it would be about 4 to 6 inches deep. So it takes about 40 gallons just to cover the bottom of the pool to a depth of about 4 to 6 inches. You want the water to be about five times this high. You estimate that it would take about $40 \times 5 = 200$ gallons of water to fill this pool to a depth of 2 feet.

Recheck your work on the problem. Perhaps the given fact that there are 231 cubic inches in a gallon is incorrect. Visualize a gallon jug and some cubic-inch blocks. If you have worked with cubic-inch blocks, you will agree that it would take slightly more than 200 cubic-inch blocks to fill a gallon jug. The given fact appears reasonable. By visualizing two layers of 3 cubic feet by 5 cubic feet, it also seems reasonable that there are 30 cubic feet of water in the pool. The problem must be in the conversion from cubic feet to cubic inches. You multiplied by a factor of 12. But, how many cubic inches are in a cubic foot? Visualize a cubic foot. It is 12 inches long, 12 inches wide, and 12 inches tall. Thus, a cubic foot contains $12 \times 12 \times 12 = 1,728$ cubic inches. So the pool contains $30 \times 1,728 = 51,840$ cubic inches of water. Because $51,840 \div 231$ is approximately 224, there are approximately 224 gallons of water in the pool. This number appears reasonable according to your estimate.

Step 5: *Extend the problem.* This problem has natural real-world connections. Children may be surprised to find out how many gallons of water it takes to take a bath or to fill a pool. Similar problems could easily be devised by changing the numbers or situation.

In the solution to the last problem a deliberate error was made to stress the importance of the looking back step. If children are not taught to look back and to consider their answers, they may arrive at the answer of 1.6 and move on to the next problem without giving it a second thought. The looking back step is essential to the premise that mathematics does make sense. It is also important in encouraging students to take ownership of their work and ideas. It is especially important, then, that you the teacher have acquired the habit of looking back.

Example 2-7: Jodi writes a secret message to Jeremy. Decode the message.

22-14-14-3   22-14   18-23   3-17-1   25-10-1-20

Step 1: *Understand the problem.* Each different number must stand for a different letter. The code is unknown. It is possible that the code is sequential: $A = 1$, $B = 2$, $C = 3$, and so on. The code may use skip counting: $A = 1$, $B = 6$, $C = 11$, $D = 16$, and so forth. It may begin with an assignment for A other than the value 1: $A = 5$, $B = 6$, $C = 7$. The code may use backward counting: $Z = 1$, $Y = 2$, $X = 3$. It may use any combination of the above ideas, or may even use random choices: $A = 7$, $B = 19$, $C = 15$, and so on.

Step 2: *Devise a plan.* It is clear that some guess and check work will be involved. You may also solve a smaller problem by considering the words separately or by focusing on one of the words. Each word must contain a vowel, so you may assume that each word contains one of the letters A, E, I, O, U, or Y. Also notice that number 14 occurs the most often. You might guess that $E = 14$.

Step 3: *Carry out the plan.* You may wish to begin by writing out the alphabet, leaving enough space to write numbers underneath.

A B C D E F G H I J K L M N O P Q R S T U V W X Y Z
        14   17

You already have guessed that $E = 14$. Notice that this is the last letter of a three-letter word. Perhaps this word is "the"; this would mean that $H = 17$. This seems to indicate that the code is sequential. Fill in the rest of the numbers noting that 1 comes after 26. This seems to verify your guess that $T = 3$ and the fourth word is "the" as surmised. You can now decipher the remaining words in the message: *MEET ME IN THE PARK.*

A B C D E F G H I J K L M N O P Q R S T U V W X Y Z
10 11 12 13 14 15 16 17 18 19 20 21 22 23 24 25 26 1 2 3 4 5 6 7 8 9

Step 4: *Look back.* The message makes sense. It seems that you have cracked the code.

Step 5: *Extend the problem.* It is easy to create similar problems. Young children may be given a message and the code; the problem becomes an exercise in one-to-one correspondence. Older children will enjoy writing and breaking codes on their own.

Problem Set 2.1

For Your Understanding

In solving problems in this section, include the five-step problem-solving process in your solution. Write a specific related problem as part of step 5 of the process.

1. Find all three-digit numbers that meet these criteria: all digits are distinct, one digit is odd, and the sum of the digits is five.

2. Solve Example 2-2b.

3. Solve Example 2-3b.

4. Suppose it takes 45 minutes to paint the square chimney part of the house shown in Example 2-5. How long would it take to paint the entire wall?

5. A doll's swimming pool is 8 inches by 1 foot. It is filled with 6 inches of water. How many gallons of water are in the pool?

6. Place the numbers 1 through 7 in the circles so that the sums along each of the three line segments passing through the center are equal.

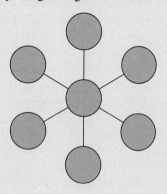

7. Frank asks Irene for her phone number. She gives him a slip of paper that has *P-H-O-N-E-M-E* written on it. Can you determine Irene's phone number?

8. Teresita writes a secret message below. Decode the message.

   7-19-22   25-22-26-7-15-22-8   9-12-24-16!

9. Li buys a used CD for $5. He sells it to Chandler for $10. Then Joey finds out that Ross wants the CD. Joey buys the CD from Chandler for $15 and sells it to Ross for $20. How much money did Joey make or lose on these transactions?

Applications in the Classroom

1. Write and solve a problem similar to Example 2-1 that involves two-digit numbers.

2. Look up "problem solving" in the index or table of contents of an elementary-level mathematics textbook. Photocopy or copy by hand one example or problem from within the textbook that you think is interesting or unusual and indicate why. Be sure to state what grade-level textbook you are using.

3. Look up "problem solving" in the index or table of contents of an elementary-level textbook. List each problem-solving strategy that is covered in that text. For each strategy covered, give one example of a problem that can be solved using that strategy. Be sure to state what grade-level text you are using.

4. Write and solve a pattern problem that uses pattern blocks.

5. Use tangrams and create a puzzle similar to Example 2-4.

6. Write and solve a problem similar to Example 2-6.

 7. Find and print a problem-solving activity from the Web. What problem-solving strategies are used in the activity? State what grade level you think the activity would be appropriate for. What mathematical concepts or topics does the problem address?

 8. Choose one of the manipulatives—pattern blocks, attribute blocks, or tangram pieces—and read the description given in this chapter. Write a problem-solving activity that uses this manipulative, or find such an activity on the Web or in an activities manual.

2.2 PROBLEM SOLVING IN THE EARLY CHILDHOOD CLASSROOM

Encourage an Atmosphere That Fosters Problem Solving

There are several things that a teacher can do to encourage an atmosphere that fosters problem solving. It is vital to maintain an open environment where children are not afraid to make mistakes. A wrong answer can be viewed as a learning opportunity. In problem solving, a failed attempt can be used to gain information that may lead to a successful next attempt. Children should be expected to explain their solutions and ideas; in doing so, they may use their own language and notations. Eventually the children will need to learn correct, precise mathematical terminology and notations. The teacher may include these ideas only if they do not detract from the child's solution. It may be possible to use other students to inject correct terminology, as in the following situation.

Example 2-8: A plane ticket from Cleveland to Dallas costs $139. Estimate how much it would cost for a family of four to fly from Cleveland to Dallas.

Ivan: I estimated $600.

Teacher: Good. How did you get that?

Ivan: Well, $139 is close to $150. And four hundreds is $400 and four fifties is another $200. So $600.

Teacher: I like the way you made the multiplication easier by breaking down $150 to $100 and $50. Is there a name for the property that you used to do that?

Ivan: I call it the "make math easy by breaking it down" property.

Dacia: Is that called the distributive property?

Teacher: Yes, **Dacia**. That is called the distributive property. The factor of 4 is multiplied by $100 and by $50 and when the results are added, you have the answer to $4 \times \$150$. Stu is correct. The distributive property does make multiplication easy by breaking down one of the factors. Did anybody have a different estimate?

Manipulatives, Technology, and Collaborative Learning Enhance Problem Solving Manipulatives and technology are often valuable in problem-solving situations. Research indicates that collaborative learning is useful in expanding children's repertoires of strategies and exposing them to more than one way of thinking about a problem (Noddings, 1985). It is essential to remember that problem solving takes time, and not every group or child will work at the same pace. Give your students the time they need. Many problems will not be solved in a single session or even in a single week. The extend the problem step of the problem-solving process gives a teacher related problems to have on hand for students or groups that finish a task early. Open-ended problems or problems where students are to find as many answers as they can are especially useful when it is known that some students will require more time than others.

🐜 Using Literature in the Mathematics Classroom

Grades 3–6

Math Curse

By J. Scieszka and L. Smith
Penguin Books USA, 1995

A math teacher makes the statement "You know, you can think of almost everything as a math problem." From this point on, the girl in the book sees math problems everywhere, even in her dreams. The book is filled with colorful real-life math problems. Will she ever be free of the math curse?

Classroom Activity

This book is a bit long to read all in one setting. If you read a few pages a day and have students figure out the answers to the math problems as you read, it will last approximately 1 week. Put your own "math curse" on students. Challenge students to find math in their everyday lives and to bring the problems into the classroom.

Pupils at early grade levels were shown a picture of a group of birds and a smaller number of worms. The children were asked the traditional question: How many more birds than worms are there? Responses were collected. Then the children were told and asked: Suppose the birds all race over and each tries to get a worm! Will every bird get a worm? . . . How many birds won't get a worm?

Striking differences in the amounts of correct answers are shown in the table.

	Percent of correct responses when a problem is asked two different ways	
	How many more birds than worms?	How many birds won't get a worm?
Nursery school	17%	83%
Kindergarten	25%	96%
First grade	64%	100%

Hembree & Marsh, 1993, pp. 155–156

 Teaching Connections

Search for Good Problem-Solving Problems A teacher should not rely on the textbook alone as a source of problems. Many excellent problem-solving resources are available. Several of the problems given in this chapter were adapted from a variety of resources (Currie, 1994; Goodnow & Hoogeboom, 2000; Polya, 1945; Reardon, 2001; Stenmark, 1995). The students in a classroom also provide an excellent resource for problems. Teachers should be on the lookout for problems that have multiple solutions or multiple solution methods and open-ended problems, as these types of problems provide excellent problem-solving situations. Children can be encouraged to share real-life or everyday situations involving mathematics.

One advantage to student-created problems is that these problems are likely to contain student-friendly language and situations and may be more interesting to other students than textbook problems. The statement and language of a problem often play a large role in whether students will correctly solve the problem. In *Research Ideas for the Classroom* (see the box on p. 33) Hembree and Marsh illustrate this idea.

The example illustrates that children are more apt to correctly solve a problem when the problem is stated in a manner that captures their interest or provides some motivation for a solution. In Activity 2-1, an alternate version of the problem: "In how many ways can four tiles of different colors be arranged in a row?" is presented.

Capture Children's Interest and Provide Motivation for Problem Solving Do you notice a difference between the appearance of Activities 2-1 and 2-2, and Activity 2-3? Cute, colorful animals appear in Activities 2-1 and 2-2. In these activities a problem situation is described that provides a reason or motivation to find a solution for the problem. In Activity 2-3, the problem is merely stated; no graphics or real-life situation or purpose or motivation for a solution is given. Of the three activities shown above, which activity do you think children will find most engaging?

Children are usually more motivated to solve mathematical problems that appear in real-life situations than those that are contrived and artificial. Research indicates

---

 **Assessment**   **Grades 2–4**
Writing in Mathematics

Curly has 14 pencils. Larry has 20 pencils. Mo has 24 pencils.

    Write and solve as many problems as you can using this information.

 Activity 2-1   Grades 1–3

Coloring Caterpillars—Finding Permutations

Materials: Caterpillar body handouts; four colors of crayons or markers for each group.

Teacher Statement: Each group will get four colors to color the caterpillars with. You must use all four colors for each caterpillar. These caterpillars like to be unique or different, so make sure that within your group, all the caterpillars are different. Before you start coloring, talk about how you will be sure that your group will not color two caterpillars exactly the same. Try to find as many different caterpillars as you can.

    Yellow-green-red-blue  is different than yellow-green-blue-red.

Source: Currie, 1994

 Activity 2-2   Grades 1–4

Don't Cross My Path—Matching Objects

Materials: Pencils, Don't Cross My Path handouts:

Teacher Statement: The handout shows a room with a dog, a cat, a mouse, and a bird. There is also a birdhouse, a piece of cheese, a bone, and a ball of yarn. Draw a path from each animal to the object that belongs with it. The trick is that the animals don't get along, so none of the paths can cross. The paths must stay in the room.

Problem Extensions:
1. Find all solutions to the given path puzzle.
2. Ask children to draw their own path puzzles for other children to solve.

Source: Currie, 1994

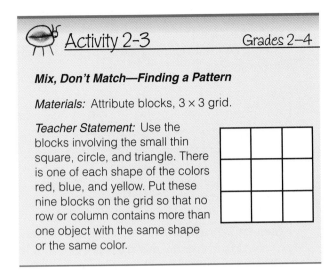

Activity 2-3   Grades 2–4

Mix, Don't Match—Finding a Pattern

Materials: Attribute blocks, 3 × 3 grid.

Teacher Statement: Use the blocks involving the small thin square, circle, and triangle. There is one of each shape of the colors red, blue, and yellow. Put these nine blocks on the grid so that no row or column contains more than one object with the same shape or the same color.

that children often naturally demonstrate a great capacity for high-level thinking in nonschool settings and that out-of-school performance is often better than school performance (Lester, 2002; Resnick, 1989, Silver & Smith, 2002). Children may use their own language and notation in the solution of an out-of-school problem; they may have more familiarity with the situation and a vested interest in the solution. To generate interest in school mathematics, teachers should include real-life student-friendly situations and examples whenever possible. Children can be asked to create their own problems and examples regarding a given topic. Creating problems generates interest in finding solutions and gives students a better insight into underlying ideas and relationships.

Example 2-9: Trisha goes to the mall. In the video store she spends half of her money on a DVD. She spends $12 on a shirt from a clothing store. Then Trisha spends half of her remaining money on lunch, and $3 at the arcade. When she leaves the mall she has $2 left. How much money did she have to begin with? Solve the problem for

yourself before reading the solution given on the bottom of this page.

Step 1: *Understand the problem.* You are to calculate the amount of money Trisha had when she went to the mall. It is difficult to estimate how much money Trisha began with because in the first store she spent half of her money. There is no easy way to judge the size of this amount at this time. The sequence of spending is shown in the figure on the bottom of this page.

You must make the assumption that all of Trisha's purchases were listed. You also assume that the given amounts include taxes.

Step 2: *Devise a plan.* It might be possible to solve this problem using guess and check. However, there is a sequence of events that may be reversed. This indicates the strategy of working backward.

Step 3: *Carry out the plan.* After lunch, Trisha had $2 + $3 = $5. Because her lunch cost half of the money that she had before buying it, she must have had $10 before buying lunch. The shirt cost $12, so after purchasing the DVD she had $22. The DVD cost half of the money that she had before buying it, so she had $44 before buying the DVD. Trisha must have begun with $44.

Step 4: *Look back.* To check the answer you can work forward. If Trisha began with $44 and spent half on a DVD, she would have $22. Spending $12 on a shirt, she would have $10 left. Half of that amount for lunch would be $5 for lunch, which leaves $5. Spending $3 in the arcade, she would have $2 when she left the mall. The answer checks.

Step 5: *Extend the problem.* This problem has natural real-life connections. Amounts spent or fractions could be changed to make the problem easier or harder. At the very earliest grade levels, this type of problem could be used without fractions. Working backward reinforces the inverse relationship between addition and subtraction (and multiplication and division).

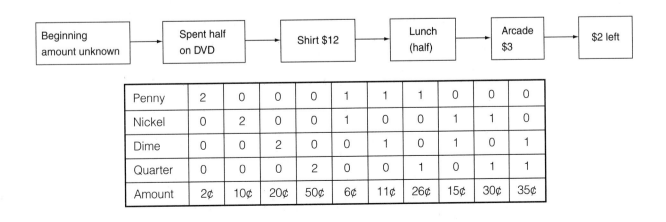

| Beginning amount unknown | Spent half on DVD | Shirt $12 | Lunch (half) | Arcade $3 | $2 left |

Penny	2	0	0	0	1	1	1	0	0	0
Nickel	0	2	0	0	1	0	0	1	1	0
Dime	0	0	2	0	0	1	0	1	0	1
Quarter| 0	0	0	2	0	0	1	0	1	1
Amount	2¢	10¢	20¢	50¢| 6¢	11¢	26¢	15¢	30¢	35¢

Making Connections Among Problem Solving, Other Subjects, and Real Life

Problem solving is not a stand-alone topic useful in solving isolated problems. Problem solving can and should be used in conjunction with other required topics of mathematics as well as other subject areas. Children are introduced to the strategy *make a table* at around the first-grade level. This strategy is important in collecting and organizing information. A table helps to ensure that all possibilities have been considered. Making all possible combinations and considering all possibilities are abilities that are frequently necessary in problem-solving activities and in real-life situations. Counting and determining money amounts is a critical skill in the early childhood curriculum. The following example combines these ideas.

Example 2-10: Jamal has two coins in his pocket. Neither coin is worth more than a quarter. What are the possibilities for the amount of money that Jamal has? Solve the problem for yourself before reading the solution given.

> **Step 1:** *Understand the problem.* You need to determine the total value of two coins. The possible types of coins are: penny, nickel, dime, or quarter.
>
> **Step 2:** *Devise a plan.* You can make a table of all possible coin combinations, systematically listing all combinations. Jamal might have two of the same coin; he might have two different types of coins. Be sure that you consider all of the possibilities.
>
> **Step 3:** *Carry out the plan.* See the table on p. 35.
>
> **Step 4:** *Look back.* The 10 amounts listed satisfy the problem stipulations. There are two coins and neither coin is worth more than a quarter. You were careful to consider all cases. This solution could be checked using manipulatives.
>
> **Step 5:** *Extend the problem.* The problem as given is approximately first- or second-grade level. It could be made more difficult by including more coins or more possible coin values. It could be made easier by restricting to fewer types of coins. There is a natural real-world connection that may be stressed.

In a similar type of problem, children use a grid to solve a puzzle from given clues. This type of problem is popular with students; several books and game magazines contain these kinds of problems. To solve these problems, it is necessary to use logical reasoning and to eliminate possibilities.

Example 2-11: Mario, Jean, and Kayla each own one pet. The pets are: cat, dog, fish. Use the clues to determine who owns which pet: (1) Mario does not own the dog; and (2) Mario and Kayla both put leashes on their pets to take them for a walk.

> **Step 1:** *Understand the problem.* You must figure out which pet belongs to which person. You may make

the assumption that you would not put a leash on a fish to take it for a walk.

> **Step 2:** *Devise a plan.* You can use a grid and eliminate possibilities.

	cat	dog	fish
Mario		X	X
Jean			
Kayla			X

> **Step 3:** *Carry out the plan.* Using the first clue you know that Mario does not own the dog. Place an *X* in the Mario/dog square. From the second clue you know that neither Mario nor Kayla own the fish. Place *X*'s in these squares to record this information. The grid shows that Mario must own the cat, and the fish must belong to Jean. Record this on the grid using smiling faces. You may place *X*'s in the open spaces in the Jean row and in the cat column, because these associations have already been determined. You can then determine that Kayla must be the owner of the dog.

	cat	dog	fish
Mario	☺	X	X
Jean	X	X	☺
Kayla	X		X

> **Step 4:** *Look back.* The solution is: Mario owns the cat, Jean owns the fish, and Kayla owns the dog. This solution fits the given clues—Mario does not own the dog and Mario and Kayla could leash their pets for a walk.
>
> **Step 5:** *Extend the problem.* It would be easy for a teacher to create such problems using student information. In this manner, the problem would be directly related to the students. Problems could be made easier or more difficult, and students could create their own puzzles for other students to solve.

The hands-on nature and teddy bear counters make Activity 2-4 enjoyable for students. Activity 2-4 also provides experience in using manipulatives such as counters and a balance scale. The particular set of counters used here contains Papa bears, Mama bears, and Baby bears. The counters are sized and weighted so that one Papa bear is equivalent to three Baby bears, and one Mama bear is equivalent to two Baby bears. If a set is used where these particular relationships do not hold, the questions in the activity will need to be appropriately modified.

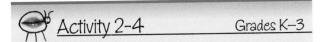

Activity 2-4   Grades K–3

Balance the Bears—Finding Equivalences

Materials: Weighted teddy bear counters, balance scale.

Teacher Statement: Use the balance scale and find a combination of bears that will balance with the given information.

1. 1 Mama bear = ___ Baby bears.
2. 1 Papa bear = ___ Baby bears.
3. 1 Papa bear and 1 Mama bear = ___ Baby bears.
4. 2 Papa bears = ___ Mama bears.
5. 1 Papa bear = ___ Mama bears and ___ Baby bears.

Rather than merely determining equivalences, the problem could be stated in a more motivating manner as follows: There are some Papa bears, some Mama bears, and some Baby bears at a picnic. A Papa bear weighs as much as three Baby bears. A Mama bear weighs as much as two Baby bears. If the bears are to play on the seesaw and wish to have an even amount of weight on each side, how many Baby bears should sit on one side if a Mama bear is on the other side? What combinations of bears could play on the seesaw with a Mama bear and a Papa bear on one side? and so on.

Posing Problems

In posing problems, a teacher should strive to make the problems interesting to the students. The teacher must ensure that the problems posed are grade-level and developmentally appropriate for the students. The above seesaw problem, although interesting, is wordy and could not be used in printed form with students who are not reading on at least a second- or third-grade level. It could, however, be modified to use with lower level students by presenting the situation and the questions in a more visual format. With such modifications, and with the help of a balance scale, first-grade children could enjoy success at solving such problems.

Another consideration in posing problems is that the problems must be well formulated. This is not to say that problems should have a unique answer or a unique method of solution. In fact, problems with more than one answer or more than one solution method often make the best problem-solving examples. A problem that is well formulated is grammatically correct, mathematically accurate, and can be understood (with perhaps some effort) by the students for whom it is intended.

It is up to you to make problem solving a rewarding, exciting experience for your students. You should strive to meet the challenge set forth by the NCTM to preserve and encourage a disposition that values problem solving. . . . In classrooms that focus on the goals of the NCTM standards, children . . . are encouraged to build their math power. They do not sit passively, listening to a teacher who controls the way they do math, nor do they watch quietly while a few highly verbal children dominate class discussions. They spend little time memorizing arithmetical algorithms and rules that they don't understand. Instead, they create or adapt procedures that they do understand and can use efficiently. These students are provided with multiple situations that build, and build on, their mathematical backgrounds and personal interests. Students in these classrooms are allowed to solve problems in ways that are meaningful to them: they receive guidance through insightful teacher questioning; and have ample time and opportunity for thought, reflections, and discourse. Consequently, the children see themselves as doers of mathematics—as mathematicians (Rowan & Bourne, 2001, p. 3).

Problem Set 2.2

For Your Understanding

In solving problems in this section, include the five-step problem-solving process in your solution. Write a specific related problem as part of step 5 of the process.

1. Solve Activity 2-1.

2. The picture shows a beehive. The bees that want to live in this hive aren't very friendly. They all refuse to live in a cell next to another bee. So if one bee lives in a cell, then no bee may live in any adjacent cell.
   a. What is the largest number of bees that can live in this hive?
   b. Is there a way to arrange fewer bees than the answer found in question (a) so that no more can move in?

   > You can't bee my neighbor!

3. A camera cost $20 more than a CD player. Together they cost $120. How much does the camera cost?

4. Your grandfather tells you that he has four coins in his pocket. He has no pennies, and no coin is

worth more than a quarter. Calculate all the possible amounts. If Grandpa offers to give you the coins if you are able to guess the amount within ten cents, what is your guess?

5. I have seven coins that are worth thirty-seven cents all together. What are the coins?

6. A container has 25 red, 25 blue, 25 green, and 25 yellow counters. You are to remove some counters without looking at the colors. How many counters must you remove to be sure that you have removed at least 5 of the same color?

7. A drawer has 10 black socks and 8 brown socks all mixed up.
   a. How many socks must you remove to be sure that you have a pair of the same color?
   b. How many socks must you remove to be sure that you have a pair of brown socks?

Applications in the Classroom

1. Create a handout that could be used with a problem like problem 2 in "For Your Understanding." If you have access to a computer, the technology section in the appendices "Microsoft Word Drawing Tools" may be useful in creating this handout.

2. Create a handout that could be used with Activity 2-2. If you have access to a computer, the technology section in the appendices "Microsoft Word Drawing Tools" may be useful in creating this handout.

3. Solve Activity 2-3. Write new directions for this activity that would make it more interesting for students.

4. Write a story problem that involves spending money (see Example 2-9) and include the solution. Indicate the approximate grade level of your problem.

5. Write a logic puzzle similar to Example 2-11.

6. Write a coin problem (see problems 4 and 5 in "For Your Understanding") and include the solution. Indicate the approximate grade level of your problem.

2.3 Assessing Student Understanding

Three Types of Evaluation: Diagnostic, Formative, and Summative

Student evaluation or assessment is essential to help a teacher determine whether teaching objectives have been

met. Researchers have identified three different types of assessment—diagnostic, formative, and summative (Bloom, Madaus, & Hastings, 1981; Linn & Gronlund, 1995). Before teaching a lesson or concept, the teacher should perform a *diagnostic evaluation* to determine whether students have the prerequisite skills and understand any prerequisite concepts or ideas. In the lesson plan format presented in the Appendices, the diagnostic evaluation is called the *set*. The second type of evaluation identified by researchers, *formative evaluation,* uses a variety of ongoing assessment tools such as tests, quizzes, interviews, observations, and student work or portfolios to measure students' learning and comprehension during instruction and throughout a grading period. Examples of formative evaluation are given throughout the text. Finally, *summative evaluation* occurs at the end of a unit or grading period when a grade is assigned or a report of student progress is completed. Summative evaluations are based on results collected during formative evaluations and may involve finding averages or percentages involving these results. The topics of averages and percentages are discussed later in this textbook.

The Need for a Variety of Assessment Techniques

There are many excellent references describing various assessment techniques. (See, for example, Bush, 2001; Charles, Lester, O'Daffer, 1987; Stenmark, 1989; Stenmark, 1991; Webb, 1993.) Several articles in the *NCTM 1993 Yearbook: Assessment in the Mathematics Classroom* (Webb, 1993) particularly address assessment and diversity issues within the early childhood classroom. Seven types of formative evaluations, many considered "alternative assessment" techniques, are summarized from these sources and will be described and illustrated within this section. First, we will consider why such alternative assessment techniques are necessary.

Standardized tests and worksheets come with many student textbook series. You will probably also administer standardized state or national proficiency tests in your classroom. Why, then, is there a need for assessment tools and techniques beyond those that are provided for you? In many cases standardized tests and worksheets are answer oriented and may not reflect today's teaching methodology that encourages a conceptual understanding of topics and processes. When available standardized tests and materials fail to properly assess student knowledge and achievement or do not reflect current teaching methodologies, "to ensure alignment between instruction and assessment, mathematics teachers may need to develop their own assessments based on the rich variety of alternative methods, such as open-ended tasks, checklists, interviews, extended investigations, and portfolios" (Cain & Kenney, 1992, p. 613).

For example, cooperative learning is a large part of today's classroom. Individual standardized testing does not take this group learning into account. If you use cooperative learning in your classroom, you should be prepared to assess this learning. You may wish to use a scoring combination that considers both group effort and individual retention and achievement: "[T]eachers must be vigilant to ensure that assessments developed for cooperative learning account for both the group environment and individual achievement" (Cain & Kenney, 1992, p. 614). Although one example of the assessment of cooperative learning is presented below, a detailed discussion is beyond the scope of this textbook and may be found in Davidson (1990), Kagan (1994), or Kroll, Masingila, and Mau (1992).

In today's classroom the problem-solving process is considered to be a vital part of the learning experience. For this reason many examples are presented here for which student thinking and the problem-solving process are more heavily weighted than the final answer to a problem. Two excellent sources that further describe the assessment of problem solving and problem-solving skills are Krulik (1980) and Charles, Lester, and O'Daffer (1987).

Seven Types of Assessment

1. *Rubric:* A rubric is a scale that rates student performance on a particular item. It is not a count of correct answers on a set of exercises, but an indication of student performance based on a range of criteria or performance indicators. A rubric may use a three-point scale: 1—complete misunderstanding; 2—partial or incomplete understanding; 3—full or complete understanding (Charles, Lester, & O'Daffer, 1987). A four-point scale would indicate the following: 1—Novice; 2—In Progress; 3—Meets Expectations; 4—Exceeds Expectations (Bush, 2001). You could even use a five- or six-point scale. Specific criteria or performance indicators may be given, but these criteria "should allow for the unusual responses that are often seen in open investigative work by students" (Stenmark, 1989, p. 17). The following rubric could be used to solve a problem such as Example 2-2a. Use the rubric to score the student's work for each of the examples shown in Figure 2-2. See Example 2-2 for a problem statement.

2. *Checklist:* A checklist is similar to a rubric in that a list of specific items is required for a complete solution. The student receives a check for each of the items present in his or her work. The following checklist could be used to solve a problem such as Example 2-9.

____ Considered the fact that Trisha had $2 when she left the mall.

____ Considered the fact that Trisha spend $3 in the arcade.

____ Considered the fact that Trisha spent half of her money (at the time) on lunch.

____ Considered the fact that Trisha spent $12 on a shirt.

____ Considered the fact that Trisha spent half of her money (at the time) on a DVD.

____ Chose a reasonable plan to solve the problem.

____ Correctly sequenced the spending events.

____ Correctly computed the amounts when "half" was spent.

____ Correctly computed the other amounts spent.

____ Correctly stated the answer.

____ Displayed evidence of checking the answer.

3. *Observation Log:* A teacher may wish to use an organized worksheet to record observations and student results. An observation log may be completed during a one-on-one student interview or questioning period, or at a time when students are working either collaboratively or independently at their seats. Observation logs are especially useful when a student may be able to solve a problem but may not have the skill or expertise necessary to record the answer. The observation log shown on the next page could be used to solve a problem such as Example 2-10.

Example Observation Log: In a first-grade classroom, students may have difficulty recording their results for this activity. The teacher could observe students as they worked at their desks with manipulatives, and could ask students to verbally state the amount for each two-coin combination that they illustrate.

Understanding the Problem	0: Complete misunderstanding of the problem 1: Part of the problem misunderstood or misinterpreted 2: Complete understanding of the problem
Planning a Solution	0: No attempt, or totally inappropriate plan 1: Partially correct plan based on part of the problem being interpreted correctly 2: Plan could have led to a correct solution if implemented properly
Getting an Answer	0: No answer, or wrong answer based on an inappropriate plan 1: Copying error; computational error; partial answer for a problem with multiple answers 2: Correct answer and correct label for the answer

Source: Charles, Lester, & O'Daffer, 1987.

Draw a picture and use it to answer the question.
Do all of your work inside the box.
Write your first name and your age inside the box.

Sarah lives in an apartment building that has several floors.
Sarah leaves her apartment and walks down two flights of stairs to visit a neighbor.
She then walks up three flights of stairs to visit her grandmother.
Sarah's grandmother lives on the fifth floor.
What floor does Sarah live on?

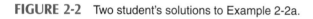

Draw a picture and use it to answer the question.
Do all of your work inside the box.
Write your first name and your age inside the box.

Sarah lives in an apartment building that has several floors.
Sarah leaves her apartment and walks down two flights of stairs to visit a neighbor.
She then walks up three flights of stairs to visit her grandmother.
Sarah's grandmother lives on the fifth floor.
What floor does Sarah live on?

FIGURE 2-2 Two student's solutions to Example 2-2a.

	two pennies	two nickels	two dimes	two quarters	penny and nickel	penny and dime	penny and quarter	nickel and dime	nickel and quarter	dime and quarter
Jarad showed the coins	✓	✓	✓	✓	✓		✓		✓	✓
Jarad stated the amount	✓		✓	✓	✓		✓			✓

Note: *Jarad missed some combinations and showed some difficulty calculating amounts, especially when the quantity involved a nickel.*

4. ***Performance Assessment or Worksheet:*** A teacher may need to create a worksheet to record student performance for a skill or topic not covered by the standardized worksheets included with a textbook series. For example, suppose that a state or district framework included the first-grade objective "The student will be able to extend a pattern involving two attributes," but the textbook series used included only examples where patterns involving one attribute were extended. The teacher must create examples for this topic, teach the topic, and then determine whether the objective had been met. The following performance assessment worksheet could be used to solve a problem such as Example 2-3b.

Draw the next elements in the pattern.

etc.

5. *Writing:* Writing in mathematics was discussed in Chapter 1. It is not uncommon for students in the elementary grades to keep a classroom journal in which they record classroom ideas, examples, problems, and solutions. In the very early grades these journals may involve more pictorial than verbal or symbolic examples and solutions. Teachers may provide writing stems or prompts for the students to address or may ask students to create their own examples or problems for a topic that was studied. Student-created examples and problems may lend insight into student difficulties or misconceptions in a particular area or topic. Students may write about how they feel about a particular topic or may indicate their understanding of how the topic is useful in real-world applications. The use of student journals also provides a method to encourage all students to participate. A student who is normally shy in contributing to a classroom discussion may agree to share some of his or her journal entries with classmates. The following writing prompt could be used with Example 2-1: Suppose that in a third-grade classroom, students have been solving number riddles involving two- or three-digit numbers. The teacher may ask students to write their own such number riddle. These number riddles may be exchanged and solved by other students in the class.

6. *Self-Assessment:* "In order to appropriate mathematics as their own, students must assume an active role in their own learning by becoming aware of what they know about mathematics and by being able to evaluate their attainment of mathematical power" (Kenney & Silver, 1993, p. 229). Student journals, as mentioned above, are an important component in student self-assessment. Students may also fill out specific questionnaires or worksheets regarding a particular activity or assignment, reflecting on how they solved a problem, whether they cooperated well within a collaborative learning experience, or how they felt about an activity or exercise. In the very early grades, the teacher may read the questions and students may mark a happy, neutral, or frowning face as appropriate. The following self-assessment could be used with solve a problem such as Example 2-4.

- I enjoy solving tangram puzzles.
- I like to use the tangram pieces.
- I can name the shapes in a tangram set.

7. *Collaborative Learning Assessment:* In a collaborative learning situation, there are several ways to assign student scores. Some teachers assign each student in a group the score of that group and do not consider or evaluate individual results, whereas other teachers assess both the group score and the individual score. Some teachers assign each student a score based on the sum of their group score and their individual score; others assign each student in a group the sum of the group score and the average of the individual scores for the members of that group. The following collaborative learning assessment could be used with an activity such as Activity 2-1:

Each student will earn up to 8 points on the group project and up to 5 points on an individual follow-up problem.

Group scoring rubric:

- Understand the problem:
  - 2 points—used each color exactly once on each caterpillar, no duplicate caterpillars.
  - 1 point—some part of problem misunderstood.
  - 0 points—problem completely misunderstood.
- Explain the plan:
  - 2 points—clear explanation of how the group worked together to ensure that each caterpillar used each color exactly once and that no duplicate caterpillars were created.
  - 1 point—part of explanation incomplete or unclear.
  - 0 points—little or no coherent explanation given.
- Get an answer:
  - 4 points—found all 24 caterpillars with no duplicates.
  - 3 points—found most of the caterpillars or had some duplicates.
  - 2 points—found some of the caterpillars or had several duplicates.
  - 1 point—found very few caterpillars and had several duplicates.
  - 0 points—little or no work shown.

Follow-up problem, to be completed individually (include a handout with several three-layer snowmen for students to color): Use the colors red, white, and blue. How many three-layer snowmen can you color so that each snowman uses each color exactly once? The snowmen all like to be different, so be sure that you do not include any duplicates.

The individual problem would be graded on the following categories: Understand the problem (0, 1, or 2 points, as above) and Get an answer (0, 1, 2, or 3 points—this problem has fewer answers than the caterpillar problem, so a smaller range of points for the final answer should suffice).

Suppose that a group received these scores: Understanding—2, Explanation—1 (didn't explain how they checked that they were finding all the caterpillars), and Answer—3 (missed a few caterpillars) for a total group score of 6. On the subsequent individual problem, the students' scores were as follows:

	Abe	Beth	Corinne	Duane
Understanding	2	1	2	2
Answer	3	2	2	2

If the teacher chooses to assign each student the sum of the group score and the student's individual score, the student scores are: Abe = 11, Beth = 9, Corinne = 10, and Duane = 10 out of a total of 13 possible points

See Chapter 9 for a detailed discussion on calculating averages.

each. If the teacher chooses to assign each student the sum of the group score and the average of the students' individual scores, the teacher must first calculate that average: $5 + 3 + 4 + 4 = 16$, and $16 \div 4 = 4$. Each student in the group then receives the score of 10 out of a total of 13 possible points. When the first method is used, a student's score reflects both the group's score and his or her individual work. When the second method is used, students in a group may make more of an effort to ensure that each group member understands the process and the problem because each score is dependent on the others.

Assessing Logical Arguments

Only a few brief ideas are covered here relating to logic. The Appendices include a more in-depth look at the topic.

The seven types of assessment will be illustrated throughout this textbook as content topics are developed. In this section we consider the assessment of logical arguments. Logic is not a topic that is covered in the early childhood curriculum. However, logic forms the basis for any sound mathematical argument and underlies the process of assessment. Anyone who teaches mathematics must have an understanding of the basic ideas of logic. Ideas of logic are necessary for the presentation of clear, precise, valid mathematical arguments. When children have difficulties in mathematics or present incorrect mathematical arguments, logic is necessary to assess and remediate the errors.

If an argument uses valid reasoning, it should produce a valid conclusion. However, in some cases the mathematical reasoning used on a particular argument is flawed, thus the conclusion reached is invalid. In these cases, a knowledge of logic is useful to help discover the error, explain how and why the presented solution or conclusion is incorrect, and to produce a correct solution or conclusion. Given statements are often called *premises*. Any given premises should be accepted as true, and you must determine whether the given conclusion can be reached from the given premises.

Example 2-12: Determine whether the arguments given are valid or invalid.

   a. Premises:
      1. All early childhood majors are college students.
      2. Some college students dislike math.
         Conclusion: Some early childhood majors dislike math.
   b. Premises:
      1. All early childhood majors must take a math course.
      2. Some special education students major in early childhood education.
         Conclusion: Some special education students must take a math course.

Solutions:

   a. The argument is invalid, as illustrated by a Venn diagram (Venn diagrams will be discussed in further detail in Chapter 3). The first premise indicates that the set of early childhood majors is contained in the set of college students as shown. The second premise indicates that some college students dislike math. It could be the case that none of the students who dislike math are early childhood majors. There is no evidence given that any of the early childhood majors dislike math.

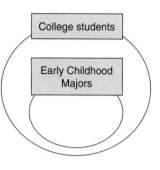

   b. The argument is valid. The second premise indicates that some special education students major in early childhood education. Because *all* early childhood majors must take a math course, those special education students who major in early childhood education must take a math course.

In general, a mathematical *statement* is a declarative sentence that is either true or false. When given as a premise or hypothesis, you assume a statement to be true. A statement may contain a *universal quantifier* such as the phrase "for every" or "for all." For example, "Every square is a rectangle." A statement may contain an *existential quantifier* such as "there exists" or "for some." For example, "Some rectangles are not square."

ꙮꙮꙮ Teaching Connections

Provide a Counterexample for Invalid Arguments and Conclusions When a student first discovers that every square is also a rectangle (around the second-grade level), the student may conjecture the converse—that every rectangle is a square. It is up to you, the teacher, to determine that this converse result is not true. You must be able to provide the student (or assist the student in finding) a *counterexample*—an example that illustrates that the conjecture is incorrect. To do this, you must be able to negate the statement. The negation of "Every rectangle is a square" is "There is a rectangle that is not a square." You should be able to produce such a drawing to convince your students that it is not true that every rectangle is a square. Further examples of common student errors and misconceptions and the logical processes necessary to remediate these errors will be discussed throughout this textbook as the corresponding content material is developed.

Problem Set 2.3

For Your Understanding

1. Determine whether the given argument is valid or invalid.
   a. Premises: If I wash my car, then it will rain. It rained on Tuesday.
   Conclusion: I washed my car on Tuesday.

2. Write the premise(s) and the conclusion for the given statement. Determine whether the argument is valid or invalid: All men are mortal; all heros are men, therefore all heros are mortal (Aristotle).

3. Determine whether the given arguments are valid or invalid.
   a. Premises: If I bring my umbrella then it will not rain. It rained today.
   Conclusion: I did not bring my umbrella today.
   b. Premises: Some students like math. Students who like math enjoy solving problems. Becky enjoys solving problems.
   Conclusion: Becky likes math.

Applications in the Classroom

1. See problems 1 and 2 in "For Your Understanding." Create your own logical argument, then give the premises and a conclusion. Indicate whether your argument is valid or invalid.

2. Create an assessment tool to be used with Example 2-5. Explain why you chose that type of assessment tool.

3. Create an assessment tool to be used with Activity 2-2. Explain why you chose that type of assessment tool.

4. Create an assessment tool to be used with Example 2-11. Explain why you chose that type of assessment tool.

5. Choose an activity from this chapter that is written as an individual student activity. Indicate how you could implement the activity as a collaborative learning experience.

6. Choose one of the books in the children's literature section of the references for this chapter. Give a brief description of the content of the book and explain how you could incorporate the book into a math lesson.

7. Make up two writing prompts or stems that fit in with material or activities from this chapter.

References

Children's Literature References

Atherlay, Sara. (1995). *Math in the bath (and other fun places, too!).* New York: Scholastic.

Birch, David. (1988). *The king's chessboard.* New York: Penguin Putnam Books for Young Readers.

Burns, Marilyn. (1975). *The I hate mathematics! book.* New York: Scholastic.

Burns, Marilyn. (1982). *Math for smarty pants.* Boston: Little, Brown.

Burns, Marilyn. (1996). *How many feet? How many tails? A book of math riddles* (Hello Math Reader Level 2). New York: Scholastic.

Law, Felicia, & Chander, Suzanne. (1980). *Mouse count.* Quarry Bay, Hong Kong: Octopus Books.

Munsch, Robert. (1987). *Moira's birthday.* Toronto Ontario: Annick Press.

Scieszka, Jon, & Smith, Lane. (1995). *Math curse.* New York: Penguin Books USA.

Time Life for Children. (1992). *How do octopi eat pizza pie?* (Pizza Math—I Love Math Series). Alexandria, VA: Time-Life.

Trimble, Irene. (1997). *Crack the code!:* New York Golden Books.

Teacher Resources

Barnett, J. C., Sowder, L., & Vos, K. E. (1980). Textbook problems: Supplementing and understanding them. In S. Krulik (Ed.). *1980 Yearbook: Problem solving in school mathematics.* (pp. 146–156). Reston, VA: National Council of Teachers of Mathematics.

Burns, M. (1996). *50 problem-solving lessons: Grades 1–6.* Sausalito, CA: Math Solutions Publications.

Bush, W. S. (Ed.). (2001). *Mathematics assessment: Cases and discussion questions for grades K–5.* Reston, VA: NCTM.

Butts, T. (1980). Posing problems properly. In S. Krulik (Ed.). *1980 Yearbook: Problem solving in school mathematics.* (pp. 146–156). Reston, VA: National Council of Teachers of Mathematics.

California Department of Education. (2000). *Mathematics Content Standards for California Public Schools.* Retrieved November 12, 2003 from http://www.cde.ca.gov/board/pdf/math.pdf

Charles, R., Lester, F., & O'Daffer, P. (1987). *How to evaluate progress in problem solving.* Reston, VA: NCTM.

Coates, G., & Stenmark, J. K. (1997). *Family math for young children.* Berkeley, CA: Regents of the University of California.

Currie, S. (1994). *Problem play.* Palo Alto, CA: Dale Seymour Publications.

Davidson, N. (1990). *Cooperative learning in mathematics.* Reading MA: Addison-Wesley Pub. Co.

Garland, T. H. (1997). *Fibonacci fun: Fascinating activities with intriguing numbers.* Parsippany, NJ: Dale Seymour Publications.

Goodnow, J., & Hoogeboom, S. (2000). *Activities for overhead manipulatives grades 1–3.* Grand Rapids, MI: Ideal School Supply.

House, P. (Ed.). (1995). *1995 yearbook: Connecting mathematics across the curriculum.* Reston, VA: National Council of Teachers of Mathematics.

Kagan, S. (1994). *Cooperative learning.* San Clemente, CA: Kagan.

Krulik, S. (Ed.). *1980 Yearbook: Problem solving in school mathematics.* Reston, VA: NCTM.

LeBlanc, J. F., Proudfit, L., and Putt I. (1980). Teaching problem solving in the elementary school. In S. Krulik (Ed.). *1980 Yearbook: Problem solving in school mathematics.* (pp. 146–156). Reston, VA: National Council of Teachers of Mathematics.

Linn, R. L., & Gronlund, N. E. (1995). *Measurement and assessment in teaching.* (7th ed.). Upper Saddle River, NJ: Merrill/Prentice Hall.

Moomaw, S., & Hieronymus, B. (1995). *More than counting: Whole math activities for preschool and kindergarten.* Saint Paul, MN: Redleaf Press.

National Council of Teachers of Mathematics. (1989). *Curriculum and evaluation standards for school mathematics.* Reston, VA: Author.

National Council of Teachers of Mathematics. (2000). *Principles and standards for teaching mathematics.* Reston, VA: Author.

Reardon, T. (2001). *Teaching problem solving strategies in the 5–12 curriculum.* Youngtown, OH: Reardon Problem Solving Gifts.

Scope and Sequence Document (2002). Unpublished document. Lisbon, OH: West Point Elementary School, Beaver Local School District.

Silver, E. A. & Smith, J. P. (1980). Think of a related problem. In S. Krulik (Ed.). *1980 Yearbook: Problem solving in school mathematics* (pp. 146–156). Reston, VA: NCTM.

Stenmark, J. K. (Ed.). (1991). *Mathematics assessment: Myths, models, good questions, and practical suggestions.* Reston, VA: NCTM.

Stenmark, J. K. (Ed.). (1995). *101 short problems from equals.* Berkeley, CA: Regents of the University of California.

Texas Education Agency. (1998). *Chapter 111. Texas Essential Knowledge and Skills for Mathematics.* Retrieved November 12, 2003 from http://www.tea.state.tx.us/rules/tac/ch111toc.html

Trudge, J., & Caruse, D. (1989). *Cooperative problem-solving in the classroom* (ERIC Digest No. ED310881).

Webb, N. L. (Ed.). (1993). *1993 Yearbook: Assessment in the mathematics classroom.* Reston, VA: NCTM.

Selected Research Books and Articles

Bley, N. S., & Thornton, C. A. (2001). *Teaching mathematics to students with learning disabilities* (4th ed.). Austin, TX: Pro-Ed.

Bloom, B. S., Madaus, G. F., & Hastings, J. T. (1981). *Evaluation to improve learning.* New York: McGraw-Hill.

Cain, R. W. & Kenney, P. A. (1992, November). A joint vision for classroom assessment. *Mathematics Teacher, 85*(8), 612–615.

Hembree, R., & Marsh, H. (1993). Problem solving in early childhood: Building foundations. In R. J. Jenson (Ed.), *Research ideas for the classroom: Early childhood mathematics* (pp. 151–170). Reston, VA: National

Council of Teachers of Mathematics, and New York: Macmillan.

Kenney, P. A., & Silver, E. A. (1993). Student self-assessment in mathematics. In N. Webb (Ed.), *1993 Yearbook: Assessment in the mathematics classroom* (pp. 229–238). Reston, VA: NCTM.

Kroll, D. L., Masingila, J. O., & Mau, S. T. (1992, November). Grading cooperative problem solving. *Mathematics Teacher, 85*(8), 619–627.

Lester, F. K. (2002). Mathematical problem solving in and out of school. In D. L. Chambers (Ed.), *Putting research into practice in the elementary grades: Readings from NCTM journals* (pp. 75–78). Reston, VA: National Council of Teachers of Mathematics.

Noddings, N. (1985). Small groups as a setting for research on mathematical problem solving. In E. Silver (Ed.), *Teaching and learning mathematical problem solving: Multiple research prospectives.* Hillsdale, NJ: Erlbaum.

Resnick, L. B. (1989, February). Developing mathematical knowledge. *American Psychologist, 44* 162–169.

Silver, E. A., & Smith, M. S. (2002). Teaching mathematics and thinking. In D. L. Chambers (Ed.), *Putting research into practice in the elementary grades: Readings from NCTM journals* (pp. 63–67). Reston, VA: National Council of Teachers of Mathematics.

Stenmark, J. K. (1989). *Assessment alternatives in mathematics: An overview of assessment techniques that promote learning.* Regents, University of California, Berkeley, CA: EQUALS.

Further Reading

Britz, J. (1993). *Problem solving in early childhood classrooms* (ERIC Digest No. ED355040).

Brown, S. (1990, October). Integrating manipulatives and computers in problem-solving experiences. *Arithmetic Teacher, 38,* 8–10.

Brownell, W. (1942). Problem solving. In N. Henry (Ed.), *The psychology of learning* (41st yearbook of the National Society for the Study of Education, Part II) (pp. 415–443). Chicago: University of Chicago Press.

Cobb, P., Wood, T., Yackel, E., Nicholls, J., Wheatley, G., Trigatti, B., et al. (1991). Assessment of a problem-centered second-grade mathematics project. *Journal for Research in Mathematics Education, 22*(1), 3–29.

Cobb, P., Yackel, E., Wood, T., Wheatley, G., & Merkel, G. (2002). Creating a problem-solving atmosphere. In D. L. Chambers (Ed.), *Putting research into practice in the elementary grades: Readings from NCTM journals* (pp. 72–74). Reston, VA: National Council of Teachers of Mathematics.

Goffin, S. G., & Tull, C. Q. (1985, March). Problem solving encouraging active learning. *Young Children, 28*–32.

Gronlund, N. E. (1995). *Stating objectives for classroom instruction* (5th ed.). Upper Saddle River, NJ: Merrill/Prentice Hall.

Hiebert, J. C., Carpenter, T. P., Fennema, E., Fuson, K. C., Wearne, D., Murray, et al. (1997). *Making sense: Teaching and learning mathematics with understanding.* Portsmouth, NH: Heinemann.

Labinowicz, E. (1987, December). Children's right to be wrong. *Arithmetic Teacher, 35,* 2, 20.

Polya, G. (1945). *How to solve it.* Princeton, NJ: Princeton University Press.

Resnick, L. B. (1987, December). Learning in school and out. *Educational Researcher, 16* 13–20.

Rowan, T. E., & Bourne, B. (2001). *Thinking like mathematicians, updated for Standards 2000: Putting the NCTM Standards into practice.* Portsmouth, NH: Heinemann.

Suydam, M. (1985). *Recent research on mathematics instruction* (ERIC/SMEAC Mathematics Education Digest No. 2., ED266019).

Warfield, J. (2001). Teaching kindergarten children to solve word problems. *Early Childhood Education Journal, 28*(3) 161–167.

Worth, J. (1990). Developing problem-solving abilities and attitudes. In J. N. Payne (Ed.), *Mathematics for the young child* (pp. 38–61). Reston, VA: National Council of Teachers of Mathematics.

3

Developing Early Concepts of Mathematics

In this chapter we develop many concepts of early childhood mathematics involving classification, patterns, and counting. Two early classification or counting activities involve using the set of whole numbers $W = \{0, 1, 2, 3, \ldots\}$ to (1) determine how many objects are in a set, and (2) compare sets. Initially children may base set comparisons on visual interpretations and may say that line A below contains more stars than line B. At the kindergarten or first-grade level, a child may be able to tell you the fact that $3 + 2 = 5$ and still may state that line A contains more stars (Baroody, 1987; Copeland, 1984; Piaget, 1964).

A * * *　* *
B * * * * *

Young children may also say that there are more dogs than cats pictured below.

Children will need much practice matching objects one-to-one before they can consistently determine which set has more without making mistakes due to the size or arrangement of the objects (Ginsburg, 1983; Hiebert, 1986).

This chapter presents both conceptual and procedural sorting, as well as classification and pattern activities. These activities help children develop number sense useful for later counting tasks. Sorting, classification, and ordering skills are necessary for the later development of number skills and concepts (Gibbs & Castaneda, 1975). Finding patterns and recognizing relationships are essential skills for problem-solving tasks throughout the mathematics curriculum.

Standards

NCTM

Pre-K–2

Teachers must maintain a balance, helping students develop both conceptual understanding and procedural facility (skill). Students' development of number sense should move through increasingly sophisticated levels of constructing ideas and skills, of recognizing and using relationships to solve problems, and of connecting new learning with old. As discussed in the Learning Principle (Chapter 2 of the NCTM 2000 document), skills are most effectively acquired when understanding is the foundation for learning.

NCTM, 2000, p. 77

Standards are listed with the permission of the National Council of Teachers of Mathematics (NCTM). NCTM does not endorse the content or validity of these alignments.

Objectives

After completing Chapter 3, you will be able to

- Draw and interpret Venn diagrams and perform set operations
- Use set operations and Venn diagrams in solving application problems
- Consider activities to help develop prenumber concepts and skills in young children
- Recognize, extend, and create patterns and appropriate pattern terminology
- Recognize whether children have developed the concepts of conservation and number invariance
- Help children explore relations among sets, numbers, and numerals
- Use correct terminology and notation in describing number relations

3.1 Understanding Sets and Operations on Sets

The concepts and operations of set theory are crucial for the understanding of many mathematical topics. Children learn quantity by learning to associate numbers with how many objects are in a set. They explore topics like more, fewer, or as many as by making comparisons among sets. Many elementary textbook series do not define or explicitly mention sets; however, every elementary textbook series is filled with illustrations, examples, and problems that use sets. So, what exactly is a set?

Defining Set

One might intuitively define a *set* as a collection of objects. An object that belongs to a set is called an *element* or member of the set. With these definitions, two questions arise: (1) What is a *collection?* (2) How might one determine whether a specific object belongs in the collection? The first question is difficult to answer without running into the same semantic difficulties that arise in attempting to define a set. Therefore, we will be satisfied with the intuitive definition of *set* given above. The second question is of more importance and is discussed below.

Is it possible to determine for a given class the set of tall people in the class? It would be difficult to determine who should be included in the set of "tall people" without a precise indication of whether or not a given person should be considered tall. When a specific height is given—for example, a person is tall if he or she is at least 5 feet 8 inches— it is easy to determine who should be included in the set and who should not.

Another difficulty occurs when it is not clear which objects are to be considered. The example above specified that the people under consideration were members of a given class. What if the question had been "Can you determine the set of students who are 5 feet 8 inches tall or taller?" Which should you consider: the students in your current class, all students in your school, or all students in your town, your state, or your country? Perhaps you should consider all students in the world?

To avoid such ambiguities, sets must be well defined. This idea was promoted by pioneer of set theory Georg Cantor (1845–1918). Cantor required two things for a set to be *well defined:* (1) there must be a *universe* of objects that are allowed into consideration; and (2) each object in the universe either is an element of the set or is not an element of the set, and it is possible to determine which of these applies.

Set Notation and Symbolism

Consider the set of whole numbers that are less than 10. This set is well defined. The universe is the set of whole numbers; only whole numbers are considered. A whole number is included in the set, or is an element of the set if and only if the number is less than 10. There are two common ways of symbolically describing a set using braces:

> *Roster Notation:* $\{0, 1, 2, 3, 4, 5, 6, 7, 8, 9\}$.
> *Set Builder Notation:* $\{x \mid x$ is a whole number less than $10\}$.

The set builder notation above is read as "the set of all x such that x is a whole number less than 10." Set builder notation uses a variable and a description that characterizes elements in the set. The example above uses the variable x, although any variable may be used. The order in which elements are listed in a set is arbitrary. Thus $\{0, 1, 2, 3, 4, 5, 6, 7, 8, 9\} = \{9, 8, 7, 6, 5, 4, 3, 2, 1, 0\} = \{1, 5, 8, 2, 3, 0, 9, 7, 6, 4\}$, and so on. In order to avoid listing every element of a set, ellipses may be used to indicate that an established pattern continues. The set above may be written as $\{0, 1, 2, 3, \ldots, 9\}$.

Sets are usually denoted by capital letters, such as $S = \{0, 1, 2, \ldots, 9\}$. Some letters are generally reserved to denote specific commonly used sets. For example, the letter W is typically used for *whole numbers:* $W = \{0, 1, 2, 3, 4, \ldots\}$; N is frequently used for *natural numbers* (sometimes called the *counting numbers*): $N = \{1, 2, 3, \ldots\}$; Z for *integers:* $Z = \{\ldots, -3, -2, -1, 0, 1, 2, 3, \ldots\}$; and Q for *rational numbers:* $Q = \{a/b \mid a$ and b are integers and $b \neq 0\}$. Again, ellipses are used to indicate that a displayed pattern continues.

The set of whole numbers is infinite; there is no largest whole number. In the case of the set of integers, the pattern continues infinitely in both the positive and the negative direction. There is neither a largest nor a smallest integer. The sets W, N, Z, and Q are all infinite sets. The set $S = \{0, 1, 2, \ldots, 9\}$ is a finite set.

The *element symbol* is $\in$, so the expression $3 \in S$ is read as "3 is an element of set S." The expression $10 \notin S$ is read as "10 is not an element of set S." The expression $5 \in Z$ can be read as "5 is an element of the set of integers."

Venn Diagrams and Subsets

One way to visually represent a set and its elements is to use a *Venn diagram,* named after English logician John Venn (1834–1923). The universal set (often denoted by the letter U) is represented by a rectangle. Sets within the universal set are denoted by closed curves; elements of a set are written within the interior of the curve that represents the set. Two sets are denoted by two overlapping closed curves so that common members may be written within the overlapping region. Two sets that have no members in common are called *disjoint.* The curves that represent two disjoint sets need not overlap. Shading is useful to indicate a specific set or part of a set within a Venn diagram.

If every element of set A is also an element of set B, you can say that A is a *subset* of B, or $A \subseteq B$. You may notice a similarity between subset notation and the relational symbol $\leq$ known as "less than or equal to" which can be used to compare two numbers such as $2 \leq 4$. The sentence $A \leq B$ implies that set A is contained in set B; however, this does not necessarily mean that A is a smaller set than B. Consider the fact that every element of set A is also an element of set A. Hence, A is a subset of itself or $A \subseteq A$. This observation coincides with the numerical result $2 \leq 2$. If A is a subset of B and there is at least one element in B that is not in A, you can say that A is a *proper subset* of B and use the notation $A \subset B$.

Example 3-1: Consider universal set $S = \{0, 1, 2, 3, 4, 5, 6, 7, 8, 9\}$ and subsets $E = \{0, 2, 4, 6, 8\}$, $O = \{1, 3, 5, 7, 9\}$, and $T = \{0, 1, 2, 3\}$. You may draw various Venn diagram representations to illustrate the given sets.

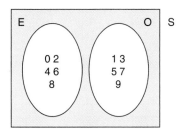

(a) E and O are disjoint subsets of set S that together contain all of the elements of S.

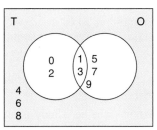

(b) T and O are not disjoint subsets. Three elements of set S, namely 4, 6, and 8, are not contained in either T or O.

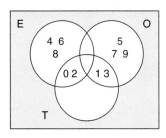

(c) This Venn diagram illustrates the relationships among the three sets E, O, and T.

Operations on Sets

If A is a subset of universal set U, the set of all elements in the universal set that are not in set A is called the *complement of A* or *A-complement*. This set, sometimes called *A-bar*, is denoted by $\overline{A}$. That is, $\overline{A} = \{x \mid x \in U \text{ and } x \notin A\}$.

Example 3-2: Let $T = \{0, 1, 2, 3\}$. Compute $\overline{T}$ when the universal set is (a) $S = \{0, 1, 2, \ldots, 9\}$, and (b) the set of whole numbers.

Solutions: (a) With universe S, the set T-complement is $\overline{T} = \{4, 5, 6, 7, 8, 9\}$. (b) With universe W, the set T-complement is $\overline{T} = \{4, 5, 6, 7, 8, 9, 10, \ldots\}$.

The *intersection* of two sets A and B, denoted $A \cap B$, is the set of all elements common to A and B. That is, $A \cap B = \{x \mid x \in A \text{ and } x \in B\}$. The *union* of two sets A and B, denoted $A \cup B$, is the set of all elements that are in either or both sets. That is, $A \cup B = \{x \mid x \in A \text{ or } x \in B\}$. An element that is in both set A and set B is written only once in a roster notation listing of the elements of A union B.

The *difference* of sets A and B, denoted $A - B$, is the set of all elements that are in set A but not in set B. That is, $A - B = \{x \mid x \in A \text{ and } x \notin B\}$. It is generally the case that $A - B \neq B - A$. The set $B - A$ denotes the difference of sets B and A, and $B - A = \{x \mid x \in B \text{ and } x \notin A\}$. You will on occasion have use for a set that contains no members, which is called an *empty set* and is denoted $\emptyset$.

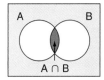 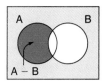

Example 3-3: Consider universal set $S = \{0, 1, 2, 3, 4, 5, 6, 7, 8, 9\}$ and subsets $E = \{0, 2, 4, 6, 8\}$, $O = \{1, 3, 5, 7, 9\}$, and $T = \{0, 1, 2, 3\}$. Find the following sets.

  a. $O \cap T$
  b. $O \cup T$
  c. $O \cap E$
  d. $O \cup E$
  e. $O - T$
  f. $T - O$
  g. $\overline{T} - O$
  h. $\overline{O}$
  i. $\overline{O \cup T}$
  j. $\overline{O} \cap \overline{T}$

Solutions: See the Venn diagrams in Example 3-1 for visual clarification of the given answers.

  a. $O \cap T = \{1, 3\}$
  b. $O \cup T = \{0, 1, 2, 3, 5, 7, 9\}$
  c. $O \cap E = \emptyset$
  d. $O \cup E = S$
  e. $O - T = \{5, 7, 9\}$
  f. $T - O = \{0, 2\}$
  g. $\overline{T} - O = \{4, 5, 6, 7, 8, 9\} - \{1, 3, 5, 7, 9\} = \{4, 6, 8\}$
  h. $\overline{O} = E$
  i. $\overline{O \cup T} = \{4, 6, 8\}$
  j. $\overline{O} \cap \overline{T} = \{0, 2, 4, 6, 8\} \cap \{4, 5, 6, 7, 8, 9\} = \{4, 6, 8\}$

The above example illustrates that a given region in a Venn diagram may have more than one symbolic representation.

For example, for the sets as given above, numerical calculations indicate that $\overline{T} - O = \overline{O} - T = \overline{O \cup T} = \overline{O} \cap \overline{T}$. The shading of this region is illustrated below.

Example 3-4: Shade the region $\overline{T} - O$ for sets T, O, and universal set S as given above.

Solution: You may begin by shading $\overline{T}$ and then eliminate set O from this shading.

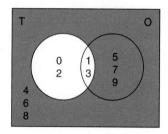

$\overline{T}$ is shaded.

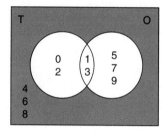

$\overline{T} - O$ is shaded.

A similar shading process could be used to verify that the shaded section of the final picture also represents $\overline{O} - T$. It is clear that the unshaded region of the final picture represents $T \cup O$ or equivalently $O \cup T$. Hence, the shaded region of this picture represents $\overline{O \cup T}$. We will leave it as an exercise to verify that this region also represents $\overline{O} \cap \overline{T}$.

One final set operation is the *Cartesian product* of two sets named after French mathematician René Descartes (1596–1650). The Cartesian product of sets A and B, denoted $A \times B$, is the set of all ordered pairs with first component an element of set A and second component an element of set B. That is, $A \times B = \{(a, b) \mid a \in A \text{ and } b \in B\}$. The number of elements in set A, sometimes called the *cardinality* of set A, may be denoted by $|A|$. If A and B are finite sets with $|A| = n$ and $|B| = m$, then $|A \times B| = n \times m$. In general $A \times B \neq B \times A$, although both of these sets will have the same number of elements.

Example 3-5: Find $T \times P$ for sets $T = \{0, 1, 2, 3\}$ and $P = \{3, 5\}$.

Solution: Note that $|T| = 4$ and $|P| = 2$ so that $|T \times P| = 4 \times 2 = 8$. The set $T \times P$ should have eight elements: $T \times P = \{(0,3), (0,5), (1,3), (1,5), (2,3), (2,5), (3,3), (3,5)\}$.

Teaching Connections

Venn Diagrams and Set Operations in the Early Childhood Classroom Venn diagrams are introduced at around the first-grade level. At this level, there may be no mention of a universal set; it is assumed or implied that the only objects under consideration are those pictured or specifically mentioned. Set notations and symbols are generally avoided; however, children may be asked questions about various parts of the diagram as in Example 3-6.

Example 3-6: A first-grade-level Venn diagram example.

a. Does Cindy own a dog? (Yes/No)
b. Which does Raúl own? (Dog/Cat/Both)
c. How many students own a dog? (___ students)
d. How many students do not own a dog? (___ students)
e. Write the names of the students who own a dog but not a cat. (_____)

Example 3-7: Making connections between teacher knowledge and student knowledge. Find the universal set for Example 3-6, and for each question asked in that example, identify the set term or knowledge required by the question.

Solution: The universal set is $U = \{$Cindy, Juanita, Raúl, Cary, Sheila, Ed, and Latasha$\}$.

a. The student must determine whether Cindy is an *element* of the set Owns a Dog.
b. Raúl is in the *intersection* of the two sets and owns both a dog and a cat.
c. The student must realize that exactly five students own a dog.
d. There are two students in the *complement* of the set Owns a Dog.
e. There are three students in the set *difference* Owns a Dog − Owns a Cat.

Example 3-8: Problem solving—drawing a diagram (third- or fourth-grade level).

Gary, Harriet, Ingrid, Jóse, and Kalayah each have at least one brother or one sister. Two of these students have both a brother and a sister. Use the clues and draw a diagram to determine which two students have both a brother and a sister. Which clues are not needed to solve the problem?

a. Kalayah has only one sibling.
b. Harriet is the only student who does not have a sister.

Math Manipulative: Color Counters

Color counters come in many shapes and sizes and can be used for sorting, classification, pattern, comparison, estimation, and counting activities. They may also be used for place value, addition and subtraction, multiplication and division, fractions, graphing, measurement, and many other types of activities that we shall discuss later. A set of color counters usually includes four, six, or eight different colors. Although a variety of figures are available, teddy bear counters and dinosaur counters appear to be especially popular with young children. Overhead versions are available for classroom demonstrations.

Another type of color counter is the two-color counter. Two-color counters are usually circular in shape, red on one side, and yellow on the other. Although there are only two colors involved, two-color counters can be used for sorting, pattern, comparison, estimation, and counting activities. The two-sided aspect makes them particularly useful in demonstrating fact families, addition and subtraction (especially involving integers), and fractions.

 ## Activity 3-1   Grades 1–3

A Floor Venn Diagram—Sorting and Classifying

Materials: Two hula-hoops, teddy bear counters, and dinosaur counters.

Directions: Overlap the hula-hoops on the floor at the front of the classroom. Place the sign "Red" on one of the hoops and the sign "Bears" on the other. Fill a bag with teddy bear and dinosaur counters. Each student picks one counter from the bag and places it in the appropriate hoop on the floor. Students should explain why they placed their counter where they did. The first student with a dinosaur counter that is not red may need reassurance that it is OK to place the counter outside of the hoops.

Note: This is a concrete developmental or reinforcement activity. It addresses the NCTM Algebra Standard: Understand patterns, relations, and functions. The related Pre-K–2 expectation is to sort, classify, and order objects by size, number, and other properties.

 ## Activity 3-2   Grades 2–4

The One-Top Pizza Shop—Finding Combinations

Materials: Several small, medium, and large circles and topping materials for each group.

Directions: Each group is to make as many different one-topping pizzas as they can. They can make small, medium, or large pizzas, but each pizza can have only one toppings. Students will use the following four toppings. Modify as necessary to use materials found in your classroom, or cut out paper toppings.

    Learning links = green peppers
    Poker chips = pepperoni slices
    Base-ten singles = sausage bits
    Unifix cubes = mushrooms

    c. Gary has a cat but not a dog.
    d. Jóse does not have a brother.
    e. Harriet takes the bus to school.

Solution: Gary and Ingrid are the two students who have both a brother and a sister. Clues (c) and (e) are not needed.

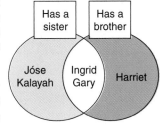

    The mathematics underlying Activity 3-2 involves the Cartesian product. The three sizes of small, medium, and large may be represented by the set $P = \{s, m, l\}$. The

four toppings may be represented by the set $T = \{g, p, s, m\}$, where g = green peppers, p = pepperoni slices, s = sausage bits, and m = mushrooms. Each one-topping pizza corresponds to an element of the Cartesian product $P \times T$. For example, a large pizza with green peppers is denoted by (l, g); the element (m, m) represents a medium mushroom pizza. Since $|P| = 3$ and $|T| = 4$, there are $|P \times T| = 12$ different one-topping pizzas.

Example 3-9: Venn diagrams and logic puzzles.
    Consider the following:

    a. No creature with eight legs is friendly.
    b. All spiders have eight legs.

Are there any friendly spiders?

Solution: Statement (a) tells you that the sets "friendly" and "eight legs" are disjoint. Statement (b) tells you that the set "spiders" is a subset of "eight legs." It is clear from the Venn diagram that there are no friendly spiders (according to the statements given in this example).

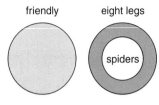

friendly   eight legs

spiders

Problem Set 3.1

For Your Understanding

1. Using set notation, write the set of states that border
   a. Florida
   b. Ohio
   c. Hawaii

2. a. Write the set of letters that are used in the sentence "math class is cool."
   b. What universal set is implied in question (a)?
   c. Draw a three-loop Venn diagram illustrating the relationships among the three sets (1) consonants, (2) vowels, and (3) the set in question (a).

3. Consider universal set N.
   a. Write in roster notation: $\{x \in N \mid x$ is a multiple of $4\}$.
   b. Write in roster notation: $\{x \in N \mid x$ is a prime number less than $20\}$.
   c. Write in set builder notation: $\{2, 4, 6, 8, 10, \ldots\}$.
   d. Write in set builder notation: $\{5, 10, 15, 20\}$.

4. Let $U = \{1, 2, \ldots, 10\}$; let $P = \{x \in U \mid x$ is a prime number$\}$; and let $E = \{x \in U \mid x$ is an even number$\}$. Draw a Venn diagram that represents these sets. Then compute each of the following:
   a. $E \cap P$
   b. $E \cup P$
   c. $\overline{P}$
   d. $P - E$
   e. $E - P$
   f. $\overline{E \cup P}$
   g. $\overline{E} - P$
   h. $\overline{E \cup P} - \overline{P}$

5. Answer *True* or *False* for each of the following. Be prepared to justify your answers.
   a. $\{m, a, t, h\} = \{h, a, t, m\}$
   b. $\{h, a, t\} \subseteq \{m, a, t, h\}$
   c. $\{h, a, t\} \subset \{m, a, t, h\}$
   d. $\{1\} \subseteq \{2\}$
   e. $\{1, 2\} \subseteq \{2, 1\}$
   f. $\{2\} \in \{1, 2\}$

   g. $2 \in \{1, 2, 3\}$
   h. $2 \subseteq \{1, 2, 3\}$

6. With a universal set of N, let $H = \{12, 24, 36, \ldots\}$ and $K = \{20, 40, 60, \ldots\}$.
   a. Describe $H \cap K$.
   b. What is the smallest element of $H \cap K$?

7. With a universal set of N, let $J = \{x \mid x$ divides 60 with no remainder$\}$ and $L = \{x \mid x$ divides 45 with no remainder$\}$.
   a. Describe $J \cap L$.
   b. What is the largest element of $J \cap L$?

8. Ang, Selma, and Tammy represent their school at a speech contest. Use subsets of $\{R, S, T\}$ to illustrate the possibilities for who among these students might win an award at the contest.

9. a. Compute the Cartesian product $\{1\} \times \{a, b\}$.
   b. Compute the Cartesian product $\{1, 2, a\} \times \{a, b\}$.
   c. The Cartesian product $S \times T$ is given. Find sets S and T.
   $S \times T = \{(x, y), (y, y), (z, y), (x, 1), (y, 1), (z, 1)\}$.

10. Use a Cartesian product to find the different ice cream sundaes that can be made with one flavor of ice cream and one topping if the ice cream flavors are $\{$chocolate, vanilla, strawberry$\}$ and the toppings are $\{$caramel, hot fudge, butterscotch$\}$.

11. Draw a three-loop Venn diagram with sets A, B, and C. Shade each of the following regions:
    a. $A \cap B$
    b. $(A \cap B) \cap C$
    c. $\overline{A \cup B}$
    d. $(A \cup B) - C$

12. Draw a three-loop Venn diagram with sets A, B, and C. Shade each of the following regions:
    a. $\overline{A}$
    b. $(A - B) - C$
    c. $A - (B - C)$
    d. $(A \cup B) \cap C$

13. Use a Venn diagram to solve the following logic puzzle:
    a. All of the pets in a house are cats or dogs.
    b. None of the yellow pets are dogs.
    c. All of the cats are smart.
    d. Cricket is yellow.

    Is Cricket smart?

14. The single-element set $\{w\}$ has two subsets: $\emptyset$ and $\{w\}$. The two-element set $\{w, x\}$ has four subsets: $\emptyset$, $\{w\}$, $\{x\}$, and $\{w, x\}$.

a. List all of the subsets of the three-element set $\{w, x, y\}$.

b. Make a conjecture about the number of subsets of a four-element set. Then find all subsets of $\{w, x, y, z\}$.

c. Make a conjecture about the number of subsets of an *n*-element set.

15. Create a Venn diagram of blood types. Human blood can be classified into four groups according to the presence or absence of proteins called antigens. A person may have antigens A or B or both A and B. This corresponds to blood types A, B, or AB, respectively. A

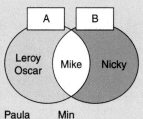

person without antigens A or B is said to have blood type O. Use the given diagram to determine the blood type of each of the people shown.

Applications in the Classroom

1. Write a logic puzzle (see Example 3-9 and problem 13) that can be solved by using a Venn diagram. Include the solution to your puzzle.

2. Problem 15 shows how a Venn diagram can be used in the area of health to illustrate human

blood types. Find another instance in which a Venn diagram is used in an elementary school subject other than math.

3. Classify the level of knowledge and the type of learning experience of Activity 3-2. What objective from the NCTM model (or from your state or district model) does the activity address?

4. Design a rubric that will measure student achievement and understanding of the problem-solving exercise presented in Example 3-8.

3.2 TEACHING PRENUMBER CONCEPTS— SORTING, CLASSIFYING, AND RECOGNIZING AND EXTENDING PATTERNS

There are several abilities and skills that children need to master before they are introduced to numerical procedures and algorithms. Activities that set the stage for later number instruction may benefit children even younger than age 3 (Fromboluti & Rinck, 1999; Wynn 1998). Sorting and classification are essential skills in the early childhood curriculum. Besides math activities, sorting and classifying are used in a number of real-world activities, such as recycling, presented at this level. Sorting and classifying activities may easily fit into many thematic units and topics and may be integrated with other subject area lessons.

 ## Lesson Plan

Bear Domino Lesson
by Cindy Morelli

While looking for new ideas to use for my bear theme, I happened upon a Web site that had a free bear dominos printable game (http://www.billybear4kids.com/clipart/clipart.htm). I was really looking for a nice clip art picture of a bear that I could print in several sizes so the children could put them in order by size, but this game was unusual because it used photographs. I immediately thought that my children would love this. I printed the game on tagboard, cut out the 36 pieces, and thought about the skills my children would be able to work on while playing the game.

Skills:

1. Matching pictures.
2. Turn taking.

3. Organization. How can they arrange the pieces so that they can find the one that they need?
4. Counting. Each child was to start with five pieces.
5. Color identification (black, brown, white).
6. Language. The game had seven different kinds of bears: polar, panda, sun, black, brown, grizzly, and a brown bear cub. I thought that I would tell the children the proper names for the bears, but they could use their own words to describe the bears when they were playing to help each other.

How the Lesson Went:

I am describing what happened in the first small group of four children to play. The other eight children were at the other stations in the room: Dramatic Play, Blocks, Sensory Table, Writing Center, and Computer. Those stations were being monitored by the classroom assistant.

continued

I first asked the children to look at the game pieces and to tell me something about them. The children answered in several ways: a growl from a child with limited verbal skills, "bears" from two of the children, and "bear faces" from one. I asked if the bear faces were the same or different. (Some were the same and some were different.) Zan said he had two bear faces on each piece. I asked again if they were the same or different. Mickey held up a piece and said "These are different." We talked about each bear and I told the children the real names for each of the bears and that pandas were not really bears. We also talked about how the bears looked. The children thought that the panda looked happy, the bear on the log looked sleepy, and that the bear with his mouth open was trying to scare someone.

We then mixed up all the pieces. I showed the children that we had to match the bear pictures with the picture on the table, put the piece on top of the matching picture, and look at the picture on the other side of the piece to see what the next person had to find. I told them that we were each to start with five game pieces, and asked them how we should make sure everyone had five. They suggested we count. So I counted out five to each child as they counted with me. The game began. I led the play by saying, "Mickey, do you have this bear? Who knows what bear is this?" while pointing to the first game piece. Zan and Daejahnae tried to explain to me which bear it was with words. Ciara held up the correct piece to show Mickey. Mickey remembered the real name, and looked through his pieces to find the match. He was very excited when he placed the matching piece. It was then Ciara's turn. She had to match Baby Bear. Because she has difficulty recalling words I asked her if it was Baby Bear or Scary Bear. She correctly replied "Baby."

The game was very active and verbal. All of the children were looking for the bear in question and wanted to put it out if they had it, even if it wasn't their turn. When a child was out of the correct piece we all enjoyed saying "OH, NO!" and covered our faces before the child drew a new piece. The next day, at playtime, I left the game pieces out for the children to direct their own games. They were again very popular. Some of the children wanted to play alone, and others played in pairs.

Skill Assessment:

1. Matching pictures: All four children were able to match the pictures.
2. Turn taking: Turn taking was sometimes confusing. All of the children were looking for the bear in question and wanted to put it out if they had it, even if it wasn't their turn.
3. Organization: The children followed my lead. As we were preparing to play, I arranged my pieces right side up in front of me. The children did this after my prompt of "fix your pieces."
4. Counting: Each child counted to five with me as I dealt the pieces.
5. Color identification: The children used the color words *white, brown,* and *black* to describe the bears.
6. Language: The children were very creative when they were describing the bears. They used "Sleepy Bear" for the one shown leaning on a branch, "Open Mouth Bear" or "Scary Bear" for the one showing his teeth, "Puppy Dog Bear" for the sun bear, and several other phrases.

Things I Can Do to Improve This Lesson:

- I wish I would have thought to enlarge one of each of the pictures; it would have made talking about them easier for everyone. Children with language difficulties could have also identified the bears by pointing to the enlarged pictures.
- I should have also made an extra picture of each bear to put with our Bear Resource Book at the Science Table so the children could look up more information about the bears we were playing with.
- I have a small bear in our teddy bear collection. That bear could have been the turn keeper by having each child hold it during his or her turn.
- The pieces were very small. I could enlarge them so that the children with fine motor difficulties would have an easier time with them, and they would also be easier to see.

Cindy Morelli is in her fifth year of teaching preschool. Her class is composed of 12 children. Half of the children have been identified with a disability, and half are in the Head Start program.

Notice the use in the above scenario of a thematic unit. Many early childhood curriculums and programs are built around such units. The activity described effectively combines objectives from language arts and mathematics and indicates a connection to science. The teacher identifies skills and objectives before the lesson is presented. The centers in the room allow her to obtain an observational assessment log on the four students playing the game while other students are occupied at other stations. She reflects on the lesson and records changes and possible alterations. Although the teacher in the above scenario had already taught a bear unit several times, she is continually on the lookout for new materials and ideas to use in the classroom. She was pleased with the students' reactions to the activity and with the success of the students in meeting the objectives. This is an activity that she will use for many years to come.

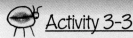

Teaching Connections

Use Your Ideas and Creativity to Make Activities Come Alive for Students In comparison with the lesson just described, the following activities may appear to be dull and uninteresting. As with many of the activities in this text, only a bare outline of the activity is given. It is up to you, the teacher, to create the lesson that successfully integrates these activities into your topic or theme and makes them come alive for the children.

Notice how Activity 3-6 can be used to reinforce the positional terms *left, middle,* and *right.* Classification activities such as this can also be used to reinforce other positional terms such as *before, between,* or *after, top, middle,* or *bottom,* or *above* and *below.* Once children have learned to identify characteristics and properties, and to select objects having given properties, they are ready for more complicated selection or sorting activities.

 ## Activity 3-3   Grades Pre-K–1

Identifying Attributes

Materials: Classroom objects or toys.

Directions: Hold up an object and ask the children to describe it.
    The scenario may go something like this:

What can you tell me about this?
    Yes, it is a square. What else?
Right, it is blue.
What properties does it have?
Good, there are four sides. What else? And so on.

Activity 3-4   Grades Pre-K–1

Classifying Based on a Single Attribute

Materials: Classroom objects or toys.

Directions: Set up a row of objects and ask the children to select the object(s) with a particular quality or property. For example, "Which of these will roll?" Continue the activity with other properties and objects.

Patterns and Pattern Terminology

Patterns are an important concept in mathematics at nearly every grade level. The study of patterns often begins at the prekindergarten level. A simple alternating pattern is sometimes called an *AB pattern.* A pattern in which two copies of a first object are followed by one copy of a

 ## Activity 3-5   Grades K–3

A Real-World Classification Activity—Recycling

Materials: Tubs or bins marked glass, plastic, paper, and trash, materials to sort.

Directions: Gather materials that children can sort into recycling bins. The number of items should be about three or four times the number of children in the class. Dump the items on the floor of the classroom and invite the children to help you sort the items and place them into the proper recycling bin or into the bin marked "Trash." If children place items in the bins simultaneously, after the sorting process each bin should be examined during a classroom discussion. Otherwise, children may place items in bins one student at a time while explaining to the class why each student chose to place the item where he or she did.

Note: This is a concrete reinforcement activity. It addresses the NCTM Connections Standard: Recognize and apply mathematics in contexts outside of mathematics.

Activity 3-6   Grades Pre-K–2

Classifying Based on More than One Attribute

Materials: Attribute blocks or geo-pieces (see Blackline Master 1 in the Appendices) for each student.

Directions: Ask students to hold up an object after you describe it. You may wish to pause in between words of the description. For instance, "Hold up a small (pause) red (pause) triangle. Hold up a large (pause) blue (pause) circle."

Alternate Directions: Show three attribute blocks or geo-pieces to the class. Tell the students to raise their left hand if the object you describe is on the left, both hands if it is in the middle, and their right hand if the object is on the right. Demonstrate to the class.

Which is the blue square?

Sample Observation Log for Assessment of Activity 3-6

	Difficulties Noted with Classification Based On			
	Three Attributes	**Two Attributes**	**One Attribute**	**No Difficulties Noted**
Mario				√
Jayliza	√	√ some correct		
Skye	√ some			

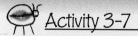 **Activity 3-7**   Grades K–2

Which Object Does Not Belong?—Problem Solving and Logical Reasoning

Materials: Objects or pictures of objects, such that one differs from the rest.

Directions: Show a set of objects to the class. Ask the students which object does not belong with the others. They must explain their answers.
Show a picture of a pen, crayon, chalk, scissors, and pencil. Which object does not belong?

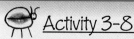 **Activity 3-8**   Grades 1–2

Which Object Does Not Belong?—Problem Solving and Logical Reasoning

Materials: Attribute blocks or geo-pieces (see Blackline Master 1 in the Appendices).

Directions: Show three or more attribute blocks or geo-pieces to the class. Ask the students which object does not belong with the others. They must explain their answers. Some problems may have more than one correct answer.

Which object does not belong?

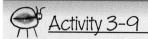 **Activity 3-9**   Grades 2–4

What Do I Like?—Problem Solving and Logical Reasoning

Materials: What do I like? puzzles and cutout materials if necessary.

Directions: Place objects or write words in the "I Like" and "I Don't Like" columns until children can figure out what properties or objects you like.

Examples:

(a) I Like	**I Don't Like**	**(b) I Like**	**I Don't Like**
		Mom	Mop
		Wow	Cow
		Pup	Cup
		Level	Revel

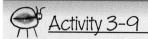 **Activity 3-10**   Grades Pre-K–2

Sorting Objects

Materials: Attribute blocks, geo-pieces, or other objects that may be sorted.

Directions:

a. Ask students to sort objects by color.
b. Ask students to sort objects by shape.
c. Ask students to sort objects by size or thickness.
d. Ask students to sort objects without specifying what characteristic to sort by. Ask the students how they sorted the objects.
e. Ask students what types of objects are sorted at home, and how these objects are sorted. Common examples include mail, laundry, groceries, toys, etc.

---

second object is called an *AAB pattern*. An *ABC pattern* involves repetition of three different objects in a given order. Other pattern types such as ABB patterns or AABB patterns may be similarly defined.

Example 3-10: Pattern types.

a. Examples of AB patterns:
(1) A B A B A B A B . . .
(2) O □ O □ O □ O . . .
(3) red blue red blue red blue . . .
(4)  . . .

b. Examples of AAB patterns:
  (1) A A B A A B A A B . . .
  (2) OO ☐ OO ☐ OO . . .
  (3) red red blue red red blue red red blue . . .
  (4) 😊😊☹️😊😊☹️😊😊☹️ . . .
c. Examples of ABC patterns:
  (1) A B C A B C A B C . . .
  (2) O ☐ ▽ O ☐ ▽ O ☐ ▽ . . .
  (3) red white blue red white blue . . .
  (4) 😊😊☹️😊😊☹️ . . .

Planning for students with special needs: Lesson plans that include activities such as 3-12 and 3-13 should include examples of simpler patterns for lower level students as well as more complicated ones for higher level students.

Children must learn to recognize patterns, duplicate a given pattern, extend a given pattern, and create their own patterns. Patterns also provide an opportunity for students to extend their logical thinking skills and diagnostic abilities.

 Teaching Connections

Help Children Learn to Recognize, Duplicate, Extend, and Create Patterns
You and your students will find a variety of patterns in your classroom. There may be patterns in the paint or wallpaper, patterns in the curtains, or patterns on the ceiling or floor tiles. For example, the squares on a carpet may alternate red, blue, red, blue, and so on. Children will find patterns in their clothing and among their belongings.

Not all patterns are visual; children also enjoy auditory patterns. Such patterns are especially effective with children who are auditory learners or who have limited verbal skills. You can begin a pattern by clapping hands or snapping fingers and children can join in when they figure out the pattern. Young children may have difficulty snapping their fingers, so other actions may need to be planned. The following pattern alternates between slapping knees and clapping hands: slap, clap, slap, clap-clap, slap, clap, slap, clap-clap and so forth.

Consider the following sequence that alternates between slapping knees and clapping hands: slap, clap, slap, clap-clap, slap, clap-clap-clap, slap, clap-clap-clap-clap, slap, . . . Notice that the number of claps increases each time. Is this a pattern? At the elementary level, a *pattern* is defined as a list of objects,

events, or ideas that repeat. Even though no terms repeat, even a sequence such as 1, 2, 3, 4, . . . may be considered a pattern. The underlying repeating idea is that each term may be found by adding one to the previous term. At around the first-grade level, children learn to continue growing patterns such as *X*0, *X*00, *X*000 and so on. Skip counting patterns such

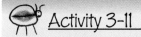 **Activity 3-11**   Grades Pre-K–2

Duplicating a Given Sequence or Pattern

Materials: Geo-pieces (Blackline Master 1) for each student.

Teacher Statement: I built a truck on the board with my geo-pieces. Let's see if you can build the same truck with your pieces at your desk.
  Repeat with other patterns and with patterns that the students themselves create.

Standards

NCTM

Pre-K–2

Patterns are a way for young students to recognize order and to organize their world and are important in all aspects of mathematics at this level. Preschoolers recognize patterns in their environment, and through experiences in school, should become more skilled in noticing patterns in arrangements of objects, shapes, and numbers and in using patterns to predict what comes next in an arrangement.

NCTM, 2000, p. 91

Standards are listed with the permission of the National Council of Teachers of Mathematics (NCTM). NCTM does not endorse the content or validity of these alignments.

Standards

North Carolina Mathematics Standards

Patterns, Relationships, and Functions for Kindergarten

3.03 Identify, copy, continue, and describe patterns.
3.04 Create patterns with actions, words and objects.

Patterns, Relationships, and Functions for Grade 2

3.03 Define, continue, and describe rules for geometric patterns.
3.04 Use patterns to continue numerical sequences; identify the rule.
3.05 Identify and correct errors in numerical and geometric patterns.

North Carolina Department of Public Instruction, 2003

Math Manipulative: Learning Links

Learning links also come in a variety of sizes and colors. They tend to be made of plastic and resemble large paperclips. Learning links may be used with many of the same types of activities as color counters. Learning links have the advantage that they may be linked together. This is especially useful in demonstrating fact families, place value concepts, and some measurement concepts.

 Activity 3-12   Grades Pre-K–2

Extending Patterns—Problem Solving

Materials: Learning links or unifix cubes.

Teacher Statement: What kind of pattern have I started? Yes, an AAB pattern. With your learning links, I want you to make the same pattern at your desk. Now add more links to the chain to continue the pattern.

Repeat with other patterns and with patterns that the students themselves create.

 Activity 3-13   Grades 2–4

Extending Patterns—Problem Solving

Materials: Geo-pieces ■ ● ▲ ■ ● ▲ ■ (Blackline Master 1) for each student.

Teacher Directions: What kind of patterns do you see? Yes, there is a pattern of shapes. What kind of pattern is this? Good, an ABC pattern. Do you see any other patterns? Yes there is also an AB pattern of colors. With your geo-pieces, I want you to make the same pattern at your desk. Now add more pieces to continue the pattern.

Repeat with other patterns and with patterns that the students themselves create.

---

as 3, 6, 9, ___, ___, 18 are also found at the first-grade level. Skip counting is a skill that will be useful in the later learning of multiplication facts.

Problem Set 3.2

For Your Understanding

1. Solve the problems given in Activity 3-14.

2. Describe each pattern using letter terminology such as AB pattern or AAB pattern. Give the next three terms of each pattern.

 Assessment   Grades 2–4
Writing in Mathematics:
A Calculator Pattern Activity

Teacher Statement: Each of you will choose a single-digit number. You will use a calculator to repeatedly multiply this number by itself and record the results. Then write in your math journal to describe any patterns or results that you discover.

Notes: Teachers may wish to specify which digit each child uses. This will ensure that children with special needs receive problems suited to their ability. An advanced student may attempt the task using a two-digit number. This activity simultaneously addresses the Communication Standard, the Algebra Standard, and the Technology Principle of the NCTM. Children can be challenged to find the last digit for products as above that are too large to be displayed by a calculator. For example, an eight-digit display calculator shows an error when the product of nine factors of eight is computed. Use such a calculator and determine the last digit of $8^9 = 8 \times 8 \times 8 \times 8 \times 8 \times 8 \times 8 \times 8 \times 8$.

3. Give the next three terms of each numerical or letter sequence.
   a. 1, 12, 123, . . .
   b. 356, 345, 334, 323, . . .
   c. 1, 2, 2, 4, 8, 32, . . .
   d. 3, 9, 4, 12, 7, 21, . . .
   e. *A, D, G, J, M,* . . .
   f. *F, S, T, F, F, S,* . . .

 4. The sequence 1, 1, 2, 3, 5, 8, 13, . . . is called the Fibonacci sequence. Use the Internet or some other source to research the history of this sequence.

5. Problem solve using a pattern. Determine the last digit of the following:
   a. 5^{20}
   b. 7^{100}

Applications in the Classroom

1. Look up "sets," "sorting," "classifying," or "patterns" in the index or table of contents of an elementary-level textbook. Photocopy or copy by hand one example or problem that you think is interesting or unusual and indicate why. What objective from the NCTM model (or from your state or district model) does the activity or problem address? Be sure to state what grade-level text you are using.

2. Find and print a sorting, classification, or pattern activity from the Web. What objective from the NCTM model (or from your state or district model) does the activity or problem address? State what grade level you think the activity would be appropriate for.

3. Create an activity similar to Activity 3-6 that reinforces positional terms other than *left, right,* and *middle*.

4. Write three "I like" puzzles that could be used with Activity 3-9.

5. Create three sequences in which more than one pattern appears. See Activity 3-13 for an example of such a sequence. Indicate how you will assess student achievement or comprehension.

6. Create five numerical or letter patterns that could be used in your classroom. Indicate how you will assess student achievement or comprehension.

7. Choose one of the manipulative color counters or learning links. Write a sorting, classification, pattern, or counting activity that uses this manipulative.

8. Suppose you wish to use the calculator pattern writing activity in your third-grade classroom. Which single-digit numbers 2–9 would be appropriate to assign to each group of students. Justify your answers.
   a. Inclusion students
   b. Average-ability students
   c. Advanced students

9. Write the directions for an activity in which children practice skip counting by orally reciting some numbers while using a noise or sound for others. For example, MMM, MMM, 3, MMM, MMM, 6, and so on.

10. Choose an activity from this section that is written as an individual student activity. Indicate how you could implement the activity as a collaborative learning experience.

11. Choose one of the books in the children's literature section of the references for this chapter. Give a brief description of the content of the book and explain how you could incorporate the book into a math lesson.

12. Make up two writing prompts or stems that fit in with material or activities from this section.

Activity 3-14   Grades 2–4

Patterns Involving Number and Letter Sequences
Problem Solving

Teacher Statement: Look at the number pattern 2, 4, 8, ___, ___, ___. Write what comes next in the blanks.

Ask students what they wrote. Accept a variety of answers. Students should give reasons for their answers. Some students may merely repeat the given numbers: 2, 4, 8, 2, 4, 8. Other students may have used a doubling process and may have written 2, 4, 8, 16, 32, 64. Other students may have used an addition process and may have written 2, 4, 8, 14, 22, 32 with the explanation that in the original sequence first 2 was added and then 4 was added, so that for the extended sequence they added 6, then 8, then 10. Many other answers are possible.

Consider the letter pattern *M, T, W, T, F,* ___, ___. Write what comes next in the blanks.

Ask students what they wrote. Many students will notice the repeating *T* and will write *T* in the first blank and then another letter in the final blank. These students should be asked to explain how they chose the final letter. Other students will notice that the letters may represent days of the week and will have written the sequence *M, T, W, T, F, S, S.*

Write the next three terms for each of the following:
a. 1, 4, 7, 10, ___, ___, ___
b. 1, 1, 2, 3, 5, 8, 13, ___, ___, ___
c. 2, 4, 3, 6, 5, 10, 9, 18, ___, ___, ___
d. *J, F, M, A, M, J,* ___, ___, ___
e. *O, T, T, F, F, S, S, E,* ___, ___, ___

3.3 EXPLORING RELATIONS AMONG SETS, NUMBERS, AND NUMERALS

Through real-life experiences, children will have developed many concepts involving *more* and *less* prior to the time that they enter school. For example, "I have more cats than dogs" or "My sister has more candy than I do." Initially, children will base their conclusions involving whether one set contains more or less than another set on visual perceptions. This may lead to errors such as those described in the chapter introduction.

 Teaching Connections

Children Construct the Idea of One-to-One Correspondence Children will need much practice matching objects one-to-one before they can consistently determine which set has more without making mistakes due to the size or arrangement of the objects. Many children will already have some real-world experience in making one-to-correspondences. Real-life experiences such as setting the table or passing out classroom materials are an invaluable aid in developing a sense of one-to-one. In initial activities, the objects matched should have some connection so that the pairing of the objects is a natural process.

Conservation and Invariance of Number

In initial activities children use a one-to-one correspondence to match objects and determine which of two sets contains more objects. Children should eventually discover and understand the property that rearranging the objects in a set does not change the number of objects in the set. Young children will not recognize this fact unless they have acquired the ideas of conservation of the equality relation and conservation of greater than or less than relations.

When presented with Activity 3-18, most children 5 or 6 years of age will respond that there are more blocks in the spread-out set (Copeland, 1984). These children have not yet reached the stage of *conservation* or *invariance of number.* Conservation is not a concept that can be taught. Children will construct this concept in their own time, when they are developmentally ready for it. Initially children rely on their visual perception. The spread-out row of blocks appears to take up more space and children will conclude that this row contains more blocks.

Activity 3-19 also tests to see whether children have acquired the concept of invariance of number—the number of objects remains the same when the objects are rearranged. In this activity children may conclude that there are more dog cards based on the relative sizes of the cards. As previously mentioned, conservation or number invariance is not a topic that can be forced or taught. Children will understand this principle when they are developmen-

---

 **Activity 3-16**   Grades Pre-K–1

More Boys or More Girls?

Materials: Students in the class.

Teacher Statement: Let's see if our class has as many boys as girls, fewer boys than girls, or more boys than girls. Before we line up and pair off, would you like to guess whether the number of boys is as many as, more then, or less than the number of girls?

 **Activity 3-17**   Grades Pre-K–1

Matching Unrelated Objects

Materials: Twelve unrelated objects, two plates, and two plate covers for each group.

Teacher Statement: Each group has two plates of objects. When I say "Go" you will remove the covers from the plates. Without moving the objects from their plates, your group should match the objects on the left plate with the objects on the right plate. Keep the objects on their original plate. When I call "More," your group will raise the plate that contains more objects. You should raise both plates if the plates have the same number of objects.

 **Activity 3-15**   Grades Pre-K–1

Matching Objects One-to-One

Materials: Envelopes containing dog cards and bone cards (see Blackline Master 12 in the Appendices).

Teacher Statement: Each group has an envelope with dog pictures and bone pictures. Match the dogs and the bones. Can you give each dog one bone? Are there more bones than dogs, fewer bones than dogs, or as many bones as dogs?

tally and maturationally ready to do so (Copeland, 1984; NAEYC, 1996, 1997; Piaget, 1952).

 Teaching Connections

Use Concrete, or Pictorial Activities to Help Children Develop the As-Many-As Relation Once children are proficient in activities comparing the number of objects in two sets, you may plan activities where children compare or order more than two sets at a time. These activities will develop and reinforce the as-many-as relation while developing the new skills of classifying and ordering according to this relation. Activities 3-20 to 3-23 rely on picture materials. You may also wish to have concrete materials such as counters available so that kinesthetic learners can act out the process using concrete manipulatives if necessary.

Learning the Numbers and Numerals for Zero Through Twelve

Although initial activities will involve counting, eventually children should come to recognize quantities in some sets without counting. They must also come to realize that collections can have the same number even though the objects are arranged in a different manner. For example, both cards shown illustrate five objects. Which card do you think young children would be quicker to name as five?

 Teaching Connections

Help Children Learn to Associate a Number With a Set Learning numbers involves both conceptual knowledge and

---

Activity 3-18   Grades K–2

Concept of Conservation

Materials: Five red blocks and five blue blocks.

Teacher Statement: On the table I have a row of red blocks and a row of blue blocks. Raise your hand if you think there are more red blocks than blue ones. Raise your hand if you think there are more blue blocks. Raise your hand if you think there are as many red blocks as blue ones. Good, we all think there are as many red blocks as blue ones. What about now? (Spread out the row of blue blocks.) Raise your hand if you think there are more red blocks. Raise your hand if you think there are more blue blocks. Raise your hand if you think there are just as many red blocks as blue ones.

Activity 3-19   Grades K–2

Concept of Invariance of Number

Materials: Envelopes containing six dog cards and seven bone cards (see Blackline Master 12).

Teacher Statement: Each group has an envelope with dog pictures and bone pictures. Match the dogs and the bones. Can you give each dog one bone? Are there more bones than dogs, fewer bones than dogs, or as many bones as dogs?

   Now sort the cards putting dog cards in one pile and bone cards in another pile. Are there more bones than dogs, fewer bones than dogs, or as many bones as dogs?

 Using Literature in the Mathematics Classroom   **Grades Pre-K–2**

Just Enough Carrots

By Stuart Murphy
MathStart Level 1, HarperCollins, 1997

A mother and son pair of rabbits go to the store. The son compares the amounts of each item they will buy to amounts that other animal customers are purchasing. The book frequently uses the terms *more*, *same*, and *fewer*.

Classroom Activity:

After reading the story, children can act out the situation described. Each child should make up a plate containing classroom objects such as blocks, learning links, etc. Dice rolls may be used to determine how many of each object each child should select. Children then compare their plates to the plates of other children using the terms *more*, *same*, and *fewer*.

Activity 3-20 — Grades Pre-K–1

Delivering Packages—Developing the as Many as Relation

Materials: Cards with pictures of one to five copies of an object (see Blackline Masters 13–14 in the Appendices).

Directions: Select five groups, with one containing one student, another containing two students and so on up to five students. Students sit with their group in various locations of the room. The remaining students will act as postal employees.

Explain to the students that each small group represents a house with that number of people. The postal employees must deliver the packages (cards) to the correct houses so that there is one item for each person in the house. For example, a card showing three shirts should be delivered to the house (group) with three members. If a postal worker attempts to deliver a package to the incorrect house, the house members must refuse delivery and return the package to the postal worker so that it may be delivered to the correct house.

 Activity 3-21 — Grades K–2

Creating More than, Less than, or as Many as Stories

Materials: Cards from Blackline Masters 13–14.

Directions: Each student will choose two cards. They must tell a story using one of the phrases *more than, less than,* or *as many as.* For example:

Ernestine has more shirts than pants.

 Activity 3-22 — Grades K–2

Using More or Less—Sorting Objects

Materials: Cards from Blackline Masters 13–14.

Directions: Separate cards by types of objects. Deal pants cards to one row of students, cookie cards to the next row of students, shirt cards to the next row of students, etc. Call students to the front one row at a time. The first two students compare cards, and decide whose card contains more objects. They place the cards on the board with the smaller card to the left. Each subsequent student in that row decides whether to place his or her card to the left, in the middle, or to the right. Reinforce correct terminology as students place their cards.

My card has more than this card and less than that one. It goes between.

 Activity 3-23 — Grades K–2

Ordering Quantities

Materials: Cards from Blackline Masters 13–14.

Directions: Each student will choose five cards, keeping the cards face down. At the given signal, students flip their cards and arrange them in order from smallest number of objects to the largest number of objects. If two cards contain the same number of objects, they are stacked. The teacher may choose several students to show their cards and explain their arrangement to the class. For example:

procedural knowledge. Children must understand the idea that a number represents a specific quantity, and they must learn the counting sequence. Many elementary textbook series present several sorting, classification, and pattern activities before presenting any activities relating a number to an amount of items in a set. In this manner children may develop number sense before numbers and numerals are formally presented.

Prekindergarten children often "count" with seemingly random sequences of word names such as "one-two-five-eight-ten." Most children enter kindergarten with the ability to use the correct word sequence to count to 10 or beyond (Fuson, Richards, & Briars, 1982). In some cases the act of counting is based on memorization of the word sequence of number names. Young children often recognize the importance of learning to count and may spontaneously invent reasons to do so.

Whereas correctly naming the terms of the counting sequence is a rote procedure, the meaning of counting is a conceptual idea that children must construct (Van de Walle, 1990). Children may need guidance in making the connection between a number and the amount of objects in a set. In Activity 3-24, concrete objects are used to illustrate counting and the process of associating a number with a set. The one-to-one correspondence is stressed by pointing to each object as it is counted. Some children will need to develop the skill of counting and pointing at the same rate. Children who point faster than they count or who count faster than they point will end the counting process at a number that does not accurately reflect the number of objects. By having children perform this activity in small groups, other children in the group can help monitor the counting process. At some point children should discover that counting objects left to right results in the same total number of objects as counting the objects right to left. This discovery provides evidence that they understand that the last number counted represents the total number of objects (Fuson et al., 1982).

The fact that a child can count a set of objects and tell the number in the set does not guarantee that the child has constructed the idea that the number stated refers to the amount of objects in the set. The child may count a set of five objects, but when asked "show me 5" may point to the last object in the set (Kamii, 1982). A teacher can plan for situations where children count specified amounts and it is clear within the context of the situation that the entire set is represented by the number counted. For example, suppose you wish to do an activity with the children in which each child needs five learning links. You may state "When I call your table number, each of you will go to the manipulative corner and count out five learning links. You will each take your five learning links with you to your seat." With much

---

Standards

Ohio Academic Content Standards K–12 Mathematics

Number, Number Sense, and Operations:

K–2 Benchmark B: Recognize, classify, compare, and order whole numbers.

Kindergarten grade-level indicator #13: Recognize the number or quantity of sets up to 5 without counting; e.g., recognize without counting the dot arrangement on a domino as 5.

Ohio Department of Education, 2001

A Glimpse into the Classroom

Counting in Preschool

One day while shopping Cindy Morelli noticed wooden figurines attached to large springs. When pulled downward and released, the figure bounced several times and then slowly came to rest. She knew that her preschool students would enjoy it, so she took the figure to school. When she showed the item to her students, with no prompting one student began to orally count the bounces, and other students readily chimed in. This turned out to be an excellent counting tool as students must match their counting speed to the speed of the bouncing figure.

Activity 3-24　　　Grades Pre-K–1

Counting Objects

Materials: Blocks or other objects to count. ▪ ▪ ▪ ▪ ▪

Teacher Statement: We can use numbers to count how many objects we have. I have some blocks on the table. Let's count together to see how many there are. One, two, three, four, five. I have five blocks.

Repeat with other quantities. Then have children practice the counting process in small groups.

---

practice and guidance, the child will come to understand that the last number stated refers to the amount of objects in the set and not merely the last object counted.

Help Children Learn to Recognize Numerals A *number* indicates a quantity. A *numeral* is the symbolic written expression of a number. For example, the word *five* represents a number that indicates a quantity; the numeral for this quantity is 5.

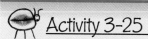 Activity 3-25   Grades Pre-K–1

Learning Numerals

Materials: Object cards and numeral cards (see Blackline Masters 13–14 in the Appendices).

Teacher Statement: We can use numbers to describe how many things we see. This picture has one shirt. This is how we write the number 1.

This picture has two shirts. We can count them: one, two. This is how we write the number 2, and so on.

 Activity 3-26   Grades K–2

Matching Quantities and Numerals

Materials: Cards from Blackline Masters 13–14 and envelopes marked 1, 2, 3, 4, and 5.

Directions: Choose five students to hold envelopes marked 1 to 5. Distribute picture cards to the remaining students. These students act as postal workers and deliver their packages (cards) to the correct envelopes. The student holding an envelope may refuse delivery of a package if it is delivered to the wrong address.

 Activity 3-27   Grades Pre-K–1

Pictorial Counting Activity

Materials: Picture that illustrates several instances of 1, 2, and 3.

Teacher Statement: We can use numbers to describe how many things we see. Who can name something that the snowman has only one of? Yes, the snowman has one hat. (Write "1 hat" on the board.)

Who can name something that the snowman has two of?

How many feathers are in the snowman's hat? and so on.

There is a natural progression in the activities above. Activity 3-24 uses concrete objects and the number names. Activities 3-25 and 3-26 use pictures of objects, and numerals are presented along with the number names. The picture in Activity 3-27 contains a variety of different objects that may be counted and the process of writing the numeral is illustrated. Later activities will help children write the numeral associated with a number of objects.

Help Children Learn to Write Numerals   Kindergarten- and first-grade-level textbooks often contain pages of exercises where students practice writing numerals. You should provide a variety of writing experiences to help maintain interest in writing. Students at this level enjoy writing on their own student-sized chalkboards or writing with their fingers in pans of sand or rice. Writing in pans of sand or rice allows the child to easily erase when mistakes are made; writing with a pencil on paper is not as forgiving.

Correctly forming numerals is a skill that requires much practice. It is common for young students to reverse certain numerals. With practice and attention, most children will outgrow this habit (Hasazi & Hasazi, 1972; Stromer 1975). Only if numeral reversal continues throughout the third- or fourth-grade level should this be a concern.

Microsoft® Word drawing tools can be useful in creating classroom handouts such as the one shown in the assessment on p. 65. See the technology section in Appendix B at the end of the textbook for an introduction to Microsoft Word drawing features.

Help Children Understand the Concept of Zero   Most elementary textbook series introduce at least the numerals for one through five before introducing the idea of zero. As with other topics of mathematics, the concept of zero should be presented before the symbolism and should be approached through familiar examples. Some children may even be surprised to learn that there is a symbol to represent zero. They may think "If zero means nothing, why write something?"

Learning About Larger Numbers

Activities similar to those given previously in this section can be used to present numerals for 6 through 12. Ten is the first number that requires more than a single symbol numeral. However, most textbook series do not make special

Assessment
Sample Assessment Worksheet

Note the relationship between the task below and Activities 3-25 and 3-26. At this point it would be inappropriate to ask the children to write the numeral. Writing numerals is covered in a later activity. The teacher should read the directions to the students and may need to provide assistance to students with limited verbal abilities to ensure that these students understand the directions given. An example is shown on the handout.

Help the dog count the bones.
Draw a line from the bones to the numeral that tells how many.

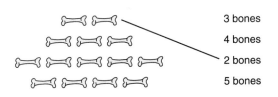

3 bones

4 bones

2 bones

5 bones

 ## Activity 3-28   Grades K–2

Introducing Zero

Materials: Plates and blocks.

Directions: Hold up a plate containing four blocks.

Teacher Statement: How many blocks are on this plate? One, two, three, four. Hold up an empty plate. How many blocks are on this plate?

There are *no* blocks on this plate. The number word for no objects is *zero.* We write the numeral 0 for zero.

We can use *zero* to describe other situations. Raise your hand if you have two sisters. Raise your hand if you have one sister. Raise your hand if you have zero sisters. What does it mean to say you have zero sisters? and so on.

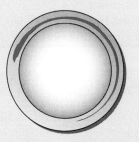

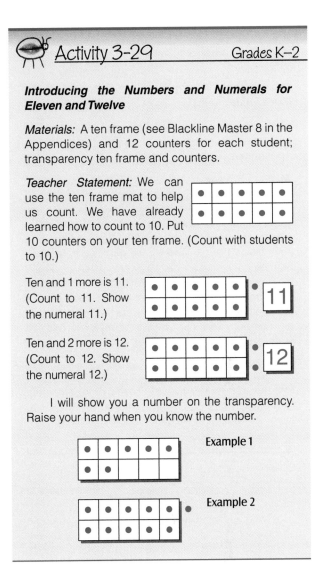

Activity 3-29   Grades K–2

Introducing the Numbers and Numerals for Eleven and Twelve

Materials: A ten frame (see Blackline Master 8 in the Appendices) and 12 counters for each student; transparency ten frame and counters.

Teacher Statement: We can use the ten frame mat to help us count. We have already learned how to count to 10. Put 10 counters on your ten frame. (Count with students to 10.)

Ten and 1 more is 11. (Count to 11. Show the numeral 11.)

Ten and 2 more is 12. (Count to 12. Show the numeral 12.)

I will show you a number on the transparency. Raise your hand when you know the number.

Example 1

Example 2

numeral 11, 12 objects with numeral 12, and so on. The place value ideas and properties can be analyzed in later activities once children are familiar and comfortable with these numbers. We will discuss place value in Chapter 4; however, the idea of regrouping, trading ten singles for a ten strip, is introduced in Activity 3-30.

Ordinal Numbers

Numbers that are used to express a quantity are called *cardinal numbers.* Children must also learn to use *ordinal numbers* to express position or order in a sequence. At around the kindergarten level, children learn the terms *first, second, third, fourth, fifth, sixth, seventh, eighth, ninth, tenth, eleventh,* and *twelfth.* You will find many everyday classroom opportunities to reinforce the use of such terms. Ordinal numbers can also be used to sequence events in the areas of social studies and science. Specific activities that stress the difference between cardinal numbers and ordinal numbers can also be planned.

mention of the place value ideas involved when first introducing symbols such as 10, 11, and 12. These textbook series allow children to become accustomed to the idea of representing 10 objects with numeral 10, 11 objects with

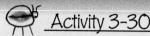 **Activity 3-30**   Grades K–2

Counting to Twenty-five—An Introduction to Place Value

Materials: Two smiley ten strips and 10 smiley singles for each student (see Blackline Master 7 in the Appendices).

Teacher Statement: We are going to use smiley faces to help us count to some pretty big numbers. Does everyone have 10 single smiley faces? Let's count them to be sure. (Count with students to make sure that each one has 10 singles.) Because we each have only 10 single smileys, we will have to regroup or trade each time we get 10 singles when we count. How many faces are on a smiley strip? You think that there are 10? Let's count them. Yes, there are 10 faces on each smiley strip. We are ready to count to big numbers now. First we will count to 25. We will start by counting smiley singles:

☺☺☺☺☺☺☺☺☺☺ → ☺☺☺☺☺☺☺☺☺☺

One, two, three, four, five, six, seven, eight, nine, ten. Regroup. Trade the 10 singles for a smiley strip. That is still 10 faces and we can keep counting.

☺☺☺☺☺☺☺☺☺☺   ☺☺☺☺☺☺☺☺☺☺
☺ eleven   ☺☺ twelve

Continue counting while sliding single smileys into view until you reach 20:

Twenty—regroup. We can trade the 10 single smileys for a smiley strip. Now we have 2 smiley strips. That is 20 faces and we can continue counting.

☺☺☺☺☺☺☺☺☺☺   ☺☺☺☺☺☺☺☺☺☺
☺☺☺☺☺☺☺☺☺☺ → ☺☺☺☺☺☺☺☺☺☺

☺☺☺☺☺☺☺☺☺☺   ☺☺☺☺☺☺☺☺☺☺
☺☺☺☺☺☺☺☺☺☺   ☺☺☺☺☺☺☺☺☺☺
☺ twenty-one   ☺☺ twenty-two

Continue counting to 25. Repeat with other numbers.

Symbols for Greater Than and Less Than

At around the second-grade level, number comparisons are made using the symbols for *greater than* (>) and *less than* (<). Although the number sentences "5 > 3" and "3 < 5" both reflect the idea that a set with five elements contains more members than a set with three elements, these number sentences do differ. The first is

---

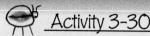 **Activity 3-31**   Grades 1–2

Comparing Cardinal Numbers and Ordinal Numbers

Materials: Cards with cardinal and ordinal numbers for half of the students.

Directions: Divide the class into two groups. Make two lines of students and review the ordinal numbers by having each student state their position (first, second, . . .) in the line of their group. Tell the students that they will play a game where they show the difference between a number that tells how many and a number that names a position.

Staying in line, all students will sit on the floor. You will read a card from the deck. If you read an ordinal card such as *third*, the third student should stand. If you read a cardinal card such as *three*, three students in the group should stand. The first group to correctly show you what is written on the card gets a point.

Example: The teacher reads the card "three." Two groups are shown. The group on the right gets a point. If the card read had been "third" the group on the left would have received the point.

read as "five is greater than three" and the second is read as "three is less than five." As the teacher, you must be careful to be correct and consistent in your usage of these symbols.

Two related symbols are *greater than or equal to* (≥) and *less than or equal to* (≤). The number sentences "5 ≥ 3" and "3 ≤ 5" are respectively "five is greater than or equal to three" and "three is less than or equal to five." The statements "5 ≤ 5" and "5 ≥ 5" are also true number sentences because "five is less than or equal to five" and "five is greater than or equal to five." To help students remem-

---

Teacher-Created Materials for Grades Pre-K–1:

Preschool teacher Cindy Morelli read the book *Over on the Farm* by Christopher Gunson (1995) to a Head Start preschool class. This book features a simple, catchy rhyme that introduces farm animals and their babies in increasing numbers—from a mother cat and her little cat 1 to a mother pig and her little piggies 10. The children loved the book! They begged Miss Morelli to read it again and again.

To capitalize on this interest, Miss Morelli created an activity set that corresponds to the book. Laminated foldout pages contain the phrases used in the book to describe the baby animals along with the correct number of Velcro-covered positions for each animal. Laminated baby animals contain Velcro strips on their backs so that they can be secured to the positions. The activity set can be used for counting, sorting, set comparison, number recognition, and for teaching ordinal numbers. The children love the activity set as much as they loved the book.

Morelli, 2003

ber how these symbols are used, teachers may introduce these relational symbols using a visualization such as a hungry mouth that always chooses to eat the larger number.

Problem Set 3.3

For Your Understanding

1. Identify the number usage as cardinal or ordinal, or identification for each of the numbers in the following sentence: Batter two in our line-up is number five who hit three home runs so far this season.

2. For each number sentence below, write the sentence in words and indicate whether it is true or false.
   a. $3 < 3$
   b. $5 > 7$
   c. $4 \leq 7$
   d. $0 \geq 1$

Applications in the Classroom

1. Write an activity that will help children discover that rearranging objects in a set does not change the number of objects in the set.

2. Design materials for a matching activity in which the objects to be matched have a natural connection such as the dog and bone materials of Blackline Master 12.

3. What is your response if a child claims there are more blue blocks than red blocks after the row of blue blocks in Activity 3-18 is spread out?

4. Design materials for a "more than, fewer than, as-many-as" activity.

5. What is your response if a student claims that the picture of pants below contains more objects than the picture of cookies?

6. Choose a grade level K, 1, or 2. Obtain an elementary-level textbook for this level. In what order are the following topics presented: sorting, classification, patterns, working with numbers?

7. How do you respond when a child counts faster than he or she points or points faster than he or she counts when counting objects?

8. Create three pictures that could be used with Activity 3-26.

9. You are watching a kindergarten student count five blocks that are in a row. The student correctly counts: one, two, three, four, five. You ask the student to pick up three blocks. The student picks up only the third block. How do you respond?

10. List five classroom situations or questions that involve the concept of zero.

11. List five classroom situations in which you can use the idea of ordinal numbers.

12. Write a lesson plan that describes how you will introduce the topic of ordinal numbers in a kindergarten classroom. Follow the format given

by your instructor or use the lesson plan format given in Appendix A.

13. Ask a student to count a pile of blocks. Cover the blocks with a piece of paper and ask the student how many blocks are under the paper. What is the purpose of the activity described?

14. Write a lesson plan that describes how you will introduce the greater than and less than symbols in a second-grade classroom. Follow the format given by your instructor or use the lesson plan format given in Appendix A.

 15. Recite the words for 1 to 30 in the English language counting sequence. List at least three difficulties that children might have when learning this sequence. See the textbook companion Web site for a discussion of languages other than English in which some of these difficulties are avoided.

References

Children's Literature References

Aker, Suzanne. (1990). *What comes in 2's, 3's, and 4's?* New York: Simon & Schuster.

Anno, Mitsumasa. (1986). *Anno's counting book.* New York: HarperCollins.

Baker, Alan & Petty, Kate. (1998). *Little rabbit's first number book.* Boston: Houghton Mifflin.

Bang, Molly. (1991). *Ten, nine, eight.* New York: William Morrow.

Bender, Robert. (1996). *The A to Z beastly jamboree.* New York: Penguin Books.

Carle, Eric. (1998). *1, 2, 3 to the zoo.* New York: Putnam.

Crew, Donald. (1986). *Ten black dots.* New York: William Morrow.

Edwards, Pamela. (2000). *Roar! A noisy counting book.* NewYork: HarperCollins.

Gunson, Christopher. (1995). *Over on the farm: A counting picture book rhyme.* New York: Scholastic.

Hard, Charlotte. (1995). *One green island. An animal counting gamebook:* Cambridge, MA: Candlewick Press.

Hayward, Linda. (1992). *I can count to ten and back again* (a Sesame Street book.) Western.

Hill, E. (1999). *Spot can count.* New York: Putnam's Sons.

Hutchings, A., & Hutchings, R. (1997). *The gummy candy counting book.* New York: Scholastic.

Keenan, Sheila. (1997). *More or less a mess* (Hello Math Reader Level 2). New York: Scholastic.

Kleinhenz, Sydnie. (1997). *More for me!* (Hello Math Reader Level 2). New York: Scholastic.

Maccarone, Grace. (1995). *Monster math* (Hello Math Reader Level 1.) New York: Scholastic.

McGrath, Barbara Barbieri. (1994). *The M&M's brand counting book.* Watertown, MA: Charlesbridge.

McGrath, Barbara Barbieri (1998). *The Cheerios counting book.* New York: Scholastic.

Murphy, Stuart (1997). *Just enough carrots* (MathStart Level 1). New York: HarperCollins.

Pallota, Jerry (1992). *The icky bug counting book.* Watertown, MA: Charlesbridge.

Dr. Seuss (1988). *One fish, two fish, red fish, blue fish.* New York: Random House.

Wilson, Anna. (1999). *Over in the grasslands.* New York: Scholastic.

Teacher Resources

Bentley, B. (1995). *Math games and activities for the primary grades (grades preK–2).* Parsippany, NJ: Fearon Teacher Aids.

McGowan, D., & Schrooten, M. (1997). *Math play: 80 ways to count & learn.* Charlotte, VT: Williamson.

McIntosh, A., Reys, B. J., & Reys, R. E. (1997). *Number sense: Simple effective number sense experiences* (Grades 1–2). White plans, NY: Cuisenaire—Dale Seymour.

National Association for the Education of Young Children. (1996, 1997). *Developmentally appropriate practice in early childhood programs serving children from birth through age 8* Washington, DC: Author.

National Council of Teachers of Mathematics. (2000). *Principles and standards for school mathematics.* Reston, VA: Author.

North Carolina Department of Public Instruction. (2003). *North Carolina Mathematics Standard Course Study and Grade Level Competencies K–12 (2003).* Retrieved November 19, 2003, from http://www.dpi.state.nc.us/curriculum/mathematics/standard2003/index.html

Ohio Department of Education. (2001). *Ohio Academic Content Standards.* Retrieved November 12, 2003 from http://www.ode.state.oh.us/academic_content_standards/pdf/MATH.pdf

Texas Education Agency. (1998). *Chapter 111. Texas Essential Knowledge and Skills for Mathematics.* Retrieved November 12, 2003 from http://www.tea.state.tx.us/rules/tac/ch111toc.html

Van de Walle, J. (1990). Concepts of number. In J. N. Payne (Ed.), *Mathematics for the young child* (pp. 63–87). Reston, VA: National Council of Teachers of Mathematics.

Whitin, D. J., Mills, H., & O'Keefe, T. (1994). Exploring subject areas with a counting book. *Teaching Children Mathematics, 1*(3), 170–177.

Young, C., & Maulding, W. (1994). Mathematics and Mother Goose. *Teaching Children Mathematics 1*(1), 36–38.

Selected Research Books and Articles

Baroody, A. J. (1987). *Children's mathematical thinking: A developmental framework for preschool, primary, and special education teachers.* New York: Teachers College Press.

Copeland, R. (1984). *How children learn mathematics: Teaching implications of Piaget's research* (4th ed.). New York: Macmillan.

Fromboluti, C. S., & Rinck, N. (1999). *Early childhood: Where learning begins—Mathematics.* Washington, DC: U.S. Department of Education.

Fuson, K. C., Richards, J., & Briars, D. J. (1982). The acquisition and elaboration of the number word sequence. In C. Brainerd (Ed.), *Children's logical and mathematical cognition: Progress in cognitive development* (pp. 33–92). Berlin Heidelberg, New York: Springer-Verlag.

Gibbs, E. G., & Castaneda, A. M. (1975). Experiences for young children. In J. N. Payne (Ed.), *37th Yearbook: Mathematics learning in early childhood* (pp. 95–124). Reston, VA: NCTM.

Ginsburg, H. (Ed.). (1983). *The development of mathematical thinking.* New York: Academic Press.

Hasazi, J. E., & Hasazi, S.E. (1972). Effects of teaching attention on digit-reversal behavior in an elementary school child. *Journal of Applied Behavior Analysis, 5,* 157–162.

Hiebert, J. (Ed.). (1986). *Conceptual and procedural knowledge: The case of mathematics.* Hillsdale, NJ: Lawrence Erlbaum Associates.

Hiebert, J. (1989). The struggle to link written symbols with understandings: An update. *Arithmetic Teacher, 36*(7), 38–44.

Kamii, C. (1982). *Number in preschool and kindergarten.* Washington, DC: National Association for the Education of Young Children.

Piaget, J. (1952). *The child's conception of number.* London: Routledge & Kegan Paul.

Piaget, J. (1964). *The child's conception of number.* London: Routledge and Kegan Paul.

Stromer, R. (1975). Modifying letter and number reversals in elementary school children. *Journal of Applied Behavior Analysis, 8,* 211.

Wynn, K. (1998). Numerical competence in infants. In C. Donlan (Ed.), *The Development of Mathematics Skills* (pp. 1–25). New York: Psychology Press.

Further Reading

Alexander, K. L., & Entwisle, D. R. (1988). Achievement in the first 2 years of school: Patterns and processes. *Monographs of the Society for Research in Child Development, 53* (2, Serial No. 218). Ann Arbor: University of Michigan.

Baratta-Lorton, M. (1976). *Mathematics their way.* Addison-Wesley.

Baroody, A. J., & Benson, A. (2001). Early number instruction. *Teaching Children Mathematics 8*(3), 154–158.

Bresser, R., & Holtzman, C. (1999). *Developing number sense.* Sausalito, CA: Math Solutions Publications.

Burns, M. (1997). How I boost my students' number sense. *Instructor 106*(7) 49–54, 73.

Burton, G., Mills, A., Lennon, C., & Parker, C. (1993). *Number sense and operations: Addenda series, grades K–6.* Reston, VA: National Council of Teachers of Mathematics.

Clements, D. H., & Callahan, L. G., (1983, November). Number or prenumber foundational experiences for young children: Must we choose? *Arithmetic Teacher 31*(3), 34–37.

Geary, D. C. (1994). *Children's mathematical development: Research and practical applications.* Washington DC.: American Psychological Association.

Gelman, R., & Meck, E. (1983). Preschoolers' counting: Principles before skill. *Cognition 13,* 343–359.

Huinker, D. (2002). Calculators as learning tools for young children's explorations of number. *Teaching Children Mathematics 8*(6), 316–321.

Maxim, G. W. (1989). Developing preschool mathematical concepts. *Arithmetic Teacher, 37*(4), 36–41.

Morelli, C. (2003). *Over the farm activity set.* Unpublished activity set for use with the children's literature selection by Christopher Gunson.

National Council of Teachers of Mathematics. Number sense [Focus issue]. *Arithmetic Teacher, 36*(6).

Naylor, M., & Naylor, P. (2001). Building and using the amazing abacus. *Teaching Children Mathematics 8*(4), 202–205.

Payne, J. N., & Huinker, D. M. (1993). Early number and numeration. In R. J. Jensen (Ed.), *Research ideas for the classroom: Early childhood mathematics* (pp. 43–71). New York: Macmillan.

Van de Walle, J. A., & Watkins, K. B. (1993). Early development of number sense. In R. J. Jensen (Ed.), *Research ideas for the classroom: Early childhood mathematics* (pp. 127–150). New York: Macmillan.

4 Understanding Place Value and Numeration Systems

The idea of *place value* is precisely what the phrase suggests: each place has a specific value. The digit written in a specific place indicates the number of units of that place value that occur, with the right-most digit indicating the number of singles or ones. For example, the number twenty-seven is represented by the symbolic expression 27. This number contains two tens and seven ones.

Place value is one of the most important concepts covered in the early childhood mathematics curriculum. Many of the difficulties that children have with later arithmetic concepts and procedures can be traced back to a lack of a solid understanding of place value concepts (Kouba, Brown, Carpenter, Lindquist, Silver, & Swafford, 1988). For example, consider the child who makes the error below.

$$\begin{array}{r} 27 \\ + 35 \\ \hline 512 \end{array}$$

It may first appear that this student has difficulty with addition problems, but the error made is not really an addition error; it is a regrouping error. The child who has a solid understanding of place value concepts (and who has learned to look back and consider whether an answer makes sense) would not make such an error or would recognize and correct it.

Because you are already quite familiar with the concepts and operations of the base-ten numeration system, we begin this chapter with an exploration of the base-four numeration system. This is intended to provide you with some insights into difficulties that early childhood students may encounter as they explore concepts and operations within the base-ten numeration system.

Standards

NCTM

Pre-K–2

It is absolutely essential that students develop a solid understanding of the base-ten numeration system and place-value concepts by the end of grade 2.

NCTM, 2000, p. 81

Standards are listed with the permission of the National Council of Teachers of Mathematics (NCTM). NCTM does not endorse the content or validity of these alignments.

Objectives

After completing Chapter 4, you will be able to

- Count forward and backward and illustrate regrouping and other place value concepts within the base-four and other base numeration systems
- Perform additions and subtractions within the base-four and other base numeration systems
- Describe how to help children develop place value concepts
- Use correct terminology and procedures in working with large numbers and rounding to a given place value
- Perform operations such as addition, subtraction, and the representation of numbers in the Egyptian and Roman numeration systems

4.1 EXPLORING BASE-FOUR AND OTHER BASE NUMERATION SYSTEMS

Although the material in this section will not be taught in the early childhood classroom, it is included to demonstrate some of the difficulties that children may have in learning concepts and processes related to place value and operations in a numeration system unfamiliar to them. As you work through each example, note any difficulties that you encounter and try to relate these to difficulties that children may have in learning about regrouping and the base-ten numeration system.

The "Package by Fours" Candy Factory Activity

Imagine that you work in a candy factory. The owner has decided that to ship candies economically, candies should always be packaged by fours. You and other factory workers have been instructed to never ship more than three of any type of package. You are to replace four units of any type by one unit of a larger type. Notations and terms used in the factory are shown in Table 4-1. The first problem to consider is to find the total number of candies in a given order.

Example 4-1: Find the total number of candies in an order.

Taffy orders ■ | | • • • candies. How many candies will she get?

Thinking it out: Since there are 4 singles in a line and 4 lines in a box, there are 16 singles in a box. Taffy will get $16 + 8 + 3 = 27$ candies.

Combining Orders Next, consider additions. When two orders are to be shipped together, you must determine what types of packages to send without violating the "Do not ship more than three of any type of package" rule. To add two amounts of candy, you could convert both amounts to singles, add the singles, and then determine what packages correspond to the total. However, a better alternative is to add without first converting to singles. Using the notations from Table 4-1, and following the "Do not ship more than three of any type of package" rule, try to determine what packages you will ship in the following example before reading the given solution.

Example 4-2: Find the total number of candies and the types of packages to ship.

TABLE 4-1 Base-four terminology and notations.

Term	Notation	Equivalent
Single	•	
Line (four single candies)			• • • •
Box (four lines)	■					
Case (four boxes)	⬡	■■■■

Taffy orders ■ | | • • • and Carmel orders ■ ■ | | | • •. How many total candies and what type of packages will you send if Taffy and Carmel place their orders together?

Thinking it out: If you rearrange the symbols and place them in order with the largest amounts first, the total amount is ■ ■ ■ | | | | | • • • • •. Replacing four singles by a line and four lines by a box, you get ■ ■ ■ ■ | | •. Replacing the four boxes by a case, you get ⬡ | | •. You should ship one case, two lines, and one single.

How many total pieces of candy is this? You already determined that a box has 16 pieces. Since there are four boxes in a case, a case has $4 \times 16 = 64$ pieces. Together Taffy and Carmel receive $64 + 8 + 1 = 73$ pieces of candy. You can check this result by noting that Taffy orders $16 + 8 + 3 = 27$ candies, whereas Carmel orders $32 + 12 + 2 = 46$ candies. Your answer of 73 checks since $46 + 27 = 73$.

Filling Out an Order Form To order an amount of candy from the factory, an order form must be filled out. An order form containing Taffy and Carmel's order is shown in Figure 4-1.

As a worker in the factory, you must be able to determine what types of packages to send when customers order various total amounts of candy. Look for patterns in Table 4-2. Do you agree with the order form amounts for each of the total pieces of candy shown? Before reading further, fill out an order form for 31, 32, . . . , 40 pieces of candy.

Regrouping Determines the Digits Used in a Given Base System

In the base-ten numeration system that is commonly used, you regroup whenever you have 10 of a single type of number. Ten ones regroups to a 10, 10 tens regroups to 100, and so on. The candy factory workers are using a base-four numeration system. They regroup whenever they have four of any type of package of candy. Candy factory workers could use numerals or digits instead of pictures or an order form to count in this system.

The base-ten system uses the digits 0, 1, . . . , 9. There is no single digit to represent ten as this number is written 10 using the place value idea of one ten and zero singles. Similarly, the base-four system uses only the dig-

> When working in a numeration system with a base other than ten, write the base as a word subscript to distinguish that the numeral represents a number in that base.

Cases	Boxes	Lines	Singles
1	0	2	1

FIGURE 4-1 Candy order form.

TABLE 4-2 Total customer orders.

Total Candies	Cases	Boxes	Lines	Singles
1				1
2				2
3				3
4			1	0
5			1	1
6			1	2
7			1	3
8			2	0
9			2	1
10			2	2
11			2	3
12			3	0
13			3	1
14			3	2
15			3	3
16		1	0	0
17		1	0	1
18		1	0	2
19		1	0	3
20		1	1	0
21		1	1	1
22		1	1	2
23		1	1	3
24		1	2	0
25		1	2	1
26		1	2	2
27		1	2	3
28		1	3	0
29		1	3	1
30		1	3	2

its 0, 1, 2, and 3. You do not need a digit to represent four as four units of any type would be regrouped into one unit of a larger type. Write four in the base-four numeration system as 10_{four}. Do you see the relationship between this symbolic expression and the idea that four single candies regroups to be one line and no singles? The following example shows the base-four numerals for the numbers 1 to 21. Can you see a relationship between these representations and the order form representations given in Table 4-2 for 1 to 21 pieces of candy?

Example 4-3: Counting to 21 in base four (see the tables below).

Use caution in reading numerals written in bases other than base ten. The numeral 10_{four} should be read as "one, zero base four" and *not* as "ten base four." The reason for this distinction is that when base-four numerals are evaluated, the result does not coincide with the visual representation if read using base-ten terminology. The numeral 10_{four} does not represent 10; it represents one unit of four and zero singles. The numeral 203_{four} is read as "two, zero, three base four."

Counting Forward and Backward One important skill in the early childhood math curriculum is learning to count both forward and backward. This requires regrouping at the appropriate places and may be difficult for young children. It is good practice for you to count forward and backward in an unfamiliar numeration system. This will give you some insight into difficulties that young children may have with counting in the base-ten system. Example 4-4 gives a base-four numeral and asks you to count forward and backward from this numeral.

Example 4-4: Given 202_{four}, count seven numbers (a) forward and (b) backward.

Solution:

a. 202_{four}, 203_{four}, 210_{four}, 211_{four}, 212_{four}, 213_{four}, 220_{four}, 221_{four}

b. 202_{four}, 201_{four}, 200_{four}, 133_{four}, 132_{four}, 131_{four}, 130_{four}, 123_{four}

Advantages of a Positional System

In a positional system the position of a digit determines the value represented by that digit. A positional system uses a fixed set of digits with no need to create new symbols. One advantage to this type of system is that any number, no matter how large, can be represented by placing the appropriate digits in the appropriate positions.

In the base-four system, a single can be represented by 1_{four}. In fact, single-digit base-four numerals can be used to represent 0, 1, 2, or 3 singles. A line is equivalent to four singles and can be represented by 10_{four}. Two-digit

Base-four numeral	1_{four}	2_{four}	3_{four}	10_{four}	11_{four}	12_{four}	13_{four}	20_{four}	21_{four}	22_{four}	23_{four}
Base-ten equivalent	1	2	3	4	5	6	7	8	9	10	11

Base-four numeral	30_{four}	31_{four}	32_{four}	33_{four}	100_{four}	101_{four}	102_{four}	103_{four}	110_{four}	111_{four}
Base-ten equivalent	12	13	14	15	16	17	18	19	20	21

base-four numerals can be used to represent any number from 4 to 15 singles as shown in Example 4-3 above. A box is equivalent to 16 singles and can be represented by 100_{four}. The largest three-digit base-four numeral is 333_{four} which is equivalent to $(3 \times 16) + (3 \times 4) + 3 = 63$ singles. In fact, any number from 15 to 63 singles can be represented by three-digit base-four numerals. A case is equivalent to 64 singles and can be represented by 1000_{four}. Four-digit base-four numerals can be used to represent any number from 64 to 255 singles. Four cases is equivalent to 256 singles and is represented by 10000_{four}. There is no need to define a new term or symbol when this quantity can be represented by the positional system already defined.

Making the Connection to Place Value

The base-four numeration system uses the idea of *place value*. Place value is precisely what the phrase suggests; each place has a specific value. The digit written in a specific place indicates the number of units of that place value that occur with the rightmost digit indicating the number of singles or ones. As mentioned, base-four numerals use only the digits 0, 1, 2, and 3. The value of a position is determined by the power of four with exponent the distance of the position from the units position. You might recall from algebra that $4^0 = 1$, so it is logical that the rightmost digit or the digit in the units position indicates the number of singles.

For example, 203_{four} represents two units of four squared, zero units of four, and three singles. This is equivalent to the base-ten number $(2 \times 4^2) + (0 \times 4) + 3 = 2 \times 16 + 3 = 35$. That is, a person ordering 203_{four} candies from the base-four candy factory would receive two boxes, no lines, and three singles for a total of 35 pieces of candy. Example 4-5 illustrates more conversions of base-four numerals to their base-ten equivalents, and Example 4-6 illustrates more conversions of base-ten numerals to base-four numerals.

Example 4-5: Convert each numeral to base ten. That is, how many single candies are in each order below?

    a. 203_{four}
    b. 3210_{four}
    c. 102030_{four}

Solutions:

    a. $203_{four} = (3 \times 1) + (0 \times 4) + (2 \times 16) = 3 + 0 + 32 = 35$.
    b. $3210_{four} = (0 \times 1) + (1 \times 4) + (2 \times 16) + (3 \times 64) = 0 + 4 + 32 + 192 = 228$.
    c. $102030_{four} = (0 \times 1) + (3 \times 4) + (0 \times 4^2) + (2 \times 4^3) + (0 \times 4^4) + (1 \times 4^5) = 0 + 12 + 0 + 128 + 0 + 1024 = 1164$.

TABLE 4-3 Values of powers of four.

Power of Four	Value
4^0	1
4^1	4
4^2	16
4^3	64
4^4	256
4^5	1,024
4^6	4,096

Example 4-6: Convert each numeral to its equivalent in base-four notation. That is, determine what packages to send to each customer who orders the number of single candies below. Refer to Table 4-3 as necessary.

    a. 40
    b. 367
    c. 2,506

Solutions:

    a. In terms of the candy factory example, a person who orders 40 single candies will not receive any cases. Since each box contains 16 candies, this person should receive 2 boxes (32 candies) and 8 additional candies. You cannot send 8 singles, so you should send 2 additional lines. Thus, a person who wants 40 candies should receive 2 boxes, 2 lines, and no singles.

       To solve such a problem using symbolic notation, first decide how many positions will be necessary. Since $16 < 40 < 64$, the numeral will have three digits. Now, $40 = (2 \times 16) + 8 = (2 \times 16) + (2 \times 4) + (0 \times 1)$. Thus, the answer is 220_{four}.

    b. Since $256 < 367 < 1,024$, the answer will have five digits. Use division to determine a digit and the remainder to determine the next digit. It may be helpful to refer to the table of powers of four shown in Table 4-3. Remember that the value of each position is determined by a power of four.

$$367 = (1 \times 256) + 111$$
$$= (1 \times 256) + (1 \times 64) + 47$$
$$= (1 \times 256) + (1 \times 64) + (2 \times 16) + 15$$
$$= (1 \times 256) + (1 \times 64) + (2 \times 16) + (3 \times 4) + (3 \times 1).$$

    The answer is 11233_{four}.

    c. Since $1,024 < 2,506 < 4,096$, the answer will have six digits.

$$2,506 = (2 \times 1,024) + 458$$
$$= (2 \times 1,024) + (1 \times 256) + 202$$
$$= (2 \times 1,024) + (1 \times 256) + (3 \times 64) + 10$$
$$= (2 \times 1,024) + (1 \times 256) + (3 \times 64) + (0 \times 16) + (2 \times 4) + (2 \times 1).$$

    The answer is 213022_{four}.

How did you do? Were you able to successfully convert numbers back and forth from base four to base ten? To help ensure greater success and your understanding, never move on to the next problem until you check your answers. You can formally check the answers from Example 4-5 using the methods of Example 4-6. You can formally check the answers from Example 4-6 using the methods of Example 4-5. Remember that the digits in base four are 0, 1, 2, and 3 and that base-four answers should use only these digits. Also, always remember to write the base on any numeral that is not a base-ten numeral.

Teaching Connections

Provide Experiences Appropriate for the Level of Development Base-four numerals were presented because your thought processes for computations within the base-four numeration system parallel the thought processes of a preschool student who is learning about base-ten numerals. There is, however, one important difference. You are an adult who has been dealing with numbers and computations your entire life. You have already developed a great deal of number sense that will help you process this material. A preschool child is encountering numbers and computation for the first time. Even so, the difficulties that you may have with this material are similar to difficulties that preschool children may have with base-ten material.

Your students will need several experiences with concrete materials before they are ready to solve problems involving just numerals and notations. You may need to solve several addition and subtraction problems using concrete base-four materials before you are ready to solve such problems numerically. Unifix cubes provide excellent concrete candy factory materials. You can also make such materials out of paper or cardboard.

Addition and Subtraction Using Base-Four Symbolic Notation

You may wish to try the following problems with concrete materials or by drawing pictorial representations before you attempt them using merely notation.

Example 4-7: Compute the problems using base-four symbolic notation.

    a. 123_{four}
       $+232_{\text{four}}$

    b. 1021_{four}
       $-\ \ 113_{\text{four}}$

    c. 302_{four}
       $-\ \ \ \ 3_{\text{four}}$

Solutions:

    a. $\overset{1\ 1}{123_{\text{four}}}$
       $+232_{\text{four}}$
       $\overline{1021_{\text{four}}}$

    b. $\overset{4\,1\,5}{\cancel{1021}_{\text{four}}}$
       $-\ \ 113_{\text{four}}$
       $\overline{\ \ 302_{\text{four}}}$

    c. $\overset{2\,3\,6}{\cancel{302}_{\text{four}}}$
       $-\ \ \ \ 3_{\text{four}}$
       $\overline{\ \ 233_{\text{four}}}$

Example 4-2 showed a pictorial representation of Example 4-7(a). Notice how the concrete or pictorial solution is especially effective in illustrating the required regroupings. Can you see the relationship between the pictorial and symbolic solutions shown below?

$$\blacksquare\ |\ |\ \bullet\bullet\bullet\ +\ \blacksquare\ \blacksquare\ |\ |\ |\ \bullet\bullet\ =\ \square\ |\ |\ \bullet$$
$$123_{\text{four}} + 232_{\text{four}} = 1021_{\text{four}}$$

Example 4-8 shows a similar pictorial representation for Example 4-7(b). You should create your own concrete or pictorial materials to illustrate the regroupings involved in Example 4-7(c).

Example 4-8: Find the number of candies left using a concrete or pictorial solution.

    Taffy and Carmel have $\square\ |\ |\ \bullet$ candies. They give $\blacksquare\ |\ \bullet\bullet\bullet$ to Peanut. How many candies do Taffy and Carmel have left?

Math Manipulative: Unifix Cubes

Unifix cubes are interlocking cubes, usually made of plastic. Sets come in a variety of quantities and colors. Unifix cubes may be used for patterns, place value, addition and subtraction, multiplication and division, fractions, graphing, measurement, and many other types of activities that we will discuss later. Their interlocking feature makes them especially useful in place value and measurement activities. This is an excellent manipulative to illustrate singles and lines in base-ten and other base numeral activities.

Thinking it out: You wish to compute ▯ | | • − ▢ | • • •. You need to regroup. Trading the case for four boxes and a line for four singles, you get ▢ ▢ ▢ ▢ | • • • • • − ▢ | • • • = ▢ ▢ ▢ • •. Taffy and Carmel will have three boxes and two single candies left. Check this answer by noting that you had already determined that Taffy and Carmel had 73 candies. If they give a box, a line, and three singles, or $16 + 4 + 3 = 23$ candies to Peanut, they will have 50 candies left. This would fill three boxes with two candies remaining since $3 \times 16 = 48$. The answer is correct.

Do you see how the regroupings in Example 4-8 are related to those in the symbolic solution in Example 4-7(b)? Can you see the relationship between the concrete or pictorial solution ▯ | | • − ▢ | • • • = ▢ ▢ ▢ • • and the notational solution $1021_{four} - 113_{four} = 302_{four}$? Some college students prefer to work these types of problems with concrete or pictorial materials, whereas others are immediately comfortable with the symbolic representation, even when regrouping is involved. Most children will need many experiences with concrete and pictorial materials before they are comfortable with the symbolic representations of addition and subtraction in the base-ten system, especially when regrouping is involved.

Exploring Other Base Numeration Systems

In the same manner that we derived the base-four system, we could derive numeration systems for other bases. For example, a base-seven system would use digits 0, 1, 2, 3, 4, 5, and 6 and would require regrouping any set of seven objects. In a base-seven system, the value of a position is determined by the power of seven with exponent the distance of the position from the units position.

A base-thirteen system would require digits 0 through 9 as well as single digits to represent the quantities 10, 11 and 12. We will use T to represent 10, E to represent 11, and W to represent 12. A base-thirteen system would require regrouping of any set of 13 objects. The value of a position in a base-thirteen system is determined by the power of 13 with exponent the distance of the position from the units position. You may use concrete materials to illustrate any of the examples below. Only a few numerical examples are shown. More examples are given in the exercises and on the textbook companion Web site.

Example 4-9: Counting in other bases.

  a. Table 4-4 shows numerals to represent 1 to 30 in bases seven and thirteen.

  b. Count forward five terms from (1) 465_{seven} and from (2) $2T8_{thirteen}$.

    1. 465_{seven}, 466_{seven}, 500_{seven}, 501_{seven}, 502_{seven}, 503_{seven}

    2. $2T8_{thirteen}$, $2T9_{thirteen}$, $2TT_{thirteen}$, $2TE_{thirteen}$, $2TW_{thirteen}$, $2E0_{thirteen}$

  c. Count backward five terms from (1) 102_{seven} and from (2) $200_{thirteen}$.

    1. 102_{seven}, 101_{seven}, 100_{seven}, 66_{seven}, 65_{seven}, 64_{seven}

    2. $200_{thirteen}$, $1WW_{thirteen}$, $1WE_{thirteen}$, $1WT_{thirteen}$, $1W9_{thirteen}$, $1W8_{thirteen}$

Example 4-10: Addition and subtraction in base seven.

  a. Compute $545_{seven} + 424_{seven}$.

Thinking it out: Draw pictures and regroup sets of seven. In a solution using concrete or pictorial materials, a line would represent 7 singles and a box would represent 7 lines, hence 49 singles, and a case would represent seven boxes. The problem might look like this: ▢ ▢ ▢ ▢ ▢ | | | | • • • • • + ▢ ▢ ▢ ▢ | | • • • •

TABLE 4-4   Counting in base seven and base thirteen.

Base ten	1	2	3	4	5	6	7	8
Base seven	1_{seven}	2_{seven}	3_{seven}	4_{seven}	5_{seven}	6_{seven}	10_{seven}	11_{seven}
Base thirteen	$1_{thirteen}$	$2_{thirteen}$	$3_{thirteen}$	$4_{thirteen}$	$5_{thirteen}$	$6_{thirteen}$	$7_{thirteen}$	$8_{thirteen}$

Base ten	9	10	11	12	13	14	15	16
Base seven	12_{seven}	13_{seven}	14_{seven}	15_{seven}	16_{seven}	20_{seven}	21_{seven}	22_{seven}
Base thirteen	$9_{thirteen}$	$T_{thirteen}$	$E_{thirteen}$	$W_{thirteen}$	$10_{thirteen}$	$11_{thirteen}$	$12_{thirteen}$	$13_{thirteen}$

Base ten	17	18	19	20	21	22	23
Base seven	23_{seven}	24_{seven}	25_{seven}	26_{seven}	30_{seven}	31_{seven}	32_{seven}
Base thirteen	$14_{thirteen}$	$15_{thirteen}$	$16_{thirteen}$	$17_{thirteen}$	$18_{thirteen}$	$19_{thirteen}$	$1T_{thirteen}$

Base ten	24	25	26	27	28	29	30
Base seven	33_{seven}	34_{seven}	35_{seven}	36_{seven}	40_{seven}	41_{seven}	42_{seven}
Base thirteen	$1E_{thirteen}$	$1W_{thirteen}$	$20_{thirteen}$	$21_{thirteen}$	$22_{thirteen}$	$23_{thirteen}$	$24_{thirteen}$

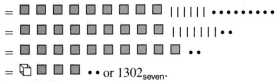

= □ □ □ □ □ □ □ □ □ ⎸⎸⎸⎸⎸⎸ • • • • • • • •

= □ □ □ □ □ □ □ □ □ ⎸⎸⎸⎸⎸⎸⎸ • •

= □ □ □ □ □ □ □ □ □ • •

= ⌂ □ □ □ • • or 1302_{seven}.

b. Compute $642_{seven} - 156_{seven}$.

Solution: To illustrate a different method, instead of using concrete or pictorial materials as above, you will convert both numbers to base ten, subtract, and then convert this answer back to base seven.

$$642_{seven} = 2 + (4 \times 7) + (6 \times 7^2) = 2 + 28 + 294 = 324$$
$$156_{seven} = 6 + (5 \times 7) + (1 \times 7^2) = 6 + 35 + 49 = 90$$

Now $324 - 90 = 234$, but this is a base-ten number. Convert it to base seven. The first few powers of seven are 1, 7, 49, and 343. You will need only three positions: $234 = (4 \times 49) + 38 = (4 \times 49) + (5 \times 7) + 3$. The answer in base seven is 453_{seven}.

Symbolic solutions for both (a) and (b) are shown below. Can you see how the regroupings in the symbolic solution are related to regroupings in the concrete or pictorial solution? Can you see how the regroupings are similar to regroupings that are performed in addition and subtraction within the standard base-ten system?

Symbolic Solutions:

a.
$$\begin{array}{r} {}^{1\,1} \\ 545_{seven} \\ +\ 424_{seven} \\ \hline 1302_{seven} \end{array}$$

b.
$$\begin{array}{r} {}^{10} \\ 53\cancel{9} \\ \cancel{6}\cancel{4}\cancel{2}_{seven} \\ -\ 156_{seven} \\ \hline 453_{seven} \end{array}$$

Example 4-11: Addition and subtraction in base thirteen.

Only the symbolic solutions are shown for (a) $578_{thirteen} + 464_{thirteen}$ and (b) $2E04_{thirteen} - W2T_{thirteen}$. These solutions could be checked either by using concrete materials and regrouping sets of 13 or by converting to base-ten numerals, performing the operation in base ten, and converting the answer to base thirteen.

Symbolic Solutions:

a.
$$\begin{array}{r} {}^{1} \\ 5\ 7\ 8_{thirteen} \\ +\ 4\ 6\ 4_{thirteen} \\ \hline T\ 0\ W_{thirteen} \end{array}$$

b.
$$\begin{array}{r} {}^{23} \\ 1\ T\ W\ 17 \\ \cancel{2}\ \cancel{E}\ \cancel{0}\ \cancel{4}_{thirteen} \\ -\ W\ 2\ \ T_{thirteen} \\ \hline 1\ E\ T\ \ 7_{thirteen} \end{array}$$

 Teaching Connections

Use Manipulatives to Illustrate Regrouping As stated earlier, the purpose of presenting this material is so that you will become aware of the difficulties that can occur among your students in working with these concepts—in particular, learning to add or subtract in base ten. Use of concrete materials helps show when regroupings must occur, what regroupings are appropriate, and exactly how they may be completed and properly denoted.

Problem Set 4.1

For Your Understanding

1. a. Juli orders ⌂ □ □ □ ⎸ from the base-four candy factory. How many candies will she get?
   b. Jeff wants 135 candies from the base-four candy factory. Draw a picture showing the packages the factory will send to him.
   c. Mark packages candies to send Jeff and Juli their order in a combined shipping. What packages does he send?

2. Use a computer to make a table like Table 4-2 that shows the proper way to fill out an order form for 31 to 70 candies ordered from the base-four candy factory.

3. Given 3322_{four}, count seven numbers (a) forward and (b) backward.

4. a. Convert the base-four numeral 2013_{four} to base-ten notation.
   b. Convert 1,739 to its equivalent in base-four notation.

5. a. Convert the base-four numeral 102030201_{four} to base-ten notation.
   b. Convert 18,740 to its equivalent in base-four notation.

6. Complete the addition and subtraction and write your answer in symbolic base-four notation. Also draw pictorial representations and show the regroupings.
   a.
   $$\begin{array}{r} 312_{four} \\ +\ 23_{four} \end{array}$$
   b.
   $$\begin{array}{r} 312_{four} \\ -\ 23_{four} \end{array}$$

7. Complete the addition and subtraction and write your answer in symbolic base-four notation. Also draw pictorial representations and show the regroupings.

a. 3021_{four}
    $+\ 2033_{four}$

b. 3021_{four}
    $-\ 2033_{four}$

8. a. List the digits that would be used in a base-five system.
    b. Write base-five numerals to represent the numbers 1 to 30.
    c. Write the base-five numerals to count forward 10 numbers from 2432_{five}.
    d. Write the base-five numerals to count backward 10 numbers from 1011_{five}.

9. a. List the digits that would be used in a base-fourteen system.
    b. Write base-fourteen numerals to represent the numbers 1 to 30.
    c. Write the base-fourteen numerals to count forward 10 numbers from $2798_{fourteen}$.
    d. Write the base-fourteen numerals to count backward 10 numbers from $101_{fourteen}$.

10. Complete the addition and subtraction and write your answer in symbolic base-five notation. Also draw pictorial representations and show the regroupings.

    a. 4303_{five}
        $+\ 224_{five}$

    b. 4303_{five}
        $-\ 224_{five}$

11. Complete the addition and subtraction and write your answer in symbolic base-fourteen notation.

    a. $9377_{fourteen}$
        $+\ 4928_{fourteen}$

    b. $9377_{fourteen}$
        $-4928_{fourteen}$

12. Complete the addition and subtraction in base thirteen.

    a. $9377_{thirteen}$
        $+4928_{thirteen}$

    b. $9377_{thirteen}$
        $-4928_{thirteen}$

13. Complete the addition and subtraction and write your answer in base-seven symbolic notation. Also draw pictorial representations and show the regroupings.

a. 635_{seven}
    $+406_{seven}$

b. 635_{seven}
    -406_{seven}

Applications in the Classroom

1. Show how you could use concrete materials to help students who make the following errors.

    a.   25
        $+37$
        ———
         512

    b.   25
        -17
        ———
          12

    c. William, a first grader, counts "twenty-eight, twenty-nine, twenty-ten."

    d. $\overset{1\ 1015}{\cancel{205}}$
        -187
        ———
          28

              2
    e.   25
        $+37$
        ———
          71

4.2 Place Value and the Base-Ten System

The numeration system that we use today is called the *Hindu-Arabic,* or *decimal system.* This system was developed by the Hindus (c. 800 BC) and brought to Western Europe by the Arabs. It is a positional system, requiring a solid understanding of place value. The Hindu-Arabic system is a base-ten system using the digits 0, 1, 2, 3, 4, 5, 6, 7, 8, and 9. Larger numbers have unique representations using appropriate combinations of these digits in the appropriate positions. Consider this set of whole numbers: $W = \{0, 1, 2, 3, 4, 5, 6, 7, 8, 9, 10, 11, 12, 13, 14, 15, 16, 17, 18, 19, 20, 21, 22, \ldots, 99, 100, 101, 102, \ldots\}$.

Defining *Place Value*

As discussed in this chapter's introduction, each place has a specific value. The digit in a place indicates the amount of that place value that occurs. For example, consider the numeral 323. The 3 on the left indicates three hundreds whereas the 3 on the right indicates three ones. Any whole number can be written in *expanded form* by considering the number as a sum of the products of each of its digits multiplied by the appropriate power of 10. Expanded form uses the idea of place value.

Example 4-12: Expanded form.

$$13{,}507 = 1 \times 10{,}000 + 3 \times 1{,}000 + 5 \times 100 + 0 \times 10 + 7 \times 1$$

$$= 1 \times 10^4 + 3 \times 10^3 + 5 \times 10^2 + 0 \times 10^1 + 7 \times 10^0$$

Exponents are usually not introduced until around the fifth-grade level, although some textbook series introduce them at the third-grade level (Larson, 1994). Generally the first format of expanded form shown above, the format not using exponents, is used in the earlier grades.

The manipulative base-ten blocks will be an extremely useful model to illustrate expanded form and place value. Concrete manipulatives such as base-ten blocks help children develop a conceptual understanding of place value, which is necessary for children to evaluate the reasonableness of their answers or to make estimations. It is never too early to encourage and develop skills in estimation.

Exponents and expanded form will be further discussed in Chapters 7 and 8.

 Teaching Connections

Use Concrete Models to Develop Ideas Such as Regrouping, Place Value, and Expanded Form Basic ideas of place value and expanded form are introduced as early as in kindergarten. At this level, children learn to write and use two-digit numerals. They must learn to think about a two-digit number as tens and ones rather than just a total number of objects. It may be easier for children to understand the symbolism 12 (one ten and two ones) than 10 (one ten and no ones).

In Chapter 3 we used tens and singles in the smiley strip model to illustrate regrouping. Concrete models such as the ten frame and base-ten blocks or smiley strips are invaluable tools for the teaching and learning of place value concepts as well. These models can be used to illustrate numbers such as 10 or 20 that have a zero in the ones or units position. Initial place value activities will involve only two-digit numbers.

Notice the variety in Activities 4-1 and 4-2. At this level, children need much practice with numerals that contain switched digits such as 23 and 32. They may also reverse numerals when writing them, for example writing ⌐ instead of 4. Such reversals are common through the second-grade level. If these difficulties persist into the third-grade level, there may be some cause for con-

cern. As a teacher, you must be careful with the terminology that you use. The number 12 may be considered as one ten and two ones. However, if you ask a first-grade child "How many ones are in 12?" it is likely that the child will answer "one."

Check for Developmental Understanding Children may have difficulty deciding which numeral in a given pair is larger, especially when the pair includes a numeral with a large number of singles. Although concrete models are useful for illustrating place value concepts, if the children do not understand how the model represents the underlying idea, they will not be able to correctly use the model. For example, suppose the task is to determine which is larger, 19 or 23. A child may set out 1 ten strip and 9 singles to represent 19 and 2 ten strips and 3 singles to represent 23 and then claim that 19 is larger than 23. If this happens, the child is viewing the model as a set of objects but does not recognize the significance of the representation of 10 singles by a ten strip. This student needs concrete developmental activities such as those presented in Chapter 3 that will help him or her acquire meaning for the model. Following such concrete activities, students should be able to understand the concepts behind determining which numeral in a pair is larger. Then drill and practice activities such as Activity 4-4 can be done.

Introducing Large Numbers

The smiley face model (see Blackline Master 7 in the Appendices) is easily extended to include hundreds. Base-ten block manipulatives usually also include cubes that represent thousands. Money can be a useful manipulative to illustrate larger numbers. At around the second-grade level, students have seen large numbers in real-life situations such as the billions of hamburgers sold by McDonalds, or the millions of dollars in a lottery jackpot.

To represent or read large numbers such as these, you need to be familiar with basic ideas of place value, be able to read three-digit numerals, and know the names for the groups. Modern convention is to separate a written numeral by three-digit groups called *periods* beginning with the

Standards

Mathematics Content Standards for California Public Schools

Number Sense, Kindergarten Level

3.0 Students use estimation strategies in computation and problem solving that involve numbers that use the ones and tens places:

3.1 Recognize when an estimate is reasonable.

California Department of Education, 2000

Math Manipulative: Base-Ten Blocks

Base-ten blocks have been used in the classroom for a number of years, and can be used at a variety of grade levels. Nearly every elementary student textbook printed after 1980, and many of the student textbooks printed in the 1970s, contains pictures of base-ten blocks. A typical set consists of 1-centimeter (cm) cubes that represent ones, sticks called "longs" or "rods" made up of 10 unit cubes that represent tens, "flats" made up of 10 longs to represent hundreds, and decimeter cubes that represent thousands.

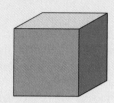

Cubes	Longs	Flat	Decimeter cube
or units	or rods		
or singles	or ten-strips		

A set may be made of plastic (which can be noisy) or foam (which is less durable). Large classroom sets are available. Transparency sets or sets that will stick to a magnetic board or chalkboard are useful for classroom demonstrations.

In the early childhood classroom, base-ten blocks can be used in counting, sorting, place value, estimation, regrouping, addition and subtraction, and multiplication and division. In the middle school classroom, they are useful for fractions, decimals, percents, and measurement.

Activity 4-1   Grades K–1

Learning to Regroup

Materials: Smiley ten strips, recording charts, and several envelopes containing 10 to 19 smiley singles each.

Directions: Divide the class into groups of three. The group tasks are regroup, exchange, and record. Repeat the activity several times so that each child performs each task at least once.

a. One group member removes the singles from an envelope and regroups them into one pile of 10 and the remaining singles in another pile.

b. The next group member exchanges the 10 singles for a ten strip.

c. The final group member records the number on the recording chart.

	tens	ones
Recording Chart:		

Note: This is a concrete developmental activity. It addresses the NCTM Number and Operations Standard: Understand numbers, ways of representing numbers, relationships among numbers, and number systems. The related Pre-K–2 expectation is to use multiple models to develop initial understandings of place value and the base-ten number system.

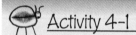
Source: Troutman & Lichtenberg, 2003, p. 139

Activity 4-2   Grades K–1

Representing Two-Digit Numbers Using Numerals

Materials: Smiley ten strips and singles, manipulative mats or plates, recording charts.

Directions: Write two-digit numbers on the board. Have students put appropriate ten strips and singles on their mats. Put some ten strips and singles on the board or transparency machine. Have students write appropriate numerals.

Notes and Variations:

a. Include reversals—"Show me 34. Now show me 43."
b. Include numbers with zero ones—"Show me 20."
c. Numbers can be given verbally.

---

ones or units position. Most written sources use commas for these separations. Some newer books use spaces rather than commas, whereas a number of computers and calculators use neither commas nor spaces. This book uses the traditional form of commas to separate the periods in a large number.

Example 4-13:

Traditional form: 12,345,678
Newer book form: 12 345 678
Computer and calculator form: 12345678

Assessment

Sample Assessment Rubric for Activity 4-2

The student will be able to show concrete representations for given numerals using base-ten materials.

4   The child is able to complete the task of showing a number using the correct amounts of tens and ones when given a two-digit numeral.

3   The child needs occasional prompting or makes occasional errors such as showing three tens and four ones when given the numeral 43.

2   The child needs frequent assistance or makes frequent errors, but recognizes that the numbers of items used in the representation should correspond to the two digits of the given numeral, (i.e., the child frequently makes the type of error described in level 3).

1   The child does not recognize that the numbers of items used in the representation should correspond to the two digits of the given numeral.

 Activity 4-3   Grades K–1

Matching Numbers and Numerals

Materials: Index cards with two-digit numerals, index cards with ten strips and singles pictured.

Directions: Pass out cards. Have students match numeral cards with picture cards.

Notes and Variations:
a. Have children compare pairs of cards—tell which is larger, which is smaller.
b. Students can play as a Go Fish or Bingo game.

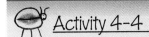 Activity 4-4   Grades 1–2

Find the Largest and Smallest Two-Digit Number

Materials: Index cards with one-digit numerals.

Directions: Students pick two cards. They state the largest number and the smallest number that can be made with the two cards.

Notes and Variations:
a. This activity can be done with dominoes.
b. Students can play this as a lineup game—each student makes the largest number that they can make. Then the entire class lines up from smallest to largest.
c. Students can play "War" using pairs of digit cards or dominoes.

Activity 4-5   Grades 2–4

How Big Is One Million?

Questions for Classroom Exploration:
a. Could we collect one million pennies?
b. How much room would one million pennies take up?
c. How much room would one million two-liter bottles take up?
d. How long in years, days, hours, and/or minutes is one million seconds?
e. How many boxes of rice would it take to get one million grains?

The number shown in Example 4-13 has three periods: millions, thousands, and ones. This number is read as "twelve million, three hundred forty-five thousand, six hundred seventy-eight." In general, the name of a period is determined by the smallest place value of that group. This is an example of *nonstandard place value*. The idea of nonstandard place value is that digits are considered as a group rather than considering each digit of a number separately. Nonstandard place value groupings do not have to occur only at a comma position. For example, a nonstandard place value interpretation of 1,200 is "twelve hundred."

Children are often fascinated by the number one million. Activity 4-5 gives a few ideas that can show children how large one million really is. Similar activities could be used in higher grades to illustrate one billion or even larger values. A typical elementary school project involves collecting one million of a specified object. This idea will be revisited in Chapter 11 when we calculate exactly how much space one million objects will take for a variety of different objects.

After children have been introduced to larger numbers, they may enjoy the following activities. Activity 4-6 is found in many math activity books including Burns (1996). Activity 4-7 describes a common calculator idea involving place value that children enjoy.

Rounding

Rounding to the nearest ten is introduced at approximately the first- or second-grade level. Some first-and

Using Literature in the Mathematics Classroom

How Much Is a Million?

By David Schwartz
Scholastic, 1985

This book explores the height of one million students standing on each other's shoulders, the time it would take to count to one million, the volume of a tank containing one million goldfish, and the number of pages it would take to draw one million stars. Each of the above situations is explored with the numbers one billion and one trillion.

Classroom Activity:

Before reading the book, have students estimate or calculate answers for each of the problems involving one million. Then read the part of the book involving one million. Compare student answers to the book answers. Then have students estimate or calculate answers to the questions involving one billion. Read the book answers

for one billion and again compare student solutions. Then have students estimate or calculate answers to the questions involving one trillion before reading the final section of the book.

Notes: This is an excellent activity for cooperative learning. Letting the same groups work together three different times on similar problems allows the groups to improve on their collaborative skills. The intermediate feedback given helps the groups to also improve on their problem-solving skills and strategies. This activity is good practice in the problem-solving skill "solve a simpler problem" as the size of the numbers increases in each round. The activity also contains connections to science. Book answers involve the size of a whale, the distance to the moon, and other interesting facts.

Because of the large numbers involved, the specific activity given is appropriate for the fourth- or fifth- grade levels. A similar classroom activity using the numbers 10, 100, and 1,000 could be designed for lower level classes.

 ## Activity 4-6   Grades 2–6

Roll the Largest Number

Materials: Large classroom dice.

Directions: Decide on the size of the numbers students will roll. For example, suppose the class has recently been introduced to thousands. Divide the class into groups of an appropriate size. For thousands, you will need groups of 4. Write a set of 4 blanks on the board for each group. Group members take turns rolling a die and deciding which blank to fill with the result. The winner is the group with the largest number after their four rolls. Be sure students are using correct terminology in naming the positions.

Group A rolls a 4 and places it in the hundreds position. Group B rolls a 2. Where should they place it?

___ , 4 ___ ___   ___ , ___ ___ ___

Source: Burns, 1996, p. 65–67

 ### Assessment   Grades 3–6
Writing in Mathematics

Suppose you are playing the Roll the Largest Number game. There are four places in the number to roll. Your first roll is a 5. In which place do you write the 5? Write an explanation that tells why you placed it in the position that you chose.

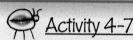 ## Activity 4-7   Grades 2–6

Calculator Wipe-Out

Materials: Calculators.

Directions: Have students enter a number such as 12345 into the calculator. Tell students to wipe out a digit such as 2 using one operation. The student must report what operation they used and use correct place value terminology—subtract 2,000. Continue with other place values and other numbers.

Note: This is a symbolic reinforcement activity. It addresses the NCTM Number and Operations Standard: Understand numbers, ways of representing numbers, relationships among numbers and number systems. The related Pre-K–2 expectation is to develop understanding of the relative position and magnitude of whole numbers.

second-grade-level textbooks avoid the word "rounding" and instead use a phrase such as "find the nearest ten." In a third-grade textbook, you might find the following definition of *rounding:* "replacing a number with a number that tells about how many or how much." If children understand the concepts and ideas underlying the process, they do not need to memorize complicated rounding rules.

A number line can be a useful visual aid in rounding. At some point children must learn the rule that if a number is exactly halfway between, it is rounded to the larger value. Number line rounding examples are shown in Example 4-14.

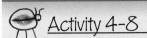

Activity 4-8　　　　　Grades 1–2

Rounding Road

Materials: Rounding road map (see Blackline Master 15 in the Appendices).

Teacher Statement: You are driving along rounding road. The gas stations are at the tens. These are the numbers that end in zero like 0, 10, 20, 30, etc. Find the nearest gas station if you are at 23. Where's the nearest gas station if you are at 37? How about 26?

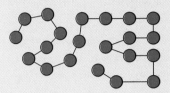

Example 4-14: Rounding on a number line.

　a. Round each of the following to the nearest ten.
　　1. 38
　　2. 21
　　3. 25

Solution: See the number line below. (1) 38 rounds to 40, (2) 21 rounds to 20, and (3) 25 rounds to 30.

　b. Round each of the following to the nearest hundred.

　　1. 149
　　2. 368
　　3. 450

Solution: See the number line below: (1) 149 rounds to 100, (2) 368 rounds to 400, and (3) 450 rounds to 500.

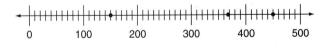

　　Once the concept of rounding is understood, larger numbers and rounding to other positions may by considered. Rounding and large numbers often occur in subjects other than mathematics. When discussing historical events, you may use rounding to place an event "about one thousand years ago." Large numbers and rounded numbers are often found in scientific applications as well.

　　This textbook will not present formal rounding rules. The idea is to find the closest "nice" number to use in calculations or as an estimation. For example, if you round

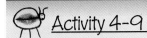

Activity 4-9　　　　　Grades 2–3

Rounding Lineup

Materials: Index cards labeled 0 to 100

Directions: Eleven children sit in a row of chairs at the front of the class holding cards 0, 10, 20, . . ., 100 (in order) so that the rest of the class can see them. A student not in the lineup picks a card from the remainder of the deck. This student must correctly name the two students who have the cards with the number on the picked card between those two numbers. Those two students stand. If the student who picked the card then correctly identifies which of these tens the number rounds to, they may take the place of that student in the lineup. Play continues with another student not in the lineup.

Variation—Blind Rounding Lineup: In this variation, the student who picks a card does not look at it but shows it to the students in the lineup. The two students in the lineup with the cards that the number is between must stand. The student holding the tens card that the number rounds to steps forward. The student who picked the card must guess the number on the card that he or she picked in three guesses or fewer in order to take the place of the student in the lineup.

368 to the nearest 25, the answer is 375. Only when rounding to a specific position will all the digits in smaller positions be replaced by zeros.

Example 4-15: Rounding to a specific position.

　　a. Round 145,396 to the nearest ten.
　　b. Round 145,396 to the nearest hundred.
　　c. Round 145,396 to the nearest thousand.
　　d. Round 145,396 to the nearest ten-thousand.
　　e. Round 145,396 to the nearest hundred-thousand.

Solutions:

　　a. 145,400
　　b. 145,400
　　c. 145,000
　　d. 150,000
　　e. 100,000

Notice how the idea of nonstandard place value can be used in rounding. For example, to round to the nearest ten-thousand, look at the number 145,396 as 14 ten-thousands and 5,396. Since 5,396 is more than halfway to 10,000 you round up to obtain 15 ten-thousands or 150,000.

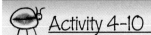 Activity 4-10   Grades 2–6

What's My Number?—Problem Solving to Eliminate Possibilities

Teacher Statement:

a. Grade 2: I am thinking of a two-digit number. The sum of the digits is 9. If I round the number to the nearest ten, I get 40. What is my number?

b. Grade 4: I am thinking of a number. Rounded to the nearest ten, my number is 240. My number has only one odd digit. The three digits of my number can be rearranged to fill in the multiplication fact ___ × ___ = ___. What is my number?

Problem Set 4.2

For Your Understanding

1. Write 302,047,019 in expanded form without using exponents.

2. Write the word expression for 302,047,019.

3. Round 2,995,036 to the nearest
   a. ten
   b. hundred
   c. thousand
   d. ten-thousand
   e. hundred-thousand
   f. million

4. Round 3,049,872 to the nearest
   a. ten
   b. hundred
   c. thousand
   d. ten-thousand
   e. hundred-thousand
   f. million

5. It takes your mother 3 seconds to say the phrase "clean your room." How long would it take her to say this 10,000 times if she said it over and over at the same rate without stopping?

6. Estimate how many breaths you have taken in your lifetime.

7. A printer used 1,266 digits to number the pages of a book, beginning with a page numbered 1. How many pages are in the book?

Applications in the Classroom

1. Write a word explanation of how nonstandard place value can be useful in rounding 3,197 to the nearest ten and to the nearest hundred.

2. Classify the level of knowledge and the type of learning experience of Activity 4-3. What objective from the NCTM model (or from your state or district model) does the activity address?

3. Devise an activity using ten frames (see Blackline Master 8 in the Appendices) that teaches children how to write a numeral for a given set of 10 to 19 counters.

4. Create a magnetic set of smiley tenstrips and singles that could be used on any magnetic surface.

5. Write an activity similar to Activity 4-1 that uses unifix cubes.

6. If you ask a first-grade child "How many ones are in 12?" he or she may answer "one." What is a better way to ask this question?

7. Read Activity 4-5. Create three more questions or projects involving one million that you think an elementary school student would enjoy.

8. Solve the riddles given in Activity 4-10.

9. Write three riddles similar to those in Activity 4-10. Indicate the approximate grade level of your riddles, and provide all answers.

10. Some common student errors are given. For each error given describe the error and what can be done to help the student making such an error.
    a. $25 + 5 = 210$
    b. Teacher directs student to "Write five hundred two." Student writes 5002.
    c. Teacher directs student to "Write in expanded form 4073." Student writes $4 \times 100 + 7 \times 10 + 3 \times 1$.

11. Create an assessment tool to be used with Activity 4-4. Explain why you chose that type of assessment tool.

4.3 Ancient Numeration Systems— Egyptian and Roman Numerals

This section covers the Egyptian and Roman numeration systems. Children are often fascinated by these unfamiliar numeration systems and are eager to learn how ancient systems compare to the system that they use. It is easy to imagine the need of ancient civilizations to formalize the notion of numeration and counting, to embody the concept of "how many." The need for written symbols to record "how many" naturally follows the need for a word or phrase to express this idea.

A discussion of and exercises involving the Mayan numeration system may be found at the textbook companion Web site.

The earliest convention of recording numbers was to use tally marks. For example, | | | | | | | | | | | | could be used to express 12. Tally marks are still used today in many mathematical instances. A common convention is to group tally marks by groups of five for ease of reading. For example, ⊥⊥⊤ ⊥⊥⊤ | | also represents 12 and is much easier to read than the first representation presented. Bone artifacts bearing precise, grouped notches indicate that the people of the Stone Age used a system of tallying by groups as early as 30,000 BC (Burton, 1998).

The Egyptians' Base-Ten System

Hieroglyphics found on stone tablets indicate that as early as 3400 BC the Egyptians used a base-ten system for recording numbers. The choice of a base-ten system is a natural one: it is easy to calculate using your hands in a base-ten system. The Egyptian system contained separate numerals for powers of 10 as shown in Table 4-5.

The Egyptian System Was an Additive System Although generally symbols for larger numbers were written before those representing smaller numbers, the Egyptian system did not require such place value considerations. Hence a number such as 21 is usually written as ∩∩| but may also be written as ∩|∩ or as |∩∩. Some advantages to a place value system are clear when you consider that up to nine copies of a single symbol may be necessary to designate a single place value. When more than four copies of a symbol are required, it is convenient to place them in two rows. Example 4-16 illustrates conversions between the Egyptian system notation and standard notation.

Example 4-16: Converting between standard notation and Egyptian notation.

  a. Write 103,296 in Egyptian notation.

  Solution: The Egyptian system is an additive system. You simply need to write as many symbols for each place value as necessary.

TABLE 4-5 Egyptian Symbols for Powers of 10

Power of 10	Symbol	Description
$10^0 = 1$	|	Vertical staff
$10^1 = 10$	∩	Heel bone
$10^2 = 100$	୨	Coiled rope
$10^3 = 1,000$	⚘	Lotus flower
$10^4 = 10,000$	⌇	Pointed finger
$10^5 = 100,000$	⤝	Fish (or tadpole)
$10^6 = 1,000,000$	⤲	Astonished man

b. What number is represented by the Egyptian numeral shown?

Solution: $2,000,000 + 70,000 + 4 = 2,070,004$.

Adding and Subtracting Using Egyptian Notation Because the Egyptian system is an additive system, additions and subtractions can be shown by joining together or removing the appropriate symbols. It is sometimes necessary to regroup to simplify an addition answer or to perform a subtraction. Regrouping is based on standard base-ten principles such as ten ones may be exchanged for a ten, a hundred may be exchanged for ten tens, and so on. Example 4-17 illustrates additions and subtractions using Egyptian notation.

Example 4-17: Addition and subtraction using Egyptian notation.

  a. Show $1,685 + 3,018$ using Egyptian notation only.

  Solution:

You must do some regrouping to simplify this answer.

Answer:

b. Subtract 417 from 2,043 using Egyptian notation only.

Thinking it out: You represent 2,043 by

There are not enough staffs or coiled ropes to take away

so you must regroup. You can exchange a heel bone for 10 staffs, and a lotus flower for 10 coiled ropes.

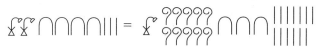

After the regroupings, you take away the required amounts.

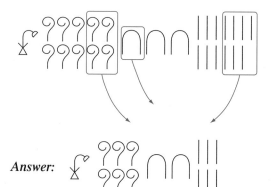

Answer:

Multiplying and Dividing Using Egyptian Notation As the Egyptian system is an additive system, multiplications and divisions must be shown by repeated additions or subtractions. These calculations quickly become tedious. Some fairly simple illustrations are shown in Example 4-18.

Example 4-18: Multiplication and division using Egyptian notation.

a. Show 107×4 using Egyptian notation.

Thinking it out: The number 107 is represented by

so 107×4 is represented by four copies of this representation.

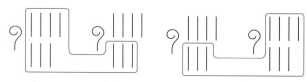

You can regroup sets of 10 staffs to form heel bones and get the answer.

Answer:

b. Show $107 \div 4$ using Egyptian notation.

Thinking it out: You need to split the coiled rope and seven staffs into four equal sets. Begin by regrouping the coiled rope.

You now have

You can distribute two heel bones and a staff to each of the four sets.

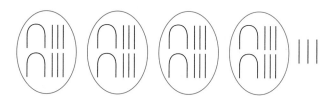

You must regroup the heel bones in order to continue.
You may then distribute an additional five staffs to each set.

Answer (in conventional notation is): $107 \div 4 = 26$ R3.

Teaching Connections

The Presentation of Egyptian Numerals in an Early Childhood Classroom The Egyptian numeration system may be a topic not covered in the traditional early childhood curriculum. When it is presented, it is likely that only numerals, place value, and addition is covered. Some examples of multiplication and division were included here because the additive methods illustrated provide a natural means by which to view concretely the multiplication and division processes.

> In Chapter 6, when developing multiplication and division algorithms within the standard Hindu-Arabic numeration system, we will use methods similar to those used in Example 4-18.

The Presentation of Roman Numerals in an Early Childhood Classroom You are probably already familiar with the Roman system of numeration. This system is still used today on many clocks and to record dates or page numbers. Telling time is an important component of the early childhood math curriculum. The first three Roman numeral symbols shown in Table 4-6 are often introduced at about

Activity 4-11   Grades 3–4

Uncover a Numeration System—Problem Solving Through Guess and Check

Teacher Statement. Suppose you were on a scientific expedition and you found a cave with evidence of a long ago forgotten population. You determine that the population did not use place value. You also determine that they used the symbols E, 0, and ∇ to represent one, ten, and one hundred, but you don't know which symbol represents which number. You find the subtraction problem shown drawn on the cave wall. Use guess and check to figure out which symbol represents which number. Then write an addition or subtraction problem using the given symbols for the rest of the class to solve.

$$\begin{aligned}
&\nabla 0E\nabla 0\nabla 0E\nabla\\
-\ &0\nabla 0\nabla 00\nabla 0\nabla 00\nabla 0\\
\hline
&0\nabla\nabla 0\nabla\nabla E\nabla\nabla 0\nabla 0\nabla 0
\end{aligned}$$

TABLE 4-6 Roman numerals.

Roman Symbol	I	V	X	L	C	D	M
Modern Equivalent	1	5	10	50	100	500	1,000

the first- or second-grade level. All of the symbols shown can be found in elementary school textbooks at around the third- or fourth-grade level. Larger numbers are represented by placing bars above the symbols shown. For our purposes, the seven symbols shown will suffice.

Roman Numerals

In some cases, five copies of a single symbol may be exchanged for a single copy of a larger valued symbol. In other cases, only two copies of a symbol are necessary to make an exchange. For example, IIIII = V and VV = X. The system is not strictly a base-ten system, nor is it strictly a base-five system. Initially the Roman system was additive like the Egyptian system.

Example 4-19: Representation in the Roman system before the introduction of the subtractive principle.

a. Write 1994 using Roman numerals.

Solution: MDCCCCLXXXXIIII.

b. What number does MDCCXXXXVIII represent?

Solution: 1,000 + 500 + 200 + 40 + 5 + 3 = 1,748.

The Subtractive Principle A subtractive principle was later introduced that allows the representation of some numbers by a shorter notation. The idea behind the shorter notation is to avoid the consecutive use of four of any one symbol.

For example, consider the base-ten numeral 4. In the additive Roman numeral system, this is represented by IIII. To avoid the use of these four consecutive symbols, 4 is considered as 5 − 1. To indicate subtraction rather than addition, place the smaller symbol to the left of the larger symbol. That is, the Roman numeral notation for four is IV.

In general, if the symbol I is placed to the left of either V or X, then 1 is subtracted. If the symbol X is placed to the left of L or C, then 10 is subtracted. If C is placed to the left of D or M, then 100 is subtracted. In ancient times the use or nonuse of this principle was not always consistent. The Colosseum in Rome (AD c. 80) contains a doorway marked XLIIII for 44, whereas it is represented by XXXXIIII if the subtractive principle is not used and by XLIV if the subtractive principle is consistently used. In modern-day usage, the subtractive principle is used whenever possible. Example 4-20 illustrates the use of the subtractive principle.

Example 4-20: Representation in the Roman system using the subtractive principle.

a. Write 1994 using Roman numerals.

Solution: MCMXCIV.

b. Write 45 using Roman numerals.

Solution: XLV.

Note: Due to specific instances where subtractive notation is allowed, the notation VL should not be used to represent 45.

c. Write 99 using Roman numerals.

Solution: XCIX.

Note: Due to specific instances where subtractive notation is allowed, the notation IC (i.e., subtracting one from one hundred) should not be used to represent 99.

d. What number does CDLXI represent?

Solution: 400 + 50 + 10 + 1 = 461.

e. What number does MMCCCIX represent?

Solution: 2,000 + 300 + 9 = 2,309.

Adding and Subtracting Using Roman Numeral Notation
Addition and subtraction can be carried out in the Roman system much as in the Egyptian system. Regroupings are performed as necessary. To avoid complications that could arise from the use of the subtractive principle, you may wish to rewrite the numbers involved in addition and subtraction problems without using the subtractive principle before proceeding with the addition or subtraction. Because multiplications and divisions within the Roman system are quite tedious, examples of only addition and subtraction are shown in Example 4-21. Underlining and blue lettering are used to indicate the regrouping that will occur in the subsequent step of the procedure. The symbol(s) shown in blue in

Suppose you wish to randomly assign partners for a group activity. You can use Roman numerals to do this. Prepare a set of index cards with Roman numerals on half of the cards and standard numeral equivalents on the other half. Children are each dealt one card. They are paired by matching a Roman numeral to its equivalent standard numeral representation.

---

one step are replaced by the underlined symbol(s) in the following step.

Example 4-21: Addition and subtraction in the Roman system. Blue lettering and underlining are used to illustrate the changes made in each step. These markings should be omitted when solving problems on your own.

    a. Add using Roman notation: DCCCXLVII + CXCIII.

Solution: The problem may be rewritten as DCC-CXXXXVII + CLXXXXIII.

This gives DCCCCLXXXXXXXXVIIIII =
DCCCCLXXXXXXXXX$\underline{V}$$\underline{V}$ =
DCCC$\underline{C}$LXXXXXXXXX$\underline{X}$ =
DCCCC$\underline{C}$XXXX =
$\underline{DD}$XXXX =
$\underline{M}$XXXX =
M$\underline{XL}$.

    b. Subtract using Roman notation: DCCCXLVII − CXCIII.

Solution: Rewrite to eliminate subtractive notation: DCC-CXXXXVII − CLXXXXIII. Regroup as necessary: DC-C$\underline{LL}$XXXX$\underline{IIIIII}$ − CLXXXXIII. Then subtract: DCLIIII. Simplify: DCL$\underline{IV}$.

Problem Set 4.3

For Your Understanding

1. You learned three different ways to write the number 21 in Egyptian notation. How many different ways are there to write the number 22 in Egyptian notation?

2. a. Write in Egyptian notation
      1. 257,830
      2. 1,046,902
  b. Write in standard notation

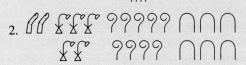

    c. Add the two numbers from part (a) using only Egyptian notation.
    d. Subtract the number shown in (2) of part (b) from the number shown in (1) of part (b) using only Egyptian notation.
    e. Calculate $4{,}827 \times 3$ using only Egyptian notation.
    f. Calculate $4{,}827 \div 3$ using only Egyptian notation.

3. Use the Internet or some other source and look up the Roman symbols for numbers larger than 1,000. Use Roman symbols to write the following numbers. Use the subtractive principle whenever possible.
    a. 1,209,304
    b. 96,952

4. a. Add using Roman notation only CMXLVIII + CCCXCIII.
    b. Subtract using Roman notation only MCDXXIX – DLXXXIII.

5. Solve Activity 4-11

Applications in the Classroom

1. Invent your own symbols for an imaginary group of people and write an activity similar to Activity 4-11.

2. List at least five ways in which Roman numerals are commonly used in today's society.

3. Do a search of the Internet or use some other source to find classroom materials and activities related to either Roman or Egyptian numerals. Create a developmental activity to introduce one of these types of numbers to a class of students.

4. While teaching a thematic unit about Rome in a third-grade class, you introduce Roman numerals. You mention that the people who live in Rome today primarily use the same digits 0 to 9 that we use. One student asks why Roman numerals are no longer widely used, even in Rome. How do you respond?

5. Prepare an I Have/Who Has deck of cards (see Activity 7-3) that practices the identification of Roman or Egyptian numerals. You may wish to have students write their Who Has expression on the board.

Example Card

```
+-------------------+
|                   |
|      I have       |
|       23          |
|                   |
|     Who has       |
|       XIV?        |
|                   |
+-------------------+
```

6. Classify the level of knowledge and the type of learning experience of Activity 4-11. What objective from the NCTM model (or from your state or district model) does the activity address?

7. Another numeration system that is occasionally introduced in the elementary school is that of Mayan numerals. This topic is discussed at the textbook companion Web site. Review this discussion and complete the activities provided.

8. Look up either "place value" or "numeration systems" in the index or table of contents of an elementary-level textbook. Photocopy or copy by hand one example or problem that you think is interesting or unusual and indicate why. What objective from the NCTM model (or from your state or district model) does the activity or problem address? Be sure to state what grade-level text you are using.

9. Find and print a place value activity from the Web. What objective from the NCTM model (or from your state or district model) does the activity address? State what grade level you think the activity would be appropriate for.

10. Choose an activity from this chapter. Indicate how you could implement the activity as a collaborative learning experience.

11. Choose one of the books in the children's literature section of the references for this chapter. Give a brief description of the content of the book and explain how you could incorporate the book into a math lesson.

12. Make up two writing prompts or stems that fit in with material or activities from this chapter.

References

Children's Literature References

Adler, David. (1975). *Base five.* New York: HarperCollins Children's Books.

Adler, David. (1976). *Roman numerals.* New York: HarperCollins Children's Books.

Carona, Philip. (1964). *The true book of numbers.* Chicago: Children's Press.

Fisher, Leonard. (1982). *Number art: Thirteen 123's from around the world.* New York: Simon & Schuster.

Gag, Wanda. (1928). *Millions of cats.* New York: Coward-McCann.

Medearis, Angela. (1996). *The 100th day of school* (Hello Reader Level 2) New York: Scholastic.

Schwartz, David. (1985). *How much is a million?* New York: Scholastic.

Sitomer, Harry, & Sitomer, Mindel. (1976). *How did numbers begin?* New York: Thomas Crowell.

St. John, Glory. (1975). *How to count like a Martian.* New York: Hill & Wang.

Wells, Robert. (1993). *Is a blue whale the biggest thing there is?* Morton Grove, IL: Albert Whitman.

Wells, Robert. (2000). *Can you count to a google?* Morton Grove, IL: Albert Whitman.

Zaslavsky, Claudia. (1989). *Zero! Is it something? Is it nothing?* New York: Franklin Watts.

Teacher Resources

Burns, M. (1994). *Place value grade 2 (math by all means).* Sausalito, CA: Math Solutions Publications.

Burns, M. (1996). *50 problem-solving lessons grades 1–6.* Sausalito, CA: Math Solutions Publications.

California Department of Education. (2000). *Mathematics Content Standards for California Public Schools.* Retrieved November 12, 2003. from http://www.cde.ca.gov/board/pdf/math.pdf

Larson, N. (1994). *Saxon Math–Grade 3.* Norman, OK. Saxon Publishers.

National Council of Teachers of Mathematics. (2000). *Principles and standards for school mathematics.* Reston, VA: Author.

Payne, J. N. (2002). Place value for tens and ones. In D. L. Chambers (Ed.), *Putting research into practice in the elementary grades: Readings from NCTM journals* (pp. 105–108). Reston, VA: National Council of Teachers of Mathematics.

Schifter, D., Bastable, V., & Russell, S. J. (1999). *Developing mathematical ideas: Numbers and operations, Part 1: Building a system of ten* (Casebook). White Plains, NY: Cuisenaire-Dale Seymour.

Troutman, A. P. & Lichtenberg, B. K. (2003). *Mathematics–A Good Beginning* 6th Edition. Wadsworth, Thomson Learning, Inc.

Selected Research Books and Articles

Burton, D. M. (1998). *The history of mathematics* (4th ed.). Newton, MA: McGraw-Hill.

Kouba, V. L., Brown, C. A., Carpenter, T. P., Lindquist, M. M., Silver, E. A., & Swafford, J. O. (1988). Results of the fourth

NAEP assessment of mathematics: Number, operations, and word problems. *Arithmetic Teacher, 35*(8), 14–19.

Further Reading

Baroody, A. J. (1990). How and when should place-value concepts and skills be taught? *Journal for Research in Mathematics Education, 21,* 281–286.

Barr, D. C. (1978, January). A comparison of three methods of introducing two-digit numeration. *Journal for Research in Mathematics Education, 9* 33–43.

Battista, M., & Clements, D. (1991). *Logo geometry.* Morristown, NJ: Silver Burdett & Ginn.

Bobis, J. F. (1991, January). Using a calculator to develop number sense. *Arithmetic Teacher, 38,* 42–45.

Campbell, P. F., & Stewart, E. L. (1993). Calculators and computers. In R. J. Jensen (Ed.), *Research ideas for the classroom: Early childhood mathematics* (pp. 251–268). Reston, VA: NCTM, and New York: Macmillan.

Clements, D. H. (1989) *Computers in elementary mathematics instruction.* Upper Saddle River, NJ: Prentice Hall.

Cowle, I. M. (1970, May). Ancient systems of numerations—Stimulating, illuminating. *Arithmetic Teacher, 17,* 413–416.

Fitch, D. (1993). *101 ideas for Logo.* Portland, ME: Terrapin Software.

Gluck, D. (1993, March). Helping students understand place value. *Arithmetic Teacher, 38,* 10–13.

Hiebert, J. C., & Wearne, D. (1992). Links between teaching and learning place value with understanding in first grade. *Journal for Research in Mathematics Education, 23,* 98–122.

Hopkins, L. (1995). Popping up number sense. *Teaching Children Mathematics, 2*(2), 82–86.

Hopkins, M. H. (1992). Wipe out refined. In J. T. Fey & C. R. Hirsch (Eds.), *Calculators in mathematics education, 1992 yearbook* Reston, VA: National Council of Teachers of Mathematics.

Kamii, C. K. (1986). Place value: An explanation of its difficulty and educational implications for the primary grades. *Journal of Research in Childhood Education, 1,* 75–86.

Lehrer, R., & Randle, L. (1987). Problem solving, metacognition and composition: The effects of interactive software for first-grade children. *Journal of Educational Computing Research, 3,* 409–427.

McNeil, S. A. (2001). The Mayan zeros. *Mathematics Teacher, 94*(7), 590.

Pattern, J. (1996). *Numbers and counting.* Vero Beach, FL: Rourke.

Payne, J. N., & Huinker, D. M. (1993). Early number and numeration. In R. J. Jensen (Ed.), *Research ideas for the classroom: Early childhood mathematics* (pp. 43–71). Reston, VA: National Council of Teachers of Mathematics, and New York: Macmillan.

Schmandt-Besserat, D. (1999). *The history of counting.* New York: Williams Morrow.

Thompson, C. (1990). Place value and larger numbers. In J. Payne (Ed.), *Mathematics for the young child* (pp. 89–110). Reston, VA: National Council of Teachers of Mathematics.

Thompson, C. S., & Van de Walle, J. (1984, November). The power of ten. *Arithmetic Teacher, 32*(3) 6–11.

5

Developing Concepts and Operations of Addition and Subtraction

Students are introduced to the basic concepts of addition and subtraction way before they ever enter school. Life in the real world is full of addition and subtraction examples: "When I had two cats and five kittens, I had seven pets. I gave away four of the kittens and then I had three pets." However, children sometimes have a difficult time making connections between the math they learn in school and everyday real-life math. School math is full of rules and usually is focused on getting an answer, and then quickly moving on to the next problem. Unless they are heartily encouraged to do so, children may not even consider whether their answer is

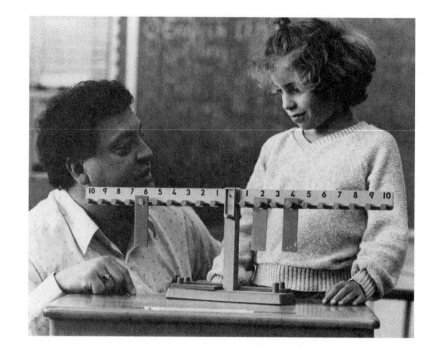

reasonable. "Teachers play an important role in helping to enable the development of these reflective habits of mind. . . . This habit should begin in the lowest grades" (NCTM, 2000, pp. 54–55).

Word problems can be used to develop and give meaning to whole number computations (Carpenter, Carey, & Kouba, 1990). By conceptually developing the algorithms for addition and subtraction, children can be shown why and how the algorithms work. If they understand the logic behind the rules, they are less likely to make mistakes when applying those rules. Providing opportunities for students to use and discuss invented procedures can increase students' number and operation sense (Carroll & Porter, 1998; Sowder, 1992). A teacher must also learn how to assess student-invented procedures to determine their validity (Campbell, Rowan, & Suarez, 1998).

This chapter introduces several concrete models that can be used to make addition and subtraction processes and properties more tangible. We will frequently refer to the base-ten block model introduced in Chapter 4 and to the number line. Students should be encouraged to use their developing number sense in solving problems and performing computations.

Standards

NCTM

Grades K–2

Teachers have a very important role to play in helping students develop facility with computation. By allowing students to work in ways that have meaning for them, teachers can gain insight into students' developing understanding and give them guidance. To do this well, teachers need to become familiar with the range of ways that students might think about numbers and work with them to solve problems.

NCTM, 2000, p. 86

Standards are listed with the permission of the National Council of Teachers of Mathematics (NCTM). NCTM does not endorse the content or validity of these alignments.

Objectives

After completing Chapter 5, you will be able to

- Describe two interpretations for addition and correctly use addition notation, terminology, and properties
- Describe five interpretations for subtraction and correctly use subtraction notation, terminology, and properties
- Describe strategies to help children develop meaning for addition and subtraction, learn basic addition and subtraction facts, and develop algorithms for whole number addition and subtraction
- Diagnose and remediate common student errors involving addition and subtraction
- Perform computations using estimation, speedy addition, and equal additions
- Use the number line and poker chip model to illustrate addition of integers

5.1 CONSTRUCTING MEANING FOR ADDITION

A child's first introduction to the concept of addition should involve real-life situations that the child can relate to, as well as concrete objects to help the child solve the problems in these situations (Carpenter et al., 1990). The child must be comfortable associating numbers with sets and with counting concrete objects.

Consider a problem such as "Jim has four blocks and Sandy has three blocks. How many blocks do they have in all?" A child operating on the concrete level might approach this problem by counting out one pile of four blocks, then counting out a separate pile of three blocks. The child might then push those two piles together and begin counting the blocks in the combined pile—one, two, three, four, five, six, seven. At around the first-grade level, some children will discover the process of *forward counting* or *counting on* and will solve the above problem by beginning with the number four and counting on: five, six, seven. Other first-grade-level students will persist in joining together the piles and beginning the count of the combined set at one. As with any concept or process that must be constructed, it is best not to insist that students use the idea of forward counting until they are developmentally ready for it (Dunn & Kontos, 1997; NAEYC, 1997).

Teaching Connections

Use Problems Involving Disjoint Sets to Illustrate Addition A relationship exists between the above process of the student pushing together the two piles of blocks and the process of taking the union of two disjoint sets. To arrive at the answer "seven blocks" you must assume that Jim's four blocks are distinct from Sandy's three blocks. That is, the sets are disjoint. As a teacher, you must be sure that the addition problems presented to students initially learning the concept of addition are clearly problems involving disjoint sets. A problem such as "Jim has four pets and his brother Sandy has three pets. How many pets do they have in all?" is inappropriate at this level because it could be the case that the sets of pets are not disjoint. However, this would be a good "consider all cases" problem-solving problem to use after children have constructed the idea of the meaning of addition as there are several possible answers and various combinations could be considered.

After several experiences in which the students encounter situations with disjoint sets of like objects that may be combined, they are ready for situations involving disjoint sets of unlike objects. Consider problems such as "Two dogs are sleeping. Three cats are playing. How many animals are there in all?" and "There are two houses on one side of the street and three houses on the other side. How many houses in all?" It is important for students to realize that concrete objects such as blocks or counters can be used to represent or model problems involving more complex objects. Students should also learn how to draw pictures or diagrams to represent such problems (see Figure 5-1).

Two Interpretations of Addition

Combination addition problems involve objects that may be combined so that the total number of objects may be counted. Combination addition problems sometimes include sets that cannot be physically combined such as "There are three trees in the front yard and four trees in the back yard. How many trees are there in all?" Once students are comfortable with the idea of addition as the combination of sets, they may be introduced to more abstract problems that require addition but do not involve set objects such as "Mary is seven years old. How old will she be three years from now?" This type of problem is often called an *incremental addition* problem.

Use a Number Line to Illustrate an Incremental Addition Problem A number line can provide a model for the student who needs concrete representation of the incremental type of addition problem. Figure 5-2a illustrates 7 + 3 on the number line. Note how this differs from the illustration of 3 + 7 shown in Figure 5-2b.

When the number line is first introduced, it is important that it begins with zero (0). Initially, number line mod-

FIGURE 5-1 Student problems involving unlike objects.

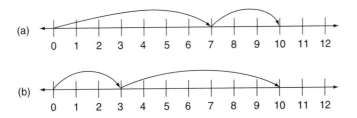

FIGURE 5-2 (a) An illustration of 7 + 3, (b) an illustration of 3 + 7.

els will not include negative integers, which are usually not introduced in the early childhood curriculum. In drawing a number line, make sure that you space the numbers evenly. This is a skill that you may need to practice. There are also commercial models of a number line that can be purchased. A floor model could involve students; students can physically act out addition and subtraction problems by walking or hopping from one number to another. A creative teacher could make up a story about frogs who live on numbered lily pads and who hop to visit other frogs.

 Teaching Connections

Teaching Addition Facts The process of learning addition facts entails several lessons over a period of several years. At the kindergarten level, students may begin to explore addition in a developmental lesson "Ways to make three" using two-color counters. A reinforcement lesson could involve having children show ways to make three using learning links, unifix cubes, or pennies. Subsequent lessons could involve "Ways to make four," "Ways to make five," and "Ways to make six" using appropriate manipulatives. Then a "joining lesson" such as a lesson centered around Activity 5-1 can be planned.

Note the use of the different colors of the learning links in Activity 5-1. By consistently using the same color to represent the objects of one set and a different color to represent the objects of the other set, you can clearly see the associated addition sentence. Note also that students are asked to both make a chain for a given addition sentence and to write or state an addition sentence and a story problem for a given chain. This variety of tasks is typical of today's elementary school curriculum. The terminology used in this activity indicates that it is a developmental activity designed to introduce the *concept* of addition. Later activities will gradually introduce the terminology and symbolization of addition. A follow-up activity could use the terminology "four plus two is the same as six" and a later activity could use "four plus two is equal to six." After the students have an idea of the concepts involved, the symbolic notation "4 + 2 = 6" may be introduced.

Consider again the problem "There are two houses on one side of the street and three houses on the other side. How many houses in all?" A preschool or kindergarten student may solve this problem by using counters or by draw-

---

Activity 5-1   Grades K–1

Using Concrete Materials to Illustrate Addition

Materials: Learning links for each student.

Directions: Write on the board and read to students: 4 and 2 more make 6.

Show students a four-link chain (all the same color) and a two-link chain (of another color). Combine the two chains and explain how this illustrates 4 and 2 more make 6.

Teacher Statement:
a. Use your links and show me (write on the board, repeat as necessary): 2 and 3 more make 5.
b. Make a chain with three links all of one color. Make another chain with four links all the same color, but a different color than your three-link chain. Link those two chains together. What addition sentence can you show? Think about or write a story to go along with your addition sentence.

Note: This activity can also be done with unifix cubes.

---

ing objects and then counting them. A first- or second-grade student may solve the same problem simply by stating "two plus three is five." In the second case, the student may have memorized the addition fact "2 + 3 = 5" and may no longer need counters or drawings to verify this.

The first addition facts that students memorize are usually the "add one" facts: 1 + 1 = 2, 2 + 1 = 3, 3 + 1 = 4, and so on. The next facts that students usually memorize are the "doubles" facts: 1 + 1 = 2, 2 + 2 = 4, 3 + 3 = 6, and so forth. Other strategies and properties useful in learning basic facts will be covered later in this chapter. Textbook series differ on exactly what facts are to be memorized and in what order they are introduced, but generally it is expected that students at the second-grade level memorize facts up to 9 + 9 = 18. Before students can memorize these facts, it is imperative that they understand the underlying concepts. Addition facts can be reinforced through many concrete classroom and real-life experiences. Drill and practice games and activities can also aid in the memorization process.

Terminology, Notation, and Properties of Addition

Terminology and Notation Most elementary student textbooks introduce the mathematically correct terminology associated with addition and addition facts. For the addition fact "2 + 3 = 5," the numbers 2 and 3 are called addends, and 5 is called the sum. An *addend* is "a number that is added" and a *sum* is "the answer to an addition problem."

At the kindergarten level, most addition and subtraction problems will be written horizontally such as 5 + 3 = ___ and 7 − 2 = ___. At the first-grade level, students should also be exposed to problems written vertically such as shown.

$$\begin{array}{r} 5 \\ +3 \\ \hline \end{array} \qquad \begin{array}{r} 7 \\ -2 \\ \hline \end{array}$$

The Commutative Property of Addition A whole number property that cuts down the number of facts to be memorized is the property of commutativity. The *commutative property of addition* states "If *a* and *b* are whole numbers, then $a + b = b + a$." For example, 2 + 3 = 3 + 2. That is, if you have memorized the fact that 2 + 3 = 5, then the fact 3 + 2 = 5 is not far behind.

You may allow students to discover this property by completing an activity such as Activity 5-2 before formally presenting it to them. Some elementary textbooks use the term "commutative property," whereas others will call it the "order property" or "turnaround facts."

The Fact Family Associated with a Given Number Some textbooks use the term *fact family* to describe the set of whole number addition facts with a common sum. For example, the 5-fact family is the set of addition facts: 0 + 5 = 5, 1 + 4 = 5, 2 + 3 = 5, 3 + 2 = 5, 4 + 1 = 5, and 5 + 0 = 5. At about the third-grade level, students can discover for themselves that there are $n + 1$ facts in the *n*-fact family (see Activity 5-3). Sometimes the term "fact family" is used in a different manner that will be explained in Section 5.2.

A homemade manipulative (see Blackline Master 6 in the Appendices) that can be used to reinforce the concepts of fact families and the commutative property is called the groovy board (Troutman & Lichtenberg, 2003). The groovy board is made of notched cardboard so that a rubber band or pipe cleaner can be used to separate one section of the board from the other. Activities 5-4 and 5-5 use the groovy board.

It is easy to create ten frame worksheets using Microsoft Word. See the Microsoft Word drawing technology section in Appendix B.

One fact family that deserves special attention is the fact family for ten. Sums that equal ten are especially important because of the base-ten numeration system. Many activities related to the 10-fact family use a device known as the ten frame. You may not recall using models such as the groovy board or the ten frame when you were learning basic addition facts in your own elementary school experience. As noted in Chapter 1, today's elementary school classrooms are probably much more hands-on than the elementary school classrooms that you experienced as a student. Activities 5-6 through 5-9 involve the 10-fact family.

After students are skilled at making sums of ten, they are ready to use this skill in order to add two numbers that have a sum greater than ten. You may first wish to review regrouping activities such as Activities 3-28, 3-29, and 4-2.

The Associative Property of Addition There is an addition property used in Activity 5-10 that deserves mention: this

---

Activity 5-2   Grades K–2

Discovering the Commutative Property of Addition

Materials: Counters, links, or unifix cubes for each student.

Directions for Students: Find each sum. You may use counters.

1. (a) 2 + 3 = ___   (b) 3 + 2 = ___
2. (a) 2 + 4 = ___   (b) 4 + 2 = ___
3. (a) 3 + 4 = ___   (b) 4 + 3 = ___
4. (a) 2 + 5 = ___   (b) 5 + 2 = ___
5. (a) 3 + 5 = ___   (b) 5 + 3 = ___

Talk About It: If you know the fact 4 + 5 = 9, how can you find the sum 5 + 4?

Using Literature in the Mathematics Classroom   Grades 1–2

The Hershey's Kisses Addition Book

By Jerry Pallotta
Scholastic, 2001

In this book, colorful clowns illustrate addition facts using Hershey's Kisses. Types of facts covered include the add-one facts, doubles facts, and adding zero. Both vertical and horizontal symbolic addition notation is used.

After reading this book, an addition or subtraction activity using Hershey's Kisses as manipulatives could be planned.

Activity 5-3 — Grades 2–3

How Many Facts Are There in an Addition Fact Family?

Materials: Counters, links, or unifix cubes for each student.

Teacher-Directed Example: There are *three* facts in the 2-fact family. They are (write on board):

$$0 + 2 = 2 \qquad 1 + 1 = 2 \qquad 2 + 0 = 2$$

Why do we call this the 2-fact family? (Accept several responses.) Let's work together to find all the facts in the 3-fact family. For example, can you give me addition facts with a sum of 3?

(Accept facts from students, then write them on the board.)

$$0 + 3 = 3, 1 + 2 = 3, 2 + 1 = 3, 3 + 0 = 3.$$

Note: For each correct fact given, point out why it belongs in the 3-fact family. Note that there are *four* facts in the 3-fact family.

Directions for Students: Find all the facts in each fact family.

1. Find the five facts in the 4-fact family. The facts will look like ___ + ___ = 4.
2. What do the facts in the 5-fact family look like? Find the six facts in the 5-fact family.
3. How many facts do you think there are in the 6-fact family? Find all the facts in the 6-fact family.
4. How many facts are in the 7-fact family? Try to answer without writing down the facts.
5. How many facts are there in the 10-fact family? Try to answer without writing down the facts.

 Activity 5-4 — Grades K–2

Using the Groovy Board to Illustrate an Addition Fact Family

Materials: Groovy boards (see Blackline Master 6) with rubber bands or pipe cleaners.

Teacher-Directed Example: Let's use the groovy board to see some addition facts.

What addition fact does this show?

Directions for Students: Use your groovy board to show the other facts in the 4-fact family.

Use the six groovy board to find all the facts in the 6-fact family.

Source: Troutman & Lichtenberg, 2003.

 Activity 5-5 — Grades K–2

Using the Groovy Board to Illustrate the Commutative Property of Addition

Materials: Groovy boards (see Blackline Master 6) with rubber bands or pipe cleaners.

Teacher-Directed Example: You can use the groovy board to show turnaround facts.

What addition fact does this show?

Use your groovy board to show the turnaround fact.

Directions for Students: Use your six groovy board to show more turnaround facts.

Note: If faces are printed on both sides of the board, showing the turnaround facts is easy.

Source: Troutman & Lichtenberg, 2003.

is the property of associativity. The *associative property of addition* states "If *a, b,* and *c* are whole numbers, then $a + (b + c) = (a + b) + c$." For example, $7 + (3 + 2) = (7 + 3) + 2$. This is sometimes called the *grouping property* in elementary textbooks. It is the associative property of addition that lets you change which addends in a sum are paired together. This allows you to group together certain addends, for instance those that sum to ten, to make the overall sum easier to find. This strategy of "making tens" can be useful for students as they are learning basic addition facts.

The Additive Identity Technology can be useful to help students discover interesting mathematical properties. One such property is that of an identity. Zero is called an *additive identity* because whenever zero is added to any whole number, that other addend is unchanged and retains

Activity 5-6 — Grades 1–2

Illustrating the 10-Fact Family with Ten Frames

Materials: Ten frame worksheets (see Blackline Master 8) and ten two-sided counters for each student; crayons or markers.

Teacher Statement: Shake your ten counters and drop them on your desk. Record on your ten frame sheet how many reds and how many yellows you get on each drop. Make an addition sentence for each drop.

Example: $4 + 6 = 10$

Activity 5-7 — Grades K–2

Illustrating the 10-Fact Family with Fingers

Teacher-Directed Examples: We can use our fingers to find facts in the 10-fact family. Hold up three fingers. How many fingers do you have folded down? Yes, seven. What 10-fact addition sentence does this show? It shows $3 + 7 = 10$, right. Now hold up two fingers. What 10-fact does this show? It shows $2 + 8 = 10$, good. Who can show me a 10-fact using four fingers? Great, $4 + 6 = 10$. What other 10-facts can we use our fingers to find?

Activity 5-8 — Grades K–2

Making Ten

Materials: Index cards with the numerals 1 to 9 (one card per student).

Directions: Pass out one card (face down) to each student. When you give the signal, students flip over their card and look at their number. They then must find a partner so that the two of them make a sum of ten.

Activity 5-9 — Grades 1–2

"Go Fish"—Making Ten

Materials: Index cards with the numerals 1 to 9 (one set per student).

Setup: Put students in groups of four to six students. Each group shuffles together as many sets of cards as there are students in the group, and deals five cards to each student. Remaining cards are placed face down in a pile in the middle of the group.

Directions for Students: When it is your turn you will look at your own cards. Using two cards at a time, make a sum of ten if you can and lay it face up in front of you. The other members of your group will check to see if your sum is correct. If you cannot lay down a sum of ten, you may ask another member of the group for a particular card, for example "John do you have a seven?" If John does have a seven he must give it to you, and you may use it to lay down a sum of ten. If he does not, he will tell you to "go fish" and you must take a card from the middle pile. If you get the card you were fishing for, you may lay it down immediately. If you get another card that helps you make a sum of ten you must wait until your next turn to lay it down. You may lay down only one sum of ten on each turn. The winner is the person with the most sums in front of him when every player of the group is out of cards.

ample such as $3 + 2 = 5$ before giving any examples involving zero.

The Closure Property One further property of whole number addition that should be mentioned is that the sum of any two whole numbers is also a whole number. This is known as a *closure property:* the set of whole numbers is closed under addition. The set of even whole numbers $E = \{0, 2, 4, 6, 8, 10, \dots\}$ is also closed under addition because the sum of any two even whole numbers is an even whole number. The set of odd whole numbers is not closed under addition. There are operations for which the set of whole numbers is not closed. Can you think of any such operations? We will study such an operation in Section 5.2, but for now we continue with our discussion of addition.

Strategies for Learning Basic Addition Facts

We have already discussed the phrase *counting on*. Counting on can also be used as a strategy for learning basic addition facts. For example, to find the sum $9 + 3$, you may start at 9 and count on three terms—10, 11, 12. One downfall to this strategy is that students may get confused about

its identity. That is, if b is any whole number, then $0 + b = b + 0 = b$. This corresponds to the set property $A \cup \varnothing = A$. One way to introduce the additive identity property of zero is with a calculator as shown in Activity 5-11.

You could also introduce the additive identity property of zero with concrete objects such as fingers. Notice how the teacher in Activity 5-12 starts with a familiar ex-

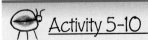 Activity 5-10   Grades 1–2

Making Ten and Adding

Materials: Base-ten blocks (or smiley sets). Each student should have at least 20 singles and 2 longs (ten strips); you will also need to make up a worksheet with appropriate problems.

Teacher-Directed Example: Show me 7 singles plus 5 singles. Can I use part of this to make a sum of 10? Yes, 7 plus 3 more is 10. If you regroup and replace the 10 singles with a ten strip, what do you have? Right, you have a 10 and 2 singles. That's 12. (Write on the board.)

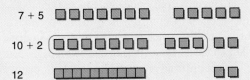

Note: If a student writes $5 + 5 = 10$, instead of $7 + 3 = 10$, you may use an alternate regrouping to the one shown above.

Directions for Students: For each problem, count the number in each set and write the numbers in the blanks. Make a ten, then find the sum. Record your work in the blanks.

$$\frac{\_\_ + \_\_ =}{10 + \_\_ =}$$

$$\_\_$$

Note: The worksheet should contain several problems similar to the one above.

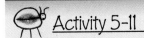 Activity 5-11   Grades K–2

Using a Calculator to Illustrate the Additive Identity

Materials: A calculator for each student.

Teacher-Directed Example: Press the buttons on your calculator. Fill in the blanks with the results shown by the calculator.

Follow-Up Questions: What happens when you add zero to another number? What do you think $5 + 0$ will be? Why do you think that? What do you think $100 + 0$ is? What do you think $0 + 88$ is?

$1 + 0 = \_\_\_$	$0 + 1 = \_\_\_$
$2 + 0 = \_\_\_$	$0 + 2 = \_\_\_$
$3 + 0 = \_\_\_$	$0 + 3 = \_\_\_$
$4 + 0 = \_\_\_$	$0 + 4 = \_\_\_$

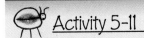 Activity 5-12   Grades K–2

Illustrating the Additive Identity

Teacher-Directed Examples: Hold up three fingers on your left hand. Hold up two fingers on your right hand. What addition sentence does this show? Right, $3 + 2 = 5$. Now hold up three fingers on your left hand and zero fingers on your right hand. What addition sentence does this show? Good, $3 + 0 = 3$. Who can show me an addition sentence for $4 + 0$? What is $4 + 0$ equal to? Great, $4 + 0 = 4$. Can anyone show me an addition sentence for $0 + 2$? What is $0 + 2$ equal to? Great, $0 + 2 = 2$.

Follow-Up Questions: What happens when you add zero to another number? What do you think $5 + 0$ will be? Why do you think that? What do you think $100 + 0$ is? What do you think $0 + 88$ is?

where the counting on begins and may make an error such as "9 + 3 is 9, 10, 11." How would you explain their error to the student who counts on in this manner?

Another strategy that can help students learn basic addition facts is that of *counting back*. This is similar to the idea of counting on. The following example illustrates the strategy of counting back: Since 8 is 2 less than 10, you can find the sum $8 + 5$ by first thinking $10 + 5$ and then counting back by 2. That is, to find $8 + 5$ you start at $10 + 5$ which is 15, and count back 14, 13. So, $8 + 5 = 13$.

Because doubles facts are often easy for children to memorize, some facts may be learned by *relating* them to doubles facts. For example $7 + 8$ is one more than the double $7 + 7$, so $7 + 8$ is 14 plus 1, which is 15. This idea of using doubles can be combined with the idea of counting on. To find the sum $6 + 9$, you could begin with the doubles fact $6 + 6 = 12$ and count on three terms, 13, 14, 15. You can also begin with a doubles fact and count back. For example, $7 + 8$ is one less than the double $8 + 8$, so $7 + 8$ is 16 minus 1, which is 15.

Teaching Connections

Present a Variety of Strategies to Help Children Learn Basic Addition Facts A variety of strategies for learning addition facts and solving addition problems have already been discussed. As a teacher, you should present as many strategies as possible to your students. Different children will learn in different ways. They will adopt a variety of rules and strategies, including those that they themselves create. When students make up their own math rules, you the teacher must be prepared to analyze their rule or strategy and determine whether it is valid. If it is not valid, you should be able to provide the student with a counterexample that shows them that their rule does not work. Armed with a variety of strategies and properties, children will eventually learn the addition facts they need. You may recall filling out addition tables such as the one shown in Figure 5-3 when you were in elementary school.

Encourage Alternate Solutions Eventually students will need to learn to solve problems involving more than two addends like 7 + 5 + 3. Calculate the answer to 7 + 5 + 3. Did you first add the 7 and the 5 to get 12 and then add 3 to get 15? Many elementary students will solve this in a dif-

ferent manner by saying "7 plus 3 is 10 and 5 more is 15." This solution uses the commutative and associative properties of addition to first add the "compatible numbers" 7 and 3. It is important that you as a teacher encourage students to find different ways of solving problems. Alternate solutions should be presented whenever possible. However, you must be sure that when a student solves a problem in a different manner than you had expected, that their solution process is valid and correct. Students should also be encouraged to check the answers to the math problems that they solve to determine whether the answers are reasonable.

Use Real-World Examples and Fun Activities to Practice Addition Facts One way to show students the importance of addition and learning addition facts is to use story problems that relate directly to the students. Students can also create their own story problems. It is easy to create games such as "Go Fish" or other matching games that help students practice addition facts without boring them with pages and pages of the vertical drill and practice-type problems that you may remember from elementary school textbooks.

Example 5-1: Problem solving by considering cases (third- or fourth-grade level).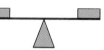

Assessment   Grades 2–3
Writing in Mathematics

An excellent writing activity that helps students organize, compare, and learn strategies for addition facts is described in *Writing in Math Class* by Marilyn Burns (1995, pp. 136–139). In this activity, a second-grade class held a class discussion of various strategies to compute a given addition fact. The teacher recorded the strategies on the board. The students then independently solved another addition problem and listed the various strategies they could use to solve the problem. All except one student were able to come up with at least three strategies for the new problem. Many of the students listed more strategies than had been recorded on the original strategy list.

 ### Activity 5-13   Grades 1–2

Creating Addition Stories

Materials: Index cards with addition problems such as 5 + 9 (one card for each student).

Directions: Pass out one card (face down) to each student. Ask students to find the answer to their addition problem and to make up a story problem that goes with their problem. They will share their story problem with the class to see if the class can solve it.

 ### Activity 5-14   Grades 1–2

Finding Addition Problems with a Common Sum

Materials: Index cards with addition problems such as 5 + 9 (one card for each student).

Directions: Pass out one card (face down) to each student. When you give the signal, students flip over their cards and solve their addition problems. They must then find all of the other students that have the same sum.

+	0	1	2	3	4	5	6	7	8	9
0	0	1	2	3	4	5	6	7	8	9
1	1	2	3	4	5	6	7	8	9	10
2	2	3	4	5	6	7	8	9	10	11
3	3	4	5	6	7	8	9	10	11	12
4	4	5	6	7	8	9	10	11	12	13
5	5	6	7	8	9	10	11	12	13	14
6	6	7	8	9	10	11	12	13	14	15
7	7	8	9	10	11	12	13	14	15	16
8	8	9	10	11	12	13	14	15	16	17
9	9	10	11	12	13	14	15	16	17	18

FIGURE 5-3 An addition table.

Note: Addends are shown in boldface. Doubles facts are circled. If you memorize or can determine the addition facts shown in black below the diagonal of doubles facts, then the addition facts above the diagonal follow from the property of commutativity.

You wish to purchase weights to use with a balance scale. You would like to be able to weigh items that are 1 pound (lb), 2 lb, . . . up to 15 lb. Weights may be used alone or with other weights. For example, if you purchase weights that are 1 lb, 5 lb, and 7 lb, you could weigh items that are any of the following weights: 1 lb, 5 lb, 7 lb, 6 lb, 8 lb, 12 lb, or 13 lb. What is the minimum number of weights that you would need to buy in order to be able to weigh all quantities from 1 to 15 lb? Which specific weights should you buy?

Partial Solution: As the above example illustrates, if you purchase only three weights, you can make at most seven different combinations of weights using the three weights purchased. You must purchase at least four weights. If the five weights 1 lb, 2 lb, 3 lb, 4 lb, and 5 lb are purchased, you could weigh all quantities from 1 to 15 lb using combinations of these five weights. It is an exercise to show that there is a solution using only four weights.

Problem Set 5.1

For Your Understanding

1. a. Sketch a number line to illustrate $5 + 4 = 9$.
   b. Sketch a number line to illustrate $4 + 5 = 9$.

2. Explain why the set of odd whole numbers is not closed under addition. Give at least one specific example in your explanation.

3. For the addition fact $3 + 6 = 9$, the numbers 3 and 6 are called ____ and the 9 is called the ____ .

4. What properties or addition strategies are used in each statement?
   a. $4 + 19$ is 20, 21, 22, 23
   b. $7 + 9 = 6 + 10 = 16$
   c. $23 + 0 = 23$
   d. $23 + 19$ is a whole number
   e. $7 + 9$ is one less than $7 + 10$, so the answer is 16
   f. $(7 + 2) + 8 = 7 + (2 + 8)$

5. Complete the following addition puzzle.

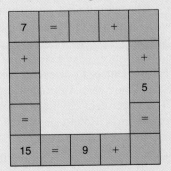

6. Find a solution to Example 5-1 that uses exactly four weights to weigh all quantities from 1 to 15 lb.

Applications in the Classroom

1. Some common student errors are given. You are the teacher. How do you respond to each student?
   a. Travis says "I can count forward to find 12 plus 3. That's 12, 13, 14."
   b. Ashanti says "$9 + 5$ is one away from $10 + 5$. That's 15, so the answer is 16."

2. Write five addition story problems that you think would be interesting to elementary school children. Classify each problem as either a combination addition problem or an incremental addition problem.

3. Complete Activity 5-3.

4. Use a computer to create a worksheet that could be used with Activity 5-10. You may wish to refer to the Microsoft Word drawing technology section in Appendix B.

5. Create a game or puzzle that could be used to help students practice their addition facts.

6. Create an assessment tool to be used with Activity 5-13. Explain why you chose that type of assessment tool.

7. Classify the level of knowledge and the type of learning experience of Activity 5-13. What objective from the NCTM model (or from your state or district model) does the activity address?

5.2 CONSTRUCTING MEANING FOR SUBTRACTION

Just as with addition, a child's first introduction to the concept of subtraction should involve real-life situations that the child can relate to, as well as concrete objects to help the child solve the problems in these situations. There are several different real-life situations that will require subtraction. It is important that students realize that subtraction is not always take-away, although this is the first type of subtraction that students usually encounter.

Five Interpretations of Subtraction

1. Take-Away The take-away interpretation of subtraction is probably the easiest and most natural for students. This is an example of a take-away type of problem: "There are six cats in a room. Two of the cats leave the room. How many cats are still in the room?" Children can use concrete objects to act out the situation. They could also draw a picture and use the picture to solve the problem. In many elementary textbooks, a picture of a situation is already drawn, and children are instructed to mark out the objects, people, or animals that "leave" with an *X*. Students should be encouraged to check their answers to see that they are reasonable.

2. Additive The additive interpretation for subtraction, sometimes referred to as the missing addend interpretation for subtraction, is useful in situations where a quantity is given that is less than the quantity that is needed or desired. The problem is to determine what must be added to reach the desired quantity. An example of this type of problem is "Carlos has 7 pennies. He needs 12 pennies to buy a toy. How many more pennies does Carlos need?" When students first encounter this type of problem, they may need to use concrete objects or pictures to solve it. They may not at first realize that the appropriate operation is subtraction; the solution process is actually more indicative of addition. To solve this problem, students might first set out or draw 7 pennies. They then continue to set out or draw pennies until they have a total of 12 pennies. They must then realize that the original 7 pennies are not part of the solution. The answer is 5, since 5 pennies must be added to the original 7 to reach a total of 12.

Students need enough practice so that upon encountering such a problem they will eventually realize that the appropriate operation is subtraction. By the third-grade level a student should be able to solve a problem like "Jan needs to sell 200 boxes of cookies to win a prize. She has already sold 42 boxes of cookies. How many more boxes of cookies does she need to sell?" To solve this problem, it would not be practical to use concrete objects. At this level, the student should realize that the appropriate operation is subtraction, and perform the operation either with a calculator or with a pen-and-paper calculation. The word "more" in the problem may lead some students to erroneously use addition instead of subtraction. Students should be encouraged to check their answers. If a student gives the answer 242, you could ask "She has to sell 242 more boxes to get the prize? Didn't she need only 200 boxes to get the prize? Why don't you try the problem again?"

3. Comparative In the comparative interpretation of subtraction, two finite set quantities are given, and the problem is to determine how much larger one set is than the other. An example of this type of problem is "Steve has six pencils and Kari has four pencils. Who has more pencils? How many more?" Initially students will solve this type of prob-

Standards

NCTM

Number and Operations Standard: Grades Pre-K–2

Expectation: In prekindergarten through grade 2 all students should understand various meanings of addition and subtraction of whole numbers and the relationship between the two operations.

NCTM, 2000, 78

Standards are listed with the permission of the National Council of Teachers of Mathematics (NCTM). NCTM does not endorse the content or validity of these alignments.

Standards

North Carolina Mathematics Standards

Number Sense, Numeration, and Numerical Operations for Grade 1

1.15 Model concept of subtraction as take-away, comparison, and missing addends.

North Carolina Department of Public Instruction, 2003

lem by using concrete objects or drawing pictures and making a one-to-one correspondence between objects in the sets. When all of the objects in the smaller set have been matched with objects in the larger set, the student can determine how many objects in the larger set were not matched.

Again, students need enough practice with this type of problem so that they will realize that the appropriate operation is subtraction. Again, the word "more" in the problem may lead some students to erroneously use the operation of addition instead of subtraction. If students have a habit of checking their answers to see if they are reasonable, they will be able to catch and correct this mistake.

4. Partitioning The partitioning interpretation of subtraction involves separating or partitioning a finite set of objects into two parts. Both the number of objects in the whole set, and the number of objects in one of the parts, are given. The problem is to determine the number of objects in the remaining part. An example of this type of problem is "There are eight children on the bus. Three of the children are girls. How many of the children are boys?" Initially, students will solve this type of problem by using concrete objects or by drawing a picture of the situation.

A typical second-grade-level problem is "There are 31 children in a class. Seventeen of the children are boys. How many are girls?" For numbers of this magnitude, it would not be practical to use concrete objects or to draw a picture. The student should realize that the appropriate operation is subtraction, and perform the operation either with a calculator or with a pen-and-paper calculation. If students check their answers to see that they are reasonable, they will not make the mistake of using addition in this type of problem.

5. Incremental Not all subtraction problems involve concrete objects that may be counted. Similar to the incremental interpretation of addition, the incremental interpretation of subtraction is useful in situations where an abstract, but measurable, quantity is increased or decreased. For example, "Last year George weighed 94 pounds. He lost 6 pounds. How much does George weigh now?" or "In Science we are growing tomato plants. The plant in the shade is three inches tall; the plant in the sun is seven inches tall. How much taller is the plant that we put in the sun?" (The first example is also a take-away subtraction problem. The second example is also a comparative subtraction problem.)

Categorizing the Type of Subtraction Problem When elementary students encounter a subtraction problem, they are not required to categorize the type of problem, but they should learn to recognize that subtraction is the required operation. You, as the teacher, should be able to categorize the problem. There are subtle differences in the thought processes involved in the recognition and solution of the five different types of problems we have discussed. If you can identify the category of a problem, you are better prepared to help a student who is having difficulty with that problem. Some of the exercises will give you practice in identifying the type of a given subtraction problem and writing subtraction problems of a specified type.

Two Models to Illustrate Subtraction

The Smiley Card Model A model that can be used with most of the interpretations of subtraction is a set of cards that are blank on one side and have some uniform design or mark on the other. Blackline Master 9 (see the Appendices) illustrates a set of smiley cards. Activity 5-15 describes how this model is used to illustrate two of the interpretations of subtraction. This is a developmental activity to introduce the concept of subtraction. Notice the lack of subtraction terminology and notation. The focus of this activity is on the idea of subtraction. Later activities can incorporate subtraction terminology and notation.

You can create smiley cards using a computer. See the Microsoft Word drawing technology section in Appendix B.

Notice that Problem 1 of Activity 5-15 is a take-away subtraction problem, but in the smiley card model, the cards are flipped and not removed. This is so that students get used to the idea of flipping cards, and the model can be used naturally with other subtraction interpretations such

Activity 5-15 — Grades 1–3

Using Smiley Card Manipulatives to Solve Subtraction Problems

Materials: Ten smiley cards (see Blackline Master 9) for each student.

Teacher-Directed Example: We can use smiley cards to help us solve math problems.

Problem 1: There are five children in a pool. Two of the children get out of the pool. How many children are still in the pool?

1. We can set out five cards for the five children in the pool.

2. We flip over two cards for the two children who get out of the pool. Now we can tell how many children are still in the pool.

Problem 2: Jim needs seven pennies for a toy. He has three pennies. How many more pennies does he need?

1. We set out seven cards for the seven pennies.

2. We flip over three cards for the pennies Jim already has. Now we can tell how many pennies he needs.

Source: Adapted from Troutman & Lichtenberg, 2003.

as in Problem 2 of Activity 5-15 (an additive subtraction problem).

Note the variety of tasks in the reinforcement Activity 5-16. Students must be able to relate a story, a model, and a number sentence. When given one of these items, they must be able to create the two missing items. These types of problems, in which students must create story problems and write number sentences, are common in today's elementary textbooks and frequently occur in real-life situations.

The Number Line Model The number line provides a model for illustrating subtraction. Figure 5-4a illustrates a mathematically precise number line depiction of the equation $7 - 4 = 3$. Notice that the head of the arrow representing 4 is positioned at the head of the arrow representing 7. Figure 5-4b shows how a number line depiction of $7 - 4 = 3$ might appear in a second- or third-grade textbook. To a mathematician, this represents $7 + (-4) = 3$ rather than $7 - 4 = 3$. Figure 5-4c shows how a number line depiction of $7 - 4 = 3$ might appear in a first-grade textbook.

The number line shown in Figure 5-4c indicates a process of counting back to solve the subtraction problem $7 - 4$. As with any counting process, care must be taken that the students understand where the process of counting must begin and exactly how far the counting should continue. Some students are excited to learn that they may check their subtraction answers with addition, an important skill for elementary students. It also reinforces the relationship between addition and subtraction.

Teaching Connections

Emphasize the Connection Between Addition and Subtraction Children may not immediately grasp the relationship between addition and subtraction. They need to develop an understanding of this relationship by working through various problems and activities. It is because of this relationship that students do not need to memorize subtraction facts. Once addition facts are known, subtraction facts follow for free. To calculate $14 - 6$, you can think $6 + \underline{\hspace{1cm}} = 14$. The addition fact $6 + 8 = 14$ gives the answer. Thus, $14 - 6 = 8$.

Another way to solve the same problem is to start by taking 4 away from 14. This leaves 10, but you still need to take away 2 so that you have taken away a total of 6. After all the work with the 10-fact family, $10 - 2 = 8$ is an easy calculation. This method of solution essentially involves regrouping, and is easy for students who have had plenty of practice with the 10-fact family. See Figure 5-5 for an illustration of the method.

Use Games and Fun Activities to Practice Addition and Subtraction Facts There are many games and fun activities available for students to use to practice addition and subtraction facts. The elementary textbook series that you will use will probably contain a variety of games and ac-

Activity 5-16   Grades 1–3

Relating the Story, the Model, and the Number Sentence

Materials: Ten smiley cards (see Blackline Master 9) for each student.

Problem 1: If we have a set of smiley cards that looks like this, what number sentence does this represent? Write a story problem that goes with this equation.

Problem 2: Show a row of smiley cards that represents the subtraction equation $7 - 5 = 2$. Write a story problem that goes with this equation.

Problem 3: Tasha has five brothers and one sister. Joe has two brothers. How many more brothers does Tasha have than Joe? Show a row of smiley cards that represents the problem. Write a number sentence that represents the problem.

Source: Adapted from Troutman & Lichtenberg, 2003.

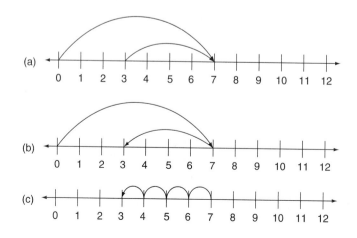

FIGURE 5-4 (a) The mathematically precise number line illustration of $7 - 4 = 3$, (b) how $7 - 4 = 3$ might appear in a third-grade textbook, (c) how $7 - 4 = 3$ might appear in a first-grade textbook.

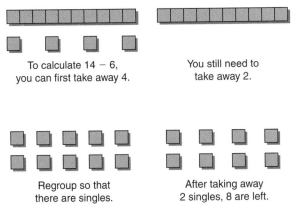

FIGURE 5-5 An illustration of 14−6.

To calculate 14 − 6, you can first take away 4.

You still need to take away 2.

Regroup so that there are singles.

After taking away 2 singles, 8 are left.

tivities. There are also several commercially published activity manuals that you may purchase, and thousands of Internet resources. Two activities that students at the second-to fourth-grade levels seem to especially enjoy are shown in Activities 5-17 and 5-18.

Activity 5-19 mentions equations that cannot be completed and gives the example 5 − 6 = ___. Technically, this equation *can* be completed. The answer, of course, is −1. However, the directions in Activity 5-19 specify that the student must write a whole number in the fourth box. The problem is that the set of whole numbers is not closed under subtraction. For example, when the whole number six is subtracted from the whole number five, the result is not a whole number. Although some elementary school curriculums introduce negative integers at the third- or fourth-grade level, most do not until the fifth-grade level. Because the focus is on whole number addition and subtraction, it is important that students who have not been introduced to negative integers recognize that there is no whole number answer to a problem such as 5 − 6. To get a whole number answer, the subtrahend must be no larger than the minuend. In other words, the amount you are subtracting cannot be larger than the amount you are subtracting from. However, you should not use phrases like "subtract the smaller from the larger" as they could lead to a common student error that will be discussed in Section 5.5. Negative integers will be covered further in Section 5.4.

Subtraction Terminology and Notation

It is common for students to encounter problems where the answer does not occur on the right side of the equal sign. The equation 4 + ___ = 7 is a typical first-grade-level example. For obvious reasons, this is called a *missing addend equation*. This type of equation helps show the relationship between addition and subtraction. Most addition sentences have two related subtraction sentences. For example, the addition sentence 3 + 4 = 7 is related to the subtraction sentences 7 − 4 = 3 and 7 − 3 = 4. It is also related to the

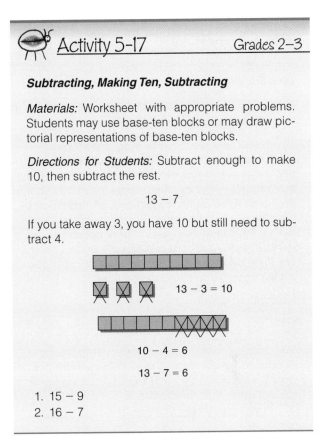

Activity 5-17   Grades 2–3

Subtracting, Making Ten, Subtracting

Materials: Worksheet with appropriate problems. Students may use base-ten blocks or may draw pictorial representations of base-ten blocks.

Directions for Students: Subtract enough to make 10, then subtract the rest.

13 − 7

If you take away 3, you have 10 but still need to subtract 4.

13 − 3 = 10

10 − 4 = 6

13 − 7 = 6

1. 15 − 9
2. 16 − 7

Activity 5-18   Grades 2–4

Beat the Calculator

Materials: Calculators, addition or subtraction flash cards (or multiplication or division flash cards).

Directions: Divide students into two teams. One team gets calculators, the other team does not. Line up the two teams. Show an addition or subtraction flash card problem to the first person in each line. The calculator student punches the problem into the calculator to get an answer. The other student computes the problem mentally. The winning team gets a point.

addition sentence 4 + 3 = 7. Some textbooks call these four related facts a *fact family*. This usage differs from the *n*-fact family discussed in Section 5.1. When dealing with a fact family, make sure that you know whether the term refers to the set of all addition facts with a common sum or the set of related addition and subtraction facts using the same set of three numbers.

Once the concept of subtraction is understood, students may be introduced to the terminology and notations

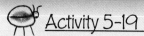

Activity 5-19   Grades 2–4

Dice Equations

Materials: Two dice for each team. Handout for each team containing ☐ ☐ ☐ = ☐ equations.

Directions: One student rolls a die and records the result in the first box. The second student writes either the plus or minus sign in the second box. The third student rolls a die and records the result in the third box. If the fourth student can, she completes the equation by writing an appropriate whole number in the fourth box. Subtraction equations are worth 2 points, addition equations are worth 1 point. The team gets no points for equations that cannot be completed.

Example:

This equation cannot be completed. If the second student had put + instead of − in the second box, the equation would be worth 1 point when the fourth student wrote 11 in the fourth box.

---

of subtraction. A problem such as 6 − 2 is read as "six minus two" which is *not* the same as "two minus six." The problem 6 − 2 can also be read as "six take away two," "two subtracted from six," or "two less than six." The problem 6 − 2 should *not* be read as "two times less than six" as this phrase could be confusing. The term "times" usually indicates multiplication, not subtraction.

There are words naming each of the terms in a subtraction expression. For the expression 6 − 2 = 4, the 6 is called the *minuend,* the 2 is called the *subtrahend,* and the 4 is called the *difference* or specifically the *difference of 6 and 2.* The words "minuend" and "subtrahend" are generally not used in the elementary school curriculum, but most elementary textbooks do use the term "difference" to indicate subtraction. The subtraction problem 6 − 2 = 4 can be related to the addition problem 4 + 2 = 6.

Because there is more than one number fact that can be written using a given set of numbers, children will need practice in choosing the correct operation and equation for a given story problem.

Example 5-2: Problem solving to choose the operation (Grades K–4).

Kindergarten Level: The teacher reads a story problem like "Six ducks are swimming. Two ducks get out of the water. How many ducks are still swimming?" Children have a picture of the situation and a fill-in-the-blank equation template. They must fill in the appropriate numbers as

well as the plus sign (+) for addition or the minus sign (−) for subtraction.

Second-Grade Level: The teacher poses a problem such as this: Kayla has nine fish. Some fish are in a big bowl. Three fish are in a small bowl. How many fish are in the big bowl? ___ fish. Did you add or subtract? ___ Write a number sentence: ___.

Problem Set 5.2

For Your Understanding

1. Which of the following are appropriate wording for the subtraction problem 8 − 3?
   a. eight minus three
   b. three minus eight
   c. eight subtracted from three
   d. three subtracted from eight
   e. eight less than three
   f. three less than eight
   g. three times less than eight

2. The following problems are similar to those that occur in second-grade textbooks. Classify the type of each problem.
   a. There are 45 pets in the pet store. Seventeen of the pets are dogs. The rest are cats. How many pets are cats?
   b. A squirrel gathered 30 nuts. It ate 6 nuts. How many more nuts are left for the squirrel to eat?
   c. Jay found 12 shells. Kay found 3 shells. How many more shells did Jay find than Kay?

3. Find the four facts in the fact family for 3 + 5 = 8. ("Fact family" in this problem refers to the set of related addition and subtraction facts.)

4. When are there fewer than four facts in a fact family? ("Fact family" in this problem refers to the set of related addition and subtraction facts.)

5. Is subtraction of whole numbers commutative? If your answer is yes, explain why. If your answer is no, give a counterexample.

6. Is subtraction of whole numbers associative? If your answer is yes, explain why. If your answer is no, give a counterexample.

Applications for the Classroom

1. Draw a number line that you could use in a third-grade classroom that illustrates 8 − 5 = 3.

2. Explain why the wording in this problem could be confusing: "Twelve people are at a party. Three people left. How many are left?"

3. Write one story problem for each of the five types of subtraction that were described. Classify the type of each of your problems.

4. Create a game or puzzle that could be used to help students practice their subtraction facts. Indicate the grade level for your game or puzzle and how it can be modified for students with special needs.

5. Write three subtraction word problems and illustrate their solutions using smiley cards. Write the associated number sentence.

6. Create an assessment tool to be used with Activity 5-17. Explain why you chose that type of assessment tool.

7. Classify the level of knowledge and the type of learning experience of Activity 5-19. What objective from the NCTM model (or from your state or district model) does the activity address?

5.3 USING ALGORITHMS FOR WHOLE NUMBER ADDITION AND SUBTRACTION

Once children understand the concepts of addition and subtraction, they can be introduced to processes or algorithms for these operations. An *algorithm* is a set of steps to perform a task. Addition and subtraction facts may be memorized for single-digit addition and subtraction problems, but for larger problems it would not be feasible to rely on memory alone. Think about how you yourself calculate answers to problems such as $25 + 37$ or $53 - 17$. Before reading any further, use a pen and paper and calculate answers to each of these problems. You probably did not have the answers to these problems memorized, but used some sort of algorithm or step-by-step process to produce the answers. Your work may look similar to that shown in Figure 5-6. Possible thought processes are also shown.

You may have had thoughts similar to the ones shown in Figure 5-6 when doing those calculations. It is possible that you were taught the addition and subtraction algorithms without ever being shown why the algorithms were reasonable. Why do you "put down" 2 and "carry" the 1? Why do you "cross out 5 and write 4"? The terms used by today's students may differ from the terms that you were taught as a student. For example, many elementary textbook series use the term "regroup" instead of the terms "borrow" and "carry." If addition and subtraction algorithms are developed using concrete manipulatives such as base-ten blocks, children can see why each step of the algorithm is reasonable and appropriate.

FIGURE 5-6 Addition and subtraction examples.

How would you compute answers to $25,467 + 3,720$ and $53,045 - 15,902$? Use a pen and paper and perform these calculations. Don't you find it amazing that to add or subtract large numbers, even very large numbers, you really need to know only basic addition and subtraction facts as well as ideas of place value and regrouping?

Teaching Connections

Use Concrete Activities to Illustrate Regrouping in Addition You can begin to develop addition and subtraction algorithms using concrete activities similar to those in Section 4.2. The first activity, Activity 5-20, will not involve regrouping, but the base-ten materials used will be an excellent means by which to show regroupings in later activities.

Illustrate the Relationship Between Concrete and Symbolic Solutions After several examples using the concrete manipulatives, with problems written horizontally as in Activities 5-20 and 5-21, children will be ready for the vertical notation that you are accustomed to. You may suggest to the children when using concrete manipulatives that you start with singles because if there are 10 or more singles, you will need to regroup. It is then natural for them to start with ones in a vertical calculation. However, forcing a child to begin with singles would be tantamount to forcing a left-handed student to write with his or her right hand. Some children invent their own strategy of beginning with tens. If they can use this strategy successfully, there is no reason to insist that they begin with singles. In some cases, by telling a child how to work a problem the teacher prevents the child from using his or her own number sense (McIntosh, 1998).

Some textbooks introduce a long form addition or an expanded form version of addition before introducing the shorthand notation of recording tens that arise from regrouping above the tens column. Figures 5-7a and 5-7b illustrate these ideas.

Once students are comfortable with the addition of two two-digit addends, other types of problems may be considered. Students must learn to add when addends have more

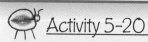

Activity 5-20 Grades 1–2

Two-Digit Addition Using Manipulatives—No Regrouping

Materials: Base-ten blocks or smiley sets for each student.

Teacher-Directed Example: Suppose there are 13 people at a party. Twelve more people come to the party. How many people are at the party in all?

Show me 13 with your blocks (smileys). Show me 12 more. How many in all? If we count singles first, we have 5 singles. We have 2 tens. How do we write this number? Yes, 25.

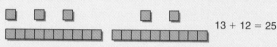

13 + 12 = 25

Activity 5-21 Grades 1–2

Two-Digit Addition Using Manipulatives—Regrouping

Materials: Base-ten blocks or smiley sets for each student.

Teacher-Directed Example: Suppose there are 17 people at a party. Fifteen more people come to the party. How many people are at the party in all?

Show me 17 with your blocks (smileys). Show me 15 more. If we start with the singles, how many singles do we have? Remember that we regroup when there are 10 or more singles. So we regroup and have 2 singles and 3 tens. How many people are there in all?

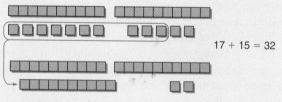

17 + 15 = 32

1. Show me 32 + 19. Don't forget to regroup if necessary. 32 + 19 = ___
2. Show me 14 + 26. Be careful when you write your answer. 14 + 26 = ___

Activity 5-22 Grades 1–2

Relating the Concrete Addition Model to Vertical Symbolic Notation

Materials: Base-ten blocks or smiley sets for each student.

Teacher Statement: We can also write our addition problems vertically.

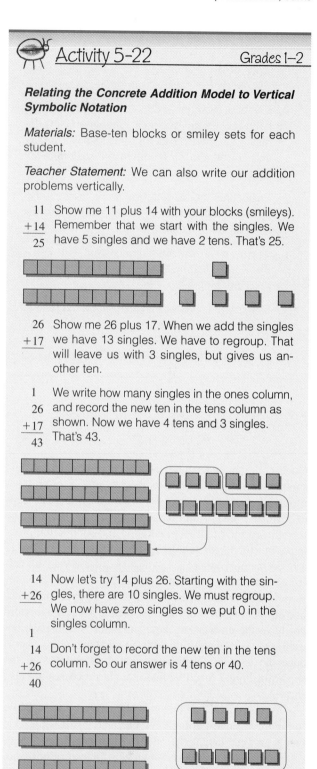

$\begin{array}{r} 11 \\ +14 \\ \hline 25 \end{array}$ Show me 11 plus 14 with your blocks (smileys). Remember that we start with the singles. We have 5 singles and we have 2 tens. That's 25.

$\begin{array}{r} 26 \\ +17 \end{array}$ Show me 26 plus 17. When we add the singles we have 13 singles. We have to regroup. That will leave us with 3 singles, but gives us another ten.

$\begin{array}{r} 1 \\ 26 \\ +17 \\ \hline 43 \end{array}$ We write how many singles in the ones column, and record the new ten in the tens column as shown. Now we have 4 tens and 3 singles. That's 43.

$\begin{array}{r} 14 \\ +26 \end{array}$ Now let's try 14 plus 26. Starting with the singles, there are 10 singles. We must regroup. We now have zero singles so we put 0 in the singles column.

$\begin{array}{r} 1 \\ 14 \\ +26 \\ \hline 40 \end{array}$ Don't forget to record the new ten in the tens column. So our answer is 4 tens or 40.

than two digits (Activity 5-23), when there are more than two addends, and when addends have different numbers of digits. Using concrete models, students realize that these types of problems are no more difficult than the two-digit, two-addend problems that they have already mastered. En-courage students to estimate the answers to these types of problems before they perform any calculations. It is especially important that students have mastered a variety of strategies for dealing with single-digit additions.

(a)   48
      +27
        15 from adding ones
      +60 from adding tens
        75

(b)   48 = 40 + 8
      +27 = 20 + 7
        60 + 15 = 60 + 10 + 5 = 70 + 5 = 75

FIGURE 5-7 (a) Long form, (b) expanded form addition.

        4
       5̶13   This notation of regrouping
      − 1 7   a ten into ten ones and using
       3 6   the original 3 to help show
                    13 ones is no longer common.

       4 13
      5̶ 3̶   Record the regrouping
      − 1 7   as shown in this example.
       3 6

FIGURE 5-8 Subtraction example 53 − 17.

Assessment

Student Self-Assessment

Checklist for Activity 5-21 (may be read to students): Circle yes, Sometimes, or No for each item.

1. It is easy to show a two-digit number with base-ten blocks.
   Yes   Sometimes   No
2. I regroup and replace ten singles with a ten when necessary.
   Yes   Sometimes   No
3. I can tell when I will have to regroup just by looking at the numbers.
   Yes   Sometimes   No
4. I can use the blocks to determine what answer to write.
   Yes   Sometimes   No
5. I checked my answers.
   Yes   Sometimes   No

Be Aware of the Computational Skills and Strategies Appropriate for Your Level of Students The progression of computational abilities and the level of competence desired as students move from one grade level to the next is evident in the standards or frameworks of many state models. Some state models explicitly mention which strategies and properties a child is to learn at each grade level.

Subtraction Algorithms

The subtraction algorithm or process can also be modeled with concrete manipulatives. Again, the first few examples should not involve regrouping. Concrete base-ten materials may be used to model the subtraction process (see Activity 5-24).

As early as first grade, students are expected to be able to verbalize when regrouping is required. You will need to devise methods for assessing this concept for English as a Second Language (ESL) students or students with limited verbal abilities. When it is clear to students that regrouping of a ten into ten singles is required when the number of singles in the amount you are trying to subtract is greater than the number of singles in the amount that you are subtracting from, they are ready for the vertical notation that you are accustomed to using. One caution about short form notation is in order. You may have learned the short form notation that regroups a ten into ten ones by writing a 1 above and to the left of the number of ones in the minuend. This notation is no longer common. The preferred method is to cross out the number of ones in the minuend and write the total number of ones after the regrouping above it. This is illustrated in Figure 5-8. Also, the term "borrow" is not commonly used today. The term "regroup" is preferred.

It is trickier than it may first appear to use a model to demonstrate the process of regrouping in subtraction and its relationship to the vertical subtraction notation. You should practice using overhead or chalkboard base-ten blocks before attempting Activities 5-25 or 5-26 in front of

> We have already discussed the ideas of compatible numbers and the commutative and associative properties mentioned in the Ohio Standards box on p. 111. The idea of compensatory numbers is discussed later in this section.

Standards

NCTM

Grades 3–5

Many students enter grade 3 with methods for adding and subtracting numbers. In grades 3–5 they should extend these methods to adding and subtracting larger numbers and learn to record their work systematically and clearly. Having access to more than one method for each operation allows students to choose an approach that best fits the numbers in a particular problem.

NCTM, 2000, p. 155

Standards are listed with the permission of the National Council of Teachers of Mathematics (NCTM). NCTM does not endorse the content or validity of these alignments.

 Activity 5-23   Grades 2–3

Adding Three-Digit Numbers

Materials: Base-ten blocks or smiley sets for each student.

Teacher-Directed Example: Let's try some addition problems with large addends.

Our first problem is 173 + 152. Let's estimate first. Our answer should be about what? Yes, by front-end estimation it will be more than 200; any other guesses? About 300? Why would you say that? That's probably a good estimate. Let's calculate it with our blocks.

Show me 173 with your blocks (smileys). Show me 152 more. Start with the singles. How many singles do we have? Right, 5. How many tens? Yes, there are 12 tens. Remember that we regroup when there are 10 or more. That will leave us with 2 tens, and give us another hundred. So, 173 + 152 = 325.

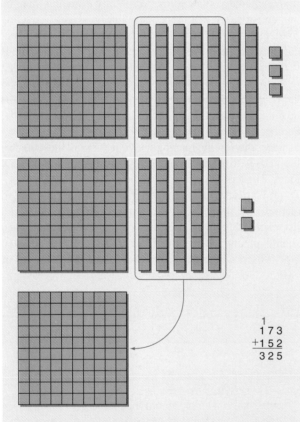

$$\begin{array}{r} 1 \\ 1\,7\,3 \\ +1\,5\,2 \\ \hline 3\,2\,5 \end{array}$$

Note: After going through one or two teacher-directed examples, give students problems to work on their own or in small groups. Make sure to include examples where regrouping of ones is required, examples where regrouping of tens is required, and examples where regrouping of both ones and tens is required. If your model includes a representation of 1,000, you may include examples where regrouping of hundreds is required.

 Activity 5-24   Grades 1–2

Two-Digit Subtraction Using Manipulatives—No Regrouping

Materials: Base-ten blocks or smiley sets for each student.

Teacher-Directed Example: There are 27 students in a classroom. Thirteen students go to the gym. How many students are still in the classroom?

Show me 27 with your blocks (smileys). Show me 13 students leaving the room. How many students are still in the room?

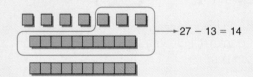

$27 - 13 = 14$

There are 27 students. Eleven students order hot dogs and the rest order pizza for lunch. How many students ordered pizza? Use your blocks to solve the problem and then write an equation.

a classroom. Your students will also need lots of practice using the vertical notation for subtraction. Remind your students that they can use estimation to see whether their answers are reasonable and they can check their answers with addition.

Teaching Connections

Use Concrete Activities to Illustrate the Process and Notation of Regrouping in Subtraction Expanded form can also be useful to demonstrate regrouping in subtraction. An expanded form subtraction example is illustrated in Figure 5-9. First you write the expanded form for each of 48 and 29. You can't take 9 singles from 8 singles. Regroup the 48 as 30 + 18, and it is easy to subtract the 20 and the 9.

Money is a useful model for addition and subtraction problems because it is easy to create real-life problems involving money. However, when money is used as a model for addition or subtraction of whole numbers, you may want to include only ones, tens, hundreds, and perhaps thousands. For example, to illustrate $39 you would use three tens and

$$\begin{array}{l} 48 = 40 + 8 = 30 + 10 + 8 = 30 + 18 \\ -29 = 20 + 9 \quad -20 + 9 \\ \hline 10 + 9 = 19 \end{array}$$

FIGURE 5-9 Expanded form subtraction 48 − 29.

nine ones instead of using any twenties or fives. This corresponds to the place value or expanded form representation of the number and allows you to focus on regrouping and other base-ten properties of whole number addition and subtraction. This also allows you to relate the concrete solution to the symbolic vertical process and notation. Money is a good model for problems that have more than two addends and for problems that involve addends having a different number of digits.

Learning how to compute with money is a major motivation for elementary schoolchildren as they can easily relate to the idea of spending money and buying objects. It is easy to create real-life money situations involving subtraction. Money examples are especially useful to demonstrate problems where more than one regrouping is required or problems where the minuend contains a zero.

Estimation and Number Sense

Remind students to use their number sense and to check their answers. Often, common mistakes can be avoided if students take the time to think about whether their answers are reasonable. Many elementary textbooks include pages of estimation and mental arithmetic exercises among the addition and subtraction exercises. Ample practice with concrete manipulatives and with estimation and mental arithmetic will provide students with a smooth transition to computations using the vertical form and notations. Estimation can also be used in other subject areas such as social studies and science. A time line in social studies is a form of a number line. Students may use this to estimate how long ago a given event occurred.

Rounding Versus Front-End Estimation

One common type of estimation involves rounding which was reviewed in Section 4.2. Another type of estimation frequently used, which is based on only the first digit of each number, is called *front-end estimation*. A true front-end estimate uses only the number determined by the first digit of each addend, regardless of what the second digit is. For example, the front-end estimation of 18 + 29 is 10 + 20 = 30.

Standards

Texas Essential Knowledge and Skills for Mathematics

Number, Operation, and Quantitative Reasoning

Grade 1:

The student recognizes and solves problems in addition and subtraction situations. The student is expected to:

- (3) (A) model and create addition and subtraction problem situations with concrete objects and write corresponding number sentences; and
  - (B) learn and apply basic addition facts (sums to 18) using concrete models.

Grade 2:

The student adds and subtracts whole numbers to solve problems. The student is expected to:

- (3) (A) recall and apply basic addition facts (sums to 18); and
  - (B) select addition or subtraction and solve problems using two-digit numbers, whether or not regrouping is necessary.

Grade 3:

The student adds and subtracts to solve meaningful problems involving whole numbers. The student is expected to:

- (3) (A) model addition and subtraction using pictures, words, and numbers; and
  - (B) select addition or subtraction and use the operation to solve problems involving whole numbers through 999.

Texas Education Agency, 1998

Standards

Ohio Academic Content Standards K–12 Mathematics

Number, Number Sense and Operations: Grade 2—Grade Level Indicator #12

The student should be able to demonstrate multiple strategies for adding and subtracting 2- or 3-digit whole numbers, such as:

a. compatible numbers;
b. compensatory numbers;
c. informal use of commutative and associative properties of addition.

Ohio Department of Education, 2001

The rounding estimate of 18 + 29 is 20 + 30 = 50. The front-end estimate of 175 + 148 is 100 + 100 = 200. If you round to the nearest tens, the estimate of 175 + 148 is 180 + 150 = 330. If you round to the nearest hundreds, the estimate of 175 + 148 is 200 + 100 = 300. Most elementary school curriculums include both rounding estimation and front-end estimation.

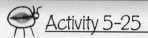

Activity 5-25 — Grades 1–2

Two-Digit Subtraction Using Manipulatives— Regrouping

Materials: Base-ten blocks or smiley sets for each student.

Teacher-Directed Example: There are 25 students in a classroom. Nineteen students go to the gym. How many students are still in the classroom?

Show me 25 with your blocks (smileys). Show me 19 students leaving the room. We have to re-group. Trade a ten for 10 singles. Now you can show 19 students leaving. How many students are still in the room?

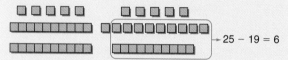

$$25 - 19 = 6$$

There are 25 students. Seventeen students order hot dogs and the rest order pizza for lunch. How many students ordered pizza? Do you have to re-group? Use your blocks to solve the problem and then write an equation.

Use your blocks to solve the following problems. The first one is done for you.

Show this many	Subtract this many	Do you have to regroup?	Solve
43	8	Yes No	43 − 8 = _35_
32	6	Yes No	32 − 6 = ___
35	17	Yes No	35 − 17 = ___
56	16	Yes No	56 − 16 = ___
40	7	Yes No	40 − 7 = ___
27	4	Yes No	27 − 4 = ___

Talk About It: When do you have to regroup in subtraction?

Activity 5-26 — Grades 2–3

Relating Concrete and Symbolic Subtraction Notation

Materials: Base-ten blocks or smiley sets for each student.

Teacher-Directed Example: We can write subtraction problems vertically.

Let's look at

$$\begin{array}{r} 25 \\ -18 \\ \hline \end{array}$$

Use your blocks and show me 25. Can we take away 8 singles?

No. We must regroup. When we trade a ten for 10 singles, what do we have? That's right, 1 ten and 15 singles. We can write this trade on our subtraction problem by crossing out 2 tens; we have only 1 ten left.

Also cross out the 5 singles and write above it that we have 15 singles.

Now we can do the subtraction. We have 15 singles and we take away 8 singles. That leaves us 7 singles. We have 1 ten, and we take away 1 ten. We won't have any tens left. Our answer is 7. This is correct since 18 + 7 is 25.

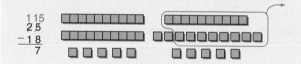

Some middle school textbooks also include a technique called *front-end estimation with adjustment,* which begins with a front-end estimate, and then uses the second digits of the addends to adjust the estimate. The front-end estimation with adjustment of 175 + 148 begins with 100 + 100 = 200 and then adjusts by 70 + 40 = 110 for a total estimate of 310.

A typical third-grade textbook definition of front-end estimation is "using the digits in the greatest place to estimate." One difficulty with this type of definition is that it is not very precise. If the numbers of digits differ, should you use the digits in the greatest place of each number or the digits in the greatest place of the largest number? For example, consider 3,680 + 715. Should the front-end estimate be 3,000 + 700 (using the digits in the greatest place of each number) or 3,000 + 0 (as the second addend has zero thousands)? This subject is currently a source of great debate among educators. Some school districts teach the first method, whereas others teach the second. In either case, the idea of front-end

Standards

Alaska Mathematics Content Standard

Between ages 8–10, students describe and use a variety of estimation strategies including rounding to the appropriate place value, multiplying by powers of 10, and using front-end estimation to check the reasonableness of solutions.

Alaska Department of Education and Early Development, 1999

Activity 5-27   Grades 2–4

Addition Using Money Manipulatives

Materials: Play money—25 ones, 20 tens, and 5 hundreds for each group of students.

Teacher-Directed Example: If we went to the mall and spent $157 on clothes, $39 on a computer game, and $15 on a CD, how much money did we spend? We'll use play money. Let's estimate first. About how much do you think we spent? 200? 250? OK, let's find out. We count out $157 and $39 and $15 for the items. We can start by counting the ones. We spent 21 ones. We could trade that in for 2 tens and 1 one. Then we have 11 tens. We trade that in for 1 hundred and a ten. We have spent $211. (Show the trading with actual bills.)

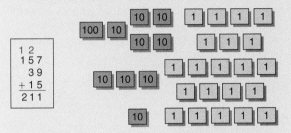

Note: Students can make up their own shopping examples and problems. Tell students that they should make up problems for which they have enough bills in front of them to show the problem solutions.

Activity 5-28   Grades 3–4

Subtraction Using Money Manipulatives

Materials: Play money—25 ones, 20 tens, and 5 hundreds for each group of students.

Teacher-Directed Example: If we went to the mall with $124 and spent $35 on a video, how much money would we have left? We'll use play money. We count out $124.

Pretend the cashier has no change, so we need exact change to give to her. We need 5 singles and 3 tens to give the cashier. We would have to break a ten to get enough singles, we would have 1 hundred, 1 ten, and 14 ones. We don't have enough tens to give the cashier 3 tens, so we break the 100 into 10 tens. Now we have 11 tens and 14 ones. We can give the cashier 3 tens and 5 ones. We will have 8 tens and 9 ones left. We will have $89 left. (Show trading with the play money. Relate to the vertical notation.)

Note: Students can make up their own shopping examples and problems. Tell students that they should make up problems for which they have enough bills in front of them to show the problem solutions.

estimation is to generate a quick estimate that can be used in real-life situations or to check the answer to a computation. Because the first method is more accurate, this textbook will adopt the convention of using the digits in the greatest nonzero place of each number in front-end estimates.

Activities to Promote Number Sense Adding and subtracting multiples of ten may easily be done on a hundreds chart. Activities like 5-31 and 5-32 promote number sense and reinforce place value ideas that are useful in developing and applying the formal addition and subtraction algorithms.

Nonstandard Place Value

The idea of nonstandard place value discussed in Chapter 4 can be used to simplify subtraction, especially when the minuend contains a zero. Figure 5–10 shows the example

305 − 147. The usual subtraction process for this problem is quite messy. The thought process for the usual method of subtraction would be something like: "We can't take 7 ones from 5 ones, so we need to regroup. We have no tens to regroup, so we cross off the 3 in the hundreds position and write a 2 above it. This gives us 10 tens; we write 10 above the tens position. We still need to regroup one of the tens, so we cross off the 10 and write 9 above the tens position. Now we have a total of 15 ones. We cross off the 5 in the ones position, and write 15 above it. We can now subtract 7 ones from 15 ones, which leaves 8 ones. Four tens from 9 tens leaves 5 tens. One hundred from 2 hundreds leaves 1 hundred. Our answer is 158." The thought process for the nonstandard place value method is "305 is 30 tens and 5 ones. This regroups as 29 tens and 15 ones. We subtract 147 which is 14 tens and 7 ones. We get 15 tens and 8 ones which is 158."

305 = 30 tens 5 ones = 29 tens 15 ones
− 147   − 14 tens 7 ones
                  15 tens 8 ones = 158

Compare this with the usual subtraction process.

2 9 10 15
3̶ 0̶ 5̶
−1 4 7
1 5 8

FIGURE 5-10 Nonstandard place value and subtraction.

Activity 5-29 — Grades 2–4

Problem Solving Using Estimation

Teacher-Directed Example: Sometimes we don't need an exact answer—an estimate will do. Here is the problem: A bus holds 60 students. There are 28 students in one class and 23 in the other. Will the two classes fit on the bus? We can use the nearest tens to estimate.

28 is close to 30.
23 is close to 20.
There are about 30 + 20 = 50 students.
Yes, the two classes will fit on the bus.

For each problem below, indicate whether an exact answer is needed or whether an estimate will do. Then solve the problem. At a concert, videos cost $27, CDs are $14, T-shirts are $42, and posters are $17.

1. Joe has $50. Can he buy a video and a CD?
2. Karen buys a T-shirt, a poster, and a CD. She pays with $100. How much change will she get?

Talk About It: What types of problems can be answered using an estimate instead of an exact calculation?

Compensatory Numbers

One final addition and subtraction strategy will be discussed here—**compensatory numbers.** The idea of compensatory numbers is to modify an addition or subtraction problem by using numbers that are easier to calculate with than the numbers given, and then to compensate as necessary. Example 5-3 illustrates this process. The modifications given are not unique.

Example 5-3: Problem solving using compensatory numbers.

a. 192 + 59
b. 192 − 59

Solutions:

a. It is easy to compute an addition problem when one of the addends is a multiple of a power of ten; for instance 200. You can easily calculate 200 + 59 = 259 and then compensate for using an addend that was larger than the one given. Because you added 8 more than you should have, you compensate by subtracting 8 from 259. Your answer is 251.

b. It is easier to subtract 60 than it is to subtract 59. You can mentally calculate 192 − 60 = 132. You subtracted 1 more than you should have, so you compensate by adding 1. Your answer is 133. You could have solved the problem by subtracting 50 from 192

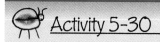

Activity 5-30 — Grades 3–4

Using Estimation

Teacher Statement: A menu has hamburgers for $1.89, fries for $1.20, soda for $0.78, and milkshakes for $1.35. If you had $5.00, could you buy a burger, fries, and a shake?

You can estimate the cost as $2 + $1 + $1 = $4. Yes, you could buy the burger, fries, and shake if you had $5.

What if you had only $4? Because your estimate is $4, you would need to calculate the exact price to make sure that your total didn't go over $4. Let's try it with mental math. The 80 cents from the burger price and the 20 cents from the fries price is an easy combination. So a burger and fries is one, two, three dollars and 9 cents. (Point to the appropriate parts of the prices as you count.) Another dollar and 35 cents for the shake makes $4.35 plus 9 cents is $4.44. No, if you only had $4, you would have to buy a soda instead of a shake.

Problems for students to solve:

1. Estimate by rounding to the nearest dollar.
   a. $2.39 + $1.75
   b. $0.48 + $2.28
   c. $0.84 + $3.55
2. Estimate by rounding to the nearest tens.
   a. 58 + 45
   b. 15 + 49
   c. 129 + 253
3. Estimate by rounding to the nearest hundreds.
   a. 280 + 368
   b. 115 + 249
   c. 129 + 253
4. Estimate using front-end estimation.
   a. 280 + 368
   b. 115 + 249
   c. 129 + 253

Talk About It: Which type of estimation do you think is the most accurate?

to obtain 142 and then subtracting an additional 9 to obtain 133.

Strategies such as compensatory numbers and properties such as commutativity and associativity can be used to sharpen students' number sense and skills. These mental arithmetic strategies are often useful in real-world situations such as shopping. Such strategies may also be used to check the results of computations and calculations.

 ## Activity 5-31 Grades 2–3

Adding or Subtracting Multiples of Ten on a Hundreds Chart

Materials: A hundreds chart for each student.

Teacher Statement: We will see how easy it is to add or subtract a multiple of ten using our hundreds chart.

1. Start at 23. What is 23 + 10? How can you find this easily on your hundreds chart?
2. How about 23 + 20? 23 + 30? And so on.
3. What is 68 − 10? Can you see this on your hundreds chart? How about 68 − 20? 68 − 30? And so on.

(Illustrate for students using a transparency or wall hundreds chart.)

1	2	3	4	5	6	7	8	9	10
11	12	13	14	15	16	17	18	19	20
21	22	23	24	25	26	27	28	29	30
31	32	33	34	35	36	37	38	39	40
41	42	43	44	45	46	47	48	49	50
51	52	53	54	55	56	57	58	59	60
61	62	63	64	65	66	67	68	69	70
71	72	73	74	75	76	77	78	79	80
81	82	83	84	85	86	87	88	89	90
91	92	93	94	95	96	97	98	99	100

Problem Set 5.3

For Your Understanding

1. Complete Activity 5-30.

2. Estimate 12,589 − 4,975 by
   a. rounding to the nearest hundreds
   b. rounding to the nearest thousands
   c. using front-end estimation

3. Show an expanded form addition for 273 + 128.

4. Show how nonstandard place value could be used in the subtraction problem 4084 − 1493.

5. Show an expanded form subtraction for 273 − 128.

6. Matthias dropped his homework in a puddle on the way to school. Several of the digits on his paper are blurred. Determine each of the missing digits.

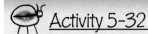 ## Activity 5-32 Grades 2–4

Paths on a Hundreds Chart—A Calculator Activity

Materials: Hundreds charts, calculators, and problem cards for each group.

Directions: Each group should have four students. There are four tasks for each round: (1) Read path card, (2) use calculator, (3) use hundreds chart, and (4) use pen and paper.

Students should alternate tasks for the various rounds. For each round, one student reads the path card while the other students solve the problem using the method they have been assigned for that round. If the three students who are solving the problem arrive at the same answer, they may move on to the next round. If they do not arrive at the same answer, they must determine the correct answer and assist any group members whose answers differed.

Example Path Card:

$$43 + 10 - 1 - 1 - 20 + 1 + 1 + 1 =$$

(a)
```
  7 ● 9
+ ● 7 ●
─────────
● ,1 0 3
```
(b)
```
  ● 4 3
- 4 ● 7
───────
  ● 1 ●
```
(c)
```
1,● 2 1
  ● 7 4 ●
───────
  8 ● 1
```

Applications in the Classroom

1. Make up a numerical addition problem that could be used with Activity 5-23 that involves regrouping of both ones and tens. Draw a base-ten block diagram that illustrates the problem and its solution. Show the regroupings in your diagram.

2. Make up a numerical subtraction problem that could be used with Activity 5-26 that involves regrouping of both tens and hundreds. Draw a base-ten block diagram that illustrates the problem and its solution. Show the regroupings in your diagram.

3. Use a computer and create a menu that you could use for an activity involving addition and subtraction of money. Also write directions for the activity and a few sample problems.

4. Create a game or puzzle that could be used to help students practice their addition and subtraction

algorithms. Indicate the grade level of your game or puzzle and how it could be modified for students with special needs.

5. Jacob (a third grader) shows his work on a subtraction problem. Explain how Jacob arrived at his answer. Will Jacob's method always work? Show how Jacob might solve $583 - 247$ using his method.

$$
\begin{array}{r}
412 \\
-147 \\
\hline
-5 \\
-30 \\
300 \\
\hline
270 \\
-5 \\
\hline
265
\end{array}
$$

6. Create an assessment tool to be used with Activity 5-27. Explain why you chose that type of assessment tool.

7. Classify the level of knowledge and the type of learning experience of Activity 5-28. What objective from the NCTM model (or from your state or district model) does the activity address?

8. Write three addition or subtraction examples that could be used in a second-grade classroom. Show solutions to each example using (a) the standard computational algorithm and (b) a nonstandard method such as nonstandard place value, expanded form, or compensatory numbers.

9. Look at either an addition chapter or a subtraction chapter in an elementary-level textbook. Photocopy or copy by hand one example or problem that you think is interesting or unusual and indicate why. What objective from the NCTM model (or from your state or district model) does the activity or problem address? Be sure to state what grade level text you are using.

10. Find and print an addition or subtraction activity from the Web. What objective from the NCTM model (or from your state or district model) does the activity address? State what grade level you think the activity would be appropriate for.

11. Make up a number line activity or game. What objective from the NCTM model (or from your state or district model) does the activity or game address? Indicate what grade level your activity is appropriate for.

12. Choose an activity from this chapter. Indicate how you could implement the activity as a collaborative learning experience.

13. Choose one of the books in the children's literature section of the references for this chapter. Write a brief description of the content of the book and explain how you could incorporate the book into a math lesson.

14. Make up two writing prompts or stems that fit in with material or activities from this chapter.

5.4 ADDING INTEGERS

Computations involving negative integers are typically introduced at the fourth- or fifth-grade level. However, some textbook series introduce these computations at the third-grade level (Larson, 1994). Integer arithmetic is usually introduced using a number line or other concrete model such as those used in this section. The TI-73 calculator contains a number line model that nicely illustrates integer addition and subtraction.

> Subtraction of integers is introduced at the fifth- or sixth-grade level and is covered in the Appendices of this textbook.

In the early grade levels, negative integers occur in the context of temperature. Consider the following: "The temperature is 2°Celsius (C). The temperature will drop by 4°C. What will the new temperature be?" Recall from Chapter 2 that the set of integers is represented by $Z = \{\ldots, -3, -2, -1, 0, 1, 2, 3, \ldots\}$ where the ellipses indicate that the set continues infinitely in each direction. You can visualize integers using a number line. You can visualize negative temperatures by looking at a thermometer that resembles a vertical number line (see Figure 5-11).

Comparing Integers

The first task with integers to consider is comparison. You should be able to fill the blanks with the symbols for greater than (>), equal to (=), or less than (<) for problems like -4 ___ 2 and 0 ___ -3. The first inequality corresponds to the real-life application: Which temperature is colder? -4°C or 2°C? When comparing integers, you can use a number line to decide which is larger. The larger integer occurs to the right of the smaller integer on a number line. The correct inequalities for the numbers above are $-4 < 2$ and $0 > -3$. Make sure that you can read these inequalities correctly. The first is read as "negative four is less than two" and the second is "zero is greater than negative three." On a thermometer, colder temperatures appear below warmer temperatures; therefore, -4°C is colder than 2°C.

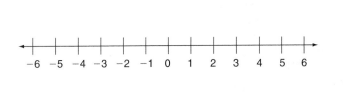

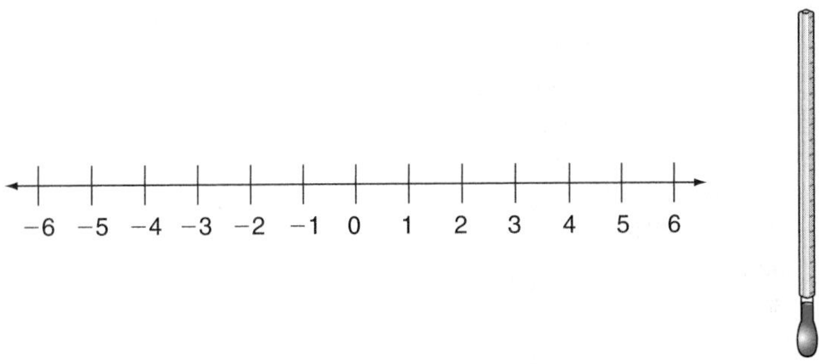

FIGURE 5-11 Integers on a number line.

Using the Poker Chip Model

Poker chips or two-sided counters can also be used as a visual aid for integer arithmetic. When poker chips are used, it is convention to use black chips ● for positive integers and red chips ○ for negative integers. This representation coincides with the phrase "in the red" meaning losing or owing money and the phrase "in the black" meaning winning or gaining money. The representation of an integer with a poker chip model is not unique. Several representations of the integer −3 are shown in Figure 5-12. In each representation of −3, there are three more red chips than there are black chips. That is, you may think of the pairing of a black chip and a red chip as canceling each other out. In other words, zero can be represented by an equal number of black and red chips.

Adding Integers Using the Number Line and Poker Chip Models

Before presenting "the rules" for adding integers, we will consider addition using the number line model and the poker chip model. Figure 5-13 illustrates several addition problems using a number line. In using the number line model to represent addition, start the arrow representing the first addend at zero and the arrow representing the second addend at the head of the first arrow. Arrows representing positive integers point to the right, and arrows representing negative integers point to the left.

Figure 5-14 illustrates several addition problems using the poker chip model. In using the poker chip model to represent addition, start with a combination of the simplest representation of each integer, pair up as many black chips with red chips as possible, and use the remaining chips to determine the answer to the problem.

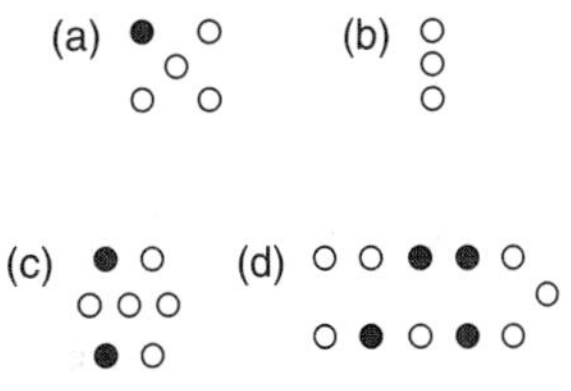

Standards

Ohio Academic Content Standard K–12 Mathematics

Number, Number Sense and Operations: Grade 2—Grade Level Indicator #13

The student should be able to estimate the results of whole number addition and subtraction problems using front-end estimation, and judge the reasonableness of the answers.

Ohio Department of Education, 2001

Standards

Mathematics Content Standards for California Public Schools

Grade Two

Number Sense, 2.3: Use mental arithmetic to find the sum or difference of two two-digit numbers.

Algebra and Functions, 1.1: Use the commutative and associative rules to simplify mental calculations and to check results.

California Department of Education, 2000

Standards

Mathematics Content Standards for California Public Schools

Grade Four

Number Sense, 1.8: Use concepts of negative numbers (e.g., on a number line, in counting, in temperature, in "owing").

California Department of Education, 2000

(a) ● ○   (b) ○
  ○ ○   ○
                ○

(c) ● ○   (d) ○ ○ ● ● ○
 ○ ○ ○   ○
 ● ○   ● ○ ● ○ ●

FIGURE 5-12 Poker chip model representations of −3.

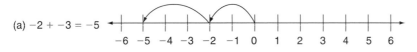

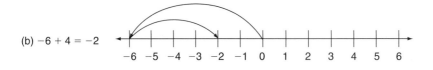

(a) $-2 + -3 = -5$

(b) $-6 + 4 = -2$

(c) $-6 + 8 = 2$

(d) $6 + -8 = -2$

FIGURE 5-13 Adding integers using a number line model.

(a) $-4 + -2 = -6$

(b) $-4 + 6 = 2$

(c) $4 + -1 = 3$

(d) $2 + -4 = -2$

FIGURE 5-14 Adding integers using a poker chip model.

When you learned how to add and subtract integers in your elementary school experience, you probably memorized rules like "If the signs are the same, add the numbers and keep the sign" and "If the signs are different, subtract the smaller from the larger and keep the sign of the larger." A mathematician reading the above "rules" might shudder at their technical incorrectness. However, the above statements are typical of the rules memorized by most students who learned these processes from the 1970s, through the early 1990s.

These days, rules such as those discussed above are never presented to elementary students. The process of adding integers is learned by considering concrete models like the number line and the poker chip model. It then makes sense that the sum of two negative integers is a negative integer. After all, combining a pile of red chips with another pile of red chips certainly gives you a pile of red chips. It also makes sense that the sum of one positive integer and one negative integer may be positive or it may be negative. This depends on whether the pile of black chips representing the positive integer is larger or smaller than the pile of red chips representing the negative integer.

Once the process is understood, problems with larger numbers can also be computed. For a problem like $-250 + -37$, you can visualize a pile of 250 red chips combined with a pile of 37 red chips which would produce a pile of 287 red chips. Thus, $-250 + -37 = -287$. For the problem $250 +$

-37, you visualize a pile of 250 black chips combined with a pile of 37 red chips. You would pair up 37 black chips with the 37 red chips which leaves you with an additional $250 - 37 = 213$ black chips. So, $250 + -37 = 213$.

The poker chip model also provides convincing arguments that adding of integers is both commutative and associative. The commutative property of addition states that for any two integers a and b, it must be true that $a + b = b + a$. To see that addition of integers is commutative, visualize switching the two piles of chips that represent the integers a and b. Using the poker chip model, can you explain why addition of integers is associative?

Teaching Connections

Negative Integers in the Early Grades Although negative integers are usually not introduced until the middle school level, with appropriate models they could be introduced much earlier. Activity 5-33 was created by a first-grade teacher. She had been showing a class of first graders how to draw smiley faces to solve problems such as $3 + 2$. On impulse she decided to take this one step further and showed the students how to draw frowning faces to represent negative integers, to cross off pairs involving one smiling face and one frowning face, and use the remaining faces to solve integer addition problems like $-3 + 2$.

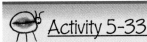

Activity 5-33   Grades 1–3

Introducing Negative Integers in the First Grade

Teacher-Directed Example: Let's draw smiley faces to figure out 3 + 2. First we draw three smiley faces, then we draw two smiley faces. How many smiley faces in all? Five, right? So, 3 + 2 = 5.

There's another type of number called a negative number. We write negative numbers by putting a dash in front of the number, like −2. The dash is called a negative sign or a minus sign. We draw frowning faces for negative numbers. So we draw −2 like this: How would we draw −5? By drawing 5 frowning faces, great.

We can add with negative numbers. How about −3 + 2. Right, that's three frowning faces and two smiling faces. We can cross out pairs of one frowning face and one smiling face. What's left? One frowning face. What number is that? Right, −1. So, −3 + 2 = −1.

Let's have you try some problems. How about 5 + −2. Remember to draw smiley faces and frowning faces and cross off pairs of one frowney and one smiley. The answer is what is left.

Note: Help individual students as necessary. Give the students more problems to try on their own.

Source: Darlene Moulin, First-Grade Teacher, Youngstown, Ohio.

Problem Set 5.4

1. Compare the integers by filling in the blanks with the less than (<) or greater than (>) symbol.
   a. −2 ___ 0
   b. −5 ___ −6
   c. 3 ___ −4

2. Write in words how each of the statements in problem 1 is read.

3. Draw (a) a number line model, and (b) a poker chip or smiley face model representation and give the answer to −4 + 5.

4. Draw (a) a number line model, and (b) a poker chip or smiley face model representation and give the answer to 4 + −5.

5. Give a poker chip model explanation in words, and give the answer for each of the following:
   a. −25 + −83
   b. −300 + 842
   c. 261 + −560

6. Give a poker chip model explanation that addition of integers is associative.

5.5 AVOIDING COMMON STUDENT ERRORS AND USING FUN MATH TRICKS

We have already discussed the importance of estimation and checking answers. If students have acquired the habit of checking their answers, they can avoid many of the common student errors that we will discuss in this section. Seven difficulties frequently occur with addition and subtraction situations and problems. Many of the errors described here and other common student errors are described in Ashlock (2002) and Troutman and Lichtenberg (2003).

Difficulties with Addition or Subtraction Story Problems

Wrong Operation It is very common for children to choose the wrong operation, especially in the case of subtraction problems. This occurs when the student doesn't take the time to think about the problem and what is occurring in the problem. As a teacher, you must give your students the time they need to think. If necessary, provide concrete objects so that the students can act out the problem. If the numbers in a problem are large, and it is not feasible to act out the problem, direct the students to create a similar problem with smaller numbers that could be modeled with concrete objects.

Wrong Information It is common for today's elementary textbooks to include problems with "extra" information (e.g., Problem 3 in Activity 5-16). Consequently, students may incorrectly use this information in solving a problem. They should be encouraged to check their answers. Do their answers use the correct information? Do their answers fit the question in the problem?

Wrong Equations When solving subtraction story problems, it is common for students to write the equation backward. That is, they may write 3 − 8 instead of 8 − 3. Remind the students of the meaning of subtraction and its relation to the number sentence. Let them know they need eight minus three, not three minus eight, that they are taking three away from eight. Do not say "take the smaller from the larger" as this may encourage another error that is later discussed. Students will need much practice in writing subtraction number sentences.

Errors in Counting On or Counting Back

Beginning the Count in the Wrong Position Children may make errors in using the counting on or counting back strategies. For example:

9 + 4, that's 9, 10, 11, 12 or 18 − 3, that's 18, 17, 16.

Use concrete objects to show them the proper place to begin the counting when counting on or counting back. Show them how to check their answers with a number line or other model.

Inappropriate Use of the Counting On or Counting Back

Strategy Some students may use counting on or counting back when it is not the best strategy to use, for instance, when the numbers involved are too large to mentally keep track of the counting. Present a variety of strategies, not just counting, for determining basic facts. Be prepared to suggest alternate strategies when children use the counting strategy inappropriately.

Basic Fact Errors

Basic addition facts must be memorized. This is not an easy task—it takes practice and diligence. Find ways to make learning and practicing basic facts fun for your students. Remind them to use the commutative property. Show them how to use the associative property to make a 10 when dealing with facts larger than 10. Remind them of the relationship between addition and subtraction to learn subtraction facts. Present as many strategies as are developmentally appropriate for your students, and encourage them to come up with their own strategies. Use concrete objects, fact families, and alternate models when appropriate.

Difficulties with Zero
Failure to Record Zero

$$40 \quad\quad 502 \quad\quad 80$$
$$\underline{+30} \quad \underline{+304} \quad \underline{-40}$$
$$7 \quad\quad 8\,6 \quad\quad 4$$

If children get the idea that "zero means nothing," then they may fail to record zeros and make errors as shown above. Encourage students to check their answers. Let them use concrete or place value models if necessary. You may also want to encourage them to write a digit for each position, and then later determine whether the 0s are necessary.

Computing $n + 0$ or $n - 0$ as 0

$$30 \quad\quad 25$$
$$\underline{+46} \quad \underline{-10}$$
$$70 \quad\quad 10$$

Children who have learned the rule $n \times 0 = 0$ may mistakenly use the rule for addition or subtraction. Encourage students to check their answers, using concrete models if necessary. Use appropriate activities to reteach the rules $n + 0 = n$, and $n - 0 = n$.

Difficulties with Regrouping
Does Not Regroup (may compute left to right)

$$57 \quad\quad 57 \quad\quad 5\overset{17}{\cancel{7}}$$
$$\underline{+25} \quad \underline{+25} \quad \underline{-28}$$
$$712 \quad\quad 72 \quad\quad 39$$

Remind students to check their answers. Addition answers may be estimated. Subtraction answers may be checked using addition. Use models to reteach the process of regrouping and the notation for accounting for regrouping.

Regroups Incorrectly

$$\overset{2}{57} \quad \overset{4\,10}{\cancel{5}2} \quad \overset{6\,12}{\cancel{5}2} \quad \overset{1}{52} \quad \overset{4\,10\,10}{\cancel{5}\cancel{0}0} \quad \overset{4\,9\,9}{\cancel{5}00}$$
$$\underline{+25} \quad \underline{-24} \quad \underline{-24} \quad \underline{+24} \quad \underline{-123} \quad \underline{-123}$$
$$91 \quad 26 \quad 48 \quad 86 \quad 387 \quad 376$$

Each of the mistakes above could be made by students who have memorized the rules of addition and subtraction algorithms, but do not understand the processes. These students should be shown with models why the processes work. Once they understand the process, students can determine logically what regrouping is necessary and what the new, or regrouped, digits should be. Research indicates that children who use their own invented procedures often produce more correct answers than those who use memorized algorithms (Kamii & Dominick, 1998).

Subtracts the Smaller Digit from the Larger Digit

$$41 \quad\quad\quad 300$$
$$\underline{-27} \quad\quad \underline{-123}$$
$$26 \quad\quad\quad 223$$

When children hear a phrase like "always subtract the smaller number from the larger number" they may make mistakes as shown above. Avoid using such phrases. Students who make this mistake should be reminded of the regrouping process of subtraction. Make sure they understand which number you are subtracting and what you are subtracting it from. You may wish to use concrete models to illustrate.

Difficulties When Numbers Have a Different Number of Digits
May Add or Subtract a Single-Digit Number to or from Each Other Digit

$$32 \quad\quad 59$$
$$\underline{+\ 4} \quad \underline{-\ 3}$$
$$76 \quad\quad 26$$

Students who make mistakes like the ones shown above are trying to follow the rules of the algorithm, but not thinking about what they are doing and what makes sense. Remind students to check their answers. Use concrete models to demonstrate the steps of the algorithms and their reasonableness.

May Not Finish the Calculation

$$
\begin{array}{r}
32 \\
+\ 4 \\
\hline
6
\end{array}
\qquad
\begin{array}{r}
59 \\
-\ 3 \\
\hline
6
\end{array}
$$

Students may think "there's nothing to add to the 3" in the first problem, or "there's nothing to take away from the 5" in the second problem. Students who make mistakes like this are trying to follow the rules of the algorithm, but are not thinking about what they are doing and what makes sense. Remind students to check their answers. Use concrete models to demonstrate the steps of the algorithms and their reasonableness.

May Add All the Digits

$$
\begin{array}{r}
32 \\
+\ 4 \\
\hline
9
\end{array}
$$

Students who make mistakes like this are not thinking about what they are doing and what makes sense. Remind students to check their answers. Use concrete models to demonstrate the steps of the algorithms and their reasonableness.

Difficulties When a Sum Involves Several Addends or When a Sum or Difference Involves Large Numbers

You should first check to see that the student does not have more basic difficulties with smaller problems. Provide assistance with any difficulties with the meaning or process of addition or subtraction. Encourage mental math, estimation, and checking answers. Have students write down the intermediate steps of an algorithm or process to simplify difficult or large problems.

Math Tricks

Two math tricks that your students may enjoy are speedy addition and equal additions. The following sections describe how the tricks work and how they can help in learning everyday math. The first trick can be found in several "fun math" activity books. In particular, it can be found in *Math for Smarty Pants* by Burns (1982, p. 104).

Trick 1: Speedy Addition Ask a member of your audience for a three-digit number. Suppose, for example, you get 408. Write it on the board and tell the audience you get to pick the next number. Write 591 below the 408. (You will learn later why you picked 591 when they picked 408.) Ask the audience for another three-digit number and write it un-

der 591. Suppose they say 912. Tell them you get to pick a number and write 87 below the 912. Ask the audience for one final three-digit number, and write it below the other four numbers. Suppose they give you the number 350. Amaze the audience by writing the sum of the five numbers 2,348 immediately.

they pick		408
you pick		591
they pick		912
you pick	+	87
they pick		350
you write immediately		2,348

What's the trick? If you pick your numbers correctly, the sum will always be 2,000 plus the last number that the audience gave you minus 2. So, you can write it down immediately after you have written down the last number from the audience. It is almost like writing down their last number again, but remember to put a 2 in front of it and to subtract 2 from it.

Why does it work? The trick is for you to pick as your number the 9s complement of the number that was just given to you by the audience. The *9s complement* means that when the two numbers are added together, their sum should be 999. If the numbers involved aren't three-digit numbers, the sum won't be 999; it will be a number whose digits are all 9s with size determined by the size of the numbers involved. It is easy to calculate the 9s complement, digit by digit, for a given number. For example, when the audience picked 408, your first digit had to be 5 since 4 + 5 = 9, your middle digit had to be 9 since 0 + 9 = 9, and your last digit had to be 1 since 8 + 1 = 9. That is, you had to pick 591. When the audience picked 912, you were forced to use a two-digit number since the hundreds digit was already 9. Do you see why you had to pick 87? If you practice the trick, you will be able to calculate 9s complements instantly. Make sure to tell your audience that they must give you three-digit numbers. Why would you be in trouble if they gave you a number that had more than three digits?

Now that you know how to choose your numbers, do you see why the sum is 2,000 plus the last audience number minus 2? It is because the first pair of addends sums to 999 and the second pair of addends also sums to 999. The sum of the first four addends is almost 2,000. In fact, it is exactly 2 less than 2,000. Thus, the sum of the five addends will be 2,000 − 2 plus the last addend. Using commutativity, this is 2,000 plus the last addend minus 2. This version of speedy addition can be used at the third-grade level and above. Easier and harder versions will be discussed in Problem Set 5.5.

Trick 2: Equal Additions The next "trick" is presented in some textbooks as a subtraction algorithm or strategy. Although the name is "equal additions," this trick may be used only on subtraction problems. It is not as flashy as speedy addition, but will be especially useful in Chapter 8 when we study fractions and decimals. The trick is based on the following properties: For any whole numbers *a, b,* and *c,*

$$a - b = (a + c) - (b + c) \text{ and } a - b = (a - c) - (b - c).$$

That is, in a subtraction problem, you may add (or subtract) the same quantity to (or from) both the subtrahend and the minuend. The purpose of this is to make the subtraction easier.

For example, consider the problem

$$\begin{array}{r} 2{,}010 \\ -1{,}983 \\ \hline \end{array}$$

This calculation would involve several regroupings. Two similar problems that are easier to calculate are

$$\begin{array}{r} 2{,}027 \\ -2{,}000 \\ \hline \end{array}$$

and

$$\begin{array}{r} 1{,}999 \\ -1{,}972 \\ \hline \end{array}$$

Both of these easier problems can be obtained from the original problem by the method of equal additions. The first is obtained by adding 17 to both the subtrahend and the minuend of the original problem. Why add 17? Adding 17 turns the subtrahend into a nice round 2,000. In other words, numbers are easy to subtract when the subtrahend has lots of zeros. What makes this easier to subtract, is it eliminates the need for regroupings. You looked at 1,983 and decided that you could make that 2,000 by adding 17. You also had to add 17 to the minuend so that the new problem is equivalent to the old one. You could have also done this problem with mental math by thinking 1,983 is 17 away from 2,000, I need 10 more to get to 2,010, so the answer is 27.

The second problem is obtained from the original by subtracting 11 from both the minuend and the subtrahend. This eliminates regroupings because the new minuend has all 9s except the first digit. It is easy to see that the answer to this is also 27, and this problem is also equivalent to the original. Why subtract 11? You chose 11 by looking at the minuend 2,010. If you had only subtracted 10, your new problem would have been

$$\begin{array}{r} 2{,}000 \\ -1{,}973 \\ \hline \end{array}$$

which is easier by mental math than the original problem, but still contains several regroupings when computed using the subtraction algorithm. The purpose of subtracting 11 was to maximize the number of 9s in the minuend. However, the choice of what to add or subtract for the method of equal additions is not unique. There are usually several good options.

 Teaching Connections

The Use of Math Tricks in Everyday Math It is easy to see how equal additions is useful in everyday math. When encountered with a subtraction problem, the method of equal additions helps simplify the problem. This can sometimes be done as a mental math process and is related to the compensatory numbers strategy discussed earlier that is usually introduced at around the second-grade level. A child using the compensatory numbers strategy would solve the problem $32 - 19$ as follows: "If I take 20 away from 32, there's 12 left. To take only 19 away, there's 13 left. So, $32 - 19 = 13$."

How is speedy addition useful? It would be unlikely to encounter in everyday math a problem or situation that precisely fit the speedy addition formula. However, the idea of pairing addends may be useful. For example, consider the addition problem $125 + 37 + 75$. The student who is used to doing math strictly by the rules would start adding left to right. However, a student who has seen the paired addend trick of speedy addition might be more apt to notice that $125 + 75$ is 200 and 37 more is 237. As well as sharpening math skills, math tricks are also good for grabbing students' attention and making them excited about mathematics.

Problem Set 5.5

For Your Understanding

1. For each problem shown, state what error the student is making. Try to determine exactly what the student was thinking. Also indicate what you as a teacher could do to help a student who makes this type of error.

   a. There are six children in a boat. Four of the children are girls. How many boys are in the boat? $6 + 4 = 10$.

   b. $$\begin{array}{r} 240 \\ +670 \\ \hline 811 \end{array}$$

   c. $$\begin{array}{r} {}^{1\,10}\!\quad 2\;\;13 \\ 30{,}387 \\ -14{,}542 \\ \hline 6{,}845 \end{array}$$

2. For each problem shown, state what error the student is making. Try to determine exactly what the student was thinking. Also indicate what you as a teacher could do to help a student who makes this type of error.

   a. $27 + 8$, that's 27, 28, 29, 30, 31, 32, 33, 34.

b. Ann has two sisters and three brothers. Bob has two brothers and one sister. Who has more brothers? How many more? Student's answer: Ann, 2.

$$\begin{array}{r} 5 \\ c.\quad 28 \\ +\,17 \\ \hline 81 \end{array}$$

$$\begin{array}{r} d.\quad 123 \\ +\,35 \\ \hline 458 \end{array}$$

e. $3 + \square = 8$; $3 + \boxed{11} = 8$

$$\begin{array}{r} f.\quad 316 \\ -\,148 \\ \hline 232 \end{array}$$

3. Explain how the speedy addition trick would work if it involved seven 3-digit addends instead of five 3-digit addends. Give an example to illustrate your explanation.

4. Explain how the speedy addition trick would work if it involved three 2-digit addends instead of five 3-digit addends. Give an example to illustrate your explanation.

5. Give at least two equivalent subtraction problems that you can find with the method of equal additions if the original problem is $352 - 174$.

References

Children's Literature References

Baker, Keith. (1999). *Quack and count.* New York: Harcourt.

Faulkner, Keith. (1997). *Magnetic math.* New York: Anytime Books, Penguin Putnam.

Gernstein, Mordicai. (1988). *Roll over.* New York: Random House Books for Young Readers.

Hewitt, Sally. (2001). *Make 10.* Wycombe, UK: Working White Limited High.

Leedy, Loreen. (1997). *Mission addition.* New York: Holiday House.

Long, Lynette. (1996). *Domino addition.* Watertown, MA: Charlesbridge.

Merriam, Eve. (1996). *12 ways to get 11.* Scott Foresman.

Murphy, Stuart. (1996). *Ready, set, hop!* (Mathstart Level 3: Building Equations.) New York: HarperCollins Children's Books.

Murphy, Stuart. (1997). *Elevator magic* (Mathstart Level 2: Subtracting). Scott Foresman.

Murphy, Stuart. (2000). *Monster musical chairs* (Mathstart Level 1: Subtracting One). New York: HarperTrophy.

Owen, Annie. (1989). *Annie's one to ten.* New York: Random House.

Pallotta, Jerry. (2001). *The Hershey's Kisses addition book.* New York: Scholastic.

Pallotta, Jerry. (2002). *The Hershey's Kisses subtraction book.* New York: Cartwheel Books.

Peek, Merle. (1999). *Roll over: A counting song.* Boston: Houghton Mifflin.

Strickland, Paul. (1997). *Ten terrible dinosaurs.* New York: Dutton Books.

Wise, William. (1993). *Ten sly piranhas: A counting story in reverse.* New York: Dial Books.

Teacher Resources

Alaska Department of Education and Early Development. (1999). *Alaska Mathematics Content Standards and Key Elements.* Retrieved December 1, 2003 from http://www.eed.state.ak.us/tls/PerformanceStandards/ math/pdf

Ashlock, R. B. (2002). *Error patterns in computation: Using error patterns to improve instruction* (8th ed.). Pearson Education, Inc.

Burns, M. (1982). *Math for Smarty Pants.* Little, Brown, and Company.

Burns, M. (1995). *Writing in math class.* Pearson Learning.

California Department of Education. (2000). *Mathematics Content Standards for California Public Schools.* Retrieved November 12, 2003 from http://www.cde.ca.gov/board/pdf/math.pdf

National Association for the Education of Young Children. (1997). *Developmentally appropriate practice in early childhood programs serving children from birth through age 8.* Washington, DC: Author.

National Council of Teachers of Mathematics. (2000). *Principles and standards for school mathematics.* Reston, VA: Author.

North Carolina Department of Public Instruction. (2003). *North Carolina Mathematics Standard Course Study and Grade Level Competencies K–12.* Retrieved November 19, 2003, from http://www.dpi.state.nc.us/curriculum/mathematics/standard2003/index.html

Ohio Department of Education. (2001). *Ohio Academic Content Standards.* Retrieved November 12, 2003 from http://www.ode.state.oh.us/academic_content_standards/pdf/MATH.pdf

Texas Education Agency. (1998). *Chapter 111. Texas Essential Knowledge and Skills for Mathematics.* Retrieved November 12, 2003 from http://www.tea.state.tx.us/rules/tac/ch111toc.html

Troutman A. P., & Lichtenberg, B. K. (2003). *Mathematics—A Good Beginning.* (6th ed.). Belmont, CA. Wadsworth, Thomson Learning, Inc.

Selected Research Books and Articles

Campbell, P., Rowan, T., & Suarez, A. (1998). What criteria for student-invented algorithms? In L. Morrow (Ed.), *The teaching and learning of algorithms in school mathematics, 1998 yearbook* (pp. 49–55). Reston, VA: National Council of Teachers of Mathematics.

Carpenter, T., Carey, D., & Kouba, V. (1990). A problem solving approach to the operations. In J. N. Payne (Ed.),

Mathematics for the young child (pp. 111–131). Reston, VA: National Council of Teachers of Mathematics.

Carroll, W., & Porter, D. (1998). Alternative algorithms for whole-number operations. In L. Morrow (Ed.), *The teaching and learning of algorithms in school mathematics, 1998 yearbook* (pp. 106–114). Reston, VA: National Council of Teachers of Mathematics.

Dunn L., & Kontos, S. (1997). Research in review: What have we learned about developmentally appropriate practice? *Young Children, 52*(5), 4–13. (Published by the National Association for the Education of Young Children, PS 526 718.)

Kamii, C. K., & Dominick, A. (1998). The harmful effects of algorithms in grades 1 through 4. In L. Morrow (Ed.), *The teaching and learning of algorithms in school mathematics, 1998 yearbook* (pp. 130–140). Reston, VA: National Council of Teachers of Mathematics.

McIntosh, A. (1998). Teaching mental algorithms constructively. In L. Morrow (Ed.), *The teaching and learning of algorithms in school mathematics, 1998 yearbook* (pp. 44–48). Reston, VA: National Council of Teachers of Mathematics.

Sowder, J. (1992). Estimation and number sense. In D. Grouws (Ed.), *Handbook of research on mathematics teaching and learning* (pp. 371–389). New York: Macmillan.

Further Reading

Balka, D. (1988). Digit delight: Problem-solving activities using 0 through 9. *Arithmetic Teacher, 36*(3), 42–45.

Baroody, A. (1985, May). Children's difficulties in subtraction: Some causes and questions. *Journal for Research in Mathematics Education, 15*, 203–213.

Baroody, A., & Standifer, D. (1990). Addition and subtraction in the primary grades. In R. J. Jensen (Ed.), *Research ideas for the classroom: Early childhood mathematics* (pp. 72–102). Reston, VA: National Council of Teachers of Mathematics, and New York: Macmillan.

Carpenter, T. P., Franke, M. L., Jacobs, V. R., Fennema E., & Empson, S. B. (1998). A longitudinal study of invention and understanding in children's multidigit addition and subtraction. *Journal for Research in Mathematics Education, 29*(1), 3–20.

Carpenter, T. P., & Moser, J. M. (1984). The acquisition of addition and subtraction concepts in grades one through three. *Journal for Research in Mathematics Education, 15*, 179–202.

Carroll, W. M., & Porter, D. (1997). Invented strategies can develop meaningful mathematical procedures. *Teaching Children Mathematics, 3*, 370–374.

Cobb, P., & Merkel, G. (1989). Thinking strategies: Teaching arithmetic through problem solving. In P. Traftan (Ed.),

New directions for elementary school mathematics, 1989 yearbook, (pp. 70–81). Reston, VA: National Council of Teachers of Mathematics.

Hasazi, J. E., & Hasazi, S. E. (1972). Effects of teaching attention on digit-reversal behavior in an elementary school child. *Journal of Applied Behavior Analysis, 5*, 157–162.

Kamii, C., & Joseph, L. (1988). Teaching place value and double-column addition. *Arithmetic Teacher, 35*(6), 48–52.

Kamii, C. K., & DeClark, G. (1985). *Young children reinvent arithmetic—Implications of Piaget's theory.* New York: Teachers College Press.

Kamii, C. K., & Joseph, L. L. (1989). *Young children continue to reinvent arithmetic 2nd grade—Implications of Piaget's theory.* New York: Teachers College Press.

Kamii, C. K., & Lewis, B. A. (1993). The harmful effects of algorithms in primary arithmetic. *Teaching K–8, 23*(5), 36–38.

Larson, N. (1994). *Saxon math 3.* Norman, OK Saxon.

Leutzinger, L., & Nelson, G. (1979, December). Using addition facts to learn subtraction facts. *Arithmetic Teacher, 27*, 8–13.

Rathmell, E. (1978). Using thinking strategies to learn basic facts. In M. Suydam & R. E. Reys (Eds.), *Developing computational skills, 1978 yearbook.* Reston, VA: National Council of Teachers of Mathematics.

Starkey, M. (1989). Calculating first graders. *Arithmetic Teacher, 37*(2), 6–7.

Stromer, R. (1975). Modifying letter and number reversals in elementary school children. *Journal of Applied Behavior Analysis, 8*, 211.

Suydam, M., & Reys, R. (Eds.) (1978). *Developing computational skills, 1978 yearbook.* Reston, VA: National Council of Teachers of Mathematics.

Thompson, C., & Dunlop, W. (1977, December). Basic facts: Do your children understand or do they memorize? *Arithmetic Teacher, 25*, 14–16.

Thompson, F. (1991, January). Two-digit addition and subtraction: What works? *Arithmetic Teacher, 38*, 10–13.

Thornton, C., & Smith, P. (1988, April). Action research: Strategies for learning subtraction facts. *Arithmetic Teacher, 35*, 9–12.

Wearne, D., & Hiebert, J. (1994). Place value and addition and subtraction. *Arithmetic Teacher, 41*(5), 272–274.

Wheatley, G., & Wheatley, C. (1978, January). How shall we teach column addition? Some evidence. *Arithmetic Teacher, 25*, 18–19.

Whitenack, J., Knipping, N., Novinger, S., & Underwood, G. (2001). Second graders circumvent addition and subtraction difficulties. *Teaching Children Mathematics, 8*(4), 228–233.

6

Developing Concepts and Operations of Multiplication and Division

L ife in the real world is full of multiplication and division examples. Young children, especially those with siblings, are accustomed to the idea of sharing equally, which is a prelude to division. Real-life examples of objects that occur in pairs, in threes, in fours, and so on provide a natural introduction to multiplication. "If you are going to visit Grandma and need to pack enough socks for three days, how many socks do you pack?" Students are formally introduced to the basic concepts of equal groups and other multiplication and division ideas as early as kindergarten.

The learning of multiplication and division is structurally similar to the learning of addition and subtraction. Children first need to develop a sound conceptual basis; basic facts can then be developed. Through concrete, developmental experiences children should see that these facts are reasonable, not just random. Eventually, the basic facts should be learned and memorized. Using just the basic facts and a few logical processes, multiplication and division of larger numbers can be considered. By conceptually developing the algorithms for multiplication and division, children can be shown why and how the algorithms work. If they understand the logic behind the rules, they are less likely to make mistakes when applying those rules.

This chapter introduces concrete models that can be used to make whole number multiplication and division processes and properties more tangible. When students understand the structure of numbers, their number sense provides a flexibility that is useful in many problem-solving and computational situations (Fuson, 1992).

Objectives

After completing Chapter 6, you will be able to

- Describe three interpretations for multiplication and correctly use multiplication notation, terminology, and properties
- Describe two interpretations for division and correctly use division notation, terminology, and properties
- Describe strategies to help children develop meaning for multiplication and division, learn basic multiplication and division facts, and develop algorithms for whole number multiplication and division
- Diagnose and remediate common student errors involving multiplication and division
- Perform computations using estimation and other ideas and properties presented within this chapter

6.1 Constructing Meaning for Multiplication

As with addition and subtraction, a child's first introduction to the concept of multiplication should involve real-life situations that the child can relate to, as well as concrete objects to help the child solve the problems in these situations. The child must be comfortable associating numbers with sets, with counting concrete objects, and with skip counting as these skills are important prerequisites to the concepts and process of multiplication.

Consider a problem such as "My three dogs each have five fleas. How many fleas do they have in all?" A child operating on the concrete level might approach this problem by counting out three piles of five blocks or counters, then counting all of the blocks or counters. A child operating on the pictorial level could solve the same problem by drawing a picture of three dogs with five fleas each and then counting the fleas in the picture. In the earliest grade levels, children could record their solution by writing $5 + 5 + 5 = 15$. The symbolism for multiplication is usually introduced at about the second-grade level. If children have had enough experience with this type of problem, they may simply state "three times five is fifteen" or write $3 \times 5 = 15$. In the following section we will discuss three interpretations of multiplication, using the problem given above to illustrate the additive interpretation.

Three Interpretations of Multiplication

Additive Given a number of sets, each with the same number of objects, find the total number of objects.

In an additive multiplication problem, it is important that the sets involved each have the same number of objects. The problem "One dog has four fleas, another has five, and the third dog has six fleas. How many fleas in all?" is not a multiplication problem. It is also important that the sets involved are disjoint. The problem "Brothers Joe, George, and Jim each have four pets. How many pets are there in all?" is not an appropriate problem because it is not clear that the sets are disjoint. The people mentioned are siblings, so the sets of pets may overlap. An early childhood teacher must learn to create or find appropriate problems to illustrate multiplication situations. An early childhood student must learn to distinguish whether multiplication is or is not the appropriate operation for such problems.

When introducing the symbolism for multiplication, it is important to be consistent in notation. In the conventional representation, the number of sets is written first and the number in each set follows the multiplication symbol. Consider the additive multiplication problem "A box of breakfast bars contains 6 packages. Each package contains two bars. How many breakfast bars are in the box?" In the early grades, before multiplication symbolism has been introduced, a child might solve this problem by using coun-

Activity 6-1   Grades 2–3

Introducing Multiplication

Materials: Counters for each student.

Teacher-Directed Examples:

a. Three students each have four pencils. How many pencils do they have all together?
   Show me with your counters. You have three piles of four. What equation do we write for this? Yes, $4 + 4 + 4 = 12$. When all the piles have the same number of objects, we can also multiply to find how many in all. We can write $3 \times 4 = 12$ for three groups with four in each group. We call the symbol $\times$ "times" so we can say this as "three times four is twelve." What's a quick way to count the objects when we have three groups of four? Yes, we could use skip counting: 4, 8, 12.

b. Four bikes each have two wheels. How many wheels in all?
   Show it with your counters. What addition sentence can we write? Yes, $2 + 2 + 2 + 2 = 8$. Four groups of two is eight. We can write the multiplication sentence $4 \times 2 = 8$. If we want to find the answer to a multiplication problem, we can use skip counting: 4×2 represents four groups of two so we count by twos and we count four times: 2, 4, 6, 8. So four times two is eight.

c. Show the multiplication sentence $2 \times 5 = 10$ with your counters. How many total counters will you need? How many groups? How many in each group? Can you write a story problem for this?

d. There are three bicycles and two tricycles. How many wheels are there all together? Can we write a multiplication sentence? Why or why not?

ters or drawing pictures and could record this solution with the equation $2 + 2 + 2 + 2 + 2 + 2 = 12$. The multiplication symbolism for this problem is $6 \times 2 = 12$; six sets, each containing 2 items, gives a total of 12 items. Although it is true that $6 \times 2 = 2 \times 6$ since both calculations result in the answer 12, the equation $2 \times 6 = 12$ should *not* be used for this problem as the equation $2 \times 6 = 12$ represents the idea that two sets, each containing 6 items, gives a total of 12 items. The commutative property of multiplication will be explored after children have acquired the concept of multiplication and are comfortable with the notation.

Notice the variety of questions and procedures in Activity 6-1. The activity begins with a previously learned skill, the writing of an addition sentence. Concrete materials are used throughout the activity. Later pictorial reinforcement activities may use the same types of problems and examples and have children draw pictures to illustrate their solutions. Activity 6-1 is a concrete developmental ac-

Assessment
Sample Assessment Rubric
for Activity 6-1:

4   The child is able to illustrate with a concrete model, write a corresponding addition sentence, and write the corresponding multiplication sentence for a given story problem.

3   The child needs occasional prompting or makes occasional errors in writing number sentences, but is generally able to model and solve the problem for a given story problem.

2   The child needs some assistance in modeling and frequent assistance in writing number sentences for a given story problem.

1   The child is not able to model the problem or write a number sentence for a given story problem.

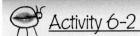

Activity 6-2   Grades 1–2

Skip Counting—An Introduction to Row by Column Multiplication

Materials: Blocks for each student.

Teacher-Directed Examples:

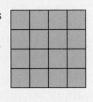

a. I made three rows with 4 blocks each.
How many blocks are there all together? Good, 12.
Is there a fast way to count the blocks? Yes, we could skip count: 4, 8, 12.

b. Make four rows with 5 blocks each. How many blocks did you use all together?
How can you use skip counting to find the total?

---

tivity to introduce the notation of multiplication. Not every problem follows the format "Given a story problem, write a multiplication sentence." Children need to learn to relate the three items—story, picture or model, and number sentence. Later reinforcement activities will provide more practice in this important skill. Children also need to be able to distinguish between problems where multiplication is appropriate and problems where it is not.

Row by Column (sometimes called the array interpretation) Given a number of rows where each row has the same number of objects, find the total number of objects.

In the row by column interpretation of multiplication, it is important that each row has the same number of objects. In the conventional symbolization of this interpretation, the number of rows is given first and the number of columns (or number in each row) follows the multiplication symbol. Here is a typical row by column example: "A boat has three rows of seats. Four people can sit in each row. How many people can sit in the boat?" A sketch of the situation is shown in Figure 6-1. The corresponding multiplication equation is $3 \times 4 = 12$. The equation $4 \times 3 = 12$ is not appropriate for the given example as this equation represents the situation of four rows each containing three people.

In the very early grades, multiplication ideas may be introduced without reference to any multiplication terms or notations. This **type of introduction** provides a concrete foundation and **provides** practice in important prerequisite ideas such as skip counting (see Activities 6-2 and 6-3).

FIGURE 6-1 Seats in a boat.

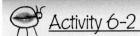

Activity 6-3   Grades 3–4

Row by Column Multiplication

Materials: Inch-squared (or centimeter-squared) paper and rubber stamps or stickers for each student.

Teacher-Directed Example:

a. I made 3 rows with 4 stamps (stickers) each.
How many stamps (stickers) all together? Good, 12.
Is there a fast way to count the stamps (stickers)? Yes, we could skip count: 4, 8, 12.
We could also use the multiplication fact $3 \times 4 = 12$ because 3 groups of 4 is 12.

Directions for Student:

a. Make 4 rows with 5 stamps each. How many stamps did you use all together?
How can you use skip counting to find the total? What multiplication sentence does this show?

b. Using a total of 12 stamps, make as many pictures as you can that have the same number of stamps in each row. Write the multiplication sentence for each of your pictures.

Combination One item is selected from each of two disjoint sets. Find the number of possible combinations.

For the combination interpretation of multiplication, it is important that the sets are disjoint and that exactly one item is chosen from each set. The following is an example of a combination problem. "Jan has four shirts and three pairs of pants. How many different outfits could she make?" Students could act out this problem using picture diagrams. They could also use a tree diagram such as in Figure 6-2. This interpretation is often the most difficult for young children because it involves two different types of objects. It is usually not introduced until around the third- or fourth-grade level. Children need many experiences where they act out, list, or draw all possible combinations before they will be comfortable in using multiplication to solve this type of problem without drawing or listing all possibilities. This idea can also be extended to more than two disjoint sets (see Activity 6-4).

Terminology, Notation, and Basic Multiplication Facts

In the multiplication sentence $a \times b = c$, the terms a and b are called *factors*, c is called the *product*, and $a \times b$ is called the *product expression* or just the *product*. The product expression $a \times b$ is read as "a times b" or "the product of a and b" or "a multiplied by b." An equation such as $3 \times \_\_\_ = 12$ or $\_\_\_ \times 4 = 8$ is called a *missing factor equation*.

The phrase "fact family" can be used to describe all whole number multiplication facts with a common product. There are four members in the multiplication fact family for 8. They are $1 \times 8 = 8$, $8 \times 1 = 8$, $2 \times 4 = 8$, and $4 \times 2 = 8$. Generally the number of members in a multi-

_____

You may remember from your own elementary school experiences completing multiplication tables such as the one shown in Figure 6-3.

_____

plication fact family for a specific number will depend on the number of divisors of that number. There are 100 basic multiplication facts where each factor is a whole number less than 10.

Concrete developmental activities can be used to show children why these facts are true and reasonable. Reinforcement activities can help solidify the connections between a symbolic numerical fact and a concrete model representation of that fact. Eventually, drill and practice activities are useful to help children gain speed and accuracy in the recollection of these facts.

One of the easiest types of facts for children to learn is the set of facts where one factor is the number 2. These

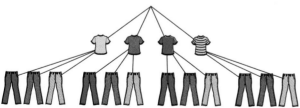

Each of the four shirts could be worn with any of the three pairs of pants. There are $4 \times 3 = 12$ possible outfits.

FIGURE 6-2   A tree diagram.

Activity 6-4   Grades 3–5

Combination Multiplication—Problem Solving by Making a List

Materials: Printed menu for each student with four entrées, five side dishes, and three types of drinks.

Directions for Students:
a. How many different types of meals could you order that consist of one entrée and a drink?
b. How many different snacks could be ordered if a snack consists of one side dish and one drink?
c. How many different Jumbo meals could you order if a Jumbo meal consists of one entrée, one side dish, and one drink?

facts are fairly easy for children to understand and remember because they may be related to doubles facts. The facts with one factor of 5 are also easy for children to understand and remember. This may be due to the fact that skip counting by fives occurs in the contexts of counting money or tally marks. Children usually receive more practice in skip counting by twos or by fives than in skip counting by any other numbers. Children may invent their own strategies for dealing with multiplication facts involving other factors. Ask a third-grade child how to multiply by four and she may answer "You just double-double." There are several properties that will reduce the number of facts that must be memorized, described in the following section.

×	0	1	2	3	4	5	6	7	8	9
0	0	0	0	0	0	0	0	0	0	0
1	0	1	2	3	4	5	6	7	8	9
2	0	2	4	6	8	10	12	14	16	18
3	0	3	6	9	12	15	18	21	24	27
4	0	4	8	12	16	20	24	28	32	36
5	0	5	10	15	20	25	30	35	40	45
6	0	6	12	16	24	30	36	42	48	54
7	0	7	14	21	28	35	42	49	56	63
8	0	8	16	24	32	40	48	56	64	72
9	0	9	18	27	36	45	54	63	72	81

FIGURE 6-3   A multiplication table.

Note: Factors are shown in bold. Square facts are circled. If you memorize or can determine the multiplication facts shown in black below the diagonal of square facts, then the multiplication facts above the diagonal follow from the property of commutativity.

Properties of Multiplication

Rather than stating a property and then giving numerical examples that illustrate the property, many of today's teachers begin with specific examples and let the students derive or discover the property. In this manner, the students become active thinkers and are more apt to assimilate the property into their own framework of knowledge. It is more meaningful to them because it is something that they themselves have thought about rather than something that they have been told.

Standards

NCTM

Grades 3–5

In grades 3-5, students' development of number sense should continue, with a focus on multiplication and division. Their understanding of the meanings of these operations should grow deeper as they encounter a range of representations and problem situations, learn about the properties of these operations, and develop fluency in whole-number computation.

NCTM, 2000, p. 149

Standards are listed with the permission of the National Council of Teachers of Mathematics (NCTM). NCTM does not endorse the content or validity of these alignments.

The Identity Element Our discussion of properties of multiplication begins with an example involving plates and cookies. This example could be acted out in the classroom with paper plates and counters. We have already discussed the idea that sets containing the same number of elements can be represented by a multiplication equation. For example, two plates of cookies with three cookies on each plate represents the equation $2 \times 3 = 6$ since two groups of three objects yields six objects. Recall that in the conventional representation, the number of groups is represented by the first factor of the equation and the number in each group is represented by the second factor of the equation.

Example 6-1:

> one plate with one cookie on the plate represents the equation $1 \times 1 = 1$.
> one plate with two cookies on the plate represents the equation $1 \times 2 = 2$.
> one plate with three cookies on the plate represents the equation $1 \times 3 = 3$.
> one plate with four cookies on the plate represents the equation $1 \times \underline{\quad} = \underline{\quad}$.
> one plate with five cookies on the plate represents the equation $\underline{\quad\quad}$.
> one plate with six cookies on the plate represents the equation $\underline{\quad\quad}$.
> one plate with $\underline{\quad}$ cookies on the plate represents the equation $\underline{\quad\quad}$.

Can you see the pattern? What would the representation of 1×20 look like? Finish the equation $1 \times 20 = \underline{\quad\quad}$. Finish the equation $1 \times 276 = \underline{\quad\quad}$. State the rule that the above example illustrates in your own words. Try to write the rule using math symbols. You may use a variable such as n to represent an unknown number.

The rule that you discovered above may have looked something like $1 \times n = n$ for any whole number n. This is part of the property that the factor 1 is an *identity element* for multiplication. That is, 1 multiplied by any element does not change the identity of that element. The other part

of this property is that it also holds that $n \times 1 = n$ for any whole number n. This can also be illustrated with a plates and cookies example similar to Example 6-1.

The Zero Element A plates and cookies example can also illustrate one part of a property that occurs when 0 is used as a factor. Recall that two plates with three cookies on each plate represents $2 \times 3 = 6$ because two groups of three cookies gives a total of six cookies. How many cookies do you have if you have two plates with zero cookies on each plate? You have zero cookies. Hence, $2 \times 0 = 0$. Example 6-2 extends this idea.

Example 6-2:

> one plate with zero cookies on the plate represents the equation $1 \times 0 = 0$.
> two plates with zero cookies on each plate represents the equation $2 \times 0 = 0$.
> three plates with zero cookies on each plate represents the equation $3 \times 0 = 0$.
> four plates with zero cookies on each plate represents the equation $4 \times \underline{\quad} = \underline{\quad}$.
> five plates with zero cookies on each plate represents the equation $\underline{\quad\quad}$.
> six plates with zero cookies on each plate represents the equation $\underline{\quad\quad}$.

Again, there is a clear pattern. Students should be able to derive the rule that $n \times 0 = 0$ for any whole number n. It is also true that $0 \times n = 0$ for any whole number n. However, Example 6-2 does not provide the best illustration of this idea. For instance, to represent 0×3 with a plates and cookies example you would have zero plates with three cookies on each plate. This is difficult to visualize. It is better to use an example where $0 \times n$ can be easily interpreted or visualized.

Example 6-3: Gina makes \$4 an hour for mowing lawns. For example, if she

> Mows three hours, she makes \$12. This illustrates $3 \times 4 = 12$.

Mows three hours, she makes $12. This illustrates
$3 \times 4 = 12$.

Mows two hours, she makes $8. This illustrates
$2 \times 4 = 8$.

Mows one hour, she makes $4. This illustrates
$1 \times 4 = 4$.

Mows zero hours, she makes $0. This illustrates
$0 \times 4 = 0$.

Notice the pattern that occurs in Example 6-3. As the first factor decreases, each product is four less than the previous product. This pattern appears to reinforce the fact that $0 \times 4 = 0$. By varying the hourly wage in Example 6-3, you could show that $0 \times 5 = 0$ or that $0 \times 12 = 0$, or that $0 \times n = 0$ for any whole number n.

Combining the two facts derived from Examples 6-2 and 6-3, you obtain the property that the factor 0 is a *zero element* for multiplication. That is, for any whole number n, both $n \times 0 = 0$ and $0 \times n = 0$ are true equations.

The Commutative Property of Multiplication Some concrete models provide good illustrations of mathematical properties. Various sizes of rectangular arrays can be cut from inch-squared (or centimeter-squared) paper (see Blackline Master 10 in the Appendices) to demonstrate various multiplication facts. Suppose you cut a three-inch by six-inch section. Held in one direction, this represents the fact $3 \times 6 = 18$. Held in another direction this represents the fact $6 \times 3 = 18$. This versatility can illustrate an important property of multiplication.

Following an activity such as Activity 6-5, the teacher could hold a classroom discussion and let students verbalize the property that they are discovering. The property that $a \times b = b \times a$, for any pair of numbers a and b, is called the *commutative property of multiplication*. Whereas some elementary school textbooks, as early as the second-grade level, do use the phrase "commutative property," others call it the *order property*.

Why is the property of commutativity important? For one thing, due to the commutativity of multiplication half of the facts in a multiplication table do not require extra effort to memorize. For example, if you know that $3 \times 6 = 18$, then the multiplication fact $6 \times 3 = 18$ follows for free. Commutativity also comes in handy in some calculations. Suppose you had to multiply $5 \times 79 \times 2$. As presented, this requires some effort in calculation. Because multiplication is commutative, you may consider the problem $5 \times 2 \times 79$ instead of the given problem. This is easily done by mental math since $10 \times 79 = 790$.

The Number Line Model for Multiplication A number line can provide a model to illustrate commutativity. Figure 6-4a illustrates 2×4 on the number line. Note how this differs from the illustration of 4×2 shown in Figure 6-4b. The figures may look different, but the end result is the same: $2 \times 4 = 8$ and $4 \times 2 = 8$. Hence, $2 \times 4 = 4 \times 2$.

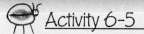

Activity 6-5 — Grades 3–4

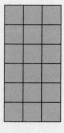

Illustrating the Commutative Property with the Rectangular Model

Materials: Rectangular arrays cut from inch-squared (or centimeter-squared) paper.

Directions: Each group gets one sheet of inch-squared (or centimeter-squared) paper. Students cut it into rectangles of different sizes (teachers may cut rectangles for students with special needs) and on the back of each rectangle, write down all the facts and equations you can find about that rectangle. When the timer rings, each group shares their results with the rest of the class.

Teacher-Directed Example: What multiplication sentence does this show? Right, $6 \times 3 = 18$

How about if I hold it this way? Yes, this shows $3 \times 6 = 18$.

So, 3×6 and 6×3 are both equal to 18. We could write the equation $3 \times 6 = 6 \times 3$.

Then, $3 \times 6 = 18$ and $6 \times 3 = 18$ and $3 \times 6 = 6 \times 3$ are three facts we can get from this rectangle.

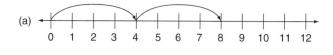

(a)

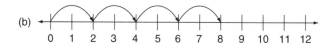

(b)

FIGURE 6-4 (a) Illustration of 2×4, (b) illustration of 4×2.

In sketching a number line model, it is important that the number line begin at zero (0). As discussed earlier, in the very early grades, negative numbers should not be included on the number line. It is also important to be consistent in spacing and numbering when drawing a number line representation. This is a skill that may require practice on your part, especially if you intend to draw number lines on a chalkboard or overhead.

The Distributive Property of Multiplication over Addition Another property that can be useful in the computation of multiplication facts is the distributive property of multiplication over addition. If a student needs to determine the answer to 6×8, but does not yet have the appropriate fact memorized, the student could use the fact that $5 \times 8 = 40$ if she knows it. Since 5 groups of 8 is 40, then 6 groups of 8 is 40 plus one more group of 8. Thus, $6 \times 8 = 48$. This method of computation uses the distributive property of multiplication over addition. In the very early grades this property is often used, for example in the same manner as it is used above, but not explicitly stated.

Formally stated, the *distributive property of multiplication over addition* is $a \times (b + c) = (a \times b) + (a \times c)$ for whole numbers *a, b,* and *c*. Because multiplication is commutative, it is also true that $(b + c) \times a = (b \times a) + (c \times a)$. The rectangular model can be used to illustrate this property as shown in Figure 6-5. When a rectangular model is drawn

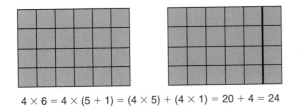

$$4 \times 6 = 4 \times (5 + 1) = (4 \times 5) + (4 \times 1) = 20 + 4 = 24$$

FIGURE 6-5 Illustration of the distributive property.

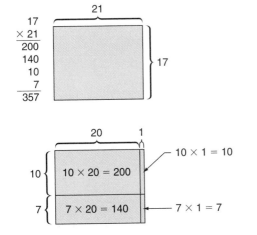

FIGURE 6-6 A rectangular model calculation of 17×21.

to illustrate a product where both factors are less than 10, it is customary to draw each individual box in the model.

The distributive property of multiplication over addition is also useful to determine products when a factor is larger than a single digit.

Example 6-4: Using the distributive property.

    a. $5 \times 14 = (5 \times 10) + (5 \times 4) = 50 + 20 = 70$.

    b. $17 \times 21 = (17 \times 20) + (17 \times 1) = 340 + 17 = 357$.

        Note that in example (b) the factor 21 is rewritten as $20 + 1$. It would also be a valid solution to rewrite the factor 17 as $10 + 7$.

    c. $17 \times 21 = (10 \times 21) + (7 \times 21) = 210 + 147 = 357$.

You could also illustrate a multiplication such as 17×21 by using a rectangular model as shown in Figure 6-6. When drawing a rectangular model to illustrate a multiplication where one or both factors are larger than 10, not every individual box in the model needs to be drawn. Begin by drawing a large rectangular box using both factors as the dimensions. Break each side into smaller components involving tens and ones and divide the rectangle into four smaller rectangles of these dimensions. Find the products associated with each of the four smaller rectangles. The answer to the original multiplication problem is the sum of these four terms. Do you see how this process uses the distributive property of multiplication over addition?

The Associative Property of Multiplication Another property that can be useful in computations is the property of associativity. Consider the following computation: $5 \times 14 = 5 \times (2 \times 7) = (5 \times 2) \times 7 = 10 \times 7 = 70$. This computation uses the associative property of multiplication. Formally stated, the *associative property of multiplication* is $a \times (b \times c) = (a \times b) \times c$, for whole numbers *a, b,* and *c*. Informally, the idea of associativity is that when multiplying three or more numbers you may associate (perform the first multiplication on) any pair of the numbers. Some elementary school textbooks, as early as the second-grade level, use the phrase "associative property." Others call it the *grouping property*. The rectangular model can be used to illustrate the associative property of multiplication as shown in Figure 6-7.

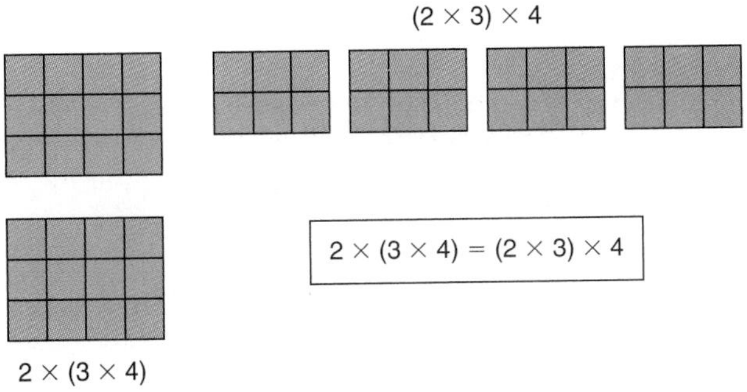

$$(2 \times 3) \times 4$$

$$2 \times (3 \times 4) = (2 \times 3) \times 4$$

$$2 \times (3 \times 4)$$

FIGURE 6-7 A rectangular model illustration of the associative property of multiplication.

The first diagram shows two pieces each having three rows and four columns. This illustrates $2 \times (3 \times 4)$ and shows a total of 24 blocks.

The second diagram shows four pieces each having two rows and three columns. This illustrates $(2 \times 3) \times 4$ and shows a total of 24 blocks.

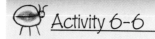

Teaching Connections

Help Children Learn Multiplication Facts If you use motivating examples and materials to guide students to discover properties or rules, you must be very patient. Do not expect precise, textbook answers from students who are asked to describe something in their own words. Student contributions may be incomplete or even incorrect. In some cases you may not understand what a student is saying or what point he is trying to make. Other students may be helpful in completing, correcting, or making sense of an imperfect student contribution.

When a student states a rule or property that is incorrect, you should either provide a counterexample yourself or challenge other students to find one. A *counterexample* to a rule is an example for which the rule does not hold. Suppose that in a classroom discussion following Activity 6-5 a student makes the statement "When you turn around the numbers in an equation, you get the same thing." First get that student and others to clarify what is meant by the statement. Some students may visualize "turn around the numbers" as writing ∂ instead of 6. Make sure it is clear that "turn around the numbers" means changing the order of the factors. Next, work on making the statement more complete. You might ask "Does this work for all equations? Can anyone think of an example of an equation where you don't get the same thing when you turn around the numbers?" Another student or you can provide a counterexample like $5 - 3 \neq 3 - 5$. The students can amend the statement to include the fact that commutativity is a property of multiplication.

Getting students to verbalize what they are doing or discovering in mathematics can be a slow and arduous process. You must provide a safe, encouraging classroom environment where students are willing to volunteer, even when they are not sure their answers are correct. An incomplete or incorrect answer can be viewed as a learning experience. Be positive, be supportive, and most of all, be patient with your students and with yourself.

Use Real-World Examples and Fun Activities to Practice Multiplication Facts After several conceptual activities are presented that help children see and understand multiplication facts, you might present drill and practice activities to help them memorize and practice the facts. There are many commercially available materials such as musical tapes that children may enjoy singing along to. Activity 6-6 is a finger activity that aids in the recollection of facts when one of the factors is 9.

Activity 6-7 lets children practice multiplication facts, relationships between facts, and predicting outcomes. There is a situation that may arise during play of the game in Activity 6-7 that is not covered by the rules given in the directions for the activity. See problem 7 of the Applica-

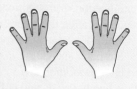

Activity 6-6 — Grades 3–4

A Factor of Nine Technique—Finger Multiplication

Teacher-Directed Example:
We can use our fingers to show us the nine facts. (Have students place their fingers on their desks. The teacher should place her fingers on the chalkboard so that students can see and imitate the action. When a finger is raised, students can see the answer to the nine fact involving the number of that finger.)

The number of tens is given by the fingers on the desk to the left of the raised finger, and the number of ones is given by the fingers on the desk to the right. See the examples given. This works for all 10 nine facts.

The raised finger, or multiplier is indicated with shading.

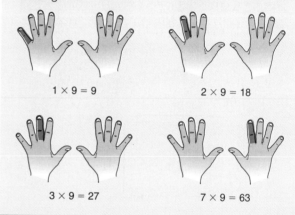

tions in the Classroom exercises for this section. You will sometimes find activities in textbooks or activity manuals that contain incomplete or incorrect directions. Often this is discovered during the first classroom presentation of the activity. As the teacher, you must occasionally make quick decisions on how to modify or amend directions so that the activity will work as planned. When this happens, be sure to make a note in your activity file so that the next time you present the activity the same problem does not occur.

Problem Set 6.1

For Your Understanding

1. Complete Activity 6-4.

2. Write a multiplication sentence and classify the type of multiplication problem for each of the following:

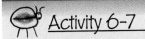

Activity 6-7

Grades 3–6

Less, Between, or More Multiplication

Materials: Multiplication flash cards (blank on the back).

Directions: A player draws three cards from the deck. The player flips over two of the cards so that two multiplication facts are showing. The player gives answers to the two multiplication facts and receives 2 points if both answers are correct, 1 point if one answer is correct, and no points if both answers are incorrect. If either answer is incorrect, make sure the player knows the correct answers before the next step of play. The player then guesses one of the following options: less, between, or more. This guess is to indicate whether the player believes the hidden fact will have an answer that is less than, between, or more than the answers to the two facts shown. The player flips the card and gives the answer. The player gets 1 point if the answer is correct, and 1 additional point if the guess about the position of the answer is correct. Play continues with the next player.

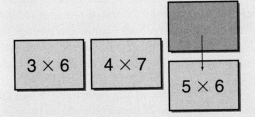

Example: Suppose the player says $3 \times 6 = 18$ and $4 \times 7 = 24$. Make sure that the player learns the correct answer $4 \times 7 = 28$ before he guesses the location of the unseen card. Suppose the player guesses "between" and flips the card. He gets a point for correctly stating $5 \times 6 = 30$, but does not get the point for answer location. This player scores 2 points.

Note: The directions are incomplete for this activity. See problem 7 in the exercises.

Source: Adapted from Troutman & Lichtenberg, 2003.

---

a. A classroom has four rows of student desks with six desks in each row. How many student desks are in the room?
b. Ken has five shirts, two pairs of pants, and one pair of shorts. How many different outfits does he have?
c. A box of snack cakes contains four packs with two cupcakes in each pack. How many cupcakes are in the box?

---

3. For the multiplication problem $6 \times 3 = 18$, the numbers 6 and 3 are called _____ and the number 18 is called the _____.

4. Is the set of even whole numbers closed under multiplication? Why or why not? Is the set of odd whole numbers closed under multiplication? Why or why not?

5. What properties are illustrated by each of the following?
   a. $4 \times 0 = 0$
   b. $4 \times 1 = 1$
   c. $4 \times 5 = 5 \times 4$
   d. $4 \times 5 = 2 \times 2 \times 5 = 2 \times 10 = 20$
   e. $4 \times 5 = 2 \times 5 + 2 \times 5 = 10 + 10 = 20$

6. Use a rectangular model calculation such as shown in Figure 6-6 to calculate 28×32.

7. Draw number line representations for (a) 3×6 and (b) 6×3.

Applications in the Classroom

1. Four different students calculate the answer to 4×6. Which of the strategies are valid? Use the strategies shown to calculate what answer each of the students would most likely get in the calculation of 4×7.
   a. $5 \times 6 = 30$, so $4 \times 6 = 30 - 6 = 24$
   b. $2 \times 6 = 12$ and $2 \times 12 = 24$
   c. $6 - 4 = 2$ and use the 4 again to get 24
   d. $2 \times 6 = 12$ and $12 + 12 = 24$

2. Write a reinforcement activity that gives children practice in relating a problem story, model, and equation for multiplication problems.

3. Create a reinforcement activity for the learning of multiplication facts. If desired, you can use an inch- or centimeter-squared grid and a manila folder cover that has appropriate windows cut out for viewing facts.

4. Create the materials for a drill and practice activity to practice multiplication facts. You can make up your own game or use previous examples such as a five-chair, Bingo, or "Go Fish."

5. Rewrite Example 6-1 to illustrate $n \times 1 = n$ instead of $1 \times n = n$.

6. Some common student errors are given. You are the teacher. How do you respond to each student?
   a. Jessica says "$5 \times 7 = 35$, so 6×7 is $35 + 6$ is 41."
   b. Jamal says "$6 \times 7 = 6 \times 3 + 4 = 18 + 4 = 22$."

c. Huong says "How come rows go up and down when you call us by row to go for recess, but you said rows always go across for row by column multiplication?"

7. Find what may happen in Activity 6-7 that isn't covered in the directions. Decide how you could change the directions to handle this situation.

8. Write multiplication word problems for each of the three interpretations of multiplication discussed.

9. Create an assessment tool to be used with Activity 6-4. Explain why you chose that type of assessment tool.

10. Suppose you have already taught a lesson in your second-grade class that included Activity 6-1. Write a lesson plan that includes a pictorial reinforcement activity similar to Activity 6-1. Follow the format given by your instructor or use the lesson plan format given in the Appendices.

11. Create an assessment tool to be used with the lesson created in problem 9 above. Explain why you chose that type of assessment tool.

6.2 CONSTRUCTING MEANING FOR DIVISION

As for the operations already discussed, division also should be introduced with concrete objects and real-life situations. Because division is inherently related to multiplication, some of the same types of multiplication examples may be used with division. Recall that for the multiplication sentence $a \times b = c$, the standard format suggests (number of sets) $\times$ (number in each set) = total number of objects. The next paragraph covers plates and cookies interpretations of the missing factor multiplication equations ___ $\times 5 = 20$ and $5 \times$ ___ $= 20$. Before reading further, try to envision a plates and cookies interpretation for each of these equations. How do the two interpretations differ?

A valid interpretation for the equation ___ $\times 5 = 20$ is the following: "There are 20 cookies. If we put 5 cookies on each plate, how many plates do we need?" A valid interpretation for the equation $5 \times$ ___ $= 20$ is as follows: "There are 20 cookies. If five plates are used and each has the same number of cookies, how many cookies are put on each plate?" Both interpretations can be

represented by the division equation $20 \div 5 =$ ___. However, there are subtle differences in how a young child with no previous knowledge of the process or notations of division would proceed in solving the two different problems. The two problems illustrate two different interpretations of division.

Two Interpretations of Division

Subtractive Given a total number of objects and how many objects are in each set, find the number of sets.

In this interpretation it is important to have the same number of objects in each set. In the previous example, there are "5 cookies on each plate." The number of plates (sets) is unknown. Another example of subtractive division is the following: "There will be 24 people at a picnic. If 6 people can sit at each table, how many tables are needed?" The reason for the terminology "subtractive division problem" is this problem may be solved by starting with a pile of 24 counters and pulling out (subtracting) piles of 6 counters each to represent each table until the number of tables is determined. Children could also solve such a problem by drawing a picture. However, concrete materials provide security in an unfamiliar situation. It is easy to experiment with ideas using concrete materials that can be returned to their initial piles and positions. To draw a picture, you must have an idea of the type of picture to draw. An appropriate missing factor multiplication equation for this problem is ___ $\times 6 = 24$. We will discuss division equations and notations shortly.

Not all division problems work out exactly. Consider the problem "There will be 22 people at a picnic. If 6 people can sit at each table, how many tables are needed?" This is still a subtractive division problem. It could be solved with counters or by drawing pictures. If 6 people are seated at the first table, there remains $22 - 6 = 16$ people to be seated. Another 6 people can occupy the second table and still $16 - 6 = 10$ people need to be seated. If 6 people sit at the third table, there are still $10 - 6 = 4$ people who require a fourth table. It is clear that four tables are needed, although not all four tables will be filled. Students should have many experiences with the concepts and ideas before being asked to write a number sentence for this type of situation. An ap-

Activity 6-8 — Grades 3–4

Concrete Illustration of Division

Materials: Plenty of plastic links for each student.

Worksheet Directions:
1. Make a big chain as long as indicated.
2. Use the big chain to make as many smaller chains as possible of the size indicated.
3. Record how many small chains you made, and the number of links left over.
4. Write a number sentence that shows your results.

Size of big chain	Size of smaller chains	Number of small chains possible	Number of links left over	Number sentence
26	8	3	2	$3 \times 8 + 2 = 26$ or $26 \div 8 = 3\,R2$
35	6			
40	8			
Etc.	Etc.			

propriate number sentence for this situation is $(3 \times 6) + 4 = 22$ or, if division notation has been introduced, $22 \div 6 = 3R4$. Once children understand the concepts behind these types of problems, they may find working with the manipulatives to be cumbersome and prefer to solve such problems numerically. Skip counting can be helpful in the solution. By skip counting 6, 12, 18 (not enough), 24 (too big) you can see that three tables will seat only 18 people and four tables will seat 24. Because there will be 22 people (which is more than 18), four tables are necessary.

Distributive Given a total number of objects and the number of sets, find how many objects are in each set.

For this interpretation it is assumed (if not explicitly stated) that each set will have the same number of objects. "There are 24 plates and 4 tables. How many plates should go on each table?" This is a "distributive division problem" because to solve the problem you could begin with a pile of 24 counters and "distribute" the counters to four smaller piles representing tables until it is determined that there will be 6 plates on each of the 4 tables. An appropriate missing factor multiplication number sentence for this problem is $4 \times \underline{\quad} = 20$.

Again, not all such division problems work out evenly: "Seventeen trading cards are to be equally shared by three children. How many cards should each get?" By distributing counters or by skip counting, you can determine that if each child gets five cards, there are two cards remaining. There are not enough cards to give each child

six cards. Because the cards were to be shared equally, perhaps an adult could hold on to the two remaining cards until more cards are available for distribution. Children should have some experience with division problems that do work out evenly before being presented with a problem that has a remainder such as the one given previously. Real-life division situations and equal sharing opportunities arise frequently. There are many children's literature selections that address these concepts.

Terminology, Notation, Properties, and Basic Division Facts

The division symbol $\div$ is usually introduced at the second-grade level. Several examples using concrete materials and pictures are shown, and nearly every problem works out evenly with no remainder. However, a second-grade-level textbook may include some examples that do have a remainder. Students are asked to discuss why the objects in such a problem cannot be shared equally, but generally do not write number sentences for problems that have a remainder at this level. Students at the second-grade level may have difficulty writing the division symbol and in a disposable textbook it may be provided, as in the following example.

Example 6-5: A division problem at approximately the second-grade level.

Eight balloons are shared by two children. Use counters to decide how many balloons each child gets.

Finish drawing the picture and write the number sentence:

$\underline{\quad} \div \underline{\quad} = \underline{\quad}$ balloons.

Division sentences with remainders and the standard computation form as in the example given below are usually introduced at the third- or fourth-grade level.

For the problem $17 \div 3$, the *standard computational form* is

$$\begin{array}{r} 5 \\ 3\overline{)17} \\ \underline{15} \\ 2 \end{array}$$

This may be recorded in a number sentence as $17 \div 3 = 5\,R2$. Although we will continue to use the phrase "standard

Using Literature in the Mathematics Classroom

The Doorbell Rang

By Pat Hutchins
Pearson Learning, 1989

Two children, Sam and Victoria, have just figured out how to fairly share Grandma's cookies when the doorbell rings. They recalculate to share the cookies with the visitors, and the doorbell rings again. This continues to happen, and each time as more people arrive, the children must again recalculate how many cookies each person should receive. At the end of the story, Grandma arrives with more cookies.

Classroom Activity:

Children can act out the story. Counters can be used to represent cookies, and students can take turns ringing the doorbell and figuring out how to distribute the cookies. For an additional challenge, you may introduce fractions by including problems that do not divide evenly. In this case, it is useful to create paper cookies for the activity.

computational form" to describe the notational process of recording division as in the previous example, it should be noted that this type of notation is "standard" only in that it is commonly the notation taught in the U.S. early childhood curriculum. Other cultures and societies may have their own "standard form" and notations that may differ from the one shown previously or from other "standard" notations as presented here. If you see children using processes and notations other than those that are familiar to you, ask them to explain their methods to you. You may learn something from the experience.

Division Terminology The 17 in the problem above is called the *dividend,* 3 is the *divisor,* 5 is the *quotient,* and 2 is the *remainder.* The problem $17 \div 3$ is read as "seventeen divided by three." Even in the format $3\overline{)17}$, the correct phrase is "seventeen divided by three" and *not* "three divided by seventeen." Most K–4 textbooks avoid using fractional notations for division such as 17 / 3 in favor of the notation above. At the third- and fourth-grade levels, division remainders are usually given as whole numbers.

When division remainders are given as whole numbers, two answers that appear to be the same may indeed be different. For example, $17 \div 3 = 5\,R2$ and $22 \div 4 = 5\,R2$. Does $5\,R2$ represent the same quantity in both cases? Is $17 \div 3 = 22 \div 4$? No, it is not. Using fractional notation, $17 \div 3 = 5\frac{2}{3}$ and $22 \div 4 = 5\frac{2}{4}$. An eight-digit display calculator will give the decimal answers $17 \div 3 = 5.6666666$ and $22 \div 4 = 5.5$. Using fractional or decimal notation it is clear that $17 \div 3 \neq 22 \div 4$, even though both calculations lead to $5\,R2$. This example illustrates that the remainder in a division calculation cannot be fully interpreted without consideration of the size of the divisor. We will revisit this idea and further discuss the effect of the remainder later in the chapter.

Using concrete, real-life examples, the meaning of division and the relationship of this meaning to the symbolic interpretation can be understood. When eight balloons are shared equally between two children, each child gets four

balloons. The division number sentence is $8 \div 2 = 4$. For a distributive division problem such as this, the dividend represents the total number of objects, the divisor represents the number of sets into which the objects are to be divided, and the answer to the division problem represents the number in each set. Can you determine the role of each of the terms in a subtractive division example?

Divisions Involving Zero The calculator is an important tool in helping students make sense of mathematical ideas, properties, and algorithms (Groves, 1994). Students may use a calculator to discover the results when divisions involving zero are performed.

Example 6-6: Use a calculator and enter each of the following equations. What do you notice?

$$\boxed{0}\ \boxed{\div}\ \boxed{1}\ \boxed{=} \qquad \boxed{1}\ \boxed{\div}\ \boxed{0}\ \boxed{=}$$
$$\boxed{0}\ \boxed{\div}\ \boxed{2}\ \boxed{=} \qquad \boxed{2}\ \boxed{\div}\ \boxed{0}\ \boxed{=}$$
$$\boxed{0}\ \boxed{\div}\ \boxed{3}\ \boxed{=} \qquad \boxed{3}\ \boxed{\div}\ \boxed{0}\ \boxed{=}$$
$$\boxed{0}\ \boxed{\div}\ \boxed{4}\ \boxed{=} \qquad \boxed{4}\ \boxed{\div}\ \boxed{0}\ \boxed{=}$$
$$\boxed{0}\ \boxed{\div}\ \boxed{12}\ \boxed{=} \qquad \boxed{12}\ \boxed{\div}\ \boxed{0}\ \boxed{=}$$

In Example 6-6, you should have discovered the pattern that $0 \div n = 0$, for n any nonzero whole number. This can be explained by considering the meaning of the equation $0 \div n =$ ___. If you had zero objects to distribute equally among n sets, each set would get zero objects. The division equation $0 \div n =$ ___ could also be related to the multiplication equations $0 = n \times$ ___ and $0 =$ ___ $\times n$. These equations have the unique solution of zero.

A pattern may also be seen in the answers to the divisions $n \div 0 =$ ___, for n any nonzero whole number. Various calculators will give various answers when calculation sequences such as in the left column of Example 6-6 are entered. Some calculator displays will show 0 and the word *error,* other calculators merely show the word *error* or *undefined.* Let's consider the meaning of the calculation $n \div 0 =$

___. If *n* objects are to be distributed equally among zero sets, the answer to the equation represents how many objects are to be in each set. But this is not an equation that can be answered. If you are not comfortable with the variable *n* in the above equation, you may prefer to analyze a specific example such as $4 \div 0 =$ ___. In this instance, four objects are to be equally distributed among zero sets. How many objects should go into each set? But there are no sets into which to distribute the objects. This is not an equation that can be answered. For this reason, division by zero is stipulated as undefined.

You could also come to the conclusion that $n \div 0$ is undefined by analyzing the related multiplication equations. The equation $n \div 0 =$ ___ is related to the equations $n = 0 \times$ ___ and $n =$ ___ $\times 0$. Or, for a more specific example, $4 \div 0 =$ ___ is related to the equations $4 = 0 \times$ ___ and $4 =$ ___ $\times 0$. It should be clear that these related multiplication equations have no solution when *n* is not zero and infinitely many solutions when *n* is zero. Thus, both $n \div 0$ for *n* any nonzero whole number and $0 \div 0$ are considered undefined.

A Divisor of One   A calculator example could also be used to discover what happens when the divisor in a division equation is equal to 1. By calculating $1 \div 1, 2 \div 1, 3 \div 1$, and so on, you will discover the rule $n \div 1 = n$. This rule can be justified by considering that when *n* objects are divided or distributed into one set, there are *n* objects in that set.

Following the presentation at the third- or fourth-grade level of the divisor of one rule above, a student may inquire whether such a rule holds for a dividend of one. Can you determine whether a general rule can be found to evaluate the expression $1 \div n$, for a nonzero value *n?*

Is Division Associative? Is Division Commutative?   A student may inquire whether division is associative or commutative. To show that division is not associative, a counterexample may be given. If division were to be associative, then it would be true that $a \div (b \div c) = (a \div b) \div c$. To show that this is not always true, consider $24 \div (6 \div 2)$ and $(24 \div 6) \div 2$. Operations within parentheses are performed first, so $24 \div (6 \div 2) = 24 \div 3 = 8$ and $(24 \div 6) \div 2 = 4 \div 2 = 2$. Thus, $24 \div (6 \div 2) \neq (24 \div 6) \div 2$.

Can you determine whether division is commutative? If you determine that division is commutative, provide a short explanation or justification. If you determine that division is not commutative, provide a counterexample.

Use Parentheses When a Calculation Involves More Than One Operation   You were probably already familiar with the convention used above that operations in parentheses are performed before operations not enclosed in parentheses. In an expression such as $3 + 12 \div 3 =$ ___ you would get different answers depending on whether you first performed the addition or first performed the division. For this equation, the division takes precedence over the addition, so the

correct answer is 7. Order of operations will be discussed in Section 7.1. Until that time, parentheses will be used when more than one operation occurs in an equation. You could rewrite the previous equation as $3 + (12 \div 3) =$ ___. Children at the third-grade level or higher often enjoy the challenge of inserting parentheses to make an equation true. The process of writing problems to match given equations allows children the opportunity to carefully analyze those equations and the order of operations involved in the computations.

The Multiplication and Division Fact Family   Most division facts are related to two multiplication facts. Thus, for a given multiplication or division fact there are usually three other multiplication or division equations in the same fact family. For example, the division fact $12 \div 3 = 4$ is in the same fact family as $12 \div 4 = 3, 3 \times 4 = 12$, and $4 \times 3 = 12$. Because of the relationship between multiplication and division, it requires no extra effort to memorize basic division facts if students have a sound command of multiplication facts.

Two Models to Illustrate Division

The Number Line Model   A number line can provide a model to illustrate division. Figure 6-8a illustrates $12 \div 4 = 3$ on the number line. Note how this differs from the illustration of $12 \div 3 = 4$ shown in Figure 6-8b. Can you explain how these illustrations differ from the number line model illustrations of 3×4 and 4×3? Can you see how the illustrations show a relationship between the operation of division and repeated subtraction?

 Activity 6-9   Grades 3–5

Insert Parentheses to Make True Equations

Materials: Teacher-made worksheet for each student.

Worksheet Directions: Insert parentheses to make true equations. Some examples follow:

$12 \div 2 + 1 = 4$
$10 - 6 - 2 = 6$
$3 + 5 \times 4 = 32$
Etc.

 Assessment   Grades 3–5
Writing in Mathematics

Write story problems for each equation:
   a. $(2 + 3) \times 6 = 30$
   b. $2 + (3 \times 6) = 20$

(a)
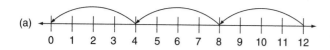

(b)
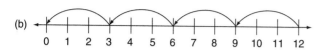

FIGURE 6-8 (a) An illustration of $12 \div 4 = 3$, (b) an illustration of $12 \div 3 = 4$.

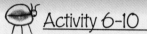 Activity 6-10   Grades 3–5

Using the Rectangular Block Model to Illustrate Operations

Materials: Blocks or inch-squared (or centimeter-squared) paper for each student.

Teacher-Directed Examples:
a. What equations can you see?

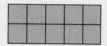

Good, $2 \times 5 = 10$. How about a division equation?
Yes, $10 \div 2 = 5$.
Any more? Great, $10 \div 5 = 2$.
b. How could we use blocks to show $(3 \times 4) - (2 \times 1)$?

Start with three rows of four—good idea.
Take away two rows of one—OK.
How is this? Can we check our answer?

Student Examples: What equations can you see in (a) and (b)? Use blocks to show the expressions in (c) and (d).
a.

b.

c. $(4 \times 3) + 2$
d. $(5 \times 3) - (2 \times 2)$

The Rectangular Model A squared paper or rectangular block model can simultaneously illustrate division as well as other operations. We have already discussed how the rectangular model can be used to represent multiplication. Can you see the relationship between a given rectangular model representation and the associated multiplication and division fact family?

 Teaching Connections

Include Variety in Your Problems, Lessons, and Activities
This section closes with some comments on writing word problems and activities to practice number skills and comprehension of operations. Remember to include variety in your problems, lessons, and activities. Not all problems should follow the format of presenting a story problem and having students calculate an answer. It is excellent practice for students to make up their own examples and problems. Try to make problems and activities fun and relevant to the students' lives and include cooperative learning and writing when possible. Be sure to include problems that have more than one solution. Elementary school textbooks typically include problems that have too much or extraneous information as well as problems that do not have enough information to find a solution. Watch out for these types of problems. Multiplication and division situations may naturally arise in other subject areas; be alert for these opportunities to stress the usefulness of mathematics in connection with other topics.

Use Games and Fun Activities to Practice Multiplication and Division Facts The 24 game is a popular game that includes practice in the four operations of addition, subtraction, multiplication, and division. There are several versions of the game available, so it may be used at many grade levels. The object of the game is to use the operations of addition, subtraction, multiplication, and division and some given numbers to make a target number. The first player to do so gets to keep that card. The sample card shown in Figure 6-9 is from the original 24 game, normally used in Grades 3–8. The target number is 24. Use the numbers 1, 3, 3, and 4 and any of the operations $(+, -, \times, \div)$ to

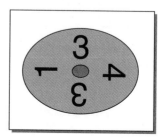

FIGURE 6-9 Example of a 24 game card.

Activity 6-11   Grades 2–5

Problem Solving by Choosing the Operation

Materials: Index cards with word problems, calculator for each student.

Teacher Statement: These cards have problems that must be solved with addition, subtraction, multiplication, or division. Read the problem, choose the operation, and use your calculator to compute the answer.

> A car drives 68 mph. How far will it go in four hours?

> Joe has $47 saved. He needs $213 to buy a TV. How much more does he need to save?

> A candy jar has 140 candies to be shared by 24 children. How many will each child get?

---

make 24. One answer is $3 \times 8 = 24$ *use* $4 + 3 + 1$ to make the 8. So, $3 \times (4 + 3 + 1) = 24$.

Can you find another answer?

It is important for students to learn how to choose which operation they will need to solve a given problem. Calculators, real-world situations, and large numbers can be used to generate interest.

Problem Set 6.2

For Your Understanding

1. Write a division sentence and a missing factor multiplication sentence for each of the following. Also classify the type of division problem.
   a. A classroom has 20 children. The teacher wishes to put them into four equal groups. How many children will be in each group?
   b. There are 20 people in line for a festival ride. If 4 people sit in each car, how many cars will be filled?

2. How should the problem $8\overline{)20}$ be read? Identify the divisor, dividend, quotient, and remainder in this example.

3. Explain the role of each of the terms "divisor," "dividend," and "quotient" in a subtractive division problem that has remainder 0.

4. Is the operation division commutative? Why or why not? Give at least one example or counterexample in your answer.

5. Complete Activity 6-10.

6. Draw number line illustrations for
   a. $12 \div 6 = 2$
   b. $12 \div 2 = 6$
   c. $6 \times 2 = 12$
   d. $2 \times 6 = 12$

   Write a few sentences to explain the differences between number line illustrations of multiplication and division.

7. Calculate $1 \div 1$, $1 \div 2$, $1 \div 3$, $1 \div 4$, and so on. Determine whether there is a general rule that can be used to evaluate the expression $1 \div n$ for n a nonzero whole number.

Applications in the Classroom

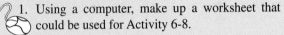

1. Using a computer, make up a worksheet that could be used for Activity 6-8.

2. Create the materials for a drill and practice activity to practice division facts. You can make up your own game or use previous examples such as five-chair, Bingo, or "Go Fish." Indicate the grade level of your game. Indicate how the game will be assessed and how it could be modified for students with special needs.

3. Make up five equations that could be used in Activity 6-9.

4. Make a set of activity cards for Activity 6-11.

5. Make up division word problems for each of the interpretations of division discussed.

6. Create an assessment tool to be used with Activity 6-8. Explain why you chose that type of assessment tool.

7. Write a formal lesson plan that includes Activity 6-8. Follow the format given by your instructor or use the lesson plan format given in the Appendices.

8. Create an assessment tool to be used with the lesson created in problem 6 above. Explain why you chose that type of assessment tool.

9. Write a formal lesson plan that includes the book *The Doorbell Rang* described in this chapter. Follow the format given by your instructor or use the lesson plan format given in the Appendices.

6.3 Using Algorithms for Whole Number Multiplication and Division

Before presenting algorithms for the operations of whole number multiplication and division, let's look at how a state or district model might specify which concepts, skills, or processes are appropriate for each of the K–2 grade levels (see the Ohio Academic Content Standards box below). Note the progression of abilities and expectations from one grade level to the next. For example, at one grade level children are expected to "model" a concept or skill, whereas at the next they are expected to "model and explain" the same concept or skill.

Standards

North Carolina Mathematics Standards

Number Sense, Numeration, and Numerical Operations for Grade 3

1.15 Solve meaningful, multi-step problems involving addition, subtraction, and multiplication using a variety of strategies.

Number Sense, Numeration, and Numerical Operations for Grade 4

1.17 Use order of operations with addition, subtraction, multiplication, and division.
1.18 Solve multi-step problems.

North Carolina Department of Public Instruction, 2003

Standards

Ohio Academic Content Standards

Number, Number Sense, and Operations

Kindergarten Grade Level Indicators:

6—Construct multiple sets of objects each containing the same number of objects.
11—Demonstrate joining multiple groups of objects, each containing the same number of objects, e.g., combining 3 bags of candy, each containing 2 pieces.
12—Partition or share a small set of objects into groups of equal size; e.g., sharing 6 stickers equally among children.

Grade 1 Grade Level Indicators:

13—Model and represent multiplication as repeated addition and rectangular arrays in contextual situations; e.g., four people will be at my party and if I want to give 3 balloons to each person, how many balloons will I need to buy?
14—Model and represent division as sharing equally in contextual situations; e.g., sharing cookies.

Grade 2 Grade Level Indicators:

7—Model, represent, and explain multiplication as repeated addition, rectangular arrays, and skip counting.
8—Model, represent, and explain division as sharing equally and repeated subtraction.

Ohio Department of Education, 2001

Multiplication Algorithms

After children understand the concepts of multiplication and division, they can be introduced to the algorithms for these operations. Multiplication and division facts may be memorized for single-digit factor facts, but larger problems will require more than memorization. For example, you probably do not have the answer to 24×13 memorized, but you most likely could use an algorithm or process to compute it.

Multiplication by a Factor of Ten The first two-digit factor type of problem that is usually introduced is multiplication by a factor of 10. Children can discover an appropriate rule by completing several problems such as in Example 6-7 below.

Example 6-7: Use a calculator to compute the following problems. What do you notice?

10	×	1	=		1	×	10	=
10	×	2	=		2	×	10	=
10	×	3	=		3	×	10	=
⋮					⋮			
10	×	9	=		9	×	10	=

Suppose that you were teaching a third-grade class, and after completing the problems in Example 6-7, a student states the rule "To multiply by 10, you add a zero at the end." How would you respond? Of course you would praise the student for finding the rule. However, there is a problem with the statement as it is given. Reread the rule as stated previously and see if you can determine the problem.

The problem is with the phrase "add a zero." Do you remember the identity property of zero for the opera-

Multiplications and divisions involving negative integers do not appear in the early childhood curriculum. However, it is a topic that should be understood by adults. Appendix A discusses operations involving integers using the number line and poker chip models introduced in Section 5.4.

tion of addition? A more correct phrase than "add a zero" would be "append or attach zero." Such a correction must be done gently. You want to encourage students to contribute, but in some cases must amend or correct their contributions.

Once the rule is correctly stated, you can use the rectangular model to show why it makes sense. Skip counting is also useful. To justify that $3 \times 10 = 30$, children could skip count (while looking at an appropriate rectangular model representation) 10, 20, 30. A 10 by 10 abacus can also be used as a visual model in this situation. Rules should never be presented and used without some justification of their validity and consideration of their appropriateness.

Students could now be encouraged to determine whether their rule works when one factor is larger than a single digit and the other factor is 10. They can do computations such as $10 \times 10 = 100$, $11 \times 10 = 110$, $12 \times 10 = 120$, ..., $20 \times 10 = 200$, and similar computations when 10 is a factor of the multiplication. They should also perform computations with larger factors such as $125 \times 10 = 1,250$ and $10 \times 300 = 3,000$. Again, reasonableness of the answers should be stressed.

Multiplication by a Multiple of a Power of Ten   Once children are comfortable with multiplication when 10 is one of the factors, you may consider multiplication when one factor is a multiple of a power of 10. Suppose a class completes the following examples:

$300 \times 4 = 1,200$ $8 \times 4,000 = 32,000$
$30 \times 40 = 1,200$ $80 \times 400 = 32,000$
$300 \times 40 = 12,000$ $800 \times 400 = 320,000$

This class might come up with a rule such as "Multiply the numbers, count, and use that many zeros." If such a rule is used without regard to the reasonableness of the answers, students will make errors such as "$50 \times 60 = 300$ since $5 \times 6 = 30$ and you need two zeros in the answer." It is extremely important that children acquire the habit of checking the reasonableness of their answers. Too often, they are in a hurry to get an answer and move on to the next problem.

The computation 4×300 could be illustrated with a base-ten model as shown in Figure 6-10. Four sets of 300 can be shown with four sets of 3 flats each. This is a total of 12 flats. Ten of the flats can be traded for one cube. A cube and 2 flats is $1,000 + 200 = 1,200$.

The computation 4×300 could also be illustrated by referencing various properties of multiplication as in Example 6-8. Each step in the computation is accompanied

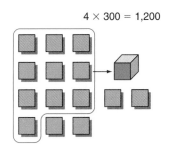

$4 \times 300 = 1,200$

FIGURE 6-10   A base ten block representation of 4×300.

by the property or concept that justifies that step. Problems might not be presented in this fashion in the early childhood classroom. However, you the teacher should understand the step-by-step process and the justifications for each step.

Example 6-8:

$$
\begin{aligned}
4 \times 300 &= 4 \times (3 \times 100) && \text{place value} \\
&= (4 \times 3) \times 100 && \text{associativity of multiplication} \\
&= 12 \times 100 && \text{basic fact} \\
&= 1,200 && \text{place value}
\end{aligned}
$$

Place value and other properties can be used to justify multiplications such as those above. For example, $80 \times 400 = 32,000$ since $8 \times 4 = 32$ and tens times hundreds is thousands. This type of calculation implicitly uses the commutative and associative properties without explicit mention. Such "nonstandard place value" ideas can also be used in calculating divisions: $1,200 \div 300 = 4$ since $12 \div 3 = 4$ and hundreds divided by hundreds is ones. This division could also be illustrated with the base-ten block model.

Let's consider two more division examples: $1,200 \div 30 = 40$ since $12 \div 3 = 4$ and hundreds divided by tens is tens, and $320,000 \div 80 = 4,000$ since $32 \div 8 = 4$ and ten thousands divided by tens is thousands. The reason for the term "nonstandard place value" is the usage of convenient place value representations such as the representation of $320,000$ as 32 ten-thousands. The trick to using this method is to find such convenient representations. One final division example: $2,000 \div 50 = 40$ since 20 hundreds divided by 5 tens is 4 tens.

Illustrate the Relationship Between Concrete and Symbolic Solutions   Before learning the formal multiplication algorithm, children should understand the interpretation of multiplication and the rectangular model. They should also be proficient in finding basic facts and performing multiple and powers of 10 computations. Initial examples of the algorithm should not require regrouping. Examples can be illustrated with concrete models as the notation is introduced.

Example 6-9:

Compute 4×21.

That's four sets of 21.

You have 4 ones and 2, 4, 6, 8 tens.

So the answer is 84.

You can show this using vertical multiplication notation:

$$
\begin{array}{r}
21 \\
\times\ 4 \\
\hline
84
\end{array}
$$

After enough examples without regrouping so that children understand the process, examples with regrouping should be presented. In the first such examples, one factor should be a single-digit factor.

Example 6-10:

Compute 4×13.

That's four sets of 13.

You have 12 ones and 4 tens.

Remember, you can regroup 10 of the ones for another ten. You have 5 tens and 2 ones. Your answer is 52.

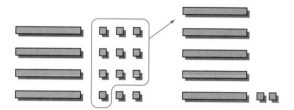

The vertical multiplication notation would look like this:

Long form notation
$$
\begin{array}{r}
13 \\
\times\ 4 \\
\hline
12 \\
40 \\
\hline
52
\end{array}
$$

Short form notation
$$
\begin{array}{r}
1 \\
13 \\
\times\ 4 \\
\hline
52
\end{array}
$$

Example 6-10 shows both a long form multiplication notation and a short form notation. Some elementary textbook series present several examples using the long form notation before introducing the short form notation, whereas others introduce short form notation immediately. Short form is a format that you as an adult have become accustomed to, but it can be very confusing for children who are seeing it for the first time. Either notation can and should be illustrated with a concrete model such as the

base-ten block model. Using concrete models can make the process of the multiplication algorithm make sense. The problem in Example 6-10 is at approximately the third-grade level.

 Teaching Connections

Promote a Conceptual Understanding In using either the long form or the short form multiplication notation, you must be very careful with the terminology that you use to explain the process. You want your students to understand what they are doing and why they are doing it, not just to blindly follow a process. Your explanations and teaching methods may differ greatly from the explanations and methods used when you were an elementary school student. Consider the rules-based explanation for the short form vertical notation associated with $13 \times 4 = 52$ given in Example 6-11.

Example 6-11: Rules-based explanation: Three times 4 is 12. Put down 2, carry the 1. One times 4 plus 1 is 5. Note: In today's elementary school textbooks, the term *regroup* is often used instead of the term *carry*.

$$
\begin{array}{r}
1 \\
13 \\
\times\ 4 \\
\hline
52
\end{array}
$$

This may be how you learned the process, but it is *not* how you should teach it. It is better to give a conceptually based explanation such as the explanation given in Example 6-10. Using the model, you can show why it is appropriate to write 2 in the ones column. You can also make sense of the fact that there are now $(1 \times 4) + 1 = 5$ tens. Several common student errors that arise when children attempt to follow rules-based explanations without understanding why or how the process works are given in Section 6.4.

Each step in the process can be justified by properties and basic concepts of multiplication and addition. Each step in the computation below is accompanied by the property or concept that justifies that step.

$4 \times 13 = 4 \times (10 + 3)$	place value (or expanded form)
$= (4 \times 10) + (4 \times 3)$	distributive property
$= 40 + 12$	basic multiplication facts
$= 40 + (10 + 2)$	place value
$= (40 + 10) + 2$	associativity of addition
$= 50 + 2$	addition fact
$= 52$	place value

Choose Appropriate Examples and Models The problem $4 \times 13 = 52$ was not the best example to begin with to illustrate a problem with regrouping where one factor is a single-digit factor. Why not? In the computation of the number of tens in the answer, there are two different ones. One of the ones represents the ten from the factor 13. The other represents the ten from the regrouping of the 12 singles. This repetition of digits may be confusing for the children and should be avoided. The problem 4×23 would have been a better example. The point is, care must be taken in selecting examples to determine whether they are suitable.

After presenting examples involving only one regrouping, you will present examples involving two regroupings. A good beginning example for this type of problem is 3×46. Can you show how this can be conceptually presented using the base-ten block model? The next type of problem to illustrate involves two 2-digit factors. This could be cumbersome with a base-ten block model and is perhaps better represented with a rectangular model calculation. Figure 6-6 of Section 6.1 showed one such example. In the example in Figure 6-11, you begin by drawing a large rectangular box using both factors as the dimensions. Break each side into smaller components involving tens and ones and divide the rectangle into four smaller rectangles of these dimensions. Find the products associated with each of the four smaller rectangles. The answer to the original multiplication problem is the sum of these four terms.

The rectangular model representation is compatible with the long form vertical notation. It is important to stress place value in the verbal explanation of the computations of this notation. The first multiplication performed is 3×4. The next multiplication performed is *not* 3×2 but 3×20. The third multiplication is *not* 1×4 but 10×4. The final multiplication is *not* 1×2 but 10×20. Some adults who have learned multiplication by fol-

$$\begin{array}{r} 24 \\ \times\ 13 \\ \hline 12 \\ 60 \\ 40 \\ 200 \\ \hline 312 \end{array}$$

lowing rules-based explanations have a habit of suppressing the zeros and may ignore place value when giving a verbal explanation of the process that they are using. This is not a habit that should be passed on. Children who are learning the process need place value ideas to make the process and the results make sense.

A sound verbal explanation including place value ideas should also be used when short form notation is introduced. The factor 24 is first multiplied by the 3 in the ones position. The 1 in the tens position of 13 indicates that the factor 24 is then multiplied by 10. The zero in 240 should be written, not suppressed.

$$\begin{array}{r} 1 \\ 24 \\ \times\ 13 \\ \hline 72 \\ 240 \\ \hline 312 \end{array}$$

Encourage Estimation and Mental Math Children should be encouraged to estimate to check the reasonableness of their answers. For the example 24×13, a reasonable (and easily calculated) estimate might be $25 \times 10 = 250$. Using front-end estimation, the estimate would be $20 \times 10 = 200$. As mentioned in Chapter 5, though, front-end estimation sometimes yields results that are far below the actual value. Nevertheless, estimation is heavily stressed in today's elementary school curriculum.

Mental calculations are also stressed in today's elementary school curriculum. Mental math can also be used when one factor is close to a "friendly" number. A friendly number is a number that is easy to use in a calculation. For example, to calculate 59×7, you could begin by thinking $60 \times 7 = 420$ and adjust this result by taking away the one set of 7 that you did not need. So, $59 \times 7 = 413$. "Compatible numbers" are numbers that work well together within a computation. For example, in the calculation of $5 \times 7 \times 2$, the product $5 \times 2 = 10$ might first be calculated. It is then easy to calculate that $10 \times 7 = 70$. The numbers 2 and 5 are compatible numbers. The following are all typical third-grade-level examples:

How could you use mental math to calculate 3×204?
Use mental math to calculate 52×8.
Use mental math to calculate $4 \times 27 \times 25$.

Division Algorithms

Before the formal introduction of a division algorithm or procedure, children must thoroughly understand division interpretations and place value concepts. They should also be proficient in basic multiplication and division facts and in estimation. Consider the following problem: 115 trading cards are to be divided equally among four children. How many cards should each child get? If this were a problem presented in a third-grade-level textbook, the first step in the solution would probably be to estimate a solution. Since $4 \times 25 = 100$ and $4 \times 30 = 120$, the answer will be between 25 and 30. The problem can be modeled with base-ten blocks and then the standard computational form of division symbolism can be related to the model as in Example 6-12.

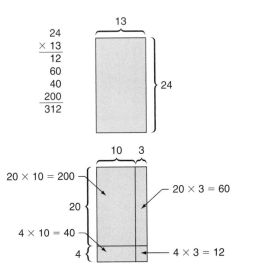

FIGURE 6-11 A rectangular model calculation of 24×13.

 Activity 6-12   Grades 3–5

Matching Pictorial and Symbolic Multiplication

Materials: Index cards, one per student, with rectangular grid representation or matching long form calculation.

Teacher Statement: When I say go, flip your card and find your partner. Go.

Example Cards:

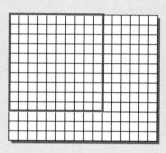

$$
\begin{array}{r}
13 \\
\times\ 16 \\
\hline
18 \\
60 \\
30 \\
100 \\
\hline
208
\end{array}
$$

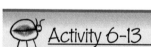 Activity 6-13   Grades 3–5

Finding Products Using Mental Math

Materials: Index cards with mental math problems.

Directions: Place students in groups of two, three, or four. Cards are placed face down, with the top card flipped over. When a member of the group knows the answer, she taps the card. The first student to tap the card states the answer and then explains how she found it. If the student is correct, she keeps that card in her pile. If she is incorrect, another student may answer that question. If two students tap a card at exactly the same time, it is a tie and the card goes back into the deck.

Example Cards:

| 38×3 | $20 \times 18 \times 5$ |

 Activity 6-14   Grades 3–5

Finding Products Using Calculators and Mental Math

Materials: Index cards with large numbers; calculator for each student.

Teacher Statement: Draw two cards, then use your calculator to find the product. The trick is, you may also need to use some mental math.

Example Cards:

| 250,000 | 32,000 |

Note: Make the numbers large enough that an eight-digit display calculator will not find the product of the numbers as given.

Example 6-12: First show 115 using base-ten blocks. Set out four plates (or draw circles) to represent four children. To share the 100, you first have to regroup. Now you have 11 longs and 5 singles.

You can put 2 longs on each plate. It remains to share 3 longs and 5 singles.

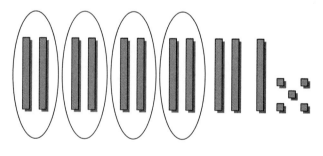

You must regroup the 3 longs.

You can distribute the 35 singles.

Putting a single on each plate takes away four at a time: 4, 8, 12 16, 20, 24, 28, 32—there are three left over.

Each plate receives 8 singles, so now has 28.

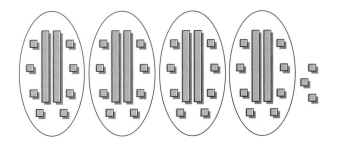

Thus, $115 \div 4 = 28\ R3$. If 115 cards are divided among four children, each gets 28 cards.

There is a convenient division notation that will show exactly what Example 6-12 shows. Instead of writing $115 \div 4$, you can write $4\overline{)115}$. This also represents 115 divided by 4. You can't share the 100 piece, so you regroup and have 11 tens and 5 ones. You put 2 tens on each plate. This takes away $2 \times 4 = 8$ tens. In the notation you write 2 above the division symbol in the tens place and subtract the 8 tens that have already been distributed from the 11 tens that were available. The notation now looks like this:

$$\begin{array}{r} 2 \\ 4\overline{)115} \\ \underline{8} \\ 3 \end{array}$$

You regrouped the 3 tens into singles and had 35 singles. In the notation you can do this by bringing down the 5 so that the notation now looks like this:

$$\begin{array}{r} 2 \\ 4\overline{)115} \\ \underline{8} \\ 35 \end{array}$$

Then you divide the 35 singles by 4, putting 8 singles on each plate. In the notation you write 8 above the division symbol in the singles position and subtract the $8 \times 4 = 32$ singles that have been distributed. There are 3 singles remaining, but this cannot be divided by 4. The notation now looks like this:

$$\begin{array}{r} 28 \\ 4\overline{)115} \\ \underline{8} \\ 35 \\ \underline{32} \\ 3 \end{array}$$

You could also write the answer as $28\ R3$, where the R stands for "remainder."

So, if 115 trading cards are divided among four children, each gets 28 cards. Are you finished with this problem? No! You should check this answer. You know it is a reasonable answer because your estimation was between 25 and 30 cards. You can formally check it by calculating $4 \times 28 = 112$ cards that were given to the children, and with the 3 cards that were left over you have accounted for all $112 + 3 = 115$ cards.

In general, because division and multiplication are inverse operations, you can always use multiplication to check the answer to a division problem. Using the general terminology and notation,

$$\text{divisor }\overline{)\text{dividend}}^{\textstyle\ quotient}$$

$$\underline{}$$
$$\textit{remainder}$$

In concrete terms, the dividend is the total number of objects, the divisor is the number of plates, the quotient is the number of objects on each plate after distribution, and the remainder is the number of objects left over. Hence, the quotient times the divisor plus the remainder should equal the dividend.

The Long Division Process After a few examples relating the standard computational form notation to a concrete model, students may be ready to tackle problems using numbers and notation alone. There are several steps in the process of long division, but if children have seen why each step makes sense, they quickly learn the process. The basic steps of the process are divide, multiply, subtract, check remainder, and bring down. An acronym that uses the first letter of each step of the process is Dawn Makes Super Chocolate Really Big Donuts. The "check remainder" step is necessary because the remainder at each step of the process must be smaller than the divisor. If it is not, then there is a mistake in a digit of the quotient. A remainder denotes how many units of a certain place value are left over. If it is larger than the divisor, then more of that place value could have been distributed. What happens when a student continues the division when a remainder was larger than a divisor will be covered when we discuss common student errors in Section 6.4.

The long division process uses the ideas of nonstandard place value and estimation. For example, consider the process that occurs in the division $29\overline{)14{,}295}$. You choose friendly numbers to estimate, 29 is approximately 30, and this divides easily into 15,000 so the answer is approximately 500. You could have chosen to estimate 14,295 as 14,000 or 14,300, but the division would not have been so easy to do with mental math. The 14 ten-thousands cannot be distributed among 29 sets, so you move on to consider 142 hundreds. You can decide how many times 29 will go into 142 by thinking "30, 60, 90, 120"—the digit of the quotient in the hundreds position is probably 4. You continue the process by multiplying $4 \times 29 = 116$ and subtracting to get

$$\begin{array}{r} 4 \\ 29{\overline{)14{,}295}} \\ \underline{116} \\ 26 \end{array}$$

Since the remainder 26 is less than the divisor 29, you bring down the 9 and continue. In concrete terms this is equivalent to placing 4 hundreds on each of 29 plates, and having 26 hundreds left that must be regrouped into tens. Because there were 9 tens originally, you are now dealing with 269 tens that must be divided by 29. Again, you can use estimation to determine the next digit of the quotient. Since $270 \div 30 = 9$, the next digit may be 9. You place 9 in the tens position of the quotient, multiply $9 \times 29 = 261$, and subtract to get

$$\begin{array}{r} 49 \\ 29{\overline{)14{,}295}} \\ \underline{116} \\ 269 \\ \underline{261} \\ 8 \end{array}$$

Again, the remainder 8 is smaller than the divisor 29, so you bring down the 5 and continue. In concrete terms you regroup the 8 tens into ones, combine them with the 5 original ones, and have 85 ones that must be now divided by 29. Suppose you estimate here as $90 \div 30 = 3$, and attempt to use 3 as the ones digit of the quotient. When you multiply $3 \times 29 = 87$ you discover a problem because 87 cannot be subtracted from 85 (without incurring negative integers). The notation at this point looks like this:

$$\begin{array}{r} 493 \\ 29{\overline{)14{,}295}} \\ \underline{116} \\ 269 \\ \underline{261} \\ 85 \\ \underline{87} \end{array}$$

Because 3×29 was too large, the ones digit of the quotient cannot be 3. You retry using a ones digit of 2 by multiplying $2 \times 29 = 58$ and subtracting to get

$$\begin{array}{r} 492 \\ 29{\overline{)14{,}295}} \\ \underline{116} \\ 269 \\ \underline{261} \\ 85 \\ \underline{58} \\ 27 \end{array}$$

The remainder 27 is less than the divisor 29 and there are no more digits to bring down. You can check this an-

swer by calculating $492 \times 29 = 14{,}268$ and $14{,}268 + 27 = 14{,}295$. The answer is correct. It is important for students to realize that they will not always choose correct digits for the quotient. Examples such as this one show them how to correct such errors. If your students see only examples for which you always choose the correct digits, they will not know how to fix an error when they choose a digit incorrectly. Estimation is a valuable tool in choosing what digits to use for the quotient, but it does not always give the correct digit on the first try.

In the above example you made the mistake of choosing a quotient digit that was too large. Students sometimes choose a quotient digit that is too small. Consider the same division example, but suppose that at this step

$$\begin{array}{r} 4 \\ 29{\overline{)14{,}295}} \\ \underline{116} \\ 269 \end{array}$$

you erroneously choose the digit 8 for the tens position of the quotient. You multiply $8 \times 29 = 232$ and subtract to get

$$\begin{array}{r} 48 \\ 29{\overline{)14{,}295}} \\ \underline{116} \\ 269 \\ \underline{232} \\ 37 \end{array}$$

You can tell that you have made an error at this point because the remainder 37 is not less than the divisor 29. In concrete terms you had 269 tens to distribute to 29 plates. Putting 8 tens on each plate left you with 37 tens. You can put an additional ten on each of the 29 plates. That is, the tens digit of the quotient should be 9 and not 8. You could correct this problem and continue as above. Again, students must be shown what types of errors can occur when choosing digits for the quotient of a division as well as how to fix such errors.

Integer Division on a Calculator Many calculators include an integer division key that is useful in performing division calculations. For example, on the Texas Instruments Explorer, the keying sequence below will yield the results shown. $\boxed{14295}$ $\boxed{\text{Int÷}}$ $\boxed{29}$ $\boxed{=}$ will result in the display.

$$\begin{array}{cc} \boxed{492} & \boxed{27} \\ Q & R \end{array}$$

The same keying sequence on a TI-15 results in the display "492 r 27." Integer division with remainders may be performed on calculators that do not include an integer division key as in Activity 6-15.

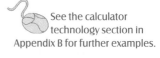

See the calculator technology section in Appendix B for further examples.

Activity 6-15   Grades 3–5

Calculator Division

Materials: Division problems; calculator for each student.

Directions for Students: Use your calculator to find the quotient and the remainder for each division problem.

Example Problem: 254 ÷ 8

Note: A calculator gives the answer 31.75 for the above problem. However, the quotient is 31 and the remainder is 6. Choose examples carefully for this activity so that children will be able to see the difference between the decimal answer given by the calculator and the division with remainder answer. They may use long division to check their answers, but must be able to explain how to use the calculator to find the answers.

Activity 6-16   Grades 3–8

Number Puzzles

Materials: Index cards with number puzzles.

Directions for Students: Find at least one answer for each puzzle. Some puzzles have more than one correct answer. If time allows, find additional answers.

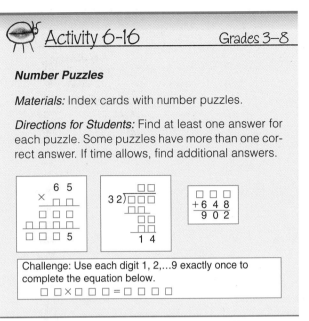

Source: Adapted from Troutman & Lichtenberg, 2003.

Interpreting the Remainder A common problem in elementary-level textbooks at the third-grade level and higher is to interpret the effect of a remainder in a division with remainder story problem. In some cases, the remainder may be ignored. In other cases, a remainder implies that the quotient of the calculation must be increased in order to provide an answer to the given problem. Consider the two problems shown in Example 6-13.

Example 6-13:

   a. 115 trading cards are to be divided equally among four children. How many cards should each child get?

   b. 115 children are in line for a ride at an amusement park. If four children ride at one time, how many times must the ride be run?

For both problems given in this example, the division sentence is $115 \div 4 = 28\ R3$. However, the answer to the problem given in (a) is that each child should get 28 cards, whereas the answer to the problem given in (b) is that the ride must be run 29 times.

 Teaching Connections

Use Games and Fun Activities to Practice Multiplication and Division Number riddles such as those presented in the two following activities can be used to reinforce relationships between operations. Children should understand and be able to use the inverse relationships of multiplication and division or addition and subtraction. Although some riddles and puzzles have a unique answer, others have many correct solutions. In constructing number riddles and

Activity 6-17   Grades 3–5

Mental Math Number Riddles

Materials: Index cards with number riddles.

Teacher Statement: I will read each riddle twice. Solve the riddle using mental math.

Example:

> If I am multiplied by 3 and then 4 is added, the result is 19. What number am I?

puzzles, it is important that you, the teacher, either know how to find all the correct answers to such riddles and puzzles or at least be able to verify whether a given answer is correct.

Problem Set 6.3

For Your Understanding

1. Estimate the computation and answer to 243 × 42 using
   a. friendly numbers
   b. front-end estimation
   c. rounding to the nearest ten

2. Show a rectangular model calculation and the associated long and short form notation for 26 × 31.

3. Jonathan dropped his homework paper in a puddle and some of the digits blurred. Determine the missing digits.

4. Give a numerical multiplication example where the rounding estimate is greater than the actual answer.

5. Write out the thought process for the two examples shown in Activity 6-13.

6. Give a justification for each step:

$$206 \times 4 = (200 + 6) \times 4$$
$$(200 \times 4) + (6 \times 4)$$
$$(200 \times 4) + 24$$
$$[(2 \times 100) \times 4] + 24$$
$$[(100 \times 2) \times 4] + 24$$
$$[100 \times (2 \times 4)] + 24$$
$$[100 \times 8] + 24$$
$$800 + 24$$
$$824$$

7. Find answers to the number puzzles in Activity 6-16.

8. Use the digits 1, 2, 3, 4, and 5 once each to create (a) the largest possible product and (b) the smallest possible product using the format shown.

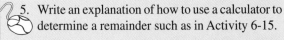

Applications in the Classroom

1. Draw base-ten block diagrams to illustrate 3×46. Show all necessary regroupings. Then write an explanation that could be used in presenting the example to a third-grade class.

2. Make a set of cards for Activity 6-12 that could be used in a class of 24 students.

3. Make a set of 20 mental math cards that could be used with Activity 6-13.

4. Draw base-ten block diagrams that illustrate the process of $1,128 \div 6$. Write an explanation of the step-by-step process of this division that could be used in presenting the example to a fourth-grade class.

5. Write an explanation of how to use a calculator to determine a remainder such as in Activity 6-15.

6. Make up a numerical division example and write two story problems using the same numbers. In one problem the remainder should be ignored and in the other problem, the remainder must be considered in the solution to the problem. Give the solutions to the problems as well.

7. Obtain a calculator that contains an integer division key. Practice using this feature until you are comfortable with it. Write a lesson plan in which you show how to use this feature to a fourth-grade class.

8. Which example would you present first in introducing division notation to a third-grade class? Explain your choice.
   a. $4\overline{)23}$
   b. $6\overline{)21}$

9. What is the best order in which to present the following multiplication examples to a third-grade class? Explain your choices.
   a. 6×23
   b. 4×14
   c. 3×20
   d. 2×32

10. Create an assessment tool to be used with Activity 6-14. Explain why you chose that type of assessment tool.

11. Write a formal third-grade-level lesson plan that introduces the vertical format of multiplication of a two-digit number by a one-digit number. Use the examples given in problem 9 above in your plan. Follow the format given by your instructor or use the lesson plan format given in the Appendices.

12. Create an assessment tool to be used with the lesson created in problem 11 above. Explain why you chose that type of assessment tool.

13. Look at either a multiplication chapter or a division chapter in an elementary-level textbook. Photocopy or copy by hand one example or problem that you think is interesting or unusual and indicate why. What objective from the NCTM model (or from your state or district model) does the example or problem address? Be sure to state what grade-level text you are using.

14. Find and print a multiplication or division activity from the Web. State what grade level you think the activity would be appropriate for. What objective from the NCTM model (or from your state or district model) does the activity address?

15. Make up a multiplication or division activity or game. What objective from the NCTM model (or from your state or district model) does the activity or game address? Indicate what grade level your activity is appropriate for.

16. Choose an activity from this chapter. Indicate how you could implement the activity as a collaborative learning experience.

17. Choose one of the books in the children's literature section of the references for this chapter. Give a brief description of the content of the book and explain how you could incorporate the book into a math lesson.

18. Make up two writing prompts or stems that fit in with material or activities from this chapter.

6.4 Avoiding Common Student Errors and Using Fun Math Tricks

As discussed in the previous chapters, if students have acquired the habit of estimating and checking answers, they can avoid many common student errors. This section focuses on seven common difficulties with multiplication and division situations and problems. Some of these difficulties and remedies are similar to difficulties that occur with addition and subtraction, as discussed in Section 5.4. Many of the errors presented here, as well as other common student errors, may be found in Ashlock (2002) and Troutman and Lichtenberg (2003).

Difficulties with Multiplication or Division Story Problems

Wrong Operation When children don't take the time to carefully consider what is going on in a problem, they may choose the wrong operation. Consider this problem: "Jose sells three times as many tickets to the school play as Sheila sells. Jose sells 147 tickets. How many tickets does Sheila sell?" A common student error for this type of problem is for the student to use multiplication instead of division. The phrase "three times as many" indicates multiplication to a child who has learned to solve problems by looking for key phrases and rules to perform rather than by thinking about the situation. As a teacher, you must give your students the time they need to think. If necessary, provide concrete objects so that the students can act out a problem. Encourage your students to check their answers and use estimation.

Wrong Information As addressed earlier, elementary textbooks commonly include problems that contain extra information or not enough information. Again, students must be encouraged to check their answers. An answer to a problem should fit the conditions of the problem, use the correct information, and answer the question asked in the problem.

Wrong Equations It is a common error in division to write digits in the wrong positions. That is, a student may intend 250 divided by 15 and may accidentally write $250 \overline{)15}$ instead of $15 \overline{)250}$. He may also make the error of writing $15 \div 250$ instead of $250 \div 15$.

Difficulty Using the Remainder in a Division Problem When a division story problem includes a nonzero remainder, children must use logical thinking to determine how the remainder affects the solution. Children should be encouraged to check their answers to determine whether they have correctly used the problem information, and whether the answer fits the conditions of the problem.

Basic Fact Errors

Incorrect Rule Usage Children who attempt to memorize rules without regard to the reasonableness of the rules may make mistakes such as $5 \times 0 = 5$. A child who makes such a mistake has probably confused the "$n \times 1 = n$" and the "$n \times 0 = 0$" rules. Rules and procedures should be justified by concrete interpretations so that they make sense to the students.

Basic Multiplication Fact Errors Before children have memorized the basic multiplication facts, they may make errors in the computations of basic facts. It takes time, practice, and patience to memorize basic multiplication facts. Make sure that students have seen a variety of strategies for computation of basic facts so that they may choose a strategy that works well for them personally. Multiplication properties, fact families, and the use of known facts may be useful in learning new facts.

Basic Division Fact Errors Children need a solid foundation in multiplication facts before they are ready to learn or memorize division facts. It is important that children understand the inverse relationship between multiplication and division.

Difficulties with Place Value or Multiple of Ten Facts

Multiplication Difficulties Children who attempt to use rules to calculate without regard to the reasonableness of their answers may make errors such as "$50 \times 600 = 3,000$ since 5×6 is 30 and the answer should have three zeros." Encourage estimation and checking of answers. Nonstandard place value ideas can also be useful in such problems.

Division Difficulties Division problems such as $50 \overline{)30,000}$ may bring about wrong answers such as 6,000 or 60. Again, estimation and checking of answers should be encouraged. Nonstandard place value ideas can also be useful in such problems.

Difficulties with Zero
Incorrect Usage of Rules Involving Zero

$$\begin{array}{r} 203 \\ \times\ 2 \\ \hline 426 \end{array} \qquad \begin{array}{r} 423 \\ 2\overline{)806} \end{array}$$

Remind students to check their answers. Use concrete materials and appropriate activities to reteach rules such as "$0 \times n = 0$" and "$0 \div n = 0$."

Omitting or Ignoring Zeros

$$\begin{array}{r} 302 \\ \times\ 4 \\ \hline 128 \end{array} \qquad \begin{array}{r} 43 \\ 2\overline{)806} \end{array} \qquad \begin{array}{r} 431 \\ 20\overline{)862} \end{array}$$

Remind students to check their answers and to use estimation. Use concrete materials and appropriate activities to reteach rules and procedures as necessary.

Difficulty Using the Distributive Property of Multiplication over Addition

$$\begin{array}{r} 23 \\ \times\ 4 \\ \hline 212 \end{array} \qquad \begin{array}{r} 23 \\ \times\ 41 \\ \hline 83 \end{array} \qquad \begin{array}{r} 23 \\ \times\ 41 \\ \hline 823 \end{array} \qquad \begin{array}{r} 21 \\ \times\ 47 \\ \hline 147 \end{array}$$

In addition and subtraction experiences, children are told to "keep their columns straight" and to add ones to ones, tens to tens, and so on. Students should be shown using concrete models such as base-ten blocks and the rectangular model why the distributive property makes sense. Otherwise, they will make errors such as those shown. They should also be encouraged to estimate and to check their answers. Long form notation can also be useful.

Difficulties with Regrouping
Does Not Regroup or Regroups Incorrectly

$$\begin{array}{r} 34 \\ \times\ 3 \\ \hline 912 \end{array} \qquad \begin{array}{r} 2\ \ \ \\ 34 \\ \times\ 3 \\ \hline 111 \end{array} \qquad \begin{array}{r} 2{,}121 \\ 3\overline{)6{,}473} \end{array}$$

Difficulties within the Long Division Process Does not complete division upon encountering a zero remainder or does not check that remainder is less than divisor.

$$\begin{array}{r} 24 \\ 3\overline{)724} \\ \underline{6} \\ 12 \\ \underline{12} \\ 0 \end{array} \qquad \begin{array}{r} 310R10 \\ 13\overline{)530} \\ \underline{39} \\ 140 \\ \underline{130} \\ 10 \end{array}$$

Uses Regrouped Digits Incorrectly

$$\begin{array}{r} 2\ \ \ \\ 34 \\ \times\ 7 \\ \hline 428 \end{array} \qquad \begin{array}{r} 2\ \ \ \\ 37 \\ \times\ 3 \\ \hline 91 \end{array}$$

Most of the errors above can be avoided if students learn to estimate and check their answers. When errors such as these are made, reteach processes using concrete materials so that children see how and why the regrouping process works.

Difficulty Aligning Partial Products

$$\begin{array}{r} 46 \\ \times\ 52 \\ \hline 92 \\ 230 \\ \hline 322 \end{array} \qquad \begin{array}{r} 65 \\ \times\ 37 \\ \hline 455 \\ 195 \\ \hline 650 \end{array}$$

Again, these kinds of errors can be avoided if students learn to estimate and check their answers. When errors such as these are made, reteach processes using concrete materials so that children see how and why the distributive process works. Do not suppress zeros when writing out partial products. Be sure to stress place value in your verbal explanation of such products. The second product in the first example is not 5×46 but 50×46. The second product in the second example is not 3×65 but 30×65.

The seven types of errors discussed cover many of the main errors that will be made when students work with multiplication and division. However, there are bound to be errors made in your classroom that have not been covered here. You must be able to diagnose and remediate such errors. Encouraging your students to explain their answers both verbally and in writing can help you discover and diagnose student errors. In some cases, a student who is working a multiplication or division problem may have troubles related to her addition or subtraction abilities. In this case you must be sure that she has learned all prerequisite skills before continuing the multiplication or division lesson.

Math Tricks

Two math tricks that your students may enjoy are evens times 5 and $n =$ blanks equals. The following sections describe how the tricks work and how they can help in learning everyday math. The first trick can be found in several "fun math" activity books.

Trick 1: Evens Times Five Challenge a member of your audience (or your students) to a multiplication race. Write a multiplication problem with the first factor a large number with all even digits, for example 244,806,462, and the second factor 5. It will take your opponent some time to do the calculation, but you immediately write the answer 1,224,032,310. Look at the examples below and see if you can spot the trick.

244,806,462	46,800,228	4,622,804	6,802
$\times$ 5	$\times$ 5	$\times$ 5	$\times$ 5
1,224,032,310	234,001,140	23,114,020	34,010

Did you see the pattern? Compare the digits of the answers to the digits of the first factor. When a number with all even digits is multiplied by 5, you may write the answer without really doing the calculation. To write the answer, append a zero and divide each of the digits of the first factor by 2. Of course, the commas in the answer must be shifted by one position due to the zero that is appended.

Why does it work? To multiply by a factor of 5 is the same as to multiply by a factor of 10 and divide by 2. After all, $5 = 10 \div 2$. By choosing all the digits of the first factor to be even, it is easy to divide this number by 2. The appending of zero takes care of multiplying by 10. Students at approximately the fourth-grade level and higher enjoy this trick.

Trick 2: *n*-Blanks Equals For this trick you need a calculator that stores the last operation performed. To check whether a calculator will do this, press $2 + 3$ and then press the equals sign ($=$) several times. If the calculator displays only 5, it does not store the last operation performed and will not be useful for this trick. If the calculator displays 5, 8, 11, 14, . . . upon repeatedly pressing the equals sign, then it can be used for this trick. Initial illustrations of the trick should involve 10 blanks as this is the easiest problem of this type to solve. Write the following sequence on the board:

$$2 + 3 = \underline{\hspace{1cm}} = \underline{\hspace{1cm}} = \underline{\hspace{1cm}} = \underline{\hspace{1cm}} =$$
$$\underline{\hspace{1cm}} = \underline{\hspace{1cm}} = \underline{\hspace{1cm}} = \underline{\hspace{1cm}} =$$
$$\underline{\hspace{1cm}} = \underline{\hspace{1cm}} .$$

Tell your audience (or your students) that you can figure out what should go into the last blank before the calculator figures it out. Write 32 in the last blank. Then have a student enter the sequence into a calculator. Fill in the blanks as the student calls out the answers. Invite other students without calculators to call out answers if they can see the pattern. The end result will look like this:

$$2 + 3 = \underline{5} = \underline{8} = \underline{11} = \underline{14} = \underline{17} = \underline{20} =$$
$$\underline{23} = \underline{26} = \underline{29} = \underline{32} .$$

Do several more examples of 10-blanks equals, so that children see the pattern and are also able to fill in the last blank before entering the sequence into a calculator or before figuring out the intermediate blanks mentally. Be sure to show examples where the numbers are entered in a different order. For example, $3 + 2$ with 10 blanks equals 23, the problem $5 + 4$ with 10 blanks equals 45, and the problem $4 + 5$

with 10 blanks equals 54. Do you see the pattern? If not, try a few more examples before reading further.

The final blank in a 10-blank example will contain the digits of the addition in reverse order. This is because the calculator repeatedly adds the second addend. With 10 blanks, the second addend will appear in the tens position whereas the first addend appears in the ones position of the final answer. After students understand how to fill the 10th blank, challenge them to figure out how to fill another position without filling in the intermediate numbers. For example, if only five blanks are used, then the fifth blank of the sequence $2 + 3$ would be filled with 17 since $5 \times 3 + 2 = 17$. The eighth blank of the $3 + 2$ sequence is 19 since $8 \times 2 + 3 = 19$. Using a little mental math, you can figure out how to fill any blank without filling in intermediate blanks. All it takes is one multiplication and one addition.

Teaching Connections

The Use of Math Tricks in Everyday Math The evens times 5 trick contains a skill that may be applied to everyday math situations. Suppose you went to the store and wanted to buy 5 widgets that each cost \$0.46. You could calculate the cost immediately by thinking that 10 widgets would cost \$4.60, so 5 widgets would cost half of that or \$2.30. Although this trick is easiest to use on numbers with all even digits, it may also be used when the first factor has odd digits. For example, if you want to buy 5 gadgets that each cost \$0.45, then 10 gadgets would be \$4.50, so 5 gadgets would be \$2.25. In general, the fewer odd digits in the first factor, the easier it is to find half of that factor. The trick may actually be used when the first factor has all odd digits. For example, $375 \times 5 = 3,750 \div 2 = 1,875$.

The *n*-blanks equals trick is useful in everyday math because it reminds you of the relationship of multiplication and repeated addition. When a problem calls for repeated addition of the same addend, multiplication can shorten the process. In general, math tricks are useful to sharpen math skills and to encourage student excitement about mathematics.

Problem Set 6.4

1. For each problem shown, state what error the student is making. Try to determine exactly what the student is thinking. Also indicate what you as a teacher could do to help a student who makes this type of error.
   a. Latisha bought a bag with 80 pieces of bubble gum. She wishes to share this with five friends by giving each friend 10 pieces. How many pieces does Latisha have left? Student's answer is 14. Student's work: $80 - 10 = 70$ and $70 \div 5 = 14$.

b.   25
  × 6
  123

   3
c.   38
  × 4
  242

        14
d. 38)4,204
     38
     164
     152
      12

2. For each problem shown, state what error the student is making. Try to determine exactly what the student is thinking. Also indicate what you as a teacher could do to help a student who makes this type of error.

   a. $5 \times 4 = 20$, so $5 \times 6 = 22$

   b. $400 \times 50 = 2,000$

   c.   603
      × 2
      126

   d.   63
       × 22
       126

         6
   e.   28
       × 7
       205

        52
   f.   28
       × 73
        84
       196
       280

          52
   g. 27)1,282
        135
         72
         54
         18

3. Without using a calculator, determine what number should appear in the specified blank for each of the *n*-blanks equals addition problems given. Then write out and fill in the appropriate number of blanks to check your answers.
   a. 7 + 2; the 10th blank equals _____
   b. 2 + 7; the 10th blank equals _____
   c. 2 + 7; the 4th blank equals _____
   d. 7 + 2; the 4th blank equals _____
   e. 7 + 2; the 15th blank equals _____
   f. 7 + 2; the 20th blank equals _____

4. Practice the evens times 5 trick by challenging other students, your friends, or family.

Note: Problems 5–7 involve Napier's bones, a middle school-level manipulative used for multiplication. A discussion of this manipulative may be found at the textbook companion Web site.

5. Use a computer to make a set of Napier's bones. Demonstrate their use to a friend or family member.

6. Write a paragraph that discusses the relationship of Napier's bones and the distributive property of multiplication over addition.

7. Explain how you could use Napier's bones to compute 144×88. Remember, a standard set has only one of each bone. Draw pictures to illustrate your explanation.

References

Children's Literature References

Appelt, Kathi. (1999). *Bats on parade*. New York: William Morrow.

Giganti, Paul. (1999). *Each orange had 8 slices: A counting book*. Blackburn, Lancashire: Mulberry Books.

Hong, Lily Toy. (1993). *Two of everything: A Chinese folktale*. Morton Grove, IL: Albert Whitman.

Hutchins, Pat. (1986). *The doorbell rang*. New York: Scholastic.

Leedy, Loreen. (1995). *2 × 2 = Boo! A set of spooky multiplication stories*. Bridgewater, NJ: Holiday House.

McGrath, Barbara. (1998). *More M&M's brand chocolate candies math*. Watertown, MA: Charlesbridge.

Murphy, Stuart. (1997). *Divide and ride* (Mathstart Level 3—Dividing). New York: HarperCollins Juvenile Books.

Neuschwander, Cindy. (1998). *Amanda Bean's amazing dream*. New York: Scholastic.

Pallotta, Jerry. (2000). *Reeses Pieces*. New York: Cartwheel Books.

Pallotta, Jerry. (2002). *The Hershey's Milk Chocolate multiplication book*. New York: Cartwheel Books.

Pinczes, Elinor. (1996). *Arctic fives arrive.* New York: Scholastic.

Pinczes, Elinor. (1999). *One hundred hungry ants.* Boston: Houghton Mifflin.

Rocklin, Joanne. (1997). *One hungry cat* (Hello Math Reader Level 3). New York: Scholastic.

Trivas, Irene. (1988). *Emma's Christmas: An old song.* New York: Scholastic.

Teacher Resources

Ashlock, R. B. (2002). *Error patterns in computation: Using error patterns to improve instruction* (8th ed.). Upper Saddle River, NJ: Pearson Education, Inc.

National Council of Teachers of Mathematics. (2000). *Principles and standards for school mathematics.* Reston, VA: Author.

North Carolina Department of Public Instruction. (2003). *North Carolina Mathematics Standard Course Study and Grade Level Competencies K-12.* Retrieved November 19, 2003, from http://www.dpi.state.nc.us/curriculum/mathematics/standard2003/index.html

Ohio Department of Education. (2001). *Ohio Academic Content Standards.* Retrieved November 12, 2003 from http://www.ode.state.oh.us/academic_content_standards/pdf/MATH.pdf

Ohio Office of Early Childhood Education and Office of Curriculum and Instruction. (2003). *Ohio Early Learning Content Standards.* Retrieved December 1, 2003 from http://www.ode.state.oh.us/ece/ pdf/Mathematics/pdf

Troutman A. P., & Lichtenberg, B. K. (2003). *Mathematics—A Good Beginning* (6th ed.). Belmont, CA: Wadsworth, Thomson Learning, Inc.

Selected Research Books and Articles

Fuson, K. C. (1992). Research on learning and teaching addition and subtraction of whole numbers. In *Analysis of arithmetic for mathematics teaching* (pp. 52–188). G. Leinhardt, R. Putnam, & R. Hattrup (Eds.). Hillsdale, NJ: Erlbaum.

Groves S. (1994, April). *Calculators: A learning environment to promote number sense.* Paper presented at the annual meeting of the American Educational Research Association, New Orleans.

Further Reading

Anghileri, J. (1989). An investigation of young children's understanding of multiplication. *Educational Studies in Mathematics, 20,* 367–385.

Baek, J. (1998). Children's invented algorithms for multidigit multiplication problems. In L. Morrow (Ed.), *The teaching and learning of algorithms in school mathematics, 1998 Yearbook* Reston, VA: National Council of Teachers of Mathematics. (pp. 151–160).

Behrend, J. L. (2001). Are rules interfering with children's mathematical understanding? *Teaching Children Mathematics, 8*(1), 36–40.

Burns, M. (1989). Teaching for understanding: A focus on multiplication. In P. R. Trafton (Ed.), *New directions for elementary school mathematics* (pp. 123–133). Reston, VA: National Council of Teachers of Mathematics.

Burns, M. (1995). *Math by all means: Multiplication, grade 3.* Sausalito, CA: Math Solution Publications.

Cantlon, D. (1998). Kids + conjecture = mathematics power. *Teaching Children Mathematics, 5,* 108–112.

Carroll, W. M., & Porter, D. (1998). Alternative algorithms for whole number operations. In L. Morrow (Ed.), *The teaching and learning of algorithms in school mathematics, 1998 Yearbook* (pp. 106–114). Reston, VA: National Council of Teachers of Mathematics.

Clark, F. B., & Kamii, C. K. (1996). Identification of multiplicative thinking in children in grades 1–5. *Journal for Research in Mathematics Education, 27,* 41–51.

Dubitsky, B. (1988, November). Making division meaningful with a spreadsheet. *Arithmetic Teacher, 36,* 18–21.

Graeber, A. O., & Baker, K. M. (1992). Little into big is the way it always is. *Arithmetic Teacher, 39*(8), 18–21.

Hall, W. D. (1983, November). Division with base-ten blocks. *Arithmetic Teacher,* 21–23.

Hosmer, P. C. (1986). Students can write their own problems. *Arithmetic Teacher, 34*(4), 10–11.

Huinker, D. M. (1989). Multiplication and division word problems: Improving students' understanding. *Arithmetic Teacher, 37*(2), 8–12.

Killion, K., & Steffe, L. P. (1989). Children's multiplication. *Arithmetic Teacher, 37*(1), 34–36.

Kouba, V. L. (1989, March). Children's strategies for equivalent set multiplication and division word problems. *Journal for Research in Mathematics Education, 20,* 147–158.

Kouba, V. L., & Franklin, K. (1995). Multiplication and division: Sense making and meaning. In R. J. Jensen (Ed.). *Research ideas for the classroom: Early childhood mathematics* (pp. 103–126). New York: Macmillan.

Ohanian, S., & Burns, M. (1995). *Math by all means: Division, grades 3–4.* Sausalito, CA: Math Solution Publications.

Quintero, A. H. (1985, November). Conceptual understanding of multiplication: Problems involving combination. *Arithmetic Teacher, 33,* 36–39.

Suydam, M. N. (1985, March). Improving multiplication skills. *Arithmetic Teacher, 32,* 52.

Thornton, C. A. (1989). *Basic number facts—Strategies for teaching and learning. Book 11: Multiplication and division. An Activity Based Book.* (ERIC Document Reproduction Service No. ED316426)

7

Exploring Number Theory Concepts and Operations

This chapter begins with a discussion of order of operations and arithmetic and algebraic calculators. To successfully use a calculator, you must be familiar with the logic used by the calculator. Calculator usage in the elementary classroom has increased tremendously in the last decade. "Technology can be used in the elementary grades to enhance a concrete, experimental approach to mathematical topics, enabling students to have greater success with a more symbolic, abstract approach later in school" (Flores, 2002, p. 308).

This chapter also discusses factors, multiples, divisors, divisibility, and primes. Children are usually intrigued by the fact that there are an infinite number of prime numbers and that new prime numbers are continually being discovered. At first glance it may appear that these topics are too sophisticated for the early childhood curriculum. However, many of the number theory ideas presented here are specifically for the early grades. It is never too early to foster an appreciation of number properties and patterns.

Number theory can be a fun topic for children. Many number theory problems challenge a child's problem-solving and logical thinking skills. Number theory can also be a fun topic for you, the future teacher. It is hoped that you find many ideas within this chapter that you will carry with you into the classroom.

Standards

NCTM

Students' understanding of properties of numbers develops gradually from preschool through high school. While young children are skip counting by twos, they may notice that the numbers they are using end in 0, 2, 4, 6, and 8; they could then use this algebraic observation to extend the pattern.

NCTM, 2000, p. 38

Standards are listed with the permission of the National Council of Teachers of Mathematics (NCTM). NCTM does not endorse the content or validity of these alignments.

Objectives

After completing Chapter 7, you will be able to

- Describe two types of calculator logic and determine the result of entering a given expression into a calculator of a given type
- Calculate expressions using order of operation rules
- Discuss how children develop concepts of number theory such as parity, factors and multiples, prime, and composite
- Use appropriate tests to determine whether a number is divisible by 2, 3, 4, 5, 6, 9, or 10
- Draw a factor tree, draw the factor rainbow, and find the prime factorization of a given number
- Compute the greatest common factor or least common multiple of a set of numbers and solve word problems involving these ideas

7.1 Calculator Expressions and Order of Operations

At approximately the third-grade level, children encounter word problems in which more than one operation is necessary for the solution. A typical third-grade-level example is given below.

Example 7-1: Tickets to a movie cost $5 for each adult and $3 for each child. How much does a family of two adults and three children pay to get into the movie?

Solution: The family pays $19 since $2 \times 5 + 3 \times 3 = 19$.

At this level, students have not yet learned the rules for order of operations. Formal rules for order of operations are usually presented at the fifth-grade level. However, it is logical for this problem to first perform the multiplications to find that the adults' tickets cost $10 and the children's tickets cost $9, and then to add these quantities. A third- or fourth-grade student may even write this expression using parentheses as $(2 \times 5) + (3 \times 3) = 19$.

Two Types of Calculator Logic— Arithmetic and Algebraic

If the expression $\boxed{2}\ \boxed{\times}\ \boxed{5}\ \boxed{+}\ \boxed{3}\ \boxed{\times}\ \boxed{3}\ \boxed{=}$ were entered into a calculator, the calculator might display the answer 19. If the same expression were entered into a different calculator, this second calculator might display the answer 39. Why would two different calculators give two different answers for the same keying sequence? There are two types of logic used in common handheld calculators. A calculator that uses *algebraic logic* will (in the absence of parentheses) perform multiplications before additions and follow other standard order of operations conventions. A calculator that uses *arithmetic logic* will perform operations as they are entered without regard to the standard order of operations conventions. Which calculator is correct? It depends on the situation. Consider the following example.

See the calculator technology section in Appendix B for further discussion of various calculators.

Example 7-2: Five couples and three single students go to a dance. Tickets to the dance cost $3 each. How much money is collected in tickets?

Solution: There are $2 \times 5 + 3 = 13$ students going to the dance. Each pays $3, and $13 \times 3 = 39$. Because you first must find the total number of students and then multiply that total by 3, the expression could be written using parentheses as $(2 \times 5 + 3) \times 3 = 39$. A total of $39 in ticket money to the dance is collected.

If the expression $\boxed{2}\ \boxed{\times}\ \boxed{5}\ \boxed{+}\ \boxed{3}\ \boxed{\times}\ \boxed{3}\ \boxed{=}$ were entered into a calculator that used algebraic logic, the calculator would display the correct answer to the problem in Example 7-1, but not the correct answer to the problem in Example 7-2. If the same expression were entered into a calculator that used arithmetic logic, the answer displayed would be the correct answer to the problem in Example 7-2, but not the correct answer to the problem in Example 7-1. This illustrates that to correctly use a calculator to solve a problem, you cannot merely punch in the numbers as they appear in the problem. You must know what type of calculator you are using and whether it will perform operations in the order that they are needed for the problem. In fact, you often need more knowledge to be able to solve a problem using a calculator than you would need to solve the problem without it. We will discuss calculator usage later in this section.

Formal Order of Operations Rules

As you have already discovered, when the expression $2 \times 5 + 3 \times 3$ is evaluated by first performing the multiplications and then performing the addition the result is different than when it is evaluated by performing the operations as they occur. In order that two different people evaluating such an expression get the same answer, mathematicians have established rules for priority of operations. You may remember learning the phrase "*P*lease *E*xcuse *M*y *D*ear *A*unt *S*ally." This is a pneumonic, a phrase that is easily remembered where the first letters of the words are the same as the first letters of the words of an expression that is not as easily remembered. In this case, the pneumonic represents the priority rules "*P*arentheses, *E*xponents, *M*ultiplication, *D*ivision, *A*ddition, *S*ubtraction." One problem with memorizing a pneumonic such as this is that you must be sure that you can use it properly. There are actually only four levels of priority represented by this six-term phrase.

1. Operations within parentheses are performed before other operations.
2. Exponents (and single-number operations such as square roots) are computed.
3. Multiplications and divisions are completed (before additions and subtractions).
4. Additions and subtractions are completed.

Many students who have memorized the phrase "Please Excuse My Dear Aunt Sally" believe incorrectly that multiplications must be performed before divisions and additions must be performed before subtractions. However, according to the official mathematical rules, multiplications and divisions are operations of the same level and must be performed left to right as they occur in the problem. Additions and subtractions are also of the same level and must be performed left to right as they occur. If you wish to use the pneumonic above, you may wish to think of "My Dear" as a single adjective phrase describing a single person "Aunt Sally." The four levels of priority (parentheses, exponents, multiplications and divisions, and additions and subtractions) are then appropriately represented by "<u>P</u>lease <u>Excuse</u> <u>My Dear</u> <u>Aunt Sally</u>." Several examples of the use of the rules of priority are given in Example 7-3.

Example 7-3: Evaluate each of the following expressions.

a. $24 \div 6 \times 2 + 3$
b. $24 \div (6 \times 2) + 3$
c. $15 - 7 - 2$
d. $2 + 4 \times 3^2 - 7$
e. $\sqrt{49} - 2 \times 3$
f. $12 - 4 + 6$
g. $\sqrt{9 + 16}$
h. $\dfrac{-7 - \sqrt{7^2 - 4 \times 6 \times 1}}{2 \times 6}$
i. $\dfrac{(7 + 4 \times 2) \times 2}{30 \div 2 - 5}$

Solutions:

a. $24 \div 6 \times 2 + 3 = 4 \times 2 + 3 = 8 + 3 = 11$
b. $24 \div (6 \times 2) + 3 = 24 \div 12 + 3 = 2 + 3 = 5$
c. $15 - 7 - 2 = 8 - 2 = 6$
d. $2 + 4 \times 3^2 - 7 = 2 + 4 \times 9 - 7 = 2 + 36 - 7 = 38 - 7 = 31$
e. $\sqrt{49} - 2 \times 3 = 7 - 2 \times 3 = 7 - 6 = 1$
f. $12 - 4 + 6 = 8 + 6 = 14$
g. $\sqrt{9 + 16} = \sqrt{25} = 5$
h. $\dfrac{-7 - \sqrt{7^2 - 4 \times 6 \times 1}}{2 \times 6} =$

$\dfrac{-7 - \sqrt{49 - 24}}{2 \times 6} =$

$\dfrac{-7 - \sqrt{25}}{12} = \dfrac{-7 - 5}{12} = \dfrac{-12}{12} = -1$

i. $\dfrac{(7 + 4 \times 2) \times 2}{30 \div 2 - 5} = \dfrac{(7 + 8) \times 2}{30 \div 2 - 5} =$

$\dfrac{15 \times 2}{30 \div 2 - 5} = \dfrac{30}{15 - 5} = \dfrac{30}{10} = 3$

The expressions given in parts (h) and (i) of Example 7-3 are more complicated than those that would typically occur in an early childhood classroom situation. These examples are included to illustrate that sometimes parentheses are implied by mathematical operations. For example, an expression under a square root symbol must be evaluated before the square root is taken. The division line in a fraction effectively acts as two sets of parentheses because both the numerator and denominator must be completely evaluated before the division can be performed.

Expressions Involving Exponents Special care must be taken in evaluating expressions involving exponents. In an exponential expression with a positive exponent, the *exponent* tells how many times the *base* is to be used as a factor. For the expression 2^4, the base is 2 and the exponent is 4. This expression is read as "two to the fourth" or "two to the fourth power." The expression is evaluated as $2 \times 2 \times 2 \times 2 = 16$.

It is common for students to mistakenly evaluate an expression such as 3^2 as 6. To evaluate an expression involving a positive exponent, you must realize that the base is not multiplied by the exponent, but that the exponent indicates the number of times the base should be multiplied by itself. For example, $3^2 = 3 \times 3 = 9$ and $2^3 = 2 \times 2 \times 2 = 8$. An exponent of two is generally read as "squared." An exponent of three is read as "cubed." An exponent of n, where n is greater than three, is read as "to the nth" or "to the nth power."

Example 7-4: Evaluate the expressions and indicate how each expression is read.

a. 6^2
b. 4^3
c. 3^4
d. 2^5

Solutions:

a. Six squared equals $6 \times 6 = 36$.
b. Four cubed equals $4 \times 4 \times 4 = 64$.
c. Three to the fourth (or three to the fourth power) equals $3 \times 3 \times 3 \times 3 = 81$.
d. Two to the fifth (or two to the fifth power) equals $2 \times 2 \times 2 \times 2 \times 2 = 32$.

Using Calculators to Evaluate Expressions Involving More than One Operation

The use of technology, including use of calculators, is becoming increasingly widespread in elementary education. Some state proficiency exams include calculator questions at the third-grade and higher levels. At the fourth- or fifth-grade level, students are expected to be familiar and proficient with both types of calculators. The following is a typical fourth- or fifth-grade-level example.

Example 7-5: Using calculators.

Both Juan and Marge enter the following keying sequence into their calculators.

$$\boxed{4}\ \boxed{+}\ \boxed{3}\ \boxed{\times}\ \boxed{6}\ \boxed{=}$$

Juan's calculator gives the answer 22. Marge's calculator gives the answer 42. What answers will be given by Juan's calculator and by Marge's calculator if they both enter the sequence below?

$$\boxed{6}\ \boxed{+}\ \boxed{8}\ \boxed{\div}\ \boxed{2}\ \boxed{=}$$

Solution: Juan's calculator is using algebraic logic. It will give the answer of $6 + 4 = 10$ for the given keying sequence. Marge's calculator is using arithmetic logic. It will give the answer $14 \div 2 = 7$ for the given keying sequence.

To use a calculator to evaluate an expression involving more than one operation, you must first determine whether the calculator uses algebraic logic or arithmetic logic. You must then determine a keying sequence so that the calculator that you intend to use will correctly evaluate the expression.

In some cases, there are a variety of keying sequences that will suffice. Some calculator models include keys that represent parentheses; other models do not. In Example 7-6, keying sequences for various calculators are determined so that expressions are evaluated according to standard order of operations rules.

Example 7-6: Determining a valid keying sequence. Determine a valid keying sequence for each expression using an arithmetic calculator and an algebraic calculator.

a. $24 \div 6 \times 2 + 3$
b. $24 \div (6 \times 2) + 3$
c. $150 - (71 - 26)$
d. $(26 + 18) \div 2$
e. $5 + 3 \times 2^4 - 7$

Solutions:

a. The keying sequence given below can be used with either an arithmetic calculator or an algebraic calculator.

$$\boxed{24}\;\boxed{\div}\;\boxed{6}\;\boxed{\times}\;\boxed{2}\;\boxed{+}\;\boxed{3}\;\boxed{=}$$

b. If the calculator includes parentheses keys, the keying sequence below can be used.

$$\boxed{24}\;\boxed{\div}\;\boxed{(}\;\boxed{6}\;\boxed{\times}\;\boxed{2}\;\boxed{)}\;\boxed{+}\;\boxed{3}\;\boxed{=}$$

Otherwise, it must first be calculated that $6 \times 2 = 12$ and then the sequence below may be entered.

$$\boxed{24}\;\boxed{\div}\;\boxed{12}\;\boxed{+}\;\boxed{3}\;\boxed{=}$$

c. If the calculator includes parentheses keys, this keying sequence can be used.

$$\boxed{150}\;\boxed{-}\;\boxed{(}\;\boxed{71}\;\boxed{-}\;\boxed{26}\;\boxed{)}\;\boxed{=}$$

Otherwise, it must first be calculated that $71 - 26 = 45$ and then this sequence may be entered.

$$\boxed{150}\;\boxed{-}\;\boxed{45}\;\boxed{=}$$

d. On a calculator with arithmetic logic, the following sequence will suffice.

$$\boxed{26}\;\boxed{+}\;\boxed{18}\;\boxed{\div}\;\boxed{2}\;\boxed{=}$$

On a calculator with algebraic logic, either parentheses must be inserted or the expression below may be used. Pressing the equals sign partway through a computation will perform all calculations up to that point.

$$\boxed{26}\;\boxed{+}\;\boxed{18}\;\boxed{=}\;\boxed{\div}\;\boxed{2}\;\boxed{=}$$

e. If the calculator has an exponentiation key and uses algebraic logic, the sequence below may be used.

With no exponentiation key, each multiplication must be entered separately. A valid sequence for an algebraic calculator without an exponentiation key is shown below.

On an arithmetic calculator, these multiplications must be performed first.

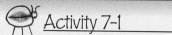

Teaching Connections

Classroom Activities Activities 7-1 to 7-4 illustrate how equations and operations may be presented in the classroom. The "I Have/Who Has" game in Activity 7-3 is a common idea found in many activity manuals and sources. In making an "I Have/Who Has" deck, you must be certain that each of the "I have" expressions is unique. The card sequence is cyclic in that the "Who has" question on the last card is answered by the "I have" question on the first card. Extra cards may be distributed to students who would like to play more than one card or may be kept by the teacher. Complicated expressions may be written on the board or on transparency slides. Game cards may be printed on transparency film rather than on index cards. This saves time in

---

Activity 7-1   Grades 2–6

Making a Group Equation

Materials: Envelopes containing index cards with numerals and symbols that can be used to make an equation.

Directions: Place students in groups of four or five. At the given signal, each group removes the cards from their envelope and distributes one card to each group member (in a group of four, the equals symbol will go to the student who is holding the answer to the equation). The students must arrange themselves to create a true equation.

$$\boxed{7}\;\boxed{=}\;\boxed{-}\;\boxed{2}\;\boxed{5}$$

Example Cards (second-grade level):

Note: Equations for higher grade levels may be more complicated and may include parentheses cards. Students take two cards each and trade cards with other members of their group until they are able to line up and illustrate a valid equation holding one card in each hand.

Example Cards (fifth-grade level):

Activity 7-2 — Grades 3–6

Making Equations

Materials: Envelopes containing index cards with numerals and symbols that can be used to make several equations.

Directions: Place students in groups of four or five. At the given signal, each group removes the cards from their envelope and arranges the cards into equations. Each card may be used in at most one equation. The groups should try to use all the cards in their envelope.

Activity 7-3 — Grades 3–6

"I Have/Who Has" Game

Materials: "I Have/Who Has" card deck.

Directions: Mix the cards and distribute one to each student. The teacher begins with one of the remaining cards by reading the "Who has" statement. The student who has the answer to that statement stands up and says "I have ___" and continues by reading the "Who has" statement on the card.

| I have 15. Who has $7 + (3 \times 4)$? | I have 19. Who has $18 \div 2 - 3$? | I have 6. Who has $4 \times 6 - 2$? |

Note: For games involving more complicated expressions, the students may write their "Who has" statement on the board instead of stating it orally.

that the students do not have to write their expressions. They merely lay their slip on the overhead projector to show it to the class. If no student claims that he has the answer to the current problem, the student who posed the problem should begin to explain the calculation. For example, suppose a student posed the question: Who has $3 + 7 \times 4$? If there are no replies, the student who posed the question would state that the first step is to multiply 7×4 and get 28. At this point a student in the audience may jump in with "Oh, I have 31."

Problem Set 7.1

For Your Understanding

1. Evaluate each of the following expressions.
   a. $12 + 36 \div 2 \times 3$
   b. $(12 + 36) \div 2 \times 3$

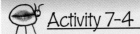

Activity 7-4 — Grades 4–6

Matching Stories, Equations, and Calculators

Materials: Index cards with story problems, keying sequences, and calculator types.

Directions: Mix the cards and distribute one to each student. Students form groups of three with each group having a story, an equation, and a calculator. After evaluating the equation, groups present their problem and its solution to the class.

Example:

At a picnic there are 10 children and 6 adults. Each adult eats 3 hot dogs. Each child eats 2 hot dogs. How many hot dogs were eaten?

$10 \times 2 + 6 \times 3 =$

Pick up a calculator with algebraic logic.

c. $5 \times 2^2 - 3 \times 4$
d. $30 - 14 - 3 + 7$

2. Evaluate each of the following expressions.
   a. $30 - 2 \times 5 + 6$
   b. $30 - (2 \times 5 + 6)$
   c. $\dfrac{4 \times 6 - 2^3}{2 \times 5 - 6}$
   d. $\sqrt{20 - 8 - 2}$

3. Evaluate the expressions and indicate how each expression is read.
   a. 7^2
   b. 5^3
   c. 2^6

4. Both Chris and Kerry enter the following sequence into their calculators:

Chris's calculator gives the answer 3 and Kerry's calculator gives the answer 10. What answers will be given by Chris's and Kerry's calculators if they both enter this sequence:

$$\boxed{4}\ \boxed{+}\ \boxed{6}\ \boxed{\times}\ \boxed{2}\ \boxed{-}\ \boxed{6}\ \boxed{\div}\ \boxed{2}\ \boxed{=}$$

5. Determine valid keying sequences for each expression below using (1) an algebraic calculator and (2) an arithmetic calculator. Assume that neither calculator has parentheses keys.
   a. $12 + 36 \div 2 \times 3$
   b. $(12 + 36) \div 2 \times 3$
   c. $5 \times 2^2 - 3 \times 4$
   d. $30 - 2 \times 5 + 6$

Applications for the Classroom

1. Write a pair of word problems. The word problems should have different answers but the same keying sequence. This keying sequence should give the correct answer to one of the word problems when typed into an algebraic calculator, and the correct answer to the other problem in the pair when typed into an arithmetic calculator.

2. Choose one activity from Activities 7-1, 7-2, 7-3, or 7-4. Make a classroom set of materials that could be used with this activity.

3. Create an assessment tool to be used with Activity 7-2. Explain why you chose that type of assessment tool.

4. Some common student errors are given. Describe how the student got her answer and calculate the correct answer for each problem.
   a. $\sqrt{9 + 16} = 7$
   b. $30 - 14 - 3 + 7 = 6$
   c. $12 + 36 \div 2 \times 3 = 8$

5. Classify the level of knowledge and the type of learning experience of Activity 7-3.

7.2 FACTORS, MULTIPLES, AND PRIMES

Number theory topics such as those covered in this section are useful in many problem-solving applications and in computer programs such as Logo. Factors, multiples, and primes are specifically mentioned in many of the state standards at the upper end of the early childhood years.

Developing Concepts of Even and Odd

When people hear the phrase "number theory," many envision topics such as we've just discussed. However, the study of numbers typically begins much earlier. One of the first number theory results that children encounter is the idea that a number is either even or odd. Children can often

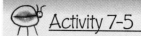

Activity 7-5   Grades K–1

Even or Odd—Using Students in the Class

Materials: Students in the class.

Teacher Statement: Today we are going to learn about even and odd. With *even* numbers we can make pairs. With *odd* numbers there is one left over when we make pairs. Let's see if the number of children in class today is even or odd.

Directions: Have children make pairs. If the number of children is odd, make sure the child who is not paired doesn't feel left out. Repeat the process of making pairs with the children a few times so they see that with different pairings the overall number of children is still even or still odd. You can also see if the number of boys and the number of girls is even or odd.

Note: If the number of boys and the number of girls and the total number of children are all even, include yourself in one of the groupings so that an example of odd is given.

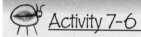

Activity 7-6   Grades K–1

Even or Odd—Using Blocks or Counters

Materials: Enough blocks or counters so that each student can have a small handful.

Teacher Statement: Today we are going to learn about even and odd. With even numbers we can make pairs. With odd numbers there is one left over when we make pairs. Everyone will grab a handful of blocks and we'll see if your handful is even or odd.

Directions: Have the children take a handful of blocks or counters and make pairs to determine whether the handful that they grabbed is even or odd. This activity may be repeated.

Extension Activity: Have students count the number of blocks in their handful. This will provide good practice in counting by twos. Go around the class and have students report their total number and whether it was even or odd.

determine whether a number is even or odd before they can even count to that number or name it. This is illustrated in Activities 7-5, 7-6, and 7-7.

Using concrete materials, primary-grade children can discover and learn simple number theory results. There is a well-known Chinese proverb regarding how people learn:

I hear; I forget.
I see; I remember.
I do; I understand.

To illustrate this proverb, consider the number theory result "odd + odd = even." If a teacher were to tell this result to a class, many of the children would be likely to forget it. If she were to show it to them using concrete visuals, they should remember it. However, if the children in the class were to discover the principle themselves, they would not only remember it, but they would also understand it. In Activity 7-8, students discover "odd + odd = even" and other number theory results. In addition to finding these results, students should also discuss why the results make sense.

Even numbers and odd numbers have convenient representations using variables. In algebraic notation, a single even number can be represented by $2n$ and a single odd number can be represented by $2n + 1$ where n is a whole number. If an even number and an odd number were to be used in the same problem, unless it was known that the odd number was exactly one larger than the

Standards

Florida Sunshine State Standards

Mathematics Grades 3–5: Number Sense, Concepts, and Operations

Standard 5: The student understands and applies theories related to numbers. (M.A.A.5.2).
1. understands and applies basic number theory concepts, including primes, composites, factors, and multiples.

Florida Department of Education, 1996

Standards

Alaska Mathematics Content Standards

Between ages 8–10, students know and are able to do everything required at earlier ages.
Mathematics Standard A1: Numeration

A1.2.6: Identify and describe factors and multiples including those factors and multiples common to a pair or set of numbers.

Mathematics Standard A4: Functions and Relationships

A4.2.1: Use patterns and their extensions to make predictions and solve problems; describe patterns found in the number system including those formed by multiplies, factors, perfect squares, and powers of 10.

Alaska Department of Education and Early Development, 1999

even number, different variables must be used. In this case, you could represent the even number by $2n$ and the odd number by $2m + 1$ where m and n are whole numbers. If you wished to discuss two different even numbers, you would also need to use two distinct variables such as $2n$ and $2m$. Theorem 7-1 gives a formal mathematical proof of one of the results from Activity 7-8. Can you use algebraic notation and give formal mathematical proofs of the remaining three results?

Theorem 7.1: The sum of two even whole numbers is an even whole number.

Proof of Theorem 7.1: Let $2m$ and $2n$ represent two arbitrary even whole numbers. The sum is $2m + 2n$, which by the distributive property of multiplication over addition is equal to $2 \times (m + n)$. Now m and n are whole numbers, so by the property of closure under addition, $m + n$ is a whole number. Hence $2m + 2n = 2(m + n)$ is even since it is a multiple of two. Therefore, the sum of any two even whole numbers is an even whole number.

Algebraic notation also appears in the early curriculum. We have already discussed that "missing addend" equations such as $5 + \underline{\quad} = 8$ are common at the first-grade level. There is a natural progression of difficulty over a series of grade levels in the abstraction of algebraic examples, ideas, and notation used (see the standard box on p. 166).

 Activity 7-7   Grades 1–3

Even or Odd—Using Smiley Strips

Materials: Even/odd smiley strips (see Blackline Master 16 in the Appendices).

Directions: Have students cut out a set of smiley strips. On the back of each strip they should write the numeral that the strip represents.
a. Students discuss even and odd numbers, illustrating their ideas with the strips.
b. Students put all their strips numeral side up and then sort the strips into an even pile and an odd pile.

Example:

Source: Adapted from Troutman & Lichtenberg, 2003.

Factors and Multiples

Even numbers have a common property: they can all be evenly divided by 2. You could say that any even number is a multiple of 2, or that 2 is a factor of any even number. The terms "factor" and "multiple," introduced at the second- or third-grade level, are easily confused by students. You, the teacher, must be careful that you use these terms correctly. "Factor" was used in Chapter 6, and "multiple" in Theorem

 Activity 7-8   Grades 1–3

Adding Even and Odd Numbers

Materials: Even/odd smiley strips (see Blackline Master 16 in the Appendices).

Teacher Statement: We can use our even/odd smiley strips to find out some interesting properties about even and odd numbers. Use your smiley strips to find the answers to all the problems in a column and then answer the question at the bottom of the column by writing an appropriate word in the blank.

4 + 6 = ___	4 + 5 = ___
6 + 2 = ___	2 + 3 = ___
even + even = ___	even + odd = ___
1 + 4 = ___	3 + 5 = ___
3 + 6 = ___	1 + 7 = ___
odd + even = ___	odd + odd = ___

Example: 3 + 5 = 8

7.1. Now it is time for some formal mathematical definitions. Recall that the set of whole numbers is $W = \{0, 1, 2, \ldots \}$.

Definition 7-1: *For whole numbers* n *and* m,
    a. the number n is a *factor* of m if there is a whole number p with $p \times n = m$.
    b. the number m is a *multiple* of n if n is a factor of m.

Example 7-7: From the expression $3 \times 4 = 12$, you have the following relationships.

    a. 3 is a factor of 12.
    b. 4 is a factor of 12.
    c. 12 is a multiple of 3.
    d. 12 is a multiple of 4.
    e. 3 is *not* a multiple of 12.
    f. 12 is *not* a factor of 3.

Every whole number has an infinite number of multiples. For example, the multiples of 4 are 0, 4, 8, 12, 16, 20, and so on. Can you see why 0 is a multiple of 4? It is because $0 = 4 \times 0$. Other multiples of 4 can also be written as a product where 4 is one of the factors of the product. So it is relatively easy to find multiples of a given number. It takes a bit more work to find factors of a given number. Activity 7-9 is a concrete hands-on activity for finding factors of a given number.

If the group activity described in Activity 7-9 is completed, a class of n students will have drawn rectangle sheets for each of the numbers $1, 2, 3, \ldots, n + 1$. During discussion of the rectangle sheets, students will notice that the sheet for 1 is the only sheet that has exactly one rectangle. They will also notice several sheets that have exactly two rectangles. There is a special fact concerning the sheets that have an odd number of rectangles drawn on them. You should draw rectangle sheets for 1 to 10 yourself, and then study the sheets and see what patterns and results you can find. Can you see how making a rectangle sheet for a given number is related to finding the factors of the number?

Using Literature in the Mathematics Classroom

Even Steven and Odd Todd

By Kathryn Cristaldi
A Hello Math Reader, Level 3, Scholastic, 1996

Even Steven likes only even numbers. All the numbers in his life are even. He has 4 pets. He makes 12 pancakes for breakfast, and so on. Steven's cousin Odd Todd comes to visit. At first the two personalities clash; in the end they work things out.

Classroom Activities:

Grade 1: Ask students questions like—Which cousin owns four pairs of shoes? Which cousin owns five pairs?

Grade 2: Even Steven makes 10 muffins. Odd Todd eats 3 muffins. Draw a picture and determine how many muffins are left.

Grade 4: Even Steven buys some apples; you decide how many. Odd Todd eats some of the apples. Which cousin is happier about the number of apples left? Try this problem using different numbers and see if you can explain the result (D. Pollack, personal communication, 1995).

Activity 7-9 — Grades 3-5

Rectangle Sheets—Problem Solving Using Cases

Materials: Blocks or square tiles and inch- or centimeter-squared paper for each group.

Teacher Statement: Each group will get an envelope that contains three numbers and the three job cards—block arranger, number writer, and rectangle drawer. You must switch jobs for each of the three numbers that your group has to do, so that everybody does each job once.

Let's do one example together. Let's look at the number 8. The block arranger arranges eight tiles into rectangles. The rectangle drawer draws the rectangles on the sheet, and the number writer writes the multiplication sentences on the sheet.

How could we arrange eight blocks in a rectangle? We could make a rectangle with one long row and eight blocks like ▭▭▭▭▭▭▭▭ or a rectangle with two rows like ⊞⊞⊞⊞. Can we make a rectangle with three rows? Not with eight blocks. How about a rectangle with four rows? Yes, ▯. Can we make a rectangle with five rows? Etc.

Extension Activity: Hang the completed rectangle sheets in order in the room. Let students study the sheets and then discuss them.

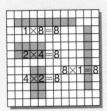

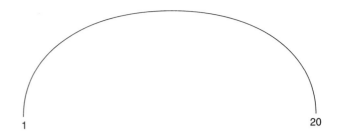

The next number to consider is 2. Two is a factor of 20 since $2 \times 10 = 20$. The following arch represents this factor pair.

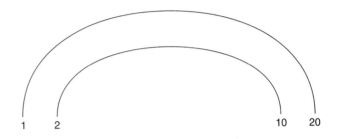

Next, consider 3. Three is not a factor of 20 since 20 is not evenly divided by 3, so there is no arch beginning with 3. However, 4 is a factor since $4 \times 5 = 20$; you can draw an arch representing this factor pair.

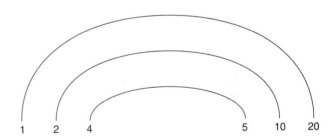

The next number to consider would be 5; but you have already found the factor pair involving 5. There are no larger factors other than the ones you have already found. Therefore, the factor rainbow for 20 is complete.

b. Draw a factor rainbow for 16.

Solution: The smallest factor of 16 is 1, which is paired with the factor 16. You can draw an arch for this factor pair.

Teaching Connections

A Rainbow Diagram of Factors Every whole number greater than one has at least two factors. A rainbow drawing can be used to visualize factors of a given number. The method of drawing a rainbow design of factors is introduced in Troutman and Lichtenberg (2003, pp. 310–311). This idea is based on the fact that factors occur in pairs. Thus, you can draw a rainbow of paired factors. Example 7-8 shows two rainbow diagrams.

Example 7-8:

a. Draw a factor rainbow for 20.

   Solution: The smallest factor of 20 is 1, and 1 is paired with the largest factor 20 since $1 \times 20 = 20$, draw an arch representing this pair of factors.

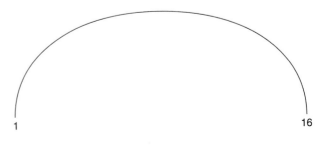

The next number to consider is 2. Two is a factor of 16 since $2 \times 8 = 16$. You can draw an arch to represent this factor pair.

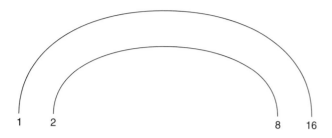

Next, consider 3. This is not a factor since 16 does not divide evenly by 3. Thus, there is not an arch for 3. Four, on the other hand, is a factor since $4 \times 4 = 16$. You place the numeral 4 in the center of the rainbow because there will be no larger factors other than those that you have already found. The finished rainbow is shown below.

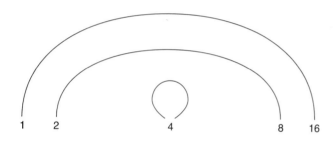

Notice the difference between the rainbow diagram for 16 and the rainbow diagram for 20. The number 16 is a perfect square since $16 = 4 \times 4$. There is a number in this rainbow diagram that has a loop because it is paired with itself in the factoring. In general, m is a *perfect square* if $m = n \times n$ for some whole number n. Rainbow diagrams for numbers that are perfect squares will have a loop at the center number. There is also a special characterization of numbers that are perfect squares when factors are represented by rectangle diagrams such as in Activity 7-9. This is explored further in problem 6 of Problem Set 7.2.

If a number is not a perfect square, it will not have an exact center numeral in the rainbow diagram. In general, the central numeral is the square root of the overall number. By taking the square root of a number, you can find out how many numbers must be checked to look for factors. For example, $\sqrt{150}$ is approximately 12.2. Thus to find all factors of 150, you need to check for divisibility only by the numbers 1 through 12. Numbers from 1 to 12 that are factors of 150 would occur on the left side of a 150-rainbow diagram. Any factor of 150 larger than 12 would be paired with one of these smaller factors and would occur on the right side of the 150-rainbow diagram.

Prime Numbers and Composite Numbers

Every whole number greater than one has at least the two factors, one and itself. If these are the only two factors of a number, the number is called *prime*. If a whole number has more than two factors, it is called *composite*. The number 1 is neither prime nor composite. It is the only number that has exactly one factor. The number 2 is the only even prime number; all other prime numbers are odd. However, not all odd numbers are prime. Example 7-9 lists all prime numbers and composite numbers less than 50. The definitions for "prime" and "composite" are usually given at the third- or fourth-grade level. Students at this level can use the Eratosthenes's sieve to find primes (see Activity 7-10).

Example 7-9:

Prime Numbers: 2, 3, 5, 7, 11, 13, 17, 19, 23, 29, 31, 37, 41, 43, 47, . . .

Composite Numbers: 4, 6, 8, 9, 10, 12, 14, 15, 16, 18, 20, 21, 22, 24, 25, 26, 27, 28, 30, 32, 33, 34, 35, 36, 38, 39, 40, 42, 44, 45, 46, 48, 49, . . .

Standards

Florida Sunshine State Standards

Grades Pre-K–2: Algebraic Thinking

Standard 2: The student uses expressions, equations, inequalities, graphs, and formulas to represent and interpret situations. (MA.D.2.1)
1. Understands that geometric symbols (●, ■, ▲) can be used to represent unknown quantities in expressions, equations, and inequalities.
2. Uses informal methods to solve real-world problems requiring simple equations that contain one variable.

Grades 3–5 Algebraic Thinking, Standard 2
The student uses expressions, equations, inequalities, graphs, and formulas to represent and interpret situations. (MA.D.2.2)
1. Represents a given simple problem situation using diagrams, models, and symbolic expressions translated from verbal phrases, or verbal phrases translated from symbolic expressions, etc.
2. Uses informal methods, such as physical models and graphs, to solve real-world problems involving equations and inequalities.

Florida Department of Education, 1996

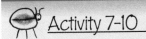 Activity 7-10   Grades 3–4

Using Eratosthenes's Sieve to Find Primes

Materials: Hundreds chart for each student.

Teacher Statement: We can find all the prime numbers less than 100 by using a method that is over 2,000 years old. This method was invented by a mathematician named Eratosthenes and is called the *Sieve of Eratosthenes.*

Circle the first prime number on your hundreds chart. That's 2, right. Now cross off all the larger multiples of 2 like 4, 6, 8, 10, and so forth. All of these are not prime because they have a factor of 2.

Circle the next prime number on your chart. That's 3, right. Now cross off all the larger multiples of 3 like 6, 9, 12, and so forth. Count by threes to find the numbers to cross off if you need to. All of these are not prime because they have a factor of 3.

What's the next prime number? Yes, 5. Circle 5 and cross off the multiples of 5. Is there an easy way?

Note: Continue the process. When finished, all primes less than 100 will be circled and all the composite numbers will be crossed off.

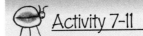 Activity 7-11   Grades 4–5

Goldbach's Conjecture

Materials: Handouts that indicate which numbers each group is to work on.

Teacher Statement: We have already talked about making mathematical conjectures. One very famous conjecture is called Goldbach's conjecture. Goldbach's conjecture is that every even number greater than two can be written as the sum of two prime numbers. This was stated in 1742 in a round of letters between Goldbach and Euler, and no one has been able to prove or disprove it yet.

Let's look at some examples. How could we write 4 as the sum of two primes? $4 = 3 + 1$? No, what is wrong with this? Of course, 1 is not a prime. How about $4 = 2 + 2$? Yes this is a way to write 4 as a sum of two primes. How about 6? Good, $6 = 3 + 3$. What about 8? Yes, $8 = 3 + 5$. And $10 = 5 + 5$. Each group will receive a list of even numbers. The group should try to write each of those numbers as the sum of two primes. Together we will see if this result holds for all the even numbers up to 100.

It is an interesting fact of number theory that there are an infinite number of primes. To determine whether a number is prime or composite, you need only check for divisibility by primes less than the square root of the number. For example, 150 is clearly composite because it is evenly divisible by 2. Let's check to see whether 151 is prime or composite. Since $\sqrt{151}$ is approximately 12.3, you need to check 151 for divisibility by primes less than 12. The number 151 is not divisible by 2 because 151 is an odd number. You can check by calculator or by long division to see that 151 is not divisible by 3. (We will discuss an alternate method to check for divisibility by 3 in Section 7.3.) You do not need to check for divisibility by 4 because 4 is not prime. The number 151 is not divisible by 5. Can you give a reason why it is not? You can check by calculator or by long division to see that 151 is not divisible by 7 or by 11. Thus, you can conclude that 151 is a prime number.

Prime numbers are the focus of many unsolved math problems and conjectures. A *conjecture* is a statement that

Standards

NCTM

Grades 3–5:

Students in grades 3–5 should frequently make conjectures about mathematical relationships, investigate those conjectures, and make mathematical arguments that are based on their work. They need to know that posing conjectures and trying to justify them is an expected part of students' mathematical activity.

NCTM, 2000, p. 191

Standards are listed with the permission of the National Council of Teachers of Mathematics (NCTM). NCTM does not endorse the content or validity of these alignments.

Standards

Alaska Mathematics Content Standards

Between ages 5–7, students
Mathematics Standard D: Reasoning
   D1.1.1 Draw conclusions about mathematical problems.
   D1.1.2 Find examples that support or refute mathematical statements.

Alaska Department of Education and Early Development, 1999

is believed to be true, but which has yet to be proven. Conjectures are an important part of both the mathematics and science curriculums in today's elementary schools.

It is important for students to realize that giving examples that support a conjecture does not prove that the conjecture is true. To prove a conjecture, you must give a valid argument that shows that the statement will always hold. However, to disprove a conjecture, it is enough to give one example for which it does not hold true. This type of example is called a *counterexample.* Giving examples, drawing conclusions, and making generalizations are very much a part of the early childhood curriculum and specifically mentioned in many state frameworks and models.

Problem Set 7.2

For Your Understanding

1. Answer *true* or *false* to each of the following.
   a. 15 is a factor of 3.
   b. 15 has a factor of 3.
   c. 3 is a factor of 15.
   d. 3 is a multiple of 15.
   e. 15 is a multiple of 3.

2. List all prime numbers between 50 and 100.

3. Draw a factor rainbow diagram for
   a. 36
   b. 40
   c. 140

4. Complete Activity 7-8. Give a word explanation and a proof using algebraic notation of the four results discovered in this activity.

5. When the band members march in rows of two, there is one person left over. When they march in rows of three, there are two people left over. When they march in rows of four, there are three people left over. When they march in rows of five, there are four people left over. What is the minimum number of people in the band?

6. Draw rectangle sheets (see Activity 7-9) for the numbers 1 through 10. Explain how you could determine whether a number was a perfect square or not just by looking at the rectangle sheet for the number. Explain how you could determine whether a number was prime or composite just by looking at the rectangle sheet for the number.

7. Complete the table below below for each of the numbers 7 through 20. In the classification column, use the following classifications: prime, prime squared, product of two distinct primes, and other.

Number	Factors	Classification
1	1	Other
2	1, 2	Prime
3	1, 3	Prime
4	1, 2, 4	Prime squared
5	1, 5	Prime
6	1, 2, 3, 6	Product of two primes
. . .		

8. Describe the factor rainbow drawing for (a) a prime number, (b) a number that is a prime squared, and (c) a number that is the product of two distinct primes.

9. Determine whether 1,357 is prime or composite. Use a calculator. Explain how you got your answer.

Applications for the Classroom

1. Describe two ways that you could convince a young child that zero (0) is an even number.

2. Look up Thwaites's conjecture in a library or on the Internet and write an activity where students explore this conjecture.

3. Write a lesson plan that describes how you will introduce the topic of even and odd numbers in a kindergarten classroom. Follow the format given by your instructor or use the lesson plan format given in Appendix A.

4. Create an assessment tool to be used with Activity 7-8. Explain why you chose that type of assessment tool.

5. Read Activity 11-11 in Chapter 11. Explain how this activity could be used as an introduction to prime numbers.

7.3 DIVISIBILITY TESTS, PRIME FACTORIZATION, AND FACTOR TREES

In Section 7.2 we discussed that to determine whether a number is prime or composite, you need to check that number for divisibility only by primes less than the square root of the number. In this section some simple tests are developed to determine whether one number is divisible by another. Some of this material is appropriate for Grades 4–6 and may be used to help you develop your own number sense and an appreciation for relationships among numbers.

Definition of *Divisible*

It is easy to determine whether a number is divisible by 2. A number is divisible by 2 if and only if it is even. This statement contains two parts: if a number is even, then it is divisible by 2; if a number is odd, then it is *not* divisible by 2. So to determine whether a number is divisible by 2, you need to look only at the last digit of the number to determine whether it is even or odd. This type of "divisibility test" and other such tests will be discussed below. We begin by discussing terminology.

Definition 7-2: *For whole numbers* m *and* n,
  a. the number *m* is *divisible* by *n* if there is a whole number *p* with $p \times n = m$.
  b. the number *n divides* the number *m* if *m* is divisible by *n*. This is sometimes denoted by $n \mid m$. The notation $n \mid m$ is read as "*n* divides *m*" and *not* as "*n* divided by *m*."

Example 7-10: Answer *true* or *false* to each of the following.

  a. 34 is divisible by 2.
  b. 34 divides 2.
  c. 34 is divisible by 4.
  d. $34 \mid 2$.
  e. 4 is divisible by 36.

Solutions:

  a. True.
  b. False. However, it is true that 2 divides 34.
  c. False. Since $34 \div 4 = 8\ R2$, it is not true that 34 is evenly divisible by 4. To say that one number divides another, the remainder when the division is performed must be 0.
  d. False; 34 does not divide 2. Using notation, this can be written $34 \nmid 2$. However, it is true that 2 divides 34. So, it is true that $2 \mid 34$.
  e. False. However, 36 is divisible by 4.

Example 7-11: Justify each of the following statements.

  a. *m* is divisible by *n* if *n* is a factor of *m*.
  b. Any whole number is divisible by 1.
  c. No nonzero whole number is divisible by 0.

Justifications:

  a. Compare Definition 7-1 and Definition 7-2.
  b. If *m* is any whole number, then $m \times 1 = m$.
  c. If *m* is a nonzero whole number, the equation $p \times 0 = m$ has no solution.

Divisibility Tests for 2, 3, 4, 5, 6, 9, and 10

It has already been mentioned that to determine whether a number is divisible by 2, you need to look only at the last digit or the units digit of the number. You can also determine whether a number is divisible by 5 or by 10 merely by looking at the last digit of the number. These "last digit" divisibility tests are usually introduced at the second- or third-grade level.

Theorem 7.2: A whole number n *is divisible by 2 if, and only if, its units digit is 0, 2, 4, 6, or 8.*

Mathematical Proof of Theorem 7.2: You can use the idea of nonstandard place value to write a whole number n *as* n = 10a + b, *where* b *is the units digit of the number* n. *Now 10 is divisible by 2, so* 10a *is divisible by 2. Thus, the number* n *will be divisible by 2 if and only if* b *is. The only single-digit numbers that are divisible by 2 are 0, 2, 4, 6, and 8. Therefore,* n *is divisible by 2 if and only if its units digit is 0, 2, 4, 6, or 8.*

The formal mathematical proof of Theorem 7.2 above would never be presented to children. In fact, some adults have difficulty following formal mathematical arguments such as the one given above. However, the idea of this proof could be used with a specific example to illustrate a concrete instance indicating why the rule makes sense.

 Assessment
Writing in Mathematics

In Grades 3 or 4, after the divisibility test for 2 has been discussed, but before presenting a divisibility test for 5, it is an excellent exercise for students to make a conjecture regarding what numbers are divisible by 5.

Activity:
Write in your journal 10 numbers that are evenly divisible by 5. Do you see a pattern? Make a conjecture or statement about numbers that are divisible by 5. How will you test your conjecture?

Example 7-12: Why do you need to check only the last digit to check for divisibility by 2?

Suppose you wished to check the number two hundred thirty-something for divisibility by 2. To check 23? for divisibility by 2, you could consider 23? = 230 + ?. The 230 part is divisible by 2, so the overall number can be divided by 2 if the last digit can be divided by 2.

You could give either a formal mathematical argument or a more intuitive specific instance argument to prove or illustrate a similar result involving the last-digit divisibility test for divisibility by 5 given in Theorem 7.3 below. Together Theorems 7.2 and 7.3 imply Theorem 7.4 regarding a last-digit divisibility test for divisibility by 10. This follows from the fact that a number is divisible by 10 if, and only if, it is divisible by both 2 and 5.

Theorem 7.3: A whole number n *is divisible by 5 if, and only if, its units digit is 0 or 5.*

Theorem 7.4: A whole number n *is divisible by 10 if, and only if, its units digit is 0.*

Divisibility tests for 3, 4, 6, and 9 typically are at the third- or fourth-grade levels. Justifications are provided for some of these tests below; other justifications and divisibility tests will be covered in the exercises at the end of this section.

Theorem 7.5: A whole number n *is divisible by 3 if, and only if, the sum of its digits is divisible by 3.*

Justification of Theorem 7.5 (When n *is a Three-Digit Number): Suppose that* n *is a three-digit number with digits* a, b, *and* c. *In expanded form,* $n = 100a + 10b + c$. *This can be decomposed as* $n = 99a + a + 9b + b + c$. *Since 3 divides* 99a *and* 9b, *it will divide* n *if it divides* $a + b + c$. *That is, 3 will divide the number if, and only if, it divides the sum of the digits. A similar argument could be used for numbers that have more than three digits.*

Theorem 7.6: A whole number n *is divisible by 4 if, and only if, the number formed by the last two digits of* n *is divisible by 4.*

Mathematical Proof of Theorem 7.6: Again, use the idea of nonstandard place value. Any number n *can be written as*

$n = 100a + b$, *where* b *represents the last two digits of the original number. Since 4 divides 100, it also divides* 100a. *Thus 4 divides* n *if and only if it divides* b. *That is, 4 divides* n *if and only if it divides the number represented by the last two digits of* n.

Theorem 7.7: A whole number n *is divisible by 6 if, and only if, it is divisible by both 2 and 3.*

Theorem 7.8: A whole number n *is divisible by 9 if, and only if, the sum of its digits is divisible by 9.*

Example 7-13: Check each number given in the table below for divisibility by 2, 3, 4, 5, 6, 9, and 10. For each instance, state "Yes" or "No" and then give a short reason that indicates that you are correctly using the appropriate divisibility test.

Factor Trees and Prime Factorization

The divisibility tests discussed above can be useful in finding the prime factorization of a given number. The *prime factorization* of a number is a product of primes and powers of primes equal to that number. The *fundamental theorem of arithmetic* states that every whole number greater than 1 is a prime or can be expressed as a product of primes, and that disregarding the order of the factors, this prime factorization is unique. A *factor tree* can also be useful in finding the prime factorization.

To draw a factor tree, begin with the given number at the top level. Factor this number, write the two factors on the next level, and draw branches to these numbers. Continue the process for each number that is composite. Branches end in prime numbers only. The prime factorization can be found by collecting the primes at the end of the branches. It is convention to write the primes in a prime factorization in increasing order. Examples of factor trees and prime factorizations are shown in Example 7-14.

Example 7-14:

   a. Factor trees and prime factorizations for 105 and 140. It is easy to recognize at a glance that 105 has a factor of 5, and that 140 can be factored as $140 = 14 \times 10$. The two factor trees shown are the result of these observations.

The number →	45	300	1424
Divisible by 2?	No; last digit = 5.	Yes; last digit = 0.	Yes; last digit = 4.
Divisible by 3?	Yes; sum of digits = 9.	Yes; sum of digits = 3.	No; sum of digits = 11.
Divisible by 4?	No; 45 ÷ 4 = 11 *R*1.	Yes; 00 ÷ 4 = 0 *R*0.	Yes; 24 ÷ 4 = 6 *R*0.
Divisible by 5?	Yes; last digit = 5.	Yes; last digit = 0.	No; last digit = 4.
Divisible by 6?	No; not divisible by 2.	Yes; both 2 and 3.	No; not divisible by 3.
Divisible by 9?	Yes; sum of digits = 9.	No; sum of digits = 3.	No; sum of digits = 11.
Divisible by 10?	No; last digit not 0.	Yes; last digit = 0.	No; last digit not 0.

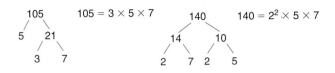

You could also build a factor tree in a more systematic manner by using the divisibility tests discussed. For example, by the last digit test, 105 is not divisible by 2. Since the sum of the digits is 6, the number 105 is divisible by 3 and can be factored as $105 = 3 \times 35$. Now 35 is not divisible by 2 or 3, but is divisible by 5 as $35 = 5 \times 7$.

The number 140 is divisible by 2 as $140 = 2 \times 70$. The number 70 is again divisible by 2 as $70 = 2 \times 35$. As above, 35 is not divisible by 2 or 3, but $35 = 5 \times 7$. The factor trees obtained by this systematic use of divisibility tests are shown below. Notice that the prime factorizations obtained below are the same as the prime factorizations obtained when the factor trees were generated by using randomly chosen factors above.

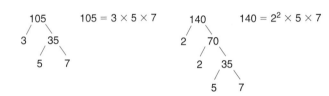

b. Different factor trees for 36. Notice that when the convention of writing primes in increasing order is followed, different factor trees yield the same prime factorization. This is what is meant by the component of the fundamental theorem of arithmetic that states that the prime factorization is unique. Prime factorizations and factor trees are introduced at around the fourth- or fifth-grade levels.

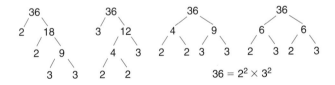

Example 7-15: Using the prime factorization to find factors of 36.

The prime factorization $2^2 \times 3^2$ can be used to determine the factors of 36. Each factor of 36 contains the prime 2 to the power 0, 1, or 2 and the prime 3 to the power 0, 1, or 2. Hence, there are nine different factors. This uses the combination principle of multiplication in that the three different ways to choose an exponent for the prime 2 are combined with the three different ways to choose an exponent for the prime 3. The factors are $2^0 \times 3^0$, $2^0 \times 3^1$, $2^0 \times 3^2$, $2^1 \times 3^0$, $2^1 \times 3^1$, $2^1 \times 3^2$, $2^2 \times 3^0$, $2^2 \times 3^1$, and $2^2 \times 3^2$. In evaluated form, the factors are 1, 3, 9, 2, 6, 18, 4, 12, and 36.

Teaching Connections

Help Students Recognize Patterns and Make Generalizations The ideas of factors, multiples, and perfect squares are useful in some problem-solving and pattern situations.

Example 7-16:

a. A pattern begins with one row of one dot. Each new element of the pattern increases the number of rows and columns by one. How many dots are there in the *n*th element of the pattern?

   Solution: The *n*th item of the pattern has n^2 dots.

b. A pattern begins with one row of two dots. Each new element of the pattern increases the number of rows and columns by one. How many dots are there in the *n*th element of the pattern?

   Solution: The *n*th item in the pattern has *n* rows and $n + 1$ columns; it has $n \times (n + 1)$ dots.

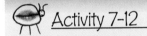

Activity 7-12   Grades 4–5

What Primes Are We? Problem Solving to Eliminate Possibilities

Directions: Assign each student in the class a prime number. Students must not reveal their numbers to each other. Each week throughout the year you will draw a number from a jar. The students who have been assigned the primes corresponding to the prime factors of the number drawn must come to the front of the room. Each student will keep track of these clues in their journal. The student who is first able to identify the primes assigned to each of the students in the class wins.

Example: Suppose 20 is drawn from the jar. The students who have been assigned the primes 2 and 5 must come to the front of the room. These two students should be able to determine what prime the other has been assigned; other students will only be able to infer that these two represent 2 and 5. Suppose these students are Mae and Anthony. If in a subsequent week the number 35 is drawn and Mae and Jill come to the front of the room, then all students should be able to determine that Mae's prime is 5, Jill's prime is 7, and Anthony's prime is 2.

Problem Set 7.3

For Your Understanding

1. Answer *true* or *false* for each of the following. If a statement is false, give a counterexample or indicate why it is false.
   a. 3 is divisible by 21.
   b. 3 | 21.
   c. Because 7 is a prime, it is not divisible by any whole numbers.
   d. Any nonzero whole number is divisible by itself.

2. Prove Theorem 7.2.

3. Devise a test for divisibility by 8. *Hint:* First look at the tests for divisibility by 2 and by 4. Explain why the test works and use it to check 23,816 and 16,405 for divisibility by 8.

4. Prove Theorem 7.8 for the case of a four-digit number.

5. Test (a) 965 and (b) 1,422 for divisibility by 2, 3, 4, 5, 6, 9, and 10. Give a reason for each of your answers to show that you are using the correct divisibility test.

6. Test 1,000,000,662 for divisibility by 2, 3, 4, 5, 6, 9, and 10. Give a reason for each of your answers to show that you are using the correct divisibility test.

7. Answer *true* or *false* for each of the following. If a statement is false, give a counterexample or indicate why it is false.
   a. A number is divisible by 12 if, and only if, it is divisible by both 3 and 4.
   b. A number is divisible by 12 if, and only if, it is divisible by both 2 and 6.
   c. If n is a whole number and $9 \mid n$, then $3 \mid n$.

8. Devise a test for divisibility by 25. Explain why the test works and use it to check 1,705 and 2,400 for divisibility by 25.

9. Draw a factor tree and find a prime factorization for 180.

10. Look in a seventh- or eighth-grade math textbook and find a test for divisibility by 11. Use the test to check 14,927 and 239,487 for divisibility by 11.

11. Find the prime factorization for 63,000,000.

12. Just by looking at the prime factorization of a number, how could you tell whether the number is a perfect square or not? Give examples to illustrate your explanation.

13. Fill in the missing digit so that 138,242,73 ___ is divisible by 6. Is there more than one solution?

14. How many different factors does the number $2^4 \times 3 \times 7^2$ have?

Applications for the Classroom

1. Create and solve a dot pattern problem similar to Example 7-16.

2. Cameron claims that if a number is divisible by both 2 and 10, then it will be divisible by 20. You are the teacher. How do you respond?

7.4 LEAST COMMON MULTIPLES AND GREATEST COMMON FACTORS

Teaching Connections

A Problem-Solving Approach to Greatest Common Factor and Least Common Multiple Problems The principles of least common multiple and greatest common factor (or divisor) will be used frequently in Chapter 8 in adding and simplifying fractions. Problems involving common multiples or factors can be introduced at about the third-grade level. However, the phrases "least common multiple" and "greatest common factor" or "greatest common divisor" are often confusing to children and are usually not introduced until the fourth- or fifth-grade level. Before children learn the terms and procedures involved in least common multiple and greatest common factor problems, they must use logical thinking and other problem-solving strategies to solve such problems (see Figure 7-1).

Example 7-17: Problem solving using logical reasoning (third- or fourth-grade level).

a. Hamburger buns are sold in packs of six, and hot dog buns are sold in packs of eight. What is the smallest amount that you could buy to have the same number of hamburger and hot dog buns?
b. Kim has 18 candy bars and 15 packs of gum. She wants to make bags of treats with an equal number of candy bars and an equal number of packs of gum in each bag. She will use all the candy bars and packs of gum. How many treat bags can she make?
c. Kari e-mails her cousin every 4 days and her pen-pal every 3 days. In a month with 30 days, how often does she send e-mail to her cousin and her pen-pal on the same day?

Solve each of the problems above before reading the solutions.

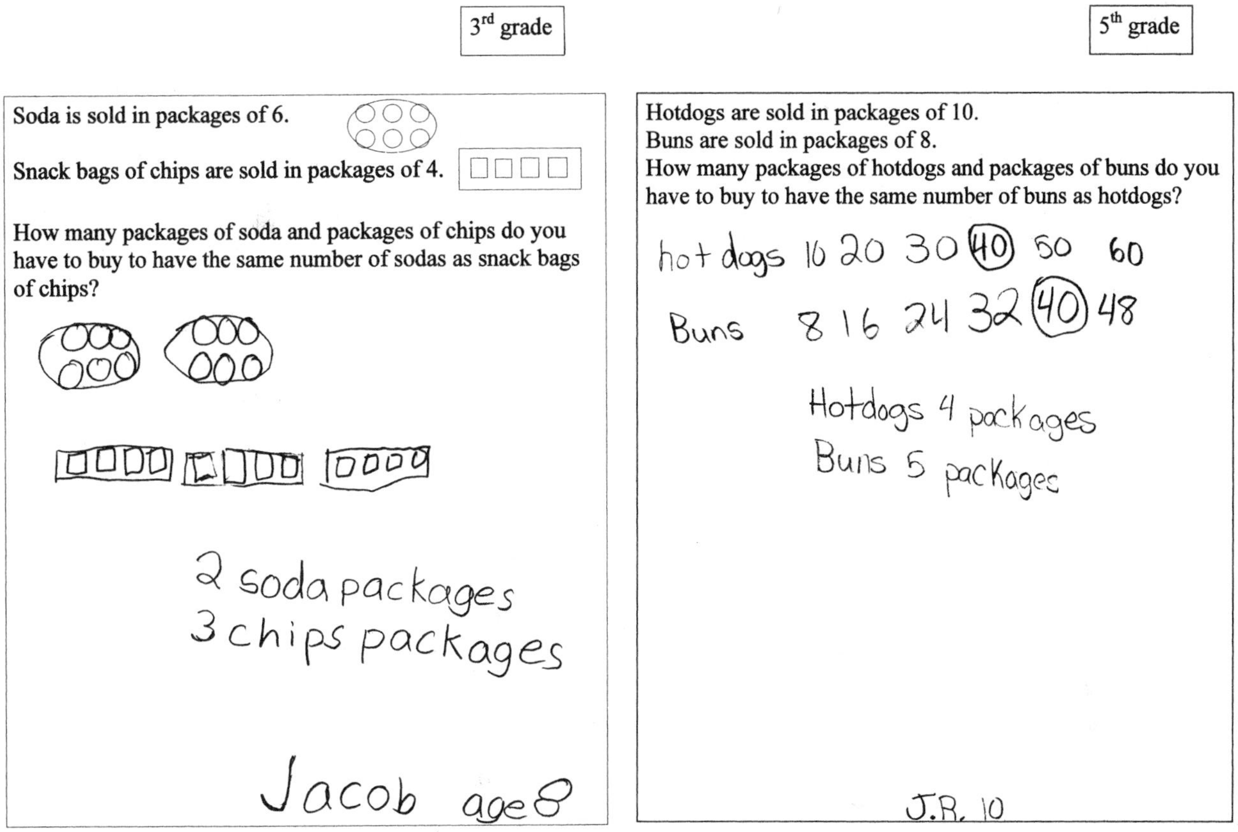

3rd grade

5th grade

Soda is sold in packages of 6.

Snack bags of chips are sold in packages of 4.

How many packages of soda and packages of chips do you have to buy to have the same number of sodas as snack bags of chips?

2 soda packages
3 chips packages

Jacob age 8

Hotdogs are sold in packages of 10.
Buns are sold in packages of 8.
How many packages of hotdogs and packages of buns do you have to buy to have the same number of buns as hotdogs?

hot dogs 10 20 30 ④ 50 60

Buns 8 16 24 32 ④ 48

Hotdogs 4 packages
Buns 5 packages

J.R. 10

FIGURE 7-1 A third-grade student may solve a least common multiple problem by drawing a picture, and a fifth-grade student may solve such a problem symbolically using numeric multiples.

Solutions:

a. Hamburger buns can be purchased in quantities of 6, 12, 18, 24, 30, 36, . . . and other multiples of 6. Hot dog buns can be purchased in quantities of 8, 16, 24, . . . and other multiples of 8. The smallest amount that you can buy to have the same number of hamburger and hot dog buns is 24 of each.

b. Kim could distribute 18 candy bars evenly among 1, 2, 3, 6, 9, or 18 bags. She could distribute 15 packs of gum evenly among 1, 3, 5, or 15 bags. Therefore, Kim could make 1 treat bag containing all 18 candy bars and all 15 packs of gum. She could not make 2 treat bags because 15 is not evenly divisible by 2. If she made 3 treat bags, there would be 6 candy bars and 5 packs of gum in each bag. There is no larger number of bags that she could make that would distribute all of the candy bars and all of the gum because 15 and 18 could not both be distributed evenly among a larger number of bags. To use all of the candy and distribute it evenly, Kim could make at most 3 treat bags.

c. Kari sends her cousin e-mail on days 4, 8, 12, 16, 20, 24, and 28 of the month. She e-mails her pen-pal on days 3, 6, 9, 12, 15, 18, 21, 24, 27, and 30.

Kari will send e-mail to both her cousin and her pen-pal twice—on days 12 and 24.

The Least Common Multiple

The problems given in Example 7-17 are typical common multiple and common factor problems. In Example 7-18a, you found the least common multiple of the numbers 6 and 8. Notice the process that is used. First, a few multiples of each number are listed. Then the lists are compared and the least common multiple, the smallest multiple common to both lists, is found. Formal definitions are given below.

Definition 7-3:

a. *Common multiple*—a nonzero number that is a multiple of two or more different numbers.

b. *Least common multiple (LCM)*—the least nonzero number that is a multiple of two or more different numbers.

In the definitions of "common multiple" and "least common multiple" it is important that only nonzero multiples are considered. Otherwise, because zero is a multiple of every whole number, zero would be a common multiple for any pair of numbers. It would also be the least common multiple for any pair of numbers. To avoid this trivial case, zero is excluded from consideration. The part of the phrase "least common multiple" that children often find misleading is the adjective *least*. Because the phrase begins with the word "least," some children erroneously expect the least common multiple to be a small number. They must remember that the least common multiple is a *multiple* of each of the numbers considered. In general, the least common multiple is at least as large as the largest of the numbers considered and no larger than the product of the numbers.

The Greatest Common Factor

In Example 7-17b you found the greatest common factor of the numbers 15 and 18. Notice the process that is used. First, the factors of each number are listed. Then the lists are compared and the common factors are found. The greatest common factor is the largest of these common factors. In some texts the phrase "greatest common divisor" is used instead of "greatest common factor." Formal definitions are given below.

Definition 7-4:
   a. *Common factor*—a number that is a factor of two or more different numbers.
   b. *Greatest common factor (GCF)*—the largest number that is a factor of each of two or more different numbers.

In the definition of "greatest common factor," it is not necessary to include the stipulation that the factor be nonzero. Zero is not a factor of any natural number. Recall that 1 is a factor of every natural number. In some cases, 1 will be the greatest common factor of a pair of numbers. In other cases, the greatest common factor will be larger than 1. For example, as determined in Example 7-17b, the GCF (15, 18) = 3. The adjective *greatest* in the phrase "greatest common factor" may mislead children into thinking that the GCF will be a large number. In general, the greatest common factor will be between 1 and the smallest of the numbers considered. After all, it must be a *factor* of each number.

Example 7-18: Compute each of the following.

   a. LCM (36, 48)
   b. LCM (45, 50, 90)
   c. GCF (36, 48)
   d. GCF (45, 50, 90)
   e. GCF (15, 16)

Solutions:

   a. Some multiples of 36 are 36, 72, 108, 144, 180, 216, 252, etc. Some multiples of 48 are 48, 96, 144, 192, 240, etc. The least common multiple is the smallest number common to these lists. LCM (36, 48) = 144.
   b. First find multiples of each of the numbers. Some multiples of 45 are 45, 90, 135, 180, 225, 270, 315,

360, 405, 450, etc. Some multiples of 50 are 50, 100, 150, 200, 250, 300, 350, 400, 450, 500, etc. Some multiples of 90 are 90, 180, 270, 360, 450, etc. LCM (45, 50, 90) = 450.
   c. Begin by listing factors of each number. The factors of 36 are 1, 2, 3, 4, 6, 9, 12, 18, and 36. The factors of 48 are 1, 2, 3, 4, 6, 8, 12, 16, 24, and 48. The common factors are 1, 2, 3, 4, 6, and 12. GCF (36, 48) = 12.
   d. Begin by listing factors of each number. The factors of 45 are 1, 3, 5, 9, 15, and 45. The factors of 50 are 1, 2, 5, 10, 25, and 50. The factors of 90 are 1, 2, 3, 5, 6, 9, 10, 15, 18, 30, 45, and 90. The only factors common to all lists are 1 and 5. GCF (45, 50, 90) = 5.
   e. Begin by listing factors of each number. The factors of 15 are 1, 3, 5, and 15. The factors of 16 are 1, 2, 4, 8, and 16. The only common factor is 1; hence, GCF (15, 16) = 1.

Using the Prime Factorization to Find the LCM or GCF

Instead of listing multiples to find the LCM or factors to find the GCF you could use the prime factorizations of the numbers involved. To be a multiple, a number must include all primes and powers of primes involved in the prime factorizations of the numbers. To be a divisor, a number includes only primes and powers of primes involved in each prime factorization. These ideas are illustrated in Example 7-19.

Example 7-19: Use prime factorizations to compute each of the following.

   a. LCM (36, 48) and GCF (36, 48)
   b. LCM (45, 50, 90) and GCF (45, 50, 90)
   c. LCM (15, 16) and GCF (15, 16)

Solutions:

   a. The prime factorizations are $36 = 2^2 \times 3^2$ and $48 = 2^4 \times 3$. Any number that is a multiple of both of these numbers must include at least four factors of 2 and two factors of 3. Thus, LCM (36, 48) = $2^4 \times 3^2 = 16 \times 9 = 144$. A factor of both numbers includes at most two factors of 2 and at most one factor of 3. Thus, GCF (36, 48) = $2^2 \times 3 = 12$.
   b. The prime factorizations are $45 = 3^2 \times 5$, and $50 = 2 \times 5^2$, and $90 = 2 \times 3^2 \times 5$. A number that is a multiple of all three of these numbers must include at least two factors of 3, two factors of 5, and one factor of 2. Hence, LCM (45, 50, 90) = $2 \times 3^2 \times 5^2 = 2 \times 9 \times 25 = 450$. A common factor cannot include the prime 3 because this is not a prime in each factorization. In particular, the prime 3 does not occur in the prime factorization of 50. A common factor cannot include the prime 2 because this is not a

prime in the prime factorization of 45. The prime 5 occurs only to the first power in one of the factorizations, but does occur in each factorization. Hence, a common factor can include at most one power of the prime 5: GCF (45, 50, 90) = 5.

c. The prime factorizations are $15 = 3 \times 5$ and $16 = 2^4$. A multiple of both of these must include each of these factors. Thus, LCM (15, 16) = $2^4 \times 3 \times 5 = 240$. Note that there are no common primes in the factorizations, hence GCF (15, 16) = 1.

Problem Set 7.4

For Your Understanding

1. The sponsor of the debate club wants to form debating teams so that each team includes both girls and boys. She wants each team to include the same number of girls and the same number of boys as each of the other teams. If 24 girls and 18 boys sign up for the debate club, what is the largest number of debating teams that can be made?

2. A store is giving away grand opening prizes. Every 8th customer gets a free pen. Every 10th customer gets a free keychain. How many of the first 200 customers will get both prizes?

3. The principal of a school puts presents in some of the lockers before the first day of school. She puts a magnet in every 8th locker, a notebook in every 12th locker, and a pen set in every 9th locker. What is the first locker number that will get all three presents?

4. Bob goes jogging every other day. Jim jogs every third day. Angie goes jogging every fourth day. If all three go jogging on April 1, list the next three days that they will all go running on the same day.

5. A room is 18 feet by 30 feet. The floor is to be covered by square tiles that are a whole number of feet on each side. If no tile is to be cut or broken, what are the different sizes of tiles that could be used?

6. A posterboard is 12 inches by 20 inches. It is to be covered by colored squares. All squares in a covering must be the same size and squares may not overlap. What sizes of squares could be used so that the board is entirely covered?

7. Compute each of the following.
   a. LCM (18, 60)
   b. LCM (36, 49)
   c. LCM (12, 40, 15)

8. Compute each of the following.
   a. LCM (75, 60)
   b. LCM (8, 45)
   c. LCM (72, 60, 126)

9. Compute each of the following.
   a. GCF (18, 60)
   b. GCF (36, 49)
   c. GCF (12, 40, 15)

10. Compute each of the following.
    a. GCF (75, 60)
    b. GCF (8, 45)
    c. GCF (72, 60, 126)

11. An adult, a child, and a duck all start walking from the same point. They each start off with their left foot. The adult takes two steps (left, right), the child takes three steps (left, right, left), and the duck takes five steps to cover the same amount of distance. At what distance did all three simultaneously land on their left foot?

12. When is the LCM of a pair of numbers equal to the product of the numbers?

13. LCM $(a, b) = 270$ and GCF $(a, b) = 9$. Find all possible values of a and b.

14. Sasha can run around a track in 60 seconds. It takes Jade 72 seconds to run around the track. How long will it take for Sasha to lap Jade?

15. During a field trip a teacher buys milkshakes for all 24 students in her class. When she later looks at the receipt, she notices that one of the digits is blurred. The receipt shows \$4 ● .96. The teacher recalls that the shakes were less than \$2.00 each. What is the missing digit, and what is the price for each shake?

16. The Euclidean algorithm is a method used to calculate the greatest common factor of a pair of numbers that has been around since approximately 300 BC. Read the discussion involving the Euclidean algorithm on this textbook's companion Web site. Use the Euclidean algorithm to calculate each of the following.
    a. GCF (11,025, 7,000)
    b. GCF (12,769, 5,040)
    c. GCF (1,674, 45,450)

Applications for the Classroom

1. Jackson asks whether you can find the "least common factor" for a pair of numbers. You are the teacher. How do you respond?

2. Milan asks whether you can find the "greatest common multiple" for a pair of numbers. You are the teacher. How do you respond?

3. Write two word problems appropriate for the third-grade level with solutions that involve the idea of common factors.

4. Write two word problems appropriate for the third-grade level with solutions that involve the idea of common multiples.

5. Look up "number theory" in the index or table of contents of an elementary-level textbook. Photocopy or copy by hand one example or problem that you think is interesting or unusual and indicate why. What objective from the NCTM model (or from your state or district model) does the example or problem address? Be sure to state what grade-level text you are using.

6. Find and print a number theory activity from the Web. State what grade level you think the activity would be appropriate for. What objective from the NCTM model (or from your state or district model) does the activity address?

7. Choose one of the books in the children's literature section of the references for this chapter. Write a brief description of the content of the book and explain how you could incorporate the book into a math lesson.

8. Make up two writing prompts or stems that fit in with material or activities from this chapter.

References

Children's Literature References

Anno, Masaichiro, & Mitsumasa, Anno. (1999). *Anno's mysterious multiplying jar.* New York: Penguin Putnam Books.

Cristaldi, Kathryn. (1996). *Even Steven and odd Todd.* New York: Scholastic.

Hulme, Joy. (1993). *Sea squares.* New York: Hyperion Books.

Losi, Carol. (1997). *The 512 ants on Sullivan Street* (Hello Math Reader Level 4). New York: Scholastic.

Mathews, Louise. (1978). *Bunches and bunches of bunnies.* New York: Scholastic.

Murphy, Stuart. (2000). *Missing mittens* (Mathstart Level 1, Odd and Even Numbers). New York: HarperCollins.

Pinczes, Elinor. (1995). *A remainder of one.* New York: Scholastic.

Teacher Resources

Alaska Department of Education and Early Development. 1999. *Alaska Mathematics Content Standards and Key Elements.* Retrieved December 1, 2003 from http://www.eed.state.ak.us/tls/PerformanceStandards/math.pdf

Bezuszka, S. J. (1985, October). A test for divisibility by primes. *Arithmetic Teacher, 33,* 36–39.

Brown, G. W. (1984, December). Searching for patterns of divisors. *Arithmetic Teacher, 32,* 32–34.

Burton, G. M., & Knifong, J. D. (1980). Definitions for prime numbers. *Arithmetic Teacher, 27*(6), 44–47.

Florida Department of Education. (1996). *Florida Sunshine State Standards.* Retrieved December 8, 2003 from http://www. firn.edu/doe/curric/prek12/ frame2.htm

Jensen, R. J. (1987, December). Teaching mathematics in technology: Common multiples activities on and off the computer. *Arithmetic Teacher, 35,* 35–37.

National Council of Teachers of Mathematics. (2000). *Principles and standards for school mathematics.* Reston, VA: Author.

Texas Education Agency. (1998). *Chapter 111. Texas Essential Knowledge and Skills for Mathematics.* Retrieved November 12, 2003 from http://www.tea.state.tx.us/rules/tac/ch111toc.html

Troutman A. P., & Lichtenberg, B. K. (2003). *Mathematics—A Good Beginning* (6th ed.). Belmont, CA: Wadsworth, Thomson Learning, Inc.

Selected Research Books and Articles

Campbell, P., & Clements, D. (1990). Using microcomputers for mathematics learning. In J. Payne (Ed.), *Mathematics for the young child* (pp. 265–283). Reston, VA: National Council of Teachers of Mathematics.

Campbell, P. F., & Stewart, E. L. (1993). Calculators and computers. In R.J. Jensen (Ed.), *Research ideas for the classroom: Early childhood mathematics* (pp. 251–261). New York: Macmillan.

Flores, A. (2002, February). Learning and teaching mathematics with technology. *Teaching Children Mathematics, 8*(6) 308–310.

8

Developing Concepts and Operations of Fractions and Decimals

Fractions are part of a mathematical system called the *rational number system* where a *rational number* represents the set of fractions equivalent to a given fraction. These terms are not generally used in the elementary school curriculum, so we will avoid their use in this textbook. There is a natural relationship between fractions, decimals, ratios, and percents. Ratios and percents are topics usually covered in the middle school years. To present more comprehensive coverage of these number topics and their relations, ratios and percents are discussed in the Appendices. In this chapter we will focus on fractions and decimals.

Many activities and examples for the conceptual introduction of fractions, decimals, and fraction and decimal computations and procedures are presented in this chapter. Students will have many real-world fraction and decimal experiences even before they enter their school-age years (Baroody, 1992; Gelman, 1994). Real-world examples and experiences can and should be used in the formal introduction to fraction and decimal concepts. Fractions can easily be used in connection with other subjects and topics. For example: "This morning we wrote down three of the nine words on our new spelling list. What fraction can we use to describe the amount of words we have written? What fraction describes the amount of words we still need to learn?"

By presenting fractions and decimals conceptually, students are able to build the necessary framework for later work with fraction and decimal algorithms and procedures. Current research indicates that children who approach fraction and decimal tasks conceptually perform better on posttests and retention tests than children who rely on standard, rote procedures in solving these problems (Cramer, Post, & delMas, 2002). Real-world connections and experiences promote appreciation for fraction ideas and confidence in fraction abilities. Concrete experiences can make fractions make sense.

Objectives

After completing Chapter 8, you will be able to

- Correctly use fraction notation, terminology, and models
- Use models to illustrate equivalent fractions, mixed numbers and improper fractions, and fraction computations
- Perform fraction computations and solve word problems involving fractions
- Correctly use decimal notation, terminology, and models
- Perform decimal computations and solve word problems involving decimals
- Describe strategies to help children develop meaning for fractions and decimals, learn basic fraction and decimal facts, and develop algorithms for fraction and decimal computations
- Diagnose and remediate common student errors involving fractions and decimals

8.1 CONSTRUCTING MEANING FOR FRACTIONS

Formal instruction in fraction concepts begins even earlier than the first-grade level, although fraction notations and terminology are sometimes avoided at these early levels as shown in Activities 8-1 through 8-4. A formal lesson plan designed around Activity 8-2 is included in the Appendices.

Notations, Symbolism, and Terminology

Fraction notations and symbolism are introduced at around the first-grade level. In the early grades, it is typical to write fractions using vertical notation only. That is, the fraction one half would be written as $\frac{1}{2}$ and not as 1/2. The latter notation is generally not introduced until the fourth- or fifth-

grade level. However, if you intend to use fraction calculators in your classroom, you may need to introduce the slanted line notation in earlier grades if the calculator that you choose to use displays fractions in this manner.

See the fraction calculator technology section in Appendix B for an introduction to some of the fraction calculators commonly used in the elementary grades.

Activity 8-1   Grades Pre-K–K

Find Equal Parts

Materials: Handouts with various items or shapes pictured.

Directions for Students: Circle the objects that are divided into equal parts.

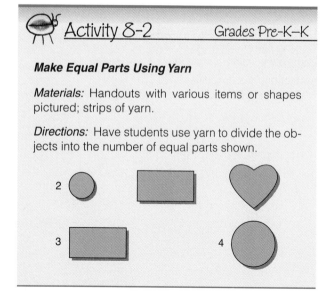

Activity 8-2   Grades Pre-K–K

Make Equal Parts Using Yarn

Materials: Handouts with various items or shapes pictured; strips of yarn.

Directions: Have students use yarn to divide the objects into the number of equal parts shown.

Activity 8-3   Grades Pre-K–K

Make Equal Groups Using Concrete Objects

Materials: Handout and counters for each student.

Directions: Tell students to place two counters on the numeral 2 on their handout. Then have the students make equal groups on the plates using these counters only. Repeat for 4, 6, 8, and 10 counters.

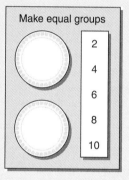

Activity 8-4   Grades K–1

Make Equal Groups Drawing a Picture

Materials: Handouts.

Directions: The large plate has several items pictured. Students draw pictures on the smaller plates to show equal groups.

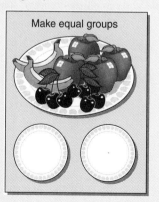

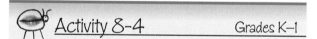

Example 8-1:

a. A first-grade-level example involving equal and unequal parts.
    You and your brother are going to split a pizza.
    He cuts the pizza into two pieces.
    He gives you the piece on the left.
    Did you get half of the pizza?
    Explain why or why not.

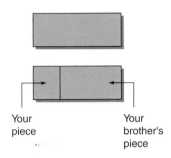

Your piece   Your brother's piece

b. Appropriate terminology and notations for fractions in first grade.
    Three equal parts are thirds.
    One out of three equal parts is shaded.
    One third is shaded.
    $\frac{1}{3}$ is shaded.

In the earliest grades, fraction examples typically involve simple diagrams or concrete objects. At this level, it is important to stress that the object, drawing, or set must have equal parts in order to determine a fraction. As students gain experience in making and recognizing equal sets, examples and diagrams become more complicated or abstract and may include *dotpaper* or *geoboard fractions* such as the one shown in Activity 8-5.

Example 8-2: Problem solving by drawing a picture (second- or third-grade level).

Jose eats $\frac{2}{3}$ of a sandwich. How much of the sandwich does he have left?

Example 8-3: Number line fractions (second-grade level).

Write the missing fraction.

By about the second or third grade, the words "numerator" and "denominator" are introduced. In the fraction $\frac{a}{b}$, the *numerator a* tells how many parts are shaded or otherwise indicated and the *denominator b* tells into how many parts the whole is divided. When dealing with fractions, it is important that it is clear what the "unit" object or size is. For example, half of a 12-inch pizza is smaller than half of a 16-inch pizza. In some cases, it does not matter what size or shape is used to represent a unit. For example, if three fourths of a pizza is eaten, you can determine that one fourth of the pizza is left regardless of the size or the shape of the pizza.

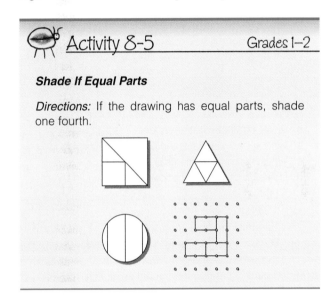

Activity 8-5   Grades 1–2

Shade If Equal Parts

Directions: If the drawing has equal parts, shade one fourth.

Standards

Ohio Academic Content Standards K–12 Mathematics

Number, Number Sense and Operations: Grade 2—Grade Level Indicator #5

The student should be able to represent fractions (halves, thirds, fourths, sixths and eighths), using words, numerals and physical models. For example:

a. Recognize that a fractional part can mean different amounts depending on the original quantity.

Ohio Department of Education, 2001

Standards

Mathematics Content Standards for California Public Schools
Number Sense, Grade 2

4.0 Students understand that fractions and decimals may refer to parts of a set and parts of a whole.

California Department of Education, 2000

Activity 8-6   Grades 3–4

Relating Division and Fractions

Materials: Strings of appropriate lengths for each group of students.

Teacher Statement: Let's see how fractions and division are related. If I take a string that is 1 foot long and fold it into four pieces, how long is each piece? You think it is $\frac{1}{4}$ of a foot? Let's check it with a ruler. Yes, you are correct. Folding the string represents $1 \div 4$, so we are saying that $1 \div 4$ is the same as $\frac{1}{4}$.

How about a string that is 3 feet long, divided into four pieces? Or 5 feet long divided into eight pieces? Or 5 feet long divided into four pieces? Check these within your groups, then figure out how to use string to answer the questions and later we will discuss your results.

a. Write a fraction that represents $2 \div 3$.
b. Write a division that is the same as $\frac{3}{8}$.
c. What fraction represents $5 \div 4$?
d. Use string to model $\frac{2}{4}$ and $\frac{1}{2}$. What do you notice?

By the third grade or so, fractions can be related to division. The fraction $\frac{1}{4}$ represents $1 \div 4$. The relationship between fractions and division can easily be modeled using string or using a number line model as in Activity 8-6.

Fraction Models and Equivalent Fractions

Using string or a number line model, it is easy to show that $\frac{2}{4}$ of a given unit is the same as $\frac{1}{2}$ of the same unit. Fraction equivalence can also be easily demonstrated with a shaded area model, a set model, or the fraction piece model as shown in Example 8-4.

Example 8-4: Models that illustrate the equivalence of $\frac{2}{4}$ and $\frac{1}{2}$.

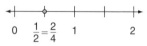

(a) Number Line Model

(b) Shaded Area Model

(c) Set Model

(d) Fraction Piece Model

The concrete and pictorial methods shown are excellent means by which to introduce the idea of equivalent fractions. This concept can be found as early as in first- or second-grade-level textbooks, although a formal definition is usually deferred. A third-grade-level textbook might contain the following definition: "*Equivalent fractions*—fractions that name the same amount. Example $\frac{2}{4}$ and $\frac{1}{2}$."

Example 8-5: Use the set model to find a fraction equivalent to $\frac{4}{10}$.

First, draw a set model representation of $\frac{4}{10}$. Upon consideration of this representation, you discover that two out of every five circles are shaded. That is, $\frac{4}{10}$ is equivalent to $\frac{2}{5}$. This can also be illustrated by adding lines to the diagram as shown. Two of the five sections contain shaded set objects.

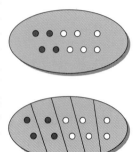

How would you determine the equivalence or nonequivalence of a pair of fractions such as $\frac{3}{5}$ and $\frac{5}{9}$? A number line or shaded area model is not feasible because the unit interval or figure would need to be divided into 5 equally spaced subintervals to represent fifths as well as into 9 equally spaced subintervals to represent ninths. Such models could be used to show that $\frac{3}{5}$ is approximately equal to $\frac{5}{9}$; however, further precision is required to state whether these quantities are equivalent. The fraction piece model cannot be used because commercial fraction piece model sets typically do not include both fifths and ninths. The set model is not an option as it is difficult to compare the sets as is shown in the following diagram.

In fact, a common misinterpretation of this diagram is "$\frac{3}{5}$ is equal to $\frac{5}{9}$ because the set models both have one more than half shaded." This is untrue.

Because fractions are related to division, a calculator could be used to discover that $\frac{3}{5} = 3 \div 5 = 0.6$ and $\frac{5}{9} = 5 \div 9 = 0.55555555 \ldots = 0.\overline{5}$. It is true that the quantity $0.55555555\ldots$ rounded to the nearest tenth is 0.6. Is this enough to say that $\frac{3}{5}$ is equivalent to $\frac{5}{9}$? No, it is not. Equivalent fractions must name the same amount—*precisely* the same amount.

By approximately the fourth-grade level, student textbooks printed prior to the mid-1980s usually included the following rule: $\frac{a}{b} = \frac{c}{d}$ if and only if $a \times d = b \times c$. You may remember learning and using this "cross-product" rule. It is

Math Manipulative: Fraction Pieces

A standard fraction tile set is made of hard plastic about 1/8 of an inch in thickness, and contains 51 pieces representing one whole as well as halves, thirds, fourths, fifths, sixths, eighths, tenths, and twelfths. Fraction manipulative sets are also available in paper-thin plastic strips, labeled or unlabeled fraction square sets, and labeled or unlabeled fraction circle sets. Fraction tower sets contain blocks of various sizes labeled with appropriate fractions. These blocks fit together much like unifix cubes. These other types of fraction manipulative sets may contain fewer or more pieces than the 51-piece fraction tile set mentioned above. Transparency versions or manipulative sets that will stick to a chalkboard or magnetic board are also widely available.

Commercial fraction manipulative sets are usually more durable than the homemade versions. They are also more costly; lost pieces may be easily replaced when using a homemade set. Most elementary textbook series contain photos of commercial fraction manipulatives that illustrate fraction operations such as identifying fractions, ordering fractions, finding equivalent fractions, adding and subtracting fractions, and computing with mixed numbers. A manipulative set is essential in developing the concept that a common denominator is necessary in order to add or subtract two fractions.

---

easy to use this rule to determine that $\frac{3}{5} \neq \frac{5}{9}$, since $3 \times 9 = 27$ and $5 \times 5 = 25$ and $27 \neq 25$. However, you *may not* use this rule with today's fourth-grade students unless they understand how and why it works. This illustrates one instance of how you will need to learn to teach differently from the ways that you were taught. We will revisit the process of determining whether a pair of fractions is equivalent in Section 8.2.

Each of the models shown in Example 8-4 can be found in early childhood student textbooks. It is becoming increasingly common for the unit in a shaded area model to be a rectangle or a square rather than a circle. This may be due to the fact that many teachers (and students) find rectangles easier than circles to divide into equal parts. If you were asked to draw a shaded area model to represent $\frac{3}{4}$, you might draw one of the figures shown in Example 8-6. Now draw shaded area models using units of (a) a circle, (b) a square, and (c) a rectangle to represent $\frac{2}{5}$. What type of unit is the easiest to divide into 5 equal parts? What type of unit do you think would be easiest to divide into 16 equal parts? As a teacher, you must think about what type of representation to draw to best illustrate a given fraction. For example, you should *not* begin a drawing to represent sixths with the following figure:

Example 8-6: Shaded area representations of $\frac{3}{4}$ using various unit shapes.

a.

b.

c.

Example 8-7 illustrates two conventions that are sometimes useful in solving fraction problems. Answer the questions given in this example before reading further.

Example 8-7: What part of each square is shaded (third- or fourth-grade level)?

a.

b.

If you answered $\frac{1}{3}$ for figure (a) or $\frac{2}{3}$ for figure (b), reconsider your answers as both of these are incorrect. The two conventions illustrated by these figures are as follows: (a) Sometimes drawing additional lines on a given figure will make equal parts easier to recognize, and (b) sometimes parts have the same size without having the same shape. Keeping these principles in mind, you may wish to reconsider your answers to Example 8-7 before reading further.

The correct answers of the amounts shaded in Example 8-7 are (a) $\frac{3}{8}$ and (b) $\frac{1}{2}$ or $\frac{2}{4}$. It is easy to see why these answers are correct if additional lines are drawn on the figures. The choice of where to position these additional lines is not unique. One possibility is shown below.

a.

b.

One of the examples in Activity 8-6 involved the fraction $\frac{5}{4}$. If you consider a string example, or plot this fraction on a number line, the result is shown below.

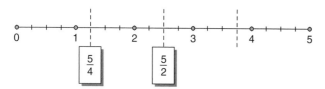

Notice that the fraction $\frac{5}{4}$ is equivalent to $1\frac{1}{4}$ and is plotted one fourth of the way between the integers 1 and 2. Fractions larger than 1 are also easily represented with a fraction piece model when enough pieces are available. One advantage to having students make their own sets of fraction pieces (see Blackline Master 17 in the Appendices) is that you can control how many of each piece is available for each student. The fraction piece model shown in Figure 8-1 is useful for Activity 8-7 in which students discover how many of a fraction of a given size it takes to make one whole.

1				$\frac{1}{4}$
$\frac{1}{4}$	$\frac{1}{4}$	$\frac{1}{4}$	$\frac{1}{4}$	$\frac{1}{4}$

FIGURE 8-1 Fraction piece model.

Activity 8-7
Grades 2–4

How Many Parts in a Whole?

Materials: Handout with questions, fraction pieces for each student or group.

Teacher-Directed Example: Use your fraction pieces. We'll do the first couple together. How many halves does it take to make a whole? Two, right. Three _____s make one whole. What piece does it take three of to make one whole? Yes, thirds. See if you can answer the rest of the questions.

a. ____2____ halves make one whole.

b. Three _thirds_ make one whole.

c. _____ eighths make one whole.

d. Five _____ make one whole.

e. Four _____ make one whole.

f. _____ sixths make one whole.

Do you see a pattern? Let's try a couple that we don't have fraction pieces for.

a. Seven _____ make one whole.

b. _____ elevenths make one whole.

The Pattern Block Model Pattern blocks also make good manipulatives for illustrating fraction relationships and concepts (see Activity 8-8). Paper pattern block representations may be made in the classroom so that each student has a set. A pattern block die for the Ellison machine is available. The Ellison machine is like a cookie cutter for paper. You insert the pattern block die, press the lever, and paper pattern block pieces are created. Many other dies are available. You may make your own handouts for this type of activity using Microsoft Word drawing tools to draw the pattern blocks (see Appendix B). When us-

> See Blackline Master 4 for a pattern block template and Blackline Master 19 for the handout shown in Activity 8-8, both in the Appendices.

ing a standard pattern block set to represent fractions, you must omit the squares and the tan rhombus pieces as these do not have convenient fraction interpretations.

The pattern block model may be used only to illustrate fractions for which there are associated pattern block pieces. In the conventional pattern block representation, the hexagon represents one whole, the trapezoid represents one half, the blue rhombus represents one third, and the triangle represents one sixth. The fraction $\frac{3}{2}$ is represented by three of the trapezoid one-half pieces. The fraction $\frac{3}{8}$ cannot

Activity 8-8
Grades 2–4

Pattern Block Fractions

Materials: Handout with questions; pattern blocks for each student or group.

Teacher-Directed Example: Use your pattern blocks. This (hold up a hexagon) will represent one whole. How many of these (hold up red trapezoid) does it take to make a whole? Yes, two. So what should we call this? Good, we'll call it a half. Write the word "half" on this shape on your handout. Figure out the fraction words for the other shapes shown and write them on the other shapes too. Now use your pattern blocks to answer the questions on the handout.

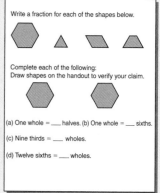

Write a fraction for each of the shapes below.

Complete each of the following:
Draw shapes on the handout to verify your claim.

(a) One whole = ___ halves. (b) One whole = ___ sixths.

(c) Nine thirds = ___ wholes.

(d) Twelve sixths = ___ wholes.

Example Questions:

One whole = ___ sixths.

Twelve sixths = ___ wholes.

be represented by the pattern block model because there is no pattern block piece that corresponds to an eighth.

Mixed Numbers and Improper Fractions

Two of the fractions discussed previously, $\frac{5}{4}$ and $\frac{3}{2}$, are improper fractions. Mixed numbers and improper fractions first appear at around the third-grade level. Some typical third-grade-level textbook definitions are as follows: *mixed number*—a number that has a whole number and a fractional part; *improper fraction*—a fraction in which the numerator is greater than or equal to the denominator. In using mixed numbers, it is generally assumed that the fractional part is a *proper fraction*—a fraction in which the numerator is less than the denominator. Note that in later grade levels, once negative numbers have been introduced, these definitions must be appropriately modified.

Example 8-8: Mixed numbers and improper fractions.

Write a mixed number for each of the following improper fractions.

a. $\dfrac{5}{4}$

b. $\dfrac{8}{3}$

c. $\dfrac{9}{6}$

Write an improper fraction for each of the following mixed numbers.

d. $1\dfrac{1}{3}$

e. $2\dfrac{5}{6}$

f. $3\dfrac{2}{4}$

Solutions:

a. Refer back to Figure 8-1. This fraction piece model indicates that $\frac{5}{4} = 1\frac{1}{4}$.

b. You can draw a shaded area model diagram. To represent a fraction that is larger than 1 using a shaded area model, more than one copy of the unit figure is necessary. Each unit must be divided into thirds, then eight thirds are shaded. From this diagram it is clear that $\frac{8}{3} = 2\frac{2}{3}$.

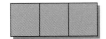 

c. You can use a pattern block model. It takes six sixths to complete the first whole unit. Another

three sixths cover half of a second unit. Thus, $\frac{9}{6} = 1\frac{3}{6} = 1\frac{1}{2}$.

 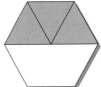

d. You can use the fraction piece model. To make an improper fraction, replace the unit bar with an equivalent amount of fraction pieces all of a common size. Because the original expression contains a one-third piece, replace the unit bar with three thirds. You can then see that $1\frac{1}{3} = \frac{4}{3}$.

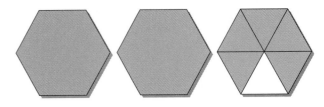

e. You can use the pattern block model. The expression $2\frac{5}{6}$ is represented by two shaded or covered whole units and $\frac{5}{6}$ of a third unit shaded or covered. You draw appropriate lines on the diagram or cover each unit hexagon with six sixths to discover that the mixed fraction is equivalent to seventeen sixths. Hence, $2\frac{5}{6} = \frac{17}{6}$.

f. You can draw a shaded area model diagram. The mixed fraction $3\frac{2}{4}$ is represented by three whole units and $\frac{2}{4}$ of another unit. You may choose any shape of unit that may be divided into fourths. If you use a square unit, the mixed fraction $3\frac{2}{4}$ is shown below.

To convert to an improper fraction, divide each of the whole unit squares into four fourths. Looking at this new diagram you can see that $3\frac{2}{4} = \frac{14}{4}$.

![bee illustration] Teaching Connections

Use a Variety of Fraction Models in Your Classroom A variety of models were used in the solutions to Example 8-8. For any given problem, there may be several models that would be appropriate for use in the solution. You should practice using a variety of models, and encourage your students to experiment with various models. At around the second-grade level, students may be asked to solve fraction problems without being told what type of model to use in the solution.

Beginning at the first-grade level, students are often asked to use estimation in many types of fraction problems and situations. A *benchmark* is a known or common measurement used to estimate other measurements. Students may use benchmarks like $\frac{1}{4}$, $\frac{1}{3}$, $\frac{1}{2}$, $\frac{2}{3}$, and $\frac{3}{4}$ to estimate fractional amounts. The combination of estimation and fractions will often allow you to incorporate real-world examples and make connections between mathematics and other subject areas.

Figure 8-2 shows how benchmarks are used at the second-grade level. Notice that in the first two examples, the student is to determine how much of the food or drink is *left,* whereas in the second example, the student is to determine how much of the food is *eaten.* The figure also illustrates a real-world example of equivalent fractions.

Example 8-9: Estimating fractions (first- or second-grade level).

We have been studying different countries. Look at the flags that we have hanging at the front of the room. Which flag is the flag of Italy? About how much of the flag of Italy is green? Which flag is Poland's? How much of Poland's flag is red? How about the U.S. flag? About how much of the U.S. flag is blue?

Example 8-10: Problem solving by drawing a picture (third- or fourth-grade level).

You and your friends decide to skate to the park and back. You leave your house at 9:00 A.M. It takes $\frac{1}{2}$ of an hour to skate $\frac{3}{4}$ of the way to the park. If you always skate at the same speed, and you do not stop, can you make it back to your house by 10:30 A.M.?

Solution: Yes, you can make it back by 10:30 A.M. Draw a picture below.

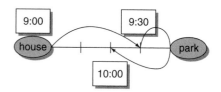

A good problem extension for the problem given above is to ask how long the skaters could stay at the park and still make it home by 10:30. By looking at the illustra-

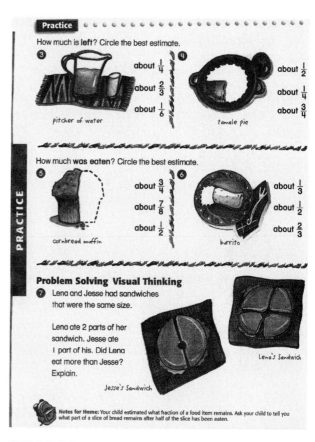

FIGURE 8-2 School book page using fraction estimation. *Source:* Page 472 from *Scott Foresman—Addison Wesley Math Grade (2).* Copyright © 1999 by Addison Wesley Longman, Inc. Reprinted by permission of Pearson Education, Inc.

![bee illustration] Using Literature in the Mathematics Classroom **Grades K–2**

Fraction Action

By Loreen Leedy
The Trumpet Club, Inc., 1994

This is a delightful book in which a collection of animal pupils learn fraction concepts from Miss Prime the teacher (a slender hippopotamus?). The pupils in the book provide many examples of various fractions and solve problems posed by Miss Prime. This provides the classroom teacher several opportunities to pause and ask similar questions of the class. The book covers halves, thirds, fourths, and fifths. It illustrates the concepts of fractions of objects, fractions of sets, ordering of fractions, and equal sharing.

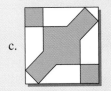

Assessment   Grades 2–3

Writing Activity

Show the class the picture book *Eating Fractions* by Bruce McMillan (Scholastic, 1991).

<u>Directions for Students:</u>

Write a story or problem about a food that you would eat only part of. Use a fraction in your story or problem to tell how much of the food that you would eat.

Note: You may provide students with a writing stem and ask them to draw a picture to illustrate. For example, I can eat _____ of a _____.

tion, you determine that each segment of one fourth of the distance to the park takes 10 minutes to skate. If the skaters left the park immediately, they would be home at 10:20. To get home exactly at 10:30, they could spend 10 minutes at the park. This extended problem illustrates the problem-solving strategy of working backward.

Problem Set 8.1

For Your Understanding

1. Use each of the models below to illustrate the equivalence of the fractions $\frac{3}{6}$ and $\frac{1}{2}$.
   a. The number line model
   b. The shaded area model
   c. The set model
   d. The fraction piece model
   e. The pattern block model

2. Write a fraction to represent the shaded amount for each of the following.

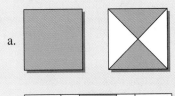

a.

b.

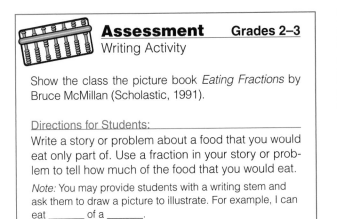

c.

3. a. Plot A and B on a number line.

   (A) $\frac{3}{5}$ (B) $\frac{5}{3}$

b. Write a fraction for C.

$$\vdash\!\!\diamond\!+\!+\!\diamond\!+\!+\!\diamond\!+\!+\!\diamond\!+\!\dashv$$
$$0 \qquad 1 \qquad 2 \quad C\ 3$$

4. Margaret had some jellybeans. She gave half of them to Debbie. Debbie divided her jellybeans into four equal sets. She ate one set and gave the other three sets to Michelle, Crystal, and Yvonne. Michelle gave half of her jellybeans to Destinee. Destinee got 6 jellybeans. How many jellybeans did Margaret have originally?

5. Draw a model appropriate for each of the following.
   a. Write a mixed number that is equivalent to $\frac{11}{4}$.
   b. Write a mixed number that is equivalent to $\frac{7}{3}$.
   c. Write an improper fraction that is equivalent to $3\frac{5}{8}$.
   d. Write an improper fraction that is equivalent to $2\frac{1}{6}$.

6. You need $3\frac{1}{4}$ cups of water for a recipe, but have measuring cups for only $\frac{3}{4}$ cup and $\frac{1}{2}$ cup. How can you use these to measure the water you need?

7. You have a large box of raisins. You give $\frac{1}{2}$ to a friend. Then you give $\frac{1}{2}$ of what is left to another friend. Then you give $\frac{1}{2}$ of what is left to a third friend. How much of the box do you have for yourself?

8. Carl's car has a 20-gallon gas tank and gets about 30 miles per gallon. Estimate the amount of gas in the tank for each of the gauge readings below. Then estimate the number of miles Carl could drive before he would have to stop for gas.

a.

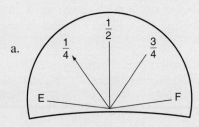

b.

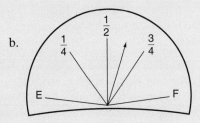

9. Ella has a habit of estimating. When using fractions, she uses convenient numbers in her estimations so that the result is a common fraction. For example, Ella has read 147 pages in a book that has 304 pages. She estimates by using the fraction $\frac{150}{300}$ and claims that she has read about $\frac{1}{2}$ of the book. What fractions will Ella use for each of the following?

   a. 19 of 30 students returned their permission forms for a field trip.

   b. 9 of 35 teachers volunteered to be judges in the science fair.

   c. Of the 787 students in a school, 105 were designated as honor roll students.

10. Estimate the amount shaded in each of the following.

   a.
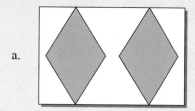

   b.
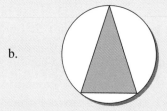

11. Show that any whole number can be represented by a fraction.

Applications for the Classroom

1. When is it easier to use a square model than a rectangular one in drawing a shaded area representation?

2. List the number of each size of piece contained in a typical fraction tile set. There are 51 pieces in the set representing one whole, halves, thirds, fourths, fifths, sixths, eighths, tenths, and twelfths.

3. Describe advantages and disadvantages to using a labeled fraction manipulative set versus an unlabeled set.

4. Create a handout that could be used with Activity 8-1. You may wish to review the instructions given in Appendix B for using the Microsoft Word drawing toolbar.

5. Ian makes the following claim: "The fractions $\frac{3}{5}$ and $\frac{5}{9}$ are equivalent because if a set model is drawn, each set has one more than half the circles shaded." You are the teacher. How do you respond?

6. Malcolm makes the following claim: "The fractions $\frac{7}{3}$ and $\frac{9}{4}$ are equivalent since $\frac{7}{3} = 7 \div 3 = 2$ $R1$ and $\frac{9}{4} = 9 \div 4 = 2\,R1$." You are the teacher. How do you respond?

7. Consider the five different types of models: (a) number line, (b) shaded area, (c) set, (d) fraction piece, and (e) pattern block. Then consider the five fractions $\frac{2}{3}, \frac{3}{2}, \frac{14}{25}, \frac{11}{6}$, and $\frac{5}{12}$. For each model type choose one of the fractions and represent it using that model. Use each fraction only once.

8. Chenise wishes to plot the fraction $\frac{2}{5}$ on a number line. She draws this illustration. You are the teacher. How do you respond?

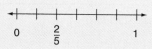

$$0 \qquad \frac{2}{5} \qquad\qquad 1$$

9. Problem: Jack divides a pie into 6 equal amounts and Jill divides a pie into 8 equal amounts. Both eat one piece of their pie. Who eats more pie?

   Dawn's Solution: Jill eats more because her pie has more pieces.

   You are the teacher. How do you respond?

10. The geoboard is a math manipulative not described within this text. Do research at the library or on the Internet to find information on geoboards, then write a math manipulative description in the same format as those given in this text.

11. Create a handout that could be used with Activity 8-5. You may wish to review the instructions given in Appendix B for using the Microsoft Word drawing toolbar.

12. Create two examples of using benchmarks or estimation and fractions (see Example 8-9) that you could use in your classroom.

13. Classify the level of knowledge and the type of learning experience of Activity 8-7. What objective from the NCTM model (or from your state or district model) does the activity address?

14. Design a rubric that will measure student achievement and understanding of Activity 8-7.

15. Write a lesson plan that describes how you could use pattern blocks to represent fractions in a third-grade classroom (see Activity 8-8). Follow the format given by your instructor or use the lesson plan format given in the Appendix A.

16. Look up "fractions" in the index or table of contents of an elementary-level textbook. Photocopy or copy by hand one example or problem that you think is interesting or unusual and indicate why. What objective from the NCTM model (or from your state or district model) does the activity or problem address? Be sure to state what grade-level text you are using.

8.2 Constructing Meaning for Fraction Computations and Algorithms

Imagine that you are teaching in a fourth-grade class and a student writes $\frac{1}{2} + \frac{2}{3} = \frac{3}{5}$. Which of the following should you *not* do?

    a. Tell the student she needs to find a common denominator to add fractions.

    b. Ask the student if she used estimation to check her answer.

    c. Ask the student to show you the addition using fraction tiles or other manipulatives.

    d. Tell the student to draw a picture to represent the computation.

The worst thing for you to do is (a). You should *not* merely tell the student that she needs a common denominator. This illustrates a major difference in the teaching methods of today compared to the teaching methods of years ago. Students should be held accountable to determine whether their answers are correct or reasonable. The student who uses estimation will know that the above calculation is incorrect. Manipulatives or pictures will guide the student to realize that a common denominator is necessary and will help her correctly finish the calculation.

Students should not be introduced to fraction computations and algorithms until they have developed some fraction sense. It will take many experiences with concrete and pictorial models before children are ready to deal with fractions at a purely symbolic level. For example, if a first- or second-grade student were shown the two symbols $\frac{1}{2}$ and $\frac{1}{3}$ and asked which represented the larger fraction, the student might answer $\frac{1}{3}$ (because 3 is larger than 2). If the same student were shown a picture of two sandwiches (of the same shape and size) and asked to draw lines on the picture to indicate one half of the first sandwich and one third of the second sandwich and then asked which is larger $\frac{1}{2}$ or $\frac{1}{3}$, with the aid of this visual experience, the student is likely to correctly answer $\frac{1}{2}$.

Using the Fraction Piece Model to Illustrate Computations and Algorithms

Before students learn algorithms and processes, it is important that they understand the concepts underlying these processes. In Section 8.1 we used a variety of models in developing the concept of fractions. However, in developing fraction procedures and algorithms, we will consistently use the fraction piece model in order to avoid unnecessary distractions that could arise from switching between various models. This use of a single model allows you, the future teacher, to easily compare and contrast the difficulty levels and procedures in the activities presented. When teaching fraction procedures you will use various models as necessary. Different students will respond better to different models.

It is vital that students understand the concrete representations of the procedures. Once the students are able to perform a computation using the concrete model, they may attempt such problems by drawing pictures to represent the model. Finally, the students will be ready to attempt such problems symbolically. By first learning to perform the procedures using a concrete model, the student has a basis for comparison and can use visualization of the model to make the steps of the symbolic computation make sense and to recall what the next step of the computation entails.

You must first be sure that your students understand how fractions may be represented using the fraction piece model (see Activity 8-9). Then ideas such as addition of fractions with a common denominator, equivalent fractions, or ordering of fractions can be presented (see Activities 8-10 and 8-11).

Equivalent Fractions The concept of equivalent fractions was introduced in Section 8.1 using a variety of models. The fraction piece model may be used to further develop this concept. Activity 8-11 may be done with actual fraction pieces or with uncut copies of Blackline Masters 17 and 18 in the Appendices.

Once students understand the concept of equivalent fractions and realize that a single fraction can have several names, you may work on developing the procedure of using multiplication or division to generate equivalent fractions. This procedure is based on the fact that if $\frac{a}{b}$ is any rational

Activity 8-9 — Grades 2–3

Representing Fractions

Materials: A plate or manipulative mat and a fraction piece set for each student (see Blackline Master 17 in the Appendices).

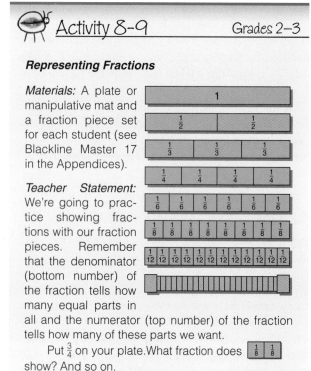

Teacher Statement: We're going to practice showing fractions with our fraction pieces. Remember that the denominator (bottom number) of the fraction tells how many equal parts in all and the numerator (top number) of the fraction tells how many of these parts we want.

Put $\frac{3}{4}$ on your plate. What fraction does [1/8 1/8] show? And so on.

Extension: The initial setup can use fraction bars that are flipped over so that the fraction symbols are not showing.

Activity 8-10 — Grades 2–4

Modeling Addition of Fractions

Materials: A plate or manipulative mat and a fraction piece set for each student (see Blackline Master 17 in the Appendices).

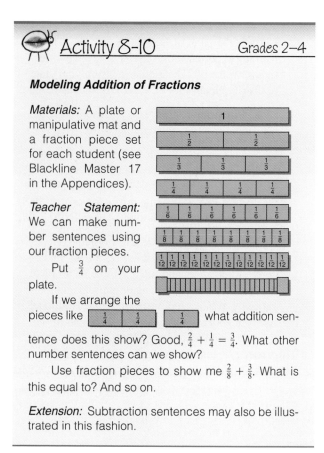

Teacher Statement: We can make number sentences using our fraction pieces.

Put $\frac{3}{4}$ on your plate.

If we arrange the pieces like [1/4 1/4] [1/4] what addition sentence does this show? Good, $\frac{2}{4} + \frac{1}{4} = \frac{3}{4}$. What other number sentences can we show?

Use fraction pieces to show me $\frac{2}{8} + \frac{3}{8}$. What is this equal to? And so on.

Extension: Subtraction sentences may also be illustrated in this fashion.

number and c is any nonzero whole number, then the fraction $\frac{a \times c}{b \times c}$ is equivalent to the fraction $\frac{a}{b}$. That is, $\frac{a}{b} = \frac{a \times c}{b \times c}$ for all whole numbers a, b, and c such that b and c are nonzero. As a teacher it is important that you understand why this rule holds and how it will be used in later fraction computations and procedures.

Example 8-11: An informal justification of the rule or fact $\frac{a}{b} = \frac{a \times c}{b \times c}$.

The fraction $\frac{a}{b}$ can be represented by dividing an appropriate number of unit strips each into b equal pieces of size $\frac{1}{b}$ and shading or otherwise indicating a of these pieces.

b pieces total in each unit strip

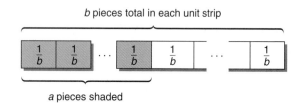

a pieces shaded

If each of the pieces in this representation is subdivided into c equal parts, the result is a representation for which

$a \times c$ pieces are shaded and each unit strip is divided into $b \times c$ equal pieces of size $\frac{1}{b \times c}$. That is, the result is a representation of the fraction $\frac{a \times c}{b \times c}$. The shaded amount did not change; hence $\frac{a}{b} = \frac{a \times c}{b \times c}$.

The justification shown in Example 8-11 of the equivalent fraction rule would not be presented to elementary students. However, students at the third- or fourth-grade level could be led to discover this equivalent fraction rule by using paper folding or by using patterns. Following the completion of the table in Activity 8-12, students should discuss their results. A similar activity could be designed so that students could discover that dividing both the numerator and denominator of a given fraction by the same nonzero whole number also results in an equivalent fraction.

Ordering Fractions Ordering of fractions is another process that can be readily accomplished when fraction strips are available. In the very early grades, you may wish to create a simpler version of the fraction strips as shown in Activity 8-13.

The "Write About It" components of Activity 8-14 are of central importance to the activity. Students use fraction pieces to derive the rules, but they must also think about why the rules make sense. By forming their own

Sample observation log for assessment of Activity 8-10:

	Using fraction pieces to illustrate a given addition sentence	Writing an addition sentence for a given set of fraction pieces	No difficulties noted
		Difficulties noted with	
Jordan		√	
Diamond			√
Derek	√ needs practice with fraction piece model	√	

Activity 8-11   Grades 2–4

Modeling Equivalent Fractions

Materials: Rulers and a fraction piece set for each student (see Blackline Masters 17 and 18).

Teacher Statement: We have already discovered that some fractions have more than one name. For example, we discovered that one half is the same as two fourths or (write the symbols) $\frac{1}{2} = \frac{2}{4}$.

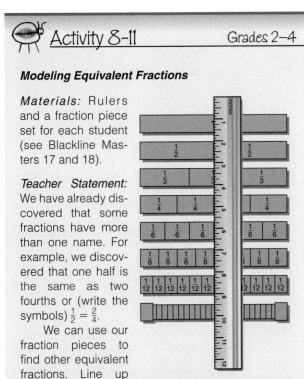

We can use our fraction pieces to find other equivalent fractions. Line up your fraction pieces and use your ruler. Can you explain why one half is the same as two fourths? Can you find other fractions that are the same as one half or two fourths? Good, three sixths is the same as two fourths. How about one half and three sixths? Are these the same? Yes, they are. So (write) $\frac{1}{2} = \frac{2}{4} = \frac{3}{6}$. Which fraction name is the simplest name for this amount? Can you find more fractions that are equivalent to one half? (Write fractions on the board as students find them. Repeat for other fractions such as two thirds, etc.)

Activity 8-12   Grades 3–4

Using Multiplication to Generate Equivalent Fractions

Materials: A fraction piece set and handout for each student (see Blackline Masters 17, 18, and 20).

Teacher Statement: We are going to find out what happens when you multiply both the numerator and denominator of a fraction by the same whole number. Complete the table below. Use your fraction strips to compare the fractions.

Original fraction	Multiply both numerator and denominator by the number given	New fraction	Compare the fractions
$\frac{1}{2}$	2	$\frac{1 \times 2}{2 \times 2}$	$\frac{2}{4}$	$\frac{1}{2} = \frac{2}{4}$
$\frac{1}{2}$	3	$\frac{1 \times 3}{2 \times 3}$		
$\frac{1}{2}$	4			
$\frac{1}{2}$	6			
$\frac{1}{3}$	2			
$\frac{1}{3}$	4			
$\frac{1}{3}$	8			
$\frac{3}{4}$	2			
$\frac{3}{4}$	3			

Write About It: What happens when you multiply both the numerator and the denominator of a fraction by the same nonzero whole number?

---

rules and then thinking about why these rules make sense, if a student were to forget a rule, she would be more apt to be able to recreate it correctly than if she were to merely memorize a given set of rules. Errors that occur when children try to memorize rules and procedures without

consideration of how and why these rules and procedures work are given in Section 8.4. It is up to you to ensure that rules and algorithms that the students create are correct and complete. Understanding how and why a rule works also will be essential in moving from performing a procedure using concrete manipulatives to performing the procedure symbolically.

 Activity 8-13   Grades 1–2

Comparing Fraction Sizes

Materials: A double-sided fraction strip for each student (see below).

Teacher Statement: Everybody has a strip that is the same size. We will find out what happens when the strip is folded into different numbers of pieces. Group 1 will fold their strips into two pieces. That is, Group 1 will fold their strips in half. Group 2 will fold their strips into three pieces or thirds. Group 3 will fold their strips into four pieces or fourths.

    Which group will have the largest pieces? Which group will have the smallest pieces?

    Let's check. Start folding.

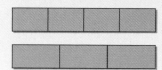

One side is marked in four equal parts, the other side is marked in three equal parts.

    Let's see if our answers make sense. Which is larger—one half of a pizza or one third of a pizza? Yes, one half of a pizza is larger than one third. Which is larger, one third of a pizza or one fourth? Etc.

Example 8-12: Use fraction strips (see Blackline Masters 17 and 18 in the Appendices) to order the fractions $\frac{1}{2}, \frac{5}{4}, \frac{3}{4}, \frac{2}{6}, \frac{5}{24}, \frac{1}{3}, 1$, and $\frac{3}{5}$ from least to greatest.

Solution: Cut fraction strips from Blackline Masters 17 and 18. It is easily seen using these fraction strips that $\frac{5}{24} < \frac{2}{6} = \frac{1}{3} < \frac{1}{2} < \frac{3}{5} < \frac{3}{4} < 1 < \frac{5}{4}$.

Adding and Subtracting Fractions with Unlike Denominators Using concrete models, children can see why it is necessary to have a common denominator to add or subtract fractions. They should already be skilled in using the model to find equivalent fractions. This skill enables them to write each fraction as an equivalent fraction using the common denominator. The fractions may then be added or subtracted as desired (see Activities 8-15 and 8-16).

 Teaching Connections

Use Developmental, Reinforcement, and Drill and Practice Activities Most of the activities presented in this chapter so far have been developmental activities designed to introduce fraction concepts and procedures. Following many developmental activities, you will wish to use reinforcement activities to reinforce these concepts (see Activities 8-17 and 8-18). Reinforcement activities may also

---

 Activity 8-14   Grades 3–4

Comparing Fractions with Like Denominators or Numerators

Materials: A fraction piece set for each student (see Blackline Masters 17 and 18).

Teacher Statement: Use fraction strips to order each set of fractions. Then answer the questions.

a. $\dfrac{3}{8}, \dfrac{6}{8}, \dfrac{5}{8}, \dfrac{2}{8}, \dfrac{4}{8}$

b. $\dfrac{11}{12}, \dfrac{6}{12}, \dfrac{8}{12}, \dfrac{7}{12}, \dfrac{4}{12}$

Write About It: When fractions have the same denominator, how can you use the numerator to order the fractions? Why does this method work?

a. $\dfrac{3}{8}, \dfrac{3}{6}, \dfrac{3}{5}, \dfrac{3}{10}, \dfrac{3}{4}$

b. $\dfrac{4}{2}, \dfrac{4}{6}, \dfrac{4}{4}, \dfrac{4}{3}, \dfrac{4}{5}$

Write About It: When fractions have the same numerator, how can you use the denominator to order the fractions? Why does this method work?

Teacher Statement: Order the following sets of fractions without using fraction pieces.

a. $\dfrac{4}{7}, \dfrac{4}{13}, \dfrac{4}{9}, \dfrac{4}{11}, \dfrac{4}{5}$

b. $\dfrac{3}{11}, \dfrac{6}{11}, \dfrac{9}{11}, \dfrac{2}{11}, \dfrac{4}{11}$

Write About It: Which is easier, ordering a set of fractions that have the same numerator or ordering a set of fractions that have the same denominator? Explain your answer.

---

introduce additional models. Finally, drill and practice activities (see Activity 8-19) are useful to help children develop skill and speed in fraction computations.

Performing Fraction Procedures Without Using Concrete Objects

Many of the activities presented in this chapter are based on the children using concrete fraction pieces. Eventually children must learn to perform fraction procedures symbolically without the concrete representations. Many experiences and activities using concrete representations are essential so that students understand the underlying concepts and procedures. This also provides a solid frame of reference. When performing symbolic calculations, children may need to visualize fraction pieces or other concrete materials to remind themselves of the correct procedures.

Activity 8-15   Grades 3–4

Adding Fractions with Unlike Denominators

Materials: Fraction strips for each student and uncut fraction strip sheets (see Blackline Master 17).

Teacher Statement: We've already seen how easy it is to use fraction strips to add fractions that have the same denominators. We can also use fraction strips to add fractions like $\frac{1}{2} + \frac{1}{3}$. First put together the fraction strips that represent these fractions. Then find on

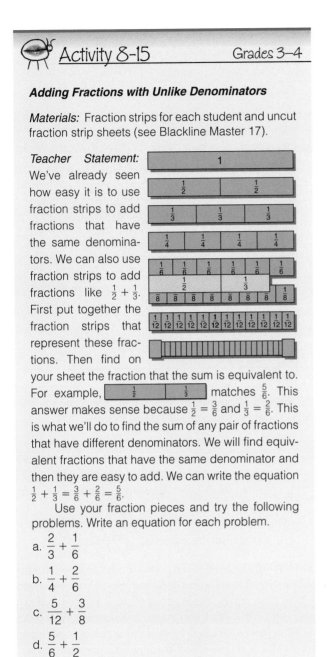

your sheet the fraction that the sum is equivalent to. For example, $\boxed{\frac{1}{2}\ \ \ \frac{1}{3}}$ matches $\frac{5}{6}$. This answer makes sense because $\frac{1}{2} = \frac{3}{6}$ and $\frac{1}{3} = \frac{2}{6}$. This is what we'll do to find the sum of any pair of fractions that have different denominators. We will find equivalent fractions that have the same denominator and then they are easy to add. We can write the equation $\frac{1}{2} + \frac{1}{3} = \frac{3}{6} + \frac{2}{6} = \frac{5}{6}$.

Use your fraction pieces and try the following problems. Write an equation for each problem.

a. $\frac{2}{3} + \frac{1}{6}$

b. $\frac{1}{4} + \frac{2}{6}$

c. $\frac{5}{12} + \frac{3}{8}$

d. $\frac{5}{6} + \frac{1}{2}$

Activity 8-16   Grades 3–4

Subtracting Fractions with Unlike Denominators

Materials: Fraction strips for each student and uncut fraction strip sheets (see Blackline Master 17).

Teacher Statement: We've already seen how easy it is to use fraction strips to add fractions. We can also use fraction strips to subtract fractions. When the fractions have the same denominator, this is easy. For example, $\frac{3}{4} - \frac{1}{4} = \frac{2}{4}$.

We can also use fraction strips to subtract fractions that don't have the same denominator, like $\frac{3}{4} - \frac{1}{3}$. Overlap the fraction strips that represent these fractions. Then find on your sheet the fraction that the difference is equivalent to. We can use equivalent fractions to write an equation so that the subtraction makes sense.

$$\frac{3}{4} - \frac{1}{3} = \frac{9}{12} - \frac{4}{12} = \frac{5}{12}$$

Use your fraction pieces and try the following problems. Write an equation for each problem.

a. $\frac{2}{3} - \frac{1}{6}$

b. $\frac{3}{4} - \frac{1}{8}$

c. $\frac{5}{12} - \frac{3}{8}$

d. $\frac{5}{6} - \frac{1}{2}$

Converting Between Mixed and Improper Fractions
The first procedure to consider is the conversion between mixed numerals and improper fractions. In presenting this procedure, it is important to stress the underlying ideas. When given an improper fraction, you must determine how many whole units are present and then determine the remaining fraction. When given a mixed number, you must convert each whole unit to the appropriate fractional units and count the total number of fractional units. This process was illustrated using concrete and visual models in Example 8-8 of Section 8.1. No di-

agrams or models are shown in the example below. Use visualization as necessary.

Example 8-13: Mixed numbers and improper fractions.

a. Convert $\frac{19}{5}$ to a mixed number.

b. Convert $3\frac{2}{7}$ to an improper fraction.

Solutions:

a. Because each whole unit will contain 5 fifths you count by fives—5, 10, 15—to determine that $\frac{19}{5}$ will

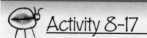

Activity 8-17 — Grades 3–4

Matching the Story, the Model, and the Equation

Materials: Deck of matching fraction problems.

Teacher Statement: Everybody will get a card. Some of the cards have story problems, some have pictures of fraction strips, and some have fraction equations. When I say go, you need to find the others in your group. Your group will explain to the class why you are a match.

Note: If cards are printed on transparency material, it is easy for students to share their results.

> Maria has one half of a pound of candy. Carlos has one third of a pound of candy. How much candy do they have together?

$$\frac{1}{2} + \frac{1}{3} = \frac{3}{6} + \frac{2}{6} = \frac{5}{6}$$

$\frac{1}{2}$		$\frac{1}{3}$	
$\frac{1}{6}$	$\frac{1}{6}$	$\frac{1}{6}$	$\frac{1}{6}$	$\frac{1}{6}$

Activity 8-18 — Grades 3–4

Writing Story Problems and Equations

Materials: Fraction pictures.

Directions: For each picture shown, have students write an equation and a story problem to go with the picture.

a.

b.

c.

Activity 8-19 — Grades 3–4

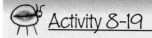

Fastest Fractions—Ordering

Materials: An envelope with fractions to order for each student; one set of large index cards with the fractions.

Teacher Statement: Place your cards face down. When I say go, flip your cards and order them from smallest to largest. If you have trouble ordering the fractions, visualize that amount of a pizza or a candy bar. (Walk around room and give the large index cards to the first students who have correctly ordered their fractions. Students with the index cards go to the front of the room to show the solution to the rest of the class by standing in the correct order and showing the large index cards.)

$\frac{1}{2}$	$\frac{1}{3}$	$\frac{2}{3}$	$\frac{1}{4}$	$\frac{3}{4}$

Formal algorithms or rules for the conversion procedures shown in Example 8-13 are as follows:

1. To convert the improper fraction $\frac{a}{b}$ to a mixed number, perform the indicated division to obtain a quotient q and remainder r. For example, $\frac{a}{b} = a \div b = qRr$. The equivalent mixed number is $\frac{a}{b} = q\frac{r}{b}$.

2. An equation to convert the mixed number $q\frac{r}{b}$ to an improper fraction is $q\frac{r}{b} = \frac{qb + r}{b}$.

Simplifying Fractions Next, consider the process of simplifying fractions. The fraction $\frac{a}{b}$ is in *simplest form* if a and b have no common factors greater than 1. Prior to Activity 8-12, you learned that dividing both the numerator and the denominator of a fraction by the same nonzero whole number produces an equivalent fraction. The quickest method to simplify a fraction is thus to divide both the numerator and the denominator by their greatest common factor.

Example 8-14: Write each fraction in simplest form as a mixed number.

a. $\dfrac{20}{12}$

b. $\dfrac{46}{9}$

Solutions:

a. GCF (20, 12) = 4. So $\frac{20}{12} = \frac{5 \times 4}{3 \times 4} = \frac{5}{3}$ and $\frac{5}{3} = 1\frac{2}{3}$. Note that you could have first written the fraction as a mixed number and then simplified: $\frac{20}{12} = 1\frac{8}{12}$ and GCF (8, 12) = 4 so that $\frac{20}{12} = 1\frac{8}{12} = 1\frac{2 \times 4}{3 \times 4} = 1\frac{2}{3}$.

contain three whole units and a remainder of $\frac{4}{5}$. Thus, $\frac{19}{5} = 3\frac{4}{5}$.

b. Each whole unit will be divided into 7 sevenths. Three whole units includes 7, 14, 21 sevenths and the additional $\frac{2}{7}$ implies that $3\frac{2}{7} = \frac{23}{7}$.

b. Since GCF $(46, 9) = 1$, the fraction $\frac{46}{9}$ is already in simplest form. Write it as a mixed number. First determine the number of whole units by counting 9, 18, 27, 36, 45; there are five whole units. Then $\frac{46}{9} = 5\frac{1}{9}$.

Ordering Fractions The next procedure to consider is that of ordering fractions. Activity 8-14 shows that it is easy to order fractions if they have the same numerator or the same denominator. Most students (and teachers) will find it easier to order fractions that have the same denominator than fractions that have the same numerator. Fractions that have the same denominator can be represented by the same size fraction pieces. The numerators tell how many of the pieces are under consideration. For example, $\frac{5}{9}$ is larger than $\frac{4}{9}$ since $\frac{5}{9}$ is represented by 5 one-ninth pieces and $\frac{4}{9}$ is represented by 4 one-ninth pieces. You can use this idea along with the idea of equivalent fractions to order any pair of fractions, consequently one new definition is required: Given a pair of fractions $\frac{a}{b}$ and $\frac{c}{d}$, the *least common denominator* is the least common multiple LCM (b, d). Thus, the least common denominator is the smallest natural number divisible by both b and d. The phrase "least common denominator" is descriptive in that this number is the smallest possible denominator for which equivalent fractions to both original fractions can be found.

Example 8-15: Order the fractions $\frac{5}{8}$ and $\frac{11}{20}$.

Solution: Since LCM $(8, 20) = 40$, find fractions with a denominator of 40 that are equivalent to the given fractions. To solve $\frac{5}{8} = \frac{}{40}$ and $\frac{11}{20} = \frac{}{40}$, recall that multiplication can be used to generate equivalent fractions. Since $8 \times 5 = 40$, calculate $5 \times 5 = 25$ to get the numerator of the first fraction. Also, $20 \times 2 = 40$ implies the numerator of the second fraction is $11 \times 2 = 22$. Thus, you have $\frac{5}{8} = \frac{25}{40}$ and $\frac{11}{20} = \frac{22}{40}$. Now $\frac{22}{40} < \frac{25}{40}$ and so $\frac{11}{20} < \frac{5}{8}$.

Adding and Subtracting Fractions The concepts of least common denominator and equivalent fractions are also used in adding or subtracting fractions that do not already have a common denominator. This parallels the methods used in Activities 8-15 and 8-16 where fraction pieces were used for such calculations. Calculate answers to each of the problems given in Example 8-16 before reading the solutions given.

Example 8-16: Calculate each of the following.

a. $\dfrac{5}{8} + \dfrac{4}{9}$

b. $\dfrac{5}{6} - \dfrac{4}{9}$

c. $\dfrac{1}{4} + \dfrac{5}{6} + \dfrac{3}{4}$

Solutions:

a. LCM $(8, 9) = 72$, so you calculate equivalent fractions each with denominator 72. You find that $\frac{5}{8} = \frac{45}{72}$ and $\frac{4}{9} = \frac{32}{72}$. Thus $\frac{5}{8} + \frac{4}{9} = \frac{45}{72} + \frac{32}{72} = \frac{77}{72}$.

b. LCM $(6, 9) = 18$, so you calculate equivalent fractions each with denominator 18. You find that $\frac{5}{6} = \frac{15}{18}$ and $\frac{4}{9} = \frac{8}{18}$. Thus $\frac{5}{6} - \frac{4}{9} = \frac{15}{18} - \frac{8}{18} = \frac{7}{18}$.

c. Did you first calculate the least common denominator LCM $(4, 6, 4) = 12$ and then compute equivalent fractions with a denominator of 12 for each of the three addends? If so, reconsider the sum $\frac{1}{4} + \frac{5}{6} + \frac{3}{4}$. The quickest way to perform this calculation is to use the properties of commutativity and associativity of addition. This problem is easily solved with mental math using "compatible numbers." Since $\frac{1}{4} + \frac{3}{4} = 1$, the answer to the problem $\frac{1}{4} + \frac{5}{6} + \frac{3}{4}$ is $1\frac{5}{6}$.

In the solutions to Example 8-16, you used least common denominators in your calculations. Notice that in Example 8-16a the least common denominator happens to be the product of the two original denominators. In general, it is a consequence of problem 12 in Section 7.4 that the least common denominator of a pair of fractions will be no larger than the product of the denominators of the fractions. It is not really necessary to use the *least* common denominator when adding or subtracting fractions. Any common denominator will make the calculations possible. However, using the least common denominator ensures that the numbers used in the calculations are as small as possible. In Example 8-16b you chose to use the least common denominator LCM $(6, 9) = 18$. You could have used any multiple of 18 as the denominator. For example, you could have used the product $6 \times 9 = 54$ as the denominator. In this case the calculations become $\frac{5}{6} - \frac{4}{9} = \frac{45}{54} - \frac{24}{54} = \frac{21}{54} = \frac{7 \times 3}{18 \times 3} = \frac{7}{18}$. Notice the extra simplification that is required when a denominator other than the least common denominator is used.

Computations Involving Regrouping, Improper Fractions, or Equal Additions Notice also that the answer to Example 8-16c is a mixed number. In some cases, computations with mixed numbers will require regrouping or other additional procedures. Additions and subtractions may be written either horizontally or vertically. When regrouping is involved, the vertical format is often more convenient. In the next example the additions and subtractions are written using the vertical format. Each answer may be checked by using concrete materials or by drawing a pictorial representation.

Example 8-17: Compute each of the following.

a.
$$\begin{aligned}
&1\tfrac{4}{5}\\
+\,&2\tfrac{2}{5}\\
\hline
\end{aligned}$$

b.

$$4$$
$$- 2\frac{1}{4}$$

c.

$$3\frac{1}{3}$$
$$- 1\frac{1}{2}$$

Solutions: These notational solutions use regrouping.

a.

$$1\frac{4}{5}$$
$$+2\frac{2}{5}$$
$$3\frac{6}{5} = 4\frac{1}{5}$$

b.

$$\begin{array}{lll} 4 & & 3\frac{4}{4} \\ - 2\frac{1}{4} & = & - 2\frac{1}{4} \\ \hline & & 1\frac{3}{4} \end{array}$$

c.

$$\begin{array}{llll} 3\frac{1}{3} & 3\frac{2}{6} & 2\frac{8}{6} \\ - 1\frac{1}{2} & = - 1\frac{3}{6} & = - 1\frac{3}{6} \\ \hline & & 1\frac{5}{6} \end{array}$$

For subtraction of mixed numbers, the equal additions trick presented in Section 5.4 may be useful. This is illustrated below.

b.

$$\begin{array}{lllll} 4 & + \frac{3}{4} & & 4\frac{3}{4} \\ - 2\frac{1}{4} & + \frac{3}{4} & = & - 3 \\ \hline & & & 1\frac{3}{4} \end{array}$$

c.

$$\begin{array}{lllll} 3\frac{1}{3} & + \frac{1}{2} & & 3\frac{5}{6} \\ - 1\frac{1}{2} & + \frac{1}{2} & = & - 2 \\ \hline & & & 1\frac{5}{6} \end{array}$$

Addition and subtraction problems involving mixed numbers may also be solved by converting all mixed numbers to improper fractions. However, when the whole part is large, converting to improper fractions may involve te-dious arithmetic that may be avoided by using the regrouping or equal additions methods as shown previously.

Example 8-18: Compute $163\frac{1}{2} - 47\frac{3}{4}$ using (a) improper fractions, (b) regrouping, and (c) equal additions.

Solutions:

a. $163\frac{1}{3} - 47\frac{3}{4} = \dfrac{490}{3} - \dfrac{191}{4} =$

$\dfrac{1960}{12} - \dfrac{573}{12} = \dfrac{1387}{12} = 115\dfrac{7}{12}$

b. $163\frac{1}{3} - 47\frac{3}{4} = 163\frac{4}{12} - 47\frac{9}{12} =$

$162\dfrac{16}{12} - 47\dfrac{9}{12} = 115\dfrac{7}{12}$

c. $163\frac{1}{3} - 47\frac{3}{4} = \left(163\frac{1}{3} + \frac{1}{4}\right) - \left(47\frac{3}{4} + \frac{1}{4}\right) =$

$163\dfrac{7}{12} - 48 = 115\dfrac{7}{12}$

Multiplications Involving Fractions

At the third- or fourth-grade level, multiplications involving one factor a whole number and the other factor a fraction are introduced. Examples typically involve real-life situations that the children can understand and relate to. The format of the multiplication sentences parallels the format introduced with the multiplication of whole numbers. For example, the equation $2 \times 12 = 24$ is represented by the concrete idea that 2 sets with 12 objects in each set yields a total of 24 objects. The equation $\frac{1}{3} \times 12 = 4$ is represented by the concrete idea that one third of a set if there are 12 objects in the set is 4 of the objects. Here is a typical real-life example: (a) "A carton of eggs has 12 eggs. How many eggs are in $\frac{1}{3}$ of a carton?" Consider this example: (b) "Liam buys 6 bags of candy. Each bag contains $\frac{1}{2}$ pound of candy. How much candy did Liam buy?" This example is modeled by the equation $6 \times \frac{1}{2} = 3$. Liam has 3 pounds of candy. These examples are illustrated by the diagrams below.

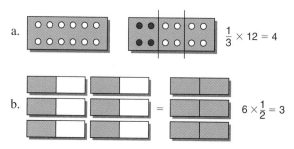

The area model can also be used to illustrate multiplication of fractions and parallels that of the array model of multiplication of whole numbers. The first factor is represented by the rows of the diagram, and the second factor is repre-

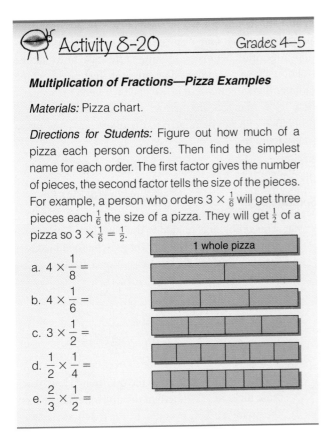

Activity 8-20   Grades 4–5

Multiplication of Fractions—Pizza Examples

Materials: Pizza chart.

Directions for Students: Figure out how much of a pizza each person orders. Then find the simplest name for each order. The first factor gives the number of pieces, the second factor tells the size of the pieces. For example, a person who orders $3 \times \frac{1}{6}$ will get three pieces each $\frac{1}{6}$ the size of a pizza. They will get $\frac{1}{2}$ of a pizza so $3 \times \frac{1}{6} = \frac{1}{2}$.

1 whole pizza

a. $4 \times \dfrac{1}{8} =$

b. $4 \times \dfrac{1}{6} =$

c. $3 \times \dfrac{1}{2} =$

d. $\dfrac{1}{2} \times \dfrac{1}{4} =$

e. $\dfrac{2}{3} \times \dfrac{1}{2} =$

sented by the columns of the diagram. The denominators of the factors indicate the total number of rows and columns, whereas the numerators of the factors indicate the number of rows and columns that are shaded. For example, to represent the multiplication $\frac{3}{4} \times \frac{2}{3}$ with an area diagram, the array contains four rows and three columns. Shading is restricted to three of the four rows and two of the three columns. Example 8-19 illustrates the area model interpretation of multiplication of fractions.

Example 8-19: Use an area model to represent (a) $\frac{3}{4} \times \frac{2}{3}$ and (b) $\frac{1}{3} \times \frac{1}{4}$.

Solutions:

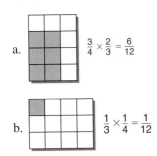

a. $\quad \dfrac{3}{4} \times \dfrac{2}{3} = \dfrac{6}{12}$

b. $\quad \dfrac{1}{3} \times \dfrac{1}{4} = \dfrac{1}{12}$

The number line model can also be used to model fraction multiplications. A number line example is illustrated in Example 8-20. This model is usually reserved for equations in which the first factor is a whole number.

Example 8-20: Illustrate $4 \times \frac{1}{2}$ using a number line model.

Solution:

$4 \times \dfrac{1}{2} = 2$

Both the number line model and the area model lend support to the following fraction multiplication rule or algorithm: If $\frac{a}{b}$ and $\frac{c}{d}$ are any two fractions, then $\frac{a}{b} \times \frac{c}{d} = \frac{a \times c}{b \times d}$. To multiply a whole number by a fraction, first convert the whole number to an equivalent fraction. For example, $n = \frac{n}{1}$. Notice that to multiply two fractions, you do *not* need to find a common denominator for the fractions before you perform the multiplication.

Two methods can be used to multiply mixed numbers. One method is to convert all mixed numbers to improper fractions and use the rule above. Another method is to use the distributive property of multiplication over addition. These methods are illustrated in Examples 8-21 and 8-22 below. Which method is easier to use depends on the numbers involved.

Example 8-21: Compute $2\frac{3}{4} \times 1\frac{4}{7}$ using (a) improper fractions and (b) the distributive property.

Solutions:

a. $\quad 2\dfrac{3}{4} \times 1\dfrac{4}{7} = \dfrac{11}{4} \times \dfrac{11}{7} = \dfrac{121}{28} = 4\dfrac{9}{28}$

b. $\quad 2\dfrac{3}{4} \times 1\dfrac{4}{7} =$

$\quad (2 \times 1) + \left(2 \times \dfrac{4}{7}\right) + \left(\dfrac{3}{4} \times 1\right) + \left(\dfrac{3}{4} \times \dfrac{4}{7}\right) =$

$\quad 2 + \dfrac{8}{7} + \dfrac{3}{4} + \dfrac{12}{28} = 3 + \dfrac{1}{7} + \dfrac{3}{4} + \dfrac{12}{28} =$

$\quad 3 + \dfrac{4}{28} + \dfrac{21}{28} + \dfrac{12}{28} = 3 + \dfrac{37}{28} = 4 + \dfrac{9}{28} = 4\dfrac{9}{28}$

Example 8-22: Compute $4 \times 23\frac{2}{5}$ using (a) improper fractions and (b) the distributive property.

Solutions:

a. $\quad 4 \times 23\dfrac{2}{5} = \dfrac{4}{1} \times \dfrac{117}{5} = \dfrac{468}{5} = 93\dfrac{3}{5}$

b. $\quad 4 \times 23\dfrac{2}{5} = (4 \times 23) + \left(4 \times \dfrac{2}{5}\right) =$

$\quad 92 + \dfrac{8}{5} = 93 + \dfrac{3}{5} = 93\dfrac{3}{5}$

Example 8-23: Use fraction pieces to illustrate $2\frac{1}{2} \times 1\frac{1}{3}$.

Solution: This product is represented by $2\frac{1}{2}$ sets with $1\frac{1}{3}$ in each set.

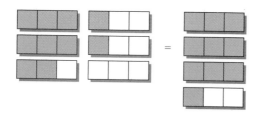

The diagram shows that $2\frac{1}{2} \times 1\frac{1}{3} = \frac{10}{3} = 3\frac{1}{3}$.

Divisions Involving Fractions

In the early childhood curriculum, divisions involving fractions may appear in problem-solving situations. These problems can be solved using diagrams and logical thinking. The symbolic representation of division of fractions is usually not presented until around the fifth- or sixth-grade level.

Example 8-24: Problem solving using a diagram (fourth-grade level).

Jamila has $2\frac{3}{5}$ cups of powdered drink mix. It takes $\frac{1}{3}$ of a cup of mix to make each serving. About how many servings can she make?

Solution: Each cup of mix will make three servings. The remaining mix will make at least one and possibly two servings. Because the question did not require an exact answer, either seven servings or eight servings would be reasonable answers.

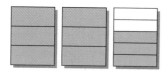

If the question had required an exact answer, you would have to be more precise. After the first two cups of mix are used, to determine whether the remaining mix will yield one or two servings, compare the fractions $\frac{3}{5}$ and $\frac{2}{3}$. The least common denominator is 15, so you compute $\frac{3}{5} = \frac{9}{15}$ and $\frac{2}{3} = \frac{10}{15}$. Then it is clear that $\frac{3}{5} < \frac{2}{3}$. That is, there is not enough mix remaining to make two additional servings. Thus only seven complete servings can be made.

By the fifth or sixth grade, students can use symbolic representations and fraction division rules to calculate $2\frac{3}{5} \div \frac{1}{3} = \frac{13}{5} \div \frac{1}{3} = \frac{13}{5} \times \frac{3}{1} = \frac{39}{5} = 7\frac{4}{5}$. This answer indicates that $7\frac{4}{5}$ servings can be made. If an exact answer is desired, the fractional part must be dropped and only 7 servings may be made.

You may remember learning the rule "to divide fractions, invert the divisor and multiply." This rule was used above in changing the problem $\frac{13}{5} \div \frac{1}{3}$ to $\frac{13}{5} \times \frac{3}{1}$. It is possible that you learned this rule without ever being shown how and why the rule makes sense. If you are teaching in an early childhood classroom, it is likely that you will never have to teach this rule. However, as a well-educated

adult, you should understand and be able to perform division of fractions. Our discussion of the division of fractions algorithm begins by looking at the case in which the fractions have a common denominator. Just as the whole number division problem $m \div n$ can be related to the question "How many ns are there in m?" the fraction division problem $\frac{a}{b} \div \frac{c}{b}$ can be related to the question "How many $\frac{c}{b}$s are there in $\frac{a}{b}$?"

Example 8-25: Use models to compute (a) $\frac{8}{3} \div \frac{2}{3}$ and (b) $\frac{1}{6} \div \frac{2}{6}$.

Solutions:

a. This problem is related to the question "How many $\frac{2}{3}$ are there in $\frac{8}{3}$?" The answer may be found using a number line (as shown below) or a fraction piece model.

$$\frac{8}{3} \div \frac{2}{3} = 4$$

b. This problem is related to the question "How many $\frac{2}{6}$ are there in $\frac{1}{6}$?" Note that the divisor is larger than the dividend. This problem is illustrated with a fraction piece model diagram.

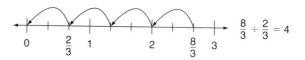

From the diagram it is clear that there is half of a $\frac{2}{6}$ region within a $\frac{1}{6}$ region. Thus $\frac{1}{6} \div \frac{2}{6} = \frac{1}{2}$.

After looking at several examples of this type, you might begin to see a pattern. By considering division as a partitioning, and by considering fraction piece and other concrete models, it eventually becomes clear that $\frac{a}{b} \div \frac{c}{b} = \frac{a}{c}$. Once this rule is discovered, you can perform divisions of fractions that do not have a common denominator by finding equivalent fractions that do have a common denominator.

Example 8-26: Calculate $\frac{8}{3} \div \frac{2}{5}$ by first finding a common denominator.

Solution: The common denominator is 15, hence $\frac{8}{3} \div \frac{2}{5} = \frac{40}{15} \div \frac{6}{15} = \frac{40}{6} = \frac{20}{3}$.

Using the procedure above, you can derive the general rule for division of fractions as $\frac{a}{b} \div \frac{c}{d} = \frac{a \times d}{b \times d} \div \frac{c \times b}{d \times b} = \frac{a \times d}{b \times d} \div \frac{c \times b}{b \times d} = \frac{a \times d}{c \times b} = \frac{a \times d}{b \times c} = \frac{a}{b} \times \frac{d}{c}$. This derivation uses the idea of equivalent fractions, the rule for multiplication of fractions, and the commutative property of multiplication. Hence, it does make sense that to divide fractions, you invert the divisor and multiply.

Example 8-27: Use fraction pieces to illustrate $1\frac{1}{2} \div \frac{3}{4}$.

Solution: The fraction $1\frac{1}{2}$ is represented by the first figure shown. Adding lines to the figure shows that there are two shaded sets of $\frac{3}{4}$. Thus, $1\frac{1}{2} \div \frac{3}{4} = 2$.

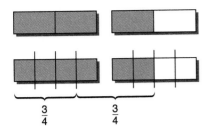

Problem Set 8.2

For Your Understanding

1. Photocopy Blackline Master 20 in the Appendices and complete Activity 8-12.

2. Complete Activity 8-14. Be sure to answer the "Write About It" questions.

3. Draw a fraction strip representation, write an equation, and complete each calculation.
   a. $\frac{1}{3} + \frac{5}{8}$
   b. $\frac{2}{3} - \frac{1}{2}$

4. Draw a fraction strip representation, write an equation, and complete each calculation.
   a. $1\frac{1}{3} - \frac{5}{6}$
   b. $1\frac{2}{3} + \frac{3}{4}$

5. a. Write $4\frac{5}{6}$ as an improper fraction.
   b. Write $\frac{31}{4}$ as a mixed number.
   c. Write $\frac{60}{24}$ in simplest form as a mixed number.
   d. Write $\frac{35}{24}$ in simplest form as a mixed number.

6. a. Write $5\frac{2}{9}$ as an improper fraction.
   b. Write $\frac{17}{3}$ as a mixed number.
   c. Write $\frac{45}{28}$ in simplest form as a mixed number.
   d. Write $\frac{66}{48}$ in simplest form as a mixed number.

7. Write the fractions $\frac{1}{2}, \frac{7}{15}$, and $\frac{13}{30}$ in order from least to greatest.

8. In the trivia tournament, Tom answers 6 out of every 7 questions correctly, J. P. answers 5 out of every 6 questions correctly, and Bill answers 22 out of every 28 questions correctly. They each answer the same number of questions. Award the prizes for first place, second place, and third place to these three contestants.

9. Compute (a) $46\frac{1}{4} + 27\frac{7}{8}$ and (b) $46\frac{1}{4} - 27\frac{7}{8}$.

10. Compute (a) $10\frac{2}{15} + 7\frac{8}{9}$ and (b) $10\frac{2}{15} - 7\frac{8}{9}$.

11. Multiply $3\frac{1}{2} \times 10\frac{4}{5}$ and show your work using (a) improper fractions and (b) the distributive property.

12. Multiply $12\frac{1}{3} \times 6\frac{3}{8}$ and show your work using (a) improper fractions and (b) the distributive property.

13. Calculate each of the following. Draw a model to illustrate each calculation.
    a. $\frac{8}{9} \div \frac{4}{9}$
    b. $2\frac{1}{2} \div \frac{3}{4}$

14. You and a friend are working on a jigsaw puzzle. You put together $\frac{3}{8}$ of the puzzle. Your friend puts together $\frac{1}{3}$ of the puzzle. Your little brother takes apart $\frac{1}{2}$ of what you and your friend have assembled. How much of the puzzle is still together?

15. A pet shop has short-, medium-, and long-haired kittens. One sixth of the kittens have long hair, three fourths have short hair, and the rest have medium hair. If there are 10 medium-haired kittens, how many have long hair?

16. A jar of marbles is half red, one third green, and the rest blue. If eight marbles are green, how many are blue?

17. Joan has $5\frac{1}{2}$ yards of ribbon. She makes bows that each take $\frac{3}{4}$ of a yard of ribbon. How many bows can she make?

18. a. Tyrel eats $\frac{1}{2}$ of a pizza. Dana eats $\frac{1}{3}$ of what Tyrel didn't eat and feeds the rest to the dog. How much of the pizza did the dog get?
    b. Dexter eats $\frac{1}{2}$ of a pizza. Dylan eats $\frac{1}{3}$ of the pizza and feeds the rest to the dog. How much of the pizza did the dog get?

19. Keisha paints $\frac{1}{3}$ of a wall. Joe paints $\frac{1}{2}$ of the remaining portion of the wall. How much is still unpainted?

20. On a map two cities are $2\frac{1}{4}$ inches apart. If each inch represents 80 miles, how far apart are the actual cities?

21. Sally has $4\frac{3}{4}$ yards of fabric. She uses $\frac{1}{2}$ of the fabric to make a shirt and then 2 yards to make a pair of matching shorts. How much fabric is left over?

22. Tai makes $4\frac{1}{2}$ cups of waffle batter. He uses $\frac{2}{3}$ of a cup of batter for each waffle. How many waffles can he make?

Applications for the Classroom

1. Solve the problems given in Activity 8-20. Give explanations for your answers that could be used in a fourth-grade classroom.

2. Choosing an appropriate model is an important teacher skill. Consider the four types of models: number line, set model, area model, and fraction piece model. Then compute the following four problems and illustrate each of the computations using one of the models listed. Use each model only once.

   a. $\frac{1}{4} \times 24$

   b. $\frac{3}{5} \times \frac{2}{3}$

   c. $6 \times \frac{1}{4}$

   d. $3\frac{1}{2} \times \frac{2}{3}$

3. Design a division activity similar to Activity 8-12 and create a handout similar to Blackline Master 20 (see the Appendices).

4. Create a set of cards that could be used with Activity 8-17.

5. Design a drill and practice activity to practice a fraction procedure and create the materials for your activity.

6. Design a paper-folding activity to help students discover various equivalent fractions.

7. Explain how the computational formula $\frac{a}{b} \times \frac{c}{d} = \frac{a \times c}{b \times d}$ can be illustrated using an area model diagram.

8. Create a handout that could be used with Activity 8-18. You may wish to review the instructions given in Appendix B for using the Microsoft Word drawing toolbar.

9. Write a word problem using fractions that could be used at the second-grade level. Indicate how your problem could be modified to be used with lower ability or higher ability students.

10. A fourth-grade student writes $\frac{5}{8} - \frac{1}{2} = \frac{4}{6} = \frac{2}{3}$. You are the teacher. How do you respond?

11. A third-grade student writes $3\frac{2}{5} = \frac{6}{5}$ and $1\frac{2}{3} = \frac{2}{3}$. You are the teacher. Describe the error the student is making. How do you respond?

8.3 Constructing Meaning for Decimals and Decimal Computations

The grade level at which decimal notation is introduced varies depending on the textbook series used. The kindergarten-level textbook of the Saxon Math series includes the lesson "Paying for items to $1.00 using dimes" as well as other lessons that use decimal notation and concepts. However, many K–2 textbook series limit money examples to amounts that are less than one dollar, using cent symbolism rather than decimal notation and symbolism (see Activities 8-21 and 8-22).

Teaching Connections

Using Money as a Decimal Model Money provides a natural introduction to the concept of decimals. Drawing on real-life experiences, most children have already been exposed to decimals prior to their formal introduction as a mathematics topic.

Estimation, especially using money amounts, is a very important skill. If children have developed the habit of using estimation, they can often detect errors they make in performing actual computations. Estimation is especially important when children are learning to use a calculator to perform a new skill or operation. When adding money amounts on a calculator, it is very easy to misplace a decimal point in one or more of the addends. If estimations are performed prior to the actual calculations, these types of errors can be easily discovered and corrected.

Decimals involving tenths and hundredths are easily modeled using money. In fact, money can be used to illustrate the reasonableness of the terms "tenth" and "hundredth." These terms could even be introduced using money examples as in Activity 8-23. A second- or third-grade textbook might include the following definitions: A *tenth* is 1 of 10 equal parts of a whole. A *hundredth* is 1 of 100 equal parts of a whole.

Money examples can also be used to illustrate the difference between equivalent decimals such as 0.6 and 0.60. The first expression, six tenths, is represented by six dimes. The second expression, sixty hundredths, is represented by sixty pennies. The equation 0.6 = 0.60 is represented by the fact that the overall value of both quantities is sixty cents.

The Base-Ten Grid Model By about the second or third grade, a base-ten or grid model can be used to illustrate dec-

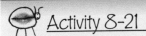

Activity 8-21 — Grades K–2

Decimal Notation Using Money

Materials: Play money for each student or group of students; transparency coins for teacher use.

Teacher Statement: One dollar is the same as 100 cents. One dollar (show a dollar bill) can be written as $1.00 (write $1.00 on the board). The dollar sign comes first, and the decimal point separates the dollars from the cents (point out various parts of the notation). Find the coins to make $1.00, then draw the coins on your handout. You will need to use skip counting so we will practice this. (Slide dimes across transparency as students count.) "Ten cents, twenty cents, thirty cents." Good, I see you remember how to skip count using dimes. Now find how many dimes make one dollar. A dollar is how many cents? Great, 100 cents.

Use all dimes.
There are ___ dimes in $1.00.

Note: Repeat for other coin values. Depending on the level of the student, other coin values may be discussed within the same lesson or in a separate lesson.

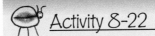

Activity 8-22 — Grades 2–4

Decimals on a Calculator

Materials: Calculators; items with prices (or handout with items and prices pictured).

Teacher Statement: For each set of items, first estimate how many dollars you would spend to buy all of the items. When you have written down all of your estimates, get a calculator and find the actual prices. The calculator doesn't have a cent sign. To put an amount like 79¢ into the calculator, we can use the decimal notation. Remember, 79¢ is the same as $0.79 so for 79 cents we press these keys: (Write 79¢ and $0.79 and the calculator keying sequence on the board.) How would we show the price of the bear with the calculator? (Write $1.25 and the correct keying sequence on the board.)

Items: toy car 79¢, stuffed bear $1.25, ruler 20¢. And so on.

1. toy car and stuffed bear
   Estimate _____
   Actual Price _____

2. toy car and ruler
   Estimate _____
   Actual Price _____

imal concepts (see Activity 8-24). You might be accustomed to reading a decimal expression such as 0.4 as "zero point four." However, in introducing this concept to elementary school children, you may wish to avoid phrases such as this in favor of the word name for such a decimal that stresses the place value involved. The expression 0.4 should be read as "four tenths."

The base-ten or grid model can also be used to illustrate hundredths (see Activity 8-25). Again, instead of reading an expression such as 0.14 as "zero point one four," this expression should be read as "fourteen hundredths." The latter expression reinforces the underlying place value ideas. Place value is a central idea in understanding and computing with decimal numbers. As a teacher you must be careful in your treatment of decimal numbers. For example, although $0.6 = 0.60$ is a true equation, there is a distinction that should be made between the symbols 0.6 and 0.60. The symbol 0.6 represents six tenths, and the symbol 0.60 represents sixty hundredths. In terms of a real-world example, although the overall amounts are the same, there is a difference between having six dimes and sixty pennies.

The Number Line Model The number line also provides a useful visual model.

Example 8-28: Plot each of the following on a number line.

 a. 0.2
 b. 0.9
 c. 1.3
 d. 1.5

Solution:

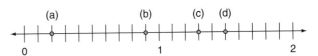

Place Value, Expanded Form, and Benchmarks

Concrete models such as money or base-ten blocks and visual models such as grids or number lines can help children understand the relationships between the place value positions of a decimal number. Ten hundredths is equivalent to one tenth; ten pennies is equivalent to one dime. Ten tenths is equivalent to one whole; ten dimes is equivalent to one dollar. One hundred hundredths is equivalent to one whole; one hundred pennies is equivalent to one dollar. The fact that we use a base-ten numeral system implies that such relationships will hold between place value positions even when concrete and visual models are not available. Expanded form can be used with such decimal numbers.

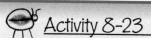

Activity 8-23   Grades 2–4

Decimal Terminology

Materials: Play money for each student.

Teacher Statement: How can we show $2.34 using only ones, dimes, and pennies? (Accept various answers.) Other answers are possible, but we are going to start with the answer 2 ones, 3 dimes, and 4 pennies.

Decide what fractions go in each blank below.

A dime is ___ of a dollar.

A penny is ___ of a dollar.

The decimal number 2.34 has three positions. We already know that the position in front of the decimal point is the ones position. We will call the position directly after the decimal point the tenths position and the position after the tenths position the hundredths position. So 2.34 has 2 ones, 3 tenths, and 4 hundredths. These position names make sense according to the fractions that we found above.

Name each of the decimals below using the terms "ones," "tenths," and "hundredths."

a. 1.58

b. 0.61

c. 0.70

d. 5.08

e. 3.11

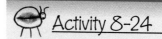

Activity 8-24   Grades 2–4

The Tenths Grid

Materials: Handouts for this activity may be made using Word drawing tools (see Appendix B).

Teacher Statement: We can show tenths using grids. 10 tenths = 1 whole. This diagram shows four tenths. We can write this as a fraction as $\frac{4}{10}$. We can write this as a decimal as 0.4.

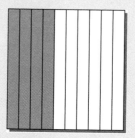

Complete the table. The first one is done for you.

Tenths grid	Fraction or mixed number	Decimal	Word name
	$1\frac{8}{10}$	1.8	One and eight tenths
			One and one tenth
		0.6	

Note: If a base-ten block model is used to illustrate decimals, the flat is considered to be one whole, and each long represents one tenth.

Example 8-29: Write 54,023.8062 in expanded form.

Solution: First write out a place value chart.

The number 54,023.8062 can be written in expanded form as $50,000 + 4,000 + 20 + 3 + \frac{8}{10} + \frac{0}{100} + \frac{6}{1,000} + \frac{2}{10,000}$, or by explicitly writing out each place value as $(5 \times 10,000) + (4 \times 1,000) + (0 \times 100) + (2 \times 10) + (3 \times 1) + (8 \times \frac{1}{10}) + (0 \times \frac{1}{100}) + (6 \times \frac{1}{1,000}) + (2 \times \frac{1}{10,000})$.

In reading a decimal number, the word "and" is used to indicate the position of the decimal point. The whole part of the number is read first. The fractional part (or part smaller than one) is generally read in terms of its smallest place value. That is, the number 2.53 is read as "two and fifty-three hundredths." When the whole part is zero, this may be omitted in reading the decimal. For example, the number 0.078 may be read simply as "seventy-eight thousandths." The number 54,023.8062 is read as "fifty-four thousand twenty-three and eight thousand sixty-two ten-thousandths."

	Ten-thousands	Thousands	Hundreds	Tens	Ones	.	Tenths	Hundredths	Thousandths	Ten-thousandths	
	5	4	0	2	3	.	8	0	6	2	

 Activity 8-25 — Grades 2–4

The Hundredths Grid

Materials: Handouts for this activity may be made using Word drawing tools (see Appendix B).

Teacher Statement: We can show hundredths using grids. 100 hundredths = 1 whole. This diagram shows fourteen hundredths. We can write this as a fraction as $\frac{14}{100}$. We can write this as a decimal as 0.14. This decimal is equivalent to one tenth and four hundredths, but is usually read as "fourteen hundredths."

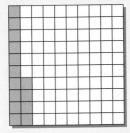

Complete the table. The first one is done for you.

Tenths grid	Fraction or mixed number	Decimal	Word name
	$1\frac{80}{100}$	1.80	One and eighty hundredths
			Two hundredths
		0.63	

Note: If a base-ten block model is used, a flat represents a whole, each long represents one tenth, and each single represents one hundredth.

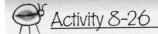 Activity 8-26 — Grades 3–5

Benchmark Basketball

Materials: Three baskets labeled 0, $\frac{1}{2}$, and 1; handouts containing fractions and decimals (handouts may be color coded for each group).

Directions:
1. Place the baskets in a row so that students can see the labels.
2. Each group receives a handout containing fractions and decimals.
3. The groups cut the handouts into sections and distribute the sections among the group members.
4. Each student wads up the sections and throws them into a basket. Other group members can collaborate on which basket the student should aim for.
5. After all the paperwads are thrown, the class sorts through each basket and determines which papers were thrown into the basket containing the closest benchmark to the fraction or decimal appearing on the paper. The group receives a point for each paper in the correct benchmark basket. The group with the most points wins.

Material involving the relationship between fractions, decimals, and percents is covered in Appendix A.

Students should be familiar with both fractions and decimals and able to convert between them. In later grades, students also relate fractions and decimals to percents. Students should also be able to compare and estimate fractions and decimals using common benchmarks such as 0, $\frac{1}{2}$, and 1.

Decimal Procedures Preliminary to Addition and Subtraction

Decimal Equivalence and Ordering One of the first decimal procedures that children learn is that of determining when two decimal quantities are equivalent. For example, 1.4 = 1.40. This may be easily shown using a concrete or visual model such as that shown in Example 8-30. The next decimal procedure that children learn is that of ordering decimals. For the first such examples, models that reinforce the underlying place value concepts should be used so that children develop meaning for this procedure.

Example 8-30: Problem solving using a number line (third- or fourth-grade level).

The meat counter has packages of hamburger labeled 1.46 lb, 1.5 lb, 1.38 lb, and 1.4 lb. Mrs. Smith wants to buy the smallest amount of hamburger that she can. Which package should she buy?

Solution:

1.38 1.4   1.46   1.5

1.30   1.40   1.50

The package marked 1.38 lb contains the smallest amount of hamburger.

Eventually children will learn to order decimals without relying on a concrete model or picture. If they have a solid foundation in using concrete and visual models, they may use visualization when necessary to assist with the ordering process.

Example 8-31: Place one of the symbols >, <, or = in each blank below.

   a. 0.38 ___ 0.6
   b. 0.38 ___ 0.06
   c. 1.5 ___ 0.98

Solutions:

   a. 0.38 < 0.6
   b. 0.38 > 0.06
   c. 1.5 > 0.98

Rounding Decimals to a Given Place Value   Another important process involving decimals is the process of rounding. As with the rounding of whole numbers, rounding may be done to any given place value. The procedure of rounding with decimals is exactly the same as the procedure of rounding with whole numbers. In the early grades, students first learn about rounding to the nearest whole number.

Example 8-32: Round decimals.

   Round the following decimals to the nearest whole number.

   a. 5.7
   b. 23.09
   c. 0.5
   d. 0.39
   e. 79.62

Solutions:

   a. 6
   b. 23
   c. 1
   d. 0
   e. 80

Example 8-33: Rounding to the given place value.

   a. Round 27.34 to the nearest tenth.
   b. Round 149.96 to the nearest tenth.
   c. Round 38.135 to the nearest hundredth.

Solutions:

   a. 27.3
   b. 150.0
   c. 38.14

Activity 8-27   Grades 3–6

Decimal Lineup

Materials: Cards with decimal word names or symbols.

Directions: Place students in small groups. Deal one card to each student. Each group should order themselves from smallest to largest according to the cards. Call one group to the front of the room to show the ordering of the group and explain how and why they ordered themselves in that way. Call other groups to the front one at a time to explain the ordering of their group. Then each student in that group takes their place in the overall ordering. At the end of the activity, the entire class will be lined up from smallest to largest.

| Twenty-three hundredths | 0.021 | Forty-two thousandths |

Standards

Florida Department of Education Sunshine State Standards

Number Sense, Concepts, and Operations: Grades 3–5

Standard 1: The student understands the different ways numbers are represented and used in the real world. MA.A.1.2.4: The student understands that numbers can be represented in a variety of equivalent forms using whole numbers, decimals, fractions, and percents.

Florida Department of Education, 1996

Standards

Ohio Academic Content Standards K–12 Mathematics

Number, Number Sense and Operations Grades 3–4

Benchmarks

B. Recognize and generate equivalent representations for whole numbers, fractions, and decimals.

D. Use models, points of reference and equivalent forms of commonly used fractions to judge the size of fractions and to compare, describe, and order them.

Ohio Department of Education, 2001

Assessment

Student Self-Assessment
for Activity 8-27

1. I participated in the group discussion to determine where I would be in the group lineup.
   Yes   Somewhat   No
2. I let the other group members tell me where to stand in the lineup.
   Yes   Somewhat   No
3. I was able to easily find my place in the overall class lineup.
   Yes   Somewhat   No
4. It is easy to order decimals that are written symbolically (e.g., 0.21).
   Yes   Somewhat   No
5. It is easy to order decimals that are written in words (e.g., twenty-one hundredths).
   Yes   Somewhat   No
6. It is easy to order decimals regardless of whether they are given in symbolic form or in word form.
   Yes   Somewhat   No
7. I know why it is important to learn about decimals.
   Yes   Somewhat   No
8. I enjoyed today's activity.
   Yes   Somewhat   No

Addition and Subtraction with Decimals

Initial activities involving addition and subtraction of decimals usually involve base-ten block or money models. As with whole number addition and subtraction, initial examples should not involve regrouping. If your intent is to illustrate the symbolic process of decimal addition and subtraction, then only bills and coins consistent with base-ten place value such as $100, $10, $1, 10¢, and 1¢ should be used. By using only these denominations, alignment of decimals can be stressed and regroupings may be modeled.

Example 8-34: Use the money model to illustrate the following.

   a. 14.6 + 1.25
   b. 3.51 − 1.38

Solutions:

a.
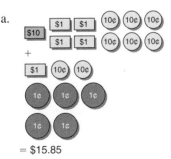

= $15.85

b. $3.51 is represented below.

In order to take away $1.38, you need to remove one dollar, three dimes, and eight pennies. You must regroup. Trading one dime for ten pennies, you have the following representation of $3.51. You can then remove $1.38 as shown.

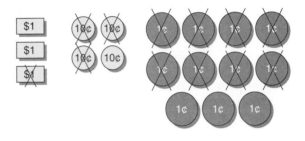

Thus, 3.51 − 1.38 = 2.13.

By using a money model with only base-ten denominations, students can see the necessity of alignment of the decimal points. Dimes must be added to dimes, pennies added to pennies. This model also illustrates that the regrouping process in addition and subtraction of decimals works exactly the same as the regrouping process in addition and subtraction of whole numbers. After a small number of examples, students are ready to tackle the vertical symbolic notation. Expanded form or the equal addition method for subtraction can be used if desired.

Example 8-35: Use vertical notation and compute each of the following.

   a. 14.6 + 1.25
   b. 3.51 − 1.38
   c. 2.35 + 4.68
   d. 4.08 − 2.19

Solutions:

a.   14.6
     + 1.25
      ─────────
       15.85

              411
b.   3.5̸1̸
     − 1.38
      ─────────
        2.13

$$\begin{array}{r} 1\ 1 \\ \text{c.}\quad 2.35 \\ +\ 4.68 \\ \hline 7.03 \end{array}$$

$$\begin{array}{r} 3\,9\,1\,8 \\ \text{d.}\quad \cancel{4.\cancel{0}\cancel{8}} \\ -\ 2.19 \\ \hline 1.89 \end{array}$$

Example 8-36: Use expanded form to calculate $2.35 + 4.68$.

Solution:

2.35	2 ones and 3 tenths and 5 hundredths
+4.68	+4 ones and 6 tenths and 8 hundredths
7.03	6 ones and 9 tenths and 13 hundredths
	6 ones and 10 tenths and 3 hundredths
	7 ones and 0 tenths and 3 hundredths

Example 8-37: Use equal additions to compute (a) $3.51 - 1.38$ and (b) $4.08 - 2.19$.

Solution: Recall that there are usually a variety of ways to choose the quantity to add or subtract in using equal additions. One answer is shown for each problem.

$$\begin{array}{lll} \text{a.}\quad & 3.51 + .02 & 3.53 \\ & -1.38 + .02 & -1.40 \\ & & \hline \\ & & 2.13 \end{array}$$

$$\begin{array}{lll} \text{b.}\quad & 4.08 + 0.81 & 4.89 \\ & -2.19 + 0.81 & -3.00 \\ & & \hline \\ & & 1.89 \end{array}$$

Multiplication and Division with Decimals

If you are teaching in a Pre-K–Grade 4 classroom, it is unlikely that you will teach formal rules and procedures for multiplication or division with decimals. At the third- or fourth-grade level these types of problems may arise in the context of real-life money examples. Such problems may be solved using logical thinking, manipulatives, or other problem-solving techniques. When a money amount is divided by a whole number, estimation and logical thinking can be used to illustrate the proper placement of the decimal point in the quotient.

Example 8-38: Problem solving using money (third- or fourth-grade).

a. Each candy bar costs 37¢. How much does it cost for three candy bars?
b. Four students had lunch at McDonald's. The total bill was $14.96. How much would each pay if they split the bill evenly?
c. A 12-pound bag of dog food costs $10.50, and a 20-pound bag costs $17.00. Which is the better buy per pound?

Solutions:

a. Money manipulatives can be used to show that $3 \times 0.37 = \$1.11$.

b. Students should be encouraged to estimate the solution before performing any calculations. For example, estimate using a "friendly" number, $\$16 \div 4 = \$4$. Each student will pay slightly less than $4. This estimation will help explain the alignment of the decimal point in the division.

The division is performed in much the same fashion as a division of whole numbers. The decimal point in the quotient is aligned directly above the decimal point in the dividend.

$$\begin{array}{r} 3.74 \\ 4\overline{)14.96} \\ \underline{12} \\ 29 \\ \underline{28} \\ 16 \\ \underline{16} \\ 0 \end{array}$$

Each student will pay $3.74.

c. You can use division to find the cost per pound of each type of bag. Estimation tells you that the cost per pound in both cases is slightly less than one dollar.

The cost in the first case is approximately 87¢ per pound. Note that at this level, if the division does not come out evenly, it is not continued. The cost in the second case is exactly 85¢ per pound.

$$\begin{array}{r} .87 \\ 12\overline{)10.50} \\ \underline{96} \\ 90 \\ \underline{84} \\ 6 \end{array} \qquad \begin{array}{r} .85 \\ 20\overline{)17.00} \\ \underline{160} \\ 100 \\ \underline{100} \\ 0 \end{array}$$

It is cheaper per pound to buy the 20-pound bag.

You may remember the following algorithm for the multiplication of decimals: "Multiply the numbers as if they were whole numbers. The number of decimal places in the product equals the sum of the number of decimal places in the factors." This rule is usually presented at the fifth-grade level. Although you may never teach this rule, as a well-educated adult, you should understand how to use it. Multiplication of fractions may be used to justify this algorithm.

Example 8-39: Compute 0.3×0.42 and show how fractions could be used to justify the rule of counting the total number of decimal places in the factors to determine where to place the decimal point in the product.

Solution:

$$\begin{array}{r} .42 \\ \underline{.3} \\ .126 \end{array}$$

$$0.3 \times 0.42 = \frac{3}{10} \times \frac{42}{100} = \frac{3 \times 42}{10 \times 100} = \frac{126}{1,000}$$

$$= 126 \text{ thousandths} = 0.126$$

To compute the fraction multiplication three tenths times forty-two hundredths, apply the fraction multiplication algorithm. The numerator is $3 \times 42 = 126$ and the denominator is $10 \times 100 = 1,000$. Using place value, it is clear that 126 thousandths should be written as 0.126 and that there are three decimal places in the answer as expected.

The first type of division problem involving decimals that is typically covered in the elementary school curriculum is the type in which the divisor is a whole number. The type of problem in which the divisor is not a whole number is presented at around the fifth-grade level. You may remember the algorithm "To divide decimals, move the decimal point in the divisor so that the divisor is a whole number. Move the decimal point of the dividend the same number of places in the same direction. Divide the numbers. Align the decimal point in the quotient above the decimal point of the dividend." Although you may never teach this algorithm, you should understand how to use it. Equivalent fractions may be used to justify this algorithm.

Example 8-40: Compute $2.583 \div 1.23$ and show how equivalent fractions can be used to justify the rule of moving the decimal points to obtain a division with a whole number divisor.

Solution:

$$1.23\overline{)2.583} = 123\overline{)258.3}$$
$$\begin{array}{r} 2.1 \\ \underline{246} \\ 123 \\ \underline{123} \\ 0 \end{array}$$

Standards

Mathematics Content Standards for California Public Schools

Number Sense, Grade 3

3.3 Students solve problems involving addition, subtraction, multiplication, and division of money amounts in decimal notation and multiply and divide money amounts in decimal notation by using whole-number multipliers and divisors.

California Department of Education, 2000

$$\frac{2.583}{1.23} = \frac{2.583 \times 100}{1.23 \times 100} = \frac{258.3}{123}$$

The division problem $1.23\overline{)2.583}$ is equivalent to the fraction $\frac{2.583}{1.23}$. To obtain a divisor that is a whole number, multiply both the numerator and the denominator by a factor of 100. This produces the equivalent fraction $\frac{258.3}{123}$. Hence, the division problem $1.23\overline{)2.583}$ is equivalent to the division problem $123\overline{)258.3}$ in which the divisor is a whole number.

Problem Set 8.3

For Your Understanding

1. You have some coins. Some of the coins are nickels and the rest are dimes. The total amount is 55¢. How many coins are nickels and how many are dimes?

2. Complete Activity 8-23.

3. Complete Activity 8-24.

4. Write 14.56035 in expanded form and write in words how this number is read.

5. Draw diagrams to illustrate the equivalence 1.3 = 1.30.

6. Place one of the symbols >, <, or = in each blank below.
   a. 2.3 ___ 1.96
   b. 3.62 ___ 3.68
   c. 4.5 ___ 4.50
   d. 0.07 ___ 0.2

7. Round each of the following to the place value given.
   a. 6.5—whole number
   b. 6.509—tenths
   c. 6.509—hundredths
   d. 0.12345—thousandths

8. Round each of the following to the place value given.
   a. 8.2—whole number
   b. 0.948—tenths
   c. 0.948—hundredths
   d. 6.54326—thousandths

9. Tickets to the zoo cost $8.25 for an adult and $5.75 for a child. You have $50. How much money will you have left after purchasing tickets for two adults and three children?

10. The price of a coat is $192.64. Each week the price will be cut by $\frac{1}{4}$ until the price is below $100. How many weeks will it take for the price to get below $100, and what will the price be at that time?

11. You and two friends pool your money to buy a CD. You each put in a $5 bill. The CD costs $11.99 plus 84¢ tax. How much change will you and each friend get?

12. a. Compute 2.06×0.58 and use fractions to illustrate why the rule of counting decimal places in the factors to determine the placement of the decimal point in the product works.
    b. Compute $135.324 \div 6.3$ and use equivalent fractions to illustrate why the rule of moving the decimal point works.

13. Terrence buys four identical candy bars and pays $3.36. Tasha buys three of the same candy bar. How much will she pay?

Applications for the Classroom

1. Write down five items and prices that could be used in Activity 8-22. Make up four problems for this activity. Give the answers to the problems that you make up.

2. Use the Microsoft Word drawing toolbar to create a handout that could be used with Activity 8-23 or Activity 8-24.

3. Create a set of cards that could be used with Activity 8-27.

4. Draw money model illustrations for
   a. $6.26 + 3.75$
   b. $6.28 - 3.75$

   Show the necessary regroupings and show all steps that you would go through to present these examples in a second- or third-grade class to illustrate the regrouping process using vertical notation.

5. Aaron uses his calculator to calculate 3.55×0.4 and gets the answer 1.42. Joshua makes the comment "This calculator must have made a mistake. There should be three decimal places in the answer. It must be 0.142." You are the teacher. How do you respond?

6. Sue uses her calculator to calculate 64.2×0.8 and gets the answer 51.36. Sue makes the comment "This calculator must have made a mistake. Multiplication makes things bigger, not smaller." You are the teacher. How do you respond?

7. Create three addition and subtraction word problems involving decimals that could be used at the third-grade level. Indicate how you could modify your problems for use with lower ability or higher ability students.

8. Create an assessment tool to be used with Activity 8-22. Indicate how you will judge whether an estimate is accurate or reasonable. Give a reason for your choice of the type of assessment tool.

9. Classify the level of knowledge and the type of learning experience of Activity 8-26. What objective from the NCTM model (or from your state or district model) does the activity address?

10. A third-grade student claims that since 6 is less than 14, it must be true that $0.6 < 0.14$. You are the teacher. How do you respond?

11. Create three multiplication word problems involving money that could be used at the third-grade level. Indicate how you could modify your problems for use with low- or high-ability students.

12. Look up "decimals" in the index or table of contents of an elementary-level textbook. Photocopy or copy by hand one example or problem that you think is interesting or unusual and indicate why. What objective from the NCTM model (or from your state or district model) does the example or problem address? Be sure to state what grade-level text you are using.

13. Find and print a decimal activity from the Web. State what grade level you think the activity would be appropriate for. What objective from the NCTM model (or from your state or district model) does the activity address?

8.4 AVOIDING COMMON STUDENT ERRORS INVOLVING FRACTIONS AND DECIMALS

The first three sections of this chapter presented a variety of ways to construct meaning for fraction and decimal concepts and algorithms. When students take the time to consider the meaning of concepts and operations, they will avoid many of the common errors that we will discuss. If a rule or algorithm is presented before children have had the time to construct meaning for the underlying concepts, they may misapply the rule or make a mistake in performing a step of the algorithm.

Repeated practice or use of incorrectly learned rote procedures tends to reinforce the error or misconception (Baroody, 1987; Moyer & Moyer, 1985). When students have such misconceptions, it is important to immediately diagnose and remediate. We begin by discussing six common errors involving fractions. Each is illustrated with diagrams or computations that show common student errors and misconceptions. Many of the errors described here and other common student errors are described in Ashlock (2002) and Troutman and Lichtenberg (2003).

Difficulties with the Concept or Meaning of a Fraction

Does Not Recognize That a Fraction Must Have Equal Parts
If a student does not recognize that a fraction must have equal parts, the child may say that $\frac{3}{5}$ of the circle or $\frac{1}{3}$ of the set shown below is shaded.

1. $\frac{3}{5}$ is shaded

2. $\frac{1}{3}$ is shaded

Considers Numerator and Denominator To Be Distinct Sets If a student does not realize that the denominator represents the number of equal parts in the whole, the child may say that $\frac{1}{3}$ of the square or $\frac{2}{3}$ of the set shown below is shaded.

1. $\frac{1}{3}$ is shaded

2. ●●○○○ $\frac{2}{3}$ is shaded

Does Not Associate a Fraction with the Correct Corresponding Division If a student does not realize that the fraction $\frac{p}{q}$ is related to the division $p \div q$, the child may make errors such as those shown below.

1. $\frac{3}{7} = 2\frac{1}{7}$ since 3 goes into 7 twice with 1 left over

2. $\frac{2}{5} = 5 \div 2$ or $2\overline{)5}$

When students make these kinds of errors, you will need to use concrete models and real-life applications such as those presented in Section 8.1 in order to reteach the following: (a) an object or set must be divided into equal parts in order to write a fraction based on that object or set; (b) the numerator of a fraction tells how many equal parts are shaded or otherwise indicated, whereas the denominator tells how many equal parts are in the whole; and (c) the fraction $\frac{p}{q}$ is related to the division $p \div q$.

Difficulties Understanding and Using the Equivalent Fraction Rule

Recall that equivalent fractions may be formed using the equation $\frac{a}{b} = \frac{a \times c}{b \times c}$ for all whole numbers a, b, and c such that b and c are not 0.

Does Not Multiply Both Numerator and Denominator by the Same Factor

1. In the example $\frac{2}{3} + \frac{1}{6} = \frac{2}{6} + \frac{1}{6} = \frac{3}{6}$, the student is not making an addition error; she is making an error involving equivalent fractions. The student realized that a common denominator was necessary. She chose to use the denominator sixths, and changed the denominator for the addend $\frac{2}{3}$ without changing the numerator for this fraction. The substitution should have been $\frac{2}{3} = \frac{4}{6}$.

2. In the example $\frac{2}{3} + \frac{4}{15} = \frac{8}{15} + \frac{4}{15} = \frac{12}{15}$, the student appears to have multiplied the numerators of the original fractions to obtain the numerator for the fraction equivalent to $\frac{2}{3}$. The substitution should have been $\frac{2}{3} = \frac{10}{15}$.

Does Not Divide Both Numerator and Denominator by the Same Factor

1. If students do not understand why dividing both the numerator and denominator of an expression by the same whole number results in an equivalent fraction, they may mistakenly think that performing other operations such as taking the square root of both the numerator and the denominator will also lead to an equivalent fraction and may make the error $\frac{25}{49} = \frac{5}{7}$. Since GCF (25, 49) = 1, the expression $\frac{25}{49}$ is already in simplest form.

2. In the example $\frac{3}{6} = 2$, the student may have divided as follows: $6 \div 3 = 2$. This student may have difficulty with the meaning of fractions as well as difficulty with equivalent fractions.

A solid understanding of equivalent fractions is essential for many of the fraction procedures and algorithms that follow. Students should be encouraged to use models until the process of finding equivalent fractions comes naturally to them. They should also be encouraged to check their answers. Reteach or review the concept of equivalent fractions using concrete models and activities such as paper folding as necessary. Be careful with terminology. The expression "reduce the fraction" that you may remember from your elementary school days has been replaced with "simplify the fraction" in many textbook series. Be sure to check your textbook series for other current terminology and expressions.

Difficulties Converting Between a Mixed Number and an Improper Fraction

Try to determine what each student may have been thinking.

1. $2\frac{3}{4} = \frac{10}{4}$
2. $2\frac{3}{4} = \frac{6}{4}$
3. $2\frac{3}{4} = \frac{14}{4}$
4. $\frac{9}{5} = 4\frac{1}{5}$
5. $\frac{23}{6} = 2\frac{3}{6}$
6. $\frac{25}{6} = 3\frac{5}{6}$

Possible Answers:

1. 2 times 3 plus 4 is 10, so $2\frac{3}{4} = \frac{10}{4}$.
2. 2 times 3 is 6, so $2\frac{3}{4} = \frac{6}{4}$.
3. 3 times 4 plus 2 is 14, so $2\frac{3}{4} = \frac{14}{4}$.
4. 9 divided by 5 is 1 with 4 left over, so $\frac{9}{5} = 4\frac{1}{5}$.
5. Move the whole part out front, so $\frac{23}{6} = 2\frac{3}{6}$.
6. 6 divided by 2 is 3, so $\frac{25}{6} = 3\frac{5}{6}$.

When students have these types of difficulties, stress the underlying concepts of whole part and fractional part. You may need to reteach ideas such as $2\frac{3}{4} = 2 + \frac{3}{4}$, which represents two whole units and three parts out of four equal parts of another unit. Use models and diagrams as necessary.

Difficulties in Ordering Fractions

Consider the following examples.

1. 2 is less than 3, so $\frac{1}{2} < \frac{1}{3}$.
2. $\frac{2}{3} < \frac{5}{8}$ since 2 < 5 and 3 < 8.

In both examples, the student is not considering the meaning of the fractions. Use concrete models to develop this meaning. In the second example, you may also wish to review the process of finding equivalent fractions to determine an ordering. In this case, $\frac{2}{3} = \frac{16}{24} > \frac{15}{24} = \frac{5}{8}$.

Difficulties Adding or Subtracting Fractions

Adds or Subtracts Without Finding a Common Denominator Can you determine how each student obtained each answer shown?

1. $\frac{1}{2} + \frac{2}{3} = \frac{3}{5}$
2. $\frac{4}{9} - \frac{1}{5} = \frac{3}{4}$

Does Not Regroup Can you determine how the student obtained the answer shown below?

$$3\frac{4}{7} - 1\frac{6}{7} = 2\frac{2}{7}$$

In each of the examples above, if students have learned to check their answers using estimation, they will detect their errors. Concrete models can be used to reinforce the necessity of common denominators and regrouping.

Difficulties Multiplying or Dividing Fractions

Does Not Distribute or Convert to Improper Fractions Can you determine how each student obtained each answer shown below?

1. $4\frac{1}{3} \times 2\frac{1}{2} = 8\frac{1}{6}$
2. $4\frac{4}{7} \div 2 = 2\frac{4}{7}$

Makes an Error in Using the Multiplication or Division Algorithm Can you determine how each student obtained each answer shown below?

1. $\frac{2}{3} \times \frac{1}{5} = \frac{10}{15}$
2. $\frac{2}{3} \div \frac{1}{5} = \frac{2}{3} \times \frac{1}{5} = \frac{2}{15}$
3. $\frac{2}{3} \div \frac{3}{4} = \frac{3}{2} \times \frac{3}{4} = \frac{9}{8}$
4. $\frac{2}{3} \div \frac{3}{4} = \frac{3}{2} \times \frac{4}{3} = \frac{12}{6}$
5. $\frac{4}{3} \div \frac{3}{2} = \frac{4}{3} \div \frac{2}{3} = \frac{2}{1}$
6. $10 \div \frac{1}{2} = 5$

The errors above arise when students attempt to apply rules before they fully understand how or why the rules work. Students should not be taught formal algorithms or rules unless they have a solid foundation in the underlying concepts. They should be shown why the rules or algorithms are reasonable and correct. Students should be encouraged to use models, estimation, or other calculation methods to check their answers.

Decimal Difficulties

Many common errors and misconceptions involving decimals stem from a lack of thorough understanding of place value concepts. Decimal algorithms and procedures parallel algorithms and procedures that are used in whole number computations. The biggest decision in a decimal algorithm or procedure is often placement of the decimal point. This should be determined using place value considerations. This section covers four common decimal difficulties that are somewhat similar to the whole number difficulties discussed in Chapter 5 and the fraction difficulties discussed above.

Difficulty with Place Value and Decimal Meaning

Suppose that you asked a school-aged child, "Which is larger, two tenths or two hundredths?" and his answer was "Two hundredths." This child has not yet developed the meaning or concept for decimal expressions. If you asked the same child "Which is more, two dimes or two pennies?" the child would be likely to answer the question correctly. If children confuse decimals such as 0.2 and 0.02, they need remediation in the meaning of decimals. Such remediation should use concrete familiar objects such as money and stress ideas of place value.

Difficulties in Ordering Decimals

A child who claims that $0.59 > 0.6$ also needs remediation in the meaning of decimals. Children must learn that decimal ordering must be based on the value, not the appearance of the decimals. Place value and equivalences (of decimals or of associated fractions) should be stressed and concrete models can be used to illustrate such equivalences. Do not say "You can add a zero after the decimal point" when illustrating an equivalence such as $0.6 = 0.60$. Recall that zero is the additive identity. Adding zero is not the same as annexing zero.

Difficulties Adding or Subtracting Decimals

Consider the following examples:

1. $0.2 + 0.6 = 0.08$
2. $0.6 - 0.2 = 4$
3. $2.4 + 0.35 = 0.59$

Children may inappropriately use a "count the number of decimal places" or "move the decimal point in both numbers" rule when adding or subtracting. They may also simply ignore the decimal point or place it at random. Reteach the concepts of place value in decimal addition and subtraction—whole units are added to whole units, tenths are added to tenths, and so on. Use models as appropriate.

Difficulties Multiplying or Dividing Decimals

Consider the following examples:

1. $0.2 \times 0.4 = 0.8$
2. $1.2 \div 0.4 = 0.3$

Children may inappropriately use a "line up the decimal point" rule when multiplying or dividing. They may also ignore the decimal point or place the decimal point in their answer at random. Reteach meanings of multiplication and division using appropriate models if necessary. Rules should be introduced *after* children understand why they are appropriate. Decimal rules for multiplication or division can be illustrated by using equivalent fractions. Children should also learn to use estimation and to check their answers.

Word Problem Difficulties

In many cases, students will have difficulty choosing an appropriate operation in the solution to a word problem. Students who attempt to solve word problems based on word clues within the problem rather than on logical thinking or other problem-solving techniques may misinterpret these word clues or use them incorrectly. Teachers should not present rules such as "of means multiply" when those "rules" are not always valid.

Example 8-41: Solve the following problem.

Jerry ate $\frac{1}{4}$ of a pizza. David ate $\frac{1}{3}$ of the pizza. How much of the pizza did Jerry and David eat?

Solution: If a student has heard the rule "of means multiply," they may give the incorrect solution $\frac{1}{4} \times \frac{1}{3} = \frac{1}{12}$ to the problem above. After all, the problem contains both of these fractions and contains the word "of" three times. Logical thinking about the situation tells you that the correct operation is addition and the correct solution is that $\frac{1}{4} + \frac{1}{3} = \frac{7}{12}$ of the pizza was eaten.

Problem Set 8.4

For Your Understanding

1. State what students might have been thinking or how they arrived at their answer for each problem shown as examples of fraction errors involving addition, subtraction, multiplication, or division (p. 210). Calculate the correct answer for each of these examples.

2. For each calculation shown below, identify the error(s) made, calculate the correct answer, and indicate what you as a teacher could do to remediate the error(s).

   a. $\frac{1}{3}$ of is shaded.

   b. Problem: Place one of the symbols $<$, $>$, or $=$ in the blank: $\frac{3}{11}$ ___ $\frac{4}{14}$. Student's Solution: $\frac{3}{11} = \frac{4}{14}$ since both are 3 *R*2.

   c. $\frac{3}{26} = \frac{1}{22}$

   d. $12\frac{2}{9} - 4\frac{1}{3} = 12\frac{2}{9} - 4\frac{3}{9} = 8\frac{1}{9} = \frac{72}{9}$

   e. $0.347 > 0.51$

   f. $\begin{array}{r} 1.2 \\ \times\ .5 \\ \hline 6.0 \end{array}$

   g. $0.4\overline{)12.20}$ with quotient 3.05

3. For each calculation shown, identify the error(s) made, calculate the correct answer, and indicate

what you as a teacher could do to remediate the error(s).

a. $\frac{2}{5} + \frac{1}{3} = \frac{2}{15} + \frac{1}{15} = \frac{3}{15} = 5$

b. $\frac{44}{12} = 2$

c. $3.2 + 1.6 = 0.48$

d. $2\frac{3}{4} \div \frac{2}{3} = \frac{6}{4} \div \frac{2}{3} = \frac{6}{4} \div \frac{3}{2} = \frac{2}{2} = 1$

e. $4\frac{2}{5} \times \frac{1}{2} = 4\frac{2}{10} = 4\frac{1}{5}$

f. $15.6 \div 1.2 = 1.3$

4. Identify the errors in the solutions to the following word problems. Give the correct answer for each problem.

   a. Problem: After a party there was $\frac{3}{4}$ of a pizza left over. Nadia ate $\frac{1}{3}$ of the leftover pizza for breakfast the next day. How much pizza is left now? Student's Solution: $\frac{3}{4} - \frac{1}{3} = \frac{9}{12} - \frac{4}{12} = \frac{5}{12}$ of the pizza is left.

   b. Candice has 10 yards of ribbon. She makes bows that each take $\frac{1}{2}$ a yard of ribbon. How many bows can she make? Student's Solution: $10 \div \frac{1}{2} = 5$ bows.

Applications for the Classroom

1. Choose one of the books in the children's literature section of the references for this chapter. Write a brief description of the book and explain how you could incorporate the book into a math lesson.

2. Make up two writing prompts or stems that fit in with material or activities from this chapter.

3. Choose an activity from this chapter that is presented as an individual student activity. Indicate how you could implement the activity as a collaborative learning experience.

References

Children's Literature References

Adler, David. (1996). *Fraction fun.* New York: Holiday House.

Bryant-Mole, Karen. (1995). *Fractions and decimals* (Usborne Math Series). Saffron Hill, London EDCP.

King, Andrew. (1998). *Making fractions.* Brookfield, CT: Millbrook Press.

Koomen, Michele. (2001). *Fractions: Making fair shares* (Vol. 1). Mankato, MN: Capstone Press.

Leedy, Loreen. (1994). *Fraction action.* New York: The Trumpet Club.

McMillan, Bruce. (1991). *Eating fractions.* New York: Scholastic.

Moncure, Jane. (1988). *How many ways can you cut a pie?* Chanhassen, MN: Childs World.

Murphy, Stuart. (1996). *Give me half* (MathStart Level 2). New York: HarperCollins.

Murphy, Stuart. (1998). *Jump, kangaroo, jump!* (MathStart Level 3). New York: HarperCollins.

Pallotta, Jerry. (1999). *The Hershey's Milk Chocolate fractions book.* New York: Scholastic.

Pinczes, Elinor J. J. (2001). *Inchworm and a half.* Boston: Houghton Mifflin.

Ziefert, Harriet. (1997). *Rabbit and hare divide an apple.* New York: Viking Penguin.

Teacher Resources

Ashlock, R. B. (2002). *Error patterns in computation: Using error patterns to improve instruction* (8th ed.). Pearson Education, Inc.

California Department of Education. (2000). *Mathematics Content Standards for California Public Schools.* Retrieved November 12, 2003 from http://www.cdeca.gov/board/pdf/math.pdf

Charles, R. I., Chancellor, D., Harcourt, L., Moore, D., Schielack, J. F., Van de Walle, J., & Wortzman, R. (1999). *Math Grade 2,* Scott Foresman—Addison Wesley.

Florida Department of Education. (1996). *Florida Sunshine State Standards.* Retrieved December 8, 2003 from http://www.firn.edu/doe/curric/prek12/ frame2.htm

National Council of Teachers of Mathematics. (2002). *Principles and standards for school mathematics.* Reston, VA: Author.

Ohio Department of Education. (2001). *Ohio Academic Content Standards.* Retrieved November 12, 2003 from http://www.ode.state.oh.us/ academic_content_standards/ pdf/MATH.pdf

Texas Education Agency. (1998). *Chapter 111. Texas Essential Knowledge and Skills for Mathematics.* Retrieved November 12, 2003 from http://www.tea.state.tx.us/ rules/tac/ch111toc.html

Troutman A. P., & Lichtenberg, B. K. (2003). *Mathematics—A good beginning* (6th ed.). Belmont, CA: Wadsworth, Thomson Learning, Inc.

Selected Research Books and Articles

Baroody, A. J. (1992). The development of basic counting number and arithmetic knowledge among children classified as mentally handicapped. In L. M. Glidden (Ed.), *International review of research in mental retardation* (pp. 51–103). New York: Academic Press.

Cramer, K. A., Post, T. R., & delMas, R. C. (2002). Initial fraction learning by fourth- and fifth-grade students: A comparison of the effects of using commercial curricula with the effects of using the rational number project curriculum. *Journal for Research in Mathematics Education, 33*(2), 111–144.

Gelman, R. (1994). Constructivism and supporting environments. In D. Tirosh (Ed.), *Implicit and explicit knowledge: An educational approach:* (Elsevier) St. Louis, MO. Vol. 6 *Human Development* (pp. 55–82). Ablex.

Langford, K., & Sarullo, A. (1993). Introductory common and decimal fraction concepts. In R. J. Jensen (Ed.), *Research ideas for the classroom: Early childhood mathematics* (pp. 223–247). New York: Macmillan.

Moyer, M. B., & Moyer, J. C. (1985). Ensuring that practice makes perfect: Implications for children with learning difficulties. *Arithmetic Teacher, 33*(1), 40–42.

Further Reading

Baroody, A. J. (1987). *Children's mathematical thinking: A developmental framework for preschool, primary, and special education teachers.* New York: Teachers College Press.

Behr, M. J., Post, T. R., & Wachsmuth, I. (1986). Estimation and children's concept of rational number size. In H. L. Schoen (Ed.), *Estimation and mental computation* (pp. 103–111). Reston, VA: National Council of Teachers of Mathematics.

Bennett, A. B. (1987). *Fractions—Concepts before symbols.* (ERIC Document Reproduction Service No. ED292630)

Bezuk, N. S. (1988). Fractions in the early childhood mathematics curriculum. *Arithmetic Teacher, 35*(6), 56–60.

Geary, D. C. (1994). *Children's mathematical development: Research and practical applications.* Washington, DC: American Psychological Association.

Haubner, M. A. (1992). Percents: Developing meaning through models. *Arithmetic Teacher, 40,* 232–234.

Hiebert, J. (1987). Research report: Decimal fractions. *Arithmetic Teacher, 34*(7), 22–23.

Huinker, D. M. (1992). Decimals and calculators make sense! In J. T. Fey (Ed.), *Calculators in mathematics education* (pp. 56–64). Reston, VA: National Council of Teachers of Mathematics.

Litwiller, B. (Ed.). (2002). *Making sense of fractions, ratios, and proportions, 2002 Yearbook* (with *Classroom Companion Booklet*). Reston, VA: National Council of Teachers of Mathematics.

Long, L. (2001). *Fabulous fractions: Games, puzzles, and activities that make math easy and fun.* Hoboken, NJ: Wiley.

Mack, N. K. (1998). Building a foundation for understanding the multiplication of fractions. *Teaching Children Mathematics, 5,* 34–38.

McBride, J. W., & Lamb, C. E. (1986). Using concrete materials to teach basic fraction concepts. *School Science and Mathematics, 86,* 480–488.

Milsaps, G. M., & Reed, M. K. (1998). Curricula for teaching about fractions. (ERIC Clearinghouse for Science Mathematics and Environmental Education ED433184)

Mitchell, C. (1999). *Funtastic math! Decimals and fractions (Grades 4–8).* New York: Scholastic Trade.

Morrow, L. J. (Ed.). (1998). *The teaching and learning of algorithms in school mathematics.* Reston, VA: National Council of Teachers of Mathematics.

Opie, B., McAvinn, D., & Jackson, L. (1999). *Fractions, ratio, probability, and standard measurement: Reproducible skill builders and higher order thinking activities based on NCTM Standards.* Nashville: Incentive Publications.

Payne, J., Towsley, A., & Huinker, D. (1990). Fractions and decimals. In J. Payne (Ed.), *Mathematics for the young child* (pp. 175–200). Reston, VA: National Council of Teachers of Mathematics.

Riddle, M., & Rodzwell, B. (2000). Fractions: What happens between kindergarten and the army? *Teaching Children Mathematics, 7*(4), 202–206.

Thompson, C. S., & Walker, V. (1996). Connecting decimals and other mathematical content. *Teaching Children Mathematics, 2,* 496–502.

Van de Walle, J., & Thompson, C. S. (1984). Let's do it: Fractions with fraction strips. *Arithmetic Teacher, 32,* 4–9.

Watanabe, T. (1996). Ben's understanding of one-half. *Teaching Children Mathematics, 2,* 460–464.

Zullie, M. (1975). *Fractions with pattern blocks.* Sunnyvale, CA: Creative Publications.

9

Exploring Graphs, Data, Statistics, and Probability

The visual nature of graphs makes them an important part of the mathematics curriculum beginning at the very earliest grade levels. Graphs can be used in conjunction with other mathematical topics such as sorting, classification, counting, and number comparison. In later grade levels, graphs may be used to introduce addition and subtraction, multiplication and division, or fractions. Examples of these uses will be given throughout this chapter.

A graph may be used to display the data resulting from a survey, and statistical measures may be used to analyze graphs and data. Graphs and statistical analysis may be easily incorporated into other subject areas. For example, you may record the results of a science experiment with a graph. Elementary social studies textbooks are filled with graphs as various populations are studied and compared. Paragraphs, poetry, and other literary works may be analyzed by sentence or line type or structure; the results may be displayed in a graph.

Graphs are also useful in displaying results of probability experiments. In recent years an increasing emphasis has been placed on data analysis and probability in the elementary grades, including in the early childhood classroom. "In prekindergarten through grade 2, the treatment of probability ideas should be informal. Teachers should build on children's developing vocabulary to introduce and highlight probability notions, for example, We'll *probably* have recess this afternoon, or It's *unlikely* to rain today. Young children can begin building an understanding of chance and randomness by doing experiments with concrete objects, such as choosing colored chips from a bag" (NCTM, 2000, p. 51).

Standards

NCTM

In prekindergarten through grade 2, students will have learned that data can give them information about aspects of their world. They should know how to organize and represent data sets and be able to notice individual aspects of the data—where their own data are on the graph, for instance, or what value occurs most frequently in the data set. In grades 3–5, students should move toward seeing a set of data as a whole, describing its shape, and using statistical characteristics of the data such as range and measures of center to compare data sets.

NCTM, 2000, p. 177

Standards are listed with the permission of the National Council of Teachers of Mathematics (NCTM). NCTM does not endorse the content or validity of these alignments.

Objectives

After completing Chapter 9, you will be able to

- Draw and interpret eight types of graphs and analyze misleading graphs
- Describe how to incorporate collecting and displaying data (conducting surveys and drawing graphs) into the early childhood curriculum
- Compute and use the statistical measures: mean, median, mode, and range
- Calculate probabilities using appropriate rules and terminology
- Describe experiments and activities that can be used in the early childhood classroom to introduce children to the concepts and processes of probability

9.1 DRAWING AND INTERPRETING GRAPHS

Most elementary school textbooks include a chapter on graphing near the beginning of the book. Graphs may then be used throughout the book as appropriate. Opportunities to draw or interpret graphs arise frequently in the areas of social studies and science. Student interest may be maintained by using student information as the subject of various graphs. Information to be graphed may be numerical: "How many people live in your house or apartment?" Students may be asked to select an option or give an opinion: "Which do you like better—cats or dogs?" Information may be obtained from the results of an experiment: "Roll your die—what number appears on the top face?" Even before they have learned to count, students can use visual clues to interpret some types of graphs.

Eight Types of Graphs

Pictographs The first types of graphs studied are usually very visual in nature. A *pictograph* is a graph that uses pictures to represent data. At the Pre-K to first-grade levels, pictures in a pictograph have a one-to-one correspondence with the data represented; each picture represents exactly one object (see Activities 9-1 and 9-2).

Students at the early grade levels enjoy helping in the construction of graphs. When young students construct a graph, an outline of the graph structure is useful to help the students with placement and aligning. Students should not be expected to draw their own graph scales until around the

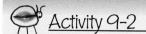

Standards

Ohio Early Learning Content Standards

Mathematics, Prekindergarten

Data Analysis and Probability (3) Select the category or categories that have the most or newest objects in a floor or table graph.

Ohio Office of Early Childhood Education & Office of Curriculum and Instruction, 2003

Activity 9-1   Grades Pre-K–Grade 1

Two-Category Pictograph

Materials: Graph outline on chalkboard, posterboard, or flannel board, and a person cutout for each student; tape or some other means of sticking cutouts to the graph.

Teacher Statement: A graph is a picture that is used to show information. We are going to make a graph showing the students in our class. You each have a person cutout with your name on it. When I call your name, you will come forward and place your person cutout in the first empty square of the appropriate row on the graph. The top row of the graph is labeled "Boys," and the bottom row is labeled "Girls." Ed, which row will you put your name in?

Do we have more boys or more girls in our class? How can you tell by looking at the graph? How many girls do we have in the class? Let's use the number line to count. And so on.

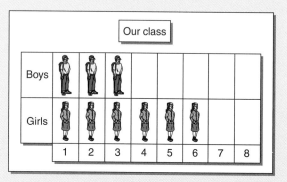

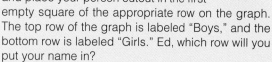

Activity 9-2   Grades 1–2

Birthday Pictograph

Materials: Birthday graph outline; a birthday cake or candle-shaped sticky note for each student.

Teacher Statement: We have studied the names of the months and are going to make a graph showing the birthdays in our class. You each have a sticky note. Write your name on the sticky note. When I call your table, you will come forward and place your note in the row of your birthday month.

What month has the most birthdays? What month has the fewest birthdays? Are there two months with the same number of birthdays? Is there a month with no birthdays? How many more birthdays were there in January than there were in March? And so on.

second- or third-grade level when the Cartesian coordinate system is introduced. The title is an important feature of a graph; it should describe what the graph is about. A number line along the bottom (or side) of a graph is used to help students identify how many objects are in each category of the graph. Initially graphs are usually constructed using horizontal rows. Once a graph is constructed, students can be asked various questions about the graph.

At the second-grade level, pictographs are introduced for which each picture represents more than a single object. A *legend* or key is used to indicate how many objects each picture represent. A partial picture may be used when necessary. Skip counting is useful in the interpretation of such a graph, making such graphs useful in the introduction of multiplication.

Example 9-1: Interpreting pictographs (second- to third-grade level).

    a. How many students write with their left hand? 5. How many students write with their right hand? 5, 10, 15. Answer: Fifteen students write with their right hand.

    b. How many students earned stars on Monday?

        Skip count by fours—4, 8, etc. Eight students earned stars on Monday. How many students earned stars on Tuesday? $4 + 2 = 6$. Six students earned stars on Tuesday. How many students earned stars on Wednesday? Four students earned stars on Wednesday.

Tally Graphs A *tally graph* is similar to a pictograph except that tally marks are used rather than pictures to record the data. Tally marks are usually drawn in groups of five with every fifth mark drawn diagonally across the preceding set of four marks. Skip counting by fives is useful in interpreting a tally graph.

Example 9-2: Example of a tally graph (first- to second-grade level).

Each student in a class flips a coin. The results are shown by a tally graph.

    a. How many students flipped heads?
    b. How many students flipped tails?
    c. How many more students flipped heads than tails?
    d. How many students are in the class?

Solutions:

    a. 5, 10, 11, 12—12 students flipped heads.
    b. 5, 6, 7, 8, 9—9 students flipped tails.
    c. $12 - 9 = 3$. Three more students flipped heads than tails.
    d. There are $12 + 9 = 21$ students in the class.

Line Plots A *line plot* uses an *X* or a similar mark to record each data point. These marks are recorded above a line depicting the possible data results. When the information to be graphed is numerical, marks are recorded above a number line as in Example 9-3.

Example 9-3: Example of a line plot (second- to third-grade level).

Students in a class were surveyed. Each student indicated the number of pets that they have at home. The results are displayed in a line plot.

    a. How many students have no pets?
    b. How many students have three pets?
    c. How many students are in the class?

Solutions:

    a. Four students have no pets.
    b. No students have exactly three pets.
    c. There are 16 results shown in the graph. Hence, 16 students in the class.

The data point in Example 9-3 that indicates that one of the students has 11 pets is called an outlier. In general, an *outlier* is a value or score that is much higher or much lower than other values in a data set. An outlier may indicate some unusual circumstance or may be due to an error in the data set. The student who indicated 11 pets may be counting her goldfish separately, whereas other students may count a bowl of fish as 1 pet. When surveys are constructed, questions must be clarified so that students in the same circumstance answer in the same manner. Otherwise, results of the survey are inaccurate. We will discuss constructing surveys further in Section 9.2.

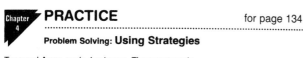

PRACTICE   for page 134

Problem Solving: Using Strategies

Tess and Amos made 4 spinners. They spun each spinner many times. They made bar graphs of their results.

Match each spinner to the bar graph that goes with it.

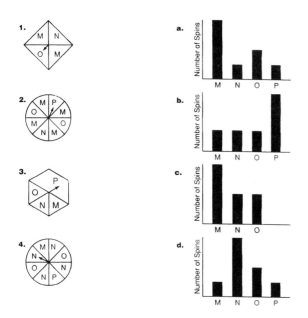

FIGURE 9-1   School book page using bar graphs.
Source: From *Heath Mathematics Connections Grade (3)* by Manfre, et al., 1996, Boston: Houghton Mifflin. Reprinted with permission.

Histograms The next type of graph is called a histogram or bar graph. In a *histogram,* bars are used to represent data. Bars may be drawn adjacent to one another, or may be separated by spaces (see Figure 9-1). The length (or height) of a bar indicates the number of objects in a given category. When the number of objects is large, it may be useful to use a scale of units other than one to number the associated number line. A histogram may also be called a *bar graph* or a *column graph.* Elementary school textbooks tend to use the phrase "bar graph" for histograms regardless of whether the bars are drawn vertically or horizontally. Software programs such as Microsoft Excel tend to use the term "bar graph" for a graph in which bars are drawn horizontally, and the term "column graph" for a graph in which bars are drawn vertically.

Example 9-4: Bar graph (histogram) variations (third- to fourth-grade level).

   a. Using a scale other than one to number the associated number line. A third-grade class sold the following numbers of candy bars: 7 Reese's cups, 20 Kit Kat bars, 23 plain M&M's, and 32 peanut M&M's. Use a bar graph to display the information.

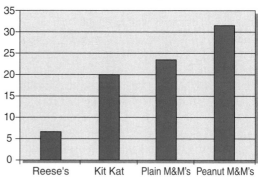

Third-Grade Candy Sales

   b. A double bar graph may be used to compare two sets of data. The double bar graph shown compares the third-grade sales with the fourth-grade sales. Use the graph to answer the following questions.

     1. Which class sold more Kit Kat bars?
     2. Did both classes sell the same number of any type of the candy bars?
     3. Which class sold more total candy bars?

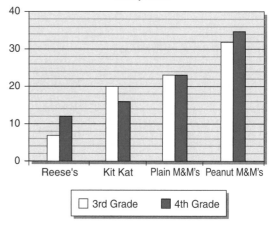

Candy Sales

   ☐ 3rd Grade   ■ 4th Grade

Solutions:

   1. The third-grade class sold more Kit Kat bars.
   2. Both classes sold the same number of plain M&M's.
   3. The third-grade class sold 7 + 20 + 23 + 32 = 82 candy bars. The fourth-grade class sold 12 + 16 + 23 + 35 = 86 candy bars. The fourth-grade class sold more candy bars.

In a histogram, a category may represent an interval of scores or values instead of a single object or value. To determine in what category a score belongs, it is important that the ranges of scores used to define the categories do not overlap. Interval ranges need not contain the same number of scores or values.

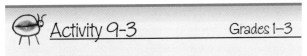

Activity 9-3   Grades 1-3

Gummy Bear Bar Graph

Materials: Bags of 15 gummy bears for each student (no more than 6 of any color in a bag); crayons or markers; gummy bear graph outline (see Blackline Master 22 in the Appendices).

Teacher Statement: We're going to make graphs with gummy bears. Do not eat any of your bears until I have checked your graph.

First, sort your bears by color. Then color one box of the graph for each bear. If you have three red bears, you will color three boxes red in the red column. (Show an example.) When I put a checkmark in the box at the bottom of your page, you may eat your bears.

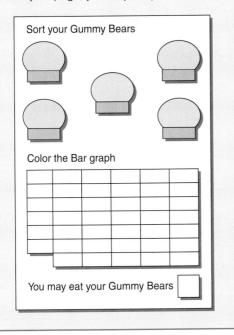

Example 9-5: Bar graph (histogram) variations (fourth- to fifth-grade level).

A physical education teacher gives a performance-based test on which students may score 0 to 60 points. In the previous year the teacher used the following scale to judge student performance: 0–20 points = poor; 21–45 points = average; 46–60 points = above average. A class of students achieves the following scores: 21, 32, 28, 41, 20, 58, 7, 36, 38, 48, 21, 46, 38, and 37. Draw a histogram using this data.

Solution: Sort the scores in increasing order and count the number of scores in each category: 7, 20 | 21, 21, 28, 32, 36, 37, 38, 38, 41 | 46, 48, 58. The number of scores in a category is sometimes called the *frequency* of that category.

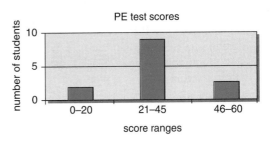

Notice that the score of 20 is only 1 point away from the two scores of 21, but it is 13 points away from the score of 7. Perhaps the two scores 7 and 20 do not belong in the same category. You can change the intervals used so that the scores of 20 and 21 fall within the same category. Changing the intervals used to define the categories will alter the histogram. Suppose the teacher used the following scale:

    0–15 = poor
    16–30 = average (low)
    31–45 = average (high)
    46–60 = above average

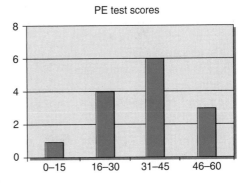

A histogram using these revised categories is shown. Do you agree that this new histogram better illustrates the results of the test for this class?

In general, when given a histogram where categories are determined by a range of scores or values, the specific scores or values cannot be determined from the graph. Consider the following double histogram that compares two different class results on the PE test. Can you tell which is the better class? What conclusions can you make? Study the graph and record any observations before reading further.

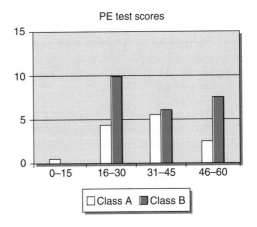

Two conclusions that can be made from this graph are: Class B had no students in the lowest category, and Class B contains more students than Class A. We will revisit this example in problem 4 of Section 9.2.

Stem-and-Leaf Plots Stem-and-leaf plots are usually introduced at around the fourth-grade level. A stem-and-leaf plot is somewhat similar in appearance to a bar graph with horizontal bars, but has the advantage that individual scores can be determined from the graph. In a *stem-and-leaf plot* using two-digit numbers, the *stem* is the part of the data that shows the tens, and the *leaf* is the part of the data that shows ones. A stem-and-leaf plot of the PE test scores given in Example 9-5 is shown in Example 9-6.

Example 9-6: Stem-and-leaf plots (fourth- to fifth-grade level).

a. Here is a stem-and-leaf plot of the scores: 21, 32, 28, 41, 20, 58, 7, 36, 38, 48, 21, 46, 38, 37.

The only score with a zero in the tens digit was 7.

There were no scores with a one in the tens digit.

The scores represented by the next row are: 21, 28, 20, and 21.

The next row represents the scores: 32, 36, 38, 38, and 37.

```
0 | 7
1 |
2 | 1 8 0 1
3 | 2 6 8 8 7
4 | 1 8 6
5 | 8
```
Stems   Leaves

The next row represents the scores: 41, 48, and 46.

The only score with 5 in the tens digit was 58.

b. A double stem-and-leaf plot can be used to compare two sets of data. Use the given graph to write the scores for Class B.

```
      Class B   |   | Class A
               | 0 | 7
          6 8 | 1 |
0 5 4 8 0 1 8 8 | 2 | 1 8 0 1
      7 1 3 9 | 3 | 2 6 8 8 7
    2 5 9 6 7 0 | 4 | 1 8 6
          3 1 9 | 5 | 8
              0 | 6 |
```

Solution: The scores for Class B are 16, 18, 20, 25, 24, 28, 20, 21, 28, 28, 37, 31, 33, 39, 42, 45, 49, 46, 47, 40, 53, 51, 59, and 60.

The score of 7 is much lower than all other scores in Class A. This score is called an outlier. As previously stated, an outlier is a value or score that is much higher or much lower than other values in a data set. An outlier may indicate some unusual circumstance or may be due to an error in the data set.

In a stem-and-leaf plot, stems are generally written vertically and leaves horizontally, as shown in Example 9-6.

Standards

North Carolina Mathematics Standards

Data, Probability, and Statistics: Grade 4

4.01 Interpret and construct stem-and-leaf plots.

North Carolina Department of Public Instruction, 2003

In some textbooks, stems are written in increasing order from the bottom of the graph to the top of the graph, whereas in others stem order may be increasing (as shown here) or decreasing (as in Example 9-6). Still other textbooks sort leaves in value before the values are written on the graph. The example shown here has sorted leaves.

```
5 | 8
4 | 1 6 8
3 | 2 6 7 8 8
2 | 0 1 1 8
1 |
0 | 7
```

Line Graphs A *line graph* is a graph in which points are joined with line segments. Line graphs are useful for continuous data and showing trends in data, or change in data, over a time period. Line graphs may be used to estimate or predict data values that are not given. Line graphs are introduced at around the second- or third-grade level.

Example 9-7: Reading and interpreting a line graph (third- to fourth-grade level).

The line graph shown gives Marsha's height in inches at ages 2 years, 4 years, and 6 years.

a. What was Marsha's height at 4 years old?
b. At what age was Marsha 32 inches tall?
c. Estimate Marsha's height at 3 years old.
d. Predict Marsha's height at 8 years old.

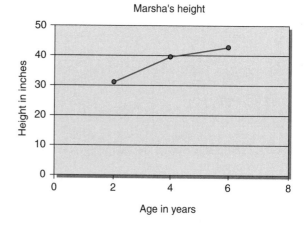

Marsha's height

Solutions:

a. 39 inches
b. 2 years
c. 35 inches
d. 45 inches

Pie Charts The next type of graph is the *pie chart* or *circle graph*. In the very early grades, circle graphs are related to simple fractions and real-world situations. In later grades, circle graphs may involve percents or more complicated fractional or decimal amounts. As with any type of graph, it is important to be careful in drawing a circle graph to ensure that the graph drawn accurately reflects the given data.

Example 9-8: Problem solving drawing and using a graph (first- or second-grade level).

In a class of students, half say that math is their favorite subject, one fourth say that science is their favorite, and the rest say that English is their favorite. Draw a circle graph to represent this information. What part of the students like English the best?

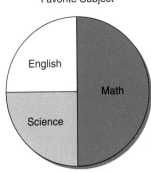

Favorite Subject

Solution: From the graph you see that one fourth of the students like English the best.

Example 9-9: A circle graph example (third- or fourth-grade level).

Angie's monthly budget: Each month Angie earns $800. She spends some on rent, some on food, some on clothing and fun items, and puts the rest in the bank. A circle graph representing Angie's budget is given. Use the graph to estimate each of the amounts spent on (a) rent, (b) food, (c) savings, and (d) clothing and fun items.

Angie's Monthly Budget

Solution: Angie has a total of $800 in her budget.

> She spends half of her money, $400, on rent.
> She spends one fourth of her money, $200, on clothing and fun items.
> She saves one eighth of her money, $100.
> She spends one eighth of her money, $100, on food.

Example 9-10: Problem solving using a graph (fifth- or sixth-grade level).

On a class assignment, 20% of the students received A's, 40% of the students received B's, 30% of the students received C's, and 3 students received grades below C. How many students received each grade of A, B, and C?

Solution: From the graph you see that the 3 students who received grades below C comprise 10% of the class. Thus, there are 30 students in the class. Since 20% of the class re-

ceived A's, 6 students received an A. Then 40% or 12 students received a B. Finally 30% or 9 students received a C. Note that $6 + 12 + 9 + 3 = 30$, so all student grades have been accounted for.

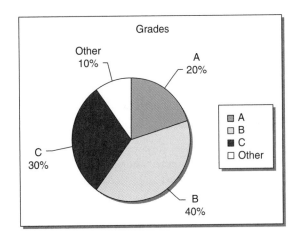

Grades

Networks Changes in math education have brought about an increased emphasis on representation in the elementary mathematics classroom. "Representations should be treated as essential elements in supporting students' understanding of mathematical concepts and relationships; in communicating mathematical approaches, arguments and understandings to one's self and to others; in recognizing connections among related mathematical concepts; and in applying mathematics to realistic problem situations through modeling" (NCTM, 2000, p. 67). We have already discussed a variety of visual representations including drawings, graphs, lists, tree diagrams, and Venn diagrams. Example 9-11 illustrates how a problem may be modeled using a network. A *network* is a series of points or nodes connected by segments or directed segments.

Example 9-11: The intercoms in an office building are malfunctioning. The following list indicates the only connections that are working. Draw a network and indicate how (or if) each office can get a message to each of the other offices using this faulty intercom system.

> Office A can send a message to office B or to office E.
> Office B can send a message to office C or to office F.
> Office C can send messages to only office E.
> Office D can send messages to only office C.
> Office E can send messages to only office A.
> Office F can send messages to only office D.

Solution: Draw the network and indicate the working connections with directed segments.

Illustrate how office A could get a message to each of the other offices.

$$A \rightarrow B$$
$$A \rightarrow B \rightarrow C$$
$$A \rightarrow B \rightarrow F \rightarrow D$$
$$A \rightarrow E$$
$$A \rightarrow B \rightarrow F$$

It is left to the reader to show how (or if) each of the remaining offices could get a message to each of the other offices.

Misleading Graphs

Many graphs that appear in newspapers, magazines, and even in textbooks are not completely accurate. By the fourth grade, students must learn to recognize and correct misleading graphs.

Example 9-12: Kendra's car had a slight oil leak and she used 20 quarts of oil in the year 2002. She repaired the leak and the car used only 10 quarts of oil in the year 2003. Kendra drew a pictograph to represent the oil used by her car in these two years. Comment on the graph.

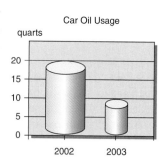

Solution: Kendra did a good job of spacing the units on the number line in her graph. She also did a nice job in labeling the graph. However, by decreasing both the height and the radius of the cylinders in the pictograph, the visual effect is that the amount of oil used in 2003 is much less than half of the oil used in 2002. Kendra should have drawn both cylinders using the same radius. The height difference then would have accurately reflected the change in oil usage.

Example 9-13: Tim uses the 2001 NFL offense statistics to draw bar graphs to compare two teams. Comment on the graphs.

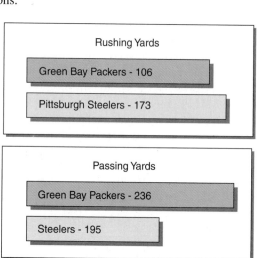

Standards

Maine Mathematics Standards

Grades 3–4

Students will understand and apply concepts in discrete mathematics. Students will be able to:

1. Create and use organized lists, tree diagrams, Venn diagrams, and networks.
2. Give examples of infinite and finite solutions.

Maine State Department of Education, 1997

Solution: It appears that Tim prefers the Green Bay Packers to the Pittsburgh Steelers. In Rushing Yards, there is an actual difference of 67 yards but the graph shows only a slight visual difference; the Green Bay bar is drawn almost as long as the Steelers bar. In Passing Yards, there is only a 41 yard difference, but the Green Bay bar is drawn nearly twice as long as the Steelers bar. In the graphs shown below, the lengths of the bars more accurately reflect the numbers given.

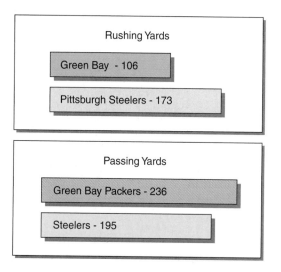

 Teaching Connections

Teach Students That a Graph Should Be Visually Accurate As discussed, when drawing any graph you must ensure that the graph accurately reflects the given data. However, many graphs that appear in newspapers, magazines, and even in textbooks are not completely accurate. At around the fourth-grade level, students must learn to recognize and correct misleading graphs. At even earlier grade levels, students should learn to check their own graphs to ensure that they accurately reflect the given data. Students must also learn how to transfer data given in one type of graph to draw a graph of another type.

Example 9-14: A third-grade student uses the given tally graph to draw a line plot. Comment on her work.

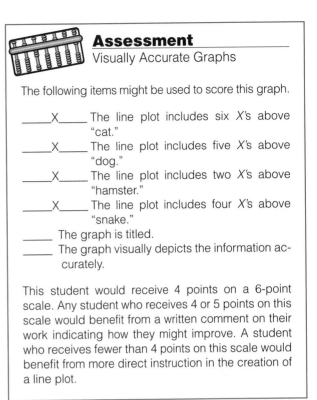

Favorite Pet	
Cat	卌 I
Dog	卌
Snake	II
Hamster	IIII

Solution: It seems that the student understands tally graphs and has some understanding of line plots. She did draw the correct number of *X*'s in each category. However, the placement and various sizing of the *X*'s in the line plot are misleading. Glancing at the line plot, one might think that the same amount of people chose hamsters as their favorite pet as dogs. However, by counting the *X*'s or looking at the tally graph, you can see that this is not so. When drawing a line plot, this student needs to be more careful that the overall height of the *X*'s in a column accurately reflects the number of *X*'s in that column. This student also needs to be reminded to title her graphs (see Activity 9-4).

Create Classroom Graphs Using a Computer Many of the graphs and illustrations in this textbook, including all of the graphs presented in this section, were created using common computer applications such as Microsoft Word or Excel. Instructions for drawing the types of graphs shown in this section are given in Appendix B at the end of this textbook. You can use these instructions to create classroom graphs using data from your students (see Activity 9-4).

At the first- and second-grade levels, children can type data into spreadsheets and interpret the resulting graphs. The click and drag process used to highlight the data used to create a graph involves some coordination and dexterity; this process can be introduced at around the third-grade level. Some children at this level may experience some frustration until they have mastered the click and drag technique. This is also a skill that you may need to practice.

See the section on using Microsoft Excel in Appendix B to learn the click and drag process necessary to create a graph using a spreadsheet.

Research indicates that with proper planning and guidance, children as young as three or four years old can benefit from computer activities (Clements, 1994; Haughland, 1999). Teachers should plan computer activities that are developmentally appropriate and have educational value. Many resources are available to help teachers select software appropriate for their grade level and objectives (for example, Kerrigan, 2002; Ozgun, 1998). The Graph Club (2003) is a software package that children

Assessment
Visually Accurate Graphs

The following items might be used to score this graph.

____X____ The line plot includes six *X*'s above "cat."

____X____ The line plot includes five *X*'s above "dog."

____X____ The line plot includes two *X*'s above "hamster."

____X____ The line plot includes four *X*'s above "snake."

_____ The graph is titled.

_____ The graph visually depicts the information accurately.

This student would receive 4 points on a 6-point scale. Any student who receives 4 or 5 points on this scale would benefit from a written comment on their work indicating how they might improve. A student who receives fewer than 4 points on this scale would benefit from more direct instruction in the creation of a line plot.

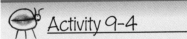

Activity 9-4   Grades 1–3

Interpreting an Excel Bar Graph

Materials: A computer with Excel.

Teacher Statement: I need three students to each give me a two-digit number. John? 23 Mary? 15 June? 38. If we draw a bar graph with these numbers, whose bar will be the tallest? Whose bar will be the shortest? Let's check.

Type the data into an Excel spreadsheet and insert a column graph.

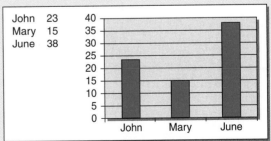

John	23
Mary	15
June	38

If Mary wanted her bar to be the tallest, what should she change her number to? You think 40? Let's change Mary's number to 40 and see what happens. What other numbers could Mary use to have the highest bar? Etc.

can use to create graphs from as early as the first-grade level. Graphs created with such software packages typically involve preprogrammed topics, sizes, styles, and data. One benefit of creating graphs with Excel or other spreadsheet programs is that classroom-generated data may be used.

Problem Set 9.1

For Your Understanding

1. In the pictograph shown, 20 more students received stars in Week 1 than in Week 3. How many students received stars in Week 2?

   Week 1: ✶ ✶ ✶ ✶
   Week 2: ✶ ✶ ✶ ✶ ✶
   Week 3: ✶ ✶

2. In the circle graph shown, 60 of the grades were A's. How many of the grades were F's?

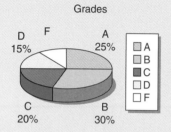

Grades

3. Consider the line graph shown.
   a. For what years was spending less than half of the rate of spending in 2000?
   b. Estimate the spending in 1985.
   c. Predict the spending in 2005.
   d. What is the percent increase in spending from 1980 to 2000?

4. 120 people are surveyed and the following data are obtained.
   a. Draw a line graph containing the data.
   b. Use the graph to estimate how many of the people surveyed were smokers in 1995.

c. Predict how many of the people will be smokers in 2002.
d. What is the percentage decrease in smokers from 1996 to 2000?

Year	# Smokers
1994	43
1996	40
1998	36
2000	30

5. The shaded bar represents 120,000. Estimate the amount represented by the unshaded bar.

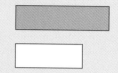

6. Write all the facts that can be determined from the graph shown. What conclusions can be made about the two classes shown?

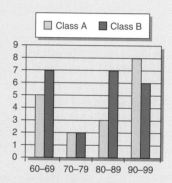

7. Draw a stem-and-leaf plot with sorted leaves for the data: 72, 60, 47, 97, 86, 65, 100, 93, 77, 82, 86, 67, 93, 80, 96, 83.

8. An angler catches fish the following lengths (in inches): 8, 10, 4, 9, 13, 14, 21, 24, 9, 22, 29, 25, 27, 13, 21, 16, 17, 14, 18, 12, 19, 21, 16, 15. Draw histograms using the following intervals. Which histogram do you think best represents the data? Explain your choice.
   a. 1 – 10, 11 – 20, 21 – 30
   b. 1 – 5, 6 – 10, 11 – 15, etc.
   c. 1 – 3, 4 – 6, 7 – 9, 10 – 12, etc.

9. Draw a line plot showing the number of letters in each of the student names: Raul, Ben, Rosalie, David, Ed, Davon, Gerry, Hanna, Latisha, Juan, and Hsu.

Applications in the Classroom

1. Rewrite Example 9-10. In the text, it is listed as a fifth-grade-level problem because of the per-

cents. Rewrite the problem (without using percents) so that it could be used at a lower grade level.

2. Connie surveys the class to find out each student's favorite color of M&M's. She finds that 6 students like yellow, 6 students like green, 12 students like red, and 16 students like blue. She draws the circle graph shown. Comment on the graph.

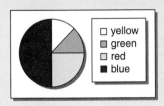

3. Jerome claims that company sales are steadily and rapidly increasing. He draws the following graph. Comment on the graph.

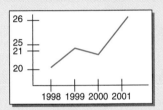

4. Make up three different questions that you could use in a kindergarten or first-grade classroom to graph data. Make up one question for each type of graph: tally, bar graph, and pictograph.

5. Make up three different questions that you could use in a second- or third-grade classroom to graph data. Make up one question for each type of graph: line plot, line graph, circle graph.

6. Create at least three problems or examples involving social studies or science topics for which you could incorporate graphs into the lesson.

7. Make up a network problem similar to Example 9-11.

8. Create an assessment tool to be used with Activity 9-2. Explain why you chose that type of assessment tool.

9. Write a lesson plan that describes how you will introduce bar graphs in a first-grade classroom. Follow the format given by your instructor or use the lesson plan format given in Appendix A.

10. Solve the problem given on the school book page shown on p. 218. Write a lesson plan that describes a lesson that you could teach involving this material. Follow the format given by your instructor or use the lesson plan format given in Appendix A.

9.2 COLLECTING AND INTERPRETING DATA

Section 9.1 concentrated on graphing data and reading or interpreting given graphs. Another important part of the graphing process is gathering the data for a graph. You have already learned that questions in a survey must be phrased so that people in similar circumstances will give similar answers. Several types of graphs and interpretations of graphs were presented so that you would have a sense of what types of graphs are available. We now focus on constructing surveys and collecting data to be used in a graph. It is good practice for children to learn how to collect data as well as how to graph and analyze it.

Teaching Connections

Constructing Surveys and Collecting Data In your lifetime you have probably seen and heard many statements such as "four out of five dentists prefer sugarless gum." Such statements are abundant in television, radio, newspapers, or magazines. How do you suppose this information is obtained? Do you think that exactly five dentists were surveyed? Do you think that every dentist in the world, or perhaps every dentist in the United States, was surveyed? If the statement was indeed the result of an actual survey, it is likely that several dentists, perhaps hundreds or thousands, were surveyed and the figure "four out of five" is an average based on the results of that survey. It would not be feasible to survey *every* dentist before making a claim about what dentists prefer.

In a survey situation, the *population* is the set about which information is desired, and the *sample* is the subset of the population that is studied. You can often make inferences or draw conclusions about an entire population based on an appropriate sample. In the above example, the population is all dentists, and the sample is the set of dentists that were surveyed. If you wish to make a statement regarding the students in your class, you may survey the entire class; both the population and the sample is the set of students in your class. In some cases, you may wish to make a statement regarding the students in your school; in this case your class alone may or may not be a representative sample. Using a sample to make conclusions regarding a population that is larger than the sample is an excellent exercise in estimation and ratios or multiplication (see Activities 9-5 to 9-7).

Using Literature in the Mathematics Classroom

A Three Hat Day

By Laura Geringer
HarperCollins, 1985

R. R. Pottle collects hats. His father collected canes, and his mother collected umbrellas. One day while wearing three hats, R. R. Pottle meets the perfect wife; she also collects hats. They marry and have a daughter who collects shoes.

Following the reading of this book, students could discuss items that they collect. They can then conduct surveys to determine how many students collect various items and can draw graphs using the survey results.

 ## Assessment
Writing in Mathematics

Directions for Students: Writing Activity—We have been discussing various graphs. To make some of the graphs, I asked the class questions to gather the information. Now it is your turn to make up a question. Think of a question that you could ask the class. Tomorrow we will conduct surveys and draw graphs showing the results of our surveys.

Write your name and your question on an index card. Tomorrow your group will draw an index card from the bowl and use that question to survey the class.

Note: Each student writes a question, but questions are not used immediately to conduct the surveys. This gives the teacher time to screen the questions to avoid duplicates or inappropriate questions.

Activity 9-5

Grades 3–5

Conducting a Classroom Survey

Materials: Questions appropriate for a class survey.

Teacher Statement: Each group will draw one question from the question bowl. First, survey your own group using that question and use a tally graph to record the results. Then your group will survey the other groups in the class. When you have surveyed the entire class, your group will draw a graph to represent the information. You may draw a bar graph, a line plot, or a circle graph. Each group member must take part in the surveying process either asking the question or recording the answer in the tally graph. Switch roles each time you survey a different group. Each group member must also draw or label some part of the final graph.

Note: You may wish to set up a schedule of interviews so that each group is certain to interview each other group. If there are six groups, you must schedule five rounds:

Round 1: Group 1 and Group 2; Group 3 and Group 4; Group 5 and Group 6.

Round 2: Group 1 and Group 3; Group 2 and Group 5; Group 4 and Group 6.

Etc.

Statistical Analysis of Data

There are several statistical methods that you could use to interpret data. The first measure that we will discuss is the average value of a set of data. In the early grade levels, students can use concrete objects or drawings to determine an average.

Example 9-15: Problem solving using objects or drawing a picture (first- or second-grade level).

Jim has 4 marbles, Joe has 8, and Jerry has 3. If they share the marbles so that each gets the same number of marbles, how many marbles will each boy get?

Solution: At the first- or second-grade level, students could use actual objects (or draw a picture) to find that there are 15 marbles. They could then distribute the marbles equally to three sets to find that each boy gets 5 marbles.

The process used in the above solution parallels the process used in a formula for the average that is typically learned at the fourth-grade level. During a problem-solving activity in which students use concrete objects and complete several examples similar to the one presented in Example 9-15, students could gain the insight that to evenly distribute or share sets of objects, to find the average of a set of given values, you must add all of the values and then divide by the total number of values. This "average" of a set of data is called the *mean*. It is also sometimes called "x-bar." The formula for this quantity is

$$\bar{x} = \frac{\text{sum of values in a data set}}{\text{number of values in the data set}}.$$

Example 9-16: Find the mean of each set of test scores (fourth- or fifth-grade level).

  a. 72, 73, 77, 72, 76
  b. 80, 83, 84, 68

 Activity 9-6   Grades 3–5

Extending Survey Results

Teacher Statement: We have discovered that 3 of the 24 students in our class write with their left hand. How many students in our school do you think write with their left hand? How can we find out? Good idea—we can survey all the classes in our school. There are 9 classes in our school, our class and 8 others. How many students would you guess are left-handed? (Record student guesses. Then send teams of 3 students each to survey all of the other classes. Following this survey, students should look up what percentage of the overall population is left-handed.)

Note: This activity can be repeated with other questions. A single class is likely to be a reasonably good representative sample to determine approximately how many students in a school write with their left hand. It may or may not be a representative sample to determine how many students in the school own home computers.

Solutions:

a. $\bar{x} = \dfrac{72 + 73 + 77 + 72 + 76}{5} = \dfrac{370}{5} = 74$

b. $\bar{x} = \dfrac{80 + 83 + 84 + 68}{4} = \dfrac{315}{4} = 78.75$

The second part of Example 9-16 illustrates that the mean is sensitive to outliers. That is, one low score can significantly lower an average. Do you think that one score that is significantly higher than the remaining scores in a data set would significantly raise the average? (See problem 6 at the end of this section.) A real-world connection involving the concept of mean or average can be made when students find the average speed of a car or other moving object given data involving various speeds traveled over various time periods.

An alternate measure of the "middle value" of a data set is the median. The definition of "median" is usually presented at the third- or fourth-grade level. To find the median, the values in the data set must be listed in increasing order. When the number of values in a data set is odd, the *median* is the middle value in the list; when the number of values in a data set is even, the *median* is the average of the two values in the middle positions of the list. Students may be introduced to the concept of median by finding the "middle" height in a line of students. In this example it is

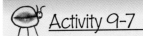 Activity 9-7   Grades 3–5

Problem Solving by Making Predictions

Materials: Container with 100 red, 150 blue, and 50 green counters; prediction handout.

Teacher Statement: In this container I have 300 counters. Some are red, some are blue, and some are green. Make a guess about how many of each color are in the container and write it in the initial guess line on your handout.

Directions: Shake or stir the counters to mix them up. Then draw a sample of 10 and have students make a new guess regarding how many of each color there are. Draw another sample of 10, so that you have drawn a sample of 20. Have students revise their predictions. Draw one more sample of 10 so that you now have a sample of 30 and repeat the prediction process. Reveal the actual number of each color, and discuss how larger samples can lead to improved predictions.

Prediction Recording Handout:

> There are 300 tiles in the container.
>
> Initial guess: ____ red, ____ blue, ____ green.
>
> Sample of 10: ____ red, ____ blue, ____ green.
>
> New guess: ____ red, ____ blue, ____ green
>
> Sample of 20: ____ red, ____ blue, ____ green.
>
> New guess: ____ red, ____ blue, ____ green
>
> Sample of 30: ____ red, ____ blue, ____ green.
>
> New guess: ____ red, ____ blue, ____ green

Standards

Nevada Mathematics Content Standards

Data Analysis: By the end of Kindergarten, students know and are able to:

5.K.1: Collect and describe data.

Nevada Department of Education, 2001

natural for the students to line up in increasing order of height. Students on each end of the lineup may remove themselves from the lineup until the student (or students) with the middle height(s) remain.

Two other definitions are needed before presenting a numerical example. The *mode* of a set of data is the value (or values) that occurs the most. A typical classroom example involving the mode is to determine the mode of the set of ages in the classroom. If each data value occurs exactly once in a set of data, we say there is *no mode*. The *range* of a set of data is the difference between the smallest and largest values in the set. You may easily calculate the range of ages of students in a classroom. These definitions are also learned at around the second- or third-grade level.

Example 9-17: Compute the mean, mode(s), median, and range for each data set.

a. 4, 6, 1, 7, 8, 5, 1
b. 6, 8, 9, 2, 6, 7, 10, 8
c. 3, 1, 2, 3, 1, 2, 3, 1, 2, 3
d. 5, 2, 9, 8, 4, 10

Solutions:

a. The ordered set of data is 1, 1, 4, $\underline{5}$, 6, 7, 8. The mode is 1. The median (indicated by underlining) is 5. The range is $8 - 1 = 7$. The mean is $\frac{32}{7}$, which rounded to the nearest tenth is 4.6.
b. The ordered set of data is 2, 6, 6, $\underline{7}$, $\underline{8}$, 8, 9, 10. The modes are 6 and 8. The median is 7.5, the range is $10 - 2 = 8$. The mean is $\frac{56}{8} = 7$.
c. The ordered set of data is 1, 1, 1, 2, $\underline{2}$, $\underline{2}$, 3, 3, 3, 3. The mode is 3. The median is 2. The range is $3 - 1 = 2$. The mean is $\frac{21}{10} = 2.1$.
d. The ordered set of data is 2, 4, $\underline{5}$, $\underline{8}$, 9, 10. There is no mode. The median is $\frac{13}{2} = 6.5$. The range is $10 - 2 = 8$. The mean is $\frac{38}{6}$, which rounded to the nearest tenth is 6.3.

Example 9-18: A small company has nine employees and one boss. The boss's salary is $110,000 per year, and each of the nine employees makes $10,000 per year. The boss states that the average salary in the company is $20,000. An employee states that the average salary in the company is $10,000. Which of the statistical measures is each using to compute these "averages"?

Solution: The boss is using the mean, the employee is using the mode or the median.

Standards

Mathematics Content Standards for California Public Schools
Statistics, Data Analysis, and Probability

Grade 2—1.3 Identify features of data sets (range and mode)
Grade 4—1.2 Identify the mode(s) for sets of categorical data and the mode(s), median, and any apparent outliers for numerical data sets.

California Department of Education, 2000

Standards

Maine Mathematics Content Standards
Elementary Grades 3–4

C. Data Analysis and Statistics:
 1. Make generalizations and draw conclusions using various types of graphs, charts, and tables.
 2. Read and interpret displays of data.

Example:
Predict the number of buttons per student in the room. Collect data on the number of buttons for each student in the room, display the data on a line plot, and analyze it to determine the average number of buttons per student.

Maine State Department of Education, 1997

Activity 9-8   Grades 3–5

Find the Mean, Mode, Median, and Range

Materials: Numbered index cards.

Directions: Divide students into three or four groups. Each group receives a set of index cards with one card for each member of the group. Each group must determine the mean, the mode, the median, and the range for their group.

Example 9-18 illustrates that as well as learning how to compute each of the measures of the average value of a data set, students should learn which measure is appropriate in a given situation. Students can then use statistical measures to analyze data from other subject areas such as science or social studies. For example, a common science experiment involves planting seeds and charting the growth of the resulting plants. Statistical measures and graphs may be used to analyze this data.

Example 9-19: Problem solving using cases (fourth- or fifth-grade level).

A teacher gives an opportunity for students to earn extra credit points. A student can earn up to 10 points. The teacher forgets to record the scores, but remembers the following: 5 students completed the extra credit assignment. There was at least one score of 10. The range of the scores was 4. The mean of the scores was 7.4. The median score was 7. The mode was either 6 or 7. Can you determine the scores?

Solution: The information that there was a score of 10 and that the range was 4 tells you that the lowest score was 6. The information that the median was 7 tells you that the middle score was 7. You now have 6, ___, 7, ___, 10. The mean is the sum of the five scores divided by 5. So the sum of the scores is $5 \times 7.4 = 37$. The two missing scores must have a sum of 14. If the mode was 6, then one of the missing scores is a 6, hence the other is 8 and the scores are 6, 6, 7, 8, 10. If the mode was 7, then one of the missing scores must have been 7, thus the other is also 7 and the scores are 6, 7, 7, 7, 10. You cannot determine the scores without knowing the mode.

 Teaching Connections

Use Computer Software to Calculate Classroom Statistics In Appendix B, instructions are given that show how to use an Excel spreadsheet to create and maintain a gradebook. Each of the statistical measures mean (average), mode, and median may be calculated with a single mouse click. You can easily calculate the average for a test or the average for a particular student. This information may be useful in your reflection about a particular test or assignment or in grade assignment.

Problem Set 9.2

For Your Understanding

1. The line plot shows the number of hours students watch TV per day. Find each of the following:
   a. number of students
   b. mean
   c. mode
   d. range
   e. median

```
    X
    X  X
  X X X      X
  X X X    X X
  0 1 2 3 4 5
```

Standards

NCTM

Grades 3–5

Students need to learn more than simply how to identify the mode or median in a data set. They need to build an understanding of what, for example the median tells them about the data, and they need to see this value in the context of other characteristics of the data.

NCTM, 2000, p. 179

Standards are listed with the permission of the National Council of Teachers of Mathematics (NCTM). NCTM does not endorse the content or validity of these alignments.

2. Find the mean, mode, range, and median for
   a. 5, 7, 6, 6, 8, 7, 9, 4, 6
   b. 1, 9, 8, 7, 3, 4, 6, 5

3. Find the mean, mode, range, and median for
   a. 4, 3, 2, 5, 4, 6
   b. 5, 7, 8, 6, 2

4. Consider the data given in Example 9-6 of Section 9.1. Find the mean, mode, range, and median for each of the two classes. What conclusions can you now make about the two classes?

5. Decide whether each of the following is sensitive to a single outlier. That is, will one outlier dramatically influence the results?
   a. range
   b. mode
   c. median

6. Determine whether one single outlier that is significantly higher than remaining values will dramatically increase the mean of the values. What will be the effect on the mean of a set of data that has one high outlier and one low one?

7. Which measure—mode, median, or mean—best describes each of the following:
   a. the average cookie contains 10 chocolate chips
   b. Rico's batting average is 0.4

8. Determine the scores from the following information. There are six scores that are each whole numbers. The lowest score is 3. The range of the scores is 6. The mode is 4. The median is 5. The mean is 5.5.

9. Shanda has already taken three tests. Her scores are 78, 74, and 81. What does she need to get on test four to have an overall average of 80?

10. Tyler had 3 hits out of 10 times at bat in his first season of little league, and 1 hit out of 2 times at bat in his second season. His mother Janet says that Tyler's batting average is 0.4 since his first season average is 0.3 and his second season average is 0.5. Tyler claims that his average is lower than 0.4. Who is correct?

Applications in the Classroom

1. Complete the scheduling of rounds that was started in Activity 9-5.

2. Write two questions that could be used with Activity 9-6. Indicate for each question whether you believe that your class will be a good representative sample for the students in the school.

3. Find three examples of survey results such as "four out of five dentists prefer sugarless gum" that you could use or discuss in your classroom.

4. Create a handout to be used with Activity 9-7. How will you assess this activity?

5. Create an activity for third- or fourth-grade students in which students solve problems similar to Example 9-15. The intent of the activity should be for students to gain an understanding of the concepts underlying the formula for calculating the mean of a set of values.

6. Write two word problems in which students calculate the average speed of a moving object.

7. Create or list one real-world application or example for each of mean, mode, range, and median.

8. Create an example in which students must determine (a) the total number surveyed, (b) the mode, (c) the median, and (d) the range from a given graph.

9. Write a lesson plan that describes how you will introduce the ideas of median, mode, and range in a third-grade classroom. Follow the format given by your instructor or use the lesson plan format given in Appendix A.

9.3 Determining Empirical and Theoretical Probability

As the following example shows, student logic and reasoning doesn't always follow the line that a teacher may desire it to follow. Probability and mathematical analysis can indicate what is likely to happen, but it is often tempting to

ꙮ A Glimpse into the Classroom

Probability in the Second Grade

Classroom teacher Miss Melissa Gibson recalls an incident that occurred during her student teaching experience in a second-grade classroom. She tossed five blue teddy bear counters and one red teddy bear counter onto the floor of the classroom and told the students, "Last night as I was preparing my math lesson, I dropped these bears on my floor. My dog Milo picked up one of the bears and brought it to me. There are five blue bears and one red bear. What color do you think the bear was that my dog picked up?" To her surprise, a chorus of students chimed "Red!" When Miss Gibson asked the students why they thought the dog would pick up the red one, they indicated that the red one was different.

Miss Gibson then placed the five blue bears and the one red bear into a paper sack. She had each student pick a counter from the sack and recorded the results in a tally graph. Students soon realized that they were more likely to pick a blue counter than the red one. The entire class cheered each time the red counter was picked.

pick the long shot or to hope for the unlikely to occur. Consider how many people routinely purchase lottery tickets or enter sweepstakes.

ꙮ Teaching Connections

Probability in the Early Childhood Classroom In the earliest grades, probability activities involve hands-on experiments that students usually enjoy (see Activities 9-9 and 9-10). Results may be displayed by graphs. Students gain experience in drawing and using graphs as well as experience involving chance and probability. Initially the language used can be informal and familiar; the word "probability" is generally not used until around the third-grade level. Ideas of probability are presented as early as the first-grade level: "It is raining today. We will probably have to stay indoors for recess." Probability terms such as "likely" and "unlikely" can be used in discussions involving other subject areas such as social studies or science. Probability can also be used in conjunction with other topics of mathematics such as time or temperature.

Terminology and Definitions

The *probability* of an event is a measure of how likely the event is to occur. Most people will agree that when you flip a coin, the likelihood that the coin will land heads up is $\frac{1}{2}$ or 50%. The event that the coin lands heads up is one of two possible outcomes—heads or tails. Does this mean that if you

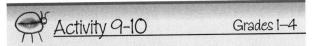

Activity 9-9 — Grades 1–3

Spinner Probability

Materials: Overhead spinner and tally graph outline.

Teacher Statement: This spinner has three colors. If every student spins once, which color do you think will occur most often? Which color do you think will occur least often? Are there two colors that should occur about the same number of times?

Note: Let each student spin once and record the results in the tally graph.

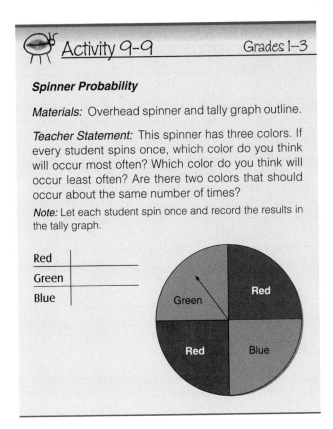

Activity 9-10 — Grades 1–4

Certain, Possible, Impossible

Materials: Sheets of paper labeled *Certain, Possible,* and *Impossible* for each student.

Teacher Statement: For each statement that I read, hold up the *Certain* sign if you think the event is certain to occur, the *Impossible* sign if you think the event is impossible or cannot occur, and the *Possible* sign if you think the event is possible but not certain.

It will snow on Christmas Day.
It will be dark outside tonight at 8 P.M.
Etc.

Note: For higher grades, you may replace *Possible* by *Likely* and *Unlikely.*

---

flip a coin two times, one of the flips will be heads and the other will be tails? Not necessarily. Although one heads and one tails is a possibility, it is also possible for two coin flips that both are heads or both are tails.

We will study two different types of probability. The *empirical probability* of an event is the probability of the event as determined from the results of experiments that are performed. If an experiment is performed n times and event E occurs r times, the empirical probability $P_e(E) = \frac{r}{n}$. The *theoretical probability* of an event is the probability of the event as determined by logical mathematical analysis and consideration of all possible outcomes.

Suppose you toss a coin 10 times and it comes up heads 4 of the 10 tosses. Then in this experiment, the empirical probability $P_e(\text{heads}) = \frac{4}{10}$. However, the theoretical probability of a coin landing heads up is $P(\text{heads}) = \frac{1}{2}$. Empirical results may not always coincide with theoretical results. It is important to remember this when performing experiments in your classroom; things may not always turn out exactly as you have planned. However, there is a mathematical theorem called the *law of large numbers* that states that if an experiment is repeatedly performed, the empirical probability of any particular outcome of the experiment will approach a fixed value. This theorem was dramatically illustrated by John Kerrich, an English mathematician who was held in a German prison during the Second World War (Long & DeTemple, 1996, p. 551). With

much time on his hands, Kerrich flipped a coin 10,000 times and recorded the results of each flip. After 100 tosses, $P_e(\text{heads})$ was 0.44; after 1,000 tosses it was 0.49. Throughout the experiment the empirical probability varied, but remained near one half. In the 10,000 tosses, heads came up 5,067 times for an overall empirical probability of approximately 0.51.

When determining theoretical probabilities, it is important that the set of all outcomes is correctly identified. For example, suppose the experiment is to toss a coin three times, and the event that you wish to find the probability of is "the coin tosses are all the same." You might think that there are only four possibilities: three heads, two heads and one tails, two tails and one heads, or three tails. In two of these possibilities, the coins are all the same. This might lead you to believe that the probability of the coins all the same when tossing a coin three times is $\frac{2}{4}$ or $\frac{1}{2}$. However, this is incorrect. The possibilities that are listed are not all equally likely. There is only one way to get three heads, that is HHH; there are three different ways to get two heads and one tails HHT, HTH, and THH. The set of all possible outcomes of the experiment is {HHH, HHT, HTH, THH, TTH, THT, HTT, TTT}.

A set of all possible outcomes of an experiment is called the *sample space* for that experiment. The eight outcomes listed above are all *equally likely;* each has the same chance of occurring. The probability that the coin tosses are the same in three tosses is $\frac{2}{8}$. Finding a sample space and using it to predict results of an experiment is presented at around the third- or fourth-grade level. The example above illustrates a general principle in calculating theoretical probabilities.

Calculating Probability

When outcomes in a sample space are equally likely, the probability of an event can be determined by dividing the number of outcomes in the event by the number of outcomes in the sample space.

Example 9-20: A single die is rolled. Find the probability that the number rolled is even.

Solution: There are six equally likely outcomes in the sample space. $S = \{1, 2, 3, 4, 5, 6\}$. In three of these rolls, the number rolled is even. Hence, the probability of an even roll is $P(\text{even}) = \frac{3}{6}$. Following this calculation, students may conduct an experiment to see whether an empirical probability close to one half is obtained for the experiment of rolling one die and recording the amount of even rolls.

Let's take a closer look at the experiment of rolling two dice and finding the sum of the numbers that appear on the top faces of the dice. As mentioned in Activity 9-11, the set of possible sums $\{2, 3, 4, 5, 6, 7, 8, 9, 10, 11, 12\}$ is not a set of equally likely outcomes, and this set should not be used as the sample space. To determine a set that may be used as the sample space, look at the actual process of the experiment. The first die may result in any of the numbers 1, 2, 3, 4, 5, or 6. Then the second die may also result in any one of the numbers 1, 2, 3, 4, 5, or 6. The sum is a combination of these two numbers. You can use the combination principle of multiplication introduced in Chapter 6 to determine that there are $6 \times 6 = 36$ such combinations. These are shown in Table 9-1.

Example 9-21: Calculating probabilities when two dice are rolled (fourth- or fifth-grade level).

Two dice are to be rolled. Find each of the following probabilities (see Table 9-1):

    a. $P(\text{sum is less than 5})$
    b. $P(\text{sum is even})$
    c. $P(\text{sum} = 13)$
    d. $P(\text{sum} > 1)$

Solutions:

    a. There are 6 outcomes where the sum is less than 5. Hence, $P(\text{sum} < 5) = \frac{6}{36}$.
    b. There are 18 outcomes where the sum is even. Thus, $P(\text{sum is even}) = \frac{18}{36}$.
    c. There are no outcomes where the sum is 13. Thus, $P(\text{sum} = 13) = \frac{0}{36} = 0$.
    d. In all of the outcomes the sum is greater than 1. Hence, $P(\text{sum} > 1) = \frac{36}{36} = 1$.

The last two parts of Example 9-21 deserve special mention. When two dice are rolled, it is impossible to obtain a sum of 13. The probability that the sum would be equal to 13 was 0. This makes sense because there is no chance that the event could happen. It is certain that when two dice are rolled the sum will be larger than 1. The probability of the sum exceeding this was found to be 1 or 100%. This result also makes sense because this event is certain to happen.

Probability Rules

In general, the following probability rules exist.

    1. An event has probability 0 if and only if it is an impossible event.
    2. An event has probability 1 if and only if it is a certain event.

TABLE 9-1 Sample space when two dice are rolled.

1,1	1, 2	1, 3	1, 4	1, 5	1, 6
2,1	2, 2	2, 3	2, 4	2, 5	2, 6
3,1	3, 2	3, 3	3, 4	3, 5	3, 6
4,1	4, 2	4, 3	4, 4	4, 5	4, 6
5,1	5, 2	5, 3	5, 4	5, 5	5, 6
6,1	6, 2	6, 3	6, 4	6, 5	6, 6

Activity 9-11 Grades 1–6

Which Wins?

Materials: "Which Wins?" handout (see Blackline Master 23 in the Appendices); two dice for each student.

Teacher Statement: We're going to play a game and see which die wins the most often. For problem 1, we will use one die only. Roll and mark an *X* in the column of the roll on your handout. If you rolled 1, mark an *X* above the 1, etc. Keep rolling until one of the columns is full of *X*s. Stop when one of the columns on your handout is full. That number hits the top and wins.

Notes: In the second game, the students roll two dice and mark an *X* in the column of the sum. They continue until one of the sums wins. Tally graphs should be used to record the results for all the students in the class. In the first game, numbers are equally likely and results should be fairly evenly distributed. In the second game, the sums are not equally likely. Students should discuss why certain sums won more than others. At the third-grade level, students should be able to list all possible combinations for each sum. At higher grade levels, theoretical probabilities can also be discussed.

3. For any event *E*, $0 \leq P(E) \leq 1$.
4. The sum of the probabilities of all outcomes in a sample space is equal to 1.
5. The probability that event *E* will not occur is $P(\text{not } E) = 1 - P(E)$.

We have already discussed the reasonableness of the first and second rules. The third rule states that all probabilities are between 0 and 1. This rule makes sense when you consider that the chance that an event will happen lies somewhere between impossible and certain. The reasonableness of rules four and five will become apparent in the examples below. Most of the probabilities calculated so far have been given in terms of fractions. However, due to the relationship between fractions, decimals, and percents, it is also possible to consider probabilities involving decimals or percents.

Example 9-22:

a. What is the probability that an earthquake will occur in your town in the next 24 hours?
b. When can the meteorologist say that the probability of rain is 100%?
c. If a spinner can result in Red, Blue, or Green, and probabilities of Red and Green are given as $P(\text{Red}) = \frac{1}{2}$ and $P(\text{Green}) = \frac{1}{3}$, determine the probability of Blue.
d. If the probability of rain is given as 0.25, what is the probability that it will not rain?

Solutions:

a. The probability of an earthquake in your town in the next 24 hours is probably near 0. You cannot say that this probability is 0 unless you are certain that the event is impossible.
b. The meteorologist should not say that the probability of rain is 100%. He can never be absolutely certain that it will rain (unless it is already raining).
c. The spinner may look something like the one shown. $P(\text{Red}) + P(\text{Green}) + P(\text{Blue}) = 1$ since one of these colors must occur.
   Then $\frac{1}{2} + \frac{1}{3} + P(\text{Blue}) = 1$, so $P(\text{Blue}) = 1 - (\frac{1}{2} + \frac{1}{3}) = 1 - \frac{5}{6} = \frac{1}{6}$.

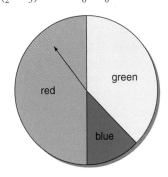

d. If the probability of rain is 0.25 or 25%, the probability that it will not rain is 0.75 or 75%.

Illustrating All Combinations

Drawing a Tree Diagram Section 6.1 of Chapter 6 discussed making a tree diagram for the illustration of various possibilities involved in the combination interpretation of multiplication. Tree diagrams are also useful in some probability situations.

Example 9-23: The numbers 3, 4, 5, and 6 are placed in a hat. Two numbers are drawn. What is the probability that the sum of the two numbers is at least 9?

Solution: Draw a tree diagram that will illustrate the possibilities. There are four ways to choose the first number. Once the first number is chosen, there are only three ways to choose the second number. There are $4 \times 3 = 12$ combinations. By looking at the tree you see that eight of these combinations have a sum of 9 or more. Thus $P(\text{sum} \geq 9) = \frac{8}{12}$. As an alternate solution, you could list the possible sets of two numbers: 3 & 4, 3 & 5, 3 & 6, 4 & 5, 4 & 6, and 5 & 6. Four of these sets have a sum of at least 9. Then $P(\text{sum} \geq 9) = \frac{4}{6}$. This answer is equivalent to the answer above, as both are equivalent to the fraction $\frac{2}{3}$.

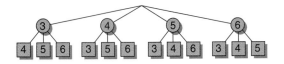

Counting Permutations and Combinations Example 9-23 considered two different ways of counting possible number combinations. When you counted the combinations and considered the order of the numbers chosen, there were 12 total combinations. When you counted only the possible resulting sets of two numbers, there were only 6 combinations. In some counting problems, the number of outcomes is too large to list or diagram all combinations.

Standards

North Carolina Mathematics Standards

Data, Probability, and Statistics: Grade 3

4.08 List arrangements (permutations) and combinations of up to three items.

North Carolina Department of Public Instruction, 2003

Example 9-24: Consider the five students Jaime, Alec, Paul, Kali, and Amelio.

  a. If these five students run a race, in how many different orders can the prizes for first, second, and third place be awarded?
  b. In how many ways can three of the students be chosen to receive a gold star for classroom participation?

Solutions:

  a. There are five possibilities for first place, four possibilities for second place, and three possibilities for third place. By the multiplication principle, there are $5 \times 4 \times 3 = 60$ different ways to award the prizes first, second, and third place. In this case the ordering of the students does matter. For example, the placement of Jaime first, Alec second, and Paul third is different than the placement of Jaime first, Paul second, and Alec third. When the arrangement of the people or items is important, the solution is called a *permutation.*
  b. In this situation, selecting Jaime, then Alec, and then Paul to receive stars gives the same set that results if the students are chosen in the order Jaime, Paul, and then Alec, or Alec, Paul, and then Jaime, or Alec, Jaime, and then Paul, and so on. In fact, for each set of three students, there are $3 \times 2 \times 1 = 6$ orderings of the students. Because there are 60 ways to choose and order three of the students, there are $60 \div 6 = 10$ different sets of three students that could receive the three gold stars.

Venn Diagrams You have already seen how graphs or tree diagrams can be useful in counting problems or in probability situations. The Venn diagram is also useful in these situations. Venn diagrams were introduced in Chapter 3 when we considered set theory. Now let's take a look at how they are used in counting or probability problems.

Example 9-25: Use Venn diagrams to solve each of the following problems.

  a. There are 30 adults in a room. Ten say they have children. Thirteen say they have pets. Fourteen say they have no children or pets. How many of the adults have both children and pets?
  b. There are 30 people in a room. Twelve own a cell phone. Five own a pager. What are the different possibilities for the number of people in the room who own neither a cell phone nor a pager?

Solutions:

  a. There are 30 people total. This is indicated by the 30 on the outside of the diagram. Since 14 people have neither children nor pets, write 14 on the outside of the two circles, and there will be 16 people included in the two circles. Since 10 of these are in the children circle, there must be 6 people in the section of the pet circle that does not overlap with the children circle. Since 13 people own pets, there must be 7 in the overlapping section. Thus, 7 people have both children and pets. You can also determine that 3 people have children but no pets.

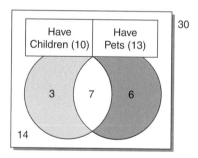

  b. There are 12 people in the cell phone circle, and 5 within the pager circle. Smallest Possible Overlap: If there is no overlap, this accounts for only 17 people, and there would be 13 people in neither circle. Largest Possible Overlap: The largest number of people that could own both a pager and a cell phone is 5. In this case, there would be 7 people who own a cell phone but not a pager, and there are only 12 people accounted for by the circles. This leaves 18 people in neither circle (see the Venn diagram below).

The number of people who own neither a cell phone nor a pager could vary from 13 to 18. This depends on the number of people who own both, which could vary from 0 to 5.

Smallest Possible Overlap   Largest Possible Overlap

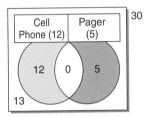
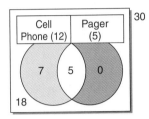

Example 9-26: The meteorologist says there is a 25% chance of rain, a 60% chance of snow, and a 15% chance that it will both rain and snow. Find the probability that (a) it will rain or snow and (b) it will neither rain nor snow.

Solutions: First place 0.15 in the circle intersection as this is the probability that it will both rain and snow. Then write $0.10 = 0.25 - 0.15$ in the section of the circle that indicates rain but no snow, and $0.45 = 0.60 - 0.15$ in the section that indicates snow but no rain. The two circles account for 0.7. There is a 70% chance that it will rain or snow. This leaves 0.3 for the section outside of the circles, and there is a 30% probability that it will neither rain nor snow.

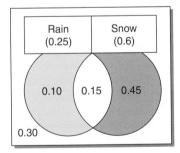

In the early grades, Venn diagrams are used in conjunction with sorting activities. The "diagram" need not be drawn as Activity 9-12 shows. A clothespin graph can help

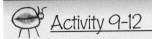

Activity 9-12   Grades 1–3

Concrete Venn Diagrams

Materials: A set of geo-pieces (see the Blackline Master 1 in the Appendices); two hula-hoops; two classification signs for each group; tape for the teacher to tape pieces to the board.

Teacher Statement: Each group will get two hula-hoops that you will overlap like the circles in our example. You will get two signs to label the hoops and a set of geo-pieces to distribute to members of your group.

Each of you will place your pieces in the appropriate part of your diagram and explain why you put them there. You will practice with your group, and then you will show the whole class. First, we will do an example on the board.

Example: Draw overlapping circles on the board. Label one circle "Green" and the other "Triangles." Hold up a green square: "Where do we place this? It is green, but not a triangle. It should go in the green circle, but not in the triangle circle." Tape the green square in an appropriate position. Repeat with a blue triangle, a red circle, a green triangle, etc.

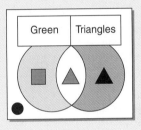

you sort your students. This illustrates the use of mathematics in a routine task such as taking a daily lunch count.

9.4 A KINDERGARTEN LESSON—CREATING A LUNCH COUNT GRAPH

Michelle Cicero is in her third year of teaching Kindergarten. Her class is composed of 1 teacher and 28 students. The children are at various learning levels. There are some children with special needs.

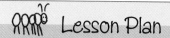

Lesson Plan

Attendance/Lunch Count Graphing Activity
by Michelle Cicero

While desperately looking for ways to help make my morning routine run a little smoother, I came across the following Web site that had a very useful graphing lesson: http://www.acorns.k12.tn.us/staffdev/curricu/lp_k_s_gml.htm.

I have 28 five-year-olds in my class and I am in charge of doing my own lunch count. In other words, I have to try and figure out who brought in money for a daily lunch, who packed their lunch, and who gets a free or reduced lunch ticket. This is a very hectic task for one person, especially in the beginning of the year. When I read over this graphing activity, I knew this was a great way to make my job a little easier.

Materials Needed:

Poster board, clothespins with students' names on them.

Preparation:

Make a graph on a large piece of poster board with one line down the center and thirty equal lines drawn across the board. Leave an inch between each line. Leave a space at the bottom of the graph. I put a picture of a lunch box and the word PACKERS on one side and a picture of a school lunch and the word BUYERS on the other side. At the top of the graph I wrote ATTEN-DANCE/LUNCH COUNT GRAPH.

Skills:

1. Name recognition
2. Turn taking
3. Counting
4. Introduction of a graph
5. Understanding of more/less

How the lesson went:

When the children arrive in the morning, they come in and sit on their assigned seats on the mat. I waited until they all settled in and explained to them that, beginning that day, they were each going to have a job to do when they come into the classroom. That immediately got their attention because they love having jobs. I brought out the graph and asked them to tell me what they saw. The children answered in several ways: "A picture of a lunch box" from one child, "A picture of a food" from another child, "My name on that wooden thing" from someone else.

I then explained to them that I was holding a graph. I told them that graphs help us learn about things. I asked if anyone could tell me what they think this graph might help us learn. Bobby immediately raised his hand and answered, "Who likes to pack." Another child answered, "It will help us learn our names." They were a little confused about the picture of the school lunch, so I asked them to think about where they might see that picture. Michael answered, "In the cafeteria." I then explained that this graph was going to help us learn how many people packed their lunch and how many were buying their lunch. I explained that it would also show us who was present in class and who was absent.

I called each row to come up and find their name and place it on the correct side. I also showed them to start at the bottom of the graph and not to skip any spaces. Almost all of them came up and placed their clothespin on the correct side. Some of them had a little trouble squeezing the clothespin. Sammy picked Simon's clothespin instead of his. He saw the S and didn't look at the rest of the letters so I asked him to try again. His second choice was successful. Overall, it went really well.

After everyone had a chance to take their turn, we talked about the graph. I had Melanie come up and count how many packers we had today and then I helped her write the number 14 above the chart on the dry erase board that the chart was hanging on. I asked Darian to come up and count how many buyers there were, she wrote the number 16 on her own. I then asked them if we had more buyers or packers today. Most of them shouted, "Buyers." I explained that 16 is more than 14, so yes we did have more buyers. I also explained that on Monday they were going to have to come up and find their name on their own and place it on the correct side so Mrs. Cicero would know who packed and who was buying their lunch. I asked them what might happen if you forgot to do your job. Carly answered, "You might think they are not here," which is exactly the answer I was looking for.

Skill Assessment:

1. Name recognition: All but 1 child was able to recognize their name, which is great at this stage in the year.
2. Turn taking: They all did a very good job, especially having to wait for 27 children to take a turn. The next time we do it, I think it will be a lot faster.
3. Counting: Most of them were able to count to 10, but I was able to identify those who had trouble counting past 10.
4. Introduction to a graph: They were able to describe what we were graphing by looking at the pictures. The picture of the lunch tray threw them off a little bit.
5. Understanding more and less: It looked pretty close because there were only two more people that

continued

bought their lunch than packers, but most of them were able to see it. Once we counted and wrote the number at the top of the graph, it was more clear.

Things I would do different:

- I am definitely going to laminate the graph because I want it to last a long time.

- The clothespins were a little difficult for some of the children to handle, but I think that will help build their fine motor skills.
- The spaces on the graph are a little small, but that's because I have 28 children. You wouldn't have to make them so small if you had a smaller class.

Notice how the teacher in the above scenario uses a real-life situation to introduce the idea of a graph to the children. Giving the children a job to do keeps them interested and involved in the daily activity. The activity described effectively combines objectives from Language Arts and Mathematics and improves fine-motor skills. The teacher identifies skills and objectives before the lesson is presented. She reflects on the lesson and records changes and possible alterations. The teacher in the above scenario is continually on the lookout for new materials and ideas to use in the classroom. She was pleased with the students' reactions to the activity and with the success of the students in meeting the objectives. This is an activity that she will continue to use.

Problem Set 9.3

For Your Understanding

1. a. Write a sample space of equally likely outcomes for the experiment of flipping a coin two times and find the probability that both flips are heads.
    b. A penny, two nickels, and a quarter are to be thrown. Find the probability that both nickels are heads.
    c. A penny, two nickels, and a quarter are to be thrown. Find the probability that two of the coins are heads.

2. Roll two dice 20 times and record the sum of the numbers appearing on the top faces.
    a. Draw a circle graph showing the results of your experiment.
    b. According to your empirical results, what is the probability of rolling a sum of 7?
    c. What is the theoretical probability of rolling a sum of 7?

3. Calculate theoretical probabilities for each of the sums 2, 3, . . . 12 when two dice are rolled and the sum is found.

4. Five red marbles numbered 1, 2, 3, 4, and 5 and five green marbles numbered 4, 5, 6, 7, and 8 are placed in a bag. One is drawn at random. Find the theoretical probability that the marble drawn is
    a. an odd-numbered marble
    b. either red or odd numbered
    c. both red and odd numbered

5. a. A player rolls two dice and finds the sum. If both dice show an even number, what is the probability that the sum is 7?
    b. A spinner has 12 equal sections labeled 1, 2, . . . 12. Find the probability that a random spin is a multiple of 4.
    c. The numbers 1 to 15 are written on slips of paper and placed in a bag. One slip is drawn. Find the probability that the slip drawn is not a multiple of 3.

6. a. You have four square tiles—one each of red, blue, green, and yellow. In how many different ways could you arrange them in a row?
    b. You have four square tiles—two red, and two blue. In how many different ways could you arrange them in a row?

7. A jar contains 10 red cubes, 4 blue cubes, 4 green cubes, and 2 yellow cubes. An experiment involves choosing a cube, recording the color, and returning the cube to the jar. The experiment is performed 30 times. How many of each color do you expect to be picked?

8. a. In a class of 31 students, 5 have both children and pets, 9 have children, and 15 have no children or pets. How many students have pets? How many students have pets but no children?
    b. In a class of 30 students, 6 own a cat and 20 own a computer. What are the possibilities for the number of students who have neither a cat nor a computer?

9. a. You and two friends go to the movies. You sit in a row of three seats. You and your best friend sit next to each other. How many different ways can your group arrange itself in the three seats?

   b. You have two 5-lb weights and three 2-lb weights. You must balance weights evenly on each end of a 10-lb bar. List the different combinations and total weights that you can use.

10. a. In a group of 30 students, 10 are taking math, 7 are taking English, and 15 are taking neither subject. How many are taking both math and English?

    b. In a room of people, 20 own a car, 5 own a truck, and 3 have both. Seven people in the room have neither a car nor a truck. How many people are in the room?

    c. In a group of 30 people, 10 say they have a brother, 7 of these have both a brother and a sister, 8 have no brothers or sisters. How many have a sister?

11. a. How many different ways are there to arrange the letters *m, a, t, h?*

    b. How many different ways are there to arrange the letters *O, H, I, O?*

12. In how many ways could you choose from six candidates
    a. two senators
    b. a president and a vice president

13. Use a Venn diagram to solve the following: 40% of the pets in a pet shop are cats, 20% of the pets in the shop have long hair, 15% of the pets in the shop are long-haired cats. What percent of the pets are neither cats nor long haired?

14. A two-player game consists of rolling two dice and finding the difference of the two numbers rolled. One player is designated "Lows" and gets a point each time the difference is 0, 1, or 2. The other player is "Highs" and gets a point each time the difference is 3, 4, or 5. Play continues until one player has 25 points. Use probability to determine whether the game is fair. If the game is unfair, which player has a better chance of winning?

Applications in the Classroom

1. Design four probability stations that you could use at the first-, second-, or third-grade level. Include directions for the stations, any necessary handouts, and a list of materials.

2. Suppose you have spinners for which $P(\text{red}) = \frac{2}{3}$ and $P(\text{blue}) = \frac{1}{3}$. You wish to design a classroom experiment where each student spins a spinner a certain number of times and records the results of their experiment to share with the class. How many times will you choose to have each student spin? Justify your answer.

3. Have your fourth-grade and higher students stand 100 pennies on their edges on a tabletop. Then jostle the table and record how many coins landed heads up. The results may surprise you.

4. Write a list of 10 statements that you could use with Activity 9-10. For each statement indicate which answer you would expect: certain, likely, unlikely, or impossible.

5. Create five Venn diagram problems or situations that you could use in a classroom. Indicate the class level of your problems.

6. Samuel (a third grader) claims that THT is more likely than HHH when a coin is tossed three times. You are the teacher. How do you respond?

7. Karlee (a first grader) claims that rolling a 1 is more likely than rolling a 6 when a die is rolled. You are the teacher. How do you respond?

8. Classify the level of knowledge and the type of learning experience of Activity 9-11. What objective from the NCTM model (or from your state or district model) does the activity address?

9. Create an assessment tool to be used with Activity 9-12. Explain why you chose that type of assessment tool.

10. Write a lesson plan that describes how you will introduce the term "probability" in a second- or third-grade classroom. Follow the format given by your instructor or use the lesson plan format given in Appendix A.

11. Write a lesson plan that describes how you will introduce the idea of determining a sample space in a third-grade or fourth-grade classroom. Follow the format given by your instructor or use the lesson plan format given in Appendix A.

12. Look up "graphs," "statistics," or "probability" in the index or table of contents of an elementary-level textbook. Photocopy or copy by hand one example or problem that you think is interesting or unusual and indicate why. What objective from the NCTM model (or from your state or

district model) does the example or problem address? Be sure to state what grade-level text you are using.

13. Find and print a graphing, statistics, or probability activity from the Web. State what grade level you think the activity would be appropriate for. What objective from the NCTM model (or from your state or district model) does the activity address?

14. Choose one of the books in the children's literature section of the references for this chapter. Write a brief description of the book and explain how you could incorporate the book into a math lesson.

15. Make up two writing prompts or stems that fit in with material or activities from this chapter.

References

Children's Literature References

Arnold, Caroline. (1984). *Charts and graphs: Fun, facts, and activities.* New York: Franklin Watts.

Bryant-Mole, Karen. (1994). *Charts and graphs* (Usborne Math Series). Saffron Hill, London: EDCP.

Cushman, Jean. (1991). *Do you wanna bet? Your chance to find out about probability.* New York: Houghton Mifflin.

Geringer, Laura. (1985). *A three hat day.* New York: HarperCollins.

Holtzman, Caren. (1997). *No fair!* (Hello Math Reader Level 2). New York: Scholastic.

Linn, Charles. (1972). *Probability.* New York: Crowell.

Markle, Sandra. (1997). *Discovering graph secrets: Experiments, puzzles, and games exploring graphs.* New York: Simon & Schuster.

Murphy, Stuart. (1997). *Lemonade for sale* (MathStart Level 3). New York: HarperCollins.

Murphy, Stuart. (1997). *The best vacation ever* (MathStart Level 2). New York: HarperCollins.

Murphy, Stuart. (2000). *Probably pistachio* (MathStart Level 2). New York: HarperCollins.

Reid, Margarette. (1990). *The button box.* New York: Penguin Putnam Books.

Srivastava, Jane Jonas. (1975). *Averages.* New York: Crowell.

Tobias, Tobi. (2000). *Serendipity.* New York: Simon & Schuster.

Whitehead, Ann. (2000). *Tiger math: Learning to graph from a baby tiger.* New York: Henry Holt.

Teacher Resources

Burns, M. (1995). *Math by all means: Probability, grades 3–4.* Sausalito, CA: Math Solutions Publications.

California Department of Education. (2000). *Mathematics Content Standards for California Public Schools.* Retrieved November 12, 2003 from http://www.cde.ca.gov/board/pdf/math.pdf

Elementary Quantitative Literacy Project. (1998). *Exploring statistics in the elementary grades: Book 1 (K–6).* White Plains, NY: Cuisenaire–Dale Seymour.

Long, C. T., & DeTemple, D. W. (1996). Mathematical reasoning for elementary teachers. New York: HarperCollins College.

Maine State Department of Education. (1997). *Maine Mathematics Standards.* Retrieved December 8, 2003 from http://www.state.me.us/education/lres/math.htm

Manfre, E., Moser, J., Lobato, J., Morrow, L. (1996). *Health mathematics connections, grade 3.* Boston: Houghton Mifflin.

National Council of Teachers of Mathematics. (2000). *Principles and standards for school mathematics.* Reston, VA: Author.

Nevada Department of Education. (2001). *Nevada Mathematics Content Standards.* (n.d.). Retrieved November 12, 2003 from http://www.leg.state.nv.us/interim/nonlegcom/academicstandards/Misc/Standards/Math.htm

North Carolina Department of Public Instruction. (2003). *North Carolina Mathematics Standard Course Study and Grade Level Competencies K–12 (2003).* Retrieved November 19, 2003 from http://www.dpi.state.nc.us/curriculum/mathematics/standard2003/index.html

Ohio Office of Early Childhood Education & Office of Curriculum and Instruction. (2003). *Ohio Early Learning Content Standards.* Retrieved December 1, 2003 from http://www.ode.state.oh.us/ ece/pdf/Mathematics.pdf

Russell, S. J., & Corwin, R. B. (1990). *Sorting: Groups and graphs* (Unit of study for grades 2–3 from *Used numbers: Real data in the classroom*). White Plains, NY: Cuisenaire–Dale Seymour.

Russell, S. J., & Stone, A. (1990). *Counting: Ourselves and our families* (Unit of study for grades K–1 from *Used numbers: Real data in the classroom*). White Plains: NY: Cuisenaire–Dale Seymour.

Shulte, A. P. (Ed.). (1981). *Teaching statistics and probability, 1981 Yearbook.* Reston, VA: National Council of Teachers of Mathematics.

Tank, B. (1996). *Math by all means: Probability, grades 1–2.* Sausalito, CA: Math Solutions Publications.

Selected Research Books and Articles

Clements, D. H. (1994). The uniqueness of the computer as a learning tool: Insights from research and practice. In J. L. Wright, & D. D. Shades (Eds.), *Young children: Active learners in a technological age.* Washington, DC: NAEYC.

Graph Club 2.0. (2003). [Computer Softwear] Tom Snyder Productions: Watertown, MA.

Haughland, S. W. (1999). What role should technology play in young children's learning? *Young Children, 54*(6), 26–31.

Kerrigan J. (2002). Powerful software to enhance the elementary school mathematics program. *Teaching Children Mathematics, 8*(6), 364–370.

Ozgun-Koca, S. A. (1998). Technology in Mathematics Education: Internet Resources. ERIC Clearinghouse for Science Mathematics and Environmental Education (ED433192).

Further Reading

Bruni, J. V., & Silverman, H. J. (1986). Developing concepts in probability and statistics—and much more. *Arithmetic Teacher, 33,* 34–37.

Brutlag, D. (1996). *Chance encounters: Probability in games and simulation.* Palo Alto, CA: Creative Publications.

Johnson, E. M. (1981). Bar graphs for first graders. *Arithmetic Teacher, 29,* 30–31.

Konold, C. (1991). Understanding students' beliefs about probability. In E. Von Glasserfeld (Ed.), *Radical constructivism in mathematics education* (pp. 139–156). Holland: Kluwer.

Landwehr, J. M., & Watkins, A. E. (1986). *Exploring data and exploring probability.* Palo Alto, CA: Dale Seymour.

Lee, H. (1999). Resources for teaching and learning about probability and statistics. (ERIC Clearinghouse for Science Mathematics and Environmental Education, ED433219).

Leutzinger, L. P. (1990). Graphical representation and probability. In J. N. Payne (Ed.), *Mathematics for the young child* (pp. 251–263). Reston, VA: National Council of Teachers of Mathematics.

Lindquist, M. M., Lauquire, J., Gardner, A., & Shekaramiz, S. (1992). *Making sense of data.* Reston, VA: National Council of Teachers of Mathematics.

Piaget, J., & Inhelder, B. (1975). *The origin of the idea of chance in children.* London: Routledge & Kegan Paul.

Russell, S. J., & Friel, S. N. (1989). Collecting and analyzing real data in the elementary classroom. In P. R. Trafton (Ed.), *New directions for elementary school mathematics* (pp. 134–148). Reston, VA: National Council of Teachers of Mathematics.

Schulte, A. P., & Choate, S. A. (1996). *What are my chances?* Palo Alto, CA: Creative Publications.

Shaughnessy, J. M. (1992). Research in probability and statistics: Reflections and directions. In D. Grouws (Ed.), *Handbook of research on mathematics teaching and learning* (pp. 465–494). New York: Macmillan.

Tarr, J. E. (2002). Providing opportunities to learn probability concepts. *Teaching Children Mathematics, 8*(8), 482–487.

University of North Carolina Mathematics and Science Education Network. (1997). *Teach-stat activities: Statistics investigations for grades 1–3.* White Plains, NY: Cuisenaire—Dale Seymour.

Uslick, J., & Barr, S. G. (2001). Children play mathematics at camp invention. *Teaching Children Mathematics, 7*(7), 392–394.

Usnick, V., McCarthy, J., & Alexander, S. (2001). Mrs. Whatsit "Socks" it to probability. *Teaching Children Mathematics, 8*(4), 246–249.

Vissa, J. M. (1988). Probability and combinations for third graders. *Arithmetic Teacher, 36,* 33–37.

Wilson, M. R., & Krapfl, C. M. (1995). Exploring mean, median, and mode with a spreadsheet. *Mathematics Teaching in the Middle School, 1*(6), 490–495.

Woodward, E. (1983). A second-grade probability and graphing lesson. *Arithmetic Teacher, 30,* 23–24.

10

Exploring Geometric Figures and Relationships

R eal-world examples and applications of geometry are abundant. Beyond the obvious examples of shapes, figures, and motions in everyday life, even a simple task such as writing involves a great deal of geometry. Think about how you would instruct a young child to draw the numeral for nine. Your instructions would probably include a circle and a line segment as well as specific directions on how to draw and connect these figures.

Children have many experiences with geometric concepts far before they enter school. "Children's first experiences in trying to understand the world around them are spatial and geometric as they distinguish one object from another and determine how close or far away an object is. As they learn to move from one place to another, they use geometric and spatial ideas regularly to solve prob-

lems and make decisions in their everyday lives" (Bruni & Seidenstein, 1990, pp. 203–204). Geometry also underlies many puzzles, patterns, and spatial activities as well as many problem-solving situations.

The NCTM Standards 2000 state, "Geometry is more than definitions; it is about describing relationships and reasoning" (p. 41). This is true for both students and teachers. In this chapter you will learn or relearn many definitions, but you also cover several applications and hands-on geometric activities. The NCTM Standards also indicate that the learning of geometry is a dynamic experience.

Standards

NCTM

Grades 3–5

The study of geometry in grades 3-5 requires thinking *and* doing. As students sort, build, draw, model, trace, measure, and construct, their capacity to visualize geometric relationships will develop. At the same time they are learning to reason and to make, test, and justify conjectures about these relationships. This exploration requires access to a variety of tools, such as graph paper, rulers, pattern blocks, geoboards, and geometric solids, and is greatly enhanced by electronic tools that support exploration, such as dynamic geometry software.

NCTM, 2000, p. 165

Standards are listed with the permission of the National Council of Teachers of Mathematics (NCTM). NCTM does not endorse the content or validity of these alignments.

Objectives

After completing Chapter 10, you will be able to

- List and describe the van Hiele levels and classify the level of a given geometric activity
- Use correct terminology and notations in describing and working with plane figures such as points, lines, rays, segments, angles, and polygons
- Plot points and determine the coordinates of plotted points in the Cartesian coordinate system
- Use correct terminology and notations in describing and working with space figures and nets of space figures
- Determine whether figures are similar or congruent
- Discuss and describe motions and symmetry
- Plan lessons and activities that incorporate geometric ideas into the early childhood classroom

10.1 The van Hiele Levels and Geometric (Plane) Figures

A widely accepted model of how children progress as they learn geometric concepts was introduced by a Dutch couple Pierre van Hiele and Dina van Hiele-Geldof in the late 1950s. This model involves five stages, known as the "van Hiele levels," through which children progress in their acquisition of spatial or geometric ideas. These five stages are described in the following section. Approximations of the student grade level at each van Hiele level are also given.

The van Hiele Levels

Level 0, Visualization: At the visualization level (pre-K–Grade 1) children use the appearance of a figure or object to classify or identify the figure or object. A child at this level may say that ⬡ is not a square.

Level 1, Analysis: At the analysis level (Grades 1–3) children begin to consider properties of a figure or object other than their immediate appearance. Children at this level are not aware of the interrelationships between figures. A child at this level may say that ◇ is a square because it has four equal-length sides and square corners. However, the child may not yet recognize that this object is also a rectangle.

Level 2, Informal Deduction: At the level of informal deduction (Grades 2–6) children can see the interrelationships between figures. Because they are able to consider the properties necessary to be included in a class of objects, they will concede that every square is also a rectangle. At this level they are capable of following and conceiving intuitive "proofs" such as the proof in Activity 10-8 that the sum of the measures of the interior angles of any triangle is 180°.

Level 3, Deduction: At the level of deduction (Grades 4–adult) students can understand and write logical proof arguments. For example, a student at this level could deduce that the sum of the measures of the interior angles of a convex quadrilateral is 360° because a quadrilateral may be divided into two triangles and each triangle has an interior angle sum of 180°.

Level 4, Rigor: The rigor level (adult) is the level of a college geometry course. The student is capable of making abstract deductions and working in an axiomatic system.

Note the overlapping of the grade-level approximations. As a teacher you must be sure that you are reaching students at their level. You will often need to modify activities and problems to accommodate students who are working at a lower or higher level than other students in the class. Many of the activities presented in this chapter may be appropriately modified as necessary. Because this text focuses on pre-K–Grade 4, the majority of activities and exercises in this chapter are Level 0–Level 2, although an occasional activity or exercise at Level 3 is also included.

Points, Lines, Rays, and Segments

One of the simplest of the geometric figures is the *point*. A third-grade textbook might define *point* as "an exact position, often marked by a dot." Even preschool children understand ideas such as pointing a finger and the point of a pencil. The infamous mathematician Euclid described a point as "that which has no part" (Krause, 1991, p. 561). Many mathematicians consider *point* to be an undefined term, however. Technically a point has no shape or dimension, but points are generally drawn as dots and labeled with uppercase letters.

•A   •Q

                    •P

You are probably familiar with the phrase "Two points determine a line." That is, given any two points, there is a unique line that contains the two points. A typical second- or third-grade textbook definition of a *line* is "a straight path that is endless in both directions." In drawing a line on paper, you use arrows to indicate that the line extends infinitely in both directions.

> Imagine the confusion the definition of *line* could cause the next time you use a phrase like "line up for lunch" or "go to the end of the line" in your classroom.

If a line contains the points P and Q it can be denoted using the notation $\overleftrightarrow{PQ}$ or $\overleftrightarrow{QP}$. If point R is a point on this line, the line may also be denoted as $\overleftrightarrow{RP}$, $\overleftrightarrow{PR}$, $\overleftrightarrow{QR}$, or $\overleftrightarrow{RQ}$. A line can be denoted using a lowercase script letter as well. The line in Figure 10-1 can be denoted by any one of the six notations mentioned above or simply by line j.

A *ray* is a subset of a line that includes one point called the endpoint of the ray and also includes all points of the line lying to one side of that endpoint. Thus, a ray extends infinitely in one direction. The arrow in the symbol for a ray is directed from left to right regardless of the direction that the actual ray is pointing. For example, the ray shown in Figure 10-2 is denoted $\overrightarrow{QP}$. This ray has endpoint Q. Note that $\overrightarrow{QP}$ and $\overrightarrow{PQ}$ do not denote the same ray. The ray $\overrightarrow{PQ}$ would have endpoint P and be directed in the opposite direction of $\overrightarrow{QP}$. Similarly, $\overrightarrow{QP}$ and $\overrightarrow{RP}$ do not denote the same ray as one has endpoint Q and the other has endpoint R. However, recall that $\overleftrightarrow{QP}$ and $\overleftrightarrow{RP}$ do denote the same line (when points P, Q, and R all lie on the same line).

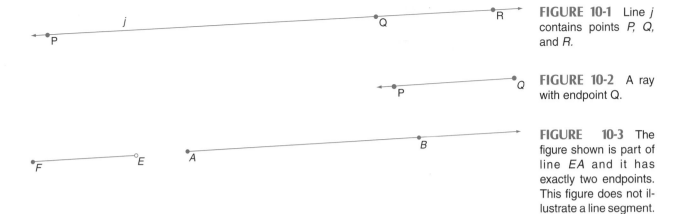

FIGURE 10-1 Line *j* contains points *P*, *Q*, and *R*.

FIGURE 10-2 A ray with endpoint Q.

FIGURE 10-3 The figure shown is part of line *EA* and it has exactly two endpoints. This figure does not illustrate a line segment.

A second- or third-grade textbook might define a *line segment* as "part of a line that has two endpoints." Mathematicians would argue that this definition is too broad, and includes such figures as the one shown in Figure 10-3.

Mathematicians and third-grade students would agree that the figure below illustrates a line segment. The notation

for the segment shown is $\overline{GH}$ or $\overline{HG}$. You may recall from a previous math course that you can illustrate an open segment, or a half-open segment by removing the endpoint(s) from a line segment. The idea of removing endpoints is generally not covered in K–4 mathematics courses, so we will not spend any more time on this concept.

Planes and Plane Figures

If two points determine a line, what do three points determine? In some cases, three points will again determine a line. For example, the points *F*, *A*, and *B* above are *collinear,* that is, they lie on the same line. If three points are *noncollinear,* they do not all lie on the same line. In this case the three points will determine three lines, which also determines a *plane.*

The term "plane" is yet another undefined term used to describe a two-dimensional region that extends infinitely in all directions (see Figure 10-4). Planes are usually denoted by capital script letters such as $\mathscr{P}$. Subsets of a plane are called *plane figures.* For the remainder of this section and in the next section, we will be concerned only with plane figures.

Parallel Lines and Intersecting Lines Two lines in a plane are *parallel* if they do not intersect. If two lines in a plane do intersect, they intersect at exactly one point. Parallel lines and intersecting lines are shown in Figure 10-5. Children will be able to recall many familiar instances of parallel lines such as railroad tracks and intersecting lines such as roads on a map. They will also be able to find instances of parallel and intersecting lines within the classroom.

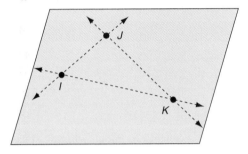

FIGURE 10-4 The points *I*, *J*, and *K* determine three lines that also determine plane $\mathscr{P}$.

Angles Intersecting lines form an *angle,* which is defined as the union of two rays with a common endpoint. When it is clear which angle is indicated, a single letter or number may be used to denote an angle, such as $\angle 1$ shown in Figure 10-5. This same angle may also be denoted by $\angle GOF$ or by $\angle FOG$. The symbol $\angle GOF$ is read as "angle G, O, F." The point O is called the *vertex* of the angle. None of the angles on the figure could be designated by simply $\angle O$ as this notation would be ambiguous. The letter O names the vertex at the intersection of the lines, and the placement of this letter on the figure is arbitrary.

Perpendicular Lines If the four angles formed by a pair of intersecting lines have the same size, the lines are *perpendicular* and the angles are called *right angles.* Later we will discuss how the measure of any right angle is 90°. A right angle is generally denoted in a drawing by a small box in the corner of the angle. Although all four angles formed by perpendicular lines are right angles, it is sufficient to mark only one as a right angle. Lines do not have to be drawn vertical and horizontal to be perpendicular. Figure 10-6 shows two pairs of perpendicular lines.

Angle Measurement It is not necessary to draw intersecting lines in order to discuss angles. As stated, an angle is the union of two rays with a common endpoint. The rays are called the *sides* of the angle, and the common endpoint is

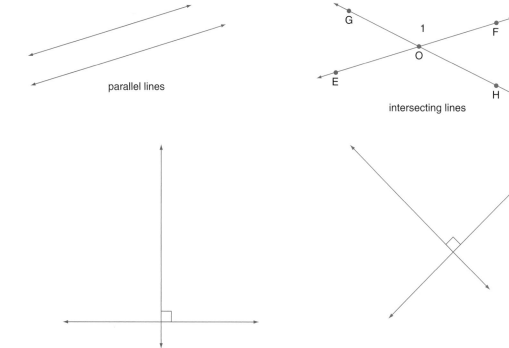

parallel lines

FIGURE 10-5
Parallel and
intersecting lines.

intersecting lines

FIGURE 10-6
Perpendicular lines.

called the vertex of the angle. To measure an angle, you do not measure the lengths of the sides of the angle, as the sides are rays of infinite length. You measure an angle by determining how far one side must be rotated about the vertex to coincide with the other side of the angle. The measure of an angle is given in degrees, with 360 degrees (written as 360°) in a full-circle rotation. If there are 360° in a full-circle rotation, then there are 180° in a half-circle rotation and 90° in a quarter-circle rotation. A quarter-circle rotation forms a square corner—that is, a right angle. Thus the measure of a right angle is 90°. The measure of $\angle A$ is denoted $m(\angle A)$.

An angle that has a measure greater than 0° and less than 90° is called *acute*. A *right angle* has a measure exactly 90°. An angle that has a measure greater than 90° and less than 180° is called *obtuse*. A *straight angle* has a measure of 180°. An angle with a measure greater than 180° and less than 360° is called a *reflex angle*. Figure 10-7 illustrates the various types of angles described above. The intended angle is indicated by drawing an arc in the interior of the angle. Note that an angle need not be in standard position. That is, it is not necessary for one ray of the angle to point directly to the right.

One tool that can be used to measure angles or to draw angles of a given measure is called a *protractor*. Protractors are generally introduced at the fourth- or fifth-grade level. In earlier grades, students may be required to classify or even draw given angles as acute, right, straight, obtuse, or reflex (see Activity 10-1). The corner of a page of paper makes a handy tool to measure or draw a right angle. By folding the corner into halves or thirds, you can also use the paper as a tool to draw 30°, 45°, or 60° angles (see problem 1 in the "Applications in the Classroom" section of Problem Set 10.1).

Activity 10-1   Grades 2–5

Pipe Cleaner Angles

Materials: Chenille wires (pipe cleaners), one for each student.

Teacher Directions: Ask students to bend their pipe cleaners to show you an acute angle, a right angle, and an obtuse angle. Then ask students to identify right, acute, and obtuse angles in the classroom and in real-world situations.

Notes: Make sure to point out the variety of sizes of acute or obtuse angles. Also tell students that angles do not have a standard fixed position. That is, an upside-down right angle is still a right angle.

Teaching Connections

Present a Variety of Illustrative Examples As the teacher you must ensure that your students are able to classify an angle even if it is not presented in the standard position with one ray pointing directly to the right. The student must be able to recognize figures such as ⌐ or ⟩ as right angles. If the only visual of a right angle that you present to your students looks like ∟ they are likely to overgeneralize and call ⌐| a "left angle" the first time they encounter it. When students are able to recognize a right angle shown in a nonstandard position, it is clear that they are beginning to rec-

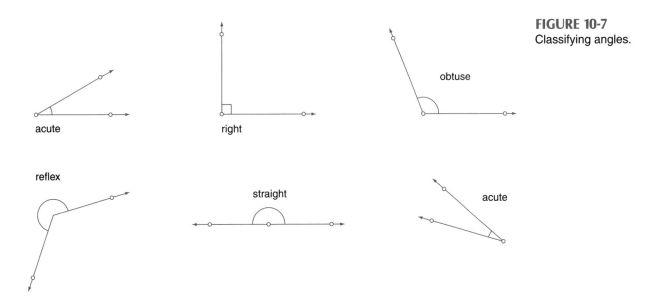

FIGURE 10-7
Classifying angles.

ognize and consider properties of a figure. They have moved beyond Level 0, the visualization level of the van Hiele model, into Level 1—analysis.

The Cartesian Coordinate System

Preliminary Ideas and Notations The ideas of parallel and perpendicular allow us to define a *rectangular coordinate system* for locating points in the plane. This concept may be introduced as a *grid*. Children first need to understand the terms *row* and *column*.

This is a row of stars: ☆ ☆ ☆ ☆ ☆

This is a column of moons: ☾
☾
☾
☾
☾

There are several interesting things to note about Activity 10-2. First, notice that the objects are drawn in the squares and not at intersections of segments. This allows the students to be introduced to the concept of locating positions without overwhelming them with the precision necessary in locating intersections of segments. Also notice that the columns are labeled with letters and the rows are labeled with numbers. This is to avoid the confusion that may be caused when both rows and columns are labeled with numbers. Note that the numbers increase from the bottom row to the top row. This is consistent with the labeling of the Cartesian coordinate system that will be defined later. There is a variety of student questions and a question with more than one correct answer is included in the activity. The process of locating items on a grid is related to the real-world application of map reading. This is a skill that will be useful not only in mathematics but also in science and social studies.

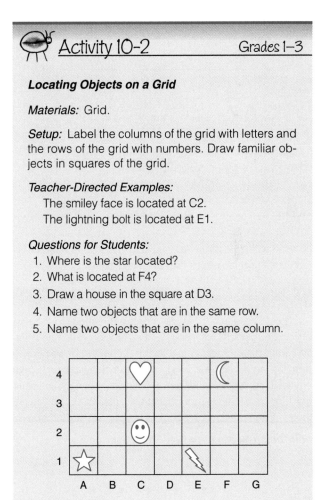

Activity 10-2   Grades 1–3

Locating Objects on a Grid

Materials: Grid.

Setup: Label the columns of the grid with letters and the rows of the grid with numbers. Draw familiar objects in squares of the grid.

Teacher-Directed Examples:
   The smiley face is located at C2.
   The lightning bolt is located at E1.

Questions for Students:
   1. Where is the star located?
   2. What is located at F4?
   3. Draw a house in the square at D3.
   4. Name two objects that are in the same row.
   5. Name two objects that are in the same column.

Ordered Pairs At the third- or fourth-grade level, students will be introduced to the *ordered pair*, which may be defined as "a pair of numbers used to locate a point where lines intersect on a grid." Ordered pairs such as (a,b) may

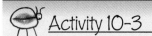

Activity 10-3   Grades 3–5

Locating Ordered Pairs on a Grid

Materials: Grid.

Setup: Label the grid with numbers. Draw familiar objects at points where lines of the grid intersect.

Teacher-Directed Examples:
  The smiley face is located at (2, 1).
  The lightning bolt is located at (5,3).

Questions for Students:
  1. Where is the star located?
  2. What is located at (6,1)?
  3. Draw a house at (4,2).
  4. Name two objects that have the same first coordinate.
  5. Name two objects that have the same second coordinate.

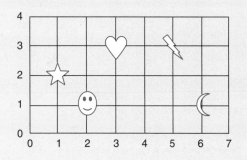

be used to locate points on a grid or in the Cartesian coordinate system (see Activities 10-3 and 10-4).

Example 10-1: Problem solving by drawing a picture (Grades 3–5).

Lost Leroy asks Longway Lou for directions to the post office. Lou says, "That's easy. Go two blocks north, turn right, and walk three blocks. Then turn right and walk one block, turn left and walk one block, then turn left and walk two blocks. Now turn left and walk two blocks, turn right and walk one block, and finally turn left and walk one block and you are there." Can you give Lost Leroy a simpler set of directions?

Solution: You can trace Lou's directions on a grid.

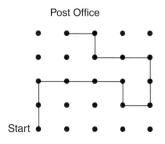

Assuming that all of the streets exist and all of the blocks are the same length, you can see that an easier set of directions would be to simply walk 4 blocks north, turn right, and walk 1 block. Lou's directions had poor Leroy walking a total of 13 blocks. With your directions Leroy walks only 5 blocks. How many other sets of directions can you find that consist of a 5-block walk?

Cartesian Coordinate System Terminology The *Cartesian coordinate system* (also referred to as a rectangular coordinate system) is comprised of two number lines called *axes.* The horizontal number line is called the x-*axis,* and the vertical number line is called the y-*axis.* The axes intersect at a point (0,0) called the *origin.* The ordered pair of coordinates of a point is determined by the distance of the point, using the scales of the number line axes, to the coordinate axes. The first number in the ordered pair is called the x-*coordinate.* The x-coordinate gives the distance of the point in the direction of the x-axis. The second number in the ordered pair is called the y-*coordinate.* The y-coordinate gives the distance of the point in the direction of the y-axis.

Negative coordinates are generally not introduced until the fifth or sixth grade, although some textbook series introduce this at the third-grade level. With the introduction of negative coordinates, you can define the four quadrants into which the axes divide the plane. Quadrants are numbered counterclockwise beginning with Quadrant I in the upper right-hand corner (see Figure 10-8). Study this illustration until you can explain the designations given that indicate positive or negative for the first coordinate and second coordinate of a point in each quadrant.

A common trick used to remember how to distinguish between the x- and y-coordinates is to recall that the letter x occurs before the letter y in the alphabet. The x-coordinate is the first coordinate of a numbered pair and the y-coordinate is the second. Also, students learn to draw horizontal number lines before they learn about vertical number lines. The horizontal axis is the x-axis and the vertical axis is the y-axis. As a teacher, it is important for you to know the difference between a horizontal line and a vertical line.

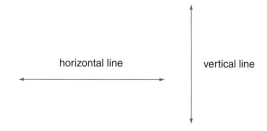

Learning to identify points on the Cartesian coordinate system is a skill that will be useful in social studies applications such as reading, following, and creating maps.

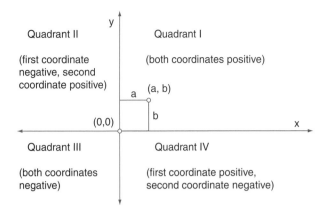

FIGURE 10-8 The axes divide the plane into four quadrants.

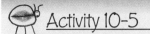

Activity 10-4 — Grades 3–6

Locating Ordered Pairs in the Cartesian Coordinate System

Materials: Cartesian coordinate system.

Teacher-Directed Examples: Explain how to obtain the coordinates of $A(2,1)$, $B(0,2)$, $C(-3,1)$, and $D(1,-2)$. Stress the idea of x-coordinate first, y-coordinate second in your explanation.

Be sure that students understand when to use positive numbers and when to use negative numbers.

Directions for Students:

1. Find the coordinates of E, F, G, and H.
2. Plot the points $I(1, 3)$, $J(-3, 0)$, $K(-2, -3)$, and $L(3, -2)$.
3. Plot and label the origin.
4. Name two points that have the same x-coordinate.
5. Name two points that have the same y-coordinate.

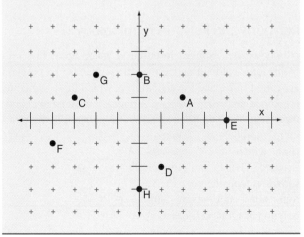

Activity 10-5 — Grades 2–6

Locating Ordered Pairs on a Geoboard

Materials: One geoboard, 2 dice, and 20 colored cubes or place markers for each pair of students. One die is marked with A, B, C, D, E, and F; the other is marked 1, 2, 3, 4, 5, 6. Each student receives 10 place markers of a common color (e.g., 10 red markers or 10 blue markers).

Directions: Label the columns of the geoboard A, B, C, D, E, and F (if only 5 columns, use only A–E), and the rows of the geoboard 1, 2, 3, 4, 5, and 6 (or 1–5). The first student rolls both dice and places a marker in the correct position. Students take turns doing this until each student has rolled 10 times. If a student rolls a coordinate that is already taken or unavailable, he or she cannot place a marker on that turn. The student with the most markers on the geoboard at the end of the game is the winner.

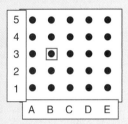

Example: If a student rolls B and 3, he places his marker on that peg.

One way to illustrate for students how to find coordinate points is to relate this skill to playing Mastermind or Battleship. You could even use your imagination to create games and puzzles to help children develop and practice this skill (see Activity 10-5).

Problem Set 10.1

For Your Understanding

1. Complete Activities 10-2, 10-3, and 10-4.

2. Draw points M, A, T, H such that no three are collinear. Then draw each of the following figures:
   a. $\overleftrightarrow{HA}$
   b. $\overrightarrow{AT}$
   c. $\overline{MH}$

3. Write the name in words for each of the figures listed in problem 2.

4. List all the valid notations for each of the figures listed in problem 2.

5. How many angles are shown by the given figure? For each angle give a three-letter name such as ∠*BAC* and classify the angle as acute, right, or obtuse.

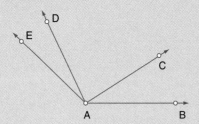

6. Draw three collinear points *A, B, C*. Sketch and name all of the rays determined by these points.

7. Draw three noncollinear points *D, E, F*. Sketch and name all of the rays determined by these points.

Applications in the Classroom

1. Explain how the corner of a page of paper or an index card could be used in a third- or fourth-grade classroom to identify or draw 30°, 45°, 60°, and 90° angles.

 2. Use Microsoft Word drawing tools (see Appendix B) to create a student handout such as this.

Fill in the blanks with an appropriate word.
a. The lines shown are _____.
b. The rays shown are _____.
c. The segments shown are _____.

 3. Use an automatic drawer such as the Geometer's Sketchpad (see Appendix B) to draw and label each of the following:

a. $\overleftrightarrow{AB}$

b. $\overrightarrow{CD}$

c. $\overline{EF}$

 4. Use Microsoft Word drawing tools to create a handout for use with Activities 10-2 or 10-3.

5. Write a "giving directions" problem similar to the problem given in Example 10-1.

6. Write an activity in which students plot a series of given points and then follow directions to connect some of the points with segments so that the result is a common word or figure. For example:

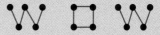

7. Classify the level of knowledge and the type of learning experience of Activity 10-3. Classify the van Hiele level of this activity. What objective from the NCTM model (or from your state or district model) does the activity address?

8. Create an assessment tool to be used with Activity 10-3. Explain why you chose that type of assessment tool.

9. Write a lesson plan that describes how you will introduce the ideas of line, ray, and segment in a second-grade classroom. Follow the format given by your instructor or use the lesson plan format given in Appendix A.

10.2 MORE PLANE FIGURES
Closed, Open, and Simple Curves

A *planar curve* is a figure that can be drawn in a plane; that is, a figure that can be drawn on a piece of paper without lifting the pencil from the paper. A curve is *closed* if its beginning and ending coincide. A curve that is not closed may be called *open*. A curve is *simple* if it does not intersect itself. Although the terms "simple" and "closed" seem to contradict one another, a *simple closed curve* may be defined as a curve that can be drawn without retracing any of its points (except the endpoints). Figure 10-9 illustrates these definitions.

A simple closed curve has an *interior* and an *exterior*. You may determine whether a point or other object lies in the interior or the exterior of a simple closed curve. Notice the similarity between Activity 10-6 and the children's puzzle of finding the path through a maze.

Polygons and Polygon Terminology

A *polygon* is a simple closed curve made up of line segments joined at their endpoints. The segments of a polygon are called *sides,* and the endpoints at which these segments are joined are called *vertices*. A polygon must have at least three sides. The number of sides of a polygon is the minimum number of segments from which it can be constructed. That is, the polygon shown is considered to have four sides, not seven. This polygon has four vertices *A, B, C,* and *D*. In general, a poly-

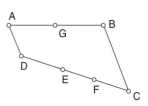

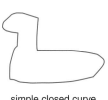

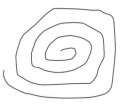

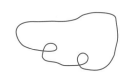

FIGURE 10-9
Closed, open and simple curves.

simple closed curve

simple curve (not closed)

closed curve (not simple)

simple curve (not closed)

simple closed curve

planar curve (not closed, not simple)

TABLE 10-1 Types of polygons.

Polygon	Number of Sides	Some Examples
Triangle	3	
Quadrilateral	4	
Pentagon	5	
Hexagon	6	
Heptagon	7	
Octagon	8	
Nonagon	9	
Decagon	10	

gon with *n* sides will have *n* vertices. When you consider an angle of a polygon, you generally are considering the interior angle. For example, ∠*A* refers to ∠*BAD* in the figure shown on p. 250.

Some polygons have special names determined by the number of sides of the polygon (see Table 10-1). A polygon with *n* sides may also be called an *n*-gon.

A *regular* polygon is one in which all sides have the same length *and* all angles have the same measure. In Table 10-1, the first example in each row illustrates a regular polygon. When two

or more sides of a polygon have the same length, this may be indicated by marking the same number of hash marks along each of the sides with the common length as shown

Standards

North Carolina Mathematics Standard

Course Study and Grade Level Competencies K–12

Spatial Sense, Measurement, and Geometry for Grade 1

2.04 Identify open and closed figures.

North Carolina Department of Public Instruction, 2003

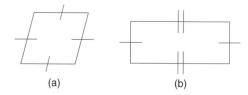

FIGURE 10-10 (a) Although this figure has four congruent sides, it is not a regular polygon. (b) Both pairs of opposite sides have equal length.

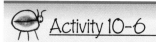

Activity 10-6   Grades 3–5

Interior or Exterior

Materials: Simple closed curves.

Teacher-Directed Examples: Shading can be used to show that point A is located *inside* the figure and point B is located *outside* the figure. (Shade the interior of the figure.)

Directions for Students: Determine whether points C, D, and E are located inside or outside the given figure.

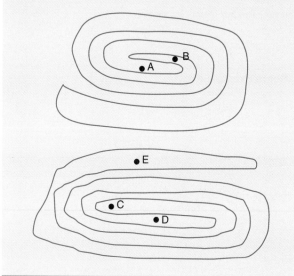

in Figures 10-10a and 10-10b. When two figures have the same size and the same shape, the figures are called *congruent*. Congruent figures will be studied in more detail in Section 10.4.

Many of the polygons above may be further classified in terms of their angles, side lengths, and other properties. For example, a triangle is called *equilateral* if all three of its sides have the same length. A triangle is called *isosceles* if at least two of its sides have the same length. A triangle is called *scalene* if none of the sides are the same length. Using the definitions given above, every equilateral triangle is also an isosceles triangle.

 Teaching Connections

Clarify Textbook Definitions as Necessary You should be aware that some textbooks define an isosceles triangle as

one in which *exactly* two sides have a common length. In those texts, an equilateral triangle is not considered isosceles. In other texts, the definition of *isosceles* is simply "a triangle with two sides of the same length." This definition is ambiguous. It does not specify whether an equilateral triangle should also be considered isosceles. As a teacher you must be precise and consistent in your use of terminology and notations. In many cases you will follow the terminology given in the textbook that you are teaching from. If a definition is incomplete or ambiguous, you may need to confer with other teachers at the same or other grade levels to determine precisely what definition is appropriate for your students.

Classifying Triangles

A triangle that includes a right angle is called a *right triangle*. Activity 10-8 will illustrate the fact that the sum of the measures of the interior angles of a triangle is 180°. Hence, a right triangle must also have two acute angles. The two acute angles of a right triangle need not have the same measure, however. A triangle that has an obtuse interior angle is called an *obtuse triangle*. An obtuse triangle also has two acute angles. If all three interior angles of a triangle are

Standards

NCTM

Grades Pre-K–2

Pre-K–2 geometry begins with describing and naming shapes. Young students begin by using their own vocabulary to describe objects, talking about how they are alike and how they are different. Teachers must help students gradually incorporate conventional terminology into their descriptions of two- and three-dimensional shapes. However, terminology itself should not be the focus of the pre-K–2 geometry program. The goal is that early experiences with geometry lay the foundations for more-formal geometry in later grades. Using terminology to focus attention and to clarify ideas during discussions can help students build that foundation.

NCTM, 2000, p. 97

Standards are listed with the permission of the National Council of Teachers of Mathematics (NCTM). NCTM does not endorse the content or validity of these alignments.

Activity 10-7 Grades 3–6

Geoboard Triangles

Materials: Geoboards and rubber bands for each student.

Teacher Directions: Ask students to show you an acute triangle with their geoboard. Then ask them to show you an acute isosceles triangle, a right scalene triangle, etc.

Notes: Make sure to point out the variety of sizes of triangles. Tell students that triangles do not have a standard fixed position. That is, an upside-down right triangle is still a right triangle.

Modification for Collaborative Learning: Students work in small groups. One student creates a geoboard shape. Other students in the group take turns naming properties of the shape. The winner of each round is the student who is able to name the most properties. Make sure that each student in the group has a turn to make a shape.

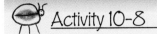

Activity 10-8 Grades 4–6

Sum of the Measures of the Interior Angles of a Triangle

Materials: Paper triangles, with *A*, *B*, and *C* written on the corners.

Teacher Directions: Instruct students to rip off two corners of their triangle. When they put the three angles together, they will discover that the three angles form a straight line. It is already known that there are 180° in a straight line. Hence, the sum of the measures of the three angles of a triangle is 180°. This demonstration works for any triangle regardless of the type or size.

acute, the triangle is called an *acute triangle.* Figure 10-11 illustrates these triangle terms. Can you explain why the figure does not show examples for an obtuse equilateral triangle or a right equilateral triangle?

Classifying Quadrilaterals

Quadrilaterals also may be classified in terms of side lengths, angles, and whether sides are or are not parallel. Some of these definitions vary from one textbook to the next. The definitions that we will use follow. In your classroom, you should use terminology and definitions that are grade appropriate for your students.

Quadrilateral A four-sided polygon. Some books require quadrilaterals to be convex. A figure is *convex* if, for any two points that it contains, it also contains the segment joining the two points. A polygon is convex if its interior is convex. Six of the figures shown in Table 10-1 are nonconvex polygons. Can you identify the polygons shown in Table 10-1 that are not convex?

Kite A quadrilateral with two distinct pairs of congruent adjacent sides, and no pair of parallel sides.

Trapezoid: A quadrilateral with exactly one pair of parallel sides.

Isosceles Trapezoid: A trapezoid whose nonparallel sides have equal length.

Parallelogram A quadrilateral with two pairs of parallel sides. Using methods usually found in a high school geometry class, you can prove that opposite sides of a parallelogram have equal length.

Rhombus: A quadrilateral with four congruent sides. Using techniques of high school geometry, you can prove that every rhombus is a parallelogram.

Rectangle: A parallelogram with a right angle. Using the fact that the sides are parallel, and the one right angle provided by the definition, you can prove that a rectangle has four right angles.

Square: A rectangle with four sides of equal length. A square may also be defined as a rhombus with a right angle.

 Teaching Connections

Use Definitions Appropriate for the Level of Your Students The level at which each term above is introduced varies widely among various textbook series. At the earliest grade levels, when students are at the visualization level, these objects may be defined with pictures rather than words. Although by definition a triangle is a polygon made up of three line segments, in practice the triangular figure made up of a triangle and its interior is generally considered a triangle. Similar comments hold for other planar figures. That is, you can cut examples of triangles, squares, rectangles, circles, and so on out of paper. For

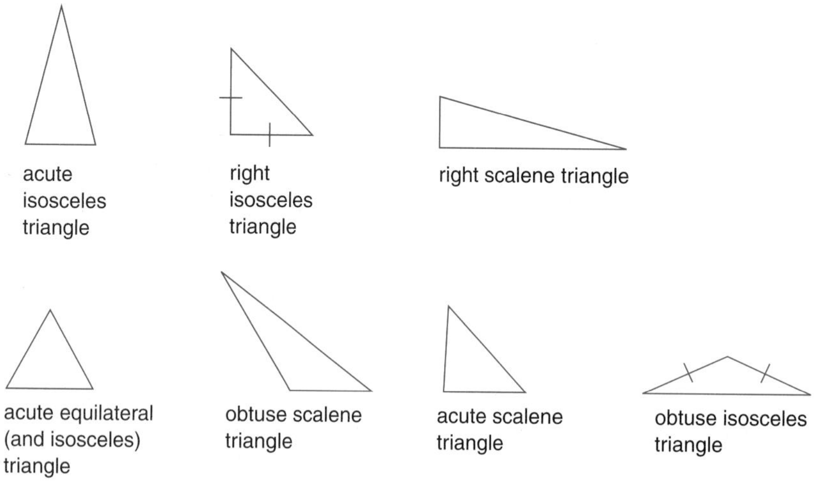

FIGURE 10-11
Classifying triangles.

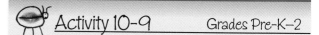

acute isosceles triangle   right isosceles triangle   right scalene triangle

acute equilateral (and isosceles) triangle   obtuse scalene triangle   acute scalene triangle   obtuse isosceles triangle

FIGURE 10-11
Classifying triangles.

instance, by definition ☐ is a square, but in practice ▨ may also be called a square.

Some elementary textbooks and math activity books do not recognize that a square is a rectangle. It is not uncommon to see an exercise with directions like "Color all squares green. Color all rectangles red. Color all circles blue." Should the student color a square both green and red in this case? Most mathematics textbooks at around the second-grade level do explicitly state that every square is a rectangle.

Students need to be able to recognize figures that have the same shape even if the shapes are oriented differently. For example, both figures shown here are squares. They are also both rhombi (the plural of *rhombus*), as every square is a rhombus. It would be acceptable for a kindergarten-level student to call the first figure a square and the second a diamond. English language learners may be allowed to identify shapes in their own language as they are learning the correct English terms. When the student recognizes that the second figure is also a square, he has moved beyond the visualization level of the van Hiele levels and has begun to consider properties of the figure; he has moved into the level of analysis.

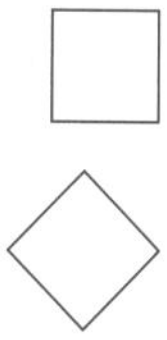

Use Concrete Manipulatives and Problem-Solving Activities The alternate directions given in Activity 10-9 provide an important experience for children. With these directions, several answers are possible. Also, students have the opportunity to vocalize, in their own words, their understanding about the objects. This provides you, the teacher, with the opportunity to discover and correct student misconceptions.

Example 10-2: Problem solving (second- or third-grade level).

How many rectangles can you find in the picture?

Activity 10-9   Grades Pre-K–2

Recognizing and Describing Geometric Figures

Materials: Geo-pieces (see Blackline Master 1) for each student.

Teacher Directions: Ask students to hold up a square, a triangle, a nonsquare rectangle, and so forth.

Alternate Directions: Hold up an object such as a rectangle. Ask students to describe the object. Repeat with other objects.

Note: You may also use pattern blocks or attribute blocks for this activity.

Extension Activity: Ask students to give real-world or classroom examples of these shapes.

Activity 10-10   Grades Pre-K–2

Sorting Figures

Materials: Geo-pieces (see Blackline Master 1) for each student.

Teacher Directions: Ask students to separate the figures so that all the pieces in a stack have the same shape. Let students discuss their choices. Ask students how stacks are the same and how they are different. Note that figures may have the same shape but not necessarily the same size.

Note: You may also use pattern blocks or attribute blocks for this activity.

Solution: First recall that a square is a rectangle, so there are 4 square rectangles in the figure. There are 3 rectangles consisting of two adjacent squares, 2 rectangles consisting of three adjacent squares, and 1 consisting of the entire figure. Hence, there is a total of 10 rectangles in the figure shown.

A typical third- or fourth-grade-level problem-solving problem, an extension of the above example, is to count the number of squares on a standard 8 × 8-inch checkerboard. The student must realize that the answer is not merely 64, but that squares larger than 1 × 1-inch must also be considered or counted. Possible strategies for solving this problem include drawing a picture or making a list. If students are having difficulty starting on the problem, you may wish to suggest the strategy of considering a simpler problem. This is an excellent problem because it is easy to modify for lower level students (consider a smaller example) or for more advanced students (challenge them to find a solution for an $n \times n$ checkerboard).

One activity to develop familiarity with shapes is to have students draw pictures using templates containing such shapes. This can also be accomplished with the help of an automatic drawer such as the Geometer's Sketchpad (see Appendix B). Activity 10-11 is a shape recognition activity that also helps children develop their visualization skills.

Be sure to have the children explain the reasoning behind their choices when they complete a sorting activity such as Activities 10-10 or 10-12. In some instances students may sort pieces differently than you had expected them to. In such instances, the student may have a valid reason for how the objects were sorted. These types of activities are good for encouraging a variety of answers.

Plane Figures That Are Not Polygons

A plane figure that has curved side(s) is not a polygon. The figure shown here should not be

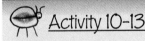

Shape Visualization

Materials: Geo-pieces (see Blackline Master 1) cut from posterboard or some other sturdy material; blindfolds.

Teacher Directions: Blindfold a student. Have the student choose a geo-piece from the table. The student should then feel the other pieces and select another piece that has the same shape.

Alternate Directions: Have the student return the chosen piece to the table and draw a picture of the piece.

called a triangle because its sides are curved. Some figures with curved sides have special names. A *circle* is the set of all points in the plane equidistant from some center point. A *chord* of a circle is a line segment from one point of the circle to another point of the circle. A *diameter* is a chord that passes through the center of the circle. A *radius* is a line segment from the center of the circle to a point on the circle. The plural of *radius* is *radii*. The term "radius" can also be used for the distance from the center to a point on the circle. Examples of these terms are shown in Figure 10-12.

Rather than giving a precise mathematical definition of the plane figure known as the *ellipse* (sometimes called an *oval*), the concept is illustrated in Figure 10-13.

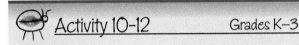

Sorting Shapes

Materials: Index cards showing geo-pieces (see Blackline Master 1) in various positions.

Teacher Directions: Ask students to separate the index cards so that all the pieces in a stack have the same shape. Let students discuss their choices. Ask students how stacks are the same and how they are different. Note that figures may have the same shape but not necessarily the same size.

Alternate Directions: Students may play a matching game where each student receives an index card and all students have to find the students who have cards with the same objects.

Identifying Shapes

Setup: Use an automatic drawer like the Geometer's Sketchpad to dray a picture using figures that you have discussed.

Directions: Identify each of the objects used in the drawing.

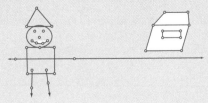

Activity 10-14   Grades K-4

Pattern Block Shapes

Setup: Draw an outline of a figure that can be made with pattern blocks.

Materials: Pattern blocks, enough so that each student has the pieces required to fill in the diagram.

Directions: Fill the pattern with pattern blocks and count how many of each type of block that you used.

Note: See Blackline Master 5 for a full-size copy of the outline of this design.

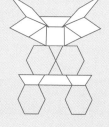

O is the center of the circle
$\overline{BC}$ is a chord
$\overline{OF}$ is a radius $\overline{OF}$, $\overline{OD}$, and $\overline{OE}$ are radii
$\overline{ED}$ is a diameter

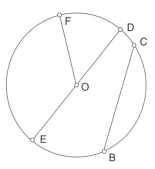

FIGURE 10-12   A circle.

FIGURE 10-13   An ellipse (oval).

Teaching Connections

Provide Experiences Using Geometric Vocabulary Children do not learn geometric terms simply to increase their vocabulary. These terms occur frequently in everyday life and applications. For example, you need a square lid to cover a square food container and a round lid to cover a round container. To buy carpet for a room, you must know the shape (and size) of the room. Shapes are important in drawing and describing objects; in science you will discuss the elliptical orbit of the planets. An example drawing lesson conducted in a preschool classroom—including shapes such as an oval, a circle, rectangles, and other plane shapes—is given below.

Lesson Plan

Drawing Lesson
by Cindy Morelli (Disability/Preschool Head Start Teacher)

I feel it is important to teach the children in my class to draw. It helps them to master the fine motor control necessary to begin writing, the planning skills necessary to complete complex tasks, and the recognition of shapes.

We start at the beginning of the school year by drawing simple objects that can be made from a single shape. We begin with drawing an apple. From there, we begin drawing more complex things, like vehicles, people, and animals. We start each lesson by finding the shapes that make up whatever it is that we are going to draw. It helps to have the actual object, a toy of the object, or a picture of the object, and a simple drawing of that object that I did myself.

I teach the drawing part of the lesson to very small groups of children. I like to have no more than four kids at a time. Once they have drawn the object, I have them finish coloring the picture independently. This gives them the opportunity to choose how they will color the picture, and to add anything else that they

wish to their pictures. It also gives me the chance to start working with another group. I make sure to keep an eye on the children who are coloring, because many preschool children will create a beautiful picture only to color over the whole thing. I sometimes have to help them recognize when to stop.

The following is a step-by-step description of what happened during our Bear Unit drawing lesson:

Four children were in this writing group: Mitchell, a 4-year-old boy identified with a disability in the area of behavior, who shows advanced cognitive skills; Belinda, a 5-year-old girl with delays in the areas of expressive language and cognition, who is very interested in fine motor tasks, including writing; Ke-Lynn, a 4-year-old girl who is typically developing, and very talented at drawing; and DeShawn, a typically developing 4-year-old boy, whose strength is his ability to foster social relationships.

We start each drawing lesson with the children getting their paper, and choosing their writing utensil. They can use pencils, crayons, markers, or gel pens.

continued

They choose their seats, and print their names on the back of the paper. DeShawn asks for his name card so he can copy his name. Belinda taps my arm and points to her work. She has "Beli" printed, and wants to know what letter is next. Even though I know what she wants, I pretend not to know, point to her letters, and say, "Wow Belinda! I love how you are printing your name!" She looks at me inquisitively. I say "Use your words. What do you want?" She says, "How?" "How do you do what, Belinda?" "How *n?*" I'm pleased; not only was she able to ask me a question, but she knew what letter comes next. I trace the motion on her paper with my finger and say, "*n* is a line and a jump." Mitchell prints his first name and I print his last name in yellow marker on his paper so he can trace and print it while he waits for everyone to finish.

Once all of the children have their names printed or traced, I show them a teddy bear, and point to its body parts, asking them to name them, and what shape we can use to draw them. I also have them point to their own corresponding body parts. I then go over a chart that I have already made (see the example chart below).

After talking about the parts of the bear, I ask the children where we should start. Mitchell says the body. I ask what shape the body is. Belinda traces an oval on her paper with her finger. I say "Wonderful, Belinda. Can we all say the name of that shape?" Together we say "oval." I notice that Belinda attempts to say it with everyone else. We all trace the oval with our fingers. I see that they are all tracing it the correct size, then I say, "Now let's all draw the oval bear body; remember, we want our bears to be big." I draw the body on my paper and hold it up for all of them to see, and watch them all draw their own. "Now what part should we draw?" I ask. DeShawn says, "Let's draw his head." KeLynn says, "My bear is going to be a girl." I say, "Wonderful, KeLynn. What shape will you use for your girl bear's head?" She answers, "I don't know." I say, "What shape is your head?" She answers, "I don't know." "Well KeLynn, go look in the mirror and see if you can tell what shape you can use." All of the children go to the mirror to look at their heads, even though I suspect they all know what shape we need, especially because we went over the chart. I

decide to let them go look because they are having fun and learning about themselves. So they all come back when I ask them to, giggling and saying "ball" and "circle." I then ask if the circle should go above or below the oval. Mitchell says "above." We all draw the circle head.

"Now what should we draw?" I ask. "Arms!" says DeShawn. "What word did we use for the bear's arms?" KeLynn says, "Paws." "Yes, KeLynn. Let's draw the bear's front paws. What shape did we use on the chart?" I point to the chart. Mitchell says, "Rectangles!" DeShawn says, "I can't draw them." I give him a scratch paper with four dots on it. I ask him to practice by connecting the dots. He does. I then use my fingers and tell him to draw a line from one finger to the next. I then say "STOP!" I move my fingers, and tell him to connect them again. When he does I say STOP again. I do this twice more until he has a nice rectangle drawn on the scrap paper. I then tell him he is ready to draw on the bear. I have him draw between my fingers for one rectangle, but on his own for the second. It is not perfect, it only has two corners, but is very close. I say, "Good job! Now let's try our bear's rear paws."

After we finish the rear paws I ask, "Now what do our bears need?" Belinda says, "Face." "Good job! Which part of the face should we draw first?" "Eyes." "Good. What shape do you use for eyes?" She traces a circle with her finger. "Yes, Belinda, it's a circle. Can you say circle?" She does. I say, "We need to draw two little circles for eyes." I draw mine, and watch as the children add their own. "Now what do you need?" I ask. KeLynn says "Triangle." "What part of the bear will the triangle be?" I ask. DeShawn says, "His nose!" "Good, DeShawn," I say. "Where will you put it?" He points to his bear. "Good! What shape is the nose?" Mitchell says, "Upside-down triangle!" "Good! Let's draw!" "Now we need the ears," says DeShawn. "Good. Where will we put them? Under his head?" "NO!" they all shout. "On top of his head," says KeLynn. "Good. Then what will you need?" "His mouth," says Mitchell. "Alright, let's all draw his ears and mouth and then you will be finished drawing and you can color your bears." While they color their bears I look for four more children to draw with.

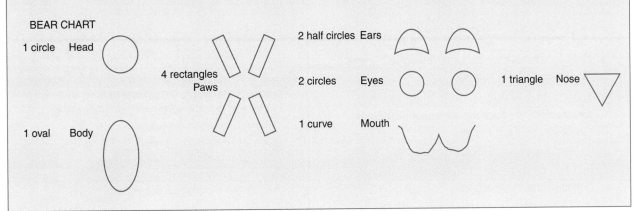

BEAR CHART

1 circle   Head

4 rectangles
        Paws

1 oval   Body

2 half circles Ears

2 circles   Eyes

1 curve   Mouth

1 triangle   Nose

Problem Set 10.2

For Your Understanding

1. Indicate simple and/or closed as appropriate for each curve shown.
   a.
   b.
   c.
   d.

2. Determine whether each point is inside or outside the figure.

   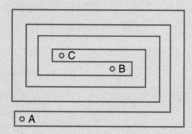

3. For each polygon shown, give the name determined by the number of sides of the polygon and determine whether or not the polygon is regular.
   a.
   b.
   c.
   d.

4. Explain why neither polygon shown in Figures 10-10a or 10-10b is regular.

5. An isosceles triangle has an angle that has a measure of 38°. Find the measures of the other two angles of the triangle.

6. An isosceles triangle has an angle that has a measure of 96°. Find the measures of the other two angles of the triangle.

7. Indicate the type(s) of triangle each figure below is.
   a.
   b.
   c.
   d.

8. Either draw the object indicated or explain why it cannot be drawn.
   a. An acute scalene triangle
   b. A right obtuse triangle
   c. An obtuse isosceles triangle

9. Indicate *all* the valid properties (names) of each quadrilateral shown.
   a.
   b.
   c.
   d.

10. Give a word name for each of the following.
    a. $\overline{OA}$
    b. $\overline{EB}$
    c. $\overline{DO}$
    d. $\overline{DC}$

    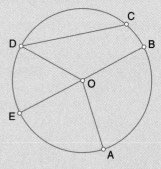

11. In a design, all rectangles are shaded. Some figures in the design are squares, whereas other figures are rhombi with nonright angles. Which of the following is *not* true:
    a. All squares are shaded.
    b. All squares are rhombi.
    c. No rhombi are shaded.
    d. Some rhombi are not square.

12. A pattern of congruent shapes that fit to-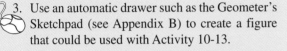
gether with no gaps or overlaps is called
a *tessellation.* For example, squares can
be used to form a tessellation.

Which of the following regular polygons could
also be used to form a tessellation?
a. triangle
b. pentagon
c. hexagon
d. octagon

Applications in the Classroom

1. Use Microsoft Word drawing tools (see Appendix B) to create a maze or drawing that could be used with Activity 10-6.

2. Make a set of index cards that you could use for Activity 10-12.

3. Use an automatic drawer such as the Geometer's Sketchpad (see Appendix B) to create a figure that could be used with Activity 10-13.

4. Obtain a set of pattern blocks. Draw a pattern that you could use with Activity 10-14. Indicate what grade level you feel your pattern is appropriate for.

5. Create an activity in which students determine the number of chords from one vertex to another of a specific regular polygon (for example, an octagon). Indicate how to modify the activity for use with lower or higher level students.

6. Classify the level of knowledge and the type of learning experience of Activity 10-11. What level of the van Heile model does the activity illustrate? What objective from the NCTM model (or from your state or district model) does the activity address?

7. Create an assessment tool to be used with Activity 10-14. Explain why you chose that type of assessment tool.

8. Write a lesson plan that describes how you will introduce the terms "trapezoid," "parallelogram," and "rhombus" in a first-grade classroom. Follow the format given by your instructor or use the lesson plan format given in Appendix A.

9. Children's development of geometric ideas often can be clearly seen in the pictures that they draw. As a class project, ask several children at various grade levels to draw you a picture. Do not give them any specific topic or instructions. Collect as many of these pictures as you can. Your class can collectively display the children's artwork and analyze it in terms of the progression of geometric and spatial ideas.

10.3 SPACE FIGURES

Figures that are not flat, and cannot be drawn in the plane, are called *space figures.* The space figures first introduced to young children are often called *solids.* A preschool textbook might give examples of solids such as spheres (sometimes called balls), rectangular prisms (sometimes called boxes), and pyramids. Mathematically, a solid includes all points on the surface of the figure as well as all points in the interior. However, a third-grade textbook definition of a *solid figure* is "a figure that has length, width, height, and volume."

Spheres

A *sphere* is defined as the set of all points in space at a constant distance from a point called the *center.* Although mathematically the sphere is not a solid, most elementary textbooks give the sphere as an example of a solid. Hence, an elementary teacher must be willing to consider both a basketball and a baseball as examples of "the solid called a sphere," although one is hollow and the other is solid.

As with the circle, the radius and diameter of a sphere can be defined. A *radius* is a segment from the center of the sphere to a point on the sphere. A *diameter* is a segment from one point of the sphere to another point of the sphere that passes through the center.

Figure 10-14 illustrates these terms.

Space Curves—Lines and Planes in Space

Just as Section 10.2 defined planar curves as curves that may be drawn in a plane, *space curves* can be defined as curves that may be drawn in space. You may think of planar figures as two-dimensional and space figures as three-dimensional. Not all of the properties that hold for planar figures are still true for space figures. For example, as planar figures, two

$\overline{AB}, \overline{AC}, \overline{AD}, \overline{AE},$ and $\overline{AF}$ are radii

$\overline{DF}$ and $\overline{BC}$ are diameters

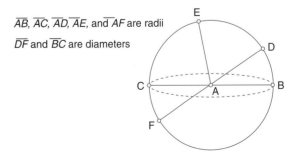

FIGURE 10-14 A sphere.

distinct lines are either parallel or they intersect at exactly one point. *Skew lines* are defined as nonparallel lines in space that do not intersect. Lines in space are *parallel* only if they are parallel in a common plane. Figure 10-15 illustrates parallel lines and skew lines in space. The box is drawn merely as an aid in visualizing the relative positions of the lines.

Parallel planes are defined as planes that do not intersect. Note that if two planes do intersect, their intersection is a line. A segment or line that intersects a region of a plane is *perpendicular to the region* if it is perpendicular to every segment of the region that passes through the point of intersection. Ideas such as parallel planes and skew lines are not generally defined until the fourth or fifth grade. Figures illustrating these definitions are shown in Figure 10-16.

Cones and Pyramids

A more familiar space object that is usually introduced at the kindergarten level or earlier is called the *cone.* Many preschool children have, at some time in their life, eaten an ice cream cone, and so are familiar with this concept. As

with the sphere, an elementary textbook may classify the cone as a "solid" regardless of whether the cone is hollow or filled. At the earliest level, the cone may be introduced by means of a picture rather than a definition. In the primary grades, children are expected to identify both hollow and filled conelike objects as cones.

Mathematically, a *cone* is a space figure that has a *base* that is any region of a plane bounded by a simple closed curve. The "side" of a cone, the *lateral surface,* is generated by line segments from the closed curve of the base to a point of the cone called the *apex.* The apex is not in the plane of the base, and is sometimes called the vertex at the "top" of the cone. Although many elementary textbooks stipulate that the base of a cone is a circle, we will follow the convention that the base may be any region. If the closed curve that surrounds the base is a polygon, the cone is called a *pyramid.* A *circular cone* then is defined as a cone in which the base is a circle. Many other space figures may be named with such a two-word description where the first word describes the base, and the second word names the object. Figures 10-17 and 10-18 show examples of cones and pyramids.

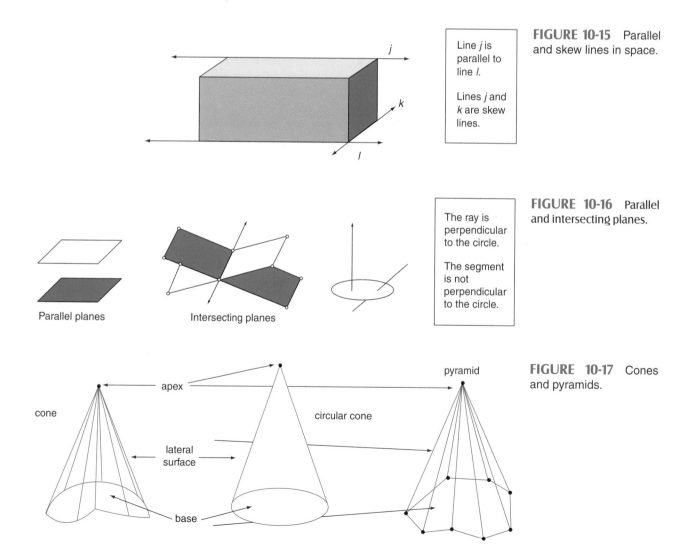

FIGURE 10-15 Parallel and skew lines in space.

FIGURE 10-16 Parallel and intersecting planes.

FIGURE 10-17 Cones and pyramids.

Faces, Edges, and Vertices

Three terms that are introduced at around the first- or second-grade level are "face," "edge," and "vertex" (see Figure 10-19). The plural of *vertex* is *vertices*. Some texts

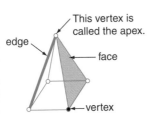

This vertex is called the apex.

edge

face

vertex

use the term "corner" instead of "vertex." The following definitions are taken from the same fourth-grade-level textbook. A *face* is "a flat surface of a solid figure." An *edge* is "a line segment where two faces of a solid figure meet." A *vertex* is "the point where two or more edges meet." A square pyramid has five faces: Four of the faces, the *lateral faces,* are triangles. The square base brings the total faces to five. A square pyramid also has five vertices: Four of the vertices are the corner points of the square base. The fifth vertex is the apex of the pyramid. The square pyramid has eight edges: Four of

the edges belong to the square base. The other four edges are found where the triangular lateral faces meet.

The fourth-grade textbook from which the above definitions were taken also defines a *cone* as "a solid figure with one circular face and one vertex". Notice how this textbook definition stipulates that the base of the cone is a circle. Notice also that according to this definition, a cone has a vertex. However, the same textbook defines a vertex as "the point where two or more edges meet," an edge as "a line segment where two faces of a solid figure meet," and a face as "a flat surface of a solid figure." It appears that the cone has only one flat surface—its base. Therefore, a cone could not have any edges because edges are lines where faces meet. If the cone has no edges, by definition it cannot have any vertices. This "paradox of definitions" occurs frequently in elementary textbooks. You are asked to resolve this paradox in problem 4 under "Applications in the Classroom" in Problem Set 10.3.

FIGURE 10-18   Pyramids.

square pyramid   triangular pyramid

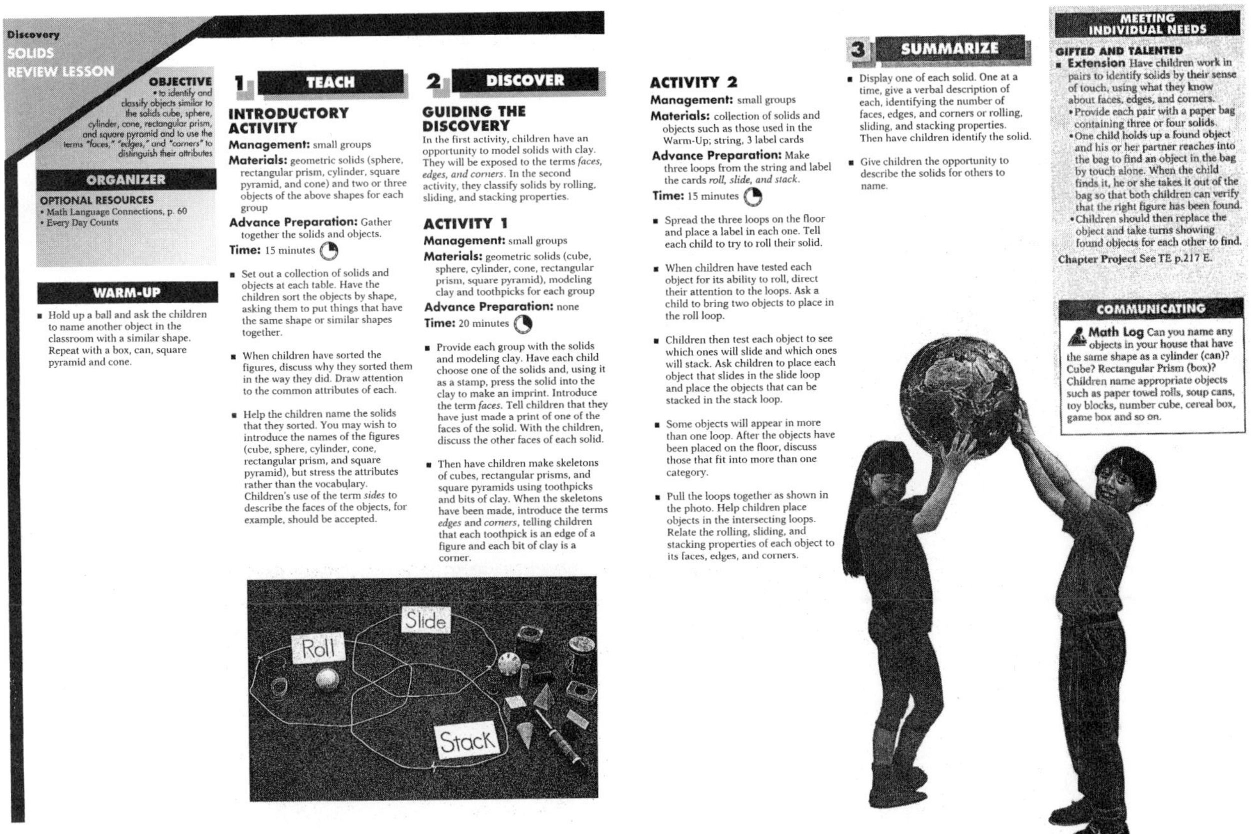

FIGURE 10-19   These Teacher's Manual pages, from a first grade textbook series, illustrate the introduction of the terms face, edge, and corner. Note also the 3-ring Venn diagram used to sort solid figures.
Source: From *Heath Mathematics Connections Teacher's Edition, Level 1* by Manfre, et al., 1994, Lexington, MA: D.C. Heath and Company. Reprinted with permission.

Cylinders and Prisms

Another space object that is usually introduced at the kindergarten level or earlier is the cylinder. In some primary textbooks this is called a *can*. As with the sphere and the cone, the cylinder is sometimes called a solid, even when the figure is hollow. Mathematically, a *cylinder* contains two congruent (same size and shape) bases. The bases lie in parallel planes and are oriented so that all the line segments joining corresponding points of the bases are parallel. These line segments comprise the lateral surface of the cylinder. Many elementary textbooks will stipulate that the bases of a cylinder be circles and that the line segments forming the lateral surface of the cylinder be perpendicular to the bases. These restrictions force the cylinder to look like a can. We will use the more general definition that allows the base region to be any region bounded by a simple closed curve. Cylinder examples are shown in Figure 10-20.

If the bases of a cylinder are congruent polygonal regions, the cylinder is called a *prism*. In a prism, the lateral faces joining the bases are parallelograms. Again, most elementary textbooks require the line segments that comprise the lateral surface of the prism to be perpendicular to the polygonal bases. This restriction forces the lateral faces to be rectangles. In fact, some textbooks define only the *rectangular prism* as "a solid figure whose six faces are all rectangles," and the *cube* as "a solid figure which has squares for its six faces." Other primary textbooks call the rectangular prism a *box*. Various shapes that are also prisms are illustrated in Figure 10-21.

As with the other solids, elementary students are required to identify, count, and describe faces, edges, and vertices of prisms. The pentagonal prism has 7 faces—the 5 lateral faces and 2 bases. It has 10 vertices—5 from each base. It has 15 edges—5 edges from each base, and 5 lateral edges. Can you find the number of faces, edges, and vertices

of the triangular prism? Activities 10-15 to 10-19 provide practice in identifying solids and properties of solids.

 Teaching Connections

Assessment—Observation Log After a class reading of the book *Captain Invincible and the Space Shapes*, the following handout (see Table 10-2, p. 265) could be used with individual students during a one-on-one student-teacher conference. The handout allows you to assess whether students are able to recognize a figure when given the figure name, as well as whether they can recall the figure name

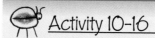

Activity 10-15　　Grades K–4

Identifying the Space Figure

Materials: Familiar objects that represent space figures (cans, balls, boxes, blocks, cone-shaped paper cups, paper towel tubes, etc.).

Directions: Using mathematical terminology appropriate for their grade level, have students identify each object as you hold it up.

Alternate Directions: Have students locate objects in the classroom as you call out the names or properties of the objects.

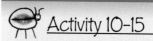

Activity 10-16　　Grades K–2

Logical Reasoning—Which Roll? Which Stack?

Materials: Objects that represent space figures (cans, balls, boxes, blocks, cone-shaped paper cups, paper towel tubes, etc.).

Directions: Have students identify which objects roll, which objects do not roll, which objects can be stacked to make a tower, which objects can be stacked to make a wall with no holes or gaps, etc.

A circular cylinder is sometimes called a can.

FIGURE 10-20 Cylinders.

FIGURE 10-21 Prisms.

cube

A rectangular prism is sometimes called a box.

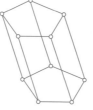

pentagonal prism

triangular prism

Math Manipulative: Power Solids (also called geosolids)

Power solids are a relatively new tool that can be purchased through a supplier that offers math manipulatives. They have been used in the classroom since approximately the mid-1980s at a variety of grade levels. A typical set is made of hollow plastic and contains a cube, cylinder, prism, hexagonal prism, rectangular prism, large triangular prism, small triangular prism, triangular pyramid, square pyramid, cone, sphere, and hemisphere. Several of the objects have congruent bases and heights—for example, the circular base of the cone is congruent to the circular base of the cylinder. Bases may be removed. Wooden or nonhollow sets are also available. Power solids are relatively inexpensive. One set can be shared by several students.

In early grades, for example K–4, the objects may be used to build vocabulary and reinforce concepts of solids and their properties. The cube may be compared

to the square, the cylinder compared to the cone, etc. Students can classify or describe objects. The objects may be used to illustrate edges, faces, and vertices. Objects may be used to develop visualization skills by having students choose objects blindfolded or from a brown paper bag.

In Grades 3–8, students can explore nets by tracing faces of the objects. Students can explore surface areas and volumes of solids. Removable bases and a hollow set allow you to fill the solids with water or rice to demonstrate volume formulas such as the cone: $V = 1/3 \pi r^2 h$, compared to the cylinder: $V = \pi r^2 h$. That is, if a cone and a cylinder have congruent bases and heights, it will take three fills of the cone to fill up the cylinder. A similar relationship between pyramids and prisms also holds.

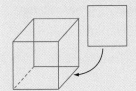

 ## Activity 10-17   Grades K–6

Identifying Solids

Materials: Power solids. Use only the objects that are appropriate for the level of the student. For example, objects that may be used at the kindergarten level include a cube, cylinder, rectangular prism, sphere, cone, and pyramid.

Directions: Using the mathematical terminology appropriate for their grade level, students should identify each object as you hold it up.

Alternate Directions: Have students hold up objects as you call out the names or properties of the objects.

Activity 10-18   Grades 2–6

Identifying Edges, Faces, and Vertices

Materials: Power solids. Use only the objects that are appropriate for the level of the student. For example, objects that may be used at the second-grade level include a cube, cylinder, rectangular prism, sphere, cone, and pyramid.

Directions: Have students identify how many edges, faces, and vertices each object has as you hold it up.

Alternate Directions: Have students hold up objects as you call out the number of edges, or faces, or vertices.

This handout and a student version showing only the diagrams of the figures can be easily made with Microsoft Word drawing tools (see Appendix B).

when shown a figure. Crossing off the words and objects as the student identifies them allows you to easily recall at the end of the session which terms and objects caused the student difficulty. The handout provides

a column for comments on the student's work. A checkmark in the comments section indicates that all the student's answers are correct.

Nets of Common Space Figures

In Activities 10-20 and 10-21, students relate solid figures to their faces. This relationship is formalized with the definition of a net or cover. A *net* or *cover* may be defined as "a flat pattern that folds into a solid." For example, a sheet of paper is a net for an open cylinder, a cylinder that has no top or bottom, because it may be rolled up into such a cylinder. Prior to being formally introduced to the idea of a net, children can use their visual skills and logical reasoning to determine whether a figure was produced by folding or curling a page of paper.

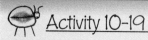

Activity 10-19   Grades 2-6

What Solid Am I? Using Visualization

Materials: Power solids; blindfolds.

Teacher Directions: Blindfold a student. Have the student choose a power solid from the table and identify it.

Alternate Directions: Have the student identify the number of faces, edges, or vertices of the solid.

Activity 10-20   Grades 2-6

Act It Out—What Imprints Will I Make?

Materials: Power solids; clay.

Setup: Choose a power solid. Make imprints in the clay of each of the faces of the solid.

Teacher Directions: Ask students to identify the solid by looking only at the tray of clay imprints.

Alternate Directions: Have the students guess what imprints a power solid will make and then test their guesses.

Activity 10-21   Grades 2-6

Guess and Check—What Solid Has These Faces?

Materials: Power solids; paper.

Setup: Choose a power solid. Trace the faces of the solid on paper.

Teacher Directions: Ask students to identify the solid by looking at the tracings of the faces. Students may cut out and tape the faces together to test their guesses.

> What solid has these faces?
> □ △ △ △ △

Alternate Directions: Have the students guess what tracings a power solid will make and then test their guesses.

Using Literature in the Mathematics Classroom   Grades 1–4

Captain Invincible and the Space Shapes

By Stuart Murphy
MathStart Level 2, HarperCollins, 2001

The book describes an adventure of a boy and his dog as the boy imagines he is "Captain Invincible—fearless spacecraft pilot." Captain Invincible battles various space obstacles using weapons that are shaped like common three-dimensional geometric objects. The text incorporates correct terminology and properties of the objects in its discourse.

Classroom Activity:

During the initial reading, children can be challenged to name properties of each object and guess how the ob-

ject will be used. "Captain Invincible is going to use a cylinder to battle the galactic beast. Who can name a property of the cylinder? What other properties does the cylinder have? How do you think the cylinder will be useful in fighting the galactic beast?"

Writing in Mathematics:

At the end of the book the boy decides that tomorrow he will be "Captain Stupendous—King of the Seas." Challenge students to create an adventure for Captain Stupendous. They should use three-dimensional shapes within the adventure they create. At the earliest levels children may draw pictures and dictate story events for you to caption instead of writing their story.

TABLE 10-2 Assessment handout.

Student name	Points to the solid diagram when given the solid name		States the name of a given solid when shown a diagram	Comments
Angie	~~Cube~~ ~~Cylinder~~ ~~Pyramid~~	~~Prism~~ ~~Cone~~ ~~Sphere~~		Called the sphere a circle
Bo	~~Cube~~ ~~Cylinder~~ ~~Pyramid~~	~~Prism~~ ~~Cone~~ ~~Sphere~~		√
Carl	~~Cube~~ ~~Cylinder~~ ~~Pyramid~~	Prism ~~Cone~~ ~~Sphere~~		Confused pyramid and prism. Called both objects prisms.

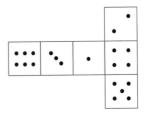

FIGURE 10-22 Three of these figures fold into a cube; one does not.

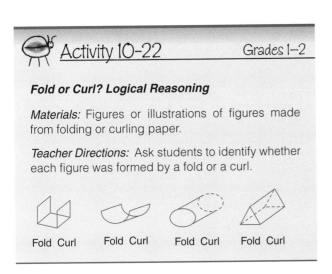

Activity 10-22   Grades 1–2

Fold or Curl? Logical Reasoning

Materials: Figures or illustrations of figures made from folding or curling paper.

Teacher Directions: Ask students to identify whether each figure was formed by a fold or a curl.

Fold Curl   Fold Curl   Fold Curl   Fold Curl

Figure 10-22 illustrates three different nets for cubes, and one figure shows six congruent squares that do not qualify as a net for a cube. Try to visualize how each of the three cube nets could be folded into a cube. Can you explain why the fourth figure is not a net for a cube? If you cannot visualize these relationships, cut the figures out of paper and fold them.

Example 10-3: Three views of a cube are given. Place dots on the cube net given so that the net will represent the cube shown.

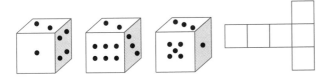

Solution: The first two views show two dots on the top face. The first view indicates that if two dots are placed in the top square of the net, then the squares with one dot and four dots are adjacent in the row of the net representing the sides of the cube. Place one and four dots accordingly and use the first view to determine that the two-dot square should contain the two dots in the bottom left and top right corners as shown.

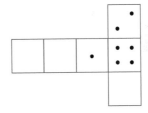

The second view indicates that the square with three dots and the square with six dots are also in the row of the net representing the sides of the cubes. The third view indicates that the bottom square of the net may be filled with five dots. The second view also indicates the correct orientations for the six and three dots, respectively. If you have difficulty visualizing these orientations, try cutting a net out of a piece of paper and using the concrete object to help you visualize them.

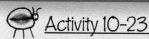 Activity 10-23   Grades 2–6

Identifying the Figure from the Net

Materials: Precut nets of solid figures (many schools have an Ellison machine and patterns for these figures).

Teacher Directions: Ask students to identify each solid by looking at the net. Have students fold and glue or tape the figures to check their guesses.

Examples of Possible Nets:

a.

b.

c.

Problem Set 10.3

For Your Understanding

1. Identify each of the solid figures used in Activity 10-23.

2. State the number of faces, edges, and vertices of each of the solids whose nets are shown below. Draw and name the solids given by the nets.

   a.

   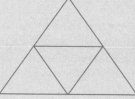

   b.

3. a. If you fold and tape edges of this cube's net, where will *A* be if *B* is on the top and *C* is on the left side?

   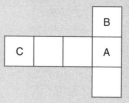

   b. If you fold and tape edges of the net shown, where will *F* be if *D* is on the left side and *E* is on the right side?

   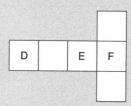

4. For each of the following, give a two-word name for the figure and tell how many faces, edges, and vertices it contains.

   a.

   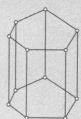

   b.

   c. The figure whose net is

   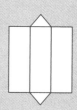

5. For each figure shown below, name the figure and then identify the shape of the cross section as the figure is cut by a plane.

6. An open cube is a cube with only five faces. Which of the following are nets for open cubes?

   a.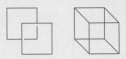

   b.

   c.

   d.

   e.

Applications in the Classroom

1. Below are some directions that you could use to sketch familiar space figures. For more accurate sketches, use a computer graphics program or a compass and a straightedge.
   a. To sketch a cube, first draw two overlapping congruent squares. Then join the vertices as shown.

   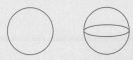

   b. To sketch a rectangular prism, follow the directions given in 1a, but use nonsquare rectangles.

   c. To sketch a sphere, first sketch a circle, then add an ellipse for depth.

   d. To sketch a cone, sketch an ellipse (or any other simple closed curve), draw a point above the ellipse for the apex, then connect the apex to the ellipse with segments.

   e. To sketch a cylinder, sketch two congruent simple closed curves, then connect the curves with line segments.

   f. To sketch a pyramid, sketch the polygonal base, draw a point above the base for an apex, then connect the apex to the base with line segments.

   Note: The lateral faces of a cone, cylinder, pyramid, or prism consist of line segments from *every* point of the lower base to the corresponding point of the upper base or to the apex. In drawing these figures, include only a few representative line segments.

2. Write a set of directions that you could follow to sketch a prism.

3. Write the directions for a pipe cleaner activity appropriate for reinforcing the concepts of skew lines and parallel lines in space.

4. Imagine you are teaching a fourth-grade class. Your textbook gives the definitions as stated earlier in this section for "face," "edge," "vertex," and "cone." Leon asks, "How can a cone have a vertex if it doesn't have any edges?" How do you respond? (*Hint:* Consider the net given in Problem 1b.)

5. Classify the level of knowledge and the type of learning experience of Activity 10-23. What level of the van Hiele model does this activity illustrate? What objective from the NCTM model (or from your state or district model) does the activity address?

6. Create an assessment tool to be used with Activity 10-17. Explain why you chose that type of assessment tool.

7. Write a lesson plan that describes how you will introduce the ideas of edges, faces, and vertices in a second-grade classroom. Follow the format given by your instructor or use the lesson plan format given in Appendix A.

10.4 CONGRUENCE AND SIMILARITY

Recognizing similarities and differences is an important skill with many real-world applications that children will be able to understand. You must replace the battery of a toy or the wheel of a bicycle with one that is the same size and shape. The cup lids at the fast-food drink counter are all the same shape, but different sizes; you must find the one that is the right size for your cup. When buying clothes, the same shirt may come in several sizes. You probably own several pairs of socks that are identical. Each of these is an example of congruence or similarity in the real world.

Two Definitions of *Congruent*

As already stated, two plane figures are congruent if they have the same shape and size. What about the two letters shown in Figure 10-23? They have the same height and the same shape because they are both the letter *F*. However, these two shapes are not considered congruent. Why not?

An alternate definition of "congruent" is that two plane figures are congruent if one can be moved so that the figures

 Microsoft Word drawing tools can be used to create handouts such as those in Activities 10-24 and 10-25. See Appendix B at the back of this textbook.

coincide. With this definition it is clear that the letters shown in Figure 10-23 are not congruent as long as you realize that in "moving" a figure, you are not allowed to alter it in any way. That is, you can slide, flip, or turn the figure, but you are not allowed to shrink or stretch any part of it.

Note the complexity of the figure in Activity 10-26. Students are to determine that each region covers exactly one square of the grid. Therefore, each region has the same size. This requires some creative visualization on the part of the student. This activity illustrates van Hiele Level 2—informal deduction.

After completing Activity 10-27, students should realize that all squares that have a common side length are congruent, but not all rhombi with a common side length are congruent. These results can be explained using methods of high school geometry and congruence properties. You may recall using congruence properties in a middle school or high school geometry course to determine whether two triangles or other plane figures were congruent.

Congruent and Noncongruent Triangles If every student in a class were to make a pipe cleaner 3-4-5 triangle (a triangle that has side lengths 3 inches, 4 inches, and 5 inches),

FIGURE 10-23 Are the letters congruent?

Activity 10-24   Grades K–1

Which Figures Match?

Setup: Draw various figures on a handout for students.

Handout Directions: Loop the shapes in each row that match (same size and same shape).

Note: If necessary, provide students with concrete cutouts of the figures in the left column.

Activity 10-25   Grades 1–6

Find the Twins

Materials: Illustrations that contain some exact duplicates. Increase the complexity for higher grade levels.

Directions: Find the twins. Explain why figures are or are not twins (first-grade-level example shown).

Activity 10-26   Grades 3–4

Congruent or Same Size?

Setup: Draw figures on a grid or on dotpaper.

Teacher Directions: Ask students which regions have the same shape, the same size, and which regions are congruent.

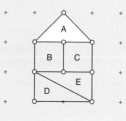

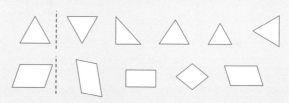

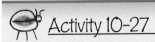 Activity 10-27 Grades 2–4

Same Size Squares and Same Size Rhombi

Materials: Chenille wires (pipe cleaners) and rulers, one for each student.

Teacher Directions: Tell students to bend their pipe cleaners to make a square where the side lengths are 3 inches each. Ask students to compare their square with the square that one of their neighbors made. What result do they find?

Tell students to make a rhombus with side lengths 3 inches each and compare it with the rhombus that another student made. What result do they find?

Note: Activity may also be conducted using centimeter lengths.

 Activity 10-28 Grades 4–6

Valid Triangles

Materials: Chenille wires (pipe cleaners) and rulers, one for each student.

Teacher Directions: Tell students to fill in the given chart with "Yes" or "No" in each box depending on whether the triangle indicated can be made by bending the pipe cleaner so that three sides of the triangle have the given lengths. Ask them if they can guess what rule must be true about the longest side of a triangle.

Note: The quickest way to complete this table is one row at a time. Each row has two common side lengths, and only the last side length need be changed.

1-1-1	1-1-2	1-1-3	1-1-4
1-2-2	1-2-3	1-2-4	1-2-5
2-2-2	2-2-3	2-2-4	2-2-5
1-3-3	1-3-4	1-3-5	1-3-6
2-3-3	2-3-4	2-3-5	2-3-6
2-4-4	2-4-5	2-4-6	2-4-7

then all the triangles would be congruent by the congruence property Side-Side-Side (SSS). If students were told to make a 2-3-30° triangle (a triangle with a side length of 2 inches, a side length of 3 inches, and a 30° angle), students might find that their triangle differs from their neighbors'. The fact that there are two such triangles, as shown in Figure 10-24, is evidence that there is not a congruence property Side-Side-Angle.

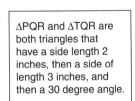 Teaching Connections

When Does a Set of Side Lengths Produce a Valid Triangle? By about the fourth grade, students are presented with another property concerning the side lengths of triangles. Even if your certification does not include fourth grade, and you may never teach this property, it is extremely important that you understand and remember it. After all, you will

draw triangles and label the side lengths beginning at the first-grade level. Complete Activity 10-28 before reading further.

Do you see any problem with drawing the following example on the board as an example of a scalene triangle in a second- or third-grade classroom? The problem with this example is that such a triangle does 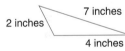 not exist! Try to construct it with a pipe cleaner or some other material that may be measured with the lengths as

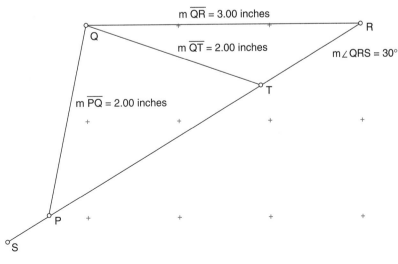

ΔPQR and ΔTQR are both triangles that have a side length 2 inches, then a side of length 3 inches, and then a 30 degree angle.

FIGURE 10-24
Two noncongruent 2-3-30° triangles.

given. You may be familiar with the old adage that "the shortest distance between two points is a straight line." Suppose we begin with a side of length 2 inches and a side of length 4 inches as shown. The shortest distance from A to C is along the direct edge from A to

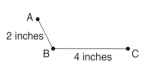

C. This distance must be *shorter* than the distance obtained by traveling from A to B and then from B to C. That is, the third side of this triangle must be less than 6 inches long. Remember this example when drawing labeled triangles to be used in the classroom to demonstrate triangle terms or for perimeter activities.

There is a similar situation that arises in drawing example right triangles with labeled side lengths. One of the figures shown below is a valid drawing of a right triangle, the other two are not. Try to determine which is a correct drawing before reading further.

Only triangle (b) above is labeled with valid side lengths. Triangles (a) and (c) violate the Pythagorean theorem: The length of the hypotenuse (longest side) of a right triangle is the square root of the sum of the squares of the lengths

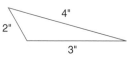

of the other two sides (legs) of the triangle. There is no right triangle with side lengths 2″-3″-4″. Appendix A shows that if a right triangle has legs of length 2″ and 3″, then the hypotenuse has the length $\sqrt{13} \approx 3.6''$. Thus, a 2″-3″-4″ triangle must be drawn as an obtuse triangle as shown.

A complete discussion of the Pythagorean theorem is given in Appendix A.

It is also a consequence of the Pythagorean theorem that the length of the hypotenuse of a right triangle exceeds the length of either of the two legs. Therefore, in any example of an isosceles right triangle, the two congruent sides must be the two legs. Example (c) above violates this principle. This is another important fact for you to remember as you prepare examples of right triangles for use in the classroom.

Similar Versus Congruent

You have seen that to be congruent, figures must have the same shape *and* the same size. If figures have the same shape, but not necessarily the same size, they are called *similar*. When two figures are similar, there is a scale factor that could be used to enlarge or reduce one figure so that it has the same size as the other. A *scale factor* is a number by which each side length of one figure may be multiplied to

obtain the side lengths of the other figure. Students may be familiar with the related idea of a scale model, a smaller replica of a larger figure.

Example 10-4: Determining the scale factor of similar squares.

For each pair of squares given, if the squares are similar, determine the scale factor from one square to the other. Square A has side lengths 2 cm, square B has side lengths 3 cm, square C has side lengths 4 cm, and square D has side lengths 3 cm.

Solution: Square A is similar to square B with scale factor from A to B of $\frac{3}{2}$ since if each side length of 2 is multiplied by $\frac{3}{2}$, the result is a square with side length 3. Square A is similar to square C with scale factor from A to C of 2. Square B is similar to square A with scale factor from B to A of $\frac{2}{3}$. Square C is similar to square A with scale factor from C to A of $\frac{1}{2}$. Square B is similar to square D with scale factor from

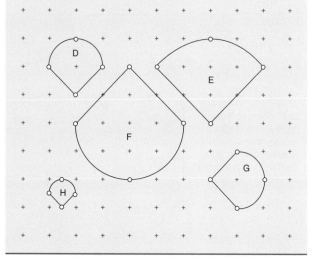

Activity 10-29   Grades 4–6

Similar, Congruent, or Neither?

Directions: For each pair of objects, determine whether the objects are congruent, similar, or neither. For objects that are similar, find the scale factor. For objects that are not similar, explain why they are not similar.

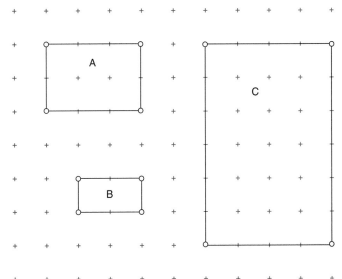

FIGURE 10-25
Similar and nonsimilar
rectanges.

Rectangle A is
similar to rectangle
C with scale factor
from A to C of 2.

Rectangle B is not
similar to either of
rectangles A or C.

Rectangle C is
similar to rectangle
A with scale factor
from C to A of 1/2.

B to *D* of 1. Whenever two figures are congruent, they are similar with scale factor 1. Can you figure the remaining comparisons?

After completing Example 10-4, you probably realize that *all* squares are similar. It is also true that all cubes are similar. You should be able to determine other classes of figures in which all figures are similar. Figure 10-25 illustrates that not all rectangles are similar.

The scale factor from *A* to *C* in Figure 10-25 is 2 since each side length of rectangle *A* must be multiplied by a factor of 2 for the resulting rectangle to have the same size as *C*. It is important that the *same* scale factor be used in each direction that a figure is stretched. This explains why rectangle *B* is not similar to rectangle *A*; there is no common scale factor that can be used to transform each side length of rectangle *B* into a side length of rectangle *A*. Try to draw rectangle *D* so that *B* and *D* are similar with a scale factor from *B* to *D* of 2.

Artists, designers, and architects use scale factors in their daily work. Students may use the idea of a scale factor to draw a room plan of their room or their house. They may use scale factors in tracing objects and drawing larger or smaller versions of a given picture.

When the concept of similar is presented in the earliest grades, a broader interpretation of the word is usually accepted. The idea of scale factor is usu-

ally not introduced until around the fourth-grade level. In earlier grades, students are allowed to rely on visual interpretations to determine whether objects are similar. It would be acceptable for a second-grade student to conclude that all of the rectangles shown in Figure 10-25 are similar. At this level, objects are declared "not similar" if there is some property that visually distinguishes them. For example, although every square is a rectangle, a square would be considered "not similar" to any nonsquare rectangle.

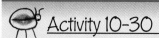 **Activity 10-30** Grades 3–6

Trace the Picture

Materials: A picture drawn on dotpaper and transferred to a transparency (dotpaper for each student).

Teacher Directions: Show the picture to the students. Ask the students to draw exactly the same picture on their dotpaper.

Alternate directions:
a. Ask students to draw the same picture but twice as large.
b. Have students place dotpaper on top of their favorite cartoon figure and use the dotpaper to trace the figure.

Source: Adapted from Troutman & Lichtenberg, 2003

Problem Set 10.4

For Your Understanding

1. Explain why the two *F*'s in Figure 10-22 are not congruent.

2. Which figures are similar? Which are congruent? Explain your answers.
   a.
   b.
   c.

d.

e.

3. a. Write a Logo procedure that will draw a square of variable size.
   b. Write a Logo procedure (see Appendix B) that will draw three similar noncongruent squares.

4. Use Logo to draw a figure that is similar but not congruent to each of the following:
   a.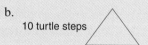

   20 turtle steps
   10 turtle steps

   b.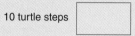
   10 turtle steps

5. a. Draw figure *B* on inch- (centimeter-) squared paper that is similar to figure *A* with scale factor from *A* to *B* of 2.

   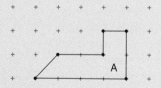

   b. Draw figure *C* on inch- (centimeter-) squared paper that is similar to figure *A* with scale factor from *A* to *C* of $\frac{1}{2}$.

6. Are figures *D* and *E* similar? Why or why not?

   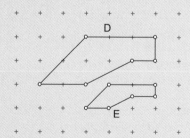

Applications in the Classroom

1. Use an automatic drawer like the Geometer's Sketchpad (see Appendix B) to draw a picture that could be used for Activity 10-29.

2. Draw and label side lengths for triangles that you could use as examples for each of the following. Make sure that all of your triangles have valid side lengths.
   a. scalene right triangle
   b. scalene obtuse triangle
   c. scalene acute triangle
   d. isosceles right triangle
   e. isosceles acute triangle
   f. isosceles obtuse triangle

3. Tangrams: Cut and label polygons of the sizes shown on Blackline Master 2 (see Appendix C). Use inch- (centimeter-) squared paper (Blackline Master 3) so that the figures are the correct sizes.
   a. Use two pieces to make a piece congruent to *F.*
   b. Use two pieces to make a piece similar but not congruent to *F.*
   c. What piece is the same size (has the same area) but is not congruent to *F?*
   d. Use three pieces to make a square.
   e. Use all the pieces to make a square.
   f. Use all the pieces to make a design that looks like a real object such as an animal.

4. Design a tangram activity such as the one above.

5. Classify the level of knowledge and the type of learning experience of Activity 10-24. What level of the van Hiele model does the activity illustrate? What objective from the NCTM model (or from your state or district model) does the activity address?

6. Create an assessment tool to be used with Activity 10-25. Explain why you chose that type of assessment tool.

7. Write a lesson plan that describes how you will introduce the idea of congruent and similar shapes in a first-grade classroom. Follow the format given by your instructor or use the lesson plan format given in Appendix A.

10.5 MOTIONS AND SYMMETRY
Motions and Symmetry in the Real World

Examples of motions are abundant in the real world. Chess and checker pieces slide across the playing board. A remote-control car performs turns as it glides along the floor. A gymnast performs flips and turns as she performs her routine. In the popular computer or arcade game Tetris, you must flip, turn, and slide the pieces to fit into the puzzle. A fan blade and other machine parts turn when the machine is properly working. Turns, flips, and slides

are useful to the artist, especially when engaged in computer drawing. Children themselves will enjoy demonstrating the motions that we will encounter within this section.

Many examples of symmetry can also be found in real life. Symmetry is apparent in the patterns of the clothing that children wear, in the shape of a snowflake, and in countless other real-world examples. Symmetry may be used in planting flowers in a garden or in creating a mask or a drawing. When children begin to recognize properties of symmetry, their drawings become more realistic and balanced. Symmetry may also be used to analyze mathematical situations. A pool player uses symmetry when he calculates the angle of a bank shot. Motions, transformations, symmetry, and other geometric ideas presented in this section appear throughout the early childhood curriculum.

Three Types of Transformations

The previous section defined congruence of two plane figures that involved moving one of the figures so that it coincided with the other figure. It also stated that in moving the figure, it could not be altered in any way. That is, the figure cannot be shrunk or stretched. This type of movement is called a *rigid motion;* in the elementary curriculum this may be called a *transformation.*

> See Appendix B for instructions in the use of the Geometer's Sketchpad. This software may be used to illustrate the three types of transformations that will be encountered in this section.

Translations (Slides) The first transformation or motion is called a *translation,* or *slide.* Figure 10-26 illustrates a translation or slide. Notice that there is no twisting or turning, as well as no shrinking or stretching, of the figure involved in a translation. The *translation vector* shows both the distance and the direction of the translation.

Rotations (Turns) The second transformation is called a *rotation,* or *turn.* Figure 10-27 illustrates a rotation or turn. Point P is called the *turn center.* A figure may also be rotated

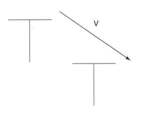

FIGURE 10-26 A translation along vector v.

FIGURE 10-27 A 45-degree rotation about point P.

Standards

Florida Sunshine State Standards

Grades Pre-K–2: Geometry and Spatial Sense

Standard 2: The student visualizes and illustrates ways in which shapes can be combined, subdivided, and changed. (MA.C.2.1)
1. Understands basic concepts of spatial relationships, symmetry, and reflections.
2. Uses objects to perform geometric transformations, including flips, slides, and turns.

Florida Department of Education, 1996

about a point that lies on the figure. In the earliest grades, the angles of rotation are usually in multiples of 90°. We will follow the convention that the angle of rotation is positive if the turn is in the counterclockwise direction. Some textbooks assign positive turn degrees to turns in the clockwise direction. Figure 10-28 illustrates more turns or rotations. The first figure shown is rotated several times 30° about the bottom left corner point to create the second figure shown. Can you explain why there are 12 copies of the original figure shown in the second figure?

Reflections (Flips) The third transformation is called a *reflection*, or *flip*. Figure 10-29 illustrates a reflection or flip. The line shown is called the *line of reflection*. The line of reflection does not need to be horizontal or vertical, although it is usually easier to draw the reflection when it is. If an object is reflected across a line that passes through the object, you must draw the resulting reflection on both sides of the line.

Figure 10-30 illustrates more flips or reflections. In example (a), the second figure illustrates a flip of the first figure across a vertical line of reflection that is not shown. Can you determine where the line of reflection should be drawn? Examples (b) and (c) show both the original figure and the end result of the reflections. This is so that you have a clear idea of what the original figure looked like. Usually when a flip or reflection is drawn, the reflection is drawn on the original figure.

Combinations of Motions

By the second or third grade, students begin to consider *combinations* of the transformations slide, turn, and flip. See the examples given in Figure 10-31 and Activity 10-32. In Figure 10-31b, the second figure can be obtained from the first by a combination of a flip and then a turn. Can you find a line of reflection and turn center that work for this transformation?

The transformations slide, flip, and turn can be useful in determining whether two plane figures are congruent. Two plane figures are congruent if there is a sequence of rigid motion transformations that moves one figure so that it coincides with the other. Both pairs of figures shown in Activity 10-32 are congruent. Transformations can also be used to create interesting designs and pictures. In particular, the mira can be used to draw the other half of a picture when half of the picture is already drawn as in the examples shown in Activity 10-33.

Symmetry

If a student draws the "other half" of a picture such as in Activity 10-33 so that the two sides of the picture match exactly, you would say that the resulting figure has symmetry. A third-grade textbook definition of *symmetry* is "a figure has symmetry if it can be folded along a line so that both parts match exactly." Activity 10-34 shows that the concept of symmetry may be introduced in the very early grades.

We will discuss three types of symmetry corresponding to the three types of transformations: line, turn, and slide.

Line Symmetry The first type of symmetry is called *line symmetry;* it corresponds to the transformation flip or reflection. A *line of symmetry* can be defined as "a line on which a figure can be folded so that both halves are congruent." This definition is misleading in that when a non-

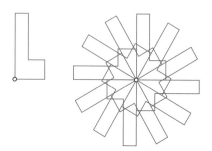

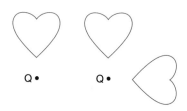

FIGURE 10-28 Turns and rotations

The figure on the right is generated by a sequence of rotations of the figure on the left about its bottom corner point.

The figure on the right shows a 270° rotation of the figure on the left about point Q. This could also be considered to be a –90° rotation.

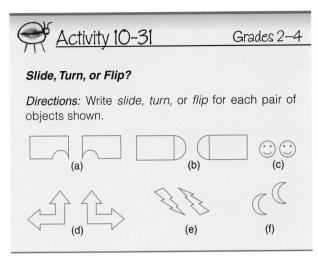

Activity 10-31 Grades 2–4

Slide, Turn, or Flip?

Directions: Write *slide, turn,* or *flip* for each pair of objects shown.

(a)   (b)   (c)

(d)   (e)   (f)

square rectangle is cut by a diagonal, the two halves are congruent. However, the diagonal of a nonsquare rectangle is not considered to be a line of symmetry of the rectangle. A more appropriate, albeit less technical, definition of "line symmetry" that would be appropriate for the third-grade level is "a line on which a figure can be folded so that both halves match exactly." Under this definition it is clear that

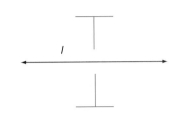

FIGURE 10-29 A reflection across line *l*.

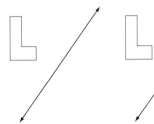

FIGURE 10-30 Flips and reflections.

(a) The figure on the right is a reflection of the figure on the left. Can you draw the line of reflection?

(b) The figure on the right is the result when the L in the figure on the left is reflected across the line shown.

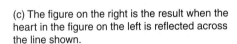

(c) The figure on the right is the result when the heart in the figure on the left is reflected across the line shown.

Math Manipulative: The Mira or Reflecta

A mira (sometimes called a reflecta) is a useful math manipulative for working with reflections. The mira or reflecta is the plastic transparent device shown below. To use a mira, place the beveled edge on the line of reflection. When a figure is drawn on one side of the mira, you may look through the mira and see its reflection on the other side. This makes it easy to draw the reflection. There are several commercially available elementary-level student activity books and math manipulative handbooks that contain mira activities.

A Mira and Mira Activity

Use the mira to help the girl try on wigs.

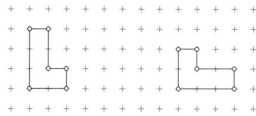

FIGURE 10-31 Combinations of transformations.

(a) A slide followed by a flip.

(b) The second figure can be obtained from the first by a flip followed by a turn.

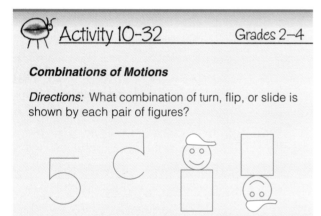

Activity 10-32   Grades 2–4

Combinations of Motions

Directions: What combination of turn, flip, or slide is shown by each pair of figures?

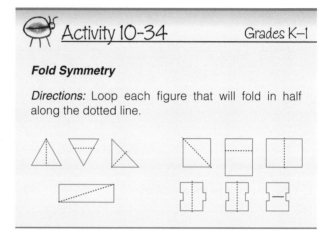

Activity 10-34   Grades K–1

Fold Symmetry

Directions: Loop each figure that will fold in half along the dotted line.

Activity 10-33   Grades 2–4

Draw the Other Half

Setup: Draw half pictures.

Materials: Miras or dotpaper for each student.

Directions to Students: Draw the other half of the given pictures.

Note: This activity can also be done with pattern blocks or attribute blocks.

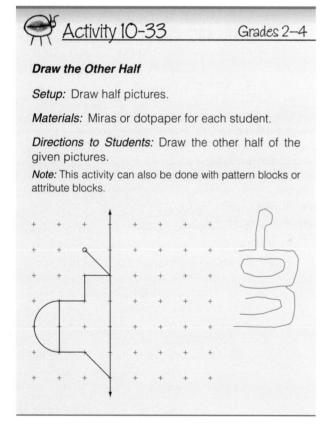

the diagonal of a nonsquare rectangle is not a line of symmetry of the rectangle. This is related to the transformation of flip or reflection in that a line of symmetry is also a line of reflection. In other words, if the figure is reflected across the line of symmetry, the result is exactly the same figure. Figure 10-32 illustrates the lines of symmetry (shown as dashed segments) for several plane figures.

Turn Symmetry The second type of symmetry is *turn symmetry,* or *rotational symmetry.* You say that a plane figure has *n*-degree turn symmetry if the figure can be rotated *n* degrees about its center and the result coincides with the original figure. Turn symmetry corresponds to the transformation turn or rotation. *Every* plane figure has 360° turn symmetry. You are usually interested in the smallest angle of turn symmetry of a figure because each whole number multiple of that angle will also give an angle of turn symmetry for that figure. Figure 10-33 gives the angles of turn symmetry for several plane figures.

Slide Symmetry The final type of symmetry corresponds to the transformation slide or translation. For both types of symmetry already discussed, the result of the corresponding transformation was precisely the original figure in its original position. So, what type of a figure would have *slide symmetry?* What type of figure could you slide so that the result was precisely the original figure in its original posi-

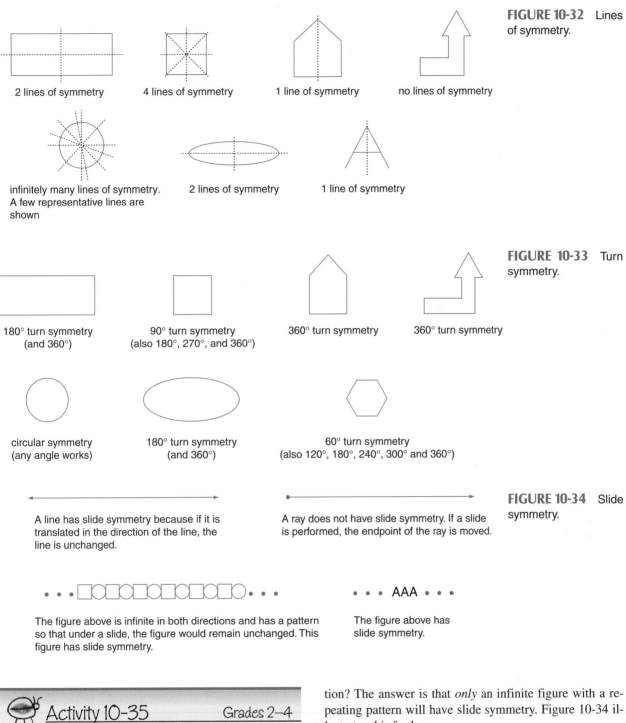

FIGURE 10-32 Lines of symmetry.

2 lines of symmetry

4 lines of symmetry

1 line of symmetry

no lines of symmetry

infinitely many lines of symmetry. A few representative lines are shown

2 lines of symmetry

1 line of symmetry

FIGURE 10-33 Turn symmetry.

180° turn symmetry
(and 360°)

90° turn symmetry
(also 180°, 270°, and 360°)

360° turn symmetry

360° turn symmetry

circular symmetry
(any angle works)

180° turn symmetry
(and 360°)

60° turn symmetry
(also 120°, 180°, 240°, 300° and 360°)

FIGURE 10-34 Slide symmetry.

A line has slide symmetry because if it is translated in the direction of the line, the line is unchanged.

A ray does not have slide symmetry. If a slide is performed, the endpoint of the ray is moved.

The figure above is infinite in both directions and has a pattern so that under a slide, the figure would remain unchanged. This figure has slide symmetry.

The figure above has slide symmetry.

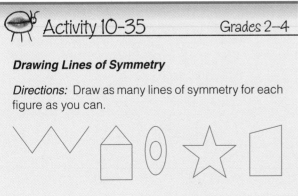

Activity 10-35   Grades 2–4

Drawing Lines of Symmetry

Directions: Draw as many lines of symmetry for each figure as you can.

tion? The answer is that *only* an infinite figure with a repeating pattern will have slide symmetry. Figure 10-34 illustrates this further.

Problem Set 10.5

For Your Understanding

1. Copy the two figures given in Figure 10-31b on dotpaper or inch- (centimeter-) squared paper. Indicate a line of reflection and turn center on the paper that will transform the first figure onto the second.

2. For each pair of figures, indicate whether the figures are or are not congruent.

a.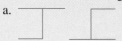

b.

c.

d.

3. For each pair of figures, indicate whether the figures are or are not congruent.

a.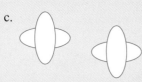

b.

c.

4. For each pair of congruent figures shown in problem 2 above, indicate what transformation(s) could be used to transform the first figure in the pair onto the second figure.

5. For each pair of congruent figures shown in problem 3 above, indicate what transformation(s) could be used to transform the first figure in the pair onto the second figure.

6. Draw all lines of symmetry for each object shown in the first column of problem 2 above.

7. Draw all lines of symmetry for each object shown in the first column of problem 3 above.

8. Find the smallest angle of turn symmetry for each object shown in the first column of problem 2 above.

9. Find the smallest angle of turn symmetry for each object shown in the first column of problem 3 above.

10. Use an automatic drawer like the Geometer's Sketchpad (see Appendix B) to draw your initials using points and line segments on one side of a line.
   a. Slide your initials.
   b. Place a point on the screen and rotate your initials about the point.
   c. Reflect your initials over the line.

11. Follow the directions below to create an Escher-like drawing. Start with a small rectangle (approximately 2 inches by 3 inches).
   a. Cut any shape from the bottom edge.
   b. Slide up and tape to the top edge.
   c. Cut a shape from the left side.
   d. Slide and tape to the right side.
   e. Place copies of figure A end-to-end and top-to-bottom, trace, and decorate.

12. Follow the directions to create an Escher-like drawing: Start with a small rectangle (approximately 2 inches by 3 inches). The diagram shown below is just an example. Your figure should look different depending on the shapes that you cut.
   a. Cut any asymmetric shape from the bottom edge.
   b. Flip and slide and tape to top edge.
   c. Cup a shape from the left side.
   d. Slide and tape to the right side.
   e. Place copies of figure B end-to-end and top-to-bottom, trace, and decorate.

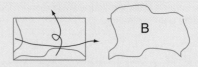

13. a. Write a Logo procedure that will draw a circle.
   b. Write a Logo procedure (see Appendix B) that will use your circle procedure to draw a figure like the figure shown.

14. A *hexomino* is formed by joining six congruent squares along edges. The figure shown is invalid because one of the squares is not joined along an edge.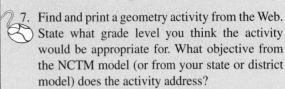

    The figures shown in Figure 10-22 are all hexominos. There are 35 different hexominos. There are 11 different hexominos that are nets for a cube. Find all 11 noncongruent hexominos that are nets for a cube. Be sure not to include any congruent copies of the same net. For example the two figures below are congruent and count only as one net.

    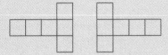

15. Write the alphabet in capital letters. For each letter determine each of the following:
    a. The lines of symmetry
    b. The smallest angle of turn symmetry
    c. Any pairs of congruent letters

16. Draw a figure that shows a 90° turn of the figure shown.

    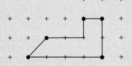

Applications in the Classroom

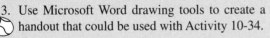

1. Create a half picture that you could use with Activity 10-33. You may use the Geometer's Sketchpad or other computer software if you wish.

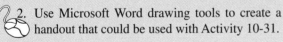

2. Use Microsoft Word drawing tools to create a handout that could be used with Activity 10-31.

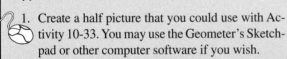

3. Use Microsoft Word drawing tools to create a handout that could be used with Activity 10-34.

4. Create an assessment tool to be used with Activity 10-35. Explain why you chose that type of assessment tool.

5. Write a lesson plan that describes how you will introduce the ideas of turn, flip, and slide in a second-grade classroom. Follow the format given by your instructor or use the lesson plan format given in Appendix A.

6. Look at the geometry chapter in an elementary-level textbook. Photocopy or copy by hand one example or problem that you think is interesting or unusual and indicate why. What objective from the NCTM model (or from your state or district model) does the example or problem address? Be sure to state what grade-level text you are using.

7. Find and print a geometry activity from the Web. State what grade level you think the activity would be appropriate for. What objective from the NCTM model (or from your state or district model) does the activity address?

8. Look at the activities in this chapter. Find at least one activity at each of the van Hiele levels from Level 0 through Level 3.

9. Choose an activity from this chapter. Indicate how you could implement the activity as a collaborative learning experience.

10. Choose one of the books in the children's literature section of the references for this chapter. Explain how you could incorporate the book into a math lesson.

11. Make up two writing prompts or stems that fit in with material or activities from this chapter.

References

Children's Literature References

Adler, David. (2000). *Shape up! Fun with triangles and other polygons.* New York: Holiday House.

Axelrod, Amy. (2000). *Pigs on the ball: Fun with math and sports.* New York: Simon & Schuster.

Baker, Alan. (1999). *Brown rabbit's shape book.* London: Larousse Kingfisher Chambers.

Burns, Marilyn. (1995). *The greedy triangle.* New York: Scholastic.

Burns, Marilyn. (1997). *Spaghetti and meatballs for all!* New York: Scholastic.

Froman, Robert. (1976). *Angles are easy as pie.* New York: HarperCollins.

Hill, Eric. (1986). *Spot looks at shapes.* New York: Putnam.

Hoban, Tana. (1995). *Shapes, shapes, shapes.* New York: William Morrow.

Murphy, Chuck. (1999). *Bow wow: A Pop-up book of shapes.* New York: Simon & Schuster.

Murphy, Stuart. (2001). *Captain Invincible and the space shapes.* New York: HarperCollins.

Neuschwander, Cindy. (1998). *Sir Cumference and the first round table.* Watertown, MA: Charlesbridge.

Onyefulu, Ifeoma. (2000). *A triangle for Adaora.* New York: Penguin Putnam.

Phillips, Jo. (1995). *Exploring triangles: Paper folding geometry.* New York: HarperCollins.

Teacher Resources

Alaska Department of Education and Early Development. (1999). *Alaska Mathematics Content Standards and Key Elements*. Retrieved December 1, 2003 from http://www.eed.state.ak.us/tls/PerformanceStandards/math.pdf

Bruni, J. V., & Seidenstein, R. B. (1990). Geometric concepts and spatial sense. In J. N. Payne (Ed.), *Mathematics for the young child* pp. 203–227. Reston, VA: National Council of Teachers of Mathematics.

Florida Department of Education. (1996). *Florida Sunshine State Standards*. Retrieved December 8, 2003 from http://www.firn.edu/doe/curric/prek12/ frame2.htm

Krause, E. F. (1991). *Mathematics for elementary teachers* (2nd ed.). D.C. Heath and Company: Lexington, MA.

Manfre, E., Moser, J. M., Lobato, J. E., & Morrow, L. (1994). *Heath mathematics connections, teacher's edition, level 1*. Lexington, MA: D.C. Heath and Company.

National Council of Teachers of Mathematics. (2000). *Principles and standards for school mathematics*. Reston, VA: Author.

North Carolina Department of Public Instruction. (2003). *North Carolina Mathematics Standard Course Study and Grade Level Competencies K-12 (2003)*. Retrieved November 19, 2003 from http://www.dpi.state.nc.us/curriculum/ mathematics/standard2003/index.html

Ohio Department of Education. (2001). *Ohio Academic Content Standards*. Retrieved November 12, 2003 from http://www.ode.state.oh.us/academic_content_standards/pdf/MATH.pdf

Troutman, A. P., & Lichtenberg, B. K. (2003). *Mathematics—A good beginning* (6th ed.). Belmont, CA: Wadsworth, Thomson Learning, Inc.

Selected Research Books and Articles

Fuys, D. J., & Liebov, A. K. (2002). Concept learning in geometry. In D. L. Chambers (Ed.), *Putting research into practice in the elementary grades: Readings from NCTM journals* (pp. 156–159). Reston, VA: National Council of Teachers of Mathematics.

Lehrer, R., Jenkins, M., & Osana, H. (1998). Longtitudinal study of children's reasoning about space and geometry. In R. Lehrer & D. Chazan (Eds.), *Designing learning environments for developing understanding of geometry and space* (pp. 137–167). Mahwah, NJ: Erlbaum.

Piaget, J., & Inhelder, B. (1964). *The child's conception of geometry*. New York: Harper & Row.

Further Reading

Battista, M. T., Wheatley, G. H., & Talsma, G. (1989). Spatial visualization formal reasoning, and geometric problem-solving strategies of preservice elementary teachers. *Focus on Learning Problems in Mathematics, 11*, 17–30.

Burger, W. F., & Shaughnessy, J. M. (1986, January). Characterizing the van Hiele levels of development in geometry. *Journal for Research in Mathematics Education,* 31–48.

Clements, D. H. (1999). Geometric and spatial thinking in young children. In J. V. Copley (Ed.), *Mathematics in the early years* (pp. 66–79). Reston, VA: National Council of Teachers of Mathematics.

Confer, C. (1994). *Math by all means: Geometry grade 1–2*. Sausalito, CA: Math Solutions Publications.

Del Grande, J. (1993). *Geometry and spatial sense: Addenda series, grades K–6*. Reston, VA: National Council of Teachers of Mathematics.

Dodwell, P. (1971). Children's perceptions and their understanding of geometrical ideas. In *Piagetian cognitive development research and mathematical education* pp. 178–188. Reston, VA: National Council of Teachers of Mathematics.

Fuys, D. J., & Liebov, A. K. (1993). Geometry and spatial sense. In R. J. Jensen (Ed.), *Research ideas for the classroom: Early childhood mathematics* (pp. 195–222). New York: Macmillan.

Hershkowitz, R. (1989). Visualization in geometry—Two sides of the coin. *Focus on Learning Problems in Mathematics, 11*(1), 61–76.

Lehrer, R., & Curtis, C. L. (2000). Why are some solids perfect? Conjectures and experiments by third graders. *Teaching Children Mathematics, 6*, 324–329.

Lindquist, M. M. (Ed.). (1987). *Learning and teaching geometry, K–12, 1987 Yearbook*. Reston, VA: National Council of Teachers of Mathematics.

Morrow, L. J. (1991, April). Geometry through the standards. *Arithmetic Teacher, 38*, 21–25.

National Council of Teachers of Mathematics. (1999). Geometry and geometric thinking [Focus issue]. *Teaching Children Mathematics, 5*(6).

Rectanus, C. (1994). *Math by all means: Geometry grades 3–4*. Sausalito, CA: Math Solutions Publications.

Thiessen, D., & Matthias, M. (1989). Selected children's books for geometry. *Arithmetic Teacher, 37*, 47–51.

van Hiele, P. M. 1986. *Structure and Insight: A Theory of Mathematics Education*. Academic Press.

Zurstadt, B. K. (1984, January). Tessellations and the art of M. C. Escher. *Arithmetic Teacher,* 54–55.

11

Developing Measurement Concepts and Operations

What things can you measure and what tools do you measure with? You can measure the length of an object with a ruler, but you can measure length with many nonstandard tools, including body parts. You measure the area of a room before purchasing carpeting for it. You estimate the volume of a milk carton as you peer into the refrigerator while making a grocery list. A weather report includes the measure of temperature, humidity, barometric pressure, and perhaps even a pollen count. During a visit to the doctor, a nurse may measure your blood pressure and body temperature. The electric and water companies measure the units of electricity and water used before sending you the monthly bills. We will discuss many other real-world applications and tools of measurement within this chapter.

This chapter explores both the U.S. customary units (inches, feet, etc.) and the metric system. As the United States gradually moves toward adopting the metric system, today's children must learn to accurately use both systems. You may need to learn or relearn metric terms and ideas. Time, temperature, and functions and relations are also covered in this chapter. Each of these areas is abundant with real-world connections and applications. A solid knowledge of these topics is necessary for survival in today's world.

Measurement has many natural connections to other branches of mathematics and other subject areas. The National Council of Teachers of Mathematics recognizes and emphasizes the significance and magnitude of measurement.

Objectives

After completing Chapter 11, you will be able to

- Use correct abbreviations, relationships, units, and terminology in measuring length, area, and volume
- Perform measurements using nonstandard measures, U.S. customary units, and metric units
- Solve measurement problems using appropriate area, perimeter, and volume formulas
- Describe how functions, time, and temperature are covered in the early childhood curriculum
- Plan lessons and activities that incorporate measurement ideas into the early childhood classroom

11.1 EXPLORING LENGTH, AREA, AND VOLUME

Prior to any formal measurement activities, children should have a variety of experiences with comparison of objects (Hiebert, 1984; Liedtke, 1990). Without measuring or otherwise determining the capacity, children can often tell which of two juice containers contains more juice. Without finding the lengths of two pencils, children can determine which pencil is longer. Without finding the heights of two students, children can determine which of the students is taller. Children may find it easier to determine which of two students is taller than to determine which of two pencils is longer. Think about why this might be so.

Comparing the Lengths of Objects

When children compare the lengths of two objects, unless one of the objects is clearly longer than the other, the children must line up the endpoints of the objects to determine which is longer (see Activity 11-1). When children compare the heights of two students, their endpoints (feet) are already lined up (on the floor). It is then a simple visual observation to determine which student is taller. Similar activities can be planned to introduce or reinforce other measurement terminology such as "wider," "farther," and so on. Notice how Activity 11-2 involves comparing distances traveled without involving the actual measurements of the distances.

Predictions and Estimations Predicting and estimating are important components of the measurement process and in developing number sense. Children can make a prediction about how far a toy car will roll or a paper airplane will fly. After the car has rolled or the airplane has flown, they can estimate the distance traveled. Using estimation they can judge the reasonableness of an answer or of the unit chosen to represent the answer. Estimation or predictions can also be used in activities that reinforce the process and terminology of object comparison.

Nonstandard Measurement Tools Prior to the introduction of standard units of measure, nonstandard measurement activities use concrete objects, such as unifix cube trains, learning links, and so on to measure other objects. Standard units of measure such as feet and inches or meters and centimeters may be introduced later. In this manner children can develop meaning for the operation and concepts of measurement before dealing with abstract measurement ideas (Hiebert, 1984). At the pre-K to first-grade level, measures are usually given in terms of the nearest whole unit. Fractional measures typically are introduced at the second- or third-grade level.

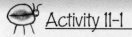 **Activity 11-1**   Grades Pre-K–2

Shortest to Longest—Ordering Objects

Materials: Bags of objects that can be linearly ordered, one bag for each group. Example objects: chalk, paper clip, comb, toothbrush, spoon, drinking straw, etc.

Teacher Statement: Each person will pick one object from the bag. Your group must decide who has the shortest object and who has the longest object. Line up the objects from shortest to longest. When two objects are almost the same length, how can you tell which one is longer? (Accept student responses. Bring out the idea that you might have to line up the endpoints of two objects to determine which is longer. Demonstrate this for the students.)

Activity Extension: Students may be asked to reach into the bag and find the shortest (or longest) object without looking. This reinforces visualization skills. If the original activity is performed first, rearrange bags so that students don't pick the shortest object based on their memory of the objects. You want them to choose the shortest based on the feel of the objects within the bag.

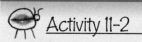 **Activity 11-2**   Grades Pre-K–2

Who Walked the Farthest?

Materials: Two or three hermit crabs, string, masking tape. (If hermit crabs are unavailable, this activity may be done with toy cars or wind-up toys.)

Teacher Statement: Today we are going to have a race and see which of our hermit crabs, Rufus, Jelly, or Bean, will walk the farthest in 10 minutes. First, let's make a prediction. You can vote only one time. Who thinks Rufus will walk the farthest? Who thinks Jelly will? Who thinks Bean will walk the farthest?

(Record the number of students who vote for each hermit crab. This information could be used to draw a graph [see Chapter 9]. Place a masking tape *X* on the starting spot. Place all crabs on the starting spot. After 10 minutes, record the final positions with masking tape. You can use masking tape crabs' initials to record which crab goes with which position. Let the children measure the distances with string. Cut the string to the appropriate lengths, so that the distances can be compared.)

Which crab walked the farthest? Did Rufus walk farther than Jelly? Did Jelly walk farther than Rufus? and so forth. Compare the results to the original predictions.

Children enjoy measuring objects with common items such as toothpicks, paper clips, or shoes. Unifix cubes are especially useful in measuring activities because these manipulatives can be naturally linked to form trains of an appropriate length. When unifix cubes (or other nonstandard units of measure) are used in measuring lengths, it is important that the unit "cubes" (or another appropriate unit) is used when describing or reporting a length. Measuring activities involving objects such as cubes, as in Activity 11-3, usually precede the introduction of formal measurement units such as inches. Most sets of unifix cubes and learning links do not contain 1-inch pieces; so in many cases it would be inaccurate to say "the calculator is 3 inches wide" when what is meant is "the calculator is 3 cubes wide."

Learning links may be used in Activities 11-3 and 11-4. These manipulatives also link together to form chains that are useful in measuring. However, the static nature of a unifix cube train makes unifix cubes easier for very young children to use in measuring activities. After such an activity, children can measure objects using a nonlinking tool like a toothpick or a shoe. Measuring with a nonlinking tool such as a pencil requires coordination in the placement of the tool and a continuous count of the number of units used. Children will need much practice to develop these skills. At the pre-K

to first-grade levels, when measures are given in terms of the nearest whole unit, you may want to carefully plan what objects children are to measure. Children should also have practice in measuring not only width or length but also height (see Activity 11-5).

Standard Abbreviations and Relationships After children have completed measurement activities with nonstandard, nonlinking measurement tools such as pencils or shoes, standard measures may be introduced. There are several abbreviations and relationships involving customary linear measurement terms that must be memorized. For example, 1 foot (ft) = 12 inches (in.), 1 yard (yd) = 3 feet, and 1 mile (mi) = 5,280 feet. Students will need practice in choosing

---

Activity 11-3   Grades K–2

Which Unifix Train Is Closest in Length?

Materials: A single cube, a 5-cube, and a 10-cube unifix train for each student; pictures of common classroom objects.

Teacher Statement: We each have three unifix trains. The shortest train has only 1 cube. We also have a medium train and a long one. Let's count the cubes in the medium train: 1, 2, 3, 4, 5. The medium train has five cubes. Let's count the cubes in the long train: 1, 2, . . . , 10. The long train has 10 cubes.

You will each get a card with a picture of an object. For example, my card has a picture of a glue stick. You must decide whether the length of the object on the card is closer to the length of the 1-cube train, the 5-cube train, or the 10-cube train. Think about the actual object, not just the picture of the object. Let's see, I know that a glue stick is about this long (show with fingers). I think it is about the same as the 5-cube train. Next, find the object in the classroom and check your prediction. Here is an actual glue stick. If I hold it up next to each train, it is closest to the 5-cube train. My prediction was correct.

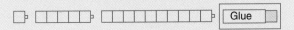

Activity 11-4   Grades K–2

Measuring with Unifix Cube Trains

Materials: Unifix cubes for each student; handout with pictures of classroom objects to be measured.

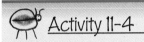

Teacher Statement: Look at the calculator that I am holding. I want to measure how wide it is. How wide do you think it is? Is it almost a 1-cube train, a 5-cube train, or a 10-cube train wide? You think it is close to a 5-cube train wide? Let's check. The 5-cube train is too long and the 1-cube train is too short. How many cubes do I need to measure how wide this calculator is? Three? Yes, I can make a 3-cube train and that is how wide the calculator is.

Using a picture of a calculator and a unifix cube, put this on the board:

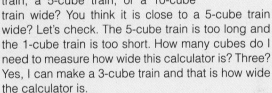

The handout shows other objects for you to measure. Fill in the blank when you find the number of cubes it takes to measure the object that is shown.

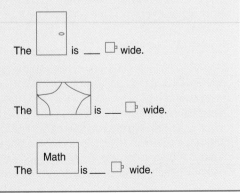

an appropriate unit of measure and in determining what objects could be measured with a given unit.

Children at the first- and second-grade levels will need assistance in learning how to use and read a standard ruler. Initially, you may want children to read the ruler to the nearest whole unit rather than introducing fractional units of measure. When an object is measured, one end of the object must be placed at the end or the zero mark of a ruler. How will you answer the student who asks why you do not measure by placing the object at the 1 mark of the ruler? After all, the counting sequence usually begins at the number 1, and measurement is a process of counting to determine how many of a unit length it takes to cover the object that is being measured.

The need for standard measures becomes obvious during measurement activities with nonstandard measures. Bert may find that that the board is six shoes wide, whereas Diamond finds that it is seven shoes wide. Which student is correct? It is quite possible that both students are correct. This type of dilemma provides a natural introduction to the need for standard units. This is also addressed in the children's literature selection *How Big Is a Foot?* (Myller, 1991) that is described in this section.

Measuring Area and Volume

Each of the measurement activities discussed thus far involves *linear measure*, that is, the measure of length along a line or curve. We will also discuss the area of a region and

---

Activity 11-5   Grades 1–3

Measuring with Nonlinking Objects

Materials: A pencil, an eraser, and a student.

Teacher Statement: We have been measuring with cubes and links. We can use other objects to measure too. I will use my pencil to measure the door. When our measuring tool doesn't have parts that stick together, we have to be careful to put a finger at the end of the tool to know where to place it next time. We can count how many pencils it takes to measure how wide the door is.

(Illustrate the process. Stress the placement of a finger to mark the subsequent placement of the pencil.)

Now let's see how many pencils tall Steven is. Steven, please come up front. Let's estimate first. How many pencils tall do you think Steven is? 4? 10? 7? Let's see which estimate is the closest.

(Use a pencil to measure the height of a student. Suppose the class finds that Steven is 6 pencils tall. Show the class an eraser that is shorter than the pencil. Ask students if it would take more or fewer than 6 erasers to measure Steven's height. They should explain their predictions. Find an object that is longer than the pencil. Ask students whether it will take more or fewer than 6 of this object to measure Steven. Again, students should explain their reasoning. Carry out these measurements.)

Assessment   Grades 2–4
Writing in Mathematics

Write the following in your journal:

a. Name two objects that would best be measured using the unit inches. Give an estimate in inches for the length of each of your objects.

b. Name two objects that would best be measured using the unit feet. Give an estimate in feet for the length of each of your objects. Then give an estimate in inches for the length of each of your objects.

🐜 Using Literature in the Mathematics Classroom   Grades 1–3

How Big Is a Foot?

By Rolf Myller
Bantam Doubleday Dell Books, 1991

The king wishes to have a bed made for the queen. Beds (and rulers) have not yet been invented, so it is a problem to determine how large to make the bed. The king has the queen lie on the floor and walks around her using his feet to measure how big the bed should be. The king tells the carpenter how many feet long and how many feet wide to make the bed. When the carpenter uses his own feet to determine how large to make the bed, it is much too small. It is decided that from that time forth, everyone should use the size of the king's foot when measuring so that all measurements are consistent and true.

Classroom Activity:

Children can act out the story. Using masking tape outlines on the floor, each group can construct a bed that is 3 feet by 6 feet (using the feet of one of the group members). Groups should compare the sizes of the beds. Groups then each construct a bed that is 3 feet by 6 feet using a foot ruler and compare this to the beds constructed by other groups.

the volume of a solid. Example 11-1 and Activities 11-6 and 11-7 provide conceptual introductions for these discussions. Before terms or formulas are presented, students can solve problems involving the underlying concepts. In this manner, they develop some concrete sense of measurement concepts before being introduced to the more abstract ideas.

Example 11-1: How many triangles of this size does it take to cover the house shown?

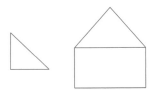

Solution: By drawing extra lines on the house, you can see that it takes two triangles to build the roof and four to build the rectangular part. It takes six triangles of the given size to cover the house.

Capacity Facts and Equivalences Activities 11-6 to 11-8 involve *capacity*—the volume that can be held in a container. A definition for *volume,* the number of cubic units needed to fill a solid figure, typically is given at the third-grade level. By first grade, children learn capacity terms such as "cup," "pint," and "quart," and in some cases "gallon." In initial activities, children identify the names of various-sized containers and indicate which container holds more when given a choice of two containers. In later activities children learn the relationships between the different sizes of containers. Most children will already have had many real-life experiences involving quantities and capacities: A package of Koolaid makes 2 quarts, you need to add 1 cup of sugar. You should memorize and be prepared to use the following facts and equivalences: 1 cup = 8 fluid ounces, 1 pint = 2 cups, 1 quart = 2 pints, and 1 gallon = 4 quarts and is approximately 231 cubic inches.

Use Square Units in Measuring Area
To cover an entire region, square units must be used. Once students understand

the relationships between cups, pints, quarts, and so on, understanding square units follows naturally. First or second graders typically are introduced to the square inch using square tiles to cover figures and determine areas. The phrase "square inch" is used until around the fifth grade, when the abbreviated notation in.^{2} is introduced. If technology such as the Geometer's Sketchpad is used with measurement activities, you may wish to introduce the exponential notation at an earlier level because programs such as this generally use exponential notation.

Use Cubic Units in Measuring Volume At around the second- or third-grade level, cubic inches are used to determine volumes. Again, the phrase "cubic inch" is used until the fifth grade or so when the abbreviated notation in.^{3} is introduced. Customary units for measuring weight and two more relations that must be memorized are: 16 ounces (oz) = 1 pound (lb) and 2,000 pounds = 1 ton (T). Technically, the term *mass* is a more accurate measurement expression than the term *weight*. However, this textbook uses the more familiar term *weight* because this is the term that is most commonly used in elementary textbooks and materials. A sample lesson plan to introduce

Standards

Florida Sunshine State Standards

Grades Pre-K–2: Measurement

Standard 2: The student compares, contrasts, and converts within systems of measurement (both standard/nonstandard and metric/customary). (MA.B.2.1)

1. Uses direct (measured) and indirect (not measured) comparisons to order objects according to some measurable characteristics (length, weight).
2. Understands the need for a uniform unit of measure to communicate in real-world situations.

Florida Department of Education, 1996

Standards

Texas Essential Knowledge and Skills for Mathematics: 111.13

Mathematics for Grade 1

(7) Measurement. The student uses nonstandard units to describe length, weight, and capacity. The student is expected to:

a. estimate and measure length, capacity, and weight of objects using nonstandard units; and
b. describe the relationship between the size of the unit and the number of units needed in a measurement.

Texas Education Agency, 1998

 Activity 11-6 — Grades 2–6

Candy Estimation

Materials: Candy estimation handout; see-through jar filled with candy; cup measure.

Teacher Statement: I have a big jar of candy. How many pieces of candy do you think are in the jar? Estimate or guess how many pieces of candy are in the jar. Write your estimate in the first blank.

Now I'll fill up a measuring cup with pieces of candy. Estimate how many pieces are in the cup and write your estimate in the second blank.

Let's count the actual number of pieces in the cup. Write that number in the third blank.

Now that you know how many pieces are in a cup, you may wish to revise your estimate of the number of pieces in the jar. Estimate how many pieces are in the jar and write the number in the fourth blank.

(Continue to fill the cup measure with candy from the jar and count how many times you fill the cup measure. The number of cups in the jar goes in the fifth blank. Students can use this information along with the number of pieces in a cup to again revise their estimate of the number of pieces in the jar. This revised estimate is written in the sixth blank. Then count the actual number of pieces in the jar. Point out how additional information [number of pieces in a cup, number of cups in the jar] can lead to improved estimates.)

Candy Estimation:

Estimate how many pieces of candy are in the jar.	_____
Estimate how may pieces in a cup	_____
Actual number of pieces in a cup	_____
Revised estimate, number of pieces in jar	_____
The number of cups in the jar	_____
Revised estimate, number of pieces in jar	_____
The actual number of pieces	_____

---

volume at the second- or third-grade level is given in Appendix A.

Example 11-2: Determine the appropriate quantities and units.

    a. $1 \text{ yd}^2 = \underline{\quad} \text{ ft}^2$
    b. $1 \text{ ft}^2 = \underline{\quad} \text{ in.}^2$
    c. $1 \text{ ft}^3 = \underline{\quad} \text{ in.}^3$
    d. $1 \text{ yd}^3 = 27 \underline{\quad}$

 ## Assessment
Assessing Activity 11-6

Suppose Activity 11-6 is performed at the third- or fourth-grade level. Possible objectives of the activity are as follows:

- The students will be able to make a reasonable estimate of the number of candies in the jar.
- The students will be able to make a reasonable estimate of the number of candies that fit into a cup.
- The students will be able to use their estimate of the number of candies in a cup to revise (if necessary) their estimate of the number of candies in the jar.
- The students will use the number of cups in the jar and the number of pieces in a cup to revise (if necessary) their estimate of the number of candies in the jar.

Suppose the jar of candy held 83 pieces, the cup held 15 pieces, and it was found that there were about $5\frac{1}{2}$ cups of candy in the jar. The students could be assessed as follows:

1. Original estimate:

63–103	3 points (gives students a 20-piece leeway)
43–62 or 104–124	2 points
23–42 or 125–145	1 point
below 23 or above 145	0 points

2. Estimate of number of pieces in a cup:

10–20	2 points
5–9 or 21–25	1 point
below 5 or above 25	0 points

3. Revised estimate of number of pieces in the jar. (At this point students know that a cup holds about 15 pieces. They should be able to estimate that the jar holds 5 or 6 cups. Revised estimates of the number of pieces in the jar should reflect this although a 5-point leeway is given.)

70–95	2 points
55–69 or 96–110	1 point
below 55 or above 110	0 points

4. After determining that there were $5\frac{1}{2}$ cups in the jar and 15 pieces in the first cup, students should be pretty accurate in their estimates.

80–85	2 points
70–79 or 86–95	1 point
below 70 or above 85	0 points

Total score:

7–9 good estimation skills

4–6 needs some estimation practice

0–3 needs extensive review and practice in estimation skills

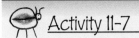

Activity 11-7   Grades Pre-K–1

Recognizing Cups, Pints, and Quarts

Materials: Several quart, pint, and cup containers; packing peanuts or other material that may be used to fill the containers.

Teacher Statement: I have several containers in this bag. Some are this size (hold up a cup). Do you know what a container of this size is called? Right, this is called a cup. Some of the containers are this size (hold up a pint container), and so on.

    (Continue to identify the pint and the quart container. Set all three containers on a desk or table in front of you with the cup on the left, the pint in the middle, and the quart on the right [from the student's point of view]. Instruct students to raise their hands to indicate where other containers from the bag should be placed—left hand for cup, both hands for pint, right hand for quart. Review terms as you pull objects from the bag and students identify where they should be placed. Ask students to predict how many cups in a pint. Use packing peanuts to verify. Repeat for the number of pints in a quart and the number of cups in a quart.)

Activity 11-8   Grades 3–4

How Many Cups in a Gallon? Using Manipulatives

Materials: Several gallon, quart, pint, and cup containers.

Teacher Statement: Your task is to find out how many cups are in a gallon. I want you to use the relationships that you do know. We have learned how many cups are in a pint, how many pints are in a quart, and how many quarts are in a gallon. You can use the containers to explain your solution.

e. $2 \text{ yd}^3 = \underline{\hspace{1.5em}} \text{ ft}^3$

f. $432 \text{ in.}^2 = 3 \underline{\hspace{1.5em}}$

g. $330 \text{ in.} = \underline{\hspace{1.5em}} \text{ ft} \underline{\hspace{1.5em}} \text{ in.}$

Solutions:

a. Visualize a square yard. It is 3 feet long and 3 feet wide. This contains a total of $3 \times 3 = 9$ square feet. So, $1 \text{ yd}^2 = 9 \text{ ft}^2$.

b. Visualize a square foot. It is 12 inches long and 12 inches wide.

This contains a total of $12 \times 12 = 144$ square inches. So, $1 \text{ ft}^2 = 144 \text{ in.}^2$.

c. A cubic foot is 1 foot long, 1 foot wide, and 1 foot tall. That is, $12 \times 12 \times 12 = 1,728 \text{ in.}^3$.

d. A cubic yard is 3 feet by 3 feet by 3 feet. Hence, $1 \text{ yd}^3 = 27 \text{ ft}^3$.

e. Two cubic yards is represented by two of the above diagrams, so $2 \text{ yd}^3 = 54 \text{ ft}^3$.

f. Visualize 432 square inches. Wow, that's a bunch of square inches. But if you arranged them in big squares that were 12 inches by 12 inches, each big square is 1 square foot and uses 144 square inches. There are three big squares: $432 \text{ in.}^2 = 3 \text{ ft}^2$.

g. There are 12 inches in a foot. If you perform the division $330 \div 12$ on a standard calculator, the result is $330 \div 12 = 27.5$. However, it is not true that 330 inches equals 27 feet, 5 inches. You must use caution in interpreting the decimal. Recall that $0.5 = \frac{1}{2}$, so that $330 \text{ in.} = 27\frac{1}{2} \text{ ft}$ or $330 \text{ in.} = 27 \text{ ft}, 6 \text{ in.}$ If the division is performed on a calculator that contains an integer division key (see Appendix B) the result is $330 \boxed{\text{Int}\div} 12 = 27 \, r \, 6$, which effectively illustrates the answer 27 ft, 6 in.

Teaching Connections

Use Real-World Situations and Problem Solving to Motivate and Maintain Interest in Measurement Think about the first hour or so of your daily routine. You use measurement when you estimate how much milk to pour on your cereal or use in a breakfast recipe. You measure a line of toothpaste for your toothbrush, and consider the daily temperature in choosing clothing for the day. You watch the clock to ensure that you will leave for school on time. Measurement is used throughout the day in activities such as these. Several problem-solving measurement activities are given below.

Example 11-3: Problem solving by drawing a picture (third- or fourth-grade level).

A rectangular playground area that is 24 feet wide and 30 feet long needs new grass. Each piece of sod is 3 feet long and 3 feet wide. How many pieces of sod will it take to cover the playground?

Solution: Draw a rectangle to represent the playground. The sides should be marked in 3-foot increments. It might be helpful to draw the rectangle on centimeter-squared paper. Each centimeter can represent 3 feet.

    Each square centimeter represents a piece of sod. There are 8 rows of sod with 10 pieces in each row. A total of 80 pieces of sod is needed.

Math Manipulative: Square Tiles and One-inch Cubes

A standard size of tiles is 1 square inch. These are usually made of plastic but they also come in a quieter foam material. Overhead and magnetic sets are available. There are usually several colors of tiles in a set, making this a useful manipulative for counting, sorting, pattern activities, and probability experiments. Square tiles can also be used in addition, subtraction, multiplication, division, or other number operation activities. One major advantage of square tiles lies in their usefulness in measurement activities. These manipulatives may be used in calculating lengths and perimeters, and they are particularly suited for area activities.

One-inch cubes are especially useful for volume activities. A set may be made of wood, plastic, or foam material. Some sets come in a single color; others come in a variety of colors. When purchasing blocks especially for measurement activities, be sure to check the size of the blocks. Some block sets contain blocks that are $\frac{1}{2}$-inch or $\frac{3}{4}$-inch cubes. These would not be especially useful in an activity where the volume was to be measured in cubic inches. A manipulative that is useful in measuring volume within the metric system is a set of centimeter cubes. The single units contained in a base-ten block set are often cubic centimeters.

You can check the answer with calculations. The area of the playground is $24 \times 30 = 720$ ft². Each piece of sod is 9 ft². It makes sense that 80 pieces are required.

Example 11-4: Problem solving by making a table (fourth- or fifth-grade level).

A bunny hops 66 inches in 15 seconds. What is his speed in miles per hour? How long would it take him to hop 1 mile at this rate?

Distance	Time
66 inches	15 seconds
132 inches	30 seconds
264 inches	1 minute
15,840 inches	1 hour
1,320 feet	1 hour
5,280 feet	4 hours

Solution: You are given information in inches and seconds and wish to convert this to information in terms of miles and hours. Make a table using ratios or multiplication. The bunny hops 66 inches in 15 seconds; this speed is equivalent to 132 inches in 30 seconds and 264 inches in 1 minute. There are 60 minutes in an hour, so the bunny hops 15,840 inches in 1 hour at this speed. There are 12 inches in a foot, so 15,840 inches is 1,320 feet. One mile is 5,280 feet, 1,320 feet is one fourth of a mile, and the rabbit's speed is 0.25 mph. Thus, it would take the bunny 4 hours to go 1 mile at his rate.

Problem Set 11.1

For Your Understanding

1. You have a five-cup measuring cup and a two-cup measuring cup that have no other markings and one large bowl of rice. Explain how you could use these two measuring cups to measure exactly three cups of rice.

2. You have a 9-cup measuring cup and a 4-cup measuring cup that have no other markings and one large bowl of rice. Which of the quantities from 1 cup to 10 cups can be measured using only these two tools?

3. Complete Activity 11-8.

4. Four pounds of apples cost $3.00, eight ounces of kiwis cost 50¢. Which fruit costs less per pound?

5. How many 10-ounce servings are in a 2-gallon jug of Koolaid?

6. a. 2 yd² = _____ ft² = _____ in.².
   b. 5 yd³ = _____ ft³.
   c. 2 ft² = 288 _____.

7. A fish swims 300 feet in 3 seconds. What is her speed in miles per hour?

8. Scott runs 100 yards in 10 seconds. What is his speed in miles per hour?

9. A weed grows 12 feet in 14 days. If the rate of growth is constant, how many minutes does it take for the weed to grow 1 inch?

10. A turtle takes 176 hours to walk 1 mile at a constant rate. How long in minutes does it take the turtle to walk 1 foot?

11. The scale of a map shows that 1 inch on the map is 60 miles in actual distance. If two cities are $3\frac{3}{4}$ inches apart on the map, how many miles apart are the cities?

12. The tops and sides of the cakes are iced. Which of the cakes are cut so that the four pieces have equal amounts of icing?

a.

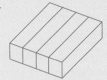

b.

c.

d.

13. Approximately what value is the arrow pointing to?

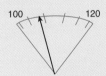

14. An architect's drawing has a scale of 1 inch for every 12 feet. What are the dimensions of a room that is 1.5 inches by 2 inches on the drawing?

15. A three-piece set of suitcases contains a total volume of 5 cubic feet. The large suitcase contains twice as much as the medium suitcase, and the medium suitcase contains three times as much as the small one. Find the volume of each of the cases.

Applications in the Classroom

1. Explain the difference between 2 square inches and a square with side length of 2 inches.

2. Choose one of the square tiles or 1-inch cubes manipulatives. Write a measurement activity that uses this manipulative.

3. Consider Activity 11-1. How many students will you place in each group? Write a specific

materials list indicating what items you will use and which items you will place into each bag.

4. Create a set of cards to be used with Activity 11-3.

5. Create a handout that could be used with Activity 11-4.

6. Create an assessment tool to be used with Activity 11-4. Explain why you chose that type of assessment tool.

7. Create an activity using tangrams, pattern blocks, or square tiles where children explore the number of pieces required to cover given figures. Create any handouts necessary for your activity.

8. Write a word problem similar to problem 11 under "For Your Understanding." Include the solution to your problem. How might you modify the problem to be used for students with special needs?

9. Create an activity where children measure objects in both feet and inches to reinforce the idea that there are 12 inches in a foot. Indicate exactly what objects the children will measure.

10. What modifications or adaptations will you make if a student has difficulty measuring with an object such as a pencil or a shoe?

11. Tai asks you why the ruler begins with 0 instead of 1. He says that the ruler should have a 1 on the end because that's what you start counting with. How do you respond?

12. Write a lesson plan that describes how you will help children discover the relationships between cups, pints, and quarts in a first-grade classroom. Follow the format given by your instructor or use the lesson plan format given in Appendix A.

11.2 THE SI METRIC SYSTEM

Teaching Both the U.S. Customary System of Measurement and the Metric System

This section focuses on the SI metric system. "SI" is the abbreviation for the *Système International d'Unités,* the modernized version of the metric system. The United States and other nations have agreed to use this system in trade and commerce. The United States is the *only* industrialized country in the world not officially using the metric system as a primary measurement system, but it has been making slow, steady progress in the past several decades. Two acts passed by Congress, the *Metric Conversion Act* of 1975 and the *Omnibus Trade and Competitiveness Act* of 1988, outline the importance and necessity of this conversion. Guidelines set by the NCTM standards reinforce the notion that even young children must learn to use this system.

Elementary schools in the United States typically teach both U.S. customary units and metric units. Students often find the metric system easier to learn and use than the U.S. customary system because all units for a given quantity within the metric system are related by factors of 10. It is a simple process of multiplying or dividing by 10, 100, 1,000, and so on, or simply moving the decimal point in an answer to convert from one unit to another. For example, 1 meter = 10 decimeters and 1 decimeter = 10 centimeters; thus 1 meter = 100 centimeters. In the U.S. customary system additional relationships such as 1 foot = 12 inches, 1 yard = 3 feet, and so forth must be memorized and used.

Measuring Length Using Metric Units

The basic unit of length in the SI system is called the *meter*. The terms "meter" and "centimeter" are usually presented at around the first-grade level. Initial activities (see Activity 11-9) involve choosing the appropriate unit and estimation using these units. Other units of length, their symbols, their relations to the meter, and common approximations or rough equivalences to customary units are shown in Table 11-1.

To convert from one metric length unit to another, you need to know only the sequence Kilo-Hecto-Deca-___-Deci-Centi-Milli. There are many pneumonics that help students remember this sequence. The blank is filled in with the current basic unit for the type of quantity to be measured. One such pneumonic is **K**ing **H**enry **D**rinks **M**ilk **D**uring **C**ouncil **M**eetings. The first letter of each word provides the first letter of the unit. When length is the quantity to be measured, the *M* in *Milk* stands for "meter." This pneumonic must be slightly altered to supply the appropriate base unit when the quantity measured is volume or weight.

Example 11-5: Fill in each blank with the appropriate numerical quantity or symbol.

    a. 250 cm = _____ m

    b. 500 m = _____ dm
    c. 400 dam = 4 _____

Solutions:

    a. Visualizing a centimeter (about the width of a small finger) and a meter (about a yard) and noting that meter is two units above centimeter in the table, you determine that there are 100 centimeters in a meter. Thus, 250 centimeters is equivalent to 2 full meters and $\frac{1}{2}$ of a meter, and 250 centimeters =

TABLE 11-1 Metric units of length.

Unit	Symbol	Relation to Meter	Common Approximation
Kilometer	km	1 km = 1,000 m	1 kilometer is approximately 5/8 of a mile.
Hectometer	hm	1 hm = 100 m	
Decameter	dam	1 dam = 10 m	
Meter	m		1 meter is approximately 39 inches (slightly longer than a yard).
Decimeter	dm	1 dm = 0.1 m	The length of a cassette tape is approximately 1 dm (slightly less than 4 inches).
Centimeter	cm	1 cm = 0.01 m	The width of your small finger is approximately 1 cm (slightly less than $\frac{1}{2}$ inch).
Millimeter	mm	1 mm = 0.001 m	The width of a wire paper clip is approximately 1 mm.

 Activity 11-9   Grades 1–2

Measure with Meters or Centimeters?

Materials: Cards with the words "Meter" and "Centimeter" for each student; classroom objects.

Teacher Statement: You each have a card with the word "Meter" and a card with the word "Centimeter." I will hold up or point to an object. You should hold up your "Meter" card if I should use meters to measure that object and your "Centimeter" card if I should use centimeters to measure that object. We will also be estimating how many meters or centimeters long the objects are.

(Hold up a chalkboard eraser. Ask students to show you either their "Meter" card or their "Centimeter" card. Pick a few students to estimate the length of the eraser in centimeters. Measure the eraser [or have a student measure it]. Continue with other objects.)

2.5 meters. This answer can also be found by moving the decimal point in 250 two units to the left.

b. Visualizing a meter (about a yard) and a decimeter (about 4 inches) and noting that the meter is one unit above the decimeter in the table, you determine that 1 meter = 10 decimeters. Thus, 500 meters = 5,000 decimeters.

c. Using the prefix sequence or the table you determine that 10 decameters = 1 hectometer and 100 decameters = 1 kilometer. Then, 400 decameters = 4 kilometers.

Measuring Volume (Capacity) and Weight

Common approximations and rough equivalences typically are used in measuring volume or weight. The basic unit of capacity measure is the *liter* (L). One liter is slightly more than a quart. Many drinks are sold in quantities marked in liters; a standard 12-ounce can of soda is approximately one third of a liter. One liter of water occupies 1,000 *cubic centimeters* (cm³) of space, whereas a *milliliter* (mL) of water occupies only 1 cubic centimeter of space.

The basic unit of metric weight measure is the *gram* (g). A nickel weighs approximately 5 grams. One *kilogram* (kg) is 1,000 grams and is the weight of 1 liter of water. One kilogram is approximately 2.2 pounds, and a *metric ton* (t) is 1,000 kilograms.

Example 11-6: Fill in the blank with an appropriate metric symbol or numerical quantity.

a. My cat weighs 5 _____.
b. The child's swimming pool is 2 _____ wide.
c. The child's cough medicine label says that one dose is 8 _____.
d. Sixty miles is approximately _____ kilometers.
e. One ft is approximately _____ centimeters.
f. Twenty-five kg is approximately _____ pounds.

Solutions:

a. The basic unit of weight measure is the gram. However, 5 grams is not much weight at all, certainly not enough for the weight of a cat. The one reference to standard weights given is that 1 kilogram is equivalent to 2.2 pounds. Thus, 5 kilograms is equivalent to 5 × 2.2 = 11 pounds. That is a reasonable weight for a cat. My cat weighs 5 kilograms.

b. The basic unit of length measurement is the meter. Two meters is slightly longer than 6 feet, a reasonable width for a child's pool. Two decimeters would be only about 8 inches, much too small for the width of a child's pool. The child's pool is 2 meters wide.

c. The basic unit of capacity or liquid measurement is the liter. A dose of cough medicine would be a very small amount, perhaps about a spoonful. One milliliter of liquid takes up 1 cubic centimeter of space. Eight milliliters would fill one or two large spoons. Thus, the child's dose is 8 milliliters.

d. The only given reference is that 1 kilometer equals $\frac{5}{8}$ of a mile. Thus, 8 kilometers equals 5 miles. Now 60 miles is 12 of these 5-mile stretches. Hence, 60 miles = 96 kilometers.

e. You are given that a decimeter (10 centimeters) is slightly less than 4 inches. So one estimate is that a foot is approximately 30 centimeters. Another given reference is that 1 meter (100 centimeters) is approximately 39 inches. Hence, 13 inches is approximately 33 centimeters. So 1 foot, or 12 inches, is approximately 30 or 31 centimeters.

f. You are given the reference that 1 kilogram equals 2.2 pounds. Thus, 5 kilograms = 11 pounds and 25 kilograms = 55 pounds.

Common Metric Notation Errors

There are several common mistakes in metric notation and usage that you, the teacher, should avoid. The short forms for SI units are called *symbols,* not abbreviations. SI symbols do not end with a period unless they are the last word of a sentence. The meaning of a symbol is altered if a capital letter is inadvertently used. For example, 1 millimeter is denoted by 1 mm; the symbol 1 Mm stands for 1 megameter which is equivalent to 1 million meters. However, the symbol for liter may be either capital or lowercase. In the United States, Canada, and Australia, the capital *L* is preferred; most other nations use the lowercase *l.* In the United States the spellings *meter* and *liter* are commonly used, whereas other countries tend to use *metre* and *litre.* The letter *p* is not used as a symbol for "per," so *kph* or *kmph* are incorrect whereas *km/h* is the correct way to denote "kilometers per hour." The word "kilometer" is pronounced *KILL-oh-meet-ur* and not *kill-AHM-it-ur.*

This summary of common errors is taken from an article posted on the U.S. Metric Association (USMA), Inc. Web site (2003). A link to the USMA Web site can be found at the textbook companion Web site.

Incorrect metric notation usage can often be found on products and packaging located on store shelves and in the home. The following project idea may contribute to

fewer packaging errors and simultaneously combines research, letter writing, and learning the correct metric symbols.

Problem Set 11.2

For Your Understanding

1. Maureen walks 5 meters in 10 seconds. Calculate her speed in kilometers per hour, then estimate her speed in miles per hour.

2. Four children step onto a scale two at a time in all possible combinations. The resulting weights are in kilograms: 56, 61, 62, 63, 64, and 69. Suppose the weights of the children are all whole numbers of kilograms, and that none of the children weighs more than 35 kilograms. Find the weights of the four children.

3. a. $3 \text{ m}^2 = $ _____ cm^2
   b. $2 \text{ cm}^3 = $ _____ mm^3
   c. $5 \text{ km}^2 = $ _____ m^2

4. a. 50 mm = _____ cm
   b. 2 km = _____ m
   c. 20 m = 2,000 _____

5. Place one of the symbols >, <, or = in each blank.
   a. 400 cm _____ 4 m
   b. 50 kg _____ 100 lb
   c. 3 dm _____ 35 cm

6. Choose an appropriate metric symbol for each blank.
   a. My cat's tail is 20 _____ long.
   b. The kids at the party drank 15 _____ of soda.
   c. A ball-point pen weighs about 10 _____.

7. Find the errors in the following story. Joe walked 800 mtrs to the store. He bought 2 Kg. of grapes, 3 Ls of apple juice, 5 G sunflower seeds, and a 20cm stick of taffy.

8. a. 20 km = _____ mi
   b. 33 lb = _____ kg

Applications in the Classroom

1. A second grader looks at the following diagram and claims that the measure is 6 centimeters. You are the teacher. How do you respond?

2. A decimeter is stated as approximately the length of a cassette tape. Although you are probably familiar with this parallel, children of today may be exposed to CDs and not to cassette tapes. Devise common approximations (other than those given)

that would be appropriate for today's students for meter, decimeter, centimeter, and millimeter.

3. In problem 5 under "For Your Understanding," pairs of units are compared using the symbols <, >, or =. Write an exercise similar to this where children compare pairs of units. Include motivating or real-world examples to make the problem more interesting to students. For example: My dog Charlie is 3 decimeters tall; my cat Cricket is 35 centimeters tall. Who is taller—Charlie or Cricket?

4. Write an exercise similar to problem 6 under "For Your Understanding." Include the solutions to your exercise.

5. Create a handout for an activity where children estimate and then measure objects using centimeters.

6. Create an assessment tool to be used with the activity described in problem 4 above. Explain why you chose that type of assessment tool.

7. Write an activity where children must choose liters or milliliters to measure given quantities. Indicate what examples and materials you will use in your activity.

8. Write an activity where children must choose grams or kilograms to measure given quantities. Indicate what examples and materials you will use in your activity.

11.3 AREA, PERIMETER, AND VOLUME FORMULAS

Discovering Area Concepts and Formulas

In beginning area activities, children cover objects with copies of other objects. Geoboards, tangrams, or dotpaper are useful for these types of activities. Later activities introduce specific measures and units. Some area formulas and properties may be discovered by students.

Example 11-7: Figure *F* can be covered with _____ units of figure *H*.

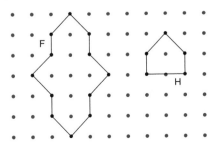

The dotpaper shown is centimeter squared. The area of figure *H* is ___ square centimeters. The area of figure *F* is ___ square centimeters. What relationship do you notice? Explain your answers.

The previous example illustrates the following *dissection property:* If region *R* is divided into nonoverlapping subregions, then the area of *R* is the sum of the areas of the subregions. This property will be useful in calculating areas and in deriving some common area formulas. The dissection property is especially useful in deriving formulas for the area of a parallelogram and the area of a triangle. The dissection property underlies Activity 11-10 in which children can be led to discover the formula for the area of a rectangle. This activity also reinforces the idea that area is measured in square units.

Formula: The Area of a Rectangle If a rectangle has length *l* and width *w*, the area *A* of the rectangle is the product of the length and the width. That is, $A = l \times w$. This can also be viewed as base times height.

Finding the Area of a Parallelogram Consider a parallelogram that has base length *b* and height *h*. Recall that the height of a parallelogram refers to the length of a segment perpendicular to the base as shown.

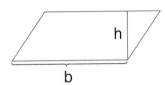

If the parallelogram is cut along the altitude and the triangular region is moved to the opposite side, a rectangle with base length *b* and height *h* is formed. The area of the rectangle is $b \times h$. Hence, the area of the parallelogram is

---

Activity 11-10   Grades 2–4

Measuring Area with Inch-Square Tiles

Materials: Various-sized index cards and rectangles and inch-square tiles or blocks for each student.

Teacher Statement: Let's start with the 3 by 5 index card. How many inch-square tiles will it take to cover this card? Let's get some predictions or estimates first. 12? 15? 10? Cover your 3 by 5 card with the tiles and let's see how many it takes.

(Repeat with the 4 by 6 card. Ask students to estimate and to cover and check. Then repeat for a 5 by 7 card and other sizes of rectangles of known dimensions in inches.)

also $b \times h$. This demonstration will hold for any parallelogram. The following formula may be used:

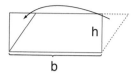

Formula: The Area of a Parallelogram If a parallelogram has base length b and height (of an altitude) h, the area A of the parallelogram is the product of the lengths of the base and the height. That is, $A = b \times h$ or $A = bh$.

Finding the Area of a Triangle A similar cut-and-paste demonstration can be used to derive a formula for the area of a triangle. Consider a triangle with base length b and height (of altitude) h. The vertices of the triangle are labeled A, B, and C (see Figure 11-1a). This labeling will help illustrate the cut-and-paste procedure. Cut the triangle parallel to the base at the level of $\frac{1}{2}h$. Label the two remaining vertices of the smaller triangle P and Q. When this triangle is moved to the position shown in Figure 11-1b, the result is a parallelogram with base length b and height $\frac{1}{2}$ h. By the formula above, the area of this parallelogram is $A = b \times \frac{1}{2}h$. Due to the commutative property of multiplication, this may be rewritten as $A = \frac{1}{2} \times b \times h$. Thus, the area of the original triangle is one half base times height; that is, $A = \frac{1}{2}bh$.

Formula: The Area of a Triangle If a triangle has base length b and height (of an altitude) h, the area A of the triangle is one half of the product of the lengths of the base and the height. That is, $A = \frac{1}{2} \times b \times h$, or $A = \frac{1}{2}bh$.

Example 11-8: Find the missing altitude or side length (fourth- to sixth-grade level).

The area of a triangle is 20 square inches. The base length is 8 inches. Find the height of the triangle.

Solution: At the fourth-grade level, a student could use the strategy of guess and check, plug values into the formula, and determine the correct height. At higher grade levels students will have enough experience with formulas and variables to use this formula—$20 = \frac{1}{2} \times 8 \times h$, or $20 = 4h$—to determine that $h = 5$ inches. This can be checked with the calculation $\frac{1}{2} \times 8 \times 5 = 4 \times 5 = 20$.

Estimation Second or third graders are expected to estimate area quantities. Estimation is especially important in

measurement problems because estimation can indicate when formulas have been incorrectly applied.

Example 11-9:

a. Each square shown represents 1 square mile. The lake pictured covers approximately _____ square miles.

b. If a person were to begin at some point on the shore of the lake and walk all the way around the lake, approximately how far would she walk? _____ miles.

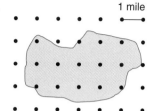

Exploring Perimeter Concepts

Example 11-9b involves an estimation of *perimeter*—the distance around a figure. Perimeter is introduced in the first or second grade using figures drawn on inch-squared or centimeter-squared paper (see Figure 11-2). Initial examples involve concrete ideas and counting; later examples involve standard units of measurement. In some cases, not all side lengths are given and students must calculate missing lengths before calculating perimeter and/or area. The dissection property is useful in finding the area of an irregular figure.

Example 11-10: Calculating perimeter and area (first- or second-grade level).

A bug builds the house shown. The house covers _____ square units. If the bug begins at one corner of the house and walks around the outside of the house and returns to the same corner, the bug walks _____ units.

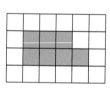

Teaching Connections

Use Caution with Slanted Line Segments Suppose that you are teaching in a third-grade classroom and you request that students draw a figure on grid paper that has a perimeter of six units. A student draws the figure shown in Figure 11-3. What is the perimeter of the figure shown? It is *not* six units.

Using the Pythagorean theorem (see Appendix A), Figure 11-3 shows a perimeter of $4 + 2\sqrt{2}$ units or approximately 6.8 units. A quick review of the Pythagorean

FIGURE 11-1
Finding the area of a triangle.

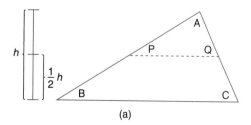

(a)

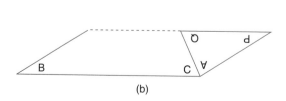

(b)

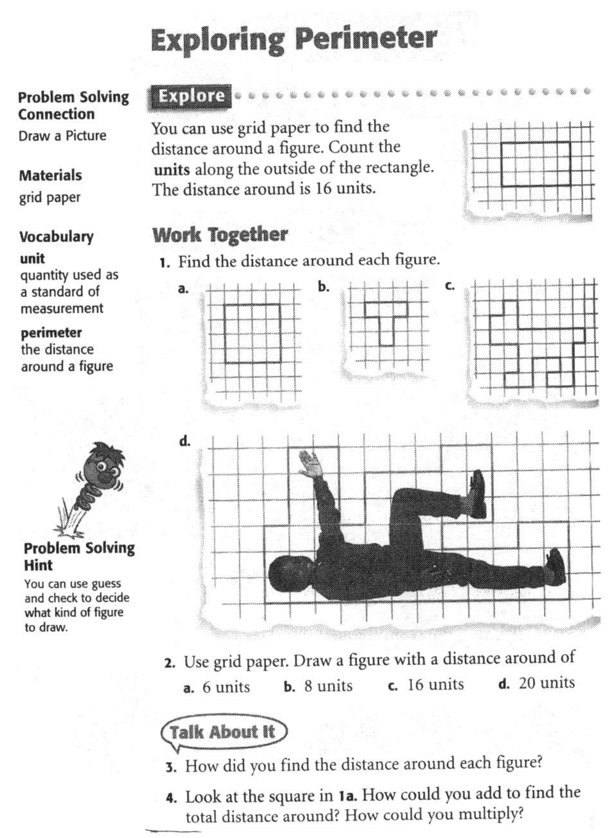

Exploring Perimeter

Problem Solving Connection
Draw a Picture

Materials
grid paper

Vocabulary
unit
quantity used as a standard of measurement

perimeter
the distance around a figure

Problem Solving Hint
You can use guess and check to decide what kind of figure to draw.

Explore •

You can use grid paper to find the distance around a figure. Count the **units** along the outside of the rectangle. The distance around is 16 units.

Work Together

1. Find the distance around each figure.

a.   b.   c.

d.

2. Use grid paper. Draw a figure with a distance around of
   a. 6 units   b. 8 units   c. 16 units   d. 20 units

(**Talk About It**)

3. How did you find the distance around each figure?

4. Look at the square in **1a**. How could you add to find the total distance around? How could you multiply?

FIGURE 11-2 School book page—exploring perimeter (third grade level).
Source: Page 340 from *Scott-Foresman—Addison Wesley Math Grade (3).* Copyright © 1999 by Addison Wesley Longman, Inc. Reprinted by permission of Pearson Education, Inc.

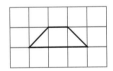

FIGURE 11-3 This figure does *not* have a perimeter of 6 units.

theorem should be enough to convince you that in drawing a grid paper figure to calculate the perimeter by counting line segments, all lines must be drawn either horizontally or vertically. Students can use a ruler to verify that the diagonal of a square is longer than the side length of the square. They can also use a ruler to verify that a line drawn diagonally on grid paper (from the corner of one square to the corner of another) is longer than the number of squares the line crosses. In some textbook series, it is not mentioned in either the student textbook or the teacher's manual that lines on grid paper figures should be drawn horizontally or vertically. In early grade levels, you must remember to caution students to draw only horizontal or vertical lines if they wish to find the perimeter by counting line segments. Alternately, students can use rulers to measure approximately the length of line segments to calculate a perimeter. (The

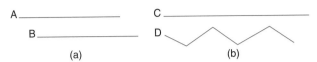

FIGURE 11-4 Which line segment is longer, *A* or *B*?

FIGURE 11-5 (a) Which line segment is longer, *A* or *B*? (b) Which path is longer, *C* or *D*?

Pythagorean theorem is necessary to calculate the exact perimeter of a grid paper figure when some of the lines are drawn diagonally. Although this theorem is usually not presented until about the sixth-grade level, it is discussed further in Appendix A.)

Children Rely on Their Visual Intuition As stated, young children will not learn the Pythagorean theorem. They will often rely on their visual perceptions and will make mistakes such as the one shown in Figure 11-3. It is up to you to help students realize that their visual intuition is not always accurate. The example shown in Figure 11-4 is one that people of all ages tend to answer inaccurately when they base their answer on visual perception alone.

A child at the preconservation stage of development might say that line segment *B* of Figure 11-5a is longer than line segment *A*. The child may be able to "measure" both segments and state that each segment is three paper clips long, and still may conclude that segment *B* is longer than segment *A*. The child may also say that path *C* is longer than path *D* in Figure 11-5b. Overcoming misleading visual interpretations can be a lengthy and difficult process (Petitto, 1990).

Understanding Invariance and Consistency Properties of Length and Distance

Conservation of length is necessary so that children are able to conceptualize and understand the process of measurement. Conservation of area is needed for use of the dissection property and in measuring the area of irregular figures. There is a well-known experiment in which water is poured from a tall, thin glass into a short, wide glass and vice versa. A child who has not yet achieved conservation of volume may claim that one of the glasses contains more liquid than the other. Three other properties that deal with the invariance and consistency of length and distance are described below.

Reflexive: An object has the same length as itself.
Symmetric: If one object has the same length as a second object, then the second object has the same length as the first. For example, if an eraser has the same length as a pencil, then the pencil has the same length as the eraser.

Transitive: If one object has the same length as a second object, and the second object has the same length as the third, then the first object has the same length as the third. For example, if an eraser has the same length as a pencil and the pencil has the same length as a glue stick, then the eraser has the same length as the glue stick.

The terms "reflexive," "symmetric," and "transitive" actually refer to properties that a given relation may or may not possess. The property of transitivity is valid for length inequalities. For example, if Bob is taller than Carolyn, and Carolyn is taller than Debbie,

See Section 11.4 for further discussion of reflexive, symmetric, and transitive properties.

then Bob is taller than Debbie. The symmetric property is not valid with length inequalities. For example, if Bob is taller than Carolyn, it is not true that Carolyn is taller than Bob. The length inequality relation is not reflexive when dealing with strict inequalities: Bob is not taller than himself.

Calculating Area and Perimeter

Example 11-11: Calculating perimeter and area (third- or fourth-grade level).

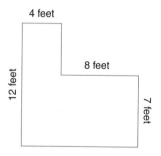

Find the perimeter and the area of the room shown.

Solution: First use the given measurements to determine that the unlabeled bottom wall has length 12 feet and the unlabeled side wall has length 5 feet.

The perimeter is then $12 + 12 + 7 + 8 + 5 + 4 = 48$ feet. Three different solutions for calculating the area are shown below. There are also other methods.

a. $4 \times 5 + 7 \times 12 = 20 + 84 = 104$ square feet.

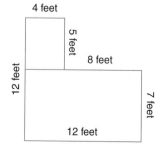

b. $4 \times 12 + 8 \times 7 = 48 + 56 = 104$ square feet.

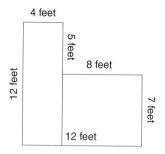

c. $12 \times 12 - 5 \times 8 = 144 - 40 = 104$ square feet.

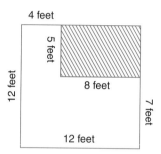

Example 11-11 illustrates that calculation of area is additive, whereas perimeter is not. In Example 11-11a the small rectangle has perimeter 18 feet and the large rectangle has perimeter 38 feet; the figure has perimeter $48 \neq 38 + 18$ feet. Can you explain why you cannot add the perimeters of the two rectangles to find the perimeter of the overall figure? Students can be led to discover facts and properties such as this. At around the third- or fourth-grade level, students can make generalizations and conjectures regarding perimeter and area. Students may discover that the perimeter of a rectangle is given by $P = 2 \times l + 2 \times w$ where l denotes the length and w denotes the width of the rectangle. Another good example at this level is for students to calculate the perimeter of regular hexagons with side lengths 1 inch, 2 inches, 3 inches, and so on and then predict and calculate the perimeters of larger regular hexagons. By noticing a pattern, students can write a formula for the perimeter of a regular hexagon that has side length n inches. Students can also answer inverse questions such as the following: "The perimeter of a regular hexagon is 48 inches. How long is each side of the hexagon?"

Exploring Volume

Initial volume activities involve students determining the number of cubic units in a stack of 1-inch cubes or estimating the quantity of a container. A sample lesson plan to introduce volume in the second or third grade is given in Appendix A. Can you write lesson plans to introduce the topics of area and perimeter?

How many cubes? _____ cubes.

How many cubes will fit in the box?

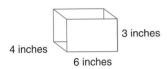

Inch cubes can be used to derive or explain the formula for the volume of a rectangular prism. Consider a rectangular prism that is 6 inches long, 4 inches wide, and 3 inches tall. This prism can be built with 1-inch cubes. It takes $6 \times 4 = 24$ cubes to build each layer. There are three layers to build. It takes $24 \times 3 = 72$ cubic inches to build the prism. The volume of this prism is 72 in.[3]. Notice that this number is the product of the length, width, and height values. It is also the product of the area of the base and the value of the height. This demonstration could be generalized for any size of rectangular prism, giving the following formula.

Formula: The Volume of a Rectangular Prism If a rectangular prism has length *l*, width *w*, and height *h*, the volume *V* of the prism is the product of the length, the width, and the height. That is, $V = l \times w \times h$. This can also be viewed as base area times height. That is, $V = B \times h$ where *B* is the area of the base.

In the late early childhood and early middle school grades, children learn to calculate the volume and surface area of more complicated figures and solids. Several such figures are discussed in the Appendices.

Activity 11-11 — Grades 4–6

Rolling Areas

Materials: Dice and handout to record width and length of rectangles.

Directions: Each team rolls two dice and uses the results to form a two-digit number. The team members then find all of the rectangles with sides measured in whole numbers of inches such that the area of each rectangle is the two-digit number (in square inches). The teams find the perimeters for each of these rectangles and get as many points as distinct perimeters found. Each team plays the same number of rounds, and the team with the total highest score wins.

Example: Round 1, Team A rolls 3 and 5, Team B rolls 5 and 5, Team C rolls 3 and 5. Team A decides to use the number 35, Team B must use 55, and Team C decides to use 53.

Team B's scorecard for round 1.

Round 1 Area = 55		Score = 2
Width	**Length**	**Perimeter**
1 inch	55 inches	112 inches
5 inches	11 inches	32 inches
11 inches	5 inches	32 inches
55 inches	1 inch	112 inches

Notes: This activity provides an excellent review of factors and multiples. It can also be used as an introduction to prime numbers.

Children will soon notice that it is not always beneficial to choose the larger number.

A similar game, Rolling Perimeters, can also be played. In this version, if both dice rolled are odd, no rectangles can be formed with perimeter either possible two-digit number.

Problem Set 11.3

For Your Understanding

1. How many small triangles does it take to cover the large triangle?

2. Play the rolling area game in Activity 11-11. Find your total score for three rolls. Indicate for each roll the two-digit number that you choose to use.

3. Answer *true* or *false* for each of the following.
   a. Two congruent regions must have the same area.
   b. Regions that have the same area must be congruent.

c. Rectangles that have the same area must have the same perimeter.

d. Congruent regions have the same perimeter.

4. The Dole family has a rectangular in-ground pool that is 8 feet wide, 12 feet long, and 6 feet deep.

a. How many gallons of water will the pool hold if it is filled to 1 foot below ground level?

b. Mr. Dole wishes to buy a tarp to cover the pool. It should extend 1 foot beyond each side of the pool. What size of tarp should he buy? What is the area of the tarp?

5. What is the area of the shaded region? The large figure is a square with 6-inch sides.

6. A rectangle has a height of 6 inches and a perimeter of 42 inches. What is the width of the rectangle?

7. See the figures drawn on centimeter dotpaper.

a. How many units of *A* will fit into a 4-centimeter by 4-centimeter square?

b. Find the area and perimeter of *A*.

c. Find the area of figure *B*.

d. Estimate the area of figure *C*.

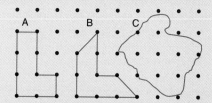

8. Which of the following have the same perimeter?

a.

b.

c.

d.

e.

9. The length of $\overline{AB}$ represents 0.2 mile. Approximate the length of the road shown from points *C* to *D*.

10. Find the perimeter and the area of the given figure.

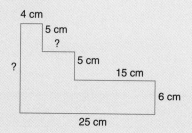

11. A rectangle has the dimensions 9 inches by 12 inches. The area of the rectangle is at least three times the area of a square. What is the largest possible side length of the square?

12. The solid has dimensions as shown. It is made of congruent blocks of what dimensions?

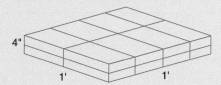

13. A square has side length *x* inches. The width is doubled, and the length is halved. Calculate the area of the new figure.

14. Find the volume of a prism that has a height of 8 centimeters and a rectangular base with the dimensions 5 centimeters by 6 centimeters.

15. Calculate the volume of a box that is 3 inches wide, 1 foot long, and 4 inches tall.

16. You wish to tile the floor of a room that has dimensions as shown. Tiles are 2 feet by 2 feet and are sold in boxes of 12. How many boxes do you need to buy?

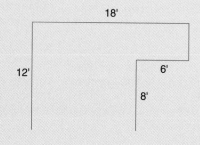

17. Find the area of the parallelogram shown.

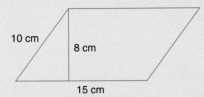

18. A rectangle has an area of 36 square feet. All the side lengths are given in whole numbers. List all of the possibilities for the perimeter of the rectangle.

19. A rectangular garden is to be fenced using 40 feet of fencing. What are the dimensions of the garden of largest area if the sides are measured in whole number units of feet?

20. Jamal buys a square piece of poster board that is 1 foot by 1 foot. How many rectangular pieces can he cut from the board if he only cuts pieces that are the following dimensions:
    a. 3 inches by 4 inches
    b. 3 inches by 5 inches

Applications in the Classroom

1. The formula for the area of a trapezoid with parallel base lengths a and b and height h is $A = \frac{1}{2}(a + b)h$. Describe a cut-and-paste process that will verify this formula.

2. Use either Microsoft Word drawing tools or the Geometer's Sketchpad to create a handout with a grid measurement example such as Example 11-10.

3. Use dotpaper or centimeter-squared paper (see Blackline Master 3 in Appendix C) and create a diagram that could be used in an area and perimeter measurement activity.

4. You ask your students to draw their initials on dotpaper and find the area and perimeter. Ann Ferguson draws her initials as follows. What problems will she encounter in calculating the area and perimeter? How might you clarify your directions for this activity so that the same problems don't occur next year?

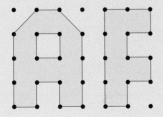

5. Olivia says, "It is easy to calculate perimeter of a figure on a grid; you just count the boxes on the outside. For this figure it is 14." How do you respond?

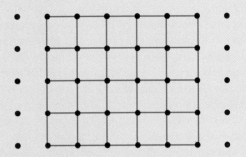

6. Chang says, "The crayon is 2.3 inches long." How do you respond?

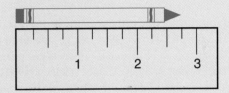

7. Give real-world implications for the calculation of the area and perimeter of a room.

8. Give counterexamples for each of the false statements in problem 3 under "For Your Understanding."

9. Martina says, "Calculating a perimeter is easy. All you have to do is add up all the numbers." How do you respond?

10. Write and solve a real-world application example such as problems 4 or 16 under "For Your Understanding."

11. Create an assessment tool to be used with Example 11-9. Explain why you chose that type of assessment tool. Your assessment tool should address the range of acceptable estimates.

12. Write a lesson plan that describes how you will introduce the topic of area in a first-grade classroom. Follow the format given by your instructor or use the lesson plan format given in Appendix A.

13. Write a lesson plan that describes how you will introduce the topic of perimeter in a second-grade classroom. Follow the format given by your instructor or use the lesson plan format given in Appendix A.

11.4 Relations, Functions, Time, and Temperature

Definition of *Relation*

The words "relation" and "function" do not appear in the early childhood curriculum, but problems involving these ideas certainly do. Intuitively, *relation* suggests a connection, such as the relation "is a brother of." Mathematical relations can describe how two objects compare (or not) or are connected (or not). Formally, a relation R that relates elements of set S to elements of set T is a subset of $S \times T$. The relation is a set of ordered pairs; each ordered pair of the relation gives one element of S and one element of T that are connected or comparable according to the relation. When $S = T$, you can say that R is a relation on set S. Several examples are given below.

Example 11-12: Relations involving various sets. See the table below.

The RST Properties Notice the variety in the examples given in Example 11-12: numbers can be related to other numbers, numbers can be related to sets, sets can be related to other sets, geometric figures can be related to other geometric figures, geometric figures can be related to numbers, and so on. The possibilities for the types of objects involved in a relation are endless. Section 11.3 mentioned that the relation "has equal measure" is reflexive, symmetric, and transitive, whereas the relation "is taller than" is transitive but not reflexive or symmetric. Here are more general definitions of these properties that may or may not apply to any given relation on a given set S.

Reflexive: A relation on set S is reflexive if a is related to a for all $a \in S$.

Symmetric: A relation on set S is symmetric if for all elements $a, b \in S$; whenever a is related to b it is also true that b is related to a.

Transitive: A relation on set S is transitive if for all elements a, b, and $c \in S$; whenever a is related to b and b is related to c, it is also the case that a is related to c.

Teaching Connections

Functions in the Early Childhood Classroom A function is a special type of relation. A *function* is a relation from S to T such that every element $a \in S$ is related to exactly one element $b \in T$. Most of the relation examples found in early childhood materials are functions. Functions may be presented in many forms. The forms of functions most often used in the early childhood classroom include tables, diagrams, graphs, and formulas. Several examples are presented throughout this textbook that involve functions of some form. Some function examples are shown below.

Example 11-13: George has 12 wheels. How many bikes and how many trikes can he make? Find as many answers as you can (first- to third-grade level).

Solution: Students need to understand that a bike has 2 wheels and a trike has 3 wheels. Common strategies include using counters to act out the problem, drawing a picture, or making an organized list. This is a function example because the number of bicycles that can be made depends on the number of tricycles that are made. There are five possible answers.

Example 11-14: I am thinking of a number. If I double my number and then add one, the result is 13. What is my number (second- or third- grade level)?

Solution: Some students will use the strategy of guess and check for this problem. Others will recognize that the strategy of working backward may be appropriate. Other students may wish to solve the algebraic equation $2n + 1 = 13$.

	Relation	Symbol	Description	Example	Nonexample
(a)	Less than	$<$	The whole number a is related to the whole number b, if $a < b$.	$3 < 5$ $(3,5) \in R$	$5 \not< 3$ $(5,3) \notin R$
(b)	Divides	|	The whole number a is related to the whole number b, if $a \mid b$.	$3 \mid 6$ $(3,6) \in R$	$6 \nmid 3$ $(6,3) \notin R$
(c)	Element	$\in$	The whole number a is related to the set A if $a \in A$.	$2 \in \{1,2\}$ $(2,\{1,2\}) \in R$	$3 \notin \{1,2\}$ $(3,\{1,2\}) \notin R$
(d)	Subset	$\subseteq$	The set A is related to the set B, if $A \subseteq B$.	$\{1\} \subseteq \{1,2\}$ $(\{1\},\{1,2\}) \in R$	$\{3\} \not\subseteq \{1,2\}$ $(\{3\},\{1,2\}) \notin R$
(e)	Similar	$\sim$	The geometric figure F is related to the geometric figure G if F is similar to G.	$\bigcirc \sim \bigcirc$ $(\bigcirc,\bigcirc) \in R$	$\bigcirc \not\sim \square$ $(\bigcirc,\square) \notin R$
(f)	Angle measure	$m(\angle \_)$ $= \_\_^\circ$	The angle A is related to the real number x if $m(\angle A) = x^\circ$.	$A\lfloor$ $m(\angle A) = 90^\circ$ $(A, 90) \in R$	$A\lfloor$ $(A, 45) \notin R$

In any case, the unknown number is related to the result 13 by the relation "double then add one." This type of relation is a function. The answer to this particular riddle is six. Young children tend to enjoy both making up and solving these types of riddles (see Activity 11-12).

Example 11-15: Joe and Fred are 40 miles apart headed toward each other on the same road. Joe is walking at the rate of 4 miles per hour. Fred is riding a bicycle at the rate of 12 miles per hour. If they begin walking or biking at the same time, and both maintain a constant rate of speed, how long does it take until they meet (fourth- or fifth-grade level)?

Solution: Distance is a function of both rate and time. A college algebra student might be tempted to solve this type of problem by using the distance formula $d = rt$. However, there are two different rates to consider that complicate the issue. A student in third or fourth grade might solve this problem by using a table or diagram.

Time	Joe Has Walked	Fred Has Biked	Total Distance Traveled
1 hour	4 miles	12 miles	16 miles
2 hours	8 miles	24 miles	32 miles
3 hours	12 miles	36 miles	48 miles—they've already passed each other
$2\frac{1}{2}$ hours	10 miles	30 miles	40 miles

It is clear from the initial diagram that the pair has not met after 2 hours have passed, but they will meet before 3 hours have passed. The diagram shows that after 2 hours, there are only 8 miles left to cover. In an additional half hour, Joe will go 2 more miles, bringing him to mile marker 10, and Fred will go 6 additional miles also bringing him to mile marker 10. They will meet after $2\frac{1}{2}$ hours of travel.

Time

Two important functions that are covered in the early childhood curriculum are time and temperature. Young children generally recognize the importance of learning to tell time, and are often excited to begin learning this skill. Early expe-

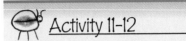

Standards

Florida Sunshine State Standards

Grades 3–5: Algebraic Thinking

Standard 1: The student describes, analyzes, and generalizes a wide variety of patterns, relations, and functions. (MA.D.1.2)
1. describes a wide variety of patterns and relationships through models such as manipulatives, tables, graphs, rules using algebraic symbols.
2. generalizes a pattern, relation, or function to explain how a change in one quantity results in a change in another.

Florida Department of Education, 1996

Activity 11-12   Grades 2–6

Guess My Rule

Materials: Index cards with math operations or rules.

Teacher Statement: I will draw a card with a math rule on it. You will give me numbers and I will tell you what the results are when the math rule is applied to your numbers. The first person to guess the rule gets to draw the next card.

Directions: The teacher draws the card "multiply by 3." The first student gives the input 2 and the teacher replies with 6. Students continue to give input values until a student is able to guess the rule.

riences entail the use of terms such as "before" and "after" and the sequencing of events. At around the kindergarten level, children write numerals on a circular clock face and learn to tell time to the hour. At this level, children learn the difference between an *analog* clock (one that has a minute hand and an hour hand) and a *digital* clock (one that has a digital display). Without looking at a clock, can you recall which is longer, the minute hand or the hour hand?

Measurement requires a certain degree of accuracy or precision that even for a routine or everyday activity is sometimes overlooked. Let's illustrate with an example. If there is a clock in the room with you, do not look at it. On a scrap piece of paper, draw a clock face with hands that illustrate the

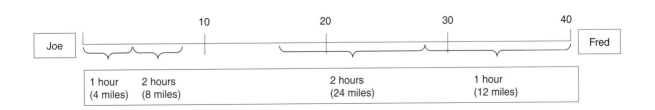

🐝 A Glimpse into the Classroom

Telling Time in Preschool

On this particular day, preschool teacher Miss Cynthia Morelli did not plan to give a lesson on telling time in her disability/Head Start classroom. However, following the third query of a certain child "Is it time for lunch yet?" she decided that because it was not yet time for lunch, it was time for a lesson about telling time.

Miss Morelli set a model clock for the correct time to go to lunch and placed it near the classroom clock. She told the students that the model clock was set for the time to go to lunch, and when the classroom clock matched the model clock, it would be time to go. She was not interrupted by any more time queries until later when the hungry student excitedly exclaimed, "They match; it's time! It's time for lunch!" Indeed, the clocks did match and it was lunchtime.

time 4:30. Did your clock face resemble the one shown here? What is incorrect or inaccurate about this face?

When asked to draw a clock that represents a given digital time, many adults will draw the hour hand of the clock pointing directly at the given hour regardless of the number of minutes in the expression. To accurately reflect the time 4:30, the hour hand should point between the 4 and the 5. How will you explain to students how to read a clock when the hour hand is not directly pointed to a numeral?

You may wish to remember this example when purchasing clock materials to use in your classroom. Some student practice clocks are geared so that once a time is correctly set, the hour hand moves in conjunction with the minute hand. For example, if the clock was set at 4:00 by pointing the hour hand directly at the 4 and the minute hand at the 12, when the minute hand is moved so that it points at the 6, the hour hand automatically moves and the time 4:30 is accurately displayed. Nongeared student clocks do not offer this feature. However, if you cannot afford to purchase enough geared student clocks for each student to have one, many teaching manuals include instructions for making a clock using a paper plate, cutout hands, and a wire brad to fasten the hands to the clock. If clocks are handmade, every student will have one to use.

Children typically learn to tell time to the half hour by the first grade. At around the second-grade level, children learn to tell time at 5-minute intervals. You must be sure that children are proficient at the skill of skip counting by fives before beginning this type of lesson. The phrases "half past," "quarter past," and "quarter to" are introduced. Time equivalences also are discussed—"The time 'two forty-five' is equivalent to 'quarter to three.' " The number of minutes between two given events can be calculated—"Lunch begins at quarter past eleven and ends at quarter to twelve. How many minutes do we have to eat lunch?" The symbols A.M. for times from midnight to noon and P.M. for times from noon to midnight are introduced. A timed event such as "How many stars can you draw in 1 minute" both reinforces place value and counting principles and familiarizes students with the length of a 1-minute interval.

By the third grade, students learn to tell time to the nearest minute. They learn to solve problems involving elapsed time that deal with both hours and minutes. Such problems may include both A.M. and P.M. times. Fourth graders are introduced to time zones and more complicated word problems: "Carol gets on a plane in Cleveland, Ohio at 7:50 A.M. When she gets off the plane in Dallas, Texas, a local clock shows the time as 9:50 A.M. How long was the flight?" (The answer is *not* 2 hours.) A similar type of problem at this level involves the number of days between two events. Students must learn the number of days in each month even in the case of a leap year.

Temperature

In initial temperature activities children learn terms such as "hot" and "cold." At the preschool or kindergarten level children learn to sequence or order the seasons of the year and discuss what types of temperatures to expect during each season. The thermometer is introduced at around the first-grade level. School thermometers are usually marked in both degrees Celsius (C) and degrees Fahrenheit (F). A beginning activity might involve children matching a picture of a thermometer showing a temperature such as 80 °F (27 °C) to a scene of either a sunny summer day or a blustery winter day. The topic of temperature can be useful in introducing other mathematical topics such as decimals. Almost every first-grade child can explain the significance of 98.6 °F.

By the second grade, children learn to read specific temperatures from a given picture or model of a thermometer. They also perform activities such as coloring thermometers to illustrate a given temperature and use subtraction to calculate changes in temperature. Many third-grade textbook series introduce negative temperatures such as −10 °C. At this level children learn the facts that water freezes at 32 °F (0 °C) and boils at 212 °F (100 °C). They also learn to estimate using temperatures without looking at a thermometer—"It is 25 °C outside. Which is more appropriate: a coat or shorts?" With no thermometer to look at, this decision must be based on an interpretation of the numerical temperature alone.

At around the fourth- or fifth-grade level, children learn to use ratios to calculate the temperature on one scale when given a numerical value on another scale. Example 11-16 illustrates this process. This problem is further discussed in Problem Set 11.4.

Example 11-16: Problem solving by logical reasoning (fourth- or fifth-grade level).

Without using a thermometer, give the Fahrenheit equivalent of 50° Celsius.

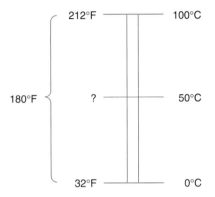

Solution: You know that 32 °F = 0 °C and 212 °F = 100 °C. Mark these facts on a diagram. Both temperature units use consistent, evenly spaced scales, so 50 °C, which is exactly halfway between 0 °C and 100 °C, will correspond to the temperature exactly halfway between 32 °F and 212 °F. This is a range of 180°. The halfway point is 90° warmer than 32 °F. Thus, 50 °C = 122 °F.

Both topics, time and temperature, will provide natural connections to other subjects. Temperature is often used in science experiments. Time lines occur frequently in social studies. It is a common exercise to calculate the length of time between two historical events. Students can research information on time zones when studying other states and countries. You will find many other natural occurrences of these topics in real-life situations and within the classroom curriculum.

Problem Set 11.4

For Your Understanding

1. Determine whether relations (a), (b), (d), and (e) of Example 11-12 are reflexive, symmetric, or transitive.

2. Determine whether each of the following are reflexive, symmetric, or transitive relations on the set of people in your class.
   a. Is the same weight as
   b. Is a different age than
   c. Has more children than

3. Shirley buys one candy bar and three packs of gum for $1.55. Ed buys three candy bars and one pack of gum for $1.85. If Laura wants to buy one candy bar and one pack of gum, how much will she spend?

4. You have an unlimited amount of 3¢ and 7¢ stamps. No package will cost less than 34¢ to mail. What amounts of postage from 34¢ to $1.00 can you form?

5. January 1, 2004, falls on Thursday. Calculate the day of the week of January 1, 2005, and January 1, 2006.

6. A bus trip left Reno, Nevada, at 10:00 A.M. headed for Chicago, Illinois. Two drivers took turns driving and sleeping so that the bus could continue moving. The trip took 30 hours. What was the local time in Chicago, Illinois, when the bus arrived?

7. Cindy gets on a plane in Cincinnati, Ohio, at 7:30 P.M. When she arrives in Frankfurt, Germany, a local clock shows the time as 11:55. What time is shown on Cindy's watch if it is still set on Ohio time? How long was the flight?

8. Use ratios or logical reasoning to complete the table of temperature equivalences. Do not look at a thermometer.

50 °C	122 °F	110 °C	
40 °C		100 °C	
30 °C		90 °C	
20 °C		80 °C	
10 °C		70 °C	
0 °C	32 °F	60 °C	

9. Find the temperature equivalences without looking at a thermometer. You may wish to extend the table from problem 8 above.
   a. 248 °F = _____ °C
   b. −10 °C = _____ °F
   c. 25 °C = _____ °F
   d. 59 °F = _____ °C

10. Between 11:30 A.M. on Monday and 12:30 P.M. on Tuesday, how many times does the minute hand pass the hour hand of an analog clock?

11. At what different times of the day does the time on a digital clock appear exactly the same forward and backward? Do not consider the colon separating hours and minutes. For example, 8:18 is one such time.

12. Fill each blank with C (Celsius) or F (Fahrenheit).
    a. You wear mittens when it is 28 °_____.
    b. You need a fan when it is 38 °_____.
    c. The surface temperature of Mars ranges from −200 °_____ to 30 °_____.

Applications in the classroom

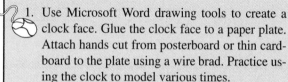

1. Use Microsoft Word drawing tools to create a clock face. Glue the clock face to a paper plate. Attach hands cut from posterboard or thin cardboard to the plate using a wire brad. Practice using the clock to model various times.

2. Problem: Klee Ning began cleaning his room at 1:57. He finished at 4:13. How long did Klee spend cleaning?

   Sally's Solution:

   $$\begin{array}{r} 3\ 10\ 13 \\ \cancel{4\!:\!1\,3} \\ -\ 1\!:\!5\ 7 \\ \hline 2\!:\!5\ 6 \end{array}$$

   Sally's answer is 2 hours and 56 minutes. You are the teacher. How do you respond?

3. Problem: It takes Mo Vie 15 minutes to drive to the theater. He estimates that he will spend 90 minutes watching the film before driving home. How long will the entire trip take?

   Leann's Solution:

   $$\begin{array}{r} 1\ \ 1 \\ :15 \\ +\ :90 \\ \hline :15 \\ 1:20 \end{array}$$

   Leann's answer is that the trip will take 1 hour and 20 minutes. You are the teacher. How do you respond?

4. Write and solve two word problems involving time, dates, and/or historical events. Indicate the grade level of your problems.

5. Make up three temperature situations such as in problem 12 under "For Your Understanding."

6. Find or draw four pictures, one for each season, that could be used for temperature activities.

7. Create materials for Activity 11-12. Indicate what grade level your materials are appropriate for.

8. Create or find a game to practice time or temperature skills. What objective from the NCTM model (or from your state or district model) does the game address? Be sure to state what grade level your game is appropriate for.

9. Choose a grade level from K–3. Create and solve three "I am thinking of a number" riddles appropriate for that grade level. Make one riddle for each level of student: below-grade-level ability, average ability, above-grade-level ability.

10. Create and solve a function example involving money such as problems 3 or 4 under "For Your Understanding."

11. Create an assessment tool to be used with the "I am thinking of a number" riddles that you created in problem 9 above. Explain why you chose that type of assessment tool.

12. Write a lesson plan that describes how you will introduce the topic of reading a thermometer in a second-grade classroom. Follow the format given by your instructor or use the lesson plan format given in Appendix A.

13. Look up any measurement topic in an elementary-level textbook. Photocopy or copy by hand one example or problem that you think is interesting or unusual and indicate why. What objective from the NCTM model (or from your state or district model) does the example or problem address? Be sure to state what grade-level text you are using.

14. Find and print a measurement activity from the Web. State what grade level you think the activity would be appropriate for. What objective from the NCTM model (or from your state or district model) does the activity address?

15. Choose an activity from this chapter that is written as an individual student activity. Indicate how you could implement the activity as a collaborative learning experience.

16. Choose one of the books in the children's literature section of the references for this chapter. Give a brief description of the content of the book and explain how you could incorporate the book into a math lesson.

17. Make up two writing prompts or stems that fit in with material or activities from this chapter.

References

Children's Literature References

Adams, Pam. (1989). *Ten beads tall.* Swindon, Wiltshire: Child's Play International.

Carle, Eric. (1977). *The grouchy ladybug.* New York: HarperCollins.

Conboy, Fiona. (1997). *Forgetful Ted: A book about telling time.* Hauppauge, NY: Brainwaves Limited.

Derubertis, Barbara. (2000). *Lulu's lemonade.* New York: Kane Press.

Hightower, Susan. (1997). *Twelve sails to one lizard.* New York: Simon & Schuster.

Keenan, Sheila. (1996). *The biggest fish* (Hello Math Reader Level 3). New York: Scholastic.

Leedy, Loreen. (2000). *Measuring Penny.* New York: Henry Holt.

Ling, Bettina. (1997). *The fattest, tallest, biggest snowman ever* (Hello Math Reader Level 3). New York: Scholastic.

Lionni, Leo. (1960). *Inch by inch.* New York: Scholastic.

Myller, Rolf. (1991). *How big is a foot.* New York: Bantam Doubleday Dell.

Pluckrose, Henry. (1987). *Big and little (think about).* London: Franklin Watts.

Schreiber, Anne. (1995). *Slower than a snail* (Hello Math Reader Level 2). New York: Scholastic.

Walter, Marion. (1971). *Make a bigger puddle: Make a smaller worm.* New York: Scholastic.

Wells, Rosemary. (2001). *How many, how much.* New York: Penguin Putnam.

Teacher Resources

Charles, R. I., Chancellor, D., Harcourt, L., Moore, D., Schielack, J. F., Van de Walle, J., & Wortzman, R. (1999). *Math grade 3.* Scott Foresman: Addison Wesley.

Florida Department of Education. (1996). *Florida Sunshine State Standards.* (n.d.). Retrieved December 8, 2003 from http://www.firn.edu/doe/curric/prek12/ frame2.htm

Liedtke, W. W. (1990). Measurement. In J. N. Payne (Ed.), *Mathematics for the young child* (pp. 229–249). Reston, VA: National Council of Teachers of Mathematics.

National Council of Teachers of Mathematics. (2000). *Principles and standards for school mathematics.* Reston, VA: Author.

Texas Education Agency. (1998). *Chapter 111. Texas Essential Knowledge and Skills for Mathematics.* Retrieved November 12, 2003 from http://www.tea.state.tx.us/rules/ tac/ch111toc.html

Selected Research Books and Articles

Hiebert, J. (1984). Why do some children have difficulty learning measurement concepts? *Arithmetic Teacher, 31*(7), 19–24.

Nitabach, E., & Lehrer, R. (2002). Developing spatial sense through area measurement. In D. L. Chambers (Ed.), *Putting research into practice in the elementary grades: Readings from NCTM journals* (pp. 183–187). Reston, VA: National Council of Teachers of Mathematics.

Further Reading

Benswanger, R. (1988, September). Discovering perimeter and area with Logo. *Arithmetic Teacher, 36,* 18–25.

Hart, K. (1984). Which comes first—Length, area, or volume? *Arithmetic Teacher, 31*(9), 16–18, 26.

Higgins, J. (Ed.). (1979). *A metric handbook for teachers.* Reston, VA: National Council of Teachers of Mathematics.

Johnson, G. L. (1988, October). Using a metric unit to help preservice teachers appreciate the value of manipulative materials. *Arithmetic Teacher, 35,* 14–20.

Petitto, A. L. (1990). Development of numberline and measurement concepts. *Cognition and Instruction, 7,* 55–78.

Rectanus, C. (1998). *Math by all means: Area and perimeter, grades 5–6.* Sausalito, CA: Math Solutions Publications.

Rhone, L. (1995). Measurement in a primary-grade integrated curriculum. In P. A. House (Ed.), *Connecting mathematics across the curriculum* (pp. 124–133). Reston, VA: National Council of Teachers of Mathematics.

Shaw, J. M., & Cliatt, M. J. P. (1989). Developing measurement sense. In P. R. Trafton (Ed.), *New directions for elementary school mathematics* (pp. 149–155). Reston, VA: National Council of Teachers of Mathematics.

Taloumis, T. (1975, November). The relationship of area conservation to area measurement as affected by sequence of presentations of Piagetian area tasks to boys and girls in grades one through three. *Journal for Research in Mathematics Education,* 232–242.

Wilson, P. S., & Osborne, A. (1988). Foundational ideas in teaching about measure. In T. R. Post (Ed.), *Teaching mathematics in grades K–8* (pp. 78–110). Boston: Allyn & Bacon.

Wilson, P. S., & Rowland, R. (1993). Teaching measurement. In R. J. Jensen (Ed.), *Research ideas for the classroom: Early childhood mathematics* (pp. 171–194). New York: Macmillan.

Answers to Selected Problems

CHAPTER 2

Problem Set 2.1

1. 104, 140, 203, 230, 302, 320, 401 and 410.

3. There are eight different solutions. The first missing object is either the large blue circle or the large red square. The second missing object is either the small blue square or the large blue triangle. The third missing object is either the small yellow triangle or the large blue triangle.

5. Approximately 2.5 gallons.

7. 746-6363

9. Joey made $10 on the transaction. Chandler made $5.

Problem Set 2.2

1. There are 24 different combinations.

3. The camera cost $70 and the player cost $50.

5. Two dimes, three nickels, and two pennies

7. a. 3
   b. 12

Problem Set 2.3

1. a. Invalid

3. a. Valid
   b. Invalid

CHAPTER 3

Problem Set 3.1

1. a. {Alabama, Georgia}
   b. {Michigan, Indiana, Kentucky, West Virginia Pennsylvania}
   c. Ø

3. a. {4, 8, 12, 16, 20, . . . }
   b. {2, 3, 5, 7, 11, 13, 17, 19}
   c. $\{x \in N \mid x \text{ is even}\}$
   d. $\{x \in N \mid x \text{ is a multiple of five that is less than 25}\}$

5. a. True
   b. True
   c. True
   d. False
   e. True
   f. False
   g. True
   h. False

7. a. $J \cap L = \{1, 3, 5, 15\}$
   b. 15 is the greatest common divisor

9. a. $\{(1, a), (1, b)\}$
   b. $\{(1, a), (2, a), (a, a), (1, b), (2, b), (a, b)\}$
   c. $S = \{x, y, z\}$ $T = \{y, 1\}$

11. a. $A \cap B$

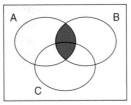

    b. $(A \cap B) \cap C$

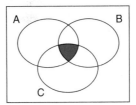

c. $\overline{A \cup B}$

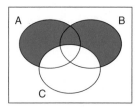

d. $(A \cup B) - C$

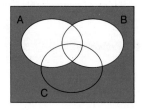

13. Yes, Cricket is smart.

15. Type A, Leroy, Oscar; Type B, Nicky; Type AB, Mike; Type O, Paula, Min

Problem Set 3.2

1. a. 13, 16, 19
   b. 21, 34, 55
   c. 17, 34, 33
   d. *J, A, S*
   e. *N, T, E*

3. a. 1234, 12345, 123456
   b. 312, 301, 290
   c. 256, 8192, 2,097,152
   d. 16, 48, 43
   e. *P, S, V*
   f. *S, E, N*

5. a. 5
   b. 1

Problem Set 3.3

1. Two, ordinal; five, identification; three, cardinal

CHAPTER 4

Problem Set 4.1

1. a. $64 + (3 \times 16) + 4 = 116$
   b. $135 = 2 \times 64 + 4 + 3 =$
   c. Three cases, three boxes, two lines, and three singles

3. a. 3323_{four}, 3330_{four}, 3331_{four}, 3332_{four}, 3333_{four}, 10000_{four}, 10001_{four}
   b. 3321_{four}, 3320_{four}, 3313_{four}, 3312_{four}, 3311_{four}, 3310_{four}, 3303_{four}

5. a. $1 + (2 \times 4^2) + (3 \times 4^4) + (2 \times 4^6) + 4^8 = 74,529$
   b. $18,740 = 16,384 + 2,048 + 256 + 48 + 4 = 4^7 + (2 \times 4^5) + 4^4 + (3 \times 4^2) + 4^1 = 10210310_{four}$

7. a.
$$\begin{array}{r} 1\,1 \\ 3\,0\,2\,1_{four} \\ +\,2\,0\,3\,3_{four} \\ \hline 1\,1\,1\,2\,0_{four} \end{array}$$

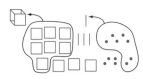

   b.
$$\begin{array}{r} 2\,3\,5\,5 \\ \not{3}\not{0}\not{2}\not{1}_{four} \\ -\,2\,0\,3\,3_{four} \\ \hline 3\,2\,2_{four} \end{array}$$

9. a. 0, 1, 2, 3, 4, 5, 6, 7, 8, 9, *T, E, W, H*
   b. $1_{fourteen}$, $2_{fourteen}$, $3_{fourteen}$, $4_{fourteen}$, $5_{fourteen}$, $6_{fourteen}$, $7_{fourteen}$ $8_{fourteen}$, $9_{fourteen}$, $T_{fourteen}$, $E_{fourteen}$, $W_{fourteen}$, $H_{fourteen}$, $10_{fourteen}$, $11_{fourteen}$, $12_{fourteen}$, $13_{fourteen}$, $14_{fourteen}$, $15_{fourteen}$, $16_{fourteen}$, $17_{fourteen}$, $18_{fourteen}$, $19_{fourteen}$, $1T_{fourteen}$, $1E_{fourteen}$, $1W_{fourteen}$, $1H_{fourteen}$, $20_{fourteen}$, $21_{fourteen}$, $22_{fourteen}$
   c. $2799_{fourteen}$, $279T_{fourteen}$, $279E_{fourteen}$, $279W_{fourteen}$, $279H_{fourteen}$, $27T0_{fourteen}$, $27T1_{fourteen}$, $27T2_{fourteen}$, $27T3_{fourteen}$, $27T4_{fourteen}$
   d. $100_{fourteen}$, $HH_{fourteen}$, $HW_{fourteen}$, $HE_{fourteen}$, $HT_{fourteen}$, $H9_{fourteen}$, $H8_{fourteen}$, $H7_{fourteen}$, $H6_{fourteen}$, $H5_{fourteen}$

11. a. $H\,W\,T\,1_{fourteen}$
    b. $4\,8\,4\,H_{fourteen}$

13. a.
$$\begin{array}{r} 1 \\ 6\,3\,5_{seven} \\ +\,4\,0\,6_{seven} \\ \hline 1\,3\,4\,4_{seven} \end{array}$$
    b.
$$\begin{array}{r} 2\,12 \\ 6\,\not{3}\,\not{5}_{seven} \\ -\,4\,0\,6_{seven} \\ \hline 2\,2\,6_{seven} \end{array}$$

Problem Set 4.2

1. $3 \times 100,000,000 + 2 \times 1,000,000 + 4 \times 10,000 + 7 \times 1,000 + 1 \times 10 + 9 \times 1$

3. a. 2,995,040

    b. & c. 2,995,000

    d., e., & f. 3,000,000

5. 8 hours and 20 minutes

7. 458 pages

6. How many units or how many singles.

10. a. The student is not regrouping. Use manipulatives and encourage estimation.

    b. The student is not considering place value. Use manipulatives and encourage students to check their answers.

    c. Same as (b) above.

Problem Set 4.3

1. There are 6 ways: $\cap \cap | \, |$, $\cap | \cap |$, $| \cap \, \cap |$, $\cap | \, | \cap$, $| \cap | \cap$, $| \, | \cap \cap$.

3. a. $\overline{M}\overline{C}\overline{C}\,\overline{M}\overline{X}\,CCCIV$

    b. $\overline{X}\overline{C}\overline{V}\,MCMLII$

5. $E = 100, \nabla = 10, 0 = 1$

CHAPTER 5

Problem Set 5.1

1. a.
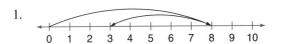

    b.

3. Addends, sum

5. Starting in the top left corner and reading clockwise, the facts are: $7 = 6 + 1$, $1 + 5 = 6$, $6 + 9 = 15$, and $15 = 8 + 7$.

Problem Set 5.2

1. Only (a), (d), and (f) are correct.

3. $3 + 5 = 8 \quad 8 + 5 = 3 \quad 8 - 3 = 5 \quad 8 - 5 = 3$

5. No, subtraction is not commutative. For example, $8 - 3$ is not equal to $3 - 8$.

1.
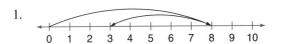

Problem Set 5.3

1. (5-30-1) (a) \$4 (b) \$2 (c) \$5
    (5-30-2) (a) 110 (b) 70 (c) 380
    (5-30-3) (a) 700 (b) 300 (c) 400
    (5-30-4) (a) 500 (b) 300 (c) 300

3. $\begin{aligned} &200 + 70 + 3 \\ &+ 100 + 20 + 8 \\ \hline \end{aligned}$
    $300 + 90 + 11 = 300 + 90 + 10 + 1 =$
    $300 + 100 + 1 = 401$

5. $\begin{aligned} &200 + 70 + 3 \\ &- (100 + 20 + 8) \end{aligned} \quad = \quad \begin{aligned} &200 + 60 + 13 \\ &- (100 + 20 + 8) \\ \hline &100 + 40 + 5 = 145 \end{aligned}$

Problem Set 5.4

1. a. $-2 < 0$

    b. $-5 > -6$

    c. $3 > -4$

3. a.
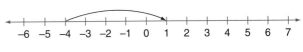

    b. ⊕ ⊕ ⊕ ⊕ $-4 + 5 = 1$
        ⊖ ⊖ ⊖ ⊖ ☺

5. a. If a pile of 25 red chips is added to a pile of 83 red chips, the result is a pile of 108 red chips. Hence, $-25 + (-83) = -108$.

    b. Start with a pile of 300 red chips and add a pile of 842 black chips. Eliminate the 300 zero pairs leaving 542 black chips. So $-300 + 842 = 542$.

    c. Combine a pile of 261 black chips with a pile of 560 red chips. Remove the 261 zero pairs leaving $560 - 261 = 299$ red chips. So $261 + (-560) = -299$.

Problem Set 5.5

1. a. The student added instead of subtracting. Have the student draw a picture to solve the problem. Emphasize the checking of answers.

    b. The student ignored the zero and doesn't regroup properly. The student should try the problems with concrete manipulatives. Emphasize estimation and checking answers.

c. The student regrouped incorrectly by equating a unit of 10,000 with 10 hundreds instead of 9 thousands and 10 hundreds. The student needs to practice problems involving a zero in the minuend. Concrete models can be used when the minuend is less than 10,000. Estimation and checking answers should be emphasized.

3. The audience picks the first number; suppose they pick 248.
The magician picks the 9s complement of the first number.
The audience picks the third number; suppose they pick 179.
The magician picks the 9s complement of this number.
The audience picks the fifth number; suppose they pick 309.
The magician picks the 9s complement of this number.
The audience picks the seventh number; suppose they pick 251.
The magician amazes the audience by immediately writing the sum. In this example the sum is
In general, the sum is 3,000 plus the last number picked by the audience minus 3.

$$
\begin{array}{r}
248 \\
751 \\
179 \\
820 \\
+\ 309 \\
690 \\
\underline{251} \\
3{,}248.
\end{array}
$$

5. Two examples are $378 - 200 = 178$ and $299 - 121 = 178$. There are other answers.

CHAPTER 6

Problem Set 6.1

1. a. $4 \times 3 = 12$ meals
   b. $5 \times 3 = 15$ snacks
   c. $4 \times 5 \times 3 = 60$ jumbo meals

3. Factors, product

5. a. Zero element
   b. Identity element
   c. Commutativity
   d. Associativity
   e. Distributive property of multiplication over addition

7. a.

b.

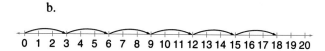

Problem Set 6.2

1. a. Appropriate equations are $20 \div 4 = 5$ and $4 \times \underline{\ \ } = 20$. The type of problem is distributive.
   b. Appropriate equations are $20 \div 4 = 5$ and $\underline{\ \ } \times 4 = 20$. The type of problem is subtractive.

3. The dividend is the total number of objects, the divisor is the number of objects in each set, and the quotient is the number of sets.

5. a. $(4 \times 5) - (2 \times 3) = 14$
   b. $(2 \times 3) + 1 = 7$
   c.

   d.

7. The rule is $1 \div n = \dfrac{1}{n}$.

Problem Set 6.3

1. a. $250 \times 40 = 10{,}000$
   b. $200 \times 40 = 8{,}000$
   c. $240 \times 40 = 9{,}600$

3. a. $48 \times 7 = 336$
   b. $307 \times 6 = 1{,}842$

5. a. One method is $40 \times 3 = 120$, take away two sets of three is 114. There are other answers.
   b. One method is $20 \times 5 = 100$, then $100 \times 18 = 1{,}800$.

7. a. There are 32 different answers.
   b. The dividend should be one of the following: 334, 366, 398, 654, 686, 718, or 974.
   c. 254

1. Let's compute 3×46. That's three sets of 46. There are 18 singles; regroup 10 of the singles. Also regroup 10 longs to get a flat (10 tens to get a hundred). The result is 1 flat, 3 longs, and 8 singles. So, $3 \times 46 = 138$.

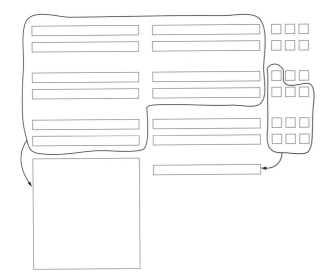

5. A calculator division is performed to determine the quotient. For example, $254 \div 8 = 31.75$. The calculator can then be used to find the remainder by multiplying the quotient and the divisor. For example, $31 \times 8 = 248$. Subtract this product from the dividend to determine the remainder. For example, $254 - 248 = 6$. Thus, $254 \div 8 = 31\ R6$.

9. c, d, b, a

Problem Set 6.4

1. a. Student interpreted the word "share" to indicate a division operation. Student should draw a picture or use concrete objects or use estimation. The correct answer is $80 - (5 \times 10) = 30$. Encourage the student to use the problem-solving process. They must *understand* the problem before performing any calculations.

   b. Student may have misplaced the 3 and the 0 in the product 30. Encourage estimation. Use concrete objects to help the student understand why the 0 is placed in the ones column and the 3 is placed in the tens column.

   c. In the tens column, student probably added $3 + 3 = 6$ and then multiplied $6 \times 4 = 24$. Use concrete objects to show student why the correct process is to multiply and then add.

   d. The student did not properly align the digits of the quotient, ignored the zero in the dividend, and has difficulty regrouping in subtraction. Use concrete objects. Make sure that students understand subtraction before introducing division.

3. a. 27
   b. 72
   c. 30
   d. 15
   e. 37
   f. 47

CHAPTER 7

Problem Set 7.1

1. a. 66
   b. 72
   c. 8
   d. 20

3. a. Seven squared is 49.
   b. Five cubed is 125.
   c. Two to the sixth power is 64.

5. a. Algebraic calculator:

   [12] [+] [36] [÷] [2] [×] [3] [=]

   Arithmetic calculator:

   [36] [÷] [2] [×] [3] [+] [12] [=]

   b. Algebraic calculator:

   [12] [+] [36] [=] [÷] [2] [×] [3] [=]

   Arithmetic calculator:

   [12] [+] [36] [÷] [2] [×] [3] [=]

   c. Algebraic calculator:

   [5] [×] [2] [×] [2] [−] [3] [×] [4] [=]

   Arithmetic calculator:

   [5] [×] [2] [×] [2] [−] [12] [=]

   d. Algebraic calculator:

   [30] [−] [2] [×] [5] [+] [6] [=]

   Arithmetic calculator:

   [30] [−] [10] [+] [6] [=]

Problem Set 7.2

1. a. False
   b. True
   c. True
   d. False
   e. True

3. a.

1 2 3 4   6   9 12 18 36

b.

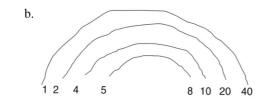

1 2 4   5   8 10 20 40

c.

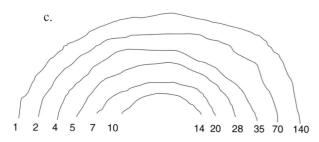

1 2 4 5 7 10   14 20 28 35 70 140

5. The smallest possible number of members in the band is 59.

7.

Number	Factors	Classification
7	1, 7	prime
8	1, 2, 4, 8	other
9	1, 3, 9	prime squared
10	1, 2, 5, 10	product of two primes
11	1, 11	prime
12	1, 2, 3, 4, 6, 12	other
13	1, 13	prime
14	1, 2, 7, 14	product of two primes
15	1, 3, 5, 15	product of two primes
16	1, 2, 4, 8, 16	other
17	1, 17	prime
18	1, 2, 3, 6, 9, 18	other
19	1, 19	prime
20	1, 2, 4, 5, 10, 20	other

9. Try dividing by 2, 3, 5, 7, 11, 13, 17, 19, and 23. You will find that $1,357 = 23 \times 59$ is composite.

Problem Set 7.3

1. a. False; 21 is divisible by 3

   b. True

   c. False; 7 is divisible by 1 and 7

   d. True

3. A whole number n is divisible by 8 if and only if the number represented by the last three digits of n is di-

visible by 8. The test works since if $n = ?abc$, then $n = ? \times 1,000 + abc$. Since 1,000 is divisible by 8, the overall number will be if the number represented by abc is divisible by 8. The number 23,816 is divisible by 8 since 816 is. The number 16,405 is not divisible by 8 since 405 is not divisible by 8.

5.

Is the number:	(a) 965	(b) 1,422
divisible by 2?	no—last digit	yes—last digit
divisible by 3?	no—sum of digits = 20	yes—sum of digits = 9
divisible by 4?	no—65 isn't divisible by 4	no—22 isn't divisible by 4
divisible by 5?	yes—last digit	no—last digit
divisible by 6?	no—not divisible by 2 and 3	yes—is divisible by 2 and 3
divisible by 9?	no—sum of digits = 20	yes—sum of digits = 9
divisible by 10?	no—last digit	no—last digit

7. a. True

   b. False; 18 is divisible by both 2 and 6 but not 12

   c. True

9.

```
        180
       /   \
     10     18
    / \    / \
   2   5  2   9        180 = 2² × 3² × 5
             / \
            3   3
```

$$180 = 2^2 \times 3^2 \times 5$$

11. $63,000,000 = 63 \times 10^6 = 7 \times 9 \times 10^6 = 2^6 \times 3^2 \times 5^6 \times 7$

13. The last digit must be 0 or 6.

Problem Set 7.4

1. $GCF(24, 18) = 6$. She can make 6 teams, each containing 4 girls and 3 boys.

3. $LCM(8, 12, 9) = 72$. The first locker to get all three presents is locker 72.

5. The tiles can be 1 by 1, 2 by 2, 3 by 3, or 6 by 6 feet each.

7. a. 180

   b. 1,764

   c. 120

9. a. 6

   b. 1

   c. 1

11. Four adult steps will put them all on the right foot.

13. The numbers are 9 and 270, or 18 and 135, or 27 and 90, or 45 and 54.

15. Each milkshake is $1.79. The total cost is $42.96.

1. Tell Jackson that this is a wonderful question. Ask Jackson to try to find the answer. Jackson should discover that the least common factor for any pair of numbers is 1.

CHAPTER 8

Problem Set 8.1

1. Models that illustrate the equivalence of $\frac{3}{6}$ and $\frac{1}{2}$:

   a. Number line model

   $$\frac{1}{2} = \frac{3}{6}$$

   b. Shaded area model

   c. Set model

   d. Fraction piece model

1					
$\frac{1}{2}$			$\frac{1}{2}$		
$\frac{1}{6}$	$\frac{1}{6}$	$\frac{1}{6}$	$\frac{1}{6}$	$\frac{1}{6}$	$\frac{1}{6}$

3. a.

   (number line with points at $\frac{3}{5}$ and $\frac{5}{3}$ between 0, 1, 2)

   b. $2\frac{2}{3} = \frac{8}{3}$

5. a. $2\frac{3}{4}$

   b. $2\frac{1}{3}$

   c. $\frac{29}{8}$

   d. $\frac{13}{6}$

7. You have $\frac{1}{8}$ of the box left for yourself.

9. a. $\frac{20}{30} = \frac{2}{3}$

   b. $\frac{9}{36} = \frac{1}{4}$ or $\frac{10}{35} = \frac{2}{7}$

   c. $\frac{100}{800} = \frac{1}{8}$

11. $n = \frac{n}{1}$

6. Ask Malcolm to show both $\frac{7}{3}$ and $\frac{9}{4}$ using the fraction piece model. Then ask if the fractions are equivalent and have Malcolm explain how each model shows 2 R1 and how to interpret the remainder in terms of the fraction piece model.

Problem Set 8.2

1. a. $\frac{1}{2} = \frac{2}{4}$

   b. $\frac{1}{2} = \frac{3}{6}$

   c. $\frac{1}{2} = \frac{4}{8}$

   d. $\frac{1}{2} = \frac{6}{12}$

   e. $\frac{1}{3} = \frac{2}{6}$

   f. $\frac{1}{3} = \frac{4}{12}$

   g. $\frac{1}{3} = \frac{8}{24}$

   h. $\frac{3}{4} = \frac{6}{8}$

   i. $\frac{3}{4} = \frac{9}{12}$

3. Equations should be accompanied by appropriate fraction model drawings:

   a. $\frac{1}{3} + \frac{5}{8} = \frac{8}{24} + \frac{15}{24} = \frac{23}{24}$

   b. $\frac{2}{3} - \frac{1}{2} = \frac{4}{6} - \frac{3}{6} = \frac{1}{6}$

5. a. $\dfrac{29}{6}$

b. $7\dfrac{3}{4}$

c. $2\dfrac{12}{24} = 2\dfrac{1}{2}$ or $\dfrac{10}{4} = \dfrac{5}{2} = 2\dfrac{1}{2}$

d. $1\dfrac{11}{24}$

7. $\dfrac{13}{30} < \dfrac{7}{15} = \dfrac{14}{30} < \dfrac{1}{2} = \dfrac{15}{30}$

9. a. $46\dfrac{2}{8} + 27\dfrac{7}{8} = 73\dfrac{9}{8} = 74\dfrac{1}{8}$

b. $46\dfrac{2}{8} - 27\dfrac{7}{8} = 45\dfrac{10}{8} - 27\dfrac{7}{8} = 18\dfrac{3}{8}$

11. a. $\dfrac{7}{2} \times \dfrac{54}{5} = \dfrac{378}{10} = 37\dfrac{8}{10} = 37\dfrac{4}{5}$

b $(3 \times 10) + \left(3 \times \dfrac{4}{5}\right) +$

$\left(\dfrac{1}{2} \times 10\right) + \left(\dfrac{1}{2} \times \dfrac{4}{5}\right) =$

$30 + \dfrac{12}{5} + 5 + \dfrac{2}{5} = 35\dfrac{14}{5} = 37\dfrac{4}{5}$

13. a. $\dfrac{8}{9} \div \dfrac{4}{9} = 2$

b. $2\dfrac{1}{2} \div \dfrac{3}{4} = 3\dfrac{1}{3}$

15. Twenty kittens have long hair.

17. Joan can make seven bows.

19. One third of the wall is unpainted.

21. There is three eighths of a yard of fabric left over.

1. a. 4 pieces each the size of $\frac{1}{8}$ of a pizza is $\frac{1}{2}$ of a pizza, so $4 \times \frac{1}{8} = \frac{4}{8} = \frac{1}{2}$.

b. 4 pieces each the size of $\frac{1}{6}$ of a pizza is $\frac{2}{3}$ of a pizza, so $4 \times \frac{1}{6} = \frac{4}{6} = \frac{2}{3}$.

c. 3 pieces each the size of $\frac{1}{2}$ of a pizza is $1\frac{1}{2}$ of a pizza, so $3 \times \frac{1}{2} = \frac{3}{2} = 1\frac{1}{2}$.

d. $\frac{1}{2}$ of a piece of pizza the size of $\frac{1}{4}$ of a pizza is $\frac{1}{8}$ of a pizza, so $\frac{1}{2} \times \frac{1}{4} = \frac{1}{8}$.

e. $\frac{2}{3}$ of a piece of pizza the size of $\frac{1}{2}$ of a pizza is $\frac{1}{3}$ of a pizza, so $\frac{2}{3} \times \frac{1}{2} = \frac{1}{3}$.

Problem Set 8.3

1. There are several possibilities: 5 dimes and 1 nickel or 4 dimes and 3 nickels or 3 dimes and 5 nickels or 2 dimes and 7 nickels or 1 dime and 9 nickels.

3. (8-24) $1\dfrac{1}{10}$ 1.1

 $\dfrac{6}{10}$ six tenths

7. a. 7

b. 6.5

c. 6.51

d. 0.123

9. $16.25

11. $0.72 each

13. $2.52

Problem Set 8.4

1. For each problem below, what the teacher could do to remediate the error should also be stated.

a. Incorrect answer: $1 + 2 = 3$ and $2 + 3 = 5$. Correct answer: Find common denominators $\frac{3}{6} + \frac{4}{6} = \frac{7}{6}$.

b. Incorrect answer: $4 - 1 = 3$ and $9 - 5 = 4$. Correct answer: $\frac{20}{45} - \frac{9}{45} = \frac{11}{45}$.

c. The student subtracted 1 from 3 and $\frac{4}{7}$ from $\frac{6}{7}$. Correct answer: $2\frac{11}{7} - 1\frac{6}{7} = 1\frac{5}{7}$.

d. Student multiplied whole parts and fractional parts, but did not distribute. Correct answer: $\frac{13}{3} \times \frac{5}{2} = \frac{65}{6} = 10\frac{5}{6}$.

e. Student did not divide fractional part by the divisor. Correct answer: $2\frac{2}{7}$.

f. Student multiplied both 2 and 3 by 5. Correct answer: $\frac{2}{15}$.

g. Student did not invert the divisor. Correct answer: $\frac{10}{3}$.

h. Student inverted the dividend instead of the divisor. Correct answer: $\frac{8}{9}$.

i. Student inverted both the dividend and the divisor. Correct answer: $\frac{8}{9}$.

j. Student forgot to change to a multiplication problem. Correct answer: $\frac{8}{9}$.

k. Student multiplied by one half, did not divide. Correct answer: 20.

3. a. The student made two errors. This student needs help with equivalent fractions and with the meaning of fractions as related to division. Fraction piece models can be used. Correct answer: $\frac{11}{15}$.

b. The student canceled 10, although this was not a factor. Stress estimation. Reteach the process of dividing out the greatest common factor. Correct answer: $\frac{7}{6}$.

c. The student counted the total number of decimal places. Use models to show the process of decimal addition. Correct answer: 4.8.

d. The student has difficulty converting to an improper fraction and difficulty with the division process. Use fraction models and stress estimation. Reteach the division process. Correct answer: $\frac{33}{8}$.

e. The student did not distribute. Stress estimation; use models. Correct answer: $2\frac{1}{5}$.

f. The student misplaced decimal point. Stress estimation. Correct answer: 13.

CHAPTER 9

Problem Set 9.1

1. 50

3. a. 1960, 1970, and 1980

   b. $15,000

   c. $30,000

   d. 150% increase

5. 90,000

7.
```
 4 | 7
 5 |
 6 | 0 5 7
 7 | 2 7
 8 | 0 2 3 6 6
 9 | 3 3 6 7
10 | 0
```

9.

2. From the graph it appears that half of the students like blue M&M's, one fourth like red, and one eighth like each of yellow and green. These numbers are slightly off according to the actual ratios. The graph should reflect the percentages more accurately: 42% blue, 32% red, 16% yellow, and 16% green. Also, the graph needs a title.

Problem Set 9.2

1. a. 12 students

   b. 1.9 hours

   c. 1 hour

   d. 5 hours

   e. 1.5 hours

3. a. Mean = 4, mode = 4, range = 4, median = 4

   b. Mean = 5.6, no mode, range = 6, median = 6

5. a. Yes

   b. No

   c. No

7. a. Median

   b. Mean

9. 87

1. Round 3: Group 1 and Group 4; Group 2 and Group 6; Group 3 and Group 5

   Round 4: Group 1 and Group 5; Group 2 and Group 4; Group 3 and Group 6

   Round 5: Group 1 and Group 6; Group 2 and Group 3; Group 4 and Group 5

Problem Set 9.3

1. a. $S = \{HH, HT, TH, TT\}$ $P(\text{both heads}) = \frac{1}{4}$

   b. $P(\text{both heads}) = \frac{4}{16}$

   c. $P(\text{two heads}) = \frac{6}{16}$

3. $P(2) = \dfrac{1}{36}, P(3) = \dfrac{2}{36}, P(4) = \dfrac{3}{36},$

 $P(5) = \dfrac{4}{36}, P(6) = \dfrac{5}{36}, P(7) = \dfrac{6}{36},$

 $P(8) = \dfrac{5}{36}, P(9) = \dfrac{4}{36}, P(10) = \dfrac{3}{36},$

 $P(11) = \dfrac{2}{36}, P(12) = \dfrac{1}{36}$

5. a. 0

 b. $\dfrac{3}{12}$

 c. $\dfrac{10}{15}$

7. In drawing 30 cubes, you would expect 15 red, 6 blue, 6 green, and 3 yellow.

9. a. Four ways

 b. 10 lb, 14 lb, 20 lb, or 24 lb

11. a. 24

 b. 12

13. 55%

3. Results of this experiment are usually between 75% and 90% heads. It may be difficult for the students to stand all 100 pennies on edge simultaneously. You may tell students that if a penny is standing on its edge and it falls, to leave that penny as it fell and count it in the total.

CHAPTER 10

Problem Set 10.1

1. (10.2.1) A1

 (10.2.2) Moon

 (10.2.4) Star and lightning or heart and moon

 (10.2.5) Heart and smiley face

 (10.3.1) (1, 2)

 (10.3.2) Moon

 (10.3.4) Not possible

 (10.3.5) Heart and lightning bolt or smiley and moon

 (10.4.1) $E(4, 0)$ $F(-4, -1)$ $G(-2, 2)$ $H(0, -3)$

 (10.4.4) B and H

 (10.4.5) B and G or A and C

3. a. Line

 b. Ray with endpoint A

 c. Line segment

5. $\angle BAC$ acute

 $\angle BAD$ obtuse

 $\angle BAE$ obtuse

 $\angle CAD$ right

 $\angle CAE$ obtuse

 $\angle DAE$ acute

 Note: Each of these is also a reflex angle.

7. There are six different rays: $\overrightarrow{DE}$, $\overrightarrow{DF}$, $\overrightarrow{EF}$, $\overrightarrow{ED}$, $\overrightarrow{FD}$, and $\overrightarrow{FE}$.

2. a. Parallel

 b. Perpendicular or intersecting

 c. Intersecting

Problem Set 10.2

1. a. Closed

 b. Neither simple nor closed

 c. Simple and closed

 d. Simple

3. a. Triangle

 b. Rectangle

 c. Regular pentagon

 d. Hexagon

5. Either one is 38° and the other is 104° or both are 71°

7. a. Right, scalene

 b. Acute, equilateral

 c. Acute, isosceles

 d. Obtuse, scalene

9. a. Square, rectangle, parallelogram, quadrilateral, rhombus

 b. Parallelogram, quadrilateral

 c. Isosceles trapezoid, quadrilateral

 d. Trapezoid, quadrilateral

11. (c) is not true.

Problem Set 10.3

1. a. Cylinder

 b. Square pyramid

 c. Rectangular prism

3. a. A is on the back face

 b. F is on the back face or on the front face

5. a. Cylinder, circle

    b. Cylinder, rectangle

    c. Cone, ellipse

Problem Set 10.4

1. The figures do not have the same size. The horizontal bars on one of the figures are longer than on the other.

3. a. to drawsquare :length
       repeat 4[fd length rt 90]
       end

    b. to drawthree :length
       repeat 3[square :length make "length :length + 10]
       end

5. Figure *B* should look similar to *A,* but each side length is twice as long. Figure *C* should look similar, but each side length is 1/2 as long.

3. *(a)* ... *(b)* ...

    (c) Either c or g

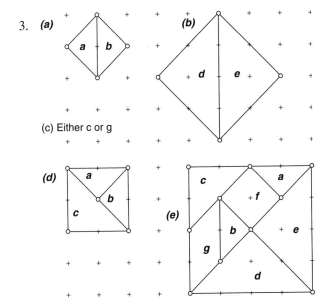

(d) ... *(e)* ...

Problem Set 10.5

3. a. Congruent

    b. Not congruent

    c. Congruent

5. a. Flip or flip and turn

    c. Turn

7. a. No lines of symmetry

    b. Five lines of symmetry

    c. Two lines of symmetry

9. a. 360°

    b. 72°

    c. 180°

11.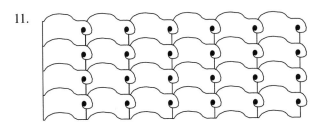

13. a. to drawcircle
       repeat 360 [fd 1 rt 1]
       end

    b. to morecircles
       repeat 6 [drawcircle rt 60]
       end

15. Answers will depend on how the letters are drawn. For example, for the two *B*'s shown, one has no line of symmetry whereas the other has one.

Chapter 11

Problem Set 11.1

1. Fill the 5-cup measure. Pour from the 5-cup measure into the 2-cup measure until it is full. What remains in the 5-cup measuring cup is exactly 3 cups of rice.

3. There are 16 cups in a gallon.

5. Two gallons is approximately 25 servings.

7. 68 mph

9. The weed grows 1 inch in 140 minutes.

11. 225 miles

13. 105

15. The small case contains $\frac{1}{2}$ cubic foot, the medium case contains $1\frac{1}{2}$ cubic feet, and the large case contains 3 cubic feet.

Problem Set 11.2

1. Maureen walks approximately 1.125 miles per hour.

3. a. 30,000

    b. 2,000

    c. 5,000,000

5. a. =

b. >

c. <

7. The correct amounts are: 800 m, 2 kg, 3 L, 5 g, and 20 cm.

Problem Set 11.3

1. 4

3. a. True

b. False

c. False

d. True

5. 27 square inches

7. a. 4

b. $A = 4 \text{ cm}^2$, $P = 10 \text{ cm}$

c. $A = 4 \text{ cm}^2$

d. 7 to 9 cm^2

9. Approximately 0.8 to 0.9 miles

11. 6 inches

13. The new area is x^2 square inches. This is the same as the original area.

15. 144 in.^{3}

17. 120 cm^2

19. 10 ft by 10 ft

Problem Set 11.4

1. a. Transitive only

b. Reflexive and transitive

c. Reflexive and transitive

d. Reflexive, symmetric, and transitive

3. $0.85

5. January 1, 2005, falls on a Saturday and January 1, 2006, falls on a Sunday.

7. 5:55 A.M., 10 hours, 25 minutes

9. a. 120

b. 14

c. 77

d. 15

APPENDIX A

Problem Set A.2

1. a.

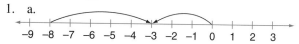

b.

c. $-3 - 5 = -8$

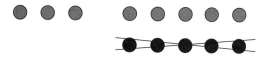

3. Start with a pile that represents a. To evaluate the equation a − (−b) you must remove −b chips from the pile that represents a. If b is negative, −b is positive. Add −b black chips and −b red chips to the pile that represents a. The new pile still represents a and you may remove the −b black chips. The remaining pile contains a plus −b red chips which, since b is negative, represents a + b.

5. The equation (a − b) − c = a − (b − c) only when c = 0.

7. a. $-5 - (2 - 3) = -5 - (-1) = -5 + 1 = -4$

b. $-5 - 2 - 3 = -10$

9. a.
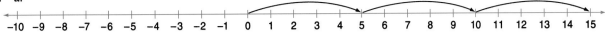

b.

c.

d.

Answers: (a) $3 \times 5 = 15$
(b) $3 \times -5 = -15$
(c) $-3 \times 5 = -15$
(d) $-3 \times -5 = 15$

13. a. 3
b. -3
c. -3
d. 3

15. a. 16
b. 16
c. 20
d. 5

Problem Set A.3

1. a. 2.38×10^6
b. 9.0×10^{-7}

3. a. 1,030,000
b. 0.0002

Problem Set A.4

1. a. not a valid ratio problem
b. 20 years

3. The recipe should use 10 cups of water to feed 15 people.

5. a. 20
b. 20
c. 75
d. 20

7. There were 14 grades of C.

9. a. $\dfrac{3}{50}$ and 0.06
b. $\dfrac{41}{2}$ and 2050%
c. 2.8 and 280%

11. a. 10% of 400 = 40 < 50% of 90 = 45 < 20% of 300 = 60 = 15% of 400 < 25% of 1000 = 250.
b. (5) only. $2.53\% = 0.0253 > 0.025 = \dfrac{25}{1000}$

13. $\dfrac{15}{45} = \dfrac{1}{3} = 33\dfrac{1}{3}\%$ are 2nd graders

15. 31 students have scheduled.

17. 20

Problem Set A.5

1. Any rectangle with length l and width w such that $lw \le 113$ and $l + w \ge 19$ works. For example, a $10''$ by $11''$ pizza has area 110 in^2 and perimeter 42 in.

3. 900 in.^{3}

5. 5 feet

7. 576 cm^3

9. The volume of the sphere is greater.

Problem Set A.6

1. $P = 32$ m, $A = (24 + 4\sqrt{48})$ m$^2 \approx 52$ m^2

3. $\dfrac{550}{3}\pi$ cm$^3 \approx 576$ cm^3

5. $A = 48$ in.^{2}, $P = (24 + 2\sqrt{20})$ in. ≈ 33 in.

Appendix A

Burris's Preparation Materials for the Praxis I(R) Tests or Exams

One main goal of this textbook is to prepare future teachers with the mathematics background necessary for teaching mathematics in an early childhood classroom. In some cases this involves content beyond that which will be taught within an early childhood classroom. For example, a teacher looking up information on the distance from the earth to the other planets may find this information given in scientific notation. To use this information in the classroom, the teacher must be able to translate it to standard notation.

Many colleges and university teacher education departments require a passing score on a national teacher examination such as the Praxis I, Pre-Professional Skills Test™ (PPST). The PPST exam covers such topics as number sense and operation sense; ratios, proportions, and percents; area, perimeter, and volume; the Pythagorean theorem; and logic. Each of these topics is covered in this appendix. The PPST exam also covers the mathematics topics found within the chapters of this textbook.

A link to the Educational Testing Service (ETS) Praxis Information site can be found at the textbook companion Web site.

Standards

Ohio Academic Content Standards

Number, Number Sense and Operation Standard, K–2 Benchmark B, Grade Level Indicator #13

Recognize the number or quantity of sets up to 5 without counting; e.g., recognize without counting the dot arrangement on a domino as 5.

Ohio Department of Education, 2001

criteria to be used to demonstrate successful or satisfactory mastery of the learning (Burdon & Byrd, 1998).

Example:

Grade level: Kindergarten.
Number, Number Sense and Operations: B: 13
The student will be able to recognize without counting and orally state the number on the top face of a die.

4. *Lesson Components*
   - *Motivation*—captures the students' attention and focuses their thought processes on the lesson topic.
   - *Set*—activates the students' prior knowledge upon which the lesson will build.
   - *New content*—details how the lesson will proceed and what examples will be used. Must include diversity and adaptation considerations. For example, an ESL student should be allowed to state the number in his or her own language. A child with limited verbal skills could point to

A.1 LESSON PLAN FORMAT AND SAMPLE LESSON PLANS

Lesson Plan Format

1. *Materials*—in list format with quantities.
2. *Vocabulary*—defined in grade-appropriate terms.
3. *Objectives*—state grade level, standard, and benchmark and grade-level indicator (if applicable).

An objective should indicate the desired outcome of learning and be expressed in terms of observable behavior or performance of the learners. The objective should describe the task to be performed and indicate

the correct numeral card or to a card containing an alternate visual representation rather than stating the quantity orally. Procedures should be outlined in step-by-step format.

- **Real-world connection**—at least one specific example of how the material learned is used or useful in a real-world or everyday context.
- **Closure**—wrap up the lesson.

5. **Assessment**—how will you determine whether the objective has been met?

Sample Lesson Plan: Fractions (Kindergarten)

1. Materials
   Paper plate with a line dividing the plate into unequal parts
   Paper plate with a line dividing the plate into equal parts
   5 large squares (with magnets on back for use on magnetic board)*
   10 pieces of yarn with length ≥ the length of the square's diagonal (magnets on ends)*
   Magnetic word cards—"one half" and "one fourth"*
   Handouts (one for each student)
   12 two-inch strips of yarn for each student (precut, prepackaged)
   Tape (one roll for each table)
2. Vocabulary
   Equal parts—each part is the same (has the same size and shape)
   One half—one of two equal parts
   One fourth—one of four equal parts
3. Objectives
   Grade level: Kindergarten
   Number, Operation, and Quantitative Reasoning (111.12.b.3a)
   The student will be able to show how a whole can be divided into two or four equal parts by placing yarn on figures.
4. Lesson Components
   Motivation: "Last night I wanted to share a pizza with my friend Juanita. She wanted to cut the pizza like this." (Show the paper plate with unequal parts.) "Is this fair? Would we both get the same amount of pizza?" (Accept various student answers.) "How do you think we should have cut the pizza so that we both got the same

Standards

Texas Essential Knowledge and Skills for Mathematics:

(3) Number, operation, and quantitative reasoning. The student recognizes that there are quantities less than a whole. The student is expected to:
   (A) share a whole by separating it into equal parts; and
   (B) explain why a given part is half of the whole.

Texas Education Agency, 1998

amount?" (Accept various student answers.) "So you think we should have cut the pizza in half, right down the middle, so that we would both get an equal amount." (Show the paper plate with equal parts.) "That is what we are going to work on in math today—sharing or dividing objects into equal parts."
Set: "Who can tell me what 'equal parts' means?"
"What word do we use when we are talking about one of two equal parts?"
"How can we tell when parts are equal?"
New content/procedures:
1. a. Place the first square on the magnetic board.
   b. Write "2 equal parts" under the square.
   c. Ask a student volunteer to place a piece of yarn (use tape or magnets) to show two equal parts.
   d. Ask students to explain how the drawing shows two equal parts.
   e. Reinforce the term "one half" as one of two equal parts.
   f. Ask students why it is important (real-world connection) to know how to divide an object into two equal parts.
2. a. Place the second square on the magnetic board.
   b. Write "2 equal parts" under the square.
   c. Ask students if there is a different way to place yarn to show two equal parts than the way shown on the last square.
   d. Ask a student volunteer to place yarn on the figure to show two equal parts. Assist the student as necessary.
   e. Reinforce the term "one half" as one of two equal parts.
   f. Ask the students to explain how the drawing shows two equal parts.
   g. Mention that there are other ways to show two equal parts as well.
3. a. Place the third square on the magnetic board.
   b. Write "4 equal parts" under the square.

*If a magnetic board is not available, squares and yarn may be taped to the board.

c. Ask a student volunteer to place yarn on the figure to show four equal parts. More than one piece of yarn will be needed. Assist the student as necessary.

d. Introduce the term "one fourth" as one of four equal parts.

e. Ask the students to explain how the drawing shows four equal parts.

f. Ask students why they might want to (real-world connection) divide an object into four equal parts.

g. Reinforce the term "one fourth."

4. a. Place the fourth square on the magnetic board.

b. Write "4 equal parts" under the square.

c. Ask students if there is a different way to place the yarn to show four equal parts than the way shown on the last square.

d. Ask a student volunteer to place yarn on the figure to show four equal parts in a different way than in the other figure.

e. Ask the students to explain how the drawing shows four equal parts.

f. Reinforce the term "one fourth."

g. Mention that there are also other ways to show four equal parts.

Note: If neither student solution given in (3) or (4) shows the method of using crossing lines to generate four equal parts, show this using the fifth square. For example, if the student solutions to (3) and (4) result in figures (a) and (b) below, you may use the fifth square to demonstrate a solution where the yarn is crossed to generate four equal parts such as in figure (c) or (d) below. Similarly, if student solutions are (c) and (d) you may use the fifth square to illustrate (a) or (b).

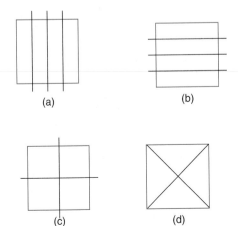

(a) (b)

(c) (d)

5. Distribute materials.

a. Students place yarn to divide the figures on the handout into the number of equal pieces shown by the numeral. Number of pieces for each figure should be orally presented to students who have difficulty reading numerals.

b. After student work is checked, yarn is taped into place.

c. Students can draw in their math journal a picture that represents a time that they used the idea of dividing an object into equal pieces in their own life.

Closure:

"Today we used yarn to divide objects into equal parts."

"What does equal parts mean?"

"How can we tell when we have equal parts?"

"What is the word we use for one of two equal parts?"

"What is the word we use for one of four equal parts?"

"If Mark divides a figure into equal parts and Leeza divides a figure into the same number of equal parts, do their pictures have to look the same? How can they each tell that they have equal parts?

"Why do you think it is important to know how to divide an object into equal parts?

5. Assessment: Students will be observed as they place yarn on their handouts. Students who are having difficulty may be assisted as necessary. The handouts provide an item that may be included in a student portfolio. The math journal also records the activity and emphasizes the natural real-world connection.

Notes: The use of yarn to divide figures rather than the use of a pencil or pen allows the teacher to help students correct their mistakes without erasing. Yarn provides a bright visual so that the teacher can quickly check student work.

Advanced students may be presented the challenge of dividing figures into other numbers of equal parts.

If students have difficulty with procedures (1) and (2), the idea of equal fourths may be deferred to a later lesson. If so, instead of introducing fourths in procedures (3) and (4) continue to present examples using the large squares of two equal parts or halves. Then the three figures at the bottom of the handout may be skipped for the majority of the class. Advanced students may be able to complete these three figures without any further instruction.

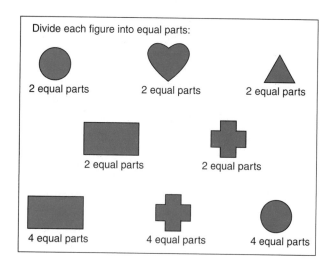

Divide each figure into equal parts:

2 equal parts   2 equal parts   2 equal parts

2 equal parts   2 equal parts

4 equal parts   4 equal parts   4 equal parts

Sample Lesson Plan: Volume
(Second or Third Grade)

1. Materials

   24 color cubes (cubic inches) for each pair of students (prepackaged for easy distribution)

   24+ color cubes for teacher demonstration

   Handouts (one for each student)

   Transparency handout for teacher demonstration

   Small box (approximately 2 by 3 by 4 inches) filled with cubic inches

   Large box (with the prepackaged cubes inside)

2. Vocabulary

   Volume—the number of cubic units in a solid figure

   Solid figure—a figure that has length, width, height, and volume (no gaps or holes)

   Cubic unit—the unit used to measure volume

   Measure—to determine the length, quantity, area, or amount

3. Objectives

   Grade level: Three

   Measurement: A.5

   The student will be able to

   a. build a solid figure having a given volume using cubic units.

   b. calculate the volume of a given or pictured solid figure.

4. Lesson Components

   Motivation: "Both of these boxes are filled with math manipulatives called cubes or cubic inches that we will use today in our math lesson. (Show two boxes: one small and one large.) Which box do you think has the most cubes in it? Why do you think this box has more in it? Today we are going to learn how to measure the amount that can fit into a box or other object. Why do you think it is important to know how much will fit into a box?"

   Set: "What is a cube?"

"How big do you think a cubic inch is? Show me with your fingers."

"What does 'measure' mean?"

"What kind of things can we measure?"

"Can we measure how much water is in a jug? How?"

New content/procedures:

1. a. Give each student one cubic unit and a handout.

   b. Pass around the small box. Tell students not to open it. Ask students to estimate how many cubic inches are in the box.

2. a. Build and show students the two figures:

   b. Ask students how many cubes it took to build each figure.

   c. Introduce the definition of *volume*—the number of cubic units in a solid figure.

   d. Write 8 in the blanks on the transparency handout and reinforce the definition of volume.

   e. Ask students if there are other solid figures that can be built with eight cubic units.

   f. Count out eight cubes and use student input or suggestions to build another solid figure with a volume of 8 cubic inches. Remind students that a solid figure does not have gaps or holes.

3. a. Pass out bags of cubic units. Each student should have a partner. Place dividers between students so that they cannot see what their partner is building.

   b. Review the definition of "solid figure." Ask each student to build a solid figure using six cubes.

   c. Ask students to remove the dividers and check to see whether their partner built a solid figure with a volume of 6 cubic units.

   d. Ask how many students built the same figure as their partner.

   e. Repeat using other numbers of units.

4. a. Ask students to find the volume of the figures on the handout. They may use cubes to help them find the answers.

   b. Advanced students, or students who finish early, may be challenged to find or build all of the different figures with a given volume.

   Closure: "Today we learned how to build figures with cubic inches."

"If I build a figure with nine cubes, what is the volume of the figure?"

"Are there different ways to build a figure with nine cubic units?"

"Why might you want to know the volume of an object or box?"

"Let's find the volume of the little box I showed you." Open the box and let the cubes slide out and form a solid figure. Ask students to count the number of cubes and compare to their original estimate.

"If I wanted to use this box to mail some 1-inch candies to my aunt, how many candies could I mail her?"

"Knowing how to find volume can help us to figure out how many things fit into a box."

5. Assessment: Students will be observed as they build solid figures. Students who are having difficulty may be assisted as necessary; partners may also assist. The handouts provide an item that may be included in a student portfolio.

> ## Standards
>
> ### Ohio Academic Content Standards
>
> *Measurement Grade 3—Grade Level Indicator 5*
>
> Estimate and measure length, weight and volume (capacity), using metric and U.S. customary units, accurate to the nearest 1/2 or 1/4 unit as appropriate.
>
> Ohio Department of Education, 2001

A.2 INTEGER ARITHMETIC

We discussed representations of integers and integer addition using the number line model and the poker chip model in Section 5.4. We are now ready to consider other operations involving integers. If you are teaching in an early childhood classroom, it is unlikely that you will teach this material. However, you will have to deal with negative integers in your own experiences as an adult.

The volume is _____ cubic units.

The volume is _____ cubic units.

Build a solid figure with 6 cubes. The figure you built has volume _____ cubic units.

Find the volume of each of the figures shown. You may use cubes to help.

The volume is _____ cubic units.

The volume is _____ cubic units.

The volume is _____ cubic units.

The volume is _____ cubic units.

Write About It: How is volume different from area?

Opposites and the Double Negative Rule

Every integer has an opposite or additive inverse. The *opposite* or *additive inverse* of an integer is the integer that must be added for a sum of zero. The equation $m + (-m) = 0$ indicates that m and $-m$ are additive inverses or opposites. The opposite of 3 is -3. The opposite of -4 is 4. This term "opposite" refers to the positions of the integers on the number line, but if you equate opposite with negative, then you can derive the "double negative" rule. An example of the double negative rule is $-(-4) = 4$. This corresponds to the idea that the opposite of -4 is 4.

Subtraction of Integers

Some textbooks simply state that subtraction is like adding a negative. For integers a and b, it holds that $a - b = a + (-b)$. Thus, you could turn any integer subtraction problem into an integer addition problem using this equation and using the double negative rule when necessary. However, this manipulation of symbols does not satisfy the need to understand how and why the process works. Again, we will use concrete models like the number line and poker chip model to illustrate the process.

The Poker Chip Model The poker chip model process is to start with a representation of the minuend and add "zero pairs" or pairs of red and black chips until it is possible to take away the subtrahend. Can you see why adding a pair of chips consisting of one black chip and one red chip does not change the original value of the representation? Several poker chip model subtraction examples are illustrated in Example A-1.

Example A-1: Subtraction of integers using a poker chip model.

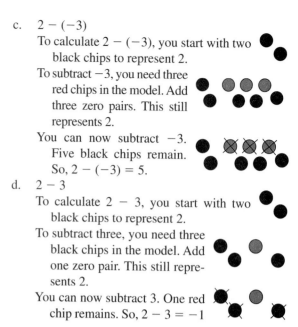

   a. $-2 - (-3)$
      To calculate $-2 - (-3)$, you start with two red chips to represent -2.
      There aren't enough red chips to take away -3, so you add a zero pair to the model. This still represents -2.
      You can now take away -3. One black chip remains. So, $-2 - (-3) = 1$.
   b. $-2 - 3$
      To calculate $-2 - 3$, you start with two red chips to represent -2.
      To subtract 3, you need three black chips. You add three zero pairs to the model. This still represents -2.
      You can now subtract 3. Five red chips remain. So, $-2 - 3 = -5$.

   c. $2 - (-3)$
      To calculate $2 - (-3)$, you start with two black chips to represent 2.
      To subtract -3, you need three red chips in the model. Add three zero pairs. This still represents 2.
      You can now subtract -3. Five black chips remain. So, $2 - (-3) = 5$.
   d. $2 - 3$
      To calculate $2 - 3$, you start with two black chips to represent 2.
      To subtract three, you need three black chips in the model. Add one zero pair. This still represents 2.
      You can now subtract 3. One red chip remains. So, $2 - 3 = -1$

The problems shown in Example A-1 illustrate an interesting property of integer subtraction. When you subtract a positive integer, the quantity that you started with decreases, but when you subtract a negative integer, the quantity that you started with increases. This is due to the double negative rule. For instance, Example A-1c shows that $2 - (-3) = 2 + 3$. You can state and prove a more general result.

Theorem A.1: For any integers a and b, $a - (-b) = a + b$.

Proof: First assume that b is positive. Start with a pile of chips that represents a.

   These chips represent a.

You can add to this b zero pairs, that is, add b black chips and b red chips.

    The black chips represent b and the patterned chips represent $-b$.

This new pile of chips still represents a. Since b is positive, $-b$ is negative. To compute $a - (-b)$ you remove the b red chips. This leaves a pile with the original representation of a as well as b black chips. That is, $a - (-b) = a + b$ when b is assumed to be positive.

Can you give poker chip model explanations of other subtraction properties including the following theorem?

Theorem A.2: For any integers a and b, $a - b = a + (-b)$.

The Number Line Model As with subtraction of whole numbers, the mathematically correct number line depiction of subtraction of integers differs from the number line illustrations that usually appear in elementary textbooks. In a mathematically precise number line illustration, the minuend is represented by an arrow from zero to the appropriate position on the number line. The subtrahend is represented by an arrow whose head is positioned at the head of the arrow representing the minuend. The arrow representing each integer points left if the integer is negative, and right if it is positive. In most elementary textbooks the arrow representing the minuend is omitted. Students are instructed to begin at the position of the minuend. They are told to move left if the subtrahend is positive, and right if it is negative. At first glance this direction appears counterintuitive because negative integers are to the left of zero and positive integers are to the right of zero on the number line. However, the directions are to "move left to subtract a positive integer." This does make sense because subtracting a positive integer will decrease the amount. To make sense of the direction "move right to subtract a negative integer," you must first establish that subtracting a negative number increases the amount. This can be accomplished using the poker chip model. It can also be rationalized by an argument such as the following which appears in a sixth grade textbook (Charles et al., 1999). "Addition and subtraction are opposite operations. When you take a number and add a negative number to it, the results get less. So when you take a number and *subtract* a negative number, the results get greater." Number line examples are shown in Examples A-2 and A-3.

Example A-2: Subtraction of integers using a mathematically precise number line model.

a. $-2 - (-3) = 1$

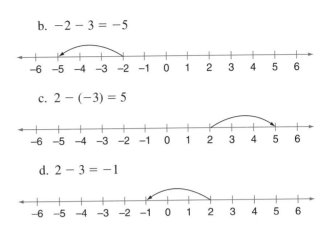

b. $-2 - 3 = -5$

c. $2 - (-3) = 5$

d. $2 - 3 = -1$

Example A-3: Subtraction of integers using a number line model as it might appear in a fifth- or sixth-grade textbook.

a. $-2 - (-3) = 1$

b. $-2 - 3 = -5$

c. $2 - (-3) = 5$

d. $2 - 3 = -1$

Computations Involving More than Two Terms You may recall that in general, subtraction is not an associative operation. That is, in most instances $(a - b) - c \neq a - (b - c)$. So when given an expression like $a - b - c$ without parentheses, it is important that you perform the operations in the correct order. When there are no parentheses, additions and subtractions are performed from left to right as in the examples below. Sometimes parentheses are used to make an equation or problem easier to read. In Example A-4a, the parentheses around the -2 are written merely to avoid the two consecutive negative signs that would appear if the parentheses were not there. Sometimes parentheses are used to indicate a precedence of operations. When grouping parentheses are present, operations within parentheses are performed prior to operations not in parentheses.

Example A-4:

a. $3 - (-2) - 4 = 5 - 4 = 1$ Do the computation $3 - (-2)$ first.
b. $-6 - 4 - (-2) = -10 + 2 = -8$ Do the computation $-6 - 4$ first.
c. $-6 - (4 + 2) = -6 - 6 = -12$ Do the computation $4 + 2$ first.
d. $-6 - (-4 - 2) = -6 - (-6) = -6 + 6 = 0$ Do the computation $-4 - 2$ first.

Multiplication of Integers

Recall that multiplication can be illustrated with an array diagram such as shown in Example A-5a. You can also represent multiplication of two positive factors with a poker chip diagram as in Example A-5b. Example A-5c shows multiplication with negative factors.

Example A-5: Representations of multiplication with two positive factors.

a. Array Model Representation of $4 \times 3 = 12$

b. Poker Chip Model Representation of $4 \times 3 = 12$

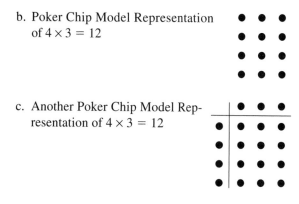

c. Another Poker Chip Model Representation of $4 \times 3 = 12$

The Poker Chip Model Using the extended poker chip model representation and the notion that $m \times n$ represents m sets of n objects each, it is easy to envision a representation of a multiplication example with the first factor positive and the second factor negative. For example, $4 \times (-3)$ represents four sets of (-3) chips each such as shown in Example A-6a. But what if the first factor is negative? Recall the idea of opposite. The multiplication $(-4) \times 3$ in concrete terms is represented by -4 sets of three black chips each. The idea of -4 sets can be represented by flipping the chips or changing the color of the chips involved. A representation of the multiplication $(-4) \times 3$ is shown in Example A-6b. This idea also provides us with a convenient representation when both factors are negative such as $(-4) \times (-3)$ shown in Example A-6c. Notice how easily this model lends itself to the development of such rules as "positive times positive gives positive," "positive times negative gives negative," "negative times positive gives negative," and "negative times negative gives positive."

Example A-6: Representations of multiplication with negative factors.

a. Poker Chip Model Representation of $4 \times -3 = -12$

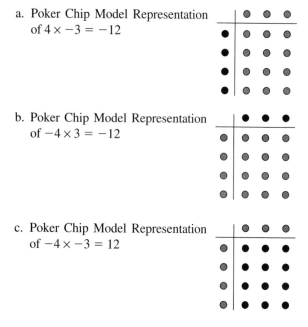

b. Poker Chip Model Representation of $-4 \times 3 = -12$

c. Poker Chip Model Representation of $-4 \times -3 = 12$

The Number Line Model The number line model can also be used to represent multiplication of integers. The first factor in a multiplication equation represents the sets, and the second factor represents the objects in a set. As with the number line representation of multiplication of positive factors, the first factor determines the number of arrows and the second factor determines the length of the arrows. The sign of the first factor is reflected by the placement of the arrows. If the first factor is positive, placement of arrows begins with the tail of the initial arrow at 0. If the first factor is negative, placement of arrows begins with the head of the initial arrow at 0. Since multiplication can be viewed as repeated addition, all arrows are placed head to tail (or equivalently tail to head). The sign of the second factor is reflected by the direction of the arrows. Examples are given in Figure A-1.

The number line illustrations shown in Figures A-1a through A-1d also support such rules as "positive times positive gives positive," "positive times negative gives negative," "negative times positive gives negative," and "negative times negative gives positive."

Division of Integers

The Number Line Model Division of integers could also be illustrated with number line representations. However, due to the limited number of interpretations of arrow direction and placement, some illustrations would represent more than one equation. In fact, we have already seen such duplication. The examples shown in Figures A-2a and A-2b were given in Figure 6-8 of Section 6.2 as illustrations of number line division. This interpretation is based on the repeated subtraction interpretation of division.

By the preceding paragraph, the illustrations shown could also be interpreted as illustrations of multiplication equations. The diagram in Figure A-2a represents $(-3) \times (-4) = 12$ as well as $12 \div 4 = 3$. The diagram in Figure A-2b represents $(-4) \times (-3) = 12$ as well as $12 \div 3 = 4$. To avoid further duplication, we will assign number line representations only to division equations involving positive dividends, divisors, and quotients.

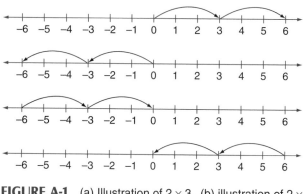

FIGURE A-1 (a) Illustration of 2×3, (b) illustration of 2×-3, (c) illustration of -2×3, (d) illustration of -2×-3.

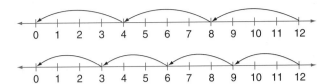

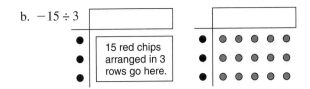

FIGURE A-2   (a) Illustration of $12 \div 4 = 3$ or $(-3) \times (-4) = 12$, (b) illustration of $12 \div 3 = 4$ or $(-4) \times (-3) = 12$.

The Poker Chip Model   We can, however, illustrate division in all cases without incurring undue duplication of illustrations using the extended poker chip model representation. The division equation $a \div b = \square$ is related to both of the multiplication equations $a = b \times \square$ and $a = \square \times b$. To avoid duplicate representations, we will use only the multiplication equation $a = b \times \square$ while using the poker chip model in considering the division equation $a \div b = \square$. This is consistent with the concrete representation of dividing a objects equally among b sets and determining how many objects are in each set. For example, the equation $15 \div 3 = \square$ is related to the equation $15 = 3 \times \square$.

If the divisor is positive, a simple poker chip model representation will suffice. The equation $15 \div 3$ is represented by dividing 15 black chips into 3 sets. This gives 5 black chips in each set, hence $15 \div 3 = 5$. Similarly, the equation $-15 \div 3$ can be represented by dividing 15 red chips into 3 sets. This gives 5 red chips in each set, hence $-15 \div 3 = -5$. This simple model does not naturally extend to division equations where the divisor is negative. These equations as well as similar equations with negative divisors are illustrated using the extended poker chip model representation in Example A-7. The divisor is used to label the rows. The dividend or total number of chips goes on the inside of the diagram arranged in rows. The answer to the division, or the quotient, is found by appropriately labeling the columns. The color of the chips used to label the columns is chosen so that the diagram is consistent with the associated multiplication diagram.

Example A-7:   Poker chip model representations of division.

a. $15 \div 3$

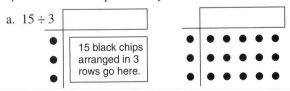

Solution: Complete the diagram by labeling the columns with 5 black chips. The chips must be black for consistency with the related multiplication diagram. This diagram represents $15 \div 3 = 5$:

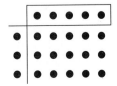

b. $-15 \div 3$

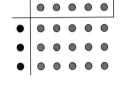

Solution: Complete the diagram by labeling the columns with 5 red chips. The chips must be red for consistency with the related multiplication diagram. This diagram represents $-15 \div 3 = -5$:

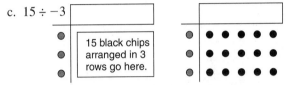

c. $15 \div -3$

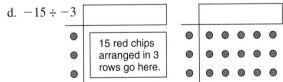

Solution: Complete the diagram by labeling the columns with 5 red chips. The chips must be red for consistency with the related multiplication diagram. This diagram represents $15 \div -3 = -5$:

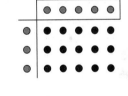

d. $-15 \div -3$

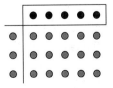

Solution: Complete the diagram by labeling the columns with 5 black chips. The chips must be black for consistency with the related multiplication diagram. This diagram represents $-15 \div -3 = 5$:

The poker chip diagrams and examples lend support to the rules "positive divided by positive gives positive,"

"positive divided by negative gives negative," "negative divided by positive gives negative," and "negative divided by negative gives positive." These correspond to the related multiplication sign rules.

Problem Set A.2

1. Draw (a) a mathematically precise number line model, (b) a number line model as it might appear in a fifth- or sixth-grade textbook, and (c) a poker chip model representation and give the answer to $-3 - 5$.

2. Draw (a) a mathematically precise number line model, (b) a number line model as it might appear in a fifth- or sixth-grade textbook, and (c) a poker chip model representation and give the answer to $-3 - (-5)$.

3. Finish the proof of Theorem A.1 by giving a poker chip model explanation of the case that b is negative.

4. Prove Theorem A.2.

5. When does $(a - b) - c = a - (b - c)$?

6. Calculate each of the following.
   a. $-4 - (8 - 2)$
   b. $-4 - 8 - 2$
   c. $-3 - (-8) - 7$
   d. $-3 - (-8 - 7)$

7. Calculate each of the following.
   a. $-5 - (2 - 3)$
   b. $-5 - 2 - 3$

8. Draw a number line model and give the answers for each of the following.
   a. 3×5
   b. 3×-5
   c. -3×5
   d. -3×-5

9. Draw a number line model and give the answers for each of the following.
   a. 5×3
   b. 5×-3
   c. -5×3
   d. -5×-3

10. Draw a poker chip model representation and give answers for each of the following.
    a. 3×5
    b. 3×-5
    c. -3×5
    d. -3×-5

11. Draw a poker chip model representation and give answers for each of the following.
    a. 5×3
    b. 5×-3
    c. -5×3
    d. -5×-3

12. Draw a number line representation for each of the following.
    a. $15 \div 5$
    b. $15 \div 3$

13. Draw a poker chip model representation and give answers for each of the following.
    a. $12 \div 4$
    b. $12 \div -4$
    c. $-12 \div 4$
    d. $-12 \div -4$

14. Draw a poker chip model representation and give answers for each of the following.
    a. $20 \div 4$
    b. $20 \div -4$
    c. $-20 \div 4$
    d. $-20 \div -4$

15. Calculate each of the following.
    a. $-4 \times (8 \div -2) =$
    b. $(-4 \times 8) \div -2 =$
    c. $-60 \div (-6 \div 2) =$
    d. $(-60 \div -6) \div 2 =$

A.3   SCIENTIFIC NOTATION

Exponents and scientific notation are generally introduced in the fifth or sixth grade. As a future early childhood educator, this may be material that you will never teach. The material is included in this textbook because you may encounter situations in your adult life for which knowledge of scientific notation is useful. In looking up information to be used in your classroom (for example, the distance to the moon) you may find numbers in magazines, journals, or other sources that are written in scientific notation. Scientific notation is useful for the expression of numbers that are either very large or very small. It is frequently used in scientific applications, thus the name *scientific notation*.

Exponential Expression Terminology

In an exponential expression with a positive exponent, the exponent tells how many times the base is to be used as a factor. For the expression 2^4, the base is 2 and the exponent is 4. This expression is read as "two to the fourth" or "two to the fourth power." The expression is evaluated as $2 \times 2 \times 2 \times 2 = 16$. Exponential expressions that have a base of 10 are easily evaluated. What patterns do you see in the base-ten expressions shown in Table A-1?

The value of an expression with a nonpositive exponent can be justified by noticing the pattern that decreasing the exponent by one effectively divides the expression by one factor of the base. You may also recall the algebraic rules $b^0 = 1$ and $b^{-n} = \frac{1}{b^n}$. For scientific notation, you use exponential expressions with a base of 10. You must be able to evaluate expressions such as those in Table A-1. One quick way to do these calculations is to notice that multiplying or dividing by a power of 10 has the effect of moving the decimal point. This is due to the fact that a base-ten numeration system is used.

Definition of *Scientific Notation*

A number is written in *scientific notation* if it is expressed as the product of two factors such that one factor is a decimal number between 1 and 10, and the other factor is a power of 10. Scientific notation is particularly useful for very large numbers and for very small numbers.

Example A-8: Write each number in scientific notation.

   a. 67,300,000
   b. 0.0024
   c. 275,640,000
   d. 20,000,000,000
   e. 0.00007
   f. 0.0001234

Solutions:

   a. Move the decimal point until you find the decimal number to use as the first factor. For 67,300,000 , the decimal 6.73 is the appropriate number to use as the first factor. This procedure also gives you the exponent. The decimal point was moved seven positions. Thus, $67{,}300{,}000 = 6.73 \times 10^7$.
   b. Move the decimal point in 0.0024 to the right to see that 2.4 is the appropriate number to use as the first factor. The decimal was moved three spaces. However, the answer is not 2.4×10^3 which represents

2,400. This example requires a negative exponent to indicate that the number is small, not large. The correct answer is $0.0024 = 2.4 \times 10^{-3}$.

   c. Moving the decimal point in 275,640,000 you see that 2.7564 is the first factor. This is a large number; the exponent on the power of 10 should be positive. Thus, $275{,}640{,}000 = 2.7564 \times 10^8$.
   d. Moving the decimal point in 20,000,000,000 you see that 2.0 is the first factor. This is a large number; the exponent on the power of 10 should be positive. Thus, $20{,}000{,}000{,}000 = 2.0 \times 10^{10}$.
   e. Moving the decimal point in 0.00007 you see that the first factor is 7 or 7.0 and the decimal is moved five places. The number is a small number; the exponent on the power of 10 should be negative. Thus, $0.00007 = 7.0 \times 10^{-5}$.
   f. Moving the decimal point in 0.0001234 you see that 1.234 is the first factor and the decimal is moved four places. The number is a small number; the exponent on the power of 10 should be negative. Thus, $0.0001234 = 1.234 \times 10^{-4}$.

Example A-9: Write each number in standard notation.

   a. 3.24×10^6
   b. 2.7×10^{-4}
   c. 6×10^{-7}
   d. 4×10^5

Solutions:

   a. $3.24 \times 10^6 = 3.24 \times 1{,}000{,}000 = 3{,}240{,}000$
   b. $2.7 \times 10^{-4} = 2.7 \times 0.0001 = 0.00027$
   c. $6 \times 10^{-7} = 6 \times 0.0000001 = 0.0000006$
   d. $4 \times 10^5 = 4 \times 100{,}000 = 400{,}000$

Calculator Expressions Many algebraic calculators will display an answer in scientific notation if it is too large or too small to be displayed otherwise. Many arithmetic calculators are not equipped for scientific notation. However, using ideas of scientific notation, some problems can be computed on an arithmetic calculator even if the initial computation gives an error.

TABLE A–1 Evaluation of some base-ten exponential expressions.

Power of 10	Evaluated Expression	Power of 10	Evaluated Expression
10^5	$10 \times 10 \times 10 \times 10 \times 10 = 100{,}000$	10^{-1}	$\frac{1}{10^1} = \frac{1}{10} = 0.1$
10^4	$10 \times 10 \times 10 \times 10 = 10{,}000$		
10^3	$10 \times 10 \times 10 = 1{,}000$	10^{-2}	$\frac{1}{10^2} = \frac{1}{100} = 0.01$
10^2	$10 \times 10 = 100$		
10^1	10	10^{-3}	$\frac{1}{10^3} = \frac{1}{1000} = 0.001$
10^0	1		

Example A-10: Compute using a calculator that supports scientific notation and another calculator that does not.

    a. $123,000 \times 2,400,000$

    b. $0.0025 \div 400,000$

Solutions:

    a. A calculator that supports scientific notation immediately gives the answer 2.952×10^{11}. On some calculators exponentiation is indicated by spacing and the display will appear as 2.952 _____ 11. On other calculators the exponent is indicated by the symbol ^ and the display will appear as $2.952 \times 10 \wedge 11$.

        A calculator that does not support scientific notation will give an error when this product is entered. However, you can write the product as $(1.23 \times 10^5) \times (2.4 \times 10^6)$ and use the calculator to find the product $1.23 \times 2.4 = 2.952$. Because multiplication is commutative and associative, you can write $(1.23 \times 10^5) \times (2.4 \times 10^6) = (1.23 \times 2.4) \times 10^5 \times 10^6 = 2.952 \times 10^{11}$.

    b. Some calculators will immediately give the exact answer using scientific notation. Other calculators display 0.000000006. A calculator that has only an eight- or nine-digit display may simply show 0. You must do part of this computation by hand to get an exact answer for many types of calculators:

$$0.0025 \div 400,000 = (2.5 \times 10^{-3}) \div (4.0 \times 10^5) = (2.5 \div 4.0) \times 10^{-8} = 0.625 \times 10^{-8} = 6.25 \times 10^{-1} \times 10^{-8} = 6.25 \times 10^{-9} = 0.00000000625.$$

Problem Set A.3

1. Write each number in scientific notation.
   a. 2,380,000
   b. 0.0000009

2. Write each number in scientific notation.
   a. 300,000
   b. 0.04901

3. Write each number in standard notation.
   a. 1.03×10^6
   b. 2×10^{-4}

4. Write each number in standard notation.
   a. 5.0×10^7
   b. 1.23×10^{-6}

5. Use a calculator that does not support scientific notation to calculate each of the following. Explain how the calculator is used in the calculations.
   a. $456,000 \times 9,200,000$
   b. $0.0003 \div 250,000$

A.4 RATIOS AND PERCENTS

Ratios

Whenever one set of objects is compared to another, a fraction can be used to illustrate this comparison. This fraction is often called a ratio. Consider the example: "There are 24 students in a class. Ten of the students are boys. Find the ratio of boys to girls." Using subtraction, you determine that 14 of the students are girls. The ratio of boys to girls is $\frac{10}{14}$. A ratio can also be expressed in words or by using notation involving a colon symbol. The above ratio can be expressed as 10 to 14 or 10:14. Using the idea of equivalent fractions, a ratio may be written in simplest form. The above ratio in simplest form is $\frac{5}{7}$ or 5 to 7 or 5:7. In many cases, expressing a ratio in simplest form makes the situation easier to visualize. Reversing the order of the sets in the comparison will reverse the ratio. For the above example, the ratio of girls to boys is 7 to 5. The two sets compared by a ratio do not have to be disjoint. The ratio of boys to students is 10 to 24 or, in simplest form, 5 to 12. Often when one ratio is given, other ratios involving the sets may be computed.

Example A-11: In a class there are 3 girls for every 2 boys. If there are 12 girls, how many boys are there?

Solution: At the lower grade levels, this could be solved with a diagram. Students could start with one row of three G's to represent 3 girls and two B's to represent 2 boys. They could add rows to the diagram until there were 12 girls represented.

    G G G B B
    G G G B B
    G G G B B
    G G G B B

From the diagram you see that when there are 12 girls, there are 8 boys.

    At a higher grade level, or when the numbers in a ratio are too large to draw an appropriate diagram, equivalent fractions can be used in the solution. When equivalent fractions are used, it is important to be consistent on which set is represented by the numerator and which set is represented by the denominator. Remember, reversing the order of the sets compared has the same effect on the ratio. Thus, inconsistency regarding which part of the fraction represents which set will lead to an incorrect answer.

Example A-12: In a school, the ratio of girls to boys is 3:2. If there are 180 boys in the school, how many girls are there?

Solution: The ratio of girls to boys is $\frac{3}{2}$. When using fractions to represent ratios, it may be a good idea to write a fraction involving words so that it is clear what each part of the fraction represents. In this case, you are using the ratio $\frac{girls}{boys}$. You are given the information that there are 180 boys.

Because the number of girls is unknown, you may use a variable in the equivalence $\frac{3}{2} = \frac{G}{180}$. Using equivalent fractions you determine that $\frac{3}{2} = \frac{270}{180}$, which implies that there are 270 girls.

In some instances, when the numbers in a ratio are too large to draw a diagram including a one-to-one representation of each number, a diagram using a visual similar to fraction strips may be used. Consider the following example.

Example A-13: An elevator indicates that it will hold 20 children or 15 adults. If there are 12 children already on the elevator, how many adults can safely board?

Solution: Since 5 is a common factor of 20 and 15, you may easily compare these quantities by fifths. Draw bars representing the children and adults, and divide each bar into fifths. There are 4 children in each section of the bar representing the children and 3 adults in each section of the bar representing the adults. It is then clear that the 12 children already on the elevator correspond to 9 adults. Thus, 6 adults may board the elevator. This solution may be checked by setting up an equivalent ratio as in the previous example and performing the calculation. Can you check this solution?

20 children

| 4 | 4 | 4 | 4 | 4 |

| 3 | 3 | 3 | 3 | 3 |

15 adults

Students should be cautioned against using ratios in situations for which they are not appropriate. Ratios should be used only in cases where sets are compared and the comparison remains valid in all other cases considered. Consider the problem: "Jan runs 2 miles in 15 minutes. How long would it take her to run 20 miles?" The original information can be expressed as the ratio $\frac{\text{miles}}{\text{minutes}} = \frac{2}{15}$. However, it is not clear that the same ratio would be valid for longer running distances. This is not a valid ratio problem unless it is stipulated that Jan will continue to run the same speed for the entire 20 miles.

Percents

In many elementary textbook series, percent is a topic that is formally introduced at the fifth-grade level. However, students will have encountered this concept many times in real-life experiences before this formal introduction. A formal definition of *percent* is "For r any real number, $r\%$ is the ratio $r/100$." Informally, you can think of 100% as the whole and compute other percents based on what part of the whole is to be considered. After all, a percent is a ratio and a ratio is a fraction.

Example A-14: Calculating percents (fifth-grade level).

A radio that normally sells for $50 is on sale for 25% off. What is the sale price?

Solution: If you didn't already recognize that 25% is equivalent to $\frac{1}{4}$, this could be computed by using the definition of "percent" since 25% =

$$\frac{25}{100} = \frac{1 \times 25}{4 \times 25} = \frac{1}{4}.$$

Once this is discovered, it is easy to compute (using division or logical thinking) that one fourth of the $50 price is $12.50. So, the sale price is $50.00 − $12.50 = $37.50.

As an alternate solution to Example A-14, you could have computed that you would have to pay $\frac{3}{4}$ of the original price. You can then compute $50 \times \frac{3}{4} = \$37.50$. Equivalent fractions, logical thinking, and diagrams are often useful in solving percent problems. Rather than presenting formal rules and equations for computations involving percent problems, this textbook relies on these more intuitive methods.

Example A-15: Solve each of the following problems.

    a. 50 is what percent of 200?
    b. 27 is 75% of what number?
    c. On a 20-question true-false test, how many questions do you need to answer correctly to score 75%?
    d. On a multiple-choice test you must get 80% or 20 questions correct in order to get a B on the test. How many questions are on the test?

Solutions:

    a. It is easy to see that 50 is $\frac{1}{4}$ of 200. Thus, 50 is 25% of 200.
    b. You must first realize (or compute) that 75% is $\frac{3}{4}$. A diagram may be useful. The shaded part represents $\frac{3}{4}$. Since this represents 27 and you must have equal parts, it is true that each part must represent 9. Then the whole number is 36. So, 27 is 75% of 36.

| 9 | 9 | 9 | 9 |

Standards

NCTM

Grades 3–5

Students should understand the meaning of a percent as part of a whole and use common percents such as 10 percent, $33\frac{1}{3}$ percent or 50 percent as benchmarks in interpreting situations they encounter.

NCTM, 2000, pp. 150–151

Standards are listed with the permission of the National Council of Teachers of Mathematics (NCTM). NCTM does not endorse the content or validity of these alignments.

c. Since $75\% = \frac{3}{4}$, you must answer an average of 3 out of each 4 questions correctly. You can use equivalent fractions to compute the ratio $\frac{3}{4} = \frac{n}{20}$ and determine that you must answer $n = 15$ questions correctly.

d. Using the definition of "percent," you find that $80\% = \frac{80}{100} = \frac{4}{5}$. You set up the ratio equivalence $\frac{4}{5} = \frac{20}{n}$ and determine that $n = 25$. There are 25 questions on the test.

Notice that if the ratio equivalence in Example A-15d had been incorrectly set up as $\frac{4}{5} = \frac{n}{20}$, an incorrect answer of $n = 16$ would have resulted. It is clear that this answer is incorrect as the problem states that 20 questions must be answered correctly. The total number of questions must then be greater than 16. The reason that the equivalence must be set up as $\frac{4}{5} = \frac{20}{n}$ is that an average of 4 out of each 5 questions must be answered correctly. So the numerator of the fraction represents the number of correct answers whereas the denominator represents the total number of questions.

Converting Between Fractions, Decimals, and Percents

In many situations a fraction will be presented when it may be more convenient to have a decimal or a percent and vice versa. We now discuss how to convert between fractions, decimals, and percents. There are six different conversions, but three of these have essentially already been discussed: (1) Any given fraction can easily be converted to a decimal by division, (2) any given decimal can be converted to a fraction by consideration of the place value properties of the decimal, and (3) any given percent can be converted to fraction by use of the definition of "percent."

Example A-16:

   a. Convert the fraction $\frac{86}{40}$ to a decimal.
   b. Convert the decimal 1.35 to a fraction.
   c. Convert the percent 56% to a fraction.

Solutions:

   a. Using long division, you find that $\frac{86}{40} = 2.15$.

$$\begin{array}{r} 2.15 \\ 40\overline{)86.00} \\ \underline{80} \\ 60 \\ \underline{40} \\ 200 \\ \underline{200} \\ 0 \end{array}$$

   b. The decimal 1.35 is one and thirty-five hundredths. This decimal is equivalent to the fraction $1\frac{35}{100}$ or in lowest terms $1\frac{7}{20}$.

c. Using the definition, you find that $56\% = \frac{56}{100}$ or in lowest terms $\frac{14}{25}$.

Combining methods (c) and (a), you have a method to convert a percent to a decimal because any given percent may be converted to a fraction and any fraction may be converted to a decimal. You may also use the definition of "percent" to derive a rule based on movement of the decimal point. Since $r\% = \frac{r}{100}$, and dividing by 100 has the effect of moving the decimal point two places to the left, you may use the fourth conversion rule: Any given percent may be converted to a decimal by moving the decimal point two places to the left. Rules such as this should not be used without consideration of how and why the rule makes sense. This rule can be illustrated with familiar examples such as $25\% = \frac{1}{4} = 0.25$ or $5\% = \frac{5}{100} = 0.05$.

Certain fractions and decimals can easily be converted to percents using the idea that 100% is one whole. Hence, $1.0 = 100\%$ and 0.5 or $\frac{1}{2} = 50\%$. If a fraction is equivalent to another fraction with denominator 100, it is also easily converted to a percent using the definition of "percent." For example, $\frac{1}{20} = \frac{5}{100} = 5\%$ and $\frac{1}{10} = \frac{10}{100} = 10\%$. When a decimal is written in terms of hundredths, it can also be converted to a percent by using the definition. For example, $0.45 = \frac{45}{100} = 45\%$ and $0.07 = \frac{7}{100} = 7\%$.

What about a fraction such as $\frac{2}{3}$ that is not easily equivalent to a fraction with denominator 100? What about a decimal such as 0.025 that is not already written in terms of hundredths? You can use logical thinking to determine how to write these quantities as a percent. The fraction $\frac{2}{3}$ should be equivalent to $\frac{2}{3}$ of 100%. Now $\frac{2}{3}$ of 100 is $\frac{2}{3} \times 100 = \frac{200}{3} = 66\frac{2}{3}$. Thus, $\frac{2}{3} = 66\frac{2}{3}\%$. The decimal 0.025 is halfway between 2% and 3%; that is, $0.025 = 2.5\%$. In general, to convert a decimal to a percent, there is another decimal point movement rule that you can use. Since $\frac{r}{100} = r\%$, you have that $r = (100 \times r)\%$. Multiplication by 100 has the effect of moving the decimal point two places to the right.

Therefore, we have the fifth conversion rule: Any decimal number may be converted to a percent by moving the decimal point in the number two places to the right. When a fraction is not easily converted to a percent by using logical arguments such as those presented above, you may use the sixth rule: Any fraction may be converted to a decimal number by division, and this may be converted to a percent by moving the decimal place in the number two places to the right.

Example A-17:

   a. Convert 3% to a decimal.
   b. Convert 0.0456 to a percent.
   c. Convert $\frac{3}{8}$ to a percent.

Solutions:

   a. $3\% = 0.03$

   b. $0.0456 = 4.56\%$

   c. $\frac{3}{8} = 0.375 = 37.5\%$

We have dealt with fractions and decimals that are larger than one. For example, $1.25 = 1\frac{25}{100} = \frac{125}{100}$. Does it also make sense to have percents that are larger than 100%? Yes, a percent that is larger than 100% is merely a quantity that is more than one whole unit. The rules for conversion still hold, for example $1.25 = 125\%$.

Example A-18: Normally the flower shop sells roses for $3.00 each. Due to the Valentine's Day rush, during the second week of February it increases the price by 150%. How much does a rose cost during this week?

Solution: You know that 100% of $3.00 is $3.00. So a 100% price increase would have changed the price from $3.00 to $6.00. This shop increased its price by even more than that. You calculate that 150% of $3.00 is the whole $3.00 plus an additional half. That is, 150% of $3.00 is $3.00 + $1.50 = $4.50. The store would increase the price by $4.50, making the new price $7.50 per rose during the week of Valentine's Day.

Problem Set A.4

1. a. A 5-month-old puppy weighs 15 pounds. How much will it weigh when it is 1 year old?
   b. On the imaginary island of Growtall, each person is 1 foot tall when she is born and grows 3 inches every year of her life. How many years will it take a citizen of Growtall to grow to 6 feet tall?

2. In a school the ratio of boys to girls in the choir is $\frac{2}{5}$. There are 20 girls in the choir.
   a. How many boys are in the choir?
   b. Express the ratio $\frac{2}{5}$ in the two alternate ratio formats discussed.
   c. What is the ratio of girls in the choir to boys in the choir?
   d. What is the ratio of girls in the choir to students in the choir?

3. A soup recipe calls for four cups of water and feeds 6 people. How many cups of water should be used if the recipe is made to feed 15 people?

4. A CD that is originally priced $12 is on sale for 20% off. What is the sale price of the CD?

5. a. 30 is what percent of 150?
   b. 30 is 150% of what number?
   c. 30 is 40% of what number?
   d. 6 is what percent of 30?

6. A radio is marked up 10%. This new price is then marked down 10%. Compare the final price to the original price.

7. The grades in a class were 25% As, 30% Bs, 10% Ds, and the rest of the grades were Cs. If four of the grades were Ds, how many of the grades were Cs?

8. a. What is the percent increase if a $40 item is marked up to $100?
   b. What is the percent decrease if an $80 item is marked down to $60?

9. Complete the following table.

	Fraction	Decimal	Percent
(a)			6%
(b)		20.5	
(c)	$2\frac{4}{5}$		

10. Complete the following table.

	Fraction	Decimal	Percent
(a)			80%
(b)		0.123	
(c)	$\frac{36}{40}$		
(d)			230%

11. a. Order the following from least to greatest.
    (1) 10% of 400
    (2) 25% of 1,000
    (3) 20% of 300
    (4) 15% of 400
    (5) 50% of 90
    b. 2.53% is greater than which of the following?
    (1) 25.3%
    (2) 0.253
    (3) 0.03
    (4) $\frac{1}{10}$
    (5) $\frac{25}{1,000}$

12. a. If 40% of *W* is 624, find *W*.
    b. 55 is what percent of 200?

13. On a bus there are 10 first graders, 15 second graders, 12 third graders, and 8 fourth graders. What percent of the students on the bus are second graders?

14. In a bag of M&M's, 10% are red, 12% are blue, 14% are green, 20% are yellow, and the rest are brown. If there are 200 M&M's in the bag, how many are there of each color?

15. 15.5% of all registered students have already scheduled for next semester. There are 200

registered students. How many have already scheduled for next semester?

16. A TV was originally priced $150. It is on sale for $120. What is the percent decrease in price?

17. To get 70% on a multiple-choice test, a student must answer 14 questions correctly. How many questions are on the test?

A.5 AREA, PERIMETER, AND VOLUME

In Section 11.3 we calculated the area, perimeter, and volume of figures and solids involving straight line segments. This section expands on those ideas to include figures involving curved or slanted sides and segments. These ideas are usually presented at the middle school level.

Area and Perimeter (Circumference) of a Circle

The perimeter of a circle, called the *circumference,* is the distance around the circle. Using an activity involving various circles and string or a tape measure, children can discover the fact that the ratio of the circumference of a circle to its diameter is always the same. This ratio, known as *pi* and symbolized by π, is approximately 3.14. At around the fifth-grade level, students are introduced to formulas for the circumference and area of a circle. The formula for the circumference of a circle follows directly from the above fact relating the circumference and the diameter. The formula for the area of a circle can be illustrated by the rearrangement of circle sectors into a figure resembling a parallelogram. If you are teaching in an early childhood classroom, you will not teach this material. However, these formulas are presented because they will be useful in later volume calculations.

Formula: The Circumference of a Circle If a circle has radius r, the circumference of the circle may be calculated using the formula $C = 2\pi \times r$ or $C = 2\pi r$.

Formula: The Area of a Circle If a circle has radius r, the area of the circle may be calculated using the formula $A = \pi \times r^2$ or $A = \pi r^2$.

Example A-19: Problem solving using formulas (fifth- or sixth-grade level).

A 10 by 12-inch rectangular pizza and a 12-inch round pizza (that have the same thickness) both sell for the same price. Which is the better value? Which pizza contains more crust?

Solution: To determine which is the better value, calculate the area (amount) of each pizza. The area of the rectangular pizza is $10 \times 12 = 120$ square inches. The area of the 12-inch round pizza can be calculated by using the formula $A = \pi r^2$. Be careful here—the radius is not 12. When a store advertises a 12-inch pizza, it is selling a pizza that has a *diameter* of 12 inches. The radius is thus 6 inches. The area of the round pizza is $A = \pi \times 6^2 = \pi \times 36 \approx 113$ square inches. The rectangular pizza contains more total pizza.

To determine which pizza contains more crust, calculate the perimeter of each pizza. The perimeter of the rectangular pizza is $P = 2 \times 10 + 2 \times 12 = 44$ inches. The perimeter of the round pizza is $P = 2 \times \pi \times 6 = 12\pi \approx 38$ inches. The rectangular pizza contains the longer crust.

Volume of a Solid

The idea used in Section 11.3 to find the volume of a rectangular prism by building each layer of the prism can be used to derive a volume formula valid for any prism, not just a rectangular prism. Any prism can be constructed by first building the bottom layer (find the area of the base) and then stacking layers up to the height of the prism. For example, the volume of a circular cylinder is $V = \pi r^2 h$, where r denotes the length of the radius and h denotes the height of the cylinder. This is based on the fact that the area of the circular base is πr^2.

Formula: The Volume of a Prism If a prism has base area B, the volume V of the prism is the product of the area of the base and the height. That is, $V = B \times h$, where B is the area of the base and h is the height.

Example A-20: A soup can has a height of 6 inches and a 4-inch diameter.

Calculate the amount of soup in the can.

Solution: The base of the can is circular. The area of the base B can be calculated using the formula $B = \pi r^2$. The diameter of the can is given as 4 inches. This implies that the radius of the can is 2 inches. Hence, the area of the base $B = \pi \times 2^2 \approx 12.56$ in.^{2}. The volume of the can is then $V = Bh \approx 12.56 \times 6 \approx 75$ in.^{3}.

Does this really answer the question? Do you know how much soup is in the can? The answer 75 in.^{3} may be the actual amount, but this answer is not intuitively satisfying. You can convert this answer to more familiar units by using the fact that a gallon contains approximately 231 in.^{3}. Another known fact is that 1 gallon contains 16 cups. Hence, a cup contains approximately $231 \div 16 \approx 14.4$ in.^{3}. The division $75 \div 14.4 \approx 5.2$ tells you that there are about 5 cups of soup in the can.

Formulas are given below for the volume of a pyramid, a cone, and a sphere. Because these formulas are not taught in the early childhood classroom, this textbook will not formally derive them. Power solids can be used to demonstrate the validity of the volume formulas for the pyramid or cone. Balloons and water can be used to demonstrate the validity of the volume formula for a sphere.

Activity A-1 Grades 5–6

Volume of a Cylinder Versus a Cone

Materials: Power solids; rice or water.

Teacher Statement: How many cones do you think it will take to fill the cylinder? Notice that the bases of both figures are congruent, and both figures have the same height. So the only difference is that the cylinder is straight up and down and the cone comes to a point. You think it will take 2 cones? $2\frac{1}{2}$ cones? 3 cones? Let's see.

(Fill the cone with water or rice and dump this into the cylinder. This will fill one third of the cylinder. Students may wish to revise their predictions at this point. It takes exactly 3 cones to fill the cylinder.)

The volume of a cylinder is given by the formula $V = \pi r^2 h$. What do you think the formula should be for the volume of a cone? Yes, it is $V = \frac{1}{3}\pi r^2 h$.

Note: A similar demonstration will show that it takes 3 pyramids to fill a cube when the bases and heights are congruent. This can be used to validate the formula for the volume of a pyramid.

Formula: The Volume of a Pyramid or Cone The volume V of a pyramid or cone is given by the formula $V = \frac{1}{3}B \times h$, where B is the area of the base and h is the height.

Example A-21: A cone has a radius of 2 inches and a height of 6 inches. Find the volume of the cone.

Solution: In Example A-20 you calculated that the volume of a cylinder with radius $r = 2$ in. and height $h = 6$ in. is $V = 75$ in.^{3}. Thus, the volume of the given cone is 25 in.^{3}.

Formula: The Circumference, Surface Area, and Volume of a Sphere If a sphere has the radius r, the circumference of the sphere is given by the formula $C = 2\pi r$; the surface area of the sphere is given by the formula $S = 4\pi r^2$, and the volume of the sphere is given by the formula $V = \frac{4}{3}\pi r^3$.

Example A-22: A water-filled spherical balloon has a diameter of 6 inches. Calculate the circumference, the surface area, and the volume. How much water does the balloon contain?

Solution: The circumference of the balloon is $C = 2\pi \times 3 = 6\pi \approx 19$ in.

The surface area of the balloon is $S = 4\pi \times 3^2 = 36\pi \approx 113$ in.^{2}.

The volume of the balloon is $V = \frac{4}{3}\pi \times 3^3 = 36\pi \approx 113$ in.^{3}.

The balloon contains 113 in.^{3} of water. This is almost one half of a gallon of water.

Notice the units used in the solution of Example A-22. Circumference is a linear measure. This can be measured with a string or tape measure. The surface area is given in square inches. Surface area measures how much surface would be covered if the balloon were popped and the balloon shell remained stretched out. Volume is measured in cubic inches. Volume measures how much can be contained within the balloon. It is the volume calculation that tells how much water a balloon contains. In this example, the numbers associated with the surface area and the volume are equal. Do you think this will be true for all spheres? See problem 2 in Problem Set A.5.

Problem Set A.5

1. Can you determine a rectangular pizza size that has less overall area, but longer crust than a 12-inch round pizza? See Example A-19.

2. Give a possible radius for each of the following, or explain why the figure does not exist.
   a. A sphere where the numerical value associated with the surface area is greater than the numerical value associated with the volume.
   b. A sphere where the numerical value associated with the surface area is less than the numerical value associated with the volume.

3. A cone has volume 300 in.^{3}. Find the volume of a cylinder that has a congruent base and the same height as the cone.

4. A swimming pool has a rectangular shape with half circles on the two ends as shown. It is filled with 5 feet of water. The length (at the longest point) is 16 feet and the width (at the widest point) is 6 feet. Find the volume of the pool and then find the number of gallons of water in the pool.

5. Rich ties an 18-foot ribbon around a tree. Two feet of the ribbon are used to make the knot and bow. Approximate the diameter of the tree.

6. A window has the shape of a rectangle topped by a semicircle and dimensions as shown. Find the area of the window.

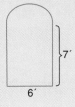
7′
6′

7. A snow cone in a paper thin cup has the shape of a cone topped by half of a sphere. Find the volume of the snow cone if the cone has a height of 12 centimeters and the hemisphere has a diameter of 10 centimeters.

8. Find the volume of the figure shown. The cylinder has a height of 15 inches and the hemisphere has a diameter of 1 foot.

9. Which has larger volume, a sphere with a radius of 5 centimeters or four cubes each with the side length of 5 centimeters?

10. A cylinder has a height of 1 foot and a volume of 942 in.^{3}. Calculate (to the nearest inch) what the radius of the cylinder is. Also, calculate the volume of a cone that has the same height and radius as the cylinder.

A.6   THE PYTHAGOREAN THEOREM

Before we discuss the Pythagorean theorem, one definition is needed. The side of a right triangle opposite the right angle is called the *hypotenuse;* the other sides of a right triangle are sometimes called *legs.* Because the right angle is the largest angle in a right triangle, the hypotenuse is the longest side in a right triangle. In general, longer sides in a triangle will be located across from larger angles. You may recall this fact from a high school geometry course. You may also recall learning the following theorem, which is presented here without proof.

The Pythagorean Theorem

For a right triangle with leg lengths a and b and hypotenuse length c, the formula $a^2 + b^2 = c^2$ holds.

Example A-23: Two side lengths of a right triangle are given. Find the side length of the third side for each triangle.

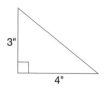

Solutions:

a. The two leg lengths are given; the length of the hypotenuse is unknown. The formula $3^2 + 4^2 = c^2$ must hold. Then, $9 + 16 = c^2$, or $25 = c^2$. Hence, $c = 5$ inches.

b. One of the given lengths is the hypotenuse length; the other is a triangle leg length. One leg length is unknown. The formula $a^2 + 8^2 = 10^2$ must hold. Thus, $a^2 + 64 = 100$, and $a^2 = 36$. Hence, $a = 6$ inches.

c. One of the given lengths is the hypotenuse length: the other is a leg length. The formula $a^2 + 2^2 = 4^2$ must hold. Thus, $a^2 + 4 = 16$, and $a^2 = 12$. There is no whole number whose square is 12; however, you can solve the equation as $a = \sqrt{12}$ inches. You can use a calculator to approximate $a \approx 3.5$ inches.

By the contrapositive of the Pythagorean theorem, if a triangle has side lengths a, b, and c (with c the longest length) such that $a^2 + b^2 \neq c^2$, then the triangle is not a right triangle. The converse of the Pythagorean theorem is also true. This result, along with the contrapositive of the Pythagorean theorem, can be used to determine whether a triangle with given side lengths is a right, an acute or an obtuse triangle.

The Converse of the Pythagorean Theorem

If the formula $a^2 + b^2 = c^2$ holds for a triangle with side lengths a, b, and c, then the triangle is a right triangle.

Example A-24: Three side lengths of a triangle are given. Determine whether each triangle is a right, acute, or obtuse triangle.

a. 5 cm, 7 cm, and 9 cm
b. 5 m, 13m, and 12m
c. 10 ft, 8ft, and 7ft

Solutions: In each case, the longest length will be used on the right side of the equation as the potential length of a hypotenuse. The first step will be to determine whether the formula $a^2 + b^2 = c^2$ holds.

a. Plugging values into the equation, you see that $5^2 + 7^2 \neq 9^2$ since $25 + 49 = 74 \neq 81$. A right triangle with leg lengths of 5 cm and 7 cm has a hypotenuse length of $\sqrt{74} \approx 8.6$ cm. A 9 cm third side will require a larger angle than the right angle shown. Hence, the 5-7-9 triangle is an obtuse triangle.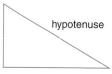

b. Plugging values into the equation, you see that $5^2 + 12^2 = 13^2$ since $25 + 144 = 169$. Hence, the 5-12-13 triangle is a right triangle.

c. Plugging values into the equation, you see that $7^2 + 8^2 \neq 10^2$ since $49 + 64 = 113 \neq 100$. A right triangle with leg lengths of 7 ft and 8 ft has a hypotenuse length of $\sqrt{113} \approx 10.6$ ft. A 10 ft third side will require a smaller angle than the right angle shown. This angle is the largest angle of the triangle because it is opposite the longest side. Hence, the 7-8-10 triangle is an acute triangle.

Example A-25: A figure is drawn on centimeter-squared paper. Find the area and the perimeter. (A smaller scale model is shown.)

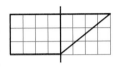

Solution: The area can be found by adding the area of the rectangle to the area of the triangle when the figure is dissected as shown. The rectangle has an area of $3 \times 4 = 12$ cm^2. The triangle has an area of $\frac{1}{2} \times 3 \times 4 = 6$ cm^2. The figure has an area of 18 cm^2.

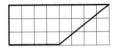

To calculate the perimeter, you must find the length of the diagonal segment. This segment is the hypotenuse of a right triangle. The formula $3^2 + 4^2 = c^2$ gives $9 + 16 = c^2$ or $25 = c^2$ and $c = 5$ cm. The perimeter is $8 + 3 + 4 + 5 = 20$ cm.

Example A-26: A square pyramid has the dimensions shown. Calculate the volume of the pyramid.

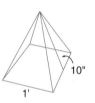

Solution: The volume formula for a pyramid is $V = \frac{1}{3}Bh$, where B is the area of the base and h is the height of the pyramid. Because one length is given in inches, and the other is given in feet, use inches in the calculations. The area of the base is $B = 12 \times 12 = 144$ in.^{2}. The 10-inch length shown is not the height of the pyramid; it is the length from the apex to the midpoint of one side of the base. To find the height, draw the triangle shown and note that the bottom leg of the triangle has a length of 6 inches (one half of the side length of the square base). This is a right triangle with a hypotenuse length of 10 inches, and you may use the Pythagorean theorem to find the missing side length, the height of the pyramid. The formula $a^2 + 6^2 = 10^2$ gives $a^2 + 36 = 100$ or $a^2 = 64$. Hence, $a = 8$ inches. Now the volume $V = \frac{1}{3}(144)(8) = 384$ in.^{3}.

Problem Set A.6

1. Find the area and the perimeter of the figure shown.

2. Find the area and the perimeter of the figure shown.

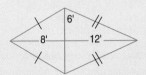

3. Find the volume of the figure.

4. Find the volume of the figure.

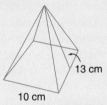

5. Find the area and the perimeter of the figure shown.

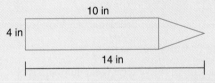

6. Calculate the perimeter of each of the following.
   a. 1 foot

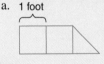

   b.

   c.

   d.

   e.

A.7 LOGIC

Logical reasoning is a problem-solving strategy that is presented as early as the first-grade level.

Inductive and Deductive Reasoning

We will discuss two types of reasoning. *Inductive reasoning* is reasoning from the particular to the general. To use inductive reasoning, you consider small or special cases and looks for a pattern. From the pattern, you attempt to induce a more general result. One drawback to this type of argument is that not all patterns will continue to hold in all larger cases.

Example A-27: Find the sum of the first 100 odd numbers.

Step 1: Understand the problem.

Be sure that you understand what is meant by "the first 100 odd numbers." The first two odd numbers are 1 and 3. The first three odd numbers are 1, 3, and 5. The first four odd numbers are 1, 3, 5, and 7. Continuing in this manner, you induce that the first 100 odd numbers are $1, 3, 5, \ldots, 199$. You recall that the sum is the answer to an addition problem. You wish to find the sum $1 + 3 + 5 + \ldots + 199$.

Step 2: Devise a plan.

Consider smaller problems and look for a pattern.

Step 3: Carry out the plan.

The sum of the first two odd numbers is: $1 + 3 = 4$.

The sum of the first three odd numbers is $1 + 3 + 5 = 9$.

The sum of the first four odd numbers is $1 + 3 + 5 + 7 = 16$.

The sum of the first five odd numbers is $1 + 3 + 5 + 7 + 9 = 25$.

The sum of the first six odd numbers is $1 + 3 + 5 + 7 + 9 + 11 = 36$.

It appears that the sum of the first k odd numbers is k^2. Predict that the sum of the first 100 odd numbers is $100^2 = 10,000$.

Step 4: Look back.

You noticed a pattern that held for $k = 2, 3, 4, 5$, and 6. You used the pattern to draw a conclusion for $k = 100$. How can

you be sure that the pattern will hold for larger values such as $k = 100$? Unless you prove that the pattern holds for larger values, you cannot be sure that your answer is correct. Perhaps there is another way to verify the answer.

You wish to calculate the sum

$$1 + 3 + 5 + \ldots + 99 + 101 + \ldots + 195 + 197 + 199.$$

Notice that if you find the sums of pairs of numbers working from the outside toward the inside, the sum of each pair is 200. There are 50 such pairs of numbers. The overall sum is then $50 \times 200 = 10,000$. It appears that the answer for $k = 100$ is correct. Does this prove that the formula will work for all larger values of k? No, it does not. But you are certain that you have correctly answered the question asked. A formal proof that the formula "The sum of the first k odd numbers is k^2" does hold for all values of k uses the principle of mathematical induction. Because this is beyond the scope of this text, it will not be addressed.

Step 5: Extend the problem.

For children in lower grade levels, you may wish to decrease the number of addends. Challenge children to find the sum of the first 50 odd numbers or the first 20 odd numbers. You could also extend the problem by asking for the sum of the first 100 even numbers or the first 100 whole numbers.

Standards

NCTM

Grades Pre-K–2

Although they have yet to develop all the tools used in mathematical reasoning, young students have their own ways of finding mathematical results and convincing themselves that they are true. Two important elements of reasoning for students in the early grades are pattern-recognition and classification skills. They use a combination of ways of justifying their answers—perception, empirical evidence, and short chains of deductive reasoning grounded in previously accepted facts. They make conjectures and reach conclusions that are logical and defensible from their perspective. Even when they are struggling, their responses reveal the sense they are making of mathematical situations.

NCTM, 2000, pp. 150–151

Example A-28:

a. Draw a circle, place two points on the circle, and draw the chord between the points. Two points divide a circle into 2 regions.

b. Place another point on the circle and draw all possible chords. Three points divide a circle into 4 regions.

c. Place another point on the circle and draw all possible chords. Four points divide a circle into 8 regions.

(1) If a fifth point is placed on the circle, and all chords are drawn, into how many regions is the circle divided? Make a conjecture and then test your conjecture.

(2) If a sixth point is placed on the circle, and all chords are drawn, into how many regions is the circle divided? Make a conjecture and then test your conjecture.

Solutions:

a. You should find 16 regions.

b. You will find at most 31 regions.

Example A-28 above shows that inductive reasoning and looking for a pattern does not always provide a solution that will work in all larger cases. Another type of logical argument is called deductive reasoning. *Deductive reasoning* involves working from a set of known facts, axioms, and statements to derive a conclusion.

Compound Statements

Statements in logic are generally denoted by small letters such as *p, q,* and *r.* You can combine statements to form *compound statements.* The first such combination that we will consider is called a conjunction. A *conjunction* combines statements with the operation "and." The compound statement "*p* and *q*," denoted $p \wedge q$, is true when both *p* and *q* are true, and false if either *p* or *q* or both is false. This corresponds to the everyday usage of the word "and." Consider the statement "It is Monday and it is raining." For this overall statement to be true, it would have to be true that (1) it is Monday *and* (2) it is raining. If either substatement happened to be false, the overall statement would be false.

The next combination is called a disjunction. A *disjunction* combines statements with the operation "or." The compound statement "*p* or *q*," denoted $p \vee q$, is true if either *p* or *q* or both is true, and false only when *p* and *q* are both false. This corresponds to the everyday usage of the word "or" in situations where both options are permissible: "Would you like salt or catsup for your fries?" "Yes, please. I'll take both." However, in other everyday situations both options are not allowed: A value menu sandwich comes with fries or onion rings; you are not allowed to choose both. You must remember that in logic, the disjunction refers to an "inclusive or" which allows both options to be true.

Example A-29: Let *p* = "5 is a prime number," and *q* = "4 is even," and *r* = "3 + 5 = 7," and *s* = "3 is a perfect square." Then *p* is true, *q* is true, *r* is false, and *s* is false. Find the truth value of each of the following.

a. $p \wedge q$

b. $p \wedge r$

c. $r \wedge p$

d. $r \wedge s$

e. $p \vee q$

f. $p \vee r$

g. $r \vee p$

h. $r \vee s$

Solutions:

a. Both *p* and *q* are true, so the statement $p \wedge q$ is true.

b. Since *r* is false, the statement $p \wedge r$ is false.

c. Since *r* is false, the statement $r \wedge p$ is false.

d. Since *r* and *s* are both false, the statement $r \wedge s$ is false.

e. Both *p* and *q* are true, so the statement $p \vee q$ is true.

f. Since *p* is true, the statement $p \vee r$ is true.

g. Since *p* is true, the statement $r \vee p$ is true.

h. Since both *r* and *s* are false, the statement $r \vee s$ is false.

The Negation of a Statement A *negation* of a statement can be formed by inserting the phrase "It is not the case that" in front of the statement. For example, if the statement is "It is raining," the negation is "It is not the case that it is raining" or simply "It is not raining." Negation has the effect of changing the truth value of a statement. If a statement is true, then its negation is false. If a statement is false, then its negation is true. Negation may be denoted by "not-*p*" or by "~*p*." Unless parentheses are present, the negation symbol applies only to the statement immediately following the symbol. For example, the negation in ~*p* ∨ *q* applies only to statement *p,* whereas the negation in ~(*p* ∨ *q*) applies to the compound statement *p* ∨ *q*.

Consider the statement "Every prime number is odd." The negation of this statement is "It is not the case that every prime is odd." If it is not the case that every prime is odd, then it must be the case that some primes are not odd, or "There is a prime that is not odd," or "There exists at least one even prime number." Notice that the original statement involved a universal quantifier whereas its negation involves an existential quantifier. The original statement is false; the negation of this statement is true. Now consider the statement "There is a whole number whose square is negative." The negation of this statement is "It is not the case that there is a whole number whose square is negative."

The effect of negation on conjunctions and disjunctions is discussed within the problem set.

If there does not exist a whole number whose square is negative, then it must be that "For every whole number, the square of the number is nonnegative." Notice that the original statement involved an existential quantifier whereas its negation involves a universal quantifier.

Truth Tables

A truth table provides a convenient notation for recording truth values. A *truth table* is a logical table that lists all possible outcomes regarding whether given statements are true or false. The truth values of compound statements can then be determined and recorded. To construct a truth table that includes two statements *p* and *q*, four cases must be considered: both *p* and *q* are true, *p* is true and *q* is false, *p* is false and *q* is true, and both *p* and *q* are false. To construct a truth table that includes three statements, eight cases must be considered (see problems 6 and 7 in Problem Set A.7). Truth tables will be useful in showing that statements are logically equivalent. Two statements are *logically equivalent* if they have the same overall truth value for all possible values of the propositions involved.

Example A-30: Construct truth tables for each of the following.

    a. *p* ∧ *q*
    b. *p* ∨ *q*
    c. ~*p* ∨ *q*

Solutions:

a.

p	*q*	*p* ∧ *q*
T	T	T
T	F	F
F	T	F
F	F	F

b.

p	*q*	*p* ∨ *q*
T	T	T
T	F	T
F	T	T
F	F	F

c.

p	*q*	~*p*	~*p* ∨ *q*
T	T	F	T
T	F	F	F
F	T	T	T
F	F	T	T

Conditional Statements

Many mathematical theorems and statements follow the pattern that the conclusion will hold only under certain conditions. Such a statement is called a *conditional* and usually has the form "If *hypothesis,* then *conclusion.*" Many statements that appear to be declarative statements may be rewritten into if/then form. For example, the statement "Every square is a rectangle" may be rewritten as "If a figure is a square, then the figure is a rectangle." The notation for a conditional statement is *p* ⇒ *q* which may be read as "*p* implies *q*" or "if *p*, then *q*." One advantage to rewriting a declarative statement into if/then form is that from this form other related statements can be determined. Next, we will discuss the related statements of converse, contrapositive, and inverse.

The Converse Statement The *converse* statement of *p* ⇒ *q* is defined as *q* ⇒ *p*. Consider the following statement regarding whole numbers: "If a product is equal to zero, then one of the factors is equal to zero." This is a true statement. Consider the converse: "If one of the factors is equal to zero, then the product is equal to zero." This is also a true statement. For another example, consider the implication *square* ⇒ *rectangle*, or "Every square is a rectangle." In if/then form, the statement is: "If a figure is a square, then the figure is a rectangle." This is a true statement. The converse is *rectangle* ⇒ *square* or, "If a figure is a rectangle, then the figure is a square." This statement is false. These examples indicate that the converse of a statement may or may not have the same truth value as the statement. Thus a statement and its converse are certainly not equivalent, although it is common for young children to treat them as equivalent.

The Contrapositive Statement The *contrapositive* of the statement *p* ⇒ *q* is defined as ~*q* ⇒ ~*p*. Consider the following statement regarding whole numbers: "If n^2 is odd, then *n* is odd." The contrapositive of this statement is: "If it is not the case that *n* is odd, then it is not the case that n^2

is odd." Or, in simpler terms, "If n is even, then n^2 is even." We will prove below that a statement and its contrapositive are logically equivalent or will always have the same truth values.

The Inverse Statement The *inverse* of statement $p \Rightarrow q$ is defined as $\sim p \Rightarrow \sim q$. It may be proven that the inverse of a statement is logically equivalent to the converse of the statement. Thus, the inverse of a statement may or may not have the same truth value as the original statement.

Before proving the logical equivalence of a conditional statement and its contrapositive, a truth table must first be devised for the conditional statement. We have stated that a valid or true hypothesis must lead to a true conclusion. What happens in the case that the hypothesis is false? Consider the example: "If it is raining, recess will be held indoors." What will happen in the case that it is not raining? That is unknown. It might be true that if it is not raining, then recess will be held outside. However, it might be too cold to hold recess outside, and recess may be held inside even when it is not raining. This example illustrates that in the case of a false hypothesis, the conclusion may be true or it may be false. The overall implication is assigned the value "true" in the case of a false hypotheses.

Example A-31: Construct and compare truth tables for each of the following.

    a. $p \Rightarrow q$
    b. $q \Rightarrow p$
    c. $\sim q \Rightarrow \sim p$

Solutions:

  a.

p	q	$p \Rightarrow q$
T	T	T
T	F	F
F	T	T
F	F	T

  b.

p	q	$q \Rightarrow p$
T	T	T
T	F	T
F	T	F
F	F	T

  c.

p	q	$\sim q$	$\sim p$	$\sim q \Rightarrow \sim p$
T	T	F	F	T
T	F	T	F	F
F	T	F	T	T
F	F	T	T	T

Notice that the truth tables for $p \Rightarrow q$ and the contrapositive $\sim q \Rightarrow \sim p$ are equivalent. In each case of possible truth

values for the propositions p and q, the corresponding overall results are the same. This shows that the statements $p \Rightarrow q$ and $\sim q \Rightarrow \sim p$ are logically equivalent. It follows that the converse statement $q \Rightarrow p$ and the inverse statement $\sim p \Rightarrow \sim q$ are also logically equivalent to each other. However, the converse and inverse are not logically equivalent to the original statement as can be seen by the fact that the truth table for $p \Rightarrow q$ is not equivalent to the truth table for the converse statement $q \Rightarrow p$. For example, when p is true and q is false, the value of $p \Rightarrow q$ is false whereas the value of $q \Rightarrow p$ is true.

Example A-32: Write the given statement as a conditional. Find the inverse, converse, and contrapositive statements. Indicate a truth value for each of the four statements.

    Given statement: All circles are similar.

Solution: If A and B are circles, then A and B are similar. (true)

> *Inverse:* If A and B are not both circles, then A and B are not similar. (false)
> *Converse:* If A and B are similar, then A and B are circles. (false)
> *Contrapositive:* If A and B are not similar, then A and B are not both circles. (true)

Necessary and Sufficient Conditions

Example A-33: Teacher's policy: If you get an A on the final, then you will pass the class.

    a. Randall passed the class. Can you conclude that Randall got an A on the final?
    b. Lucia did not pass the class. What can you conclude?

Solutions:

    a. You cannot conclude that Randall got an A on the final. Let $p =$ "get an A on the final" and $q =$ "will pass the class." Then the teacher's policy has the logical format $p \Rightarrow q$ (if p then q). The fact that a certain student passed the class does not imply that the student got an A on the final. This is the converse relation $q \Rightarrow p$, which may or may not have the same truth value as the original statement.
    b. If Lucia did not pass, then you can conclude that she did not get an A on the final. For if Lucia had gotten an A on the final, she would have passed. This illustrates the contrapositive relation. You are given the information that Lucia did not pass; this corresponds to $\sim q$. The relation $p \Rightarrow q$ is equivalent to $\sim q \Rightarrow \sim p$. So $\sim q$ (not passing) implies $\sim p$ (didn't get an A on the final).

The above example illustrates the difference between a *sufficient condition* and a *necessary condition*. The condition "get an A on the final" is sufficient to conclude "will pass the class," but it is not necessary. To "fail the class," it is necessary that "a grade of A was not attained on the final." Consider the following result: "If the last digit of a whole number is even, then the number is divisible by 2. Thus 'last digit even' is sufficient to conclude 'divisible by 2.'" However, the converse result is also true: "If a whole number is divisible by 2, then the last digit is even. Thus 'last digit even' is also a necessary condition for the conclusion 'divisible by 2.'" You may state the two results simultaneously in a single theorem.

Theorem A.3: A whole number is divisible by 2 if and only if the last digit of the number is even.

Problem Set A.7

1. a. Find the sum of the first 100 whole numbers.
    b. Find the sum of the first 100 even whole numbers.

2. Let p = "$3 \geq 3$," q = "9 is a prime number," r = "2 is the only even prime number," and s = "122 is evenly divisible by 4." Find the truth values of
    a. $p \wedge q$
    b. $p \vee q$
    c. $p \wedge r$
    d. $q \vee s$
    e. $q \wedge s$

3. a. Use truth tables to show that $\sim(p \wedge q)$ is logically equivalent to $(\sim p) \vee (\sim q)$.
    b. Use the result of part (a) to express the negation of the following statement. Use simple wording when possible. "It is Monday and it is raining."
    c. Make a conjecture regarding a statement logically equivalent to $\sim(r \vee s)$ and use truth tables to verify your conjecture.

4. Write the negation of each statement. Use simple wording when possible. Give the truth value of each statement and its negation.
    a. Every odd whole number is evenly divisible by 3.
    b. There is a whole number n such that $n^2 < n$.

5. Write the negation of each statement. Use simple wording when possible. Give the truth value of each statement and its negation.
    a. Every even whole number is evenly divisible by 2.
    b. There is a smallest whole number.

6. Construct a truth table for $\sim(p \vee q) \wedge r$.

7. Construct a truth table for $[(\sim p) \Rightarrow q] \vee r$.
    Directions for problems 8–10: Write the given statement as a conditional. Find the inverse, converse, and contrapositive of the statement.

8. All three-hour classes will meet on Monday, Wednesday, and Friday.

9. An alarm will ring if the fire door is opened.

10. You must be at least 3 feet tall to ride the carnival rides.
    Directions for problems 11–14. Explain the error in each of the following. Provide counterexamples when possible.

11. When you add 2 three-digit numbers, the result is a three-digit number.

12. If it is 50 miles from town *A* to town *B*, and 40 miles from town *B* to town *C*, then it is 90 miles from town *A* to town *C*.

13. If *a* and *b* are both whole numbers that when rounded to the nearest 10 give the same value, then the difference between *a* and *b* is at most 5.

14. When you multiply two numbers, the product is greater than either factor.

References

Burden, P. R., & Byrd, D. M. (1998). *Methods for effective teaching.* (2nd ed.). Upper Saddle River, NJ: Pearson Allyn & Bacon.

Campbell, P. F., & Stewart, E. L. (1993). Calculators and computers. In R. J. Jensen (Ed.), *Research Ideas for the Classroom: Early Childhood Mathematics* (pp. 251–268). Macmillan.

Charles, R. I., Dossey, J. A., Leinwand, S. J., Seeley, C. L., Vonder Embse, C. B. (1999). *Math Grade 6, Scott Foresman.* Menlo Park, CA: Addison Wesley.

National Council of Teachers of Mathematics. (2000). *Principles and standards for school mathematics.* Reston, VA: Author.

Ohio Department of Education. (2001). *Ohio Academic Content Standards.* Retrieved November 12, 2003 from http://www.ode.state.oh.us/academic_content_standards/pdf/MATH.pdf

Praxis I—Test at a Glance: PPST Mathematics. (n.d). Retrieved December 16, 2003 from ETS (Educational Testing Service) at http://www.ets.org/praxis/taags/prx0730.html

Texas Education Agency, (1998). *Chapter 111. Texas Essential Knowledge and Skills for Mathematics.* Retrieved November 12, 2003 from http://www.tea.state.tx.us/rules/tac/ch111toc.html

Technology in Teaching

In today's world, technology is an important part of any mathematics curriculum. Calculators and computers can and should be used in first grade and beyond. Calculator activities are included in each chapter of this text as appropriate. The main technologies discussed here are Microsoft Word drawing tools; Logo, the computer language; the Microsoft Excel Software Program; the Geometer's Sketchpad; and the TI-15 calculator. Some of this material is meant only for you as a future teacher. When these technologies are appropriate for inclusion into the early childhood curriculum, specific examples and activities are provided.

Teachers use technology in creating lesson plans and assessments. They use technology in creating handouts and materials to be used in the classroom. Some school districts require teachers to maintain a computer gradebook. Most classrooms, even at the early childhood level, come equipped with computers for both teacher and student use.

B.1 MICROSOFT WORD DRAWING

This section introduces Microsoft Word drawing features. You will find Word drawing tools useful in making handouts and materials for your classroom and for activities. Many of the illustrations in this textbook were created using Word drawing tools. With Word drawing tools, you can easily create simple shapes such as those below.

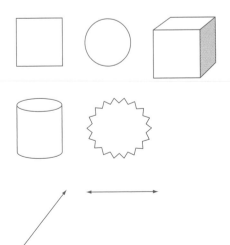

You can also create materials such as Bingo cards, 10 by 10 squares, and so on, or add text to a drawing.

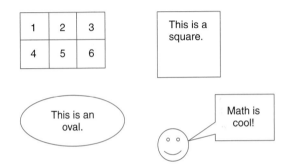

The instructions given below were written for Microsoft Word 2000. Slight modifications may be necessary if you are using a different program. Boldface print is used to emphasize the Word commands that you should select at a particular time. You should now be seated at a computer so that you can follow along with the instructions below.

How to Use the Microsoft Word Drawing Tools

Use the mouse to select (left click) the **Microsoft Word** icon from the desktop. If this icon is not on the desktop you will need to select **Start,** point to **Programs,** point to **Microsoft Office** on the pop-up menu, and then select **Microsoft Word.** You should now have a blank Word document.

The Drawing Toolbar Make sure that the Drawing toolbar is active. You should be able to see the words *Draw* and *AutoShapes* on the toolbar above the Start button at the bottom of your screen. If the toolbar does not appear, either select the drawing icon ▦ on the Standard toolbar at the top of the screen, or select View on the Menu bar, point to **Toolbars,** and click **Drawing.** Here are descriptions of some of the buttons on the Drawing toolbar.

> *The selection arrow* ▨ can be used to select an object or objects. When this is active, click on the object that you want to select. Highlighting (shown by little white boxes around an object) will indicate what object is currently selected. To select more than one object, hold down the Shift key and click on each object. You may also select more than one object by clicking outside of the objects that you wish to select and dragging a selection box to surround them while the selection arrow is activated.
>
> *The free rotate tool* ▨ is used to rotate selected objects. To rotate an object using free rotate, select the object, select Free Rotate, click on a corner dot of the object, and rotate it as you wish. There is also a Rotate or Flip option under the Draw menu.
>
> *The AutoShapes menu.* If you select a shape from the AutoShapes menu (or select one of the shapes next to the AutoShapes menu) and point to the screen you will get a new cursor ╋. A single click on the screen inserts a copy of the object in a standard predetermined size; directions for changing the size of an object are given below. You may also click where you want a shape to begin, and drag to where you want that shape to end to insert a nonstandard-sized copy of an object. Some AutoShapes objects may be altered by clicking and dragging an appropriate part of the object. For example, you may insert a smiling face ☺ and then change it to a frowning face ☹ by dragging upward the yellow diamond in the middle of the smile.

In freeform drawing (AutoShapes, Lines ◁), click each time you want the curve to change direction, and double-click when you want to stop drawing that curve. In scribble drawing (AutoShapes, Lines ⌇), click and drag to draw your object; when you let go of the mouse, you must reactivate the scribble command to continue drawing.

Practice Drawing Various Objects

1. Make copies of an object by using the selection arrow ▨ to select it. On the Menu bar choose **Edit, Copy,** and then **Edit** and **Paste.**
   Note: If you copy an object, then highlight a second object, and then choose Paste, the computer

will replace the second object by the first object. In other words, be careful when using Paste that you do not paste over and delete something that you wanted to keep.

2. Move selected objects by click and drag with the movement arrow ✛.
3. Change the size of a selected object by click and drag with ↔ or ↕ or ↗. These options are available when you point to one of the little white boxes that surrounds a selected object.
4. Delete selected objects by pressing **Delete** on the keyboard (or by selecting **Edit** and **Cut** on the Menu bar).
5. To group or ungroup objects, select the objects and then use the **Draw** menu.
6. Rotate objects. Try drawing the given picture. Note that the large girl is a copy of the small girl. You need to use grouping in order to rotate her so that she doesn't fall apart.

To add text to an object, on the Drawing toolbar select the Text Box button ▤ and click on the object. A text box will appear that you may type into. You may change the size of the textbox using the sizing arrows described above. You can hide the lines on a textbox or an object by using the Line Color tool. ▱ You can hide half of a picture by covering half with a rectangle and hiding the lines of the rectangle.

Try to draw the pictograph below:

Students who earned gold stars	
Monday	☆ ☆
Tuesday	⯨
Wednesday	☆

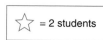

You can use the minimize button ▭ in the upper right-hand corner of the screen to minimize Word. You can then use other programs such as Microsoft Excel or the Geometer's Sketchpad to create more objects. You can copy these objects, minimize the other program, reactivate Word by clicking on Microsoft Word on the Drawing toolbar at the bottom of the screen, and then paste the new objects into your Word document.

Problem Set B.1

1. Use Microsoft Word drawing features to create each of the objects illustrated on page 347 of this section.

2. Use Word to create a 10 by 10-inch hundreds chart.

3. Use Word to draw the animal of your choice. Show that you understand the ideas of copy and paste and reducing and enlarging by making a copy of the animal and then changing its size. Demonstrate your understanding of the rotation tool by rotating one of the animals so that it is upside down.

4. Use Word drawing features to create an assessment that includes smiling and frowning faces.

5. Use Word drawing tools to create a pictograph that you could use in an early childhood classroom. You may choose one of the pictographs shown in Activity 9-1 or Example 9-1, or create your own pictograph.

6. Use Word drawing tools to draw the line plot shown in Example 9-3.

B.2 INTRODUCTION TO LOGO

Logo is a computer language that is popular with elementary school children and can be used even in the very early grades. "In the Logo context, children can hypothesize ideas, try out strategies, and validate guesses. It is a setting wherein even young children can pose and investigate mathematical problems" (Campbell & Stewart, 1993). Many student textbook series include Logo examples and exercises beginning at the first-grade level.

Before students attempt to use Logo, they should be familiar with the basics of the program. Logo is a drawing program in which a "turtle" is controlled with keyboard commands. Some versions show the turtle as a small triangle, whereas others show an image of a turtle. The turtle can be made to go forward or backward or turn to its left or its right. Typing the command **fd 50** will make the turtle go forward 50 turtle steps (approximately ¾ of an inch on a computer screen). Unless the turtle is first told to pick up his pen, he draws a line as he moves forward or backward. By changing the number after the **fd** command, you can alter the distance moved by the turtle, altering the length of the line drawn.

Typing the command **rt 90** will make the turtle turn right 90°. Turning the turtle to the right or to the left does not change the drawing, it merely points the turtle in a different direction. Right and left turns may be made in any number of degrees. For the initial introduction activity, you may wish to make all right and left turns 90°. Use caution when drawing example Logo pictures on the board. A line drawn to illustrate the command **fd 200** should appear twice as long as a line drawn to illustrate the command **fd 100.** A turn of 90° should result in a square corner in the sample picture.

Activity B-1   Grades 1–4

Introduction to Logo Commands

Materials: Small turtle figure.

Directions: Tell the students: "We are going to learn how to use a computer program called Logo. The Logo program has a turtle that will draw pictures. You tell the turtle what to do by typing the commands on the keyboard. The turtle understands only the commands for forward, backward, right, and left."

In most Logo programs, the head of the turtle initially points up.   (a)

Hold the turtle on the board with a piece of chalk. See figure (a).

"This command tells the turtle to go forward 100 turtle steps."

Write **fd 100** on the board.   (b)

Move the turtle forward, drawing a line with the chalk as in figure (b).

"This command tells the turtle to turn right."

Write **rt 90** on the board.

Turn the turtle 90° to the right as in figure (c).   (c)

"Now if we tell the turtle to go forward, will he move toward the window, toward the door, or toward the ceiling? You think he will move toward the door? Let's try it."

Write **fd 100** on the board.

Move the turtle forward, drawing a line with the chalk as in figure (d).   (d)

"If we tell the turtle to turn left, will he be pointed toward the ceiling or the floor? You think he will point to the ceiling? Let's try it."

Write **lt 90** on the board.

Turn the turtle 90° to the left as in figure (e).   (e)

Continue with various commands such as **fd 200, rt 90, bk 50,** etc. until students understand the commands **fd, bk, lt,** and **rt.** Then ask students what sequence of commands they would need to use to draw a square or a rectangle.

Example B-1: Problem solving by acting it out (second- to fourth-grade level).

What directions were given to the turtle (shown as a small triangle) to make it draw the path shown?

Solution: A small triangle can be used to act out the set of directions.

Activity B-2 Grades 1–4

Be the Turtle

Materials: Index cards with simple Logo directions.

Directions: Pass out cards. Students take turns coming to the front of the room and acting out the directions on the card. Other students list the sequence of directions as they are acted out.

Example Card:

```
fd 100
lt 90
bk 100
```

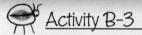

Activity B-3 Grades 1–4

Match the Turtle Path and Logo Directions

Materials: Index cards with simple Logo directions matching cards with Logo picture drawn.

Directions: Pass out cards. At the signal, students try to find the student who has the matching card. In some cases, more than one set of directions may draw the same picture. You may have more than two students in a group or you may include duplicate picture cards.

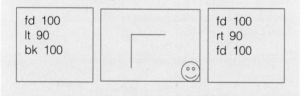

The turtle begins as a triangle in center screen, ready to travel up the screen. The first command must have been to go forward some unit of length. Use fd 100 to represent this length. The turtle turned to the right 45° and then went forward approximately the same distance as the first segment traveled. The turtle turned to the left 45° in order to be pointed up and an additional 90° to be pointed to the west. It then went forward approximately twice the original distance. One sequence of instructions that would draw the path shown is: fd 100, rt 45, fd 100, lt 135, fd 200. You could check this sequence by typing the instructions into a computer.

Notice the index card of Activity B-3 that has the Logo picture drawn on it. The smiley face in the corner is used to indicate which direction the card should be held. If this type

of signal is introduced to students early in the year, they will quickly become accustomed to it. Following initial activities such as Activities B-1, B-2, and B-3, students will be prepared to do Logo activities on the computer. The Logo instructions given in this section were written for MSWLogo (this version of the Logo is widely available on the Internet). These instructions may need to be slightly modified if other Logo programs are used. The instructions given in the remainder of this section are intended for you. They would need to be appropriately modified to be used with elementary school students. It is time for you to practice using Logo on an actual computer. Boldface print is used to emphasize instructions that you must follow or type into the computer.

See the textbook companion Web site for a link to a Logo site where this program may be downloaded for free.

How to Use Logo

Select (left click) the **MSWLogo** icon either from the desktop or by selecting **Start, Programs, MSWLogo.** You may need to press **OK** on an intermediate screen to get to the MSWLogo screen, which is a divided screen with a small triangle in the middle of the top section. This triangle represents the turtle. Click in the small white strip above the Start button. You type instructions to the turtle in this white strip. Type **fd 100** and press enter. The turtle should have moved forward 100 turtle steps. On many screens it takes 1,000 steps to move the turtle completely across the screen. Type **fd 200** and press Enter. If the turtle disappeared, you can click and drag the scroll bar on the right of the screen to see him again. If you forget the space between the forward command and the number telling the turtle how far to go, you will get an error message. Type **fd100** and press Enter to see this error message. To clear the screen, type **cs** and press Enter or select **Reset.** If you moved the scroll bar on the right of the screen, you may wish to center this so that the turtle begins in the center of the screen.

Follow the directions given below. You may press Enter after each command or you may type several commands before pressing Enter. Each command that you type appears in the Commander section of the screen. If you click on a command from the Commander section, it will appear in the white strip. Pressing Enter will then execute that command. This may save on retyping if you make a mistake in typing a command, or if you wish to use the same command several times.

cs
fd 100
rt 90
fd 100
rt 90
fd 100
rt 90
fd 100

Using Repeat Statements It is much easier to draw a square using the repeat command than typing in each command separately. Type **repeat 4[fd 100 rt 90]** in the white strip and press Enter. If you get an error message, check to see that you have included a space between each command and the number telling how far to carry out the command, also check that you are using the correct type of parentheses. If you have it typed correctly, executing this one command will draw a square. It draws a square because it repeats four times the sequence of moving forward 100 turtle steps and turning right 90°. In general, the repeat command repeats the expression within the square bracket parentheses the number of times given by the numeral outside of the parentheses.

Not All Turns Are 90° You don't always need to use 90° turns or to move forward in the same increments. First, clear the screen using **cs** or **Reset** and then type the commands **fd 30 rt 60 fd 50 lt 120 fd 100** in the white strip and press Enter. Can you see how the picture on the screen matches the commands that you typed? Clear the screen and type the command **repeat 4[fd 100 rt 60]** and press Enter. Can you see why the curve has four sides and why it is not a square?

Drawing Circles and Polygons Clear the screen and try **repeat 360[fd 1 rt 1]**. This curve looks like a circle, but it is actually a polygon with 360 sides each 1 turtle step long. You can make larger and smaller "circles" by changing the length of the sides. Side lengths do not have to be integers. Try **repeat 360[fd .5 rt 1]**. You changed the side lengths, but not the degree of the turns. You may recall the geometry fact that there are 360° in a circle. In general, to return the turtle to his original heading, he needs to turn a total of 360°. So if the inner commands are repeated 360 times, the appropriate turn is 1° to return the turtle to his original heading. To complete a polygon with turns of 60°, you would need to repeat six times. Type **repeat 6[fd 100 rt 60]**.

Moving the Turtle Without Drawing a Line You can move the turtle without drawing a line by picking up the pen. The appropriate commands are **pu** for pen up and **pd** for pen down. You can also hide the turtle with the command **ht** and show the turtle with the command **st**. Try the following:

repeat 360 [fd .2 rt 1] pu bk 50 pd
rt 120 repeat 60 [fd 1 lt 1] lt 60
pu fd 50 pd repeat 360 [fd .2 lt 1]
ht

Erasing To erase a line or curve that you have just drawn, type **pe** and then go over the region that you wish to erase. Type **ppt** to switch from erasing to drawing again. Clear the screen, type **st** to show the turtle, and practice erasing. Type **fd 100** and press Enter. Then type **pe bk 50** and press Enter. The turtle should have drawn a line that was 100 turtle steps and then erased half of the line. You must type the command **ppt** to switch from eraser mode back to drawing mode.

Elementary school students really enjoy this program. If you show them a few basic commands to get them started, they may surprise you by learning on their own things such as how to change the pen size or color. The following command summary box summarizes the Logo commands discussed so far. You may wish to photocopy this, cut out the command summary box, and paste it onto an index card for easy reference.

Some Logo Commands

Click in the white strip above Start to type your commands.

fd *x*	go forward *x* steps	ht	hide turtle	pe	pen erase
bk *x*	go backward *x* steps	st	show turtle	ppt	pen paint
rt *x*	turn right *x*°	pd	pen down	cs	clear screen
lt *x*	turn left *x*°	pu	pen up		

repeat *n*[ ] will repeat whatever you write inside [ ] *n* times

If you have a screen that you would like to print, choose the **Print** option from the **Bitmap** menu. When you are finished, choose **Exit** from the **File** menu. Unless you have a disk to save your work on, or you are working on your personal computer and wish to save your work in a file, press OK when the program tells you that your work is not saved.

Standards

NCTM

Work with virtual manipulatives (computer simulations of physical manipulatives) or with Logo can allow young children to extend physical experience and to develop an initial understanding of sophisticated ideas like the use of algorithms.

NCTM, 2000, pp. 26–27

Standards are listed with the permission of the National Council of Teachers of Mathematics (NCTM). NCTM does not endorse the content or validity of these alignments.

Logo Procedures

When you want several copies of the same figure or similar figures, writing a procedure saves typing and using variables lets you change sizes. Directions for writing and editing procedures and changing figure sizes are given at the textbook companion Web site. These skills may be useful in geometry applications to illustrate similar and congruent figures.

Problem Set B.2

1. Write a repeat statement that draws a curve that looks like a half circle.

2. Use Logo to draw your initials. Initials may use block letters or stick letters and should not be connected.

3. Write the Logo code to draw a five-sided polygon that has five equal angles and five equal sides. This figure is called a regular pentagon.

4. Write the Logo code to draw a triangle that has three equal side lengths and three equal angles. This is called an equilateral triangle.

5. Melissa, a second-grade student, is using Logo and says "The turtle just told me it doesn't know how to fd200." You are the teacher. How do you respond?

6. Use Logo to draw a picture that you think an elementary school student could use Logo to draw. Indicate the grade level of the student.

B.3   USING SPREADSHEETS—THE BASICS OF MICROSOFT EXCEL

As a teacher you may find it useful to create and maintain grade sheets using a spreadsheet utility. This section will teach you some basic techniques for entering data and using formulas in Microsoft Excel. This technology may also be used with children in the classroom; a candy store example is presented that is appropriate for Grades 2 through 4. We also explore using Excel to create charts and graphs. Boldface type is used in this section to indicate commands that you should click on or instructions for you to follow. The given directions may need to be appropriately modified if a spreadsheet utility other than Microsoft Excel is used.

How to Use Microsoft Excel

Use the mouse to select (left click) the **Microsoft Excel** icon from the desktop. If this icon is not on the desktop you will need to select **Start** (at the bottom left corner of your screen), point to **Programs,** select **Microsoft Excel** if it is on this list or point to **Microsoft Office,** and then select **Microsoft Excel.**

You should now have a blank Excel worksheet. Rows are numbered and columns are labeled with capital letters. The individual boxes on the worksheet are called cells. The dark border around cell A1 indicates that this cell is currently selected. If you were to begin typing, the results would appear in this cell. If this is your first experience working with a spreadsheet, take a few minutes to study the two rows at the top of the screen. You will frequently use these toolbars to carry out Excel commands.

Entering Data   To select a cell, use either the mouse to point to the cell and left click, or the arrow keys to move the highlighted box to the appropriate cell. Once you select a cell, you may enter data into that cell or edit the data that the cell already contains. In cell A1 (first row, first column) type **Names** and press Enter. Then type **Amy** in cell A2, **Bob** in cell A3, . . . until your worksheet contains the information shown in Table B-1. Don't worry about the spacing as long as the information is in the appropriate cell. You may notice that upon typing the *B* to begin typing *Bill* into cell A4 that Excel automatically fills that cell with the name *Bob*. Typing the letter *i* after the letter *B* will erase *Bob* and allow you to continue to enter *Bill*. Excel remembers and stores previously typed words and phrases. This feature will save typing in the event that you do want to reuse a previously typed word or phrase.

Changing the Data in a Cell   To change the data in a cell, click once on the cell and retype the correct data. Another method is to delete the contents of the cell using the **Cut** command from the **Edit** menu on the Menu bar. For this method you double-click a cell to select it, then double-click again to highlight the contents of the cell. Click on **Edit** on the Menu bar at the top of the screen and select **Cut.** Change *Bob* to *Robert* using one of the methods described above. To change only part of the data already typed into a cell, double-click on the cell, and use the arrow keys and/or the Backspace key to delete the incorrect data, and then type in the new data. See if you can change *Amy* to *Aimee.*

You May Select More than One Cell at a Time   Click cell A2 (the cell that contains *Aimee*), then hold down the Shift key and click cell F2. The *Aimee* row from *A* to *F* should now be highlighted. When selecting more than one cell, the first cell selected will appear white with a dark border and other selected cells will appear completely darkened. Another way to do this is to use click and drag to select cells in consecutive rows or columns. Click in a blank cell to unhighlight the *Aimee* row. Then click cell A2 and hold down the left mouse button and drag the mouse to the right until the row is highlighted. You may

TABLE B-1

	A	B	C	D	E	F	G
1	Names	Test 1	Test 2	Quiz 1	Quiz 2	Quiz 3	
2	Amy	80	71	8	9	7	
3	Bob	85	83	9	10	6	
4	Bill	75	78	7	8	6	
5							

also select a few cells without selecting all those in between. Click on a blank cell to undo the current highlighting, then click cell A2, hold down the Control key (Ctrl) and click cell F2. Then, still holding down the Control key, click cells C3 and then D4. Notice that you may select cells in nonadjacent rows or columns. Whenever multiple cells are selected, some may be entirely highlighted whereas others are highlighted only around the border.

Using Formulas

Calculating an Average To find the average test score for Test 1, click cell B5 (the first blank cell below the Test 1 scores), then click the Insert Function button f_* on the Formula Bar. In the select a category list, select **Statistical.** In the Select a Function box, select **AVERAGE** and then choose **OK.** You may wish to click on the Average box and drag it out of the way so that you can see the data on your worksheet. The Number 1 text box in the Function Arguments dialog box will record the numbers to be averaged as B2:B4. The colon indicates that all cells in between the two endpoints are also selected. This box indicates that the scores in B2, B3, and B4 will be averaged; choose **OK.** The average for the Test 1 scores should appear in the B5 cell. Now find the Average for Test 2 and place the value in C5.

Formatting Cells You can use the **Format** command on the Menu bar to make results in a cell (or row or column) appear as you wish. Click on **Cells** and then **Number** to indicate cells B5 and C5 should have 2 decimal places. You can also grab and drag the side of a column to make it wider. To do this, point the cursor between the letters heading the columns. When you see the double-arrow symbol $\longleftrightarrow$, press and hold down the left mouse button and drag the mouse to widen the column. Try widening the Names column so that there is room to type in last names for the students.

Creating Your Own Formulas Now let's find the average for each student. If you use the predefined Excel AVERAGE function in cell G2, it gives you the value 35 for Aimee's average. Why does it give you such a low number? A more accurate way to find Aimee's average is to add her scores and divide by 230 (the total possible number of points if tests are worth 100 points and quizzes are worth 10). If you did use the Excel average function and it placed 35 in cell G2, select this cell and use the Delete key on the keyboard to delete the current contents. Now select B2:G2 and click once on the Autosum $\boxed{\Sigma}$ button on the Standard toolbar. G2 should now contain the sum of Aimee's scores. Click cell H2, and type **=G2/230,** and press Enter. Each time you type a formula, rather than using one from the list of Excel formulas, you must remember to include the equals sign to begin your formula. H2 now contains 0.76 which seems a more reasonable average for Aimee, considering her test scores.

The concept of average is formally discussed in Chapter 9.

Copying Formulas Once you have entered a formula, you may use the Edit menu to reuse it rather than retyping it each time it is needed. Click and drag to select cells G2 and H2 (one cell will appear completely darkened; the other will merely have a dark border), then choose **Copy** from the **Edit** menu. Highlight cells G3, H3, G4, and H4 (three will appear completely dark; one will merely have a dark border) and choose **Paste** from the **Edit** menu. Note that although the sum for G2 used row 2 scores, Excel knew to use the scores from row 3 to find the sum for G3 and the scores from row 4 to find the sum for G4. In other words, when you copy a formula from one location and paste it into another location, Excel will automatically use values in the new location in its evaluation of the copied formula.

Opening, Printing and Saving a Worksheet

You may print a worksheet by selecting **Print** from the **File** menu. You should always check **Print Preview** before you select Print. You may save a worksheet to a disk by choosing **Save as** from the **File** menu and selecting drive A. Then type in an appropriate name in the File Name text box. To open a new worksheet, click on the **Sheet2** tab at the bottom of the screen. (You will need a new worksheet for the next example.)

More Tricks to Fill Rows and Columns

If you need to type the same value into several cells, type the value into one cell and press Enter. Then click to select that cell, choose **Copy** from the **Edit** menu, highlight all of the cells you wish to place the value into, and choose **Paste** from the **Edit** menu. Put the value 10 in A1, A2, ... A12 using the above method. If you accidentally double-click to select the data before choosing Copy, you may see an error message when you attempt to Paste.

You May Increase or Decrease Values in a Specific Pattern Using Formulas
Enter the value 1 in cell B1. In cell C1, type **=B1+1** and press Enter. Then click to select cell C1, choose **Copy** from the **Edit** menu, highlight cells D1, E1, ..., L1, and choose **Paste** from the **Edit** menu. The values 1, 2, ..., 11 should appear in cells B1:L1. Use a procedure similar to the above to put the odd numbers 1, 3, 5, ..., 39 into cells B1, B2, ..., B20. You can also use subtraction, multiplication, or division in formulas by using the operation symbols −, *, or /, respectively. There are also click and drag methods to input arithmetic progressions without using formulas. For information on these and other methods or shortcuts, consult a Microsoft Excel manual or the Excel Help menu.

Using Excel in the Early Childhood Classroom

Example B-2: Candy store example (second- to fourth-grade level).

Table B-2 lists several items with prices that might be found at a local candy store. This information may be typed into a spreadsheet. Appropriate formulas should be entered into column D so that cells D2 through D7 each represent the total amount spent on the item in that row, and cell D8 represents the total amount spent in all. The amount spent on a particular item depends on both the price of the item and the quantity purchased. Even after formulas are entered into column D, until quantities are entered into column C, the amounts in column D will appear as 0.00. When quantities are entered into column C, the amounts in column D will

update as appropriate. For example, if 3 is entered into cell C2, the displayed content of cell D2 should change to 0.15. For the numbers in this particular example, columns B and D should be formatted to display two decimal places. If children have not yet been introduced to the decimal format of a price given in terms of cents, the example should be modified so that items with whole dollar amount prices are given. Children may be asked to type quantities into column C and explain the resulting totals that appear in column D. Children may also be challenged to obtain specified totals.

At the second- and third-grade levels, the teacher should be responsible for typing the information shown, including column D formulas (see Problem 3 in Problem Set B.3). At around the fourth-grade level, children should have enough background with formulas and with technol-

Activity B-4   Grades 2–4

Guess and Check—Problem Solving

Materials: Example B-2 information (with appropriate formulas) typed into a spreadsheet.

Teacher Statement: Suppose I went to the candy store with $4.00. I want to spend as much of my money as possible, and buy at least one of each type of candy. If I buy two of each, the computer tells me that I have spent $3.02. Can you find a better solution?

Taffy	0.05	2	0.10
Pack of gum	0.40	2	0.80
Candy bar	0.50	2	1.00
Licorice	0.07	2	0.14
Jaw breaker	0.16	2	0.32
Mints	0.33	2	0.66
		Total	3.02

TABLE B-2

	A	B	C	D
1	Item	Price	Quantity	Total
2	Taffy	0.05		0.00
3	Pack of gum	0.40		0.00
4	Candy bar	0.50		0.00
5	Licorice	0.07		0.00
6	Jaw breaker	0.16		0.00
7	Mints	0.33		0.00
8			Grand Total	0.00

ogy that with proper guidance they could enter the data and formulas themselves. Children are usually extremely excited about using computers and computer applications. Do not be surprised when your students discover tricks and techniques for using computer applications that you did not teach them.

Drawing Graphs with Microsoft Excel

Many of the graphs shown in Section 9.1 were drawn with Microsoft Excel. The statistical measures discussed in Section 9.2 are also easily calculated using a spreadsheet utility such as Excel. Enter the bowling score data in Table B-3. Note that column A gives a possible breakdown of bowling scores, whereas columns B and C give the distributions of scores for two different classes of students.

Drawing Histograms To draw a histogram of data, first highlight the data that you want to include. For this example, highlight (click and drag the left mouse button) the data in columns A, B, and C; do not highlight empty cells. The first cell selected will appear white with a dark border; other cells appear completely darkened. If the first column selected is not a column of single numbers, Excel will use the first column that you select as the labels on the horizontal axis, and subsequent columns as frequencies on the vertical axis. Click on **Insert** on the Menu bar and select **Chart.** Select either **Column** or **Bar** as the chart type (depending on whether you want your histogram bars vertical or horizontal). Select the chart subtype as desired and press **Next.** A new box tells you the data range (the colon indicates that you are including all the data from A1 to C5). Press **Next.** A new box lets you label your chart and axes. Choose appropriate labels and then press **Next.** The final box tells you that it will insert the histogram as an object into the current sheet. Press **Finish.** You may change the size of the histogram using ↔, ↕, or similar slanted arrow images that appear when you point to a darkened box on the border of the graph. You may move the histogram by pointing to it and using click and drag when you see the symbol ↔. Study the histogram. What conclusions can you make about the bowling scores of the two classes? We will revisit this example later.

TABLE B-3

	A	B	C	D
1	**Scores**	**Class 1**	**Class 2**	
2	51–100	6	5	
3	101–150	14	12	
4	151–200	2	1	
5	201–250	1	0	
6				

Pie Charts and Pyramid, Cone, or Cylinder Graphs Click on the **Sheet 2** tag at the bottom of the Excel screen to get a clean worksheet. Consider this situation: Hannah has a monthly budget that includes the following: food, $200; rent, $300; car, $250; fun, $100; savings, $50.

Type this information into two columns (items in one column and amounts in the other). Select the information in both columns, then click **Insert** and **Chart.** Select **Pie** as the chart type in the first Chart Wizard dialog box, choose the subtype you desire (in Chapter 9 we discussed only the single circle type of pie chart), and press **Next.** Press **Next** in the Source Data dialog box. In the third Chart Wizard dialog box select a title, labels, and legend. Click on the tags to cycle through these options, change them as desired, and press **Next.** Choose **Finish** in the fourth Chart Wizard dialog box. You may click and drag to move the chart or change its size as desired. Use a similar process to draw a pyramid, cone, or cylinder graph.

Line Graphs Click on the Sheet3 tag for a clean worksheet. Type the given information into two columns. Then select the data and click on **Insert** and then **Chart.** Select **XY Scatter** as the chart type, choose a subtype with lines, and press **Next.** Press **Next** in the Source Data dialog box, type an appropriate title and axis labels, and press **Next** and then **Finish.** Resize the graph if necessary.

Hours Studied	Average Test Score
1	65
2	72
4	84
5	87

Stretching the graph vertically will change the values shown on the scale used on the vertical axis. Use the graph to predict the score for a person who studies for 3 hours or for 6 hours. Note that it is possible to draw a line graph using the Line chart type, but the procedure is more complicated than using the chart type XY Scatter.

Using Excel to Calculate Statistics

Consider the bowling data and histogram (Sheet1 of the Excel workbook) in Figure B-1.

A common misinterpretation of this data is that class 1 is better in bowling than class 2 because the histogram bars are higher. Why are the class 1 bars higher?

Use statistics calculated by Excel to figure out which class really is better. Type the following into column D of Sheet1 (do not include commas and type only one value into each cell; the data covers cells D1:D23): 108, 120, 80, 90, 130, 140, 80, 120, 130, 129, 220, 96, 105, 165, 120, 110, 126, 200, 100, 73, 145, 110, 93. In column E type 80, 90, 100, 100, 100, 110, 120, 130, 140, eight scores of 150, and one score of 200. (This data will cover cells E1:E18.)

Calculating Means Click D24 (the first empty cell below the data in column D), then click the Insert Function

Scores	Class 1	Class 2
51–100	6	5
101–150	14	12
151–200	2	1
201–250	1	0

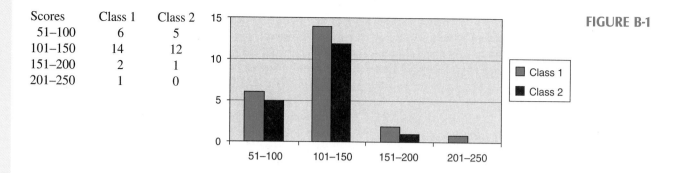

FIGURE B-1

button [f*] on the Formula Bar. In the Or select a category list, select **Statistical.** In the Select a function box, select **AVERAGE,** then click on **OK.** The Number 1 text box in the Function Arguments dialog box will record the numbers to be averaged as D1:D23. This indicates that all cells from D1 to D23 are selected. Choose **OK.** The average for the D column scores should appear in the D24 cell. Now find the Average for the E column, placing the value below the last score of the E column. You can use **Format** to make results in a cell (or row or column) appear as you wish. The average that Excel calculates is what we have been calling the *mean* or *x-bar*. Notice that the mean of the C class is actually higher than the mean of the B class. The fact that the B class bars are higher, does not mean that the B class is better. The B bars are higher because class B has more students.

Calculating Medians Click D25, then click the Insert Function button. In the Or select a category list, select **Statistical.** In the Select a function box, select **MEDIAN,** then choose **OK.** The Number 1 text box in the Function Arguments dialog box will record the numbers as D1:D24. You need to change this to D1:D23; because the D24 value wasn't really a data point, you don't want to include it in your median calculation. Choose **OK** and the median will appear in D25. Now calculate the median of the scores in the E column, and place the result under the average for the E column. Note that Excel doesn't need to have all the data values in numerical order to calculate the median.

Standard Deviation and Mode Click D26, then click the Insert Function button. In the Or select a category list, select **Statistical.** In the Select a function box, select **STDEV,** then choose **OK.** Change the Number 1 text box in the Function Arguments dialog box so that you are calculating the standard deviation of the 23 actual scores of column D. Then press **OK.** Now calculate the **MODE** following the steps above and place the result below the Standard Deviation value. How do you suppose the computer will respond when a data set has no mode or has more than one mode? This question is considered in Problem Set B.3.

Printing Charts and Graphs

You may print a worksheet by selecting **Print** from the **File** menu. Always choose **Print Preview** before you print to ensure that you are printing what you want. If a chart is selected, this will be the only item printed. To print both a chart and the data on the worksheet, you must click on a blank cell of the worksheet so that the chart is not selected. Charts may need to be repositioned or resized so that they do not exceed the page boundaries. When printing a chart, you may wish to conserve ink by eliminating the background color of the chart. This is accomplished by double-clicking on the gray background and selecting **None** as the option under the **Area** section.

Saving, Using Copy and Paste, and Exiting You may save a worksheet to a disk by choosing **Save as** from the **File** menu and selecting drive A, and then typing in an appropriate file name in the File name text blank. You may also **highlight** data or charts and **Copy** and then **Paste** them (using the **Edit** menu) into another program such as a Microsoft Word document.

When you are finished using the Excel program, choose **Exit** from the **File** menu. Say **No** when the program asks if you wish to save the changes unless you have a disk and wish to save your work as directed above or you wish to save your work onto the hard drive.

Problem Set B.3

1. Type the following information into a spreadsheet. Calculate each student's average and calculate the average score for each exam and project. The grades are based on Test 1 (100 points), Test 2 (100 points), Project 1 (50 points), Project 2 (50 points), and a Final exam (200 points). Randall's scores are: 72, 81, 39, 36, and 152. Lucia's scores are 83, 76, 41, 38, and 161. Mario's scores are 75, 76, 37, 38, and 150. Tai's scores are 68, 70, 30, 32, and 125.

2. Create a store activity for a spreadsheet that uses whole dollar prices for each item. Type the in-

formation into Excel and print an order that cost at most $20.

3. Type the information from Example B-2 into a spreadsheet. Include appropriate formulas in column D.
   a. What formula is in cell D2?
   b. What formula is in cell D8?

4. Use the data from Example B-2.
   a. Print a candy order that costs exactly $3.00.
   b. Print a candy order that costs exactly $3.00 such that no more than four of any one item are purchased.
   c. Is it possible to print a candy order that costs exactly $3.00 such that no more than two of any item are purchased? Explain why or why not.
   d. Is it possible to print a candy order that costs exactly $3.00 such that no more than three of any item are purchased? Explain why or why not.

5. Company A will give you a $5 raise every month; company B will give you a $100 monthly raise at the end of every year. If each company offers an initial salary of $1,000 per month, which is the better offer? (*Note:* Your answer will depend on the length of time that you intend to stay with the company.) Print the spreadsheet worksheet that you used to solve the problem.

6. Mary has 40 feet of fencing that she will use to enclose a rectangular garden. Each side of the garden must be a whole number of feet. What are the dimensions of the garden of largest area that Mary can plant? Print the spreadsheet worksheet that you used to solve the problem.

7. Use Excel to draw the histograms shown in Example 9-4.

8. Use Excel to draw the line graph shown in Example 9-7.

9. Use Excel to draw the circle graph shown in Example 9-9.

10. Use Excel to draw the line graph using the data in Problem 4 of Section 9-1.

11. Use Excel to draw the three histograms in Problem 8 of Section 9-1.

12. Use Excel to draw the circle graph using the data from Problem 11 of Section 9-1.

13. Use Excel to calculate the mean, mode, median, and standard deviation for each set of data in Example 9-17. Compare these results to the results calculated by hand. How does the computer handle data with no mode? How does the computer handle data with more than one mode?

14. Use Excel to calculate the mean, mode, median, and standard deviation for the data given in Problem 8 of Section 9-1.

15. Mary wants to draw a circle graph showing the colors of candies that were in her bag of M&M's. She is using the data below. She shows you her computer screen. Help Mary figure out why the computer didn't draw the graph correctly.

Color	Number in Bag
Red	4
Green	5
Blue	3
Yellow	5
Brown	6
Orange	2

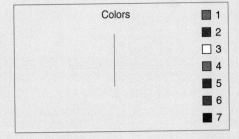

16. Draw an M&M's circle graph using the data from Problem 15 above. Single-click and then double-click on each circle sector and change each color as appropriate.

B.4 INTRODUCTION TO THE GEOMETER'S SKETCHPAD

This section gives a brief introduction to the *automatic drawer* called the Geometer's Sketchpad. This software can be used to create geometric figures, calculate measures such as the length of a segment or the area of a region, perform transformations such as those described in Section 10.5, and for many other purposes. Other automatic drawers are available including Cabri (Brooks/Cole) and Euclid's Toolbox (Addison-Wesley). You may refer to the user's guide or the Help menu of Sketchpad for instruction on the use of features not described here. If you do not have access to Sketchpad, and are using some other drawing package, the instructions given below may need to be modified for that package. Consult your user's guide as necessary.

Many of the processes used in Sketchpad will be familiar to anyone who has had some experience with other computer packages. For example, you may already know how to use Copy and Paste under the Edit menu of a Word document to duplicate a sentence or paragraph. A similar procedure will be used to copy and paste geometric figures in Sketchpad. Boldface is used in this section to emphasize the word or phrase to point to or select on the computer.

How to Use the Geometer's Sketchpad

If there is a **Sketchpad** icon on the desktop, you may select it by using the mouse to point to the icon and left clicking. Otherwise, use the mouse to point to and select (left click) **Start** (bottom left corner of screen). Point to **Programs** and a menu pops up. Point to **Sketchpad** and then select **The Geometer's Sketchpad.** Your screen should now show the sketch window.

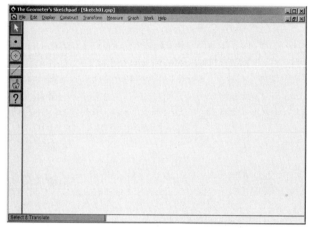

Used with permission.

The tools in the toolbox that appears along the left side of the sketch window are described below. If you click on one of these icons, you will activate it. Currently active tools are highlighted.

- **The Selection Arrow** is used to select objects. To select more than one object, hold down the Shift key and click on each object. You may also select more than one object by clicking outside of the objects that you wish to select and dragging a selection box to surround them.
  Note: The Selection Arrow tool shown above is the only selection arrow tool that will be described in this section. There are two others: the Rotate tool and the Dilate tool. See the user's guide or the Help menu for instructions on their use.
- **The Point tool** is used to create points. When this icon is highlighted, click anywhere on the sketch plane to create a point.
- **The Compass tool** is used to create circles. When this icon is highlighted, click on the sketch plane,

hold down the left mouse button, and drag the mouse. Release when your circle is the size that you want it to be.
- Creates segments. Click here and drag right to get the icons and to create rays or lines. These are known as *Straightedge tools*. When the desired icon is highlighted, click on the sketch plane and drag to create the desired object.
- **The Text tool** is used to show or hide labels, rename objects, or add text to a drawing. Practice using the tools until your screen is cluttered with points, circles of various sizes, lines, rays, segments, and labels. When you want a clean page, select **New Sketch** from the **File** menu (top left corner of screen). Several examples show how to use various features of Sketchpad. In the examples the boxes represent computer screens. If you are asked to duplicate a picture, you do not need to draw the box around the picture. Select **New Sketch** from the **File** menu before beginning each new example.

Practice Using the Geometer's Sketchpad Tools

Example B-3: Selecting, moving, stretching, shrinking, and deleting objects.

The process of using the **Selection Arrow tool** to select an object or objects is described above. You can tell what objects of the sketch plane are selected by the highlighting of the objects. To deselect objects, click on a blank part of the sketch plane. To select a line or segment, you must click on the actual line or segment and not just on the points that are on it. To select a circle, click on the circle itself, not on the center or on a point on the circle. When an object is selected, you can move the object by dragging it without changing its size. If you select only part of an object, you can shrink or stretch the object. Any parts of the object not selected will remain fixed.

To delete an object, use the **Selection Arrow tool** to select the object, then hit the **Delete** key on your keyboard. You can also select the object and use the **Cut** command under the **Edit** menu. If you want more than one copy of an object, select the object select **Edit, Copy** and then **Edit, Paste.** The copy that is pasted is often on top of the original and must be moved. As with many other computer software programs, if you copy one object, then highlight a second object and choose Paste, the computer will replace the second object by the first object. In other words, be careful when using Copy and Paste that you do not paste over and delete something that you wanted to keep. If you do make such a mistake, there is an **Undo** feature under the **Edit** menu that will let you undo your most recent actions. Draw the first picture shown. Then copy and paste the snowman, move the copy, delete the hat on the copy, and change his smile to a frown. You should then have the second picture.

 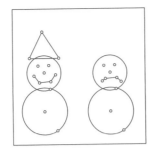

Example B-4: Segments, lines, and rays.

Using the **Straightedge tools** as described above, draw a segment, a ray, and a line all on the same sketch. Your computer screen may look like the first picture shown below. If you were to print this drawing, the printout would contain arrows on some of the segments shown as in the second drawing. Can you determine where the arrows on your drawing would appear? Check whether you were correct by looking at **Print Preview** under the **File** menu. It is always a good idea to check Print Preview before you print a file.

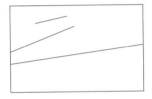 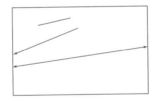

Example B-5: Drag and observe.

Use **segments** to draw a triangle. Use the **Text tool** to label the vertices. When you begin a new sketch, the first new vertex will automatically be labeled *A*, the second will be *B*, and so on. If you ever wish to change the label given by the text tool, you may do so by double-clicking on the label when the text tool is active. **Select** one side of your triangle. (Remember that to select a segment you click 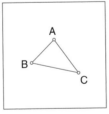 on the segment itself, not on its endpoints.) Drag it and observe what happens. Select any vertex. (Make sure you have only one vertex selected, not a vertex and a side.) Drag and observe. Select the entire triangle (use the Shift key or draw a selection box around the triangle). Drag and observe.

Example B-6: Constructing parallel lines.

Draw line $\overleftrightarrow{AB}$ and point *C* not on line $\overleftrightarrow{AB}$. Select point *C* and line $\overleftrightarrow{AB}$ (click on the line itself, not on points *A* and *B*, to select line $\overleftrightarrow{AB}$), and **construct** a line through *C* **parallel** to $\overleftrightarrow{AB}$. (If parallel is not an available

option on the construct menu, check to see that you have selected both point *C* and line $\overleftrightarrow{AB}$, and only these objects. This illustrates a feature common to many software programs. If you wish to perform a command (such as constructing a parallel line), you must first perform all of the prerequisite tasks (select a line and a point not on the line) or the command will not be available. Select point *A* and drag it and observe what happens. There is an important difference between drawing parallel lines and constructing them. If you merely draw lines that appear to be parallel, then selecting and dragging point *A* will destroy the parallel property of the lines. If you construct lines to be parallel, they will remain parallel even when dragged.

Transformations Using the Geometer's Sketchpad

The **Transform** menu allows objects to be translated, rotated, dilated and reflected. To perform a reflection (flip), use the Arrow key to select the line (or ray or segment) of reflection. Then from the **Transform** menu choose **Mark Mirror**. In the sketch plane select all the objects (and parts of objects) that you wish to reflect. Finally, from the **Transform** menu choose **Reflect**.

To translate (slide) an object, you first select it. Then from the **Transform** menu choose **Translate**. Check the "By Rectangular Vector" box in the resulting pop-up menu, type in slide coordinates (negative = left or down, positive = right or up), and press OK.

To rotate (turn) an object, you must first use the Arrow key to select a center point, then choose **Mark Center** from the **Transform** menu. Select the object(s) to rotate and choose **Rotate** from the **Transform** menu. In the menu that pops up, uncheck "by marked angle," type the degree of rotation in the "By box," and press OK.

The Dilate option lets you do size transformations to create similar figures. First mark the center (use the same process as described above), then select the object to dilate, and choose **Dilate** from the **Transform** menu. Enter the scale factor (use a decimal number like 2 or 0.5) in the resulting pop-up menu, and select OK.

Example B-7: Transformations.

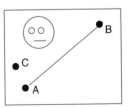

  a. Draw the given picture.
  b. Flip (reflect) the face over $\overline{AB}$.
  c. Slide (translate) the face to the left and up.
  d. Rotate the face about center point *C*.
  e. Use dilate to make a similar face that is one half of the size of the original.

Measurement Using the Geometer's Sketchpad

Example B-8: Circle measurements.

Draw a circle. Select the circle, then choose **Circumference** from the **Measure** menu. (If Circumference is not an available option, check to see that you have selected only the circle.) Select **measure** and then **area** to measure the area of the circle and then **measure** the **radius** of the circle. Select and drag one point of the circle to make it smaller or larger, and observe what happens to the measurements. (Note: You can select the measurements, drag them, and place them anywhere you like.)

Example B-9: Opposite and adjacent angles.

Create two lines $\overleftrightarrow{AB}$ and $\overleftrightarrow{CD}$ that intersect as shown.

Label the points *A*, *B*, *C*, and *D*. You may need to drag a point along the line to get one point on each side of the intersection as shown. Create the intersection point *E*. Watch the text box above the start button to ensure that the point you create is really the intersection of the lines.

Select points *C*, *E*, and *B*. If you are going to measure an angle, the order in which points are selected is important. If you want m($\angle CEB$), you may select *C* and then *E* and *B*, or *B* and then *E* and *C*. Any other order of selection will give a different angle. Choose **Angle** from the **Measure** menu. (The angle option will be available only if you have exactly three points selected. If it is not available, check to see that you have selected the correct three points.) Find the measures of each of the four angles.

m($\angle CEB$) = __

m($\angle AED$) = __

m($\angle DEB$) = __

m($\angle AEC$) = __

What do you notice about the measures of opposite angles? What do you notice about the measures of adjacent angles? Select and drag point *A* to change your drawing. Note any observations.

Example B-10: Interiors, areas, and perimeters.

Use segments to draw a pentagon. Watch the text box (above Start) to ensure that your segments are really connected to one another. Label the vertices *A, B, C, D,* and *E*. Select a side of your pentagon, and select **measure** and then **length.** Then **measure** the **length** of the other sides of the pentagon. If you want, you can select all of the sides and measure the lengths simultaneously. Select points *A* and *C*, and select **measure** and then **distance.** Compare this distance to the sum of the measures of sides $\overline{AB}$ and $\overline{BC}$.

Select points *A*, *B*, and *C*, and select **construct** and then **polygon interior.** To measure the area and perimeter of this triangle, select **measure** then **area** then **measure** then **perimeter.** Select points *A, C, D,* and *E* (in this order), **construct** the **polygon interior,** and **measure** the **area** and **perimeter** of this quadrilateral. Select points *A, B, C, D,* and *E*, **construct** the **interior,** then **measure** the **area** and **perimeter** of the pentagon. Select point *B*, and drag it until the area of *ABC* is 1.00 inch. What do you notice about the areas of *ABC, ACDE,* and *ABCDE?* Select *B* and drag it until the perimeter of triangle *ABC* is a whole number. Compare the perimeters of *ABC, ACDE,* and *ABCDE*.

Example B-11: The coordinate axes and grid.

Click on **Graph** and **Show Grid.** The axes shown are labeled with a 1-inch scale. You can change the scale by sliding the points on the axes, but for measurement purposes, we will continue to use the standard 1-inch scale. In middle and upper grade levels, this coordinate axes system is useful in teaching plotting points, predicting results of transformations, slopes and linear equations, and many other topics. Because negative coordinates are not introduced in the lower grades, you may wish to use the **Graph** menu to **hide axes.** You can then use the grid to introduce measurement topics such as the area or perimeter of a rectangle. Examples are given in Problem Set B.4.

Adding Text, Printing, and Exiting the Program

To add text other than labels to a drawing, activate the **Text tool,** and click and drag on the sketch plane. This creates a text box that you can type text into. You can select and drag the text box to any position. To print a screen, choose **Print** from the **File** menu. You should check **Print Preview** before you print. When you are finished, choose **Exit** from the **File** menu. The program will ask you if you wish to save your sketches. Unless you wish to save your sketches on a disk or in a file, choose **Don't Save.**

Problem Set B.4

1. Draw a right triangle. What happens when you drag a vertex? Now *construct* a right triangle. Draw a segment. Select the segment and one of its endpoints and **construct** a **perpendicular** line. Draw a point on that line (watch the text box), select the line, and use the **Display** menu to **hide** the line. Now draw the other two sides of the triangle. What happens now when you drag a vertex?

2. On the **Graph** menu, select **Show Grid** and then **Hide Axes.** Use segments to draw a rectangle

(with vertices at grid intersection points). Recall that the grid scale is 1 inch. Determine what the area and the perimeter of the rectangle should be. **Select** the vertices of the rectangle in clockwise order and **construct** the **polygon interior. Measure** the **area** and **perimeter.**

3. Braden shows you his computer screen and tells you that the computer must have made a mistake because the angle shown isn't a right angle. You are the teacher. How do you respond?

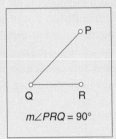

$m\angle PRQ = 90°$

4. Dexter shows you his computer screen and tells you that the computer calculations of perimeter and area of the rectangle don't look correct. How do you respond?

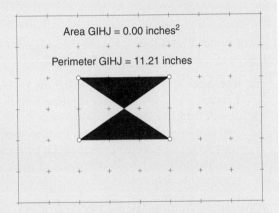

Area GIHJ = 0.00 inches²

Perimeter GIHJ = 11.21 inches

5. In Example B-9 you measured the four angles formed by a pair of intersecting lines. Complete the following sentences.

   a. Opposite angles _____.

   b. Adjacent angles _____.

6. In Example B-10 you constructed pentagon *ABCDE* and dissected it to create triangle *ABC* and quadrilateral *ACDE*. How do the measures of the areas of *ABC* and *ACDE* compare to the area of *ABCDE*? How do the measures of the perimeters of *ABC* and *ACDE* compare to the perimeter of *ABCDE*? Explain your observations.

B.5 ILLUSTRATING FRACTIONS, DECIMALS, AND PERCENTS ON THE TI-15 CALCULATOR

Many of today's calculators include fraction keys to facilitate operations using fractions. Many newer calculator models, for example the Texas Instruments TI-15, display fractions using a vertical stacked format so that a fraction such as $21\frac{5}{16}$ is displayed as $21\frac{5}{16}$. Some of the older calculator models, for example the TI-Explorer, use an underscore and a slanted bar in their display so that $21\frac{5}{16}$ is displayed as $21\text{⌴}\,{}^{5}/_{16}$. Some models, such as the Sharp EL-531R, use an entirely different display notation such as 21 r 5 r 16.

If you have a choice, you should select a calculator model that is appropriate for your classroom level, contains desired features such as fraction keys, and is easy for your students to use and understand. If the calculator that you select does not display some answers in a notation familiar to your students, you will need to spend time acquainting your students with the notations of the calculator and their relations to common classroom notations. There are many brands and models available that are suitable for the early childhood classroom. We will use the TI-15 in our discussion below. The instructions may need to be modified for use with other calculator models. For further examples and information, a link to the TI-15 guidebook is provided on the textbook companion Web site.

Fraction Keys

The fraction keys of the TI-15 calculator are described below.

Unit	Press this key after entering the whole part of a mixed number.
n̲	Press this key after entering the numerator of a fraction.
d̄	Press this key after entering the denominator of a fraction.
U$\frac{n}{d}$↔$\frac{n}{d}$	Press this key to convert a mixed number to an improper fraction and vice versa.
F↔D	Press this key to convert a fraction to a decimal and vice versa.
Frac	Press this key to display a menu so that you may choose

U$^{n}/_{d}$ to display results as mixed numbers (default), or
$^{n}/_{d}$ to display results as simple or improper fractions.

Frac ⇦	Press this key to display a menu so that you may choose

<u>Man</u> to require manual simplification of fractions (default), or
<u>Auto</u> to automatically reduce fractions to lowest terms.

When Auto is selected as the simplification option, the word *Auto* appears above results in the display. So that students see the simplification process, it is suggested that initial explorations are performed using the default manual option of simplification. When manual simplification is the selected option, the symbol $\frac{N}{D} \to \frac{n}{d}$ appears above any fraction expression that may be simplified.

$\boxed{\text{Simp}}$ Press this key to simplify fractions. You may select the factor used to simplify by typing it after pressing the Simplify key, or you may let the calculator select a factor by hitting enter immediately after pressing the key. Pressing the Factor key $\boxed{\text{Fac}}$ will then show the factor used in the simplification. Pressing this key a second time will return the display to the fractional expression. If a factor that you chose to use in the simplification process is not a common factor of both the numerator and denominator, the calculator will display the same fraction after this process as it did before the process. If the fraction is already in simplest form, the calculator will display the same fraction after pressing **Simp** and **Enter** as it did before the simplifying process.

Both the numerator and the denominator entered for a fraction must be integers; otherwise, the calculator will display "syntax error." When a denominator greater than 1,000 is used, the display will appear in decimal format. If a problem contains both fractions and decimals, results will also be displayed in a decimal format.

Example B-12: Entering fractions on the TI-15.

a. To enter the mixed number $21\frac{5}{16}$, press the following key sequence.

$\boxed{2}\ \boxed{1}\ \boxed{\text{Unit}}\ \boxed{5}\ \boxed{\text{n}}\ \boxed{1}\ \boxed{6}\ \boxed{\text{d}}$

b. To enter the improper fraction $\frac{34}{10}$, press the following key sequence.

$\boxed{3}\ \boxed{4}\ \boxed{\text{n}}\ \boxed{1}\ \boxed{0}\ \boxed{\text{d}}$

Example B-13: Fraction operations on the TI-15.

To see the simplification process at work, make sure that your calculator is in manual simplification mode. If *Auto* appears at the top of your display, press the **Frac** key and the down arrow to display the simplification options. Press the left arrow key to underline the manual option **Man,** and press **Enter** to select this option. Pressing the **Frac** key again will clear the display so that you may begin calculations.

Enter $2\frac{1}{10} + \frac{36}{15}$ using the following keying sequence.

$\boxed{2}\ \boxed{\text{Unit}}\ \boxed{1}\ \boxed{\text{n}}\ \boxed{1}\ \boxed{0}\ \boxed{\text{d}}\ \boxed{+}\ \boxed{3}\ \boxed{6}\ \boxed{\text{n}}\ \boxed{1}\ \boxed{5}\ \boxed{\text{d}}$

Pressing the Enter key $\boxed{\text{Enter}}$ will display either $4\frac{15}{30}$ or $\frac{135}{30}$ (depending on the current display mode selected). Press the

mixed to improper conversion key to alternate between these expressions. Press this key to get the expression $4\frac{15}{30}$. Notice the symbol above this that indicates that this expression may be simplified.

Press the **Simp** key and then the **Enter** key. The calculator will divide by the smallest common factor (greater than 1) to obtain $4\frac{5}{10}$. You may display this factor by pressing the **Fac** key. Press the **Fac** key again to return the display to the fractional expression. Press the **Simp** key, press **2,** and then press **Enter.** If the fraction could have been simplified by a factor of 2, this simplification would have been performed. Because 2 is not a common factor, the display still shows $4\frac{5}{10}$. Press **Simp, 5,** then **Enter.** Because 5 is a common factor, this common factor is used to simplify the expression so that the display now reads $4\frac{1}{2}$. The mixed to improper conversion key will now alternate the display between $4\frac{1}{2}$ and $\frac{9}{2}$. The fraction to decimal conversion key will alternate the display between 4.5 and $4\frac{5}{10}$.

Percent Keys

The TI-15 contains two buttons that are useful in calculations involving percents.

$\boxed{\%}$ This key is used to enter a percent.

$\boxed{>\%}$ This key is used to convert a fraction or decimal to a percent.

Example B-14: Converting between fractions, decimals, and percents on the TI-15.

a. The quantity 15% is entered using the keying sequence $\boxed{1}\ \boxed{5}\ \boxed{\%}$. If **Enter** is pressed, the display shows 0.15, the decimal equivalent to 15%. This quantity may be converted to a fraction using the fraction to decimal conversion key. Either a fraction or a decimal may be converted to a percent by pressing the conversion to percent key and then pressing **Enter.**

b. Write the keying sequence to enter the fraction $\frac{5}{4}$ and then convert this fraction to a percent.

Solution: $\boxed{5}\ \boxed{\text{n}}\ \boxed{4}\ \boxed{\text{d}}\ \boxed{>\%}\ \boxed{\text{Enter}}$

The calculator should now display 125%.

Problem Set B.5

Perform each calculation on a calculator that has fraction capabilities. For each problem, calculate an answer and use the calculator to find that answer as (a) the original calculator answer; (b) a mixed number (if applicable); (c) an improper fraction (if applicable); (d) a fraction in simplest form; (e) a decimal; and (f) a percent.

1. $3\dfrac{4}{5} - 1\dfrac{9}{10}$

2. $3\dfrac{4}{5} \times 1\dfrac{9}{10}$

3. $12\dfrac{1}{2} \div 2\dfrac{1}{4}$

4. $\dfrac{11}{18} - \dfrac{1}{9}$

5. 2.5×1.4

6. $0.186 \div 12.4$

7. $18\% \times 175$

References

Campbell, P. F., & Stewart, E. L. (1993). Calculators and computers. In R. J. Jensen (Ed.), *Research Ideas for the Classroom: Early Childhood Mathematics* (pp 251–268). Macmillan.

National Council of Teachers of Mathematics. (2000). *Principles and standards for school mathematics.* Reston, VA: Author.

Appendix C

Blackline Masters

Blackline Master 1—Geo-Pieces

For a complete set (50 pieces), use five different colors of paper—red, blue, green, yellow, and orange.

Blackline Master 2—Tangram Pieces

Blackline Master 3—Centimeter-Squared Paper

Blackline Master 4—Pattern Block Template

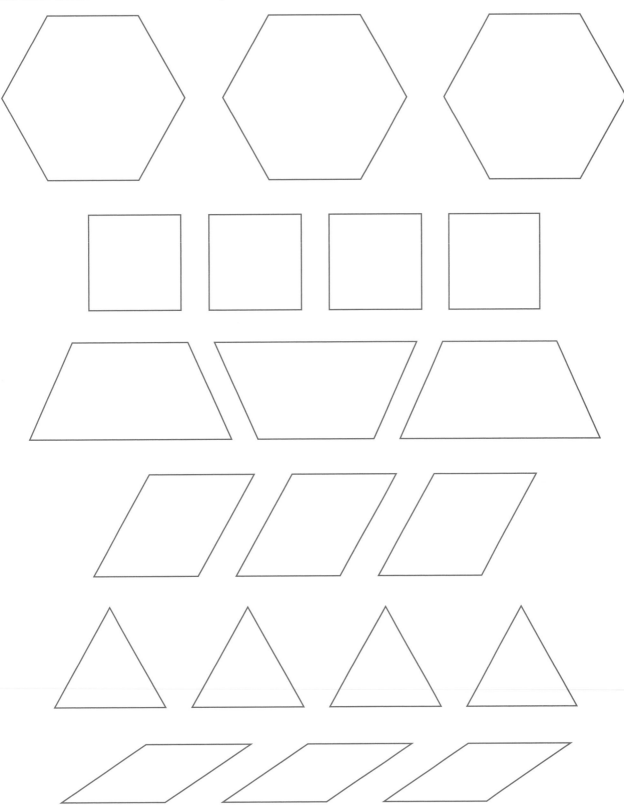

Blackline Master 5—Pattern Block Outline

Blackline Master 6—Groovy Boards

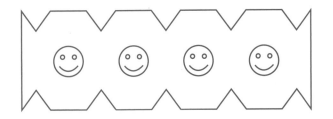

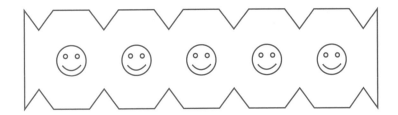

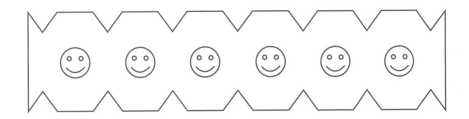

Blackline Master 7—Smiley Singles and Ten Strips
Cut smiley singles, ten strips, and hundreds as needed for activities.

Blackline Master 8—Ten Frames

Blackline Master 9—Smiley Cards

Blackline Master 10—Inch-Squared Paper

Blackline Master 11—Hundreds Chart

1	2	3	4	5	6	7	8	9	10
11	12	13	14	15	16	17	18	19	20
21	22	23	24	25	26	27	28	29	30
31	32	33	34	35	36	37	38	39	40
41	42	43	44	45	46	47	48	49	50
51	52	53	54	55	56	57	58	59	60
61	62	63	64	65	66	67	68	69	70
71	72	73	74	75	76	77	78	79	80
81	82	83	84	85	86	87	88	89	90
91	92	93	94	95	96	97	98	99	100

Blackline Master 12—Dog and Bone Cards

Blackline Master 13—Object Cards

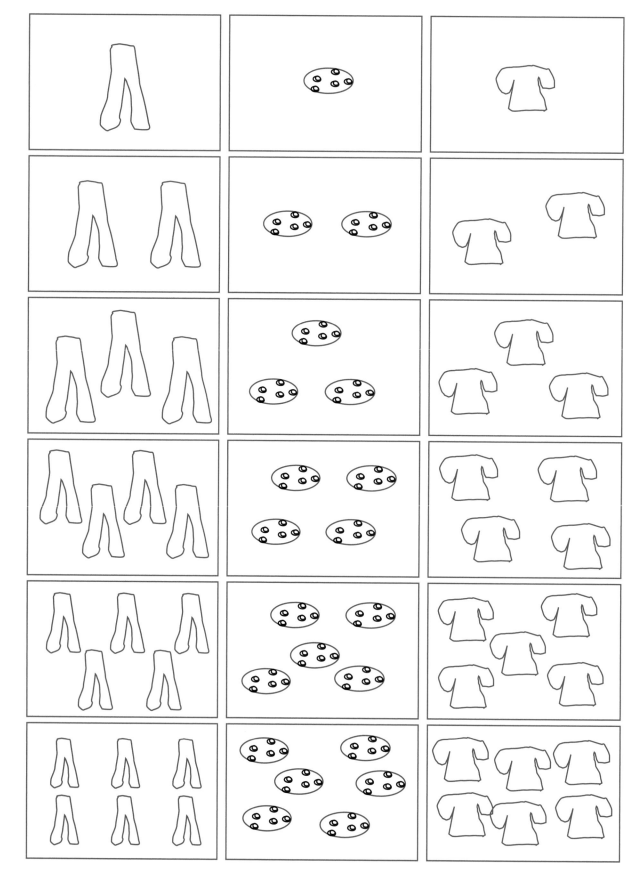

Blackline Master 14—More Object Cards

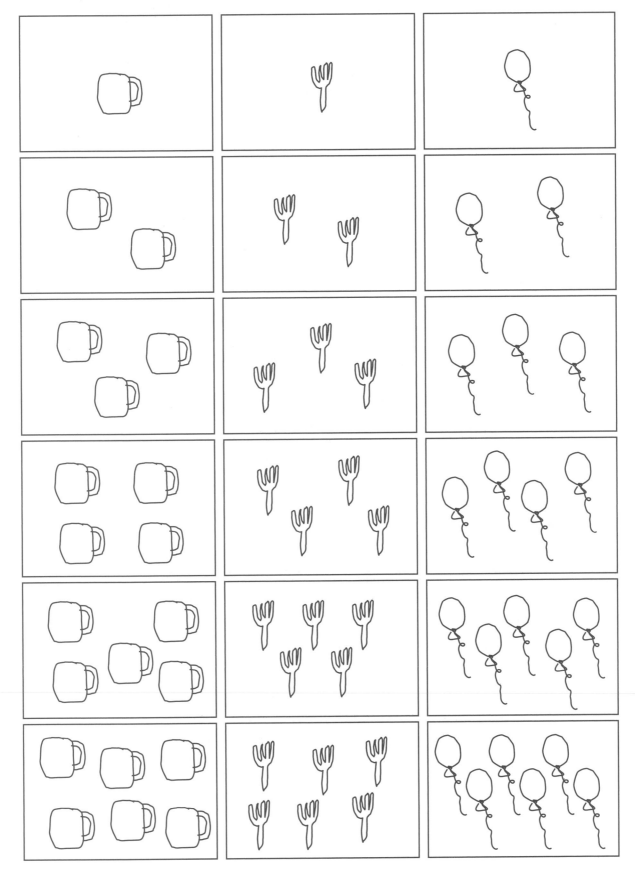

Blackline Master 15—Rounding Road Map

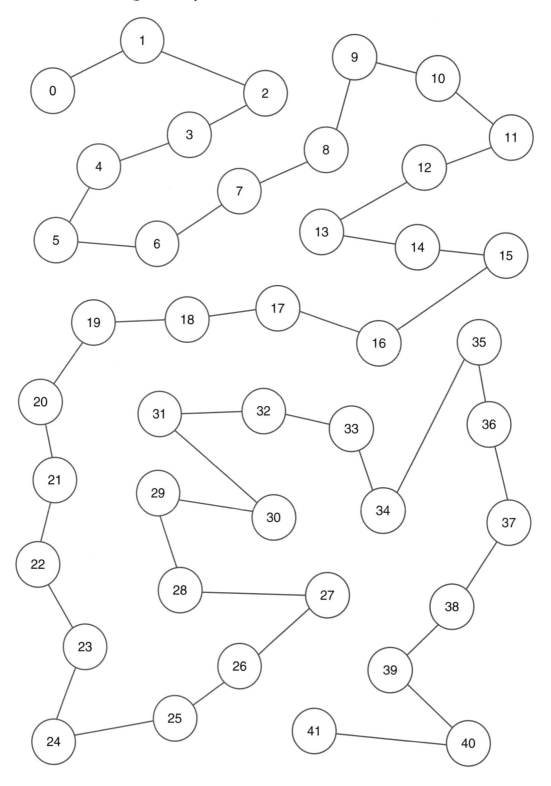

Blackline Master 16—Even/Odd Smiley Strips

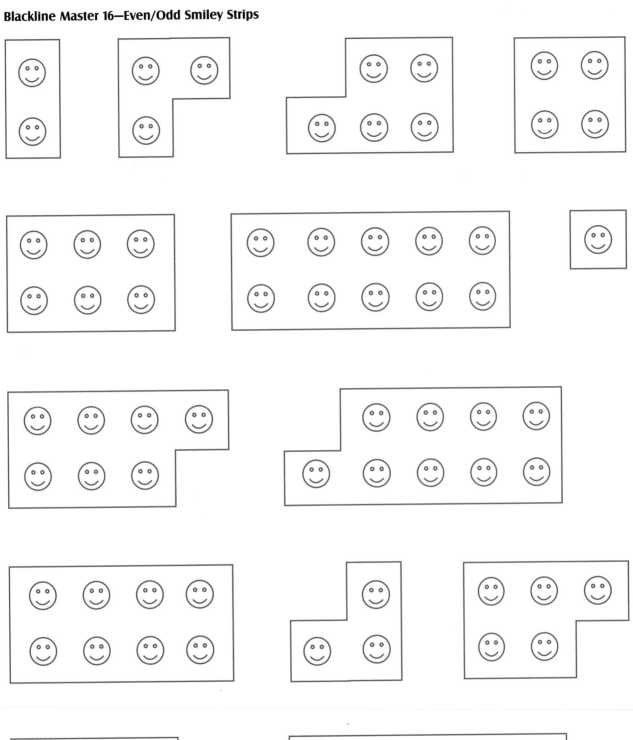

Blackline Master 17—Fraction Strips

Suggestion: Small pieces are easily lost or destroyed. You may wish to have students cut out strips but not cut the strips into individual pieces.

1

$\frac{1}{2}$	$\frac{1}{2}$

$\frac{1}{3}$	$\frac{1}{3}$	$\frac{1}{3}$

$\frac{1}{4}$	$\frac{1}{4}$	$\frac{1}{4}$	$\frac{1}{4}$

$\frac{1}{6}$	$\frac{1}{6}$	$\frac{1}{6}$	$\frac{1}{6}$	$\frac{1}{6}$	$\frac{1}{6}$

$\frac{1}{8}$	$\frac{1}{8}$	$\frac{1}{8}$	$\frac{1}{8}$	$\frac{1}{8}$	$\frac{1}{8}$	$\frac{1}{8}$	$\frac{1}{8}$

$\frac{1}{12}$	$\frac{1}{12}$	$\frac{1}{12}$	$\frac{1}{12}$	$\frac{1}{12}$	$\frac{1}{12}$	$\frac{1}{12}$	$\frac{1}{12}$	$\frac{1}{12}$	$\frac{1}{12}$	$\frac{1}{12}$	$\frac{1}{12}$

$\frac{1}{24}$	$\frac{1}{24}$	$\frac{1}{24}$	$\frac{1}{24}$	$\frac{1}{24}$	$\frac{1}{24}$	$\frac{1}{24}$	$\frac{1}{24}$	$\frac{1}{24}$	$\frac{1}{24}$	$\frac{1}{24}$	$\frac{1}{24}$	$\frac{1}{24}$	$\frac{1}{24}$	$\frac{1}{24}$	$\frac{1}{24}$	$\frac{1}{24}$	$\frac{1}{24}$	$\frac{1}{24}$	$\frac{1}{24}$	$\frac{1}{24}$	$\frac{1}{24}$	$\frac{1}{24}$	$\frac{1}{24}$

Blackline Master 18—Fraction Strips

Suggestion: Small pieces are easily lost or destroyed. You may wish to have students cut out strips but not cut the strips into individual pieces.

1

$\frac{1}{2}$	$\frac{1}{2}$

$\frac{1}{3}$	$\frac{1}{3}$	$\frac{1}{3}$

$\frac{1}{4}$	$\frac{1}{4}$	$\frac{1}{4}$	$\frac{1}{4}$

$\frac{1}{5}$	$\frac{1}{5}$	$\frac{1}{5}$	$\frac{1}{5}$	$\frac{1}{5}$

$\frac{1}{6}$	$\frac{1}{6}$	$\frac{1}{6}$	$\frac{1}{6}$	$\frac{1}{6}$	$\frac{1}{6}$

$\frac{1}{7}$	$\frac{1}{7}$	$\frac{1}{7}$	$\frac{1}{7}$	$\frac{1}{7}$	$\frac{1}{7}$	$\frac{1}{7}$

$\frac{1}{10}$	$\frac{1}{10}$	$\frac{1}{10}$	$\frac{1}{10}$	$\frac{1}{10}$	$\frac{1}{10}$	$\frac{1}{10}$	$\frac{1}{10}$	$\frac{1}{10}$	$\frac{1}{10}$

$\frac{1}{20}$	$\frac{1}{20}$	$\frac{1}{20}$	$\frac{1}{20}$	$\frac{1}{20}$	$\frac{1}{20}$	$\frac{1}{20}$	$\frac{1}{20}$	$\frac{1}{20}$	$\frac{1}{20}$	$\frac{1}{20}$	$\frac{1}{20}$	$\frac{1}{20}$	$\frac{1}{20}$	$\frac{1}{20}$	$\frac{1}{20}$	$\frac{1}{20}$	$\frac{1}{20}$	$\frac{1}{20}$	$\frac{1}{20}$

Blackline Master 19—Pattern Block Fractions

The hexagon represents one whole. What fraction describes each of the other objects? Write a fraction phrase in each object.

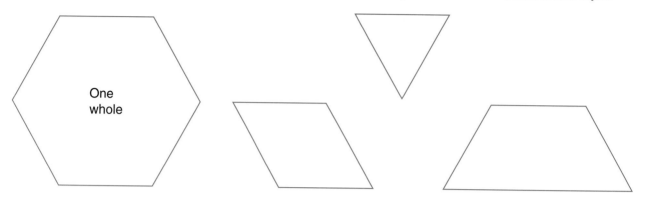

Complete each of the following. Draw shapes on the handout to verify your claim.

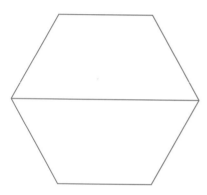

a.   One whole = _two_ halves.

b.   One whole = _____ sixths.

c.   Nine thirds = _____ wholes.

d.   Twelve sixths = _____ wholes.

Blackline Master 20—Equivalent Fractions

	Original fraction	Multiply both numerator and denominator by the number given		New fraction	Compare the fractions
(a)	$\dfrac{1}{2}$	2	$\dfrac{1 \times 2}{2 \times 2}$	$\dfrac{2}{4}$	$\dfrac{1}{2} = \dfrac{2}{4}$
(b)	$\dfrac{1}{2}$	3	$\dfrac{1 \times 3}{2 \times 3}$		
(c)	$\dfrac{1}{2}$	4			
(d)	$\dfrac{1}{2}$	6			
(e)	$\dfrac{1}{3}$	2			
(f)	$\dfrac{1}{3}$	4			
(g)	$\dfrac{1}{3}$	8			
(h)	$\dfrac{3}{4}$	2			
(i)	$\dfrac{3}{4}$	3			

Blackline Master 21—A Net for a Die
Cut along solid lines. Fold along dashed lines. Use tape or glue to secure tabs.

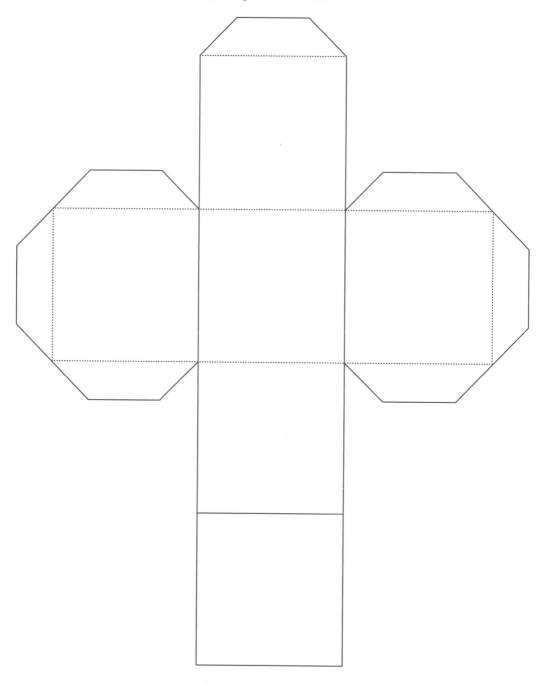

Blackline Master 22—Gummy Bear Graph Outline

Sort your Gummy Bears.

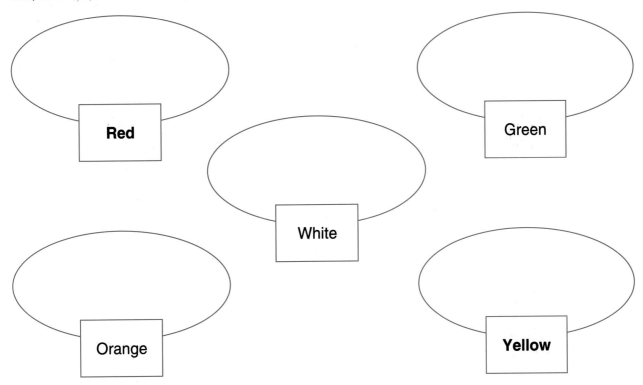

Color the Bar Graph.

6					
5					
4					
3					
2					
1					
	Red	White	Green	Yellow	Orange

You may eat your gummy bears if this box is checked. ☐

Blackline Master 23—Which Wins?

1. Roll one die. Mark a box for the number shown on the top face. Continue until one of the numbers reaches the top and wins.

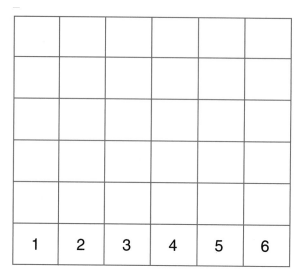

| 1 | 2 | 3 | 4 | 5 | 6 |

2. Roll two dice. Mark the box that represents the sum of the numbers shown. Continue until one of the sums reaches the top and wins.

| 2 | 3 | 4 | 5 | 6 | 7 | 8 | 9 | 10 | 11 | 12 |

Blackline Master 24—Dotpaper

Index